NEW ZEALAND CRICKETERS 1863/64 - 2010

compiled by

Tony McCarron

Published by the Association of Cricket Statisticians and Historians, Cardiff CF11 9XR
2010
Typeset by Limlow Books
Printed by City Press, Leeds
ISBN: 978 1 905138 98 2

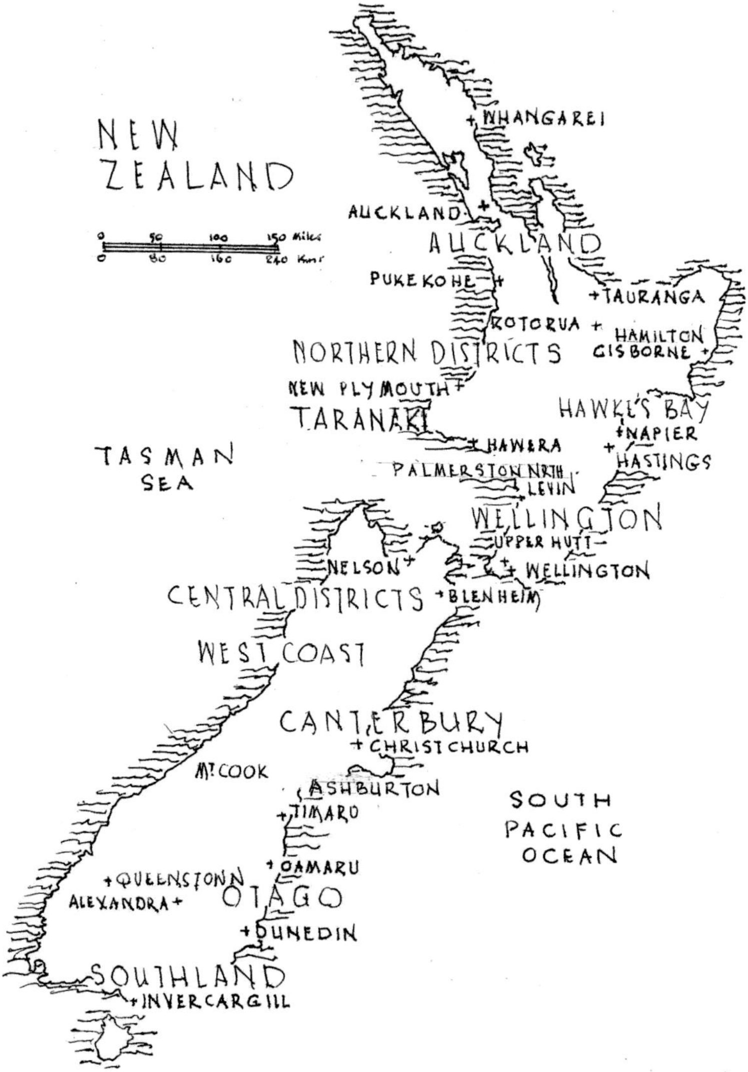
NEW ZEALAND
0 50 100 150 Miles
0 80 160 240 Kms
WHANGAREI
AUCKLAND
AUCKLAND
PUKEKOHE
TAURANGA
ROTORUA
HAMILTON
GISBORNE
NORTHERN DISTRICTS
NEW PLYMOUTH
TARANAKI
HAWKE'S BAY
NAPIER
HASTINGS
HAWERA
TASMAN SEA
PALMERSTON NRTH
LEVIN
WELLINGTON
UPPER HUTT
WELLINGTON
NELSON
CENTRAL DISTRICTS
BLENHEIM
WEST COAST
CANTERBURY
CHRISTCHURCH
MT COOK
ASHBURTON
SOUTH PACIFIC OCEAN
TIMARU
OAMARU
QUEENSTOWN
ALEXANDRA
OTAGO
DUNEDIN
SOUTHLAND
INVERCARGILL

INTRODUCTION

This book contains brief biographical details of all cricketers that have played for a New Zealand or Fijian first-class team. It gives information on prime ministers, governor generals and diplomats, as well as a multiple murderer, convicted criminals and those that weren't caught by the law. There are some excellent cricketers and other players with fewer credentials who were in the right place at the right time. The common link for the players in this book is that they have played first-class, limited overs or Twenty20 cricket for a New Zealand or Fijian team. However there is a very wide range in the amount of biographical information available for these players. For example some players were the subject of a separate biography or autobiography, whilst for over 100 players I couldn't find their birth or death details and in two cases (the Wellington players of the 1870s, England and Gouge) I couldn't locate the initial of their christian name.

The scope of the book is to include players that played first-class, limited over (List A) or Twenty20 cricket for a New Zealand national or provincial team, either in New Zealand or overseas. Fijian teams that toured New Zealand in 1894/95, 1947/48 and 1953/54 are also considered to be first-class. For completeness, Fijian cricketers who played first-class cricket on those tours have been included in this book, in a separate section.

For each player I have shown (where known) their full name, the period that they played first-class cricket, their place and date of birth and death, their batting and/or bowling style, if they were a wicket-keeper, and the teams that they played for (in chronological order; New Zealand teams are in bold). Where a player is normally known by a name other than his first name, I have underlined the name known by.

Additional information that I've included (where I could locate it) is as follows;
- the player's occupation
- the player's school
- awards and honours
- representation at other sports
- books that had been written by or about the player
- relations that have played first-class cricket (those relatives not listed in the book played first-class cricket in another country)
- batting, bowling or partnership records the player holds
- other information that I considered of interest

In regard to the school and occupation, where the player has more than one school or occupation, I've included as many as I could locate, though in many cases the occupation is that which appears in either the player's death or cemetery records.

I have no doubt also included incorrect information so any corrections or additional information, regardless of how minor, would be appreciated. Please send to me at 29 O'Rourke St, Weetangera, ACT 2614, Australia or email me at tonymccarron@grapevine.com.au.

I have taken a New Zealand focus with the biographies. For example a number of overseas-based players are included in this book, however I have generally not noted any of their records unless they are for performances in New Zealand. Similarly I have excluded overseas-based players that made a guest appearance for the New Zealand Governor General's teams in 1960/61 and 1968/69. These players are F.C.M.Alexander, I.M.Chappell, R.M.Edwards, R.C.Fredericks, J.L.Hendriks, L.A.King, R.R.Lindwall, C.H.Lloyd, C.L.Lyttelton (Lord Cobham when he played in 1960/61), C.W.Smith and K.D.Walters.

A very brief history of New Zealand cricket

Polynesians arrived in New Zealand in approximately 1200 AD and European settlement commenced 600 years later. In 1840 the Treaty of Waitangi was signed between the Māori and the British. The Treaty established a British governor in New Zealand, recognised Māori ownership of their lands and other properties, and gave Māori the rights of British subjects. In 1861 gold was discovered in Otago which led to a gold rush and with subsequent increase in population and the tour of a team of English cricketers resulted in the initial first-class match in early 1864 between Otago and Canterbury.

Prior to 1947 the Association of Cricket Statisticians and Historians (ACS) have listed all first-class cricket matches played in New Zealand (and worldwide). After 1947, first-class cricket in New Zealand was defined by the International Cricket Council (ICC) and where relevant the New Zealand Cricket Council (NZCC). The ACS book *First-class Cricket in New Zealand* lists all New Zealand first-class matches played between 1863/64 and 1980. The players that played in a match listed in that book and/or a first-class match in New Zealand from 1981/82 are the basis for inclusion in this book. For completeness all players that have also played limited over (List A) or Twenty20 cricket in New Zealand have also been included, although these players are in a separate section.

The inaugural first-class match in New Zealand was between Otago and Canterbury in the 1863/64 season. In 1873/74 Wellington and Auckland commenced playing first-class cricket. These four provinces are considered to be the major associations.

Prior to the consolidation of first-class cricket to the four major associations in 1921/22, first-class cricket was played by the following minor associations: Nelson (1873/74 to 1891/92), Taranaki (1882/83 to 1897/98), Hawke's Bay (1883/84 to 1920/21) and Southland (1914/15 to 1920/21).

In 1950/51 Central Districts was granted first-class status. Central Districts comprises eight individual minor associations: Hawke's Bay, Horowhenua-Kapiti, Manawatu, Marlborough, Nelson, Taranaki, Wairarapa and Wanganui. In 1956/57 Northern Districts was granted first-class status. Northern Districts Cricket covers an extensive area from the Far North and to the lower half of the North Island and the main minor associations include Northland, Waikato Valley, Hamilton, Counties Manakau, Bay of Plenty and Poverty Bay.

Prior to the creation of Central Districts and Northern Districts, their constituent minor associations were generally allocated to Wellington or Auckland. Since 1956/57 the four original major associations consist of the following areas:

 Canterbury includes metropolitan Christchurch as well as five minor associations - Buller,
    Canterbury Country (previously North Canterbury), Mid-Canterbury,
    South Canterbury and West Coast.
 Otago includes metropolitan Dunedin, North Otago, Central Otago and Southland.
 Wellington includes metropolitan Wellington and Hutt Valley.
 Auckland includes Auckland City metropolitan areas and the surrounding areas from Orewa,
    north of Auckland, to Manukau, south of Auckland.

Other teams have also played first-class cricket in New Zealand, for example North Island, South Island, West Coast of the North Island, and the Army. These teams are only listed in the player's details if he has not played for any other first-class team.

List A cricket commenced in New Zealand in 1970/71 with the match between Wellington and the touring MCC team, the following season an inter provincial tournament was played and has continued annually, with occasional changes to the format. The first One Day International was played by New Zealand in 1972/73 against Pakistan. New Zealand played in the initial Twenty20 international against Australia in 2004/05. Domestic New Zealand Twenty20 cricket commenced in the 2006/07 season.

This book contains biographical data up to 1st October 2010 and playing records to the end of the 2010 English season.

ACKNOWLEDGMENTS

The players listed in this book, without them this book would not be possible.

The historians of New Zealand cricket: Tom Reese, author of the History of New Zealand Cricket 1841-1914 and 1914-1936; Arthur Carman, author of the New Zealand Cricket Almanack 1948 to 1982; Francis Payne and Ian Smith, authors of the New Zealand Cricket Almanack 1983 to date; Don Neely, author of over 20 books on New Zealand cricket; the authors of histories of a range of New Zealand provincial, district and club teams; the early newspapermen, including Anders Wiren, Dan McKenzie and "Short Slip" of the *Otago Times*, their articles in newspapers on the paperspast website were a gold mine of information.

Brian Adams and Warwick Larkins for their extensive help with Canterbury and Otago cricketers respectively.

Ray Webster and Warwick Franks both of whom have given me significant help and assistance over the past 20 years.

Robin Isherwood, whose help and generosity is second to none and whose register of South African cricketers was the inspiration for the format of this book.

Andrew Samson, Philip Bailey, Peter Griffiths and John Bryant for their encouragement, statistical know how, eye for detail and general support.

Evan Watkin who has done a massive amount of research into New Zealand cricketers and has corrected a number of my errors and omissions.

Peter Wynne-Thomas, who provided the map of New Zealand.

The ACS committee for providing me with the research grant which assisted in getting this book into print.

Members of the ACS that have undertaken considerable work in locating the details of a number of players listed in this book.

The New Zealand Society of Genealogists for the work conducted by its members which was of significant assistance in developing this book.

The *New Zealand Cricket Almanack* and *Wisden Cricketers' Almanack* for the wealth of information they have provided.

The families of W.J.Garwood, W.J.Smeeton and C.S.Cross, for their helpful information.

Last but not least I would like to thank my lovely wife Allison and my beautiful children Amelie and Aidan for their support and encouragement.

Condensed Bibliography

History of New Zealand Cricket 1841-1914 and 1914-1936
New Zealand Cricket Almanack 1948-2009
Wisden Cricket Almanack 1864-2009
ACS publications including, First class cricket guides to New Zealand, England, Australia, India and South Africa, and biographical guides for innumerable first class cricket teams.
Who's Who of Cricketers
Provincial Cricket Histories for Wellington, Canterbury, Auckland, Otago, Hawkes Bay, Central Districts, Northern Districts, Taranaki and South Canterbury
Cricket Histories for a number of New Zealand district and regional teams
School Registers and/or histories including Otago Boys High, Christ College, Canterbury Boys High, Wellington College, Auckland Grammar, Takapuna Grammar and Rongatai College
NZ rugby annuals, regional and team histories and encyclopedias
NZ Dictionary of Biography
NZ Cyclopedias

Websites

paperspast.natlib.govt.nz
www.archives.govt.nz
www.bdmhistoricalrecords.dia.govt.nz
newspapers.nla.gov.au
www.cricinfo.com
www.cricketarchive.com
Websites for a number of NZ local councils which contained cemetery records and Australian state and territory births deaths and marriage websites.
www.familysearch.org
www.genealogy.org.nz

Abbreviations

b	born
c	baptised
d	died
BC	Boys College
BHS	Boys High School
CEGS	Church of England Grammar School
Coll	College
Comp Sch	Comprehensive School
Coy	Company
CS	Collegiate School
DHS	District High School
FC	First-class
GS	Grammar school
HS	High School
ICOY	Indian Cricketer of the Year
MBE	Member British Empire
NI	North Island
NZCA obit	Year that an obituary/death notice appeared in *New Zealand Cricket Almanack*
NZCA COY	*New Zealand Cricket Almanack* Cricketer of the Year

OBE	Officer British Empire
Occ	Occupation
occ wk	occasional wicket-keeper
ODI	One Day international
Q1, Q2, Q3, Q4	the quarter in the year in which the birth or death was registered
SA	South African
SACOY	South African Cricketer of the Year
Sch	School
SI	South Island
WC	West Coast of the North Island
WCOY	*Wisden Cricketers' Almanack* Cricketer of the Year
Wisden obit	Year that an obituary/death notice appeared in *Wisden Cricketers' Almanack*

Types of batsman/bowler are the standard accepted abbreviations:

RHB	right-hand bat
LHB	left-hand bat
wk	wicket-keeper
LM	left-arm medium
LMF	left-arm medium fast
OB	right-arm off-spinner
RF	right-arm fast
RM	right-arm medium
RMF	right-arm medium fast
SLA	slow left-arm orthodox spinner,

New Zealand has only been shown after birth and death when no other more specific place is known.

Notes On Career Records

It has not been possible to obtain full bowling analyses in some nineteenth century matches.

NEW ZEALAND FIRST-CLASS CRICKETERS

The cricketers given in this section are those that have played in a first-class match for a New Zealand team.

ABERCROMBIE Thomas Ralph 1920/21 b 7.12.1891 Dunedin, Otago. d 28.7.1958 Wellington. Team: **Southland.** Sch: High Street Dunedin.

ABERHART Denis Charles 1976/77-1983/84 b 23.3.1953 Motueka, Tasman. RHB RM Teams: **Central Districts, Canterbury.** Played List A in NZ. Sch: Motueka HS. Occ: Headmaster. NZ and Canterbury coach, Canterbury selector. Brother: W.M.Aberhart.

ABERHART Wayne Maurice 1985/86 b 10.5.1958 Motueka, Tasman. RHB RM Team: **Wellington.** Sch: Motueka HS. Occ: Policeman. Brother: D.C.Aberhart.

ABERNETHY Bruce 1981/82-1982/83 b 28.5.1958 Toowoomba, Queensland, Australia. RHB RM Team: **Otago.** Played List A in NZ. Occ: Professor.

ACKLAND Richard John 1976/77-1983/84 b 2.8.1958 Auckland. RHB SLA Team: **Auckland.** Played List A in NZ. Sch: Mt Albert GS. Rugby League: New Zealand.

ACKROYD Alfred Edward 1906/07-1907/08 b 22.1.1885 Dunedin, Otago. d 21.5.1952 Christchurch, Canterbury. RHB Teams: **Otago, Canterbury.** Occ: Warehouseman.

ADAMS Alan Augustus 1905/06-1907/08 b 8.5.1883 Greymouth, West Coast. d 28.7.1963 Greymouth, West Coast. Team: **Otago.** Sch: Auckland GS. Occ: Doctor. Rugby: Otago, Blackheath and England. Became a prominent rugby administrator and selector; NZRFU president in 1929.

ADAMS Andre Ryan 1997/98-2010 b 17.7.1975 Auckland. RHB RFM Teams: **Auckland, New Zealand Test, New Zealand ODI, New Zealand T20,** Essex, Nottinghamshire. Played List A in NZ; Played T20 in NZ. Sch: Westlake BHS. Occ: Cricket pro.

ADAMS Stephen Douglas 1982/83-1984/85 b 28.4.1953 Auckland. LHB RM Team: **Auckland.** Played List A in NZ. Sch: Kelston BHS.

ADAMS Thomas Daggar 1907/08 b 15.1.1884 Dunedin, Otago. d 20.11.1953 Dunedin, Otago. Team: **Otago.** Sch: Otago BHS. Occ: Professor. Book: Thomas Daggar Adams by L.Adams.

ADCOCK Joseph Mould 1891/92 b 10.3.1864 Tamworth, Staffordshire, England. d 24.1.1914 Willesborough, Ashford, Kent, England. Was appointed to a chaplaincy in Switzerland, however he contracted typhoid fever and died the following month in England. Team: **Nelson.** Sch: Bishopdale Coll, Nelson. Occ: Anglican Reverend.

ADDISON Alwin Hogarth 1909/10 b 27.10.1887 Orroroo, South Australia, Australia. d 31.7.1971 Armidale, New South Wales, Australia. LHB LM Team: **Canterbury.** Sch: Orroroo, Australia. Occ: Bank manager.

A'DEANE John Robert Bayley 1893/94 b 21.3.1865 Takapau, Hawke's Bay. d 14.3.1924 Takapau, Hawke's Bay. Team: **Hawke's Bay.** Sch: Haileybury, England. Occ: Sheep farmer.

AGER Denis Terence 1944/45 b 9.6.1919 Wairoa, Hawke's Bay. d 17.12.1979 Christchurch, Canterbury. Team: **South Island.** Occ: Accountant.

AIKEN John Maxwell 1989/90-2000/01 b 3.7.1970 Sydney, New South Wales, Australia. LHB Teams: **Wellington, Auckland.** Played List A in NZ. Occ: Psychologist. NZ U19 Test; NZ U19 ODI. Book: U-turn: putting you back into your relationship. He scored 119 on FC debut for Wellington v Canterbury in 1989/90.

AIM Gregory Martyn 1955/56-1962/63 b 4.9.1933 Wellington. d 1.4.2005 Wellington. RHB RM Teams: **Otago, Wellington.** Sch: Otago BHS. Occ: Manager. NZCA obit: 2005.

AIREY David Michael Lawson 1977/78 b 26.4.1948 Wellington. RHB Team: **Wellington.** Father: W.F.Airey.

AIREY Wilfrid Farrant 1927/28-1939/40 b 27.9.1907 Nelson. d 19.7.1980 Lower Hutt, Wellington. LHB Team: **Wellington.** Occ: Bank officer. Book: Elementary drill for the home guard. NZCA obit: 1980. Son: D.M.L.Airey.

ALABASTER Grenville David 1955/56-1975/76 b 10.12.1933 Invercargill, Southland. LHB OB Teams: **Otago, Canterbury, Northern Districts, New Zealand.** Played List A in NZ. Sch: Southland BHS. Occ: School principal. NZCA COY: 1972. NZ selector, manager and coach, Otago selector. He played for New Zealand in a FC match. He took a hat-trick for Northern Districts v Canterbury in 1962/63. Brother: J.C.Alabaster.

ALABASTER John Chaloner 1955/56-1971/72 b 11.7.1930 Invercargill, Southland. RHB LBG Teams: **Otago, New Zealand Test.** Sch: Southland BHS. Occ: Rector. Basketball: New Zealand. NZCA COY: 1960; SACOY 1962. Otago selector. Brother: G.D.Alabaster.

ALCOCK Alistair James 1992/93-1994/95 b 20.7.1972 Napier, Hawke's Bay. LHB RM Team: **Central Districts.** Played List A in NZ. Sch: Napier BHS. Occ: Fitness instructor.

ALDERSLEY William Arthur 1909/10-1922/23 b 4.12.1888 Keighley, Yorkshire, England. d 17.3.1981 Lower Hutt, Wellington. Team: **Wellington.** Sch: Mt Cook HS. Occ: Chemist. Umpired first-class cricket. NZCA obit: 1981.

ALDERSON John Dalton 1949/50-1950/51 b 3.2.1929 Auckland. RM Team: **Canterbury.** Sch: Christchurch BHS. Occ: Farmer.

ALDRIDGE Charles William 1973/74 b 12.5.1947 Balclutha, Otago. LHB RMF Teams: **Canterbury, Northern Districts (not FC).** Played List A in NZ. Sch: Christchurch BHS. Occ: Retail manager. Son: G.W.Aldridge.

ALDRIDGE Graeme William 1998/99-2009/10 b 15.11.1977 Christchurch, Canterbury. RHB RFM Team: **Northern Districts (not FC).** Played List A in NZ; Played T20 in NZ. Sch: Otumoetai Coll. Occ: Schoolteacher. He holds the Northern Districts 8th wicket partnership record of 163 with P.D.McGlashan against Canterbury in 2008/09 and the Northern Districts 10th wicket partnership record of 113* with P.D.McGlashan against Wellington in 2005/06. Father: C.W.Aldridge.

ALEXANDER Robert Edward 1933/34 b 28.6.1916 Christchurch, Canterbury. d 9.5.1988 Christchurch, Canterbury. LHB LBG Team: **Canterbury.** Sch: Christ Coll. Occ: Auctioneer.

ALINGTON William Herbert 1868/69-1869/70 b 13.12.1842 Spilsby, Lincolnshire, England. d 13.1.1938 Wandsworth, London, England. Team: **Canterbury.** Sch: Rugby, England; Uppingham, England. Occ: Farmer. Umpired first-class cricket. He died aged 95.

ALLAN Barry Clarke 1956/57 b 28.9.1928 Dunedin, Otago. d 8.1.1962 Dunedin, Otago. He died of cancer aged 33. RM Team: **Otago.** Sch: Kings HS. Occ: Salesman.

ALLAN James Matthew 1993/94-1997/98 b 3.6.1972 Waimate, Canterbury. RHB Team: **Otago.** Played List A in NZ.

ALLARD Charles Wright 1920/21 b 29.12.1885 Christchurch, Canterbury. d 2.4.1965 Kaiapoi, Canterbury. RHB Team: **Canterbury.** Sch: Christchurch BHS. Occ: Schoolmaster.

ALLARDYCE Ivan Douglas 1917/18-1918/19 b 15.4.1895 Christchurch, Canterbury. d 14.11.1967 Foxton, Horowhenua. RHB Teams: **Canterbury, Wellington.** Sch: Christchurch BHS. Occ: Hotelkeeper; clerk.

ALLCOTT Cyril Francis Walter 1920/21-1945/46 b 7.10.1896 Lower Moutere, Tasman. d 19.11.1973 Auckland. LHB SLA Teams: **Hawke's Bay, Auckland, Otago, New Zealand Test.** Sch: Blenheim HS. Occ: Bank officer. NZCA obit: 1974.

ALLEN Garry Sol 1977/78 b 11.8.1945 Wellington. LHB LM Team: **Wellington.** Played List A in NZ. Father: R.Allen.

ALLEN John 1869/70-1874/75 b 26.12.1850 Dunedin, Otago. d 29.9.1897 Dunedin, Otago. wk Team: **Otago.** Sch: Otago BHS. Occ: Farmer.

ALLEN John Henry 1944/45 b 4.2.1903 Dunedin, Otago. d 18.3.1961 Dunedin, Otago. Team: **Otago.** Occ: Insurance agent.

ALLEN Percy Frederick 1928/29-1934/35 b 7.1.1908 Mitcham, Surrey, England. d 10.12.1995 Christchurch, Canterbury. RHB wk Team: **Canterbury.** Occ: Storeman.

ALLEN Raymond 1941/42-1953/54 b 27.10.1908 Wellington. d 2.8.1979 Wellington. LHB SLA Team: **Wellington.** Occ: Coy director. NZCA obit: 1979. Son: G.S.Allen.

ALLOO Albert Peacock 1914/15 b 26.10.1893 Sydney, New South Wales, Australia. d 21.7.1955 Dunedin, Otago. LHB SLA Team: **Otago.** Sch: Otago BHS. Occ: Solicitor. Brothers: A.W.Alloo, H.C.Alloo.

ALLOO Arthur William 1913/14-1930/31 b 9.1.1892 Sydney, New South Wales, Australia. d 16.9.1950 Nelson. RHB OB Teams: **Otago, New Zealand**. Sch: Otago BHS. Occ: Schoolteacher. NZCA obit: 1950; Wisden obit: 1951. He played for New Zealand in a FC match. Brothers: A.P.Alloo, H.C.Alloo.

ALLOO Howard Cecil 1919/20-1928/29 b 28.4.1895 Sydney, New South Wales, Australia. d 23.10.1989 Timaru, South Canterbury. RHB Team: **Otago**. Sch: Otago BHS. Occ: Solicitor. Rugby: Otago. Brothers: A.W.Alloo, A.P.Alloo.

ALLOTT Geoffrey Ian 1994/95-1999 b 24.12.1971 Christchurch, Canterbury. RHB LFM Teams: **Canterbury, New Zealand Test, New Zealand ODI**. Played List A in NZ. Sch: Christchurch BHS. Occ: Cricket administrator.

ALLOTT Paul John Walter 1978-1991 b 14.9.1956 Altrincham, Cheshire, England. RHB RFM Teams: **Wellington**, England Test, England ODI, Lancashire. Played List A in NZ. Sch: Altrincham GS, England. Occ: Commentator. An English pro, played and coached in NZ.

ALPE Frank Gordon 1908/09 b 26.3.1884 Wellington. d 10.5.1958 Waikanae, Wellington. Team: **Wellington.** Occ: Farmer. Father: S.Alpe.

ALPE Samuel 1873/74-1884/85 b 29.3.1834 Swaffham, Norfolk, England. d 30.7.1918 Wellington. He died from heart disease. Teams: **Auckland, Canterbury, Wellington.** Occ: Civil servant. Son: F.G.Alpe.

AMANDEEP SINGH 2005/06-2007/08 b 17.8.1987 Punjab, India. RHB RFM Teams: **Northern Districts, Canterbury.** Sch: Tauranga BC.

ANDERSEN Leslie David 1960/61-1967/68 b 11.12.1939 Melbourne, Victoria, Australia. LHB LM Teams: **Auckland, Northern Districts.**

ANDERSON Carl James 1997/98-2000/01 b 4.10.1977 Christchurch, Canterbury. RHB SLA Team: **Canterbury.** Played List A in NZ. Sch: Shirley BHS.

ANDERSON Corey James 2006/07-2009/10 b 13.12.1990 Christchurch, Canterbury. LHB LMF Team: **Canterbury.** Played List A in NZ; Played T20 in NZ. Sch: Christchurch BHS. NZ U19 Test; NZ U19 ODI.

ANDERSON Gordon Frank 1949/50-1950/51 b 9.1.1922 Christchurch, Canterbury. RHB wk Team: **Canterbury.** Sch: Christchurch Technical Coll. Occ: Caltex Oil clerk. Uncle: W.H.R.Cunningham.

ANDERSON Hayden Thomas 1999/00 b 3.7.1980 Dunedin, Otago. RHB RM Team: **Otago**. Sch: Kaikorai Coll.

ANDERSON Ian Paul 1964/65 b 23.6.1925 Christchurch, Canterbury. d 13.8.1977 Christchurch, Canterbury. LHB wk Team: **Canterbury.** Sch: Christchurch BHS. Occ: Schoolteacher. NZCA obit: 1977.

ANDERSON James Michael 2002-2010 b 30.7.1982 Burnley, Lancashire, England. LHB RFM Teams: **Auckland,** England Test, England ODI, England T20, Lancashire. Sch: St Theodore's RCHS, Burnley, England. Occ: Cricket pro. WCOY: 2009. An English pro, played and coached in NZ.

ANDERSON Leslie Gilbert 1923/24 b 20.9.1891 Dunedin, Otago. d 18.5.1979 Dunedin, Otago. Team: **Otago.** Occ: Plumber.

ANDERSON Norman James Cecil 1909/10 b 13.9.1886 Port Ahuriri, Hawke's Bay. d 4.4.1941 Wellington. Team: **Hawke's Bay.** Occ: Clerk.

ANDERSON Peter Stewart 1977/78-1978/79 b 3.2.1950 Taihape, Rangitikei. LHB RM Team: **Northern Districts.** Played List A in NZ.

ANDERSON Robert Geoffrey 1961/62-1964/65 b 29.3.1939 Dunedin, Otago. RHB RFM Team: **Otago.** Sch: Otago BHS. Snooker: Otago champion in 1961.

ANDERSON Robert Wickham 1967/68-1981/82 b 2.10.1948 Christchurch, Canterbury. RHB LB Teams: **Canterbury, Northern Districts, Otago, Central Districts, New Zealand Test, New Zealand ODI.** Played List A in NZ. Sch: Christchurch BHS. Occ: Branch manager. NZCA COY: 1978. Father: W.M.Anderson; son: T.R.Anderson.

ANDERSON Rudolph Godfreid 1919/20 b 10.7.1888 Napier, Hawke's Bay. d 22.4.1960 Tauranga, Bay of Plenty. Team: **Hawke's Bay.** Occ: Clerk.

ANDERSON Timothy Robert 1997/98-2002/03 b 13.12.1978 Palmerston North, Manawatu. RHB LB Team: **Central Districts.** Played List A in NZ. Sch: Whangarei HS. Occ: Financial services. NZ U19 ODI. He took a hat-trick for Central Districts v Auckland in 1998/99. Father: R.W.Anderson; grandfather: W.M.Anderson.

ANDERSON William Mcdougall 1938/39-1949/50 b 8.10.1919 Westport, West Coast. d 21.12.1979 Christchurch, Canterbury. LHB LBG Teams: **Canterbury, New Zealand Test.** Sch: Christchurch BHS. NZCA obit: 1981. NZ and Canterbury selector. Grandson: T.R.Anderson; son: R.W.Anderson.

ANDREW Thomas 1872/73 b 1843 Crossgates, Fife, Scotland. d 1.6.1927 Roxburgh, Otago. Team: **Otago.** Occ: Blacksmith.

ANDREWS Bryan 1963/64-1973/74 b 4.4.1945 Christchurch, Canterbury. RHB RM Teams: **Canterbury, Central Districts, Otago, New Zealand Test.** Played List A in NZ. Sch: Christ Coll. Occ: Auctioneer. Canterbury selector. Father: S.Andrews.

ANDREWS Ernest Herbert (Sir) 1898/99 b 25.6.1873 Nelson. d 9.11.1961 Christchurch, Canterbury. Team: **Hawke's Bay.** Sch: Ashburton Coll. Occ: Schoolteacher. Books: Brief retrospect; Eventful years: anecdotes and recollections of a busy life. Knighted for his services to the community; Mayor of Christchurch.

ANDREWS Frederick Maxwell 1935/36-1942/43 b 10.7.1905 New Zealand. d 10.8.1983 Auckland. RHB RM Teams: **Auckland, Wellington.** Occ: Civil servant. Umpired first-class cricket.

ANDREWS Simon Leslie 2000/01-2006/07 b 11.7.1980 Auckland. RHB RFM Team: **Northern Districts.** Played List A in NZ; Played T20 in NZ. Sch: St Kents Coll.

ANDREWS Stanley 1933/34-1935/36 b 22.11.1912 Christchurch, Canterbury. d 4.10.1979 Christchurch, Canterbury. RHB RFM Team: **Canterbury.** Sch: West Christchurch BHS. NZCA obit: 1980. Son: B.Andrews.

ANSENNE John 1893/94 b 1860 Auckland. d 28.4.1939 Thames, Thames Valley. Team: **Auckland.** Occ: Sharebroker; solicitor.

ANSON George Edward 1879/80 b Q4 1850 Sudbury, Staffordshire, England. d 15.7.1934 Lower Hutt, Wellington. Team: **West Coast (North Island).** Sch: Eton, England. Occ: Doctor; schoolmaster. He was Chief Medical Officer for the Australian Mutual Provident Society.

ANTHONY Arnold 1905/06-1930/31 b 28.7.1886 Christchurch, Canterbury. d 14.10.1968 Auckland. RHB RM Teams: **Canterbury, Auckland.** Occ: Clerk. NZCA obit: 1969.

ARBLASTER Robert Gordon 1977/78-1979/80 b 10.4.1948 Auckland. RHB RM Team: **Auckland.** Played List A in NZ.

ARIS John 1870/71 b 12.9.1843 Croydon, Surrey, England. d 12.11.1927 Palmerston North, Manawatu. Team: **Otago.** Occ: Printer.

ARKWRIGHT Henry Fitzherbert 1920/21 b 4.1.1882 Kensington, London, England. d 29.12.1956 Marton, Rangitikei. wk Team: **Minor Assoc.** Sch: Wanganui CS. Occ: Farmer. Nephew F.G.B.Arkwright (Hampshire).

ARMITAGE Joseph Thomas Bourke 1874/75-1881/82 b 20.9.1846 Sydney, New South Wales, Australia. d Q3 1923 Steyning, Sussex, England. Team: **Wellington.** Occ: Civil servant.

ARMSTRONG Douglas Warwick 1958/59 b 13.4.1931 Wellington. RHB SLA Team: **Central Districts.** Occ: Chief exec officer.

ARNEIL John 1882/83-1893/94 b 1862 India. d 11.8.1938 Auckland. Team: **Auckland.** Sch: Auckland GS. Occ: Accountant. Rugby: Auckland. Wisden obit: 1939. President of the Auckland Rugby Union.

ARNEL Brent John 2005/06-2009/10 b 3.1.1979 Te Awamutu, Waikato. RHB RMF Teams: **Northern Districts, New Zealand Test.** Played List A in NZ; Played T20 in NZ. Sch: Te Awamatu Coll. Occ: Schoolteacher.

ARNOLD Arnold Peter 1951-1960 b 16.10.1926 Wellington. RHB RM Teams: **Canterbury,** Northamptonshire. Sch: St Bedes Coll. Occ: Cricket pro.

ARNOLD John 1877/78-1879/80 b 1849 Nelson. d 2.5.1904 Nelson. Four weeks prior to his death he was thrown from his buggy, the injuries he sustained causing his death. Team: **Nelson.** Occ: Sheep farmer.

ARNOLD William 1891/92 Team: **Nelson.**

ASHBOLT Frank Lionel 1893/94-1900/01 b 11.4.1876 Christchurch, Canterbury. d 16.7.1940 Wellington. RHB OB Teams: **Wellington, New Zealand.** Occ: Insurance agent. Wisden obit: 1941. He played for New Zealand prior to being granted Test status.

ASHBY David Alexander 1873-1889/90 b 11.6.1852 Beddington, Surrey, England. d 2.6.1934 Christchurch, Canterbury. RHB RFM Teams: **Canterbury,** Surrey. Occ: Miller. Umpired first-class cricket. Wisden obit: 1935.

ASHCROFT Peter 1905/06-1911/12 b 1873 Lancashire, England. d 5.1.1955 Bournemouth, Hampshire, England. wk Team: **Hawke's Bay.** Occ: Sharebroker. Umpired first-class cricket.

ASHENDEN Jack Gilbert 1935/36-1944/45 b 12.5.1911 Wellington. d 14.11.1992 Sydney, New South Wales, Australia. RHB RM Teams: **Wellington, New Zealand.** NZCA obit: 1993; Wisden obit: 1994. Wellington selector. He played for New Zealand in a FC match.

ASHTON William Martin 1883/84 b 1860 Manchester, Lancashire, England. d 6.7.1949 Napier, Hawke's Bay. Team: **Hawke's Bay.** Occ: Telegraphist.

ASKEW Dean Newman 1991/92-1997/98 b 15.6.1962 Hamilton, Waikato. RHB RFM Teams: **Central Districts, Auckland.** Played List A in NZ.

ASKEW James Weymss 1881/82 b 9.1.1861 Nelson. d 29.6.1952 Mt Albert, Auckland. occ wk Team: **Nelson.** Sch: Nelson Coll. Occ: Indent agent. Rugby: Nelson.

ASTLE Alec Morrison 1978/79 b 5.8.1949 Feilding, Manawatu. RHB RMF Team: **Central Districts.** Played List A in NZ. Occ: Schoolmaster. New Zealand Cricket Development Manager. Son: T.D.Astle.

ASTLE Nathan John 1991/92-2006/07 b 15.9.1971 Christchurch, Canterbury. RHB RM Teams: **Canterbury, New Zealand Test, New Zealand ODI, New Zealand T20,** Nottinghamshire, Durham, Lancashire. Played List A in NZ; Played T20 in NZ. Sch: Shirley BHS. NZ U19 Test; NZ U19 ODI. Book: Nathan Astle. NZCA COY: 1995, 1996, 2002. He holds the NZ Test 5th wicket partnership record of 222 with C.D.McMillan against Zimbabwe in 2000/01.

ASTLE Todd Duncan 2005/06-2009/10 b 24.9.1986 Palmerston North, Manawatu. RHB LB Team: **Canterbury.** Played List A in NZ; Played T20 in NZ. Sch: Christchurch BHS. NZ U19 ODI. Father: A.M.Astle.

ATKINSON Colin Maurice Hilton 1975/76-1976/77 b 6.11.1951 Taumarunui, King Country. RHB RM Team: **Central Districts.** Played List A in NZ.

ATKINSON Frederick Albert 1888/89-1891/92 b 1870 New Zealand. d 1.3.1913 Nelson. He succumbed as the result of a slight accident. He slipped on the concrete steps, dislocated his thumb and burst the skin. The injured joint was placed back in position, and he was about town, with his arm in a sling. Owing to severe pains, medical advice was then sought and he was admitted to the hospital, where he died from lock-jaw and blood poisoning. Team: **Nelson.** Occ: Omnibus proprietor.

AUCKRAM Craig Laurence 1989/90-1991/92 b 9.6.1967 Levin, Horowhenua. RHB RFM Team: **Central Districts.** Played List A in NZ. Occ: Planning consultant.

AUDINWOOD Hendrick Osborne 1906/07 b Q4 1878 Weston, Derbyshire, England. d 31.5.1950 Auckland. Team: **Hawke's Bay.** Occ: Motor assembler.

AUSTEN Michael Hubert 1982/83-1996/97 b 17.5.1964 Cape Town, Cape Province, South Africa. RHB LM Teams: **Otago, Wellington,** Western Province B, Western Province. Played List A in NZ. Sch: Rondebosch BHS, South Africa. Occ: Doctor.

AUSTIN Edmond Godwin *see GODWIN AUSTEN, E*

AUSTIN Eric 1996/97 b 5.4.1974 Wanganui. LHB wk Team: **Central Districts.** Played List A in NZ.

AUSTIN Gerald George 1896/97-1912/13 b 14.3.1875 Dunedin, Otago. d 14.10.1959 Dunedin, Otago. Team: **Otago.** Sch: Otago BHS. Occ: Coy manager. Hockey: Otago. Otago selector. Brother: T.T.L.Austin.

AUSTIN Thomas Talbert Leon 1877/78-1888/89 b 9.3.1857 Melbourne, Victoria, Australia. d 11.2.1941 Russell, Northland. occ wk Team: **Otago.** Sch: Otago BHS. Occ: Orchardist. Rugby: Otago. Otago selector. Brother: G.G.Austin.

AUSTIN-SMELLIE Joseph 2009/10 b 17.10.1989 Dunedin, Otago. RHB wk Team: **Wellington.** Played List A in NZ. Sch: Wellington Coll. NZ U19 Test; NZ U19 ODI. He scored 97 on FC debut for Wellington v Northern Districts.

AYLES Francis 1908/09 b 30.3.1880 Sandridge (now Port Melbourne), Victoria, Australia. d 18.6.1939 Newmarket, Victoria, Australia. Team: **Otago**. Australian Rules: VFL umpire. Professional coach of Otago 1908/09. He shared a 1st wicket partnership of 179 with C.G.Wilson v Hawke's Bay.
AZHAR ABBAS Haraj 1995/96-2008/09 b 1.4.1975 Khanewal, Punjab, Pakistan. RHB RM Teams: **Wellington, Auckland,** Pakistan Railways, Bahawalpur, Multan, Agriculture Development Bank of Pakistan, Sui Northern Gas Pipelines Limited. Played T20 in NZ.
BADCOCK Frederick Theodore 1924/25-1945 b 9.8.1897 Abbottabad, North-West Frontier Province, India (now in Pakistan). d 19.9.1982 South Perth, Western Australia, Australia. RHB RFM Teams: **Wellington, Otago, New Zealand Test.** Sch: Wellington Coll, England. Occ: Cricket coach. Book: Cricket - and hints on coaching. NZCA obit: 1983.
BADDELEY Rex Allen 1969/70-1971/72 b 6.11.1941 Wanganui. LHB LFM Team: **Auckland.**
BADELEY Sydney Albert Roberts 1929/30 b 7.4.1902 Auckland. d 28.12.1981 Auckland. RHB wk Team: **Auckland.** Sch: Auckland GS. Brother of C.E.O.Badeley and V.I.R.Badeley, both All Blacks in the 1920s.
BAILEY Bert 1905/06-1910/11 RHB Team: **Hawke's Bay.**
BAILEY John Frederick 1965/66 b 29.10.1941 Preston, Lancashire, England. RHB RM Team: **Northern Districts.** Nephew: M.D.Bailey.
BAILEY Mark David 1989/90-2001/02 b 26.11.1970 Hamilton, Waikato. RHB RM Teams: **Northern Districts, New Zealand ODI.** Played List A in NZ. Uncle: J.F.Bailey.
BAIN Kenneth Burns 1906/07-1913/14 b 22.6.1883 Dunedin, Otago. d 23.10.1942 Picton, Marlborough. Team: **Canterbury.** Sch: Christchurch BHS. Occ: Insurance manager.
BAIN Wallace Gordon Collingwood 1937/38-1944/45 b 1.6.1917 Auckland. d 17.6.2005 Auckland. LHB Team: **Wellington.**
BAKER Charles Kenneth 1971/72 b 7.5.1947 Christchurch, Canterbury. LHB SLA Team: **Canterbury.** Played List A in NZ. Sch: Christchurch BHS. Occ: Schoolteacher.
BAKER Edward George Huia 1919/20-1920/21 b 15.9.1895 Otaki, Horowhenua. d 15.5.1962 Christchurch, Canterbury. Team: **Wellington.** Sch: Wellington Coll. Occ: Civil servant. Brother: W.A.Baker.
BAKER Geoffrey Robert 1991/92-1994/95 b 30.7.1970 Invercargill, Southland. RHB wk Teams: **Wellington, Otago.** Played List A in NZ.
BAKER Henry Stephen 1925/26 b 26.12.1904 Melbourne, Victoria, Australia. d 7.11.1926 Dunedin, Otago. He drowned at the age of 21. Team: **Otago.** Occ: Clerk.
BAKER James 1889/90-1906/07 b 13.11.1866 London, England. d 1.2.1939 Dunedin, Otago. RHB Teams: **Otago, New Zealand.** Occ: Painter. Rugby: Otago. Wisden obit: 1940. NZ selector. He played for New Zealand prior to being granted Test status. He was born James Clark but changed his surname to that of his step-father, Baker. After the conclusion of his cricket career he reverted to using the surname of Clark. Son: J.B.Clark.
BAKER Lewis Charles 1944/45-1945/46 b 7.10.1920 Dunedin, Otago. d 12.7.1997 Dunedin, Otago. LHB Team: **Otago.** Occ: Coy director. NZCA obit: 1998.
BAKER Murray Philip 1966/67-1974/75 b 21.4.1946 Napier, Hawke's Bay. RHB LB Teams: **Central Districts, Northern Districts.** Played List A in NZ. Occ: Horse trainer.
BAKER Paul John Mark 1988/89 b 19.8.1968 Hawera, Taranaki. RHB LB Team: **Central Districts.**
BAKER Thomas Southey 1874/75-1879/80 b 29.6.1848 Cranbrook, Kent, England. d 24.6.1902 Dunedin, Otago. Team: **Canterbury.** Sch: Lancing Coll, England. Occ: Schoolmaster. Rowing: Oxford University.
BAKER Wiri Aurunui 1911/12-1929/30 b 2.4.1892 Otaki, Horowhenua. d 1.7.1966 Wellington. RHB S Teams: **Wellington, New Zealand.** Sch: Wellington Coll. Occ: Printer. NZCA obit: 1966; Wisden obit: 1967. He played for New Zealand prior to being granted Test status. Brother: G.H.Baker.
BALAJI Lakshmipathy 2001/02-2009/10 b 27.9.1981 Madras (now Chennai), Tamil Nadu, India. RHB RFM Teams: **Wellington,** India Test, India ODI, Tamil Nadu. ICOY 2002. Indian Test player who played for Wellington in order to get match practice whilst on the 2008/09 tour of NZ.
BALDWIN Scott Bruce Cameron 2006/07 b 19.11.1983 Wanganui. RHB RM Team: **Central Districts.** Sch: Wanganui CS. Father: B.C.Baldwin.

BALL Thomas Duffus 1894/95-1896/97 b 1865 Mangonui, Northland. d 17.9.1953 Auckland. Team: **Auckland**. Occ: Solicitor.

BALMAIN Louis Henry Fletcher 1880/81 b 17.1.1858 Bath, Somerset, England. d 1904 Canada. Team: **Nelson**. Occ: Soldier. He was only in NZ for a short time, during which he played FC cricket for Nelson.

BANKS John Elliott 1923/24-1925/26 b 26.5.1903 Edmonton, Middlesex, England. d 20.10.1979 Wellington. RHB Team: **Wellington**. Sch: Wellington Coll. Occ: Coy director. NZCA obit: 1980.

BANNERMAN James William Hugh 1914/15 b 20.5.1887 Ophir, Central Otago. d 23.12.1917 near Ypres, Belgium. He was killed in action aged 30. Team: **Southland**. Sch: Otago BHS. Occ: Newspaper proprietor. Books: History of Early Otago Representative Cricket; Early Cricket in Southland; Milestones, or Wrecks of Southern New Zealand. Brother: W.E.Bannerman.

BANNERMAN Wilfred Ellis 1911/12-1914/15 b 8.9.1888 Ophir, Central Otago. d 8.2.1944 Martinborough, Wairarapa. Team: **Otago**. Sch: Otago BHS. Occ: Bank officer. Brother: J.W.H.Bannerman.

BARBER Richard _Trevor_ 1945/46-1959/60 b 3.6.1925 Otaki, Horowhenua. RHB occ wk Teams: **Wellington, Central Districts, New Zealand Test**. Sch: Wellington Coll.

BARBOUR Michael _Rowan_ Harvey 1959/60 b 10.7.1922 Gisborne, Poverty Bay. d 19.5.2004 Taradale, Hawke's Bay. RHB RM Team: **Northern Districts**. Sch: Kaiti Sch. Occ: Bike shop proprietor. NZCA obit: 2004.

BARCLAY Colin Walter 1955/56 b 21.1.1937 Wellington. RHB RM Team: **Central Districts**. Sch: New Plymouth BHS. Father: W.S.Barclay.

BARCLAY Frederick 1902/03-1903/04 b Q1 1869, Northumberland, England. Team: **Auckland**. Occ: Cricket pro. He took a hat-trick for Auckland v Canterbury in 1903/04.

BARCLAY Walter Sinclair 1920/21-1925/26 b 2.5.1902 Waihola, Otago. d 1.12.1959 New Plymouth, Taranaki. RHB OB Team: **Wellington**. Occ: Civil servant. Rugby: Wellington. NZCA obit: 1960. Son: C.W.Barclay.

BARKER Charles Frederick 1873/74 b 5.7.1847 Hereford, England. d 29.11.1891 Hereford, England. Team: **Canterbury**. Sch: Christ Coll. Occ: Solicitor.

BARNES Aaron Craig 1993/94-2004/05 b 21.12.1971 Turangi, Waikato. RHB RM Team: **Auckland**. Played List A in NZ. He holds the NZ 5th wicket partnership record of 347* with M.J.Horne for Auckland v Northern Districts in 2003/04. He took a wicket with his first ball in FC cricket.

BARNES William _Edward_ Parker 1882/83-1893/94 b 1856 Kildare, Victoria, Australia. d 19.8.1897 Christchurch, Canterbury. He was found in a shed in a dying condition and expired shortly afterwards. He had been left in the shed on the previous night by some companions with whom he had been drinking. At an inquest, the jury returned a verdict of death from syncope, accelerated by drunkenness. occ wk Team: **Canterbury**. Occ: Journalist.

BARNETT David 1873/74-1877/78 b 1850 Nelson. d 14.3.1930 Nelson. Team: **Nelson**. Occ: Farmer.

BARNETT Geoffrey Edward Fulton 2004/05-2009 b 3.2.1984 Nelson. LHB RM Teams: **Central Districts,** Canada, Canada ODI, Canada T20. Played List A in NZ; Played T20 in NZ. Sch: Otago BHS. Occ: Cricket pro.

BARRETT Brian Joseph 1985-1989/90 b 16.11.1966 Auckland. RHB RFM Teams: **Auckland, Northern Districts, New Zealand,** Worcestershire. Played List A in NZ. NZ U19 Test; NZ U19 ODI. He played for New Zealand in a FC match.

BARRETT John Stephen 1913/14 b 8.9.1875 Hokitika, West Coast. d 19.2.1931 Christchurch, Canterbury. Team: **D.Reese's Canterbury XI**. Sch: Christ Coll. Occ: Solicitor. Horse Racing: owned several racehorses, including Count Cavour, a winner of the New Zealand Cup. Wisden obit: 1932. He was hon. secretary and chairman of the New Zealand Cricket Council.

BARRON Andrew 1904/05-1905/06 b 2.7.1881 Papanui, Christchurch, Canterbury. d 2.8.1915 Wellington. He underwent an operation in Dunedin in 1915, and as his health did not improve he was transferred back to Wellington three months before his death in the hope that the change of climate would prove beneficial. RHB Teams: **Canterbury, Wellington**. Sch: Otago BHS. Occ: Customs clerk.

BARRON James Runcieman 1917/18-1929/30 b 4.9.1900 Dunedin, Otago. d 22.11.1990 Dunedin, Otago. RHB Team: **Otago.** Occ: Warehouseman. NZCA obit: 1991.

BARRY Robert Deey William 1891/92-1904/05 b 7.1.1868 Christchurch, Canterbury. d 3.1.1938 Christchurch, Canterbury. Team: **Canterbury.** Sch: Christchurch Cathedral GS. Occ: Clerk. Umpired first-class cricket. He was known as R.W.Barry senior so as not to be confused with the similarly named though unrelated R.W.Barry junior.

BARRY Robert William 1901/02 b 9.9.1878 Akaroa, Canterbury. d 3.12.1915 at sea, off Gallipoli, Turkey. He died of wounds received. Team: **Canterbury.** Sch: Akaroa. Occ: Clerk. Hockey: Canterbury and Auckland. He was known as R.W.Barry junior so as not to be confused with the similarly named though unrelated R.W.Barry senior. He took part in the landing at Gallipoli and in June 1915 was erroneously reported as killed in action. He recovered from the wounds received at the landing and returned to the firing line, where he was fatally wounded.

BARTLETT Craig Edward 1996/97 b 9.10.1975 Nelson. RHB RFM Team: **Central Districts.** NZ U19 Test; NZ U19 ODI.

BARTLETT Dean Joseph 2009/10 b 10.10.1987 Auckland. RHB RMF Team: **Auckland.** Sch: Sacred Heart Coll. NZ U19 Test.

BARTLETT Gary Alex 1958/59-1969/70 b 3.2.1941 Blenheim, Marlborough. RHB RF Teams: **Central Districts, Canterbury, New Zealand Test.** Sch: Marlborough HS. Occ: Carpenter, hunter. He took a hat-trick for Central Districts v Northern Districts in 1959/60. He holds the Central Districts 10th wicket partnership record of 133 with I.A.Colquhoun against Auckland in 1959/60.

BARTON Alfred Edwin 1904/05 b 1874 Blenheim, Marlborough. d 2.4.1960 Nelson. Team: **Wellington.** Occ: Accountant.

BARTON Hamish Dymock 1995/96-2000/01 b 16.7.1976 Gisborne, Poverty Bay. LHB OB Teams: **Auckland, Canterbury.** Played List A in NZ. Sch: Kings Coll. Occ: NZC employee. NZ U19 Test; NZ U19 ODI. Father: P.H.Barton; uncle: R.H.Barton.

BARTON Paul Thomas 1954/55-1967/68 b 9.10.1935 Wellington. RHB LSM Teams: **Wellington, New Zealand Test.**

BARTON Peter Howard 1962/63-1974/75 b 28.3.1941 Gisborne, Poverty Bay. LHB RM Teams: **Northern Districts, Otago.** Played List A in NZ. Brother: R.H.Barton; son: H.D.Barton.

BARTON Richard Hugh 1957/58 b 21.11.1939 Gisborne, Poverty Bay. RHB RFM Team: **Northern Districts.** Brother: P.H.Barton; nephew: H.D.Barton.

BARTON William Edward 1879/80-1886/87 b Q4 1858 Winchester, Hampshire, England. d 15.9.1942 Christchurch, Canterbury. RHB Team: **Auckland.** Occ: Bank manager. Wisden obit: 1944. In the 1880s he was the finest batsman in New Zealand.

BASSETT-GRAHAM Jonathan Rhys McCowan 2009/10 b 28.11.1989 Auckland. RHB wk Team: **Auckland.** Sch: Kings Coll.

BATEMAN Glenn Charles 1979/80-1984/85 b 30.1.1955 Christchurch, Canterbury. RHB RM Team: **Canterbury.** Played List A in NZ. Sch: Linwood HS. Cousin: S.N.Bateman.

BATEMAN Stephen Noel 1977/78-1984/85 b 6.1.1958 Christchurch, Canterbury. RHB RMF Team: **Canterbury.** Played List A in NZ. Sch: Burnside HS. Occ: Coy director. Cousin: G.C.Bateman.

BATES Albert Edwin 1891/92-1897/98 b 16.5.1867 Christchurch, Canterbury. d 17.8.1950 Christchurch, Canterbury. Team: **Canterbury.** Occ: Furniture manufacturer.

BATES Michael David 2003/04-2009/10 b 11.10.1983 Auckland. RHB LM Team: **Auckland.** Played List A in NZ; Played T20 in NZ. Sch: Kelston BHS. NZ U19 ODI.

BATTERSBY Thomas 1914/15-1918/19 b 1878 unknown. d 16.12.1936 Invercargill, Southland. Team: **Southland.** Occ: Civil servant.

BAYLEY Bryan John 1957/58-1964/65 b 17.4.1933 Greymouth, West Coast. RHB RSM Teams: **Canterbury, Northern Districts.**

BAYLY Alfred 1891/92-1897/98 b 20.5.1866 Waitara, Taranaki. d 14.12.1907 Wanganui. He died from a heart ailment. Team: **Taranaki.** Sch: New Plymouth BHS, Wanganui CS. Occ: Farmer. Rugby: All Blacks and Taranaki; New Zealand selector and NZRFU president. In a rugby game between Taranaki and Otago in 1899, an Otago player, "Barney" Armit attempted to leap over

Bayly's tackle. Armit tripped and suffered a broken neck and died in hospital nine weeks later. It was reported that worry about this accident brought on Bayly's own death. Brothers: F.Bayly, G.T.Bayly, H.Bayly.
BAYLY Frank 1882/83 b 1860 New Plymouth, Taranaki. d 23.11.1948 Silverdale, Auckland. F Team: **Taranaki.** Sch: New Plymouth BHS. Occ: Farmer. Rugby: Taranaki. Brothers: A.Bayly, G.T.Bayly, H.Bayly.
BAYLY George Thomas 1882/83-1897/98 b 17.3.1856 New Plymouth, Taranaki. d 26.6.1938 Auckland. M Team: **Taranaki.** Sch: Wanganui CS. Occ: Farmer. Rugby: Wellington, Wanganui and Taranaki; NZRFU president in 1898. Brothers: A.Bayly, F.Bayly, H.Bayly.
BAYLY Harry 1891/92 b 1862 New Plymouth, Taranaki. d 29.5.1935 Auckland. Team: **Taranaki.** Sch: Parnell GS. Occ: Farmer. Brothers: A.Bayly, F.Bayly, G.T.Bayly.
BEAL Carl Ernest 1906/07-1914/15 b 12.7.1887 Launceston, Tasmania, Australia. d 16.8.1916 Melbourne, Victoria, Australia. He died of consumption aged 29. Teams: **Otago, Canterbury.** Occ: Clerk. Brother: W.M.Beal.
BEAL William Matthew 1909/10 b 17.3.1877 Launceston, Tasmania, Australia. d 3.8.1964 Dunedin, Otago. Team: **Otago.** Occ: Soap Manufacturer. Umpired first-class cricket. Brother: C.E.Beal.
BEALE Arthur Merritt 1893/94-1895/96 b 9.1.1858 New Zealand. d 11.10.1932 Waipiro Bay, East Coast. Team: **Hawke's Bay.** Sch: Christ Coll. Occ: Accountant. Umpired first-class cricket.
BEARD Derek Andrew 1987/88-1990/91 b 10.9.1961 Te Aroha, Thames Valley. RHB RM Team: **Northern Districts.** Played List A in NZ. Sch: Te Aroha Coll. He took a hat-trick for Northern Districts v Central Districts in 1989/90. Father: D.D.Beard.
BEARD Donald Derek 1945/46-1964/65 b 14.1.1920 Palmerston North, Manawatu. d 15.7.1982 Lancaster, Lancashire, England. RHB RM Teams: **Wellington, Central Districts, Northern Districts, New Zealand Test.** Sch: Palmerston North BHS. Occ: School principal. Rugby: Wellington, Wanganui and NZ triallist. Basketball: New Zealand. NZCA obit: 1982; NZCA COY: 1956. Son: D.A.Beard.
BEARD Leonard Alfred Douglas 1927/28 b 27.4.1895 Carterton, Wairarapa. d 21.3.1978 Palmerston North, Manawatu. RFM occ wk Team: **Wellington.** Occ: Civil servant.
BEARD Nicholas Brendan 2008/09-2009/10 b 16.9.1989 Dunedin, Otago. LHB SLA Team: **Otago.** Played List A in NZ; Played T20 in NZ. Sch: Kavanagh Coll. NZ U19 Test; NZ U19 ODI.
BEARD William Samuel 1878/79-1886/87 Teams: **Canterbury, Auckland.** Occ: Cook.
BEARE Simon Peter 2001/02-2004/05 b 2.7.1979 Hamilton, Waikato. RHB RM occ wk Team: **Otago.** Played List A in NZ. Sch: Rosehill Coll. Occ: Cricket pro.
BEATSON Terence George 1970/71-1971/72 b 3.10.1947 Motueka, Tasman. LHB LB Team: **Northern Districts.** Sch: Motukea HS.
BEBAN Mark Albert 1969/70 b 3.2.1940 Greymouth, West Coast. d 4.4.2005 Wellington. He collapsed and died on the 16th fairway of the Wainuiomata golf course in Wellington, aged 65. RHB OB Team: **Wellington.** Sch: St Patricks Coll, Wellington. Occ: Priest. NZCA obit: 2005; Wisden obit: 2006.
BECK Clement Henry 1884/85-1890/91 b 28.9.1863 Dunedin, Otago. d 11.11.1957 Dunedin, Otago. occ wk Team: **Otago.** Occ: Canister maker.
BECK John Edward Francis 1953/54-1961/62 b 1.8.1934 Wellington. d 23.4.2000 Waikanae, Wellington. LHB SLA Teams: **Wellington, New Zealand Test.** Sch: Wellington Coll. NZCA obit: 2000. He was selected for the 1953/54 tour of South Africa without having played FC cricket, made his Test debut in his 7th FC match and scored 99 run-out in his second Test.
BEEBY Victor Spearman 1919/20 b 30.9.1891 Dunedin, Otago. d 7.2.1944 Wellington. Team: **Otago.** Sch: Otago BHS. Occ: Linotype operator.
BEECHEY Ernest Mansfield 1906/07-1918/19 b 15.6.1886 Masterton, Wairarapa. d 23.12.1972 Papakura, Auckland. LHB Team: **Wellington.** Sch: Wellington Coll. NZCA obit: 1973.
BEER Gary Douglas 1962/63-1967/68 b 10.10.1941 Christchurch, Canterbury. RHB RM Teams: **Central Districts, Otago.** Sch: Christchurch West HS.

BEGG Neil Colquhoun 1939/40-1940/41 b 13.4.1915 Dunedin, Otago. d 25.6.1995 Dunedin, Otago. RHB RM Team: **Otago**. Sch: John McLashan Coll. Occ: Paediatrician. Book: The New Zealand child and his family. OBE. NZCA obit: 1995; Wisden obit: 1991. Well known paediatrician, he took a leading part in several important health campaigns, including the fluoridation of water supplies and the eradication of bovine tuberculosis and hydatid disease.

BEHRENT John David 1959/60-1967/68 b 5.7.1938 Auckland. RHB RM Teams: **Wellington, Auckland**.

BELL Arthur George Q 1888/89-1893/94 Team: **Otago**. Occ: Lawyer.

BELL F 1886/87 Team: **Hawke's Bay**. Sch: Napier BHS.

BELL Francis Henry Dillon (Sir) 1873/74-1876/77 b 31.3.1851 Nelson. d 13.3.1936 Lowry Bay, Eastbourne, Lower Hutt, Wellington. Team: **Wellington**. Sch: Otago BHS, Auckland GS. Occ: Lawyer. Book: Sir Francis Bell: his life and times. He was knighted in 1924. New Zealand's Prime Minister for 16 days from 10 May 1925 to 26 May 1925 after the death of the incumbent Prime Minister, William Massey. Wisden obit: 1937. President of the Wellington CA, and became a life member of the New Zealand Cricket Council, of which he was an early president.

BELL Matthew David 1993/94-2009/10 b 25.2.1977 Dunedin, Otago. RHB OB occ wk Teams: **Northern Districts, Wellington, New Zealand Test, New Zealand ODI.** Played List A in NZ; Played T20 in NZ. Sch: Whangarei HS. Occ: Cricket pro. NZ U19 Test; NZ U19 ODI. He holds the Northern Districts 1st wicket partnership record of 167 with M.E.Parlane against Central Districts in 1994/95; the Wellington 2nd wicket partnership record of 287 with J.D.Wells against Auckland in 1997/98 and the NZ domestic T20 8th wicket partnership record of 68* with L.J.Woodcock for Wellington v Auckland in 2008/09. He scored 303* for Northern Districts Under-20s in 1994/95.

BELL Reginald Clive 1914/15-1920/21 b 11.12.1894 Burnie, Tasmania, Australia. d 19.11.1960 Taieri Mouth, Otago. He drowned whilst on a fishing expedition on the Taieri River. Team: **Otago**. Occ: Clerk. Rugby: All Blacks and Otago.

BELL William 1949/50-1958/59 b 5.9.1931 Dunedin, Otago. d 23.7.2002 Auckland. RHB LB Teams: **Canterbury, Auckland, New Zealand Test.** Sch: Christchurch BHS. Occ: Farmer. NZCA obit: 2002; Wisden obit: 2003.

BELLAMY Francis William James 1931/32-1945/46 b 31.12.1909 Spreydon, Christchurch, Canterbury. d 19.6.1969 Invercargill, Southland. LHB SLC Teams: **Canterbury, Otago**. Occ: Publican. NZCA obit: 1969.

BELLARS Robert George 1873/74 b 5.2.1848 Calcutta (now Kolkata), Bengal, India. wk Team: **Auckland**. Occ: Farmer.

BELSHAM Selwyn Eric 1953/54-1958/59 b 26.9.1930 Auckland. RHB wk Team: **Auckland**. Occ: Real estate agent. Rugby League: New Zealand and Auckland.

BENBOW Charles Albert 1891/92-1896/97 b Q4 1870 Solihull, Warwickshire, England. d 29.3.1912 New Plymouth, Taranaki. Team: **Wellington**. Sch: Wellington Coll. Occ: Insurance agent.

BENNETT Andrew Percy 1885/86-1886/87 b 30.7.1866 Fulbourn, Cambridgeshire, England. d 3.11.1943 Hove, Sussex, England. F Team: **Nelson**. Occ: Schoolmaster; Diplomat; Counsel Gen. CMG. He played cricket for Nelson whilst a master at Nelson College. He then became a career diplomat becoming Counsel General to USA 1897-1899, Acting Counsel General to Zurich 1899-1918, Minister to Panama 1919-1923, Minister to Costa Rica 1920-1923. James Joyce named the character Sgt Bennett in his book *Ulysses* after him.

BENNETT Arthur Cochrane 1892/93-1896/97 b 22.5.1860 Edgbaston, Birmingham, Warwickshire, England. d 9.10.1932 Napier, Hawke's Bay. wk Team: **Hawke's Bay**. Sch: Rugby, England. Occ: Sheep farmer.

BENNETT Dion Rodger Turoa 1996/97 b 1.8.1974 Thames, Thames Valley. RHB RM Team: **Northern Districts**.

BENNETT Ernest Arthur 1913/14-1917/18 b 1884 Wellington. d 9.11.1918 Wellington. He died from Spanish flu. LM Team: **Wellington**. Sch: Petone Coll. Occ: Clerk.

BENNETT Hamish Kyle 2005/06-2009/10 b 22.2.1987 Timaru, South Canterbury. LHB RMF Team: **Canterbury**. Played List A in NZ; Played T20 in NZ. Sch: Timaru Boys HS; St Andrews Coll. NZ U19 ODI.

BENNETT Joseph Henry 1898/99-1919/20 b 28.2.1881 Christchurch, Canterbury. d 29.8.1947 Christchurch, Canterbury. RHB RM Team: **Canterbury, New Zealand.** Sch: West Christchurch BHS. Occ: Labourer. Wisden obit: 1949. He played for New Zealand prior to being granted Test status. He took a hat-trick for Canterbury v Wellington in 1911/12.
BENNETT Joseph Henry 1863/64 b 1835 unknown. d 28.1.1879 Christchurch, Canterbury. Team: **Canterbury.** Occ: Hotel licencee. Umpired first-class cricket.
BENNETT Neville 1950/51-1951/52 b 1.7.1928 Christchurch, Canterbury. RHB LM Team: **Canterbury.**
BENNETT Richard David 1975/76 b 1954 unknown. LFM Team: **Auckland.**
BENT W 1867/68 Team: **Canterbury.**
BERENDSEN Carl August (Sir) 1911/12 b 16.8.1890 Sydney, New South Wales, Australia. d 12.9.1973 Dunedin, Otago. wk Team: **Wellington.** Sch: Gore HS. Occ: Civil servant. Book: Mr Ambassador: Memoirs of Sir Carl Berendsen by H.Templeton. KCMG. NZCA obit: 1973. He was a New Zealand civil servant and diplomat. He was Secretary for External Affairs 1928-32, Head of the Prime Minister's Department 1932-43, and Secretary of the War Cabinet 1939-43. He attended all Imperial Conferences 1926-43, and assemblies of the League of Nations and later the United Nations. He served as the country's first High Commissioner to Australia, from 1943 until 1944. He was then transferred to Washington, D.C., where he served as Minister to the United States from 1944 to 1952.
BERESFORD Charles Henry 1882/83 b 1846 unknown. d 19.1.1906 Mangamuka, Auckland. He died whilst playing cricket: an obituary stated 'that his death should have been on the cricket field shows that his interest in the game never flagged'. RM Team: **Taranaki.** Occ: Storekeeper.
BERNAU Ernest Henry Lovell 1914/15-1927/28 b 6.4.1896 Napier, Hawke's Bay. d 7.1.1966 Wanganui. LHB LM Teams: **Hawke's Bay, Wellington, New Zealand.** Sch: Wanganui CS. Occ: Bursar. NZCA obit: 1966; Wisden obit: 1967. He played for New Zealand prior to being granted Test status.
BERRY Arthur Ernest 1955/56 b 18.9.1928 Dunedin, Otago. RHB RM Team: **Otago.** Book: Bill Bernau and the NZ cricket tour of England 1927 by Mike Batty.
BETTS Francis Matthew 1873/74 b 11.1.1844 Riverstone, New South Wales, Australia. d 15.9.1893 North Waimakariri, Canterbury. He had been missing for a few months when his body was found and it appeared he died in strange circumstances. His body was about three or four hundred yards below the Waimakarai bridge with his hands and feet tied by a small rope. A coronial jury returned an open verdict. LHB Team: **Wellington.** Sch: Kings, Parramatta, Australia. Occ: Lawyer.
BETTS John Alick 1908/09 b 3.4.1886 Wrentham, Suffolk, England. d 14.11.1959 Masterton, Wairarapa. RHB occ wk Team: **Hawke's Bay.** Sch: Framlington Coll, England. Occ: Stock agent.
BEUTH Donald 1968/69 b 6.6.1941 Gisborne, Poverty Bay. RHB RMF Team: **Central Districts.** Sch: Gisborne BHS. Brother: J.A.Beuth.
BEUTH John Anthony 1962/63-1969/70 b 27.6.1945 Gisborne, Poverty Bay. RHB RMF Team: **Northern Districts.** Sch: Gisborne BHS. Occ: Manager. Brother: D.Beuth.
BEVERIDGE Percy 1918/19 b 1875 Glebe, Sydney, New South Wales, Australia. d 31.7.1947 Coromandel, Coromandel Peninsula. Team: **Auckland.** Occ: Bank clerk.
BEYELER Fred 1985/86-1989/90 b 5.11.1965 Wellington. RHB RFM Team: **Wellington.** Played List A in NZ. Sch: Rongatai Coll. NZ U19 Test.
BEZZANT Ernest Frederic 1942/43-1943/44 b 1917 unknown. d 1.10.2002 Brisbane, Queensland, Australia. Team: **Wellington.**
BHUPINDER SINGH 2009/10 b 31.10.1986 Kurputala, Punjab, India. RHB OB Team: **Auckland.** Played List A in NZ; Played T20 in NZ. Sch: Papatoetoe HS.
BIGG-WITHER Alfred 1886/87-1887/88 b 1866 Nelson. d 11.8.1937 Nelson. wk Team: **Nelson.** Sch: Nelson Coll. Occ: Farmer. Brother: J.Bigg-Wither.
BIGG-WITHER James 1885/86-1886/87 b 1867 Nelson. d 9.10.1937 Hanmer Springs, North Canterbury. Team: **Nelson.** Sch: Nelson Coll. Occ: Solicitor; Farmer. Brother: A.Bigg-Wither.

BILBY Grahame Paul 1962/63-1976/77 b 7.5.1941 Wellington. RHB Teams: **Wellington, New Zealand Test.** Played List A in NZ. Sch: Rongatai Coll. Soccer: New Zealand. NZCA COY: 1974. Wellington selector. He scored 132 on FC debut for Wellington v Central Districts in 1962/63.
BILLCLIFF Ian Shaw 1990/91-2008 b 26.10.1972 William's Lake, British Columbia, Canada. RHB RM Teams: **Otago, Wellington, Auckland,** Canada ODI, Canada T20. Played List A in NZ. Sch: Otago BHS. Occ: Schoolteacher. NZ U19 ODI. Brother: M.R.Billcliff.
BILLCLIFF Mark Robert 1998/99 b 21.4.1977 Dunedin, Otago. RHB RFM Team: **Otago.** Played List A in NZ. Sch: Otago BHS. Brother: I.S.Billcliff.
BINNIE Nesbit Douglas 1921/22 b 1891 New Zealand. d 1969 Wellington. Team: **Wellington.** Occ: Shipping manager.
BIRCH Arthur Edwin 1909/10-1910/11 b 23.1.1888 Wellington. d 16.6.1976 Wellington. Team: **Wellington.** Sch: Wellington Coll. Occ: Importer. Brother-in-law: G.Howe.
BIRD William Gavin 1942/43 b 2.3.1916 unknown. d 31.5.1985 Hamilton, Waikato. S Team: **New Zealand Air Force.** Occ: Comm traveller.
BISHOP Harold Arthur 1903/04-1914/15 b 28.12.1883 Wellington. d 6.7.1963 Christchurch, Canterbury. Teams: **Hawke's Bay, Canterbury.** Occ: Farmer; evangelist. Brother: R.E.Bishop.
BISHOP Robert Ernest 1914/15-1920/21 b 16.4.1892 Wellington. d 6.5.1969 Waipawa, Hawke's Bay. RHB Team: **Hawke's Bay.** Occ: Clerk. Brother: H.A.Bishop.
BISHOP W 1874/75 Team: **Wellington.**
BLACK James 1895/96 b 18.9.1873 Dunedin, Otago. d 6.5.1920 Auckland. Team: **Otago.** Sch: Otago BHS. Occ: Accountant.
BLACKBOURN Peter Michael 1983/84 b 4.4.1957 Inglewood, Taranaki. RHB wk Team: **Central Districts.**
BLACKLOCK Arthur 1884/85-1895/96 b 1868 South Yarra, Melbourne, Victoria, Australia. d 20.10.1934 Wellington. Team: **Wellington.** Occ: Warehouseman. Wisden obit: 1935. Brothers: J.W.Blacklock, R.V.Blacklock; nephews: C.P.Blacklock, J.P.Blacklock.
BLACKLOCK Carne Pearson 1905/06 b 30.1.1884 Wellington. d 30.1.1924 Wellington. He died aged 40. RHB wk Team: **Wellington.** Sch: Wellington Coll. Occ: Coy director. Wisden obit: 1925. Brother J.P.Blacklock; father: J.W.Blacklock; uncles: A.Blacklock, R.V.Blacklock.
BLACKLOCK James Pearson 1904/05-1913/14 b 17.2.1883 Wellington. d 22.1.1935 Westport, West Coast. RHB Team: **Wellington, New Zealand.** Rugby: Wellington. Wisden obit: 1936. He played for New Zealand prior to being granted Test status. Brother: C.P.Blacklock; father: J.W.Blacklock; uncles: A.Blacklock, R.V.Blacklock.
BLACKLOCK James William 1877/78-1883/84 b 31.7.1855 Melbourne, Victoria, Australia. d 21.4.1907 Thorndon, Wellington. Team: **Wellington.** Occ: Accountant. Brothers: A.Blacklock, R.V.Blacklock; sons: C.P.Blacklock, J.P.Blacklock.
BLACKLOCK Robert Valder 1883/84-1895/96 b 1.4.1865 Melbourne, Victoria, Australia. d 6.10.1897 Wellington. He died aged 32. RHB Teams: **Wellington, New Zealand.** Occ: Clerk. Rugby: Wellington. He played for New Zealand prior to being granted Test status. Brothers: A.Blacklock, J.W.Blacklock; nephews: C.P.Blacklock, J.P.Blacklock.
BLACKMORE Ian Alfred 1964/65 b 13.10.1941 Nelson. RHB wk Team: **NZ Under-23s.**
BLACKMORE John Harold 1968/69-1972/73 b 1.1.1948 Hastings, Hawke's Bay. RHB RM Team: **Northern Districts.** Played List A in NZ. Son: S.J.Blackmore.
BLACKMORE Selwyn John 1991/92-2001/02 b 7.9.1972 Whangarei, Northland. RHB RM Team: **Wellington.** NZ U19 Test; NZ U19 ODI. Father: J.H.Blackmore.
BLAIN Tony Elston 1982/83-1994/95 b 17.2.1962 Nelson. RHB LB wk Teams: **Central Districts, Canterbury, New Zealand Test, New Zealand ODI.** Played List A in NZ. Sch: Nelson Coll. Book: Tony Blain testimonial magazine.
BLAIR Bruce Robert 1977/78-1989/90 b 27.12.1957 Dunedin, Otago. LHB RM Teams: **Otago, Northern Districts, New Zealand ODI.** Played List A in NZ. Sch: Otago BHS. ND and CD selector. Brother: W.L.Blair; father: R.A.J.Blair; great-uncle: J.R.Blair.
BLAIR James Robert 1926/27 b 9.11.1900 Mathinna, Tasmania, Australia. d 9.10.1961 Karitane, Otago. RHB OB Team: **Otago.** Occ: Labourer. Great-nephews: B.R.Blair, W.L.Blair; nephew: R.A.J.Blair.

BLAIR Robert 1882/83-1883/84 b 1858 Melbourne, Victoria, Australia. d 31.1.1912 Auckland. occ wk Team: **Auckland.** Occ: Timber merchant. Umpired first-class cricket.

BLAIR Robert William 1951/52-1964/65 b 23.6.1932 Petone, Lower Hutt, Wellington. RHB RFM Teams: **Wellington, Central Districts, New Zealand Test.** Occ: Linotype operator. Book: From Petone to Pretoria. NZCA COY: 1955. He took a hat-trick for Wellington v Northern Districts in 1962/63; took 9/72 for Wellington v Auckland in 1956/57 and 9/75 for Wellington v Canterbury also in 1956/57.

BLAIR Roy Alexander James 1953/54 b 13.6.1921 Dunedin, Otago. d 31.5.2002 Dunedin, Otago. LHB OB Team: **Otago.** Occ: Schoolteacher. Roller skating: 1938 Empire Games. NZCA obit: 2002. Otago selector. Sons: B.R.Blair, W.L.Blair; uncle: J.R.Blair.

BLAIR Wayne Leslie 1967/68-1990/91 b 11.5.1948 Dunedin, Otago. LHB LB occ wk Team: **Otago.** Played List A in NZ. Sch: Otago BHS. Brother: B.R.Blair; father: R.A.J.Blair; great-uncle: J.R.Blair.

BLAIR William Alexander 1920/21 b 14.8.1896 Auckland. d 29.3.1978 Gisborne, Poverty Bay. Team: **Minor Assoc.** Occ: Maybridge clerk.

BLAKE David Charles 1992/93-1998/99 b 23.4.1971 Auckland. RHB LM Teams: **Northern Districts, Central Districts.** Played List A in NZ.

BLAKE Trevor William 1964/65 b 13.3.1937 Whangarei, Northland. d 23.8.2004 Whangarei, Northland. He died from cancer. RHB Team: **Northern Districts.** Sch: Whangarei HS. Hockey: New Zealand, coach and life member of NZ Hockey. NZCA obit: 2005.

BLAKELY Douglas James 1940/41-1950/51 b 1.2.1922 Naseby, Central Otago. d 22.7.1994 Christchurch, Canterbury. RHB Team: **Otago.** NZCA Obit: 1995; Wisden obit: 1995. Brother: J.W.Blakely.

BLAKELY Geoffrey Allan Wilfred 1980/81-1984/85 b 30.10.1959 Ranfurly, Central Otago. LHB Team: **Otago.** Played List A in NZ. Sch: Otago BHS.

BLAKELY John Wilson 1940/41-1946/47 b 23.5.1914 Naseby, Central Otago. d 27.7.1985 Dunedin, Otago. LHB SLA Team: **Otago.** Occ: Sheep farmer. Brother: D.J.Blakely.

BLAMIRES Ernest Oswald 1911/12-1926/27 b 11.6.1881 Warrnambool, Victoria, Australia. d 6.6.1963 Auckland. RHB S occ wk Teams: **Wellington, Otago, New Zealand.** Sch: Wesley Coll, Melbourne, Australia. Occ: Methodist minister. Book: A Christian Core for New Zealand Education. NZCA obit: 1963; Wisden obit: 1964. His daughter was the actress Dame Pat Evison. He played for New Zealand prior to being granted Test status. Brother: H.L.Blamires.

BLAMIRES Henry Lawrence 1911/12-1913/14 b 17.4.1871 Bendigo, Victoria, Australia. d 18.8.1965 Auckland. RHB Team: **Hawke's Bay.** Sch: Wesley Coll, Melbourne, Australia. Occ: Methodist minister. Umpired first-class cricket. Brother: E.O.Blamires.

BLANDFORD John Arthur Rawdon 1932/33-1940/41 b 31.1.1913 Dunedin, Otago. d 24.12.1954 Auckland. He committed suicide by jumping out of an apartment window. RHB wk Teams: **Wellington, Auckland, New Zealand.** Sch: Melbourne CEGS, Australia. Occ: Clerk. NZCA obit: 1955; Wisden obit: 1956. He played for New Zealand in a FC match.

BLANE James Patrick 1949/50 b 21.9.1922 Auckland. d 12.7.1962 Gisborne, Poverty Bay. RHB RM Team: **Auckland.** Occ: Insurance officer.

BLINKO Roland George 1913/14 b 1.5.1886 Birmingham, Warwickshire, England. d 6.1.1917 Walton-on-Thames, Surrey, England. He died of illness aged 30. LHB Team: **Hawke's Bay.** Occ: Cabinetmaker.

BLOOMFIELD Peter James 1957/58-1958/59 b 30.6.1936 Motueka, Tasman. RHB RFM Team: **Central Districts.**

BLOXHAM Andrew Roby 1864/65 b 3.5.1839 Twycross, Warwickshire, England. d 29.7.1923 Christchurch, Canterbury. Team: **Canterbury.** Sch: Charterhouse, England. Occ: Supreme court registrar.

BLUNDELL Edward Denis 1927-1937/38 b 29.5.1907 Wellington. d 24.9.1984 Townsville, Queensland, Australia. LHB RFM Teams: **Wellington, New Zealand,** Cambridge University. Sch: Waitaki BHS. Occ: Lawyer; diplomat; Gov-Gen. GMCG, GCVO, KBE, OBE, QSO, K.St.John. NZCA obit: 1984. He was called to the bar in England in 1929, returned to New Zealand as a barrister of the Supreme Court before becoming, in 1968, his country's High Commissioner in London and Governor-General from 1972 to 1977. President of the New Zealand Cricket Board. He played for New Zealand in a FC match.

BLUNT Roger Charles 1917/18-1935 b 3.11.1900 Durham, England. d 22.6.1966 Westminster, London, England. RHB LB Teams: **Canterbury, Otago, New Zealand Test.** Sch: Christ Coll. Occ: Coy secretary. MBE. NZCA obit: 1966; Wisden obit: 1967. WCOY: 1928. He holds the NZ 10th wicket partnership record of 184 with W.Hawkesworth for Otago v Canterbury in 1931/32 - he hit 338 not out, then the highest score ever achieved by a New Zealand cricketer.

BOAM Harry Kenneth Perrott 2008/09-2009/10 b 15.10.1990 Birmingham, Warwickshire, England. RHB RM Team: **Wellington.** Played List A in NZ; Played T20 in NZ. Sch: Wellington Coll. Occ: Cricket pro. NZ U19 Test; NZ U19 ODI.

BOARD John Henry 1891-1914/15 b 23.2.1867 Clifton, Bristol, England. d 15.4.1924 at sea, on board SS Kenilworth Castle en route from South Africa to England. He died from heart failure while journeying home from his annual coaching engagement. RHB wk Teams: **Hawke's Bay, England Test,** Gloucestershire, London County. Occ: Cricket pro. Wisden obit: 1925. An English pro, played and coached in NZ.

BODDINGTON Edward Robert 1880/81-1887/88 b 29.4.1862 Wakefield, Nelson. d 9.3.1897 Perth, Western Australia, Australia. He died aged 35 years of a heart ailment. Teams: **Nelson, Wellington.** Sch: Nelson Coll. Occ: Bank clerk. Brother: H.A.Boddington.

BODDINGTON Henry Albert 1880/81-1895/96 b 15.6.1863 Kaiapoi, Canterbury. d 21.4.1938 Christchurch, Canterbury. Teams: **Nelson, Otago.** Sch: Nelson Coll. Occ: Bank manager. Brother: E.R.Boddington.

BODLE Bruce Edward 1958/59 b 30.4.1935 Papatoetoe, Auckland. d 28.6.2008 Auckland. RHB RM Team: **Auckland.** Sch: Otahuhu Coll.

BOGUE Thomas Patrick 1919/20-1920/21 b 5.12.1893 Wyndham, Southland. d 27.9.1965 Invercargill, Southland. wk Team: **Southland.** Occ: Clerk.

BOLD Edgar Harold 1919/20 b 7.10.1899 Wellington. d 9.7.1965 Auckland. Team: **Wellington.**

BOLTON Bruce Alfred 1955/56-1970/71 b 31.5.1935 Christchurch, Canterbury. RHB LB Teams: **Canterbury, Wellington, New Zealand Test.** Sch: Christchurch BHS. Occ: Admin officer.

BOLTON Samuel Frederick 1888/89 b 6.8.1858 Nelson. d 11.10.1936 Nelson. Team: **Nelson.** Occ: Butcher.

BOND K 1876/77 Team: **Wellington.**

BOND Shane Edward 1996/97-2009/10 b 7.6.1975 Christchurch, Canterbury. RHB RF Teams: **Canterbury, New Zealand Test, New Zealand ODI, New Zealand T20,** Warwickshire, Hampshire. Played List A in NZ; Played T20 in NZ. Sch: Papanui HS. Occ: Cricket pro. NZ U19 Test. NZCA COY: 2002, 2006, 2007. He took a hat-trick in a ODI for New Zealand v Australia in 2006/07; he also has the best New Zealand ODI bowling figures of 6/19 v India in 2005/06.

BOOCK Stephen Lewis 1973/74-1989/90 b 20.9.1951 Dunedin, Otago. RHB SLA Teams: **Otago, Canterbury, New Zealand Test, New Zealand ODI.** Played List A in NZ. Sch: St Pauls HS, Dunedin. Occ: Supermarket owner. Book: Boocky: cricket's a funny game. NZCA COY: 1978. He had match figures of 15/104 for Otago v Auckland in 1989/90.

BOOKER Jack Francis 1947/48 b 4.6.1915 Christchurch, Canterbury. d 17.4.2003 Waikanae, Wellington. RHB RM Team: **Canterbury.** Sch: Christchurch BHS. Occ: Branch manager. NZCA obit: 2007.

BOON Malcolm Kittson 1922/23-1927/28 b 22.7.1902 Christchurch, Canterbury. d 12.7.1988 Christchurch, Canterbury. RHB wk Teams: **Canterbury, New Zealand.** Sch: West Christchurch BHS. Lawn Bowls: New Zealand in the 1962 Commonwealth Games in Perth. NZCA obit: 1988; Wisden obit: 1989. He played for New Zealand in a FC match.

BOOTH Rex Hall 1917/18 b 9.7.1893 Christchurch, Canterbury. d 25.4.1967 Christchurch, Canterbury. Team: **Canterbury.** Sch: Christchurch BHS. Occ: Draftsman.

BOOTH Robertson Stewart 1881/82 b 1858 Livirno, Tuscany, Italy. d 8.2.1935 Nelson. Team: **Nelson.** Occ: Bank manager.

BOPARA Ravinder Singh 2002-2010 b 4.5.1985 Forest Gate, London, England. RHB RM Teams: **Auckland, England Test, England ODI, England T20,** Essex. Played List A in NZ; Played T20 in NZ. Sch: Brampton Manor, England. Occ: Cricket pro. An English pro, played and coached in NZ.

BORTON Joseph Barnes 1864/65-1865/66 b 1832 Warwickshire, England. d 24.2.1924 Dunedin, Otago. LM Team: **Otago.** Occ: Settler.

BOTTING Graham Stuart 1948/49-1953/54 b 27.6.1915 Dunedin, Otago. d 8.3.2007 Turangi, Waikato. RHB wk Teams: **Central Districts, Otago.** Sch: Otago BHS. Occ: Schoolteacher. Hockey: New Zealand. NZCA obit: 2007.

BOTTOMLEY George Robinson 1889/90 b 5.3.1846 Skelton, Yorkshire, England. Team: **Otago.** Occ: Gatekeeper.

BOTTRELL Frederick Alexander Andrew John Watsford 1912/13 b 19.3.1881 Millicent, South Australia, Australia. d 16.9.1935 Mangere, Auckland. Team: **Hawke's Bay.** Sch: Blenheim HS. Occ: Bank accountant.

BOUCH A 1876/77 Team: **Otago.** Arrived in New Zealand on 1.1.1876 and departed on 17.2.1877 but nothing else is known of him.

BOULNOIS Walter William 1912/13 b 1.7.1887 Timaru, South Canterbury. d 28.11.1960 Christchurch, Canterbury. Team: **Hawke's Bay.** Sch: Christ Coll. Occ: Hospital orderly.

BOULT Jonathan James 2008/09-2009/10 b 29.11.1985 Rotorua, Bay of Plenty. LHB OB Team: **Northern Districts.** Sch: Otumoetai Coll. Occ: Cricket pro. Brother: T.A.Boult.

BOULT Trent Alexander 2008/09-2009/10 b 22.7.1989 Rotorua, Bay of Plenty. RHB LMF Team: **Northern Districts.** Played List A in NZ; Played T20 in NZ. Sch: Otumoetai Coll. Occ: Cricket pro. NZ U19 Test; NZ U19 ODI. Brother: J.J.Boult.

BOWDEN Charles Stuart 1883/84 b 6.11.1860 Portsmouth, Hampshire, England. d 3.9.1909 Riccarton, Christchurch, Canterbury. Team: **Auckland.** Sch: Fettes, Scotland. Occ: Reverend Anglican.

BOWDEN Dewayne Jamie 2005/06-2009/10 b 27.2.1982 Wellington. LHB LFM Team: **Wellington.** Played List A in NZ; Played T20 in NZ. Sch: Wellington Coll. Occ: Cricket pro.

BOWDEN Douglas William 1950/51-1957/58 b 19.7.1927 Palmerston North, Manawatu. LHB Team: **Central Districts.** Sch: Palmerston North BHS.

BOWLES Frederick 1911/12 b Q3 1875 Maidstone, Kent, England. d 20.3.1956 Christchurch, Canterbury. Team: **Wellington.** Sch: Wellington Coll. Occ: Postal worker.

BOWLEY Edward Henry 1912-1934 b 6.6.1890 Leatherhead, Surrey, England. d 9.7.1974 Winchester, Hampshire, England. RHB LB Teams: **Auckland,** England Test, Sussex. Occ: Cricket pro. NZCA obit: 1975; Wisden obit: 1975. WCOY: 1930. An English pro, played and coached in NZ.

BOXSHALL Charles 1897/98-1914/15 b 7.7.1862 Brighton, Victoria, Australia. d 13.11.1924 Balmain, Sydney, New South Wales, Australia. RHB wk Team: **Canterbury, New Zealand.** Occ: Carpenter. Wisden obit: 1926. He was the oldest New Zealander to play first-class cricket, when aged 52 years and 189 days. He played for New Zealand prior to being granted Test status.

BOYER Timothy Andrew 1997/98-1999/00 b 11.8.1971 Wellington. RHB OB Team: **Wellington.** Played List A in NZ.

BOYLE David John 1980/81-1994/95 b 14.2.1961 Christchurch, Canterbury. RHB OB Team: **Canterbury.** Played List A in NZ. Sch: St Thomas Coll. Occ: Coy director. Brother: J.G.Boyle.

BOYLE Justin Gregory 1982/83-1990/91 b 13.4.1959 Christchurch, Canterbury. RHB LB Teams: **Wellington, Canterbury.** Played List A in NZ. Sch: St Thomas Coll. Occ: School teacher; Rector of St Bedes. Brother: D.J.Boyle.

BOYLE Tony John 1986/87 b 19.7.1957 Lower Hutt, Wellington. RHB RM Team: **Northern Districts.** Occ: Real estate agent.

BRACEWELL Brendon Paul 1977/78-1989/90 b 14.9.1959 Auckland. RHB RM Teams: **Central Districts, Otago, Northern Districts, New Zealand Test, New Zealand ODI.** Played List A in NZ. Sch: Tauranga BC. Rugby: Western Australia. Brothers: J.G.Bracewell, D.W.Bracewell, M.A.Bracewell; son: D.A.J.Bracewell.

BRACEWELL Douglas Andrew John 2008/09-2009/10 b 28.9.1990 Tauranga, Bay of Plenty. RHB RM Team: **Central Districts.** Played List A in NZ. Sch: Rathkeale Coll. NZ U19 Test; NZ U19 ODI. Father: B.P.Bracewell; uncles: J.G.Bracewell, D.W.Bracewell, M.A.Bracewell.

BRACEWELL Douglas William 1974/75-1979/80 b 20.1.1953 Auckland. RHB OB Teams: **Canterbury, Central Districts.** Played List A in NZ. Sch: Tauranga BC. Rugby: Wairarapara-Bush. Brothers: B.P.Bracewell, J.G.Bracewell, M.A.Bracewell; nephew: D.A.J.Bracewell.

BRACEWELL John Garry 1978/79-1990 b 15.4.1958 Auckland. RHB OB Teams: **Otago, Auckland, New Zealand Test, New Zealand ODI.** Played List A in NZ. Sch: Tauranga BC. Occ: Cricket coach. NZ selector and coach. Brothers: B.P.Bracewell, J.G.Bracewell, M.A.Bracewell; nephew: D.A.J.Bracewell.

BRACEWELL Mark Andrew 1977/78 b 8.10.1955 Auckland. RHB RM Teams: **Otago, Central Districts (not FC).** Played List A in NZ. Sch: Tauranga BC. Rugby: Wairarapara-Bush and Wellington. Otago selector. Brothers: B.P.Bracewell, J.G.Bracewell, D.W.Bracewell; nephew: D.A.J.Bracewell

BRADBURN Grant Eric 1985/86-2001/02 b 26.5.1966 Hamilton, Waikato. RHB OB Teams: **Northern Districts, New Zealand Test, New Zealand ODI.** Played List A in NZ. NZ U19 Test; NZ U19 ODI. Book: Grant Bradburn testimonial brochure. ND selector and coach. He holds the Northern Districts 4th wicket partnership record of 259 with M.E.Parlane against Canterbury in 1996/97. Father: W.P.Bradburn.

BRADBURN James Chalwyn 1919/20-1920/21 b 13.8.1890 unknown. d 25.1.1972 Wellington. RHB OB Team: **Hawke's Bay.** Occ: Civil servant.

BRADBURN Wynne Pennell 1957/58-1968/69 b 24.11.1938 Thames, Thames Valley. d 25.9.2008 Hamilton, Waikato. He died of a heart attack. RHB OB Teams: **Northern Districts, New Zealand Test.** NZCA obit: 2009; Wisden obit: 2009. Son: G.E.Bradburn.

BRADLEY Aaron John 1993/94-1994/95 b 3.11.1974 Whangarei, Northland. RHB OB Team: **Northern Districts.** Played List A in NZ. Sch: Whangarei HS. Occ: Mechanic. NZ U19 ODI.

BRADLEY Mark James 1987/88 b 27.10.1966 Auckland. RHB Team: **Auckland.** Played List A in NZ.

BRADLEY Martin John 1985/86-1987/88 b 27.5.1964 Auckland. RHB OB Team: **Auckland.** Played List A in NZ.

BRADLEY Roger Robert Andrew Francis 1990/91 b 30.11.1962 Wellington. RHB Team: **Northern Districts.** Occ: Sports dealer.

BRADY Dennis John 1970/71-1971/72 b 28.6.1951 Auckland. RHB Team: **Otago.** Sch: Kings HS.

BRAITHWAITE Robert 1885/86 b 1845 London, England. d 14.6.1933 Hastings, Hawke's Bay. RFu Team: **Hawke's Bay.** Occ: Civil servant.

BRAY John Harrison 1958/59-1966/67 b 18.1.1938 Wellington. RHB RM Team: **Wellington.**

BRAY William Thomas 1914/15-1920/21 b 1879 Avoca, Victoria, Australia. d 1960 Melbourne, Victoria, Australia. occ wk Team: **Wellington.** Occ: Warehouseman.

BRAZENDALE Richard Paul 1983/84 b 15.10.1960 Whangarei, Northland. RHB SLA Team: **Auckland.** Sch: Mt Albert GS.

BREEN Lindsay Charles 1993/94-1994/95 b 16.7.1971 Alexandra, Central Otago. RHB Team: **Otago.** Played List A in NZ. Sch: Southland BHS. Occ: Human resources consultant.

BREMNER Maxwell Crawford 1987/88 b 20.4.1963 Dunedin, Otago. RHB Team: **Canterbury.** Played List A in NZ. Sch: Christ Coll. Occ: Licensed bar owner.

BRENNAN Ian Nesbit 1958/59 b 17.7.1930 Petone, Lower Hutt, Wellington. LHB Team: **Wellington.**

BRIAN Donald Eric 1946/47-1955/56 b 25.10.1925 Petone, Lower Hutt, Wellington. RHB RFM Teams: **Wellington, Central Districts.**

BRIASCO Peter Scott 1982/83-1991/92 b 14.10.1958 Napier, Hawke's Bay. RHB RM Team: **Central Districts.** Played List A in NZ. Sch: Waimea Coll. Occ: Schoolteacher. Book: The Briasco File - testimonial brochure. CD selector and coach. He holds the NZ 2nd wicket partnership record of 317 with R.T.Hart for Central Districts v Canterbury in 1983/84 and the Central Districts 4th wicket partnership record of 276* with M.D.Crowe against Canterbury in 1986/87.

BRICE Alfred William Stanley 1902/03-1927/28 b 14.11.1880 South Rakaia, Canterbury. d 5.5.1959 Maraekakaho, Hawke's Bay. RHB RM Teams: **Wellington, New Zealand.** Rugby: Wellington. NZCA obit: 1959; Wisden obit: 1960. NZ and Wellington selector. He played for New Zealand prior to being granted Test status. He took 9/67 for Wellington v Auckland in 1918/19 and holds the Wellington 10th wicket partnership record of 138 with K.C.James against Otago in 1926/27.

BRIDGMAN Wallace Barkley 1954/55 b 2.4.1931 Invercargill, Southland. d 1996 Hautapu, Waikato. LHB OB Team: **Canterbury.** Sch: Southland BHS. Occ: Industrial chemist.

BRIGGS Kevin David 1959/60 b 27.1.1939 Dunedin, Otago. d 9.4.2004 Hororata, Otago. RHB Team: **Otago.** Occ: Secretary and manager of golf club. NZCA obit: 2004.
BRINSLEY William Richard 1917/18 b 9.3.1887 Dunedin, Otago. d 21.1.1959 Dunedin, Otago. Team: **Otago.** Sch: Otago BHS. Occ: Coy director. President Otago CA.
BRITTON Alan Edward Law 1945/46-1952/53 b 3.12.1922 Christchurch, Canterbury. RHB wk Team: **Canterbury.** Sch: Christchurch BHS. Occ: Headmaster.
BROAD Charles Harrington 1888/89-1899/00 b 5.10.1872 Nelson. d 7.9.1959 Nelson. RHB Teams: **Nelson, Otago.** Sch: Nelson Coll. Occ: Headmaster. NZCA obit: 1960. Brother: E.W.Broad.
BROAD Charles Lionel 1966/67 b 1.12.1945 Epsom, Surrey, England. RHB OB Team: **Canterbury.** Sch: Buller HS. Occ: Veterinarian.
BROAD Edward William 1891/92 b 30.4.1875 Nelson. d 7.4.1913 Marton, Rangitikei. He died from injuries sustained the previous day when, whilst motor cycling, he was struck by the New Plymouth express train. wk Team: **Nelson.** Sch: Nelson Coll. Occ: Land agent. Brother: C.H.Broad.
BRODIE Joshua Michael 2007/08-2009/10 b 8.6.1987 Wellington. LHB Team: **Wellington.** Sch: Wellington Coll.
BROOK J F 1913/14 Team: **Auckland.** He was selected for Auckland from Whangarei.
BROOKE Edgar William 1889/90 b 19.12.1862 England. d 3.5.1938 Auckland. Team: **Wellington.** Sch: Giggleswick, England. Occ: Farmer.
BROOKER Victor George 1947/48-1948/49 b 5.10.1924 Auckland. d 18.12.1987 Auckland. RHB RM Team: **Auckland.** NZCA obit: 1988.
BROOK-SMITH William 1904/05-1922/23 b 1.5.1885 Auckland. d 2.8.1952 Auckland. RHB RAB Teams: **Auckland, New Zealand.** NZCA obit: 1952. He played for New Zealand prior to being granted Test status. He scored 112* on FC debut for Auckland v Hawke's Bay in 1904/05.
BROOM Darren John 2009/10 b 16.9.1985 Christchurch, Canterbury. RHB RM Teams: **Canterbury (not FC), Otago.** Played List A in NZ; Played T20 in NZ. Sch: Christchurch BHS. Occ: Cricket pro. He scored 119 on FC debut for Otago v Northern Districts in 2009/10. Brother: N.T.Broom.
BROOM Neil Trevor 2002/03-2009/10 b 20.11.1983 Christchurch, Canterbury. RHB RM Teams: **Canterbury, Otago, New Zealand ODI, New Zealand T20.** Played List A in NZ; Played T20 in NZ. Sch: Shirley BHS. Occ: Cricket pro. NZ U19 ODI. He holds the Otago 3rd wicket partnership record of 306 with S.B.Haig against Central Districts in 2009/10. Brother: D.J.Broom.
BROOM Rowland Francis 1954/55 b 7.2.1925 Te Kuiti, Waikato. LHB LM Team: **Wellington.**
BROSNAHAN T 1919/20-1928/29 RHB Team: **Canterbury.**
BROUGHTON Edward Tauria 1883/84 b 1859 New Zealand. d 13.3.1894 Ngapuke, Hawke's Bay. Team: **Hawke's Bay.** Occ: Sheep farmer. He was the first known player of Maori heritage to play FC cricket.
BROUGHTON Roger Dean 1980/81-1986/87 b 7.10.1958 Gisborne, Poverty Bay. d 25.8.2004 Hiruharama, Manawatu. He was electrocuted working on powerlines. RHB OB Team: **Northern Districts.** Played List A in NZ. Sch: Gisborne BHS. NZCA obit: 2005.
BROWN Christopher Mark 1993/94-1997 b 27.3.1973 Rarotonga, Cook Islands. RHB RFM Team: **Auckland.** Played List A in NZ. NZ U19 Test; NZ U19 ODI.
BROWN Douglas Robert 1989-2006/07 b 29.10.1969 Stirling, Scotland. RHB RFM Teams: **Wellington,** England ODI, Scotland ODI, Scotland T20, Warwickshire. Played List A in NZ. Sch: West London Inst of Higher Educ, England. Occ: Cricket pro. An English pro, played and coached in NZ.
BROWN James W 1879/80-1884/85 Team: **Wellington.** Rugby: Wellington.
BROWN Kyle Vernon 1992/93 b 10.5.1973 Warkworth, Auckland. RHB LFM Team: **Auckland.** Sch: Kings Coll. NZ U19 Test; NZ U19 ODI.
BROWN Murray Thomas 1973/74-1974/75 b 9.11.1946 Inglewood, Taranaki. RHB LB Team: **Central Districts.**
BROWN Robert William 1870/71 b 15.12.1850 Dunedin, Otago. d 8.12.1934 Christchurch, Canterbury. Team: **Otago.** Sch: Otago BHS. Occ: Insurance manager.

BROWN Rodney Kirk 1988/89-1993/94 b 1.2.1968 New Plymouth, Taranaki. RHB RM Team: **Central Districts.** Played List A in NZ. NZ U19 Test; NZ U19 ODI.
BROWN Ronald Eric 1952/53-1957/58 b 18.4.1924 Auckland. d 23.3.2008 Wanganui. LHB SLA Team: **Central Districts.** Sch: Wanganui Tech Coll. NZCA obit: 2008; Wisden obit: 2009. CD selector.
BROWN Stanley Eric Vincent 1917/18 b 28.8.1885 Temuka, South Canterbury. d 21.1.1945 Invercargill, Southland. Team: **Southland.** Occ: Doctor.
BROWN Stephen William 1987/88-1994/95 b 12.10.1963 Hastings, Hawke's Bay. RHB RM Team: **Auckland.** Played List A in NZ.
BROWN Vaughan Raymond 1978/79-1989/90 b 3.11.1959 Christchurch, Canterbury. LHB OB Teams: **Canterbury, Auckland, New Zealand Test, New Zealand ODI.** Played List A in NZ. Sch: Christ Coll. Occ: Property developer.
BROWN William Jack 1944/45-1954/55 b 22.12.1917 Wanganui. RHB RFM Team: **Auckland.**
BROWNE Lionel Victor 1928/29-1930/31 b 14.12.1909 Wellington. d 22.12.1997 Auckland. RHB M Team: **Wellington.**
BROWNE Maurice Gerald 1937/38-1951/52 b 28.9.1913 Pretoria, Transvaal, South Africa. d 21.12.1980 Wellington. LHB OB Team: **Wellington.** Hockey: New Zealand. NZCA obit: 1981; Wisden obit: 1981.
BROWNETTE Sydney Cecil 1910/11-1912/13 b 1879 unknown. d 11.10.1936 Masterton, Wairarapa. Team: **Hawke's Bay.** Occ: Bootmaker.
BROWNLIE Dean Graham 2009/10 b 30.7.1984 Perth, Western Australia, Australia. RHB RM Team: **Canterbury.** Played List A in NZ; Played T20 in NZ. Sch: Lake Joondalup Baptist Coll, Western Australia, Australia. He scored 112* on FC debut for Canterbury v Northern Districts in 2009/10.
BRUCE John Alexander 1907/08-1922/23 b 11.11.1887 Wellington. d 20.10.1970 Wellington. Team: **Wellington.** Sch: Te Aro. Occ: Carpenter. Rugby: All Blacks and Wellington. NZCA obit: 1970. He became one of the few players to play for winning teams in both the Plunket Shield and Ranfurly Shield.
BRUCE Ralph Willett 1891/92-1896/97 b 3.4.1870 Woolwich, London, England. d 21.8.1952 Birch, Essex, England. LMF Team: **Hawke's Bay.** Sch: St Johns Park, Greenwich, Kent, England.
BRUGES John Stanley Beetham 1908/09-1914/15 b 18.5.1889 Christchurch, Canterbury. d 29.12.1948 Christchurch, Canterbury. RHB Teams: **Canterbury, Otago.** Sch: Christ Coll. Occ: Coy director.
BRUNTON Louis Richard 1913/14-1925/26 b 29.12.1891 Christchurch, Canterbury. d 23.3.1934 Christchurch, Canterbury. RHB wk Team: **Canterbury.** Sch: Christ Coll. Occ: Salesman.
BRYARS William 1887/88 b 1858 Belfast, Co Antrim, Ireland. d 3.11.1892 New York, United States of America. He died shortly after sustaining an injury to his eye during a storm crossing the Atlantic. He was on his way back to New Zealand after a holiday in Ireland. Team: **Canterbury.** Occ: Schoolmaster.
BRYCE John 1876/77 b 1849 Inverness, Scotland. d 13.6.1878 Wellington. He died at the age of 29. Team: **Wellington.** Occ: Compositor.
BRYDEN Thomas James 1912/13-1913/14 b 1.6.1877 Invercargill, Southland. d 12.10.1917 Ypres, Belgium. He was killed in action. Team: **Otago.** Occ: Chair maker.
BUCHAN Raymond 1943/44-1945/46 M Team: **Wellington.**
BUCHANAN James Telfer 1883/84-1884/85 b 1856 New Zealand. d 30.12.1921 Mosman, Sydney, New South Wales, Australia. Team: **Canterbury.** Occ: Wine merchant.
BUCHANAN William Beverly 1884/85 b 15.8.1863 Lyttelton, Christchurch, Canterbury. wk Team: **Hawke's Bay.**
BUCK James 1886/87-1887/88 b 1852 New Zealand. d 1928 Wellington. Team: **Hawke's Bay.** Occ: Stationmaster.
BUCKLAND William Francis 1873/74-1882/83 b 8.8.1847 Auckland. d 29.12.1915 Cambridge, Waikato. FM Team: **Auckland.** Occ: Solicitor. Umpired first-class cricket. MP. Mayor of Cambridge, Waikato.
BUIST Graham Thomas 1956/57-1957/58 b 23.7.1936 Napier, Hawke's Bay. RHB Team: **Central Districts.**

BULFIN Carl Edwin 1996/97-2000/01 b 19.8.1973 Blenheim, Marlborough. RHB RFM Teams: **Central Districts, Wellington, New Zealand ODI.** Played List A in NZ.

BULL Cranwell Leslie 1965/66-1983/84 b 19.8.1946 Auckland. RHB Team: **Canterbury.** Played List A in NZ. Sch: Christchurch BHS. Occ: Barrister. Member NZCC board, Canterbury selector.

BULLICK Anthony David 2007/08-2009/10 b 30.7.1985 Hamilton, Waikato. RHB RMF Team: **Otago.** Played List A in NZ. Sch: Kings Coll.

BURGESS Alan Thomas 1940/41-1951/52 b 1.5.1920 Christchurch, Canterbury. RHB SLA Team: **Canterbury.** Sch: Christchurch Technical Coll.

BURGESS Gordon Charles 1940/41-1954/55 b 4.10.1918 Waihi, Bay of Plenty. d 3.9.2000 Auckland. RHB Team: **Auckland.** OBE. NZCA obit: 2001. Auckland selector. Son: M.G.Burgess.

BURGESS Mark Gordon 1963/64-1980/81 b 17.7.1944 Auckland. RHB OB Teams: **Auckland, New Zealand Test, New Zealand ODI.** Played List A in NZ. Sch: Auckland GS. Soccer: New Zealand. NZCA COY: 1971. NZ selector. Father: G.C.Burgess.

BURKE Cecil 1937/38-1953/54 b 27.3.1914 Ellerslie, Auckland. d 4.8.1997 Auckland. RHB LBG Teams: **Auckland, New Zealand Test.** NZCA obit: 1998; Wisden obit: 1998. Auckland selector.

BURN Daniel 1880/81-1881/82 b 1849 Wakefield, Nelson. d 10.7.1932 Nelson. Team: **Nelson.** Occ: Plumber.

BURNES George Gordon 1883/84-1886/87 b 11.7.1866 Melbourne, Victoria, Australia. d 9.2.1949 Christchurch, Canterbury. Team: **Wellington.** Sch: Wellington Coll. Occ: Insurance manager.

BURNETT Graham Peter 1987/88-1994/95 b 7.10.1965 Tauranga, Bay of Plenty. RHB RM Teams: **Wellington, Northern Districts.** Played List A in NZ. He holds the Wellington 3rd wicket partnership record of 346 with R.A.Verry against Northern Districts in 1991/92.

BURNETTE Noel Sydney Hotham 1940/41-1945/46 b 13.6.1914 Wellington. d 29.4.1991 Wellington. RHB Team: **Wellington.**

BURNS John Campbell 1914/15 b 28.1.1880 Lawrence, Otago. d 11.6.1941 Petone, Lower Hutt, Wellington. wk Team: **Wellington.** Occ: Schoolteacher.

BURNS Kevin James 1980/81-1991/92 b 7.7.1960 Invercargill, Southland. LHB RM Team: **Otago.** Played List A in NZ. He holds the Otago 2nd wicket partnership record of 254 with K.R.Rutherford against Wellington in 1987/88 and the Otago 4th wicket partnership record of 235 with R.N.Hoskin against Northern Districts in 1987/88.

BURNS Michael 2006/07-2009/10 b 6.7.1979 Balclutha, Otago. RHB RFM Team: **Wellington.** Played List A in NZ. Sch: South Otago HS.

BURNS Robert Crosbie 1928/29-1933/34 b 24.6.1900 Templeton, Canterbury. d 10.8.1993 Christchurch, Canterbury. RHB wk Team: **Canterbury.** Sch: Christchurch BHS. Occ: Insurance manager. NZCA obit: 1994; Wisden obit: 1994. He was New Zealand's oldest first-class player when he died.

BURNS Terence Arthur 1964/65 b 15.4.1938 Lower Hutt, Wellington. RHB RM Team: **Northern Districts.**

BURROWS James Thomas 1926/27-1932/33 b 14.7.1904 Prebbleton, Canterbury. d 10.6.1991 Christchurch, Canterbury. RHB RM Team: **Canterbury.** Sch: Christchurch BHS. Occ: Headmaster; brigadier. Rugby: All Blacks and Canterbury. Book: Pathway Among Men. DSO and bar, CBE, Order of Valour (Greece). NZCA obit: 1992; Wisden obit: 1992. NZ rugby selector and coach.

BURSON Ryan David 1997/98-2007/08 b 27.8.1978 Christchurch, Canterbury. RHB RFM Team: **Canterbury.** Played List A in NZ; Played T20 in NZ. Sch: Shirley BHS. NZ U19 Test; NZ U19 ODI.

BURT David Thomas Athol 1924/25 b 28.11.1901 Auckland. Team: **Wellington.** Sch: Wellington Coll. Occ: Insurance manager.

BURT John Robert 1901/02-1908/09 b 27.8.1874 Dunedin, Otago. d 16.1.1933 Christchurch, Canterbury. Team: **Otago.** Occ: Coy manager.

BURTON Herbert Edward Ledgard 1909/10-1923/24 b 19.3.1888 Greenwich, London, England. d 24.3.1961 Auckland. RHB Teams: **Wellington, Auckland.** Occ: Merchant. NZCA obit: 1961. Father: H.G.E.L.Burton; son: J.E.L.Burton.

BURTON Herbert George Edward Ledgard 1893/94-1897/98 b 1864 Yorkshire, England. d 28.5.1910 Wellington. RHB Team: **Wellington.** Occ: Coy secretary. Grandson: J.E.L.Burton; son: H.E.L.Burton.
BURTON John Edward Ledgard 1946/47-1949/50 b 15.2.1925 Auckland. d 11.5.1910 Auckland. RHB Teams: **Wellington,** Ceylon. Sch: Auckland GS. Rugby: Auckland and Ceylon. Father: H.E.L.Burton; grandfather: H.G.E.L.Burton.
BURTON W 1940/41 Team: **Wellington.**
BURTT John Wayne 1964/65-1974/75 b 11.6.1944 Christchurch, Canterbury. RHB LB Teams: **Canterbury, Central Districts.** Played List A in NZ. Sch: Christchurch BHS. Occ: Insurance manager. CD selector. Father: N.V.Burtt; nephew: L.M.Burtt; uncle: T.B.Burtt.
BURTT Leighton Mcgregor 2006/07-2009/10 b 17.4.1984 Christchurch, Canterbury. RHB RM Team: **Canterbury.** Played List A in NZ; Played T20 in NZ. Sch: Christchurch BHS. NZ U19 ODI. Grandfather: N.V.Burtt; great-uncle: T.B.Burtt; uncle: J.W.Burtt.
BURTT Noel Vincent 1937/38-1948/49 b 10.11.1911 Christchurch, Canterbury. d 27.2.1983 Christchurch, Canterbury. RHB LBG Team: **Canterbury.** Sch: West Christchurch BHS. Hockey: Canterbury. NZCA obit: 1983. Brother: T.B.Burtt; grandson: L.M.Burtt; son: J.W.Burtt.
BURTT Thomas Browning 1943/44-1954/55 b 22.1.1915 Christchurch, Canterbury. d 24.5.1988 Christchurch, Canterbury. RHB SLA Teams: **Canterbury, New Zealand Test.** Sch: West Christchurch BHS. Occ: Furniture manufacturer. Hockey: New Zealand. NZCA obit: 1988; Wisden obit: 1989. NZCA COY: 1948. Brother: N.V.Burtt; great-nephew: L.M.Burtt; nephew: J.W.Burtt.
BUSH Benjamin John 1887/88 b 1867 Christchurch, Canterbury. d 29.6.1913 Christchurch, Canterbury. He died from a fractured skull, the result of a fall. At his inquest evidence was given that he was subject to epileptic fits. Team: **Canterbury.** Sch: Christchurch BHS. Occ: Painter.
BUSH Ronald George 1932/33-1936/37 b 3.5.1909 Nelson. d 10.5.1996 Auckland. RHB RFM Team: **Auckland.** Sch: Mt Albert GS. Occ: Indent agent. Rugby: All Blacks and Auckland. NZCA obit: 1996; Wisden obit: 1997. He became one of the few players to play for winning teams in both the Plunket Shield and Ranfurly Shield.
BUSH William Edward 1910/11 b 1883 England. d 5.8.1959 Auckland. Team: **Auckland.** Occ: Insurance manager.
BUTLER Frank 1914/15-1923/24 b 13.11.1889 Brighton, Victoria, Australia. d 8.5.1965 Kew, Melbourne, Victoria, Australia. LHB Teams: **Canterbury,** Tasmania. Sch: Mentone Coll, Australia. Occ: Insurance clerk.
BUTLER Ian Gareth 2001/02-2009/10 b 24.11.1981 Middlemore, Auckland. RHB RFM Teams: **Northern Districts, Otago, New Zealand Test, New Zealand ODI, New Zealand T20,** Gloucestershire, Kent. Played List A in NZ; Played T20 in NZ. NZ U19 Test; NZ U19 ODI. He holds the record for the best NZ T20 bowling figures of 6/28 for Otago v Auckland in 2009/10 and the NZ domestic T20 10th wicket partnership record of 29 with W.C.McSkimming for Otago against Central Districts in 2009/10.
BUTLER Keith Owen 1953/54 b 26.12.1933 Auckland. RHB RM Team: **Auckland.**
BUTLER Leslie Charles 1951/52-1967/68 b 2.9.1934 Wellington. d 21.1.2006 Clear Island Waters, Queensland, Australia. LHB SLA Teams: **Wellington, New Zealand.** Sch: Rongatai Coll. NZCA obit: 2006; Wisden obit: 2007. He played for New Zealand in a FC match.
BUTLER William Patrick 1901/02 b 8.11.1871 Dunedin, Otago. d 19.8.1953 Dunedin, Otago. Team: **Otago.** Occ: Bootmaker.
BUTLIN George Louis 1889/90 b 11.7.1861 St Pancras, London, England. d 10.7.1925 Kogarah, Sydney, New South Wales, Australia. Team: **Otago.** Occ: Commercial clerk.
BUTTERFIELD Leonard Arthur 1934/35-1945/46 b 29.8.1913 Christchurch, Canterbury. d 5.7.1999 Christchurch, Canterbury. RHB RFM Teams: **Canterbury, New Zealand Test.** Sch: Christchurch BHS. Occ: Stipendiary steward. NZCA obit: 1999; Wisden obit: 2000. In the Wellington Test match against Australia in 1945/46 he was lbw to Bill O'Reilly for 0 in both innings and did not take a wicket in what was his last first-class match.
BUTTERWORTH Thomas 1857/58-1866/67 b 1828 England. d 15.7.1877 Kensington, London, England. Teams: **Otago,** Victoria. Brother: B.Butterworth (Victoria).

BYERLEY Frederick William Alfred 1931/32 b 9.7.1910 Wellington. d 19.8.1994 Auckland. LHB SLA Team: **Auckland.** NZCA obit: 1995; Wisden obit: 1995.

CACHOPA Carl 2004/05-2006/07 b 17.5.1986 Bloemfontein, Orange Free State, South Africa. RHB RM Team: **Auckland.** Played List A in NZ. Sch: Westlake BHS. In 2004 he was awarded the inaugural New Zealand Youth Cricket Scholarship.

CAIN Jonathan Blair 1994/95 b 25.10.1969 Gore, Southland. RHB wk Team: **Auckland.** Played List A in NZ. Sch: Westlake BHS.

CAIRNS Alexander Edmond 1867/68-1870/71 b 23.4.1850 Newlands, Renfrewshire, Scotland. d 16.6.1936 Dunedin, Otago. RHB Team: **Otago.** Sch: Otago BHS. Occ: Railway employee. Brother: H.W.Cairns.

CAIRNS Bernard Lance 1971/72-1988 b 10.10.1949 Picton, Marlborough. RHB RMF Teams: **Central Districts, Otago, Northern Districts, New Zealand Test, New Zealand ODI.** Played List A in NZ. Sch: Marlborough Boys Coll. Book: Give it a heave. NZCA COY: 1976, 1983. ND selector. He shares with B.G.Cooper the record of the fastest NZ FC century, 52 minutes and 45 balls, for Otago v Wellington in 1979/80. Brother-in-law: B.L.Roberts; son: C.L.Cairns.

CAIRNS Christopher Lance 1988-2005/06 b 13.6.1970 Picton, Marlborough. RHB RFM Teams: **Northern Districts, Canterbury, New Zealand Test, New Zealand ODI, New Zealand T20,** Nottinghamshire, ICC World XI ODI. Played List A in NZ; Played T20 in NZ. Sch: Christchurch BHS. Occ: Cricket pro. NZ U19 Test; NZ U19 ODI. Book: Chris Cairns by H.McDougall. NZCA COY: 1998, 1999, 2000; WCOY: 2000, ICOY 2000. He holds the NZ Test 7th wicket partnership record of 225 with J.D.P.Oram against South Africa in 2003/04; he formerly held the world record for most sixes in Tests (87, since surpassed by Adam Gilchrist), and shared the New Zealand record for fastest century in ODIs (75 balls, since surpassed by Craig McMillan). Father: B.L.Cairns; uncle: B.L.Roberts.

CAIRNS Henry Wilson 1864/65-1869/70 b 11.12.1842 Falkirk, Stirlingshire, Scotland. d 16.12.1888 Dunedin, Otago. He died in the Dunedin asylum. Team: **Otago.** Occ: Salesman. Brother: A.E.Cairns.

CAIRNS Matthew Gordon 2001/02 b 14.6.1980 Pietermaritzburg, Natal, South Africa. RHB LB Team: **Auckland.** Sch: Auckland GS.

CAKOBAU Etuate Tuivanuavou Tugi 1930/31-1947/48 b 21.12.1908 Bau, Fiji. d 25.6.1973 Suva, Fiji. RHB RM Teams: **Auckland, Fiji.** Sch: Wanganui CS. Occ: Statesman. Rugby: Otago. KBE, MC. NZCA obit: 1973; Wisden obit: 1974. Son of King George of Tonga, he became Deputy Prime Minister of Fiji when the colony was granted independence in 1970. President of the Fiji CA and manager of the Fiji Rugby football touring team of 1964.

CALDER John Wilson 1971/72 b 5.6.1951 Waimate, South Canterbury. LHB OB Teams: **Canterbury (not FC), New Zealand Under-23s.** Played List A in NZ. Sch: Christchurch BHS. Occ: Clerk.

CALKIN David John 1969/70 b 1.3.1945 Palmerston North, Manawatu. LHB SLA Team: **Central Districts.** Sch: Rangitikei Coll.

CALLAND Roland John 1977/78 b 11.10.1946 Paeroa, Thames Valley. RHB OB Team: **Northern Districts.**

CALLAWAY Sydney Thomas 1888/89-1906/07 b 6.2.1868 Redfern, Sydney, New South Wales, Australia. d 25.11.1923 Christchurch, Canterbury. RHB RFM Teams: **Canterbury, New Zealand,** Australia Test, New South Wales. Occ: Civil servant. Umpired first-class cricket. Wisden obit: 1925. He played for New Zealand prior to being granted Test status. He has the best match figures for Canterbury when he took 15/60 against Hawke's Bay in 1903/04.

CALVERT William 1865/66-1867/68 b 1839 Sunderland, Co Durham, England. d 10.2.1894 Christchurch, Canterbury. Team: **Canterbury.** Occ: Tinsmith.

CAMERON Donald Sinclair 1930/31 b 13.1.1908 Dunedin, Otago. d 8.3.1990 Dunedin, Otago. RHB Team: **Otago.** Sch: Otago BHS. Occ: Insurance coy director. Brother: H.R.Cameron.

CAMERON Douglas Archibald 1929/30-1932/33 b 21.3.1903 Wanganui. d 10.1.1996 Wanganui. RHB RM occ wk Team: **Wellington.** Sch: Huntly School. Occ: Farmer. NZCA obit: 1996. Wisden obit: 1995.

CAMERON Ewen Henry John 1953/54-1954/55 b 1.3.1921 Dunedin, Otago. d 12.1.1997 Clyde, Central Otago. RHB LMF Team: **Otago.** Sch: Waitaki BHS. Occ: Schoolteacher. NZCA obit: 1997.

CAMERON Francis James 1952/53-1966/67 b 1.6.1932 Dunedin, Otago. RHB RM Teams: **Otago, New Zealand Test**. Occ: Schoolteacher. MBE. NZCA COY: 1962. NZ and Otago selector. He took a hat-trick for Otago v Northern Districts in 1962/63.

CAMERON Harold Raines 1939/40 b 10.10.1912 Dunedin, Otago. d 8.10.2000 Auckland. RHB Team: **Otago**. Sch: Otago BHS. Occ: Sales manager. NZCA obit: 2001. Otago selector. Brother: D.S.Cameron.

CAMERON John Nevis Allan 1917/18 b 26.9.1898 Dunedin, Otago. d 16.12.1988 Nelson. Team: **Otago**. Sch: Dunedin Normal Sch.

CAMERON Stewart Macmillan 1940/41-1955/56 b 11.2.1920 Blenheim, Marlborough. d 31.1.2001 Christchurch, Canterbury. RHB RM Team: **Canterbury**. NZCA obit: 2001.

CAMM Robert Harold John 1919/20-1920/21 b Q2 1881 Birkenhead, Cheshire, England. d 10.12.1950 Christchurch, Canterbury. Team: **Southland**.

CAMMISH James William 1950/51-1954 b 21.5.1921 Scarborough, Yorkshire, England. d 16.7.1974 Napier, Hawke's Bay. RHB LBG Teams: **Auckland,** Yorkshire. Sch: Central Sch, Scarborough, England.

CAMPBELL Colin 1920/21-1921/22 b 1884 Scotland. d 3.2.1966 Hastings, Hawke's Bay. wk Team: **Hawke's Bay.**

CAMPBELL James 1868/69 Team: **Otago.**

CAMPBELL Keith Oliver 1963/64-1978/79 b 20.3.1943 Dunedin, Otago. RHB RM occ wk Team: **Otago, New Zealand.** Played List A in NZ. Sch: Kings HS. Occ: Groundsman. He played for New Zealand in a FC match. Son: P.A.Campbell.

CAMPBELL Paul Adrian 1989/90-1994/95 b 11.2.1968 Dunedin, Otago. RHB LM wk Team: **Otago.** Played List A in NZ. Sch: Kings HS. Father: K.O.Campbell.

CAMPBELL Thomas Tasman 1894/95 b 15.8.1872 Wellington. d 15.7.1950 Patea, Taranaki. wk Team: **Taranaki.** Sch: Mt Cook HS. Occ: Farmer.

CANE Fenwick Francis 1920/21 b 30.8.1892 Christchurch, Canterbury. d 7.2.1974 Auckland. Team: **Hawke's Bay.** Sch: Napier BHS. Books: Cricket in Hawke's Bay; Cricket centenary: history of Hawke's Bay cricket. NZCA obit: 1974.

CANNEY Richard Bright 1877/78 b Q3 1852 Thanet, Kent, England. d 17.6.1887 Gunnedah, New South Wales, Australia. He died as a result of being thrown from a horse, aged 35. Team: **Nelson.** Occ: Doctor.

CANNING Davis 1893/94-1899/00 b 1.4.1871 Oakbourne, Hawke's Bay. d 28.11.1918 Hastings, Hawke's Bay. He died of Spanish flu. wk Team: **Hawke's Bay.** Sch: Clifton Coll, England. Occ: Sheep farmer.

CANNING Tamahau Karangatukituki 1998/99-2006/07 b 7.4.1977 Rose Park, Adelaide, South Australia, Australia. RHB RFM Teams: **Auckland, New Zealand ODI.** Played List A in NZ; Played T20 in NZ. Sch: Christian Brothers Coll, Fremantle, Western Australia, Australia. He played twice for the Australian Academy side on their tour of Zimbabwe in 1999/00 before being offered a place in the New Zealand Cricket Academy following some good performance in the Shell Cup. In 2000 the ICC granted him exemption from the usual four-year residential criteria and he made his one-day international debut in Pakistan in 2003/04. He took a hat-trick for Auckland v Central Districts in 1999/00.

CANT Arthur 1890/91-1900/01 b 28.3.1864 Christchurch, Canterbury. d 16.7.1949 Christchurch, Canterbury. RHB Team: **Canterbury.** Occ: Accountant. Umpired first-class cricket.

CAPSTICK John Raymond 1946/47 b 1.1.1919 Dunedin, Otago. d 24.12.1993 Wellington. Team: **Wellington.** Sch: Petone Coll.

CARGILL Archibald 1876/77-1883/84 b 20.8.1853 Melbourne, Victoria, Australia. d 18.7.1926 Porirua, Wellington. Team: **Otago.** Occ: Accountant. In 1910 he fell under a train and as a result of his injuries had his foot amputated.

CARLTON Thomas Andrew 1909/10-1931/32 b 7.12.1890 Footscray, Melbourne, Victoria, Australia. d 17.12.1973 Moreland, Victoria, Australia. LHB LM Teams: **Canterbury, Otago, New Zealand,** Victoria, South Australia. Occ: Cricket pro. NZCA obit: 1975. He played for New Zealand prior to being granted Test status. Uncles: A.R.Carlton (Victoria), J.Carlton (Victoria), W.Carlton.

CARLTON William 1898/99-1913/14 b 22.5.1876 Collingwood, Melbourne, Victoria, Australia. d 23.12.1959 North Melbourne, Victoria, Australia. RHB RAB Teams: **Auckland, Canterbury,** Victoria. Occ: Cricket coach. Umpired first-class cricket. Baseball: Victoria. Canterbury coach. Brothers: A.R.Carlton (Victoria), J.Carlton (Victoria, Queensland); nephew: T.A.Carlton.

CARRINGTON Randall Marsack 1953/54 b 31.3.1934 Whangarei, Northland. LHB SLA Team: **Auckland**. Sch: Avondale Coll.

CARRINGTON Sydney Mark 1981/82-1986/87 b 19.8.1961 Gisborne, Poverty Bay. RHB RMF Teams: **Northern Districts, New Zealand.** Played List A in NZ. Occ: Orchard manager. He played for New Zealand in a FC match.

CARSON John Ronald 1963/64-1973/74 b 8.7.1945 Auckland. LHB SLA Teams: **Auckland, Northern Districts.** Sch: Auckland GS. Uncle: W.N.Carson, great-uncle W.Carson.

CARSON William 1884/85-1887/88 b 24.9.1866 Dunedin, Otago. d 4.9.1955 Whangarei, Northland. wk Team: **Otago.** Sch: Otago BHS. Occ: Marine engineer. Nephew: W.N.Carson; great-nephew: J.R.Carson.

CARSON William Nicol 1936/37-1939/40 b 16.7.1916 Gisborne, Poverty Bay. d 8.10.1944 at sea, on board a ship between Bari, Italy and Egypt. He died of wounds received, aged 28. LHB LFM Teams: **Auckland, New Zealand.** Sch: Gisborne BHS. Occ: Warehouseman. Rugby: All Blacks and Auckland. Book: W.N.Carson, footballer and cricketer by A.H.Carman. MC. He played for New Zealand in a FC match. In his second FC match he scored 290 for Auckland v Otago in 1936/37. He holds the Auckland 3rd wicket partnership record of 445 with W.N.Carson against Otago in 1936/37at Dunedin. This partnership stood as a world record for the third wicket until 1976/77 and remains the Auckland record for any wicket. He also holds the Auckland 8th wicket partnership record of 189 with A.M.Matheson against Wellington in 1938/39 and the Auckland 10th wicket partnership record of 119 with J.Cowie against Otago in 1937/38. Nephew: J.R.Carson; uncle: W.Carson.

CARSTON Elmo Cecil 1946/47 b 19.4.1927 Christchurch, Canterbury. RHB LM Team: **Canterbury.** Sch: Home schooled. Occ: Accountant.

CARSWELL Robert Douglas 1957/58 b 19.3.1936 Gisborne, Poverty Bay. RHB Team: **Northern Districts.**

CARTER Robert Michael 1978-1984/85 b 25.5.1960 King's Lynn, Norfolk, England. RHB RM occ wk Teams: **Canterbury,** Northamptonshire. Played List A in NZ. Sch: Gaywood Park School, England. Occ: Cricket coach. Wellington and Canterbury selector and coach.

CARTWRIGHT Anthony George 1961/62-1963/64 b 8.8.1940 Timaru, South Canterbury. RHB RM Team: **Otago.**

CASEY Leonard Francis 1920/21-1922/23 b 7.5.1888 Dunedin, Otago. d 8.10.1964 Christchurch, Canterbury. RHB RFM Team: **Otago.** Occ: Insurance manager.

CATE William Alfred 1908/09-1922/23 b 22.11.1878 Upper Hutt, Wellington. d 22.10.1939 Petone, Lower Hutt, Wellington. RHB wk Teams: **Wellington, New Zealand.** Occ: Gear coy clerk. He played for New Zealand prior to being granted Test status.

CATER Stewart Bruce 1974/75-1982/83 b 4.2.1952 Nelson. d 5.2.2005 Ohakune, Manawatu. He died of a heart attack at a wedding reception aged 53. RHB RFM Team: **Wellington.** Played List A in NZ. Occ: Supermarket owner. Book: 100 years of village cricket - Johnsonville CC. NZCA obit: 2005; Wisden obit: 2006. In 1974/75 he took 9/19 in a Wellington club game.

CATO Charles Hardy 1891/92-1907/08 b 1868 Dunedin, Otago. d 20.10.1947 Gisborne, Poverty Bay. Team: **Hawke's Bay.** Sch: Napier BHS. Occ: Agent.

CAVANAGH Victor George 1927/28-1938/39 b 19.6.1909 Dunedin, Otago. d 20.7.1980 Dunedin, Otago. RHB Team: **Otago.** Sch: Otago BHS. Occ: Coy director. Rugby: Otago - noted rugby coach. NZCA obit: 1980.

CAVE Henry Butler 1945/46-1958/59 b 10.10.1922 Wanganui. d 15.9.1989 Wanganui. RHB RM Teams: **Wellington, Central Districts, New Zealand Test.** Sch: Wanganui CS. NZCA obit: 1990; Wisden obit: 1990. NZCA COY: 1957. NZ and CD selector. He holds the NZ 9th wicket partnership record of 239 with I.B.Leggat for Central Districts v Otago in 1952/53. He has the best match figures for Central Districts when he took 13/63 against Auckland in 1952/53.

CAYGILL Ernest Robson 1910/11-1913/14 b 13.12.1886 Christchurch, Canterbury. d 21.3.1971 Christchurch, Canterbury. RHB Team: **Canterbury.** Sch: Christchurch BHS. Occ: Accountant. NZCA obit: 1971. NZ selector.

CEDERMAN Duncan Robert 2004/05 b 18.10.1978 Nelson. RHB OB Team: **Central Districts.**
CEDERWALL Brian William 1973/74-1983/84 b 24.2.1952 Christchurch, Canterbury. RHB RM Team: **Wellington.** Played List A in NZ. Rugby: Wellington and New Zealand triallist. Brother: G.N.Cederwall.
CEDERWALL Grant Newton 1978/79-1990/91 b 4.7.1959 Dunedin, Otago. RHB RM Team: **Wellington.** Played List A in NZ. Sch: Rongatai Coll. Rugby: Wellington. Brother: B.W.Cederwall.
CHADWICK Charles Sydney 1912/13-1924/25 b 1.3.1880 Dunedin, Otago. d 30.10.1942 Dunedin, Otago. RHB wk Team: **Otago.** Occ: Bootmaker. Umpired first-class cricket. Brother: L.N.Chadwick.
CHADWICK Leslie Norman 1919/20 b 16.3.1889 Dunedin, Otago. d 10.10.1970 Dunedin, Otago. RHB Team: **Otago.** Occ: Accountant. Brother: C.S.Chadwick.
CHADWICK Robert John Montague 1904/05-1913/14 b 16.10.1879 Dunedin, Otago. d 11.3.1939 Napier, Hawke's Bay. Teams: **Otago, Hawke's Bay.** Occ: Engineer. Soccer: New Zealand and Otago.
CHALLIES Rex Sinclair 1946/47-1955/56 b 15.9.1924 Nelson. d 9.8.2003 Nelson. RHB LBG Teams: **Wellington, Central Districts.** Occ: Soldier. NZCA obit: 2004. He made a regular practice of catching the Cook Strait ferry from Nelson to Wellington in order to play club cricket in the capital. He would then catch the ferry home after completing his day's play with the Midland club.
CHAMBERLAIN Mark Charles 1988/89 b 12.5.1961 Leeston, Canterbury. RHB RFM Team: **Canterbury.** Sch: Lincoln HS.
CHAMBERS Kit Steven 1973/74 b 22.4.1949 Christchurch, Canterbury. LHB RM Team: **Canterbury.** Sch: St Andrews Coll. Occ: Manager.
CHAN Sunnie Percival 2006/07-2009/10 b 4.2.1982 Wellington. RHB RMF Teams: **Canterbury, Wellington.** Played List A in NZ; Played T20 in NZ. Sch: Rongatai Coll. Occ: Cricket pro.
CHANDLER Philip John Barry 1994/95-2001/02 b 6.7.1972 Wellington. LHB Team: **Wellington.** Played List A in NZ.
CHAPMAN Arthur Truman 1881/82-1891/92 b 2.6.1861 Christchurch, Canterbury. d 13.4.1950 Christchurch, Canterbury. Team: **Canterbury.** Sch: Christ Coll. Occ: Farmer. Rugby: Canterbury.
CHAPMAN Harold 1943/44-1944/45 b 28.2.1922 Ballygawley, Co Tyrone, Ireland. d 20.2.2007 Wellington. RHB RFM Team: **Wellington.**
CHAPMAN John Eli 1885/86-1886/87 b 18.1.1865 Lower Hutt, Wellington. d 16.2.1949 Wellington. wk Team: **Wellington.** Occ: Bookbinder. Rugby: Wellington.
CHAPMAN Martin 1864/65-1867/68 b 23.3.1846 Karori, Wellington. d 17.3.1924 Wellington. Team: **Otago.** Sch: Melbourne CEGS, Australia. Occ: Barrister. He was the editor of the New Zealand Law Report and a member of the Council of the Wellington Law Society.
CHAPPLE Murray Ernest 1949/50-1971/72 b 25.7.1930 Christchurch, Canterbury. d 31.7.1985 Hamilton, Waikato. RHB LM Teams: **Canterbury, Central Districts, New Zealand Test.** Occ: Schoolmaster. NZCA obit: 1985; Wisden obit: 1986. NZCA COY: 1960. NZ, Canterbury and CD selector; NZ manager.
CHARLES Leonard Andrews 1919/20 b 16.10.1898 Eketahuna, Wairarapa. d 15.9.1960 Ashburton, Mid Canterbury. Team: **Hawke's Bay.** Occ: Solicitor.
CHATFIELD Ewen John 1973/74-1989/90 b 3.7.1950 Dannevirke, Hawke's Bay. RHB RMF Teams: **Wellington, New Zealand Test, New Zealand ODI.** Played List A in NZ. Sch: Naenae Coll. Occ: Taxi driver. Book: Chats: Ewen Chatfield's life in cricket. MBE. NZCA COY: 1977. In his Test debut against England at Auckland in 1974/75, after a stubborn defensive innings at No. 11, he was struck on the temple by Peter Lever. His heart stopped and he swallowed his tongue and only mouth-to-mouth resuscitation and heart massage by England's physiotherapist, Bernard Thomas, saved his life.
CHERRY Reginald William Henry 1919/20-1931/32 b 3.10.1901 Lambeth, London, England. d 22.12.1938 Dunedin, Otago. He died as the result of complications following a minor operation. RHB Team: **Otago.** Sch: Dunedin Tech Coll. Occ: Comm traveller.

CHETTLEBURGH Verdon Joseph Thomas 1932/33-1940/41 b 19.11.1912 Dunedin, Otago. d 4.9.1960 Lower Hutt, Wellington. RHB LB Team: **Otago**. Sch: Otago BHS. Occ: Bookkeeper. NZCA obit: 1960. Member NZCC board.
CHILD Ellis Lynley 1953/54-1958/59 b 23.12.1925 Whangarei, Northland. d 8.5.2005 Auckland. RHB RM Teams: **Auckland, Northern Districts**. NZCA obit: 2005. Son: M.J.Child.
CHILD Murray John 1977/78-1986/87 b 1.9.1953 Whangarei, Northland. RHB LM Team: **Northern Districts**. Played List A in NZ. Sch: Whangarei HS. Father: E.L.Child.
CHING Ian Hamilton 1950/51-1955/56 b 25.11.1928 Te Mawhai, Waikato. d 2.2.2006 Rotorua, Bay of Plenty. LHB wk Team: **Central Districts**.
CHISHOLM Walter Edward 1885/86 b 1.8.1862 Wellington. d 1.8.1957 Dunedin, Otago. Team: **Wellington**. Occ: Telegraphist.
CHRISTOPHERSON Walter John Robert 1926/27 b 27.5.1898 Wellington. d 14.7.1979 Mount Maunganui, Bay of Plenty. Team: **Wellington**. NZCA obit: 1979.
CHURCH Basil 1871/72 b 10.1849 Kettering, Northamptonshire, England. d 31.1.1881 Melbourne, Victoria, Australia. Team: **Otago**. Occ: Schoolmaster.
CHURCHILL George Arthur 1942/43 b 1914 Dunedin, Otago. d 25.10.1961 Auckland. wk Team: **NZ Air Force**. Sch: Otago BHS. Occ: Bookkeeper.
CLAFFEY Daniel Patrick 1888/89-1889/90 b 28.11.1869 Dunedin, Otago. d 2.2.1924 Dunedin, Otago. RF Team: **Otago**.
CLARK Charles Croome 1913/14 b 13.7.1883 Auckland. d 6.8.1970 Thames, Thames Valley. Team: **Auckland**. Occ: Carpenter.
CLARK Charles Reginald 1895/96-1897/98 b 26.7.1866 Christchurch, Canterbury. d 15.9.1950 Christchurch, Canterbury. Team: **Canterbury**. Sch: Christchurch BHS. Occ: Barrister.
CLARK George H 1872/73-1879/80 Team: **Otago**. Umpired first-class cricket.
CLARK James Bernard 1933/34-1934/35 b 25.9.1910 Dunedin, Otago. d 21.1.2003 Auckland. LHB wk Team: **Otago**. Sch: Otago BHS. Occ: Accountant. NZCA obit: 2003; Wisden obit: 2004. Father: J.Baker.
CLARK Leslie Alan 1955/56-1961/62 b 16.12.1930 Wellington. RHB RM Teams: **Wellington, Otago, Auckland**. Auckland selector. Father: L.G.Clark.
CLARK Leslie Gordon 1929/30 b 30.12.1903 Christchurch, Canterbury. d 26.9.1974 Wellington. wk Team: **Otago**. Sch: Lyttleton DHS. Occ: Labourer. Umpired Test and first-class cricket. NZCA obit: 1974. Wellington selector. Son: L.A.Clark.
CLARK Michael James 1990/91-1996/97 b 7.7.1966 Auckland. LHB Team: **Auckland**. Played List A in NZ.
CLARK Trevor Leonard 1931/32 b 14.1.1908 Auckland. d 6.4.1992 Auckland. RHB Team: **Auckland**. NZCA obit: 1996.
CLARKE Alfred Edward 1889/90-1901/02 b 6.4.1868 Surry Hills, Sydney, New South Wales, Australia. d 16.9.1940 Wellington. Teams: **Otago, Wellington, New Zealand,** New South Wales. Umpired first-class cricket. He played for New Zealand prior to being granted Test status.
CLARKE Donald Barry 1950/51-1962/63 b 10.11.1933 Pihama, Taranaki. d 29.12.2002 Johannesburg, Gauteng, South Africa. He died from melanoma. RHB RFM Teams: **Auckland, Northern Districts**. Sch: Te Aroha Coll. Occ: Sales manager. Rugby: All Blacks and Waikato. Books: Boot; Don Clarke - legend. NZCA obit: 2003; Wisden obit: 2003. He became one of the few players to play for winning teams in both the Plunket Shield and Ranfurly Shield. ND selector. Brother: D.S.Clarke.
CLARKE Douglas Stewart 1957/58-1960/61 b 30.7.1932 Kaponga, Taranaki. d 31.1.2005 Morrinsville, Waikato. LHB wk Team: **Northern Districts**. Sch: Te Aroha Coll. Occ: Farmer. Rugby: Waikato. NZCA obit: 2005; Wisden obit: 2006. Brother: D.B.Clarke.
CLARKE William Vernon 1913/14 b 12.5.1894 Hastings, Hawke's Bay. d 27.8.1969 Gisborne, Poverty Bay. M Team: **Hawke's Bay**. Occ: Accountant.
CLAYFORTH Charles 1873/74 b Yorkshire, England. Team: **Auckland**. Occ: Sharebroker.
CLAYTON Daniel Louis Jarvis 1894/95-1902/03 b 28.9.1875 Auckland. d 1938 unknown. Team: **Auckland**. Occ: Accountant.
CLAYTON Frank 1893/94 b 27.7.1866 Christchurch, Canterbury. d 4.8.1941 Christchurch, Canterbury. wk Team: **Canterbury**. Occ: Painter. Umpired first-class cricket.

CLAYTON Frank Dinning 1892/93-1896/97 b 10.1.1866 Auckland. d 29.9.1944 Wellington. Team: **Otago**. Sch: Auckland GS. Occ: Bank clerk. Rugby: Auckland; selected for the NZ 1884 rugby tour of NSW but he withdrew from the team prior to the tour.

CLEAL Osmond Charles 1940/41-1951/52 b 13.12.1916 Auckland. d 8.2.1977 Auckland. RHB RM Team: **Auckland**. Sch: Auckland GS. Occ: Assistant manager. Soccer: New Zealand. Auckland selector.

CLEAVE Robert Henry 1933/34-1944/45 b 10.3.1911 Thames, Thames Valley. d 26.2.1987 Auckland. RHB Team: **Auckland**. Sch: Thames HS.

CLEVERLEY Donald Charles 1930/31-1952/53 b 23.12.1909 Oamaru, North Otago. d 16.2.2004 Southport, Queensland, Australia. LHB RFM Teams: **Auckland, Central Districts, New Zealand Test**. Occ: Publican. Boxing: National amateur champion. NZCA obit: 2004; Wisden obit: 2005. At the time of his death he was the oldest Test cricketer. He played two Tests for New Zealand, more than 14 years apart.

COATES Robert James 1917/18-1923/24 b 17.8.1881 Auckland. d 31.1.1956 Auckland. RM Team: **Auckland**. Sch: Christ Coll. Occ: Barrister.

COBCROFT Leslie Thomas 1895/96-1909/10 b 12.2.1867 Muswellbrook, New South Wales, Australia. d 9.3.1938 Wellington. RHB OB Teams: **Canterbury, Wellington, New Zealand, New South Wales**. Sch: Sydney GS, Australia. Occ: Solicitor. Umpired Test and first-class cricket. NZ selector. He played for New Zealand prior to being granted Test status.

COBDEN Alfred Palmerston 1935/36 b 9.5.1913 Christchurch, Canterbury. d 24.10.1942 El Alamein, Egypt. He was killed in action aged 29. RHB LBG Team: **Canterbury**. Sch: Christchurch BHS. Rugby: Canterbury. His brother Donald was an All Black and was also killed in WW2.

COCKBURN C 1887/88 Team: **Wellington**. Occ: Schoolmaster. Master at Wellington College.

COCKROFT William Edward 1914/15 b 24.7.1896 Lumsden, Southland. d 31.12.1964 Waipu, Northland. Team: **Southland**. Occ: Clerk.

COHEN Louis 1890/91 b 1863 Cooma, New South Wales, Australia. d 16.3.1933 Durie Hill, Wanganui. Team: **Canterbury**. Sch: West Christchurch BHS. Occ: Solicitor. Canterbury rugby selector.

COHEN N 1919/20 Team: **Hawke's Bay**.

COLE Ernest Colyer 1896/97 b 20.3.1875 Waimea South, Nelson. d 24.9.1965 Rotorua, Bay of Plenty. Team: **Taranaki**. Occ: Settler. He lived in Nelson and commuted to Taranaki to work and play cricket in summer from the 1890s until the 1920s.

COLEMAN Donald Dacre 1948/49-1957/58 b 20.5.1927 Devonport, Auckland. d 15.8.1983 Devonport, Auckland. RHB OB Team: **Auckland**. Sch: Takapuna GS. NZCA obit: 1983. Uncles: C.C.R.Dacre, L.M.Dacre.

COLES Alfred William 1873/74-1875/76 b 1849 Nelson. d 23.10.1885 Christchurch, Canterbury. Team: **Nelson**. Occ: Bookkeeper.

COLES Michael John 1965/66-1975/76 b 16.3.1944 Wellington. RHB RFM Team: **Wellington**. Played List A in NZ.

COLEY Barry David 1971/72 b 20.12.1946 Wellington. RHB Team: **Wellington**. Sch: Rangitoto Coll. Occ: Schoolteacher.

COLLIER Allen Richard 1976/77 b 23.3.1951 Paeroa, Thames Valley. RHB SLA Team: **Northern Districts**.

COLLINGE Richard Owen 1963/64-1978 b 2.4.1946 Wellington. RHB LMF Teams: **Central Districts, Wellington, Northern Districts, New Zealand Test, New Zealand ODI**. Played List A in NZ. Sch: Wairarapa Coll. NZCA COY: 1971. He holds the NZ and all nations Test 10th wicket partnership record of 151 with B.F.Hastings against Pakistan in 1972/73 (the all nations Test partnership has since been equalled by Azhar Mahmood and Mushtaq Ahmed in 1997/98), during this game he made 68 not out, the then highest score by a No. 11 in Test history (now held by Zaheer Khan with 75).

COLLINS Anthony Ernest 1977/78 b 9.6.1949 Christchurch, Canterbury. RHB LB Team: **Canterbury**. Played List A in NZ. Sch: Christchurch BHS.

COLLINS David Charles 1905/06-1926/27 b 1.10.1887 Wellington. d 2.1.1967 Tauranga, Bay of Plenty. RHB RM occ wk Teams: **Wellington, New Zealand,** Cambridge University. Sch: Wellington Coll. Occ: Doctor. NZCA obit: 1967; Wisden obit: 1968. He played for New Zealand prior to being granted Test status. Father: W.E.Collins.

COLLINS John Ulric 1884/85-1895/96 b 7.7.1868 Nelson. d 16.7.1943 Ngongotaha, Bay of Plenty. wk Teams: **Nelson, Canterbury.** Sch: Nelson Coll. Occ: Schoolmaster, Nelson Coll. Rugby: Wellington. Tennis: New Zealand and Canterbury.

COLLINS Kevin Ian 1978/79 b 6.7.1954 Christchurch, Canterbury. RHB wk Team: **Canterbury.** Played List A in NZ. Sch: Papanui HS. Occ: Housing corporation manager.

COLLINS William Edward 1887/88-1888/89 b 14.10.1853 Monghyr, Bihar, India. d 11.8.1934 Wellington. occ wk Team: **Wellington.** Sch: Cheltenham, England. Occ: Doctor. Rugby: England. MP. His nephew, A.E.J.Collins, made the highest score on record, 628 not out, in a junior house match at Clifton College in 1899. Son: D.C.Collins.

COLLINSON Edward Thomas 1868/69-1885/86 b 2.11.1849 Derby, England. d 24.9.1920 Melbourne, Victoria, Australia. occ wk Team: **Otago.** Occ: Solicitor. Umpired first-class cricket.

COLQUHOUN Ian Alexander 1953/54-1963/64 b 8.6.1924 Wellington. d 26.2.2005 Paraparaumu Beach, Wellington. RHB wk Teams: **Central Districts, New Zealand Test.** Sch: Rongatai Coll. Occ: Schoolteacher. Rugby: Wellington, Otago, Manawatu and All Black triallist. QSM. NZCA obit: 2005; Wisden obit: 2006. NZCA COY: 1963. NZ and CD selector, President of the New Zealand board. He holds the Central Districts 10th wicket partnership record of 133 with G.A.Bartlett against Auckland in 1959/60.

COLSON Henry Frederick Webster 1877/78 b 21.9.1845 Richmond, Surrey, England. d 2.3.1880 Auckland. It was reported that prior to his death his health had been failing for some time 'through a want of personal care'. wk Team: **Auckland.** Occ: Journalist.

COMAN Peter George 1962/63-1977/78 b 13.4.1943 Christchurch, Canterbury. RHB Teams: **Canterbury, New Zealand ODI.** Played List A in NZ. Sch: Christchurch BHS. Occ: Comm traveller.

CONDLIFFE James William 1909/10-1924/25 b 30.7.1888 Wellington. d 23.11.1945 Wellington. RHB wk Teams: **Otago, Wellington, New Zealand.** Sch: Mt Cook HS. Occ: Clerk. He played for New Zealand prior to being granted Test status.

CONEY Christopher John 1965/66-1966/67 b 21.8.1945 Auckland. LHB SLA Team: **Wellington.** Brother: J.V.Coney.

CONEY Jeremy Vernon 1970/71-1986/87 b 21.6.1952 Wellington. RHB RM Teams: **Wellington, New Zealand Test, New Zealand ODI.** Played List A in NZ. Sch: Onslow Coll. Occ: Schoolteacher; commentator. Book: Playing Mantis. MBE. NZCA COY: 1984, 1985, 1986; WCOY: 1984. Brother: C.J.Coney.

CONGDON Bevan Ernest 1960/61-1978 b 11.2.1938 Motueka, Tasman. RHB RM occ wk Teams: **Central Districts, Wellington, Otago, Canterbury, New Zealand Test, New Zealand ODI.** Played List A in NZ. Sch: Motukea HS. Occ: Salesman. OBE. NZCA COY: 1966.

CONNELL Thomas William Christopher 1896/97-1901/02 b 4.3.1869 Invercargill, Southland. LFM Teams: **Wellington,** New South Wales. Sch: Invercargill Sth.

CONNELLY Philip 1908/09 b 1881 Grafton, New South Wales, Australia. d 1960 Parramatta, Sydney, New South Wales, Australia. F Team: **Wellington.**

CONRADI Norris 1917/18-1925/26 b 25.8.1890 Melbourne, Victoria, Australia. d 30.7.1928 Dunedin, Otago. Team: **Otago.** Occ: Comm traveller.

CONWAY John 1861/62-1879/80 b 3.2.1842 Fyansford, Victoria, Australia. d 22.8.1909 Frankston, Melbourne, Victoria, Australia. RHB RFr Teams: **Otago,** Victoria. Sch: Melbourne CEGS, Australia. Occ: Journalist. He was manager of the 1878 Australian team to England.

COOK Allan James 1955/56-1956/57 b 30.10.1924 Lower Hutt, Wellington. d 20.3.1989 Whangarei, Northland. RHB RM Team: **Wellington.** Occ: Rigger.

COOK Reginald Frederick 1942/43-1948/49 b 11.8.1913 Christchurch, Canterbury. d 29.7.1954 Christchurch, Canterbury. OB Team: **Canterbury.** Sch: Christchurch BHS. Occ: Farmer.

COOKE Frank Herbert 1879/80-1888/89 b 22.9.1862 Northcote, Melbourne, Victoria, Australia. d 10.6.1933 Palmerston North, Manawatu. SLA Teams: **Otago, Nelson.** Sch: Tonbridge, England. Occ: Crown prosecutor. He took 9/73 for Otago v Canterbury in 1884/85; in this game he had the best match figures for Otago of 15/94.

COOKE William Arthur 1891/92 b 1869 unknown. d 21.11.1954 Auckland. Team: **Canterbury.** Occ: Chemist.
COOPER Barry George 1980/81-1994/95 b 30.11.1958 Whangarei, Northland. RHB OB Team: **Northern Districts.** Played List A in NZ. Sch: Whangarei HS. He shares with B.L.Cairns the record of the fastest NZ FC century - 52 minutes (and 66 balls) - for Northern Districts v Canterbury in 1986/87.
COOPER David Mark 1993/94-1996/97 b 18.2.1972 Wanganui. RHB RSM Team: **Central Districts.** Played List A in NZ.
COOPER Ivan Walter 1924/25-1927/28 b 28.1.1896 Auckland. d 2.8.1968 Auckland. RHB LB Team: **Auckland.** Occ: Jeweller. NZCA obit: 1968.
COOPER William Henry (Sir) 1941/42-1943/44 b 2.10.1909 Leam Farm, Derbyshire, England. d 4.9.1990 Auckland. RHB RM Team: **Auckland.** Sch: Auckland GS. Occ: Headmaster. Hockey: Auckland. Book: Henry Cooper of Auckland Grammar School by Andrew Mason. Knighted for services to the community. NZCA obit: 1991; Wisden obit: 1991. NZ cricket manager.
CORFE Charles Carteret 1871/72-1883/84 b 8.6.1847 Guernsey. d 26.6.1935 Peterborough, Northamptonshire, England. RHB Team: **Canterbury.** Sch: Elizabeth Coll, Guernsey. Occ: Schoolmaster. Athletics: Cambridge University.
CORNELIUS Cleighten James 2001/02-2004/05 b 2.6.1976 Christchurch, Canterbury. RHB RM Team: **Canterbury.** Played List A in NZ. Sch: St Bedes Coll. Occ: Winemaker. Brother: W.A.Cornelius.
CORNELIUS Wade Alfred 2000/01-2004/05 b 5.3.1978 Christchurch, Canterbury. RHB RFM Team: **Canterbury.** Sch: St Bedes Coll. Occ: Radio station employee. Brother: C.J.Cornelius.
CORNISH Charles Athelstan 1874/75 b Q2 1850 Windsor, Berkshire, England. d 27.11.1917 Auckland. Team: **Wellington.** Sch: Eton, England. Occ: Clerk.
COTTERILL Arthur James 1865/66-1873/74 b 22.1.1848 Henstead, Suffolk, England. d 3.9.1902 Napier, Hawke's Bay. He died from pneumonia. RHB occ wk Team: **Canterbury.** Sch: Christ Coll. Occ: Solicitor; Crown prosecutor. Brothers: C.N.Cotterill, E.J.Cotterill, H.Cotterill, W.J.Cotterill; sons: A.K.Cotterill, B.W.Cotterill, G.R.Cotterill.
COTTERILL Arthur Keith 1901/02 b 28.12.1881 Napier, Hawke's Bay. d 3.1.1943 Hastings, Hawke's Bay. RHB occ wk Team: **Hawke's Bay.** Sch: Christ Coll. Occ: Farmer. Brothers: B.W.Cotterill, G.R.Cotterill; father: A.J.Cotterill; uncles: C.N.Cotterill, E.J.Cotterill, H.Cotterill, W.J.Cotterill.
COTTERILL Basil Walter 1901/02-1908/09 b 6.8.1882 Wairoa, Hawke's Bay. d 7.3.1951 Dunedin, Otago. SLA Team: **Hawke's Bay.** Occ: Farmer. Brothers: A.K.Cotterill, G.R.Cotterill; father: A.J.Cotterill; uncles: C.N.Cotterill, E.J.Cotterill, H.Cotterill, W.J.Cotterill.
COTTERILL Charles Napier 1893/94 b 20.3.1865 Christchurch, Canterbury. d 20.10.1934 Timaru, South Canterbury. Team: **Hawke's Bay.** Sch: Christ Coll. Occ: Bank manager. Brothers: A.J.Cotterill, E.J.Cotterill, H.Cotterill, W.J.Cotterill; nephews: A.K.Cotterill, B.W.Cotterill, G.R.Cotterill.
COTTERILL Edward Joseph 1880/81-1895/96 b 27.6.1856 Lyttelton, Christchurch, Canterbury. d 26.4.1904 Christchurch, Canterbury. RHB Teams: **Canterbury, Auckland.** Sch: Christ Coll. Occ: Bank accountant. Rugby: Canterbury. Brothers: A.J.Cotterill, C.N.Cotterill, H.Cotterill, W.J.Cotterill; nephews: A.K.Cotterill, B.W.Cotterill, G.R.Cotterill.
COTTERILL George Robert 1899/00 b 2.11.1879 Napier, Hawke's Bay. d 28.5.1956 Hastings, Hawke's Bay. Team: **Hawke's Bay.** Occ: Sheep farmer. Brothers: A.K.Cotterill, B.W.Cotterill; father A.J.Cotterill; uncles: C.N.Cotterill, E.J.Cotterill, H.Cotterill, W.J.Cotterill.
COTTERILL Henry 1873/74-1884/85 b 16.3.1855 Lyttelton, Christchurch, Canterbury. d 2.12.1943 Christchurch, Canterbury. Team: **Canterbury.** Sch: Christ Coll. Occ: Solicitor. Rugby: Canterbury. Brothers: A.J.Cotterill, C.N.Cotterill, E.J.Cotterill, W.J.Cotterill; nephews: A.K.Cotterill, B.W.Cotterill, G.R.Cotterill.
COTTERILL William John 1881/82-1893/94 b 25.3.1863 Christchurch, Canterbury. d 30.10.1946 Timaru, South Canterbury. RHB Team: **Canterbury.** Sch: Christ Coll. Occ: Clerk. Rugby: Canterbury and was well known as a referee. Brothers: A.J.Cotterill, C.N.Cotterill, E.J.Cotterill, H.Cotterill; nephews: A.K.Cotterill, B.W.Cotterill, G.R.Cotterill.
COTTON Henry Edward 1873/74-1877/78 b Q4 1845 St Austell, Cornwall, England. d 11.8.1907 Auckland. Team: **Auckland.** Occ: Auctioneer.

COULL Gordon Graeme 1954/55-1961/62 b 15.3.1928 Christchurch, Canterbury. d 1.10.2004 Christchurch, Canterbury. RHB SLA Team: **Canterbury.** Sch: Christ Coll. Occ: Farmer. NZCA obit: 2005.

COULSTOCK Richard 1855/56-1863/64 b 1823 Surrey, England. d 15.12.1870 South Melbourne, Victoria, Australia. A benefit match was held for him in Melbourne in November 1870 as he intended to return to England but he died of a heart attack a few weeks later. RHB RFMr Teams: **Otago,** Victoria. Occ: Groundsman.

COUPER Robert Neil 1951/52 b 19.12.1927 Palmerston North, Manawatu. d 24.3.1997 Taihape, Rangitikei. RHB SLA Team: **Otago.** Sch: Christ Coll. Occ: Farmer. NZCA obit: 2002.

COUPLAND Robert John Mcqueen 1942/43 b 1918 unknown. d 8.3.1981 Titahi Bay, Wellington. Team: **North Island Army.** Occ: Manager.

COUPLAND Robert William 1930/31-1932/33 b 24.9.1904 Christchurch, Canterbury. d 29.9.1968 Sydney, New South Wales, Australia. RHB OB Team: **Otago.** Sch: West Christchurch BHS. Occ: Civil servant. NZCA obit: 1968.

COUTTS Henry Donald 1882/83-1891/92 b 14.11.1866 Kaiapoi, North Canterbury. d 30.4.1944 Onehunga, Auckland. Team: **Taranaki.** Occ: Land valuer; farmer. Rugby: Taranaki. He made his first-class debut aged 16. Whilst serving with the New Zealand Forces in the Anglo-Boer War, Coutts refused to leave a wounded comrade and galloped back to him under heavy fire. He managed to get the man on his horse and rode him about nine miles to an ambulance station. He was awarded an unusual and unique recognition of his actions in that he was presented with a woollen scarf crocheted by Queen Victoria. Eight scarves were crocheted by the Queen, four of which were awarded to imperial troops and four to colonial soldiers. Each scarf was awarded for an act of bravery and came with a gold star and clasp ordered by King Edward VII following Queen Victoria's death. The initials VRI (Victoria Regina Imperatrix) are embroidered in cotton in one corner of the scarf. In 1913, Coutts presented his scarf to the New Zealand Government and it was displayed in the Assembly Library before being presented to the New Zealand Army Museum, Waiouru, in the 1980s.

COUTTS Peter John Charles 1958/59-1972/73 b 3.11.1937 Napier, Hawke's Bay. RHB OB Teams: **Central Districts, Wellington.** Played List A in NZ.

COWIE John 1932/33-1949/50 b 30.3.1912 Auckland. d 3.6.1994 Lower Hutt, Wellington. RHB RFM Teams: **Auckland, New Zealand Test.** Sch: Takapuna GS; Mt Albert GS. Umpired Test and first-class cricket. Soccer: Auckland, Chairman of the New Zealand Football Assn council. OBE. NZCA obit: 1994. He holds the Auckland 10th wicket partnership record of 119 with W.N.Carson against Otago in 1937/38.

COWLISHAW William Patten 1864/65 b 1.11.1839 Sydney, New South Wales, Australia. d 29.3.1903 Christchurch, Canterbury. Team: **Canterbury.** Occ: Solicitor. MP.

COX Arthur 1924/25-1926/27 b 7.12.1904 Christchurch, Canterbury. d 20.9.1977 Christchurch, Canterbury. RHB Team: **Canterbury.** Sch: Christchurch BHS. Occ: Nurseryman. He scored 204 in his second FC Match, for Canterbury v Otago in 1925/26. However, eyesight problems forced his retirement shortly thereafter.

COX Keith Fortnam Sandford 1933/34 b 30.8.1903 Marton, Rangitikei. d 8.11.1977 Taupo, Waikato. Team: **Otago.** Sch: Christ Coll. Occ: Coy secretary.

COX Richard Dawson 1971/72 b 1.5.1951 Waipawa, Hawke's Bay. RHB RM Teams: **New Zealand Under-23s, Central Districts (not FC).** Played List A in NZ.

COX Theophilus Alexander 1883/84-1886/87 b Q3 1855 Edmonton, Middlesex, England. d 1908 Ryde, Sydney, New South Wales, Australia. RS Team: **Wellington.** Sch: Repton, England.

COXON Sidney William Grattan 1884/85 b Q1 1859 Marylebone, London, England. d 17.12.1937 Chelsea, London, England. Team: **Auckland.** Sch: Prior Park, England. Occ: Stockbroker.

CRABB Terry Colin 1997/98 b 23.7.1976 Auckland. LHB LM Team: **Auckland.** Played List A in NZ. Sch: Westlake BHS.

CRAFAR Carl Antony 1986/87 b 18.11.1964 Wanganui. RHB RM Team: **Central Districts.** Played List A in NZ. Occ: Civil servant.

CRAIK Emmett Duncan 1999/00 b 25.11.1974 Hastings, Hawke's Bay. RHB RM Team: **Central Districts.** Played List A in NZ.

CRAMOND Albert Alexander 1904/05 b 12.12.1881 Dunedin, Otago. d 21.6.1954 Wellington. Team: **Otago.** Occ: Merchant.

CRAWFORD Cyril Gore 1920/21-1931/32 b 13.3.1902 Christchurch, Canterbury. d 17.6.1988 Christchurch, Canterbury. RHB Teams: **Canterbury, New Zealand.** Sch: Christchurch BHS. Rugby: representative referee. NZCA obit: 1988; Wisden obit: 1989. Canterbury selector and life member of the Canterbury CA. He played for New Zealand in a FC match. Nephew: W.R.Playle.
CRAWFORD Francis Roy 1937/38-1947/48 b 23.12.1917 Wellington. d 29.7.1996 Wellington. RHB LB Team: **Wellington.** Sch: St Patricks Coll, Wellington. NZCA obit: 2004.
CRAWFORD John Neville 1904-1921 b 1.12.1886 Cane Hill, Surrey, England. d 2.5.1963 Epsom, Surrey, England. RHB RM,OB Teams: **Otago, Wellington,** England Test, Surrey, South Australia. Sch: Repton, England. Occ: Cricket pro; teacher. Books: The practical cricketer; John Crawford: His record by N.Hart. NZCA obit: 1963; Wisden obit: 1964. WCOY: 1907. An English pro, played and coached in NZ. He holds the Otago 8th wicket partnership record of 165* with A.G.Eckhold against Wellington in 1914/15. For the Australians v South Canterbury XV in 1913/14 he scored 354 out of a total of 922 for nine wickets. He and V.T.Trumper put on 298 in sixty-nine minutes for the eighth wicket and with M.A.Noble at one point added 50 in nine minutes. Brothers: R.T.Crawford (Leicestershire), V.F.S.Crawford (Surrey, Leicestershire); father: J.C.Crawford (Kent); uncle: F.F.Crawford (Kent, Natal).
CRAWSHAW Ernest Elgood 1907/08-1913/14 b 23.6.1889 Christchurch, Canterbury. d 9.10.1918 Le Cateau, France. He was killed in action, aged 29. RHB Team: **Canterbury.** Sch: Christchurch BHS. Occ: Accountant. Rugby: Canterbury.
CRAWSHAW William Joseph 1877/78-1897/98 b 1861 Melbourne, Victoria, Australia. d 11.2.1938 Caterham, Surrey, England. LHB Teams: **Otago, Canterbury, Wellington, Taranaki.** Sch: Wanganui CS; Otago BHS. Occ: Bank officer.
CREAGH Michael Clayton 1866/67 b 25.5.1845 Ireland. d 27.5.1895 Dunedin, Otago. Team: **Otago.** Occ: Solicitor.
CREED Thomas Michael 1910/11-1913/14 b 1879 Parramatta, Sydney, New South Wales, Australia. d 9.5.1950 Napier, Hawke's Bay. OB Team: **Hawke's Bay.** Occ: Machinist.
CREEKS Thomas Elliott 1886/87 b 1859 unknown. d 26.9.1917 Mt Eden, Auckland. Team: **Wellington.** Occ: Policeman.
CRENE Desmond Bruce 1966/67 b 19.8.1945 Kaitaia, Northland. LHB RM Team: **Northern Districts.** Sch: Kaitaia Coll. Occ: Sports dealer.
CRESSWELL Arthur Edward 1948/49-1951/52 b 7.8.1917 Christchurch, Canterbury. d 3.8.2002 Blenheim, Marlborough. RHB RFM Teams: **Wellington, Central Districts.** Sch: Marlborough Boys Coll. NZCA obit: 2002. NZCA COY: 1949. Brother: G.F.Cresswell.
CRESSWELL George Fenwick 1948/49-1954/55 b 22.3.1915 Wanganui. d 10.1.1966 Blenheim, Marlborough. He was found dead with a shotgun at his side. LHB RSM Teams: **Wellington, Central Districts, New Zealand Test.** Sch: Marlborough Boys Coll. Occ: Mechanic. NZCA obit: 1966; Wisden obit: 1967. NZCA COY: 1950. CD selector. Brother: A.E.Cresswell.
CROCKER Lindsay Mervyn 1982/83-1988/89 b 16.5.1958 Taumarunui, King Country. RHB RSM occ wk Team: **Northern Districts.** Played List A in NZ. Occ: Cricket administrator.
CROFT Steven John 2005-2010 b 11.10.1984 Blackpool, Lancashire, England. RHB RMF Teams: **Auckland,** Lancashire. Played List A in NZ; Played T20 in NZ. Sch: Myerscough Coll, England. An English pro, played and coached in NZ.
CROMB Ian Burns 1929/30-1946/47 b 25.6.1905 Christchurch, Canterbury. d 6.3.1984 Christchurch, Canterbury. He died in a car accident. RHB RFM Teams: **Canterbury, New Zealand Test.** Sch: Christchurch BHS. Occ: Sports shop owner; cricket coach. NZCA obit: 1984. Canterbury selector, President Canterbury CA.
CROMBIE Melville John 1900/01-1911/12 b 1876 Wellington. d 23.4.1932 Wellington. He had been playing golf on the Miramar links and was in the act of changing his shoes before going home when he fell over and died. Team: **Wellington.** Sch: St Patrick's Coll. Occ: Solicitor. NZ selector; on the Management Committees of the Wellington Rugby Union and Wellington CA.
CROOK Brendon-John 2007/08-2008/09 b 29.6.1984 Lower Hutt, Wellington. LHB RM Team: **Wellington.** Played List A in NZ; Played T20 in NZ. Sch: Hutt Valley HS.
CROOK Ronald Clarence 1930/31-1933/34 b 28.1.1907 Christchurch, Canterbury. d 17.1.1943 Tripoli, Libya. He was killed in action aged 36. RHB RF Team: **Wellington.** Wisden obit: 1944.

CROSS Christopher Smith 1873/74-1895/96 b 26.10.1852 Nelson. d 26.6.1919 Mosman, Sydney, New South Wales, Australia. F occ wk Teams: **Nelson, Wellington.** Sch: Nelson Coll. Occ: Merchant. Umpired first-class cricket. Brother: W.H.Cross.
CROSS William Henry 1875/76-1876/77 b 6.7.1850 Nelson. d 4.11.1892 Wellington. occ wk Team: **Nelson.** Sch: Nelson Coll. Occ: Clerk. Brother: C.S.Cross.
CROSSE Hugh Edward 1919/20 b 27.1.1896 Hastings, Hawke's Bay. d 28.9.1962 Napier, Hawke's Bay. wk Team: **Hawke's Bay.** Sch: Wanganui CS. Occ: Farmer. Golf: New Zealand Amateur Champion 1919. OBE.
CROWE David William 1953/54-1957/58 b 18.10.1933 Blenheim, Marlborough. d 12.5.2000 Auckland. LHB LB Teams: **Wellington, Canterbury.** Sch: Christ Coll. Book: The Crowe style. NZCA obit: 2000. Sons: M.D.Crowe, J.J.Crowe.
CROWE Jeffrey John 1977/78-1991/92 b 14.9.1958 Auckland. RHB RAB Teams: **Auckland, New Zealand Test, New Zealand ODI,** South Australia. Played List A in NZ. Sch: Auckland GS. Occ: Test match referee; manager of the New Zealand cricket team and in 2004 he became an ICC match referee. He holds the Auckland 2nd wicket partnership record of 241 with T.J.Franklin against Wellington in 1988/89 and the Auckland 4th wicket partnership record of 280 with D.N.Patel against Northern Districts in 1991/92. He scored the slowest century in NZ Test and FC matches, 516 minutes, 331 balls v Sri Lanka in 1986/87. Brother: M.D.Crowe; father: D.W.Crowe. Cousin of Russell Crowe the actor.
CROWE Martin David 1979/80-1995/96 b 22.9.1962 Henderson, Auckland. RHB RM Teams: **Auckland, Central Districts, Wellington, New Zealand Test, New Zealand ODI,** Somerset. Played List A in NZ. Sch: Auckland GS. Occ: Executive producer. Books: Out On A Limb: My Own Story; Tortured Genius by J.Romanos; Martin Crowe: His Record Innings by Innings by W.Harte. NZCA COY: 1987, 1988, 1991, 1992. WCOY: 1985. He holds the NZ 3rd wicket partnership record of 467 with A.H.Jones for New Zealand v Sri Lanka in 1990/91, at the time the highest partnership in Test history. He scored the highest New Zealand Test score of 299 in this game. He has the most Test centuries (17) for New Zealand and in all FC cricket he scored 19,608 first-class runs, with 71 centuries. He hit a record 1,676 runs in a New Zealand season in 1986/87. He also holds the Central Districts 4th wicket partnership record of 276* with P.S.Briasco against Canterbury in 1986/87. Brother: J.J.Crowe; father: D.W.Crowe. Cousin of Russell Crowe the actor.
CROWTHER John 1873/74-1881/82 b 1850 Wellington. d 17.10.1894 Wellington. Team: **Wellington.** Occ: Telegraphist.
CROXFORD William Robert James 1890/91-1893/94 b 4.9.1863 Clerkenwell, London, England. d 30.6.1950 Inch Valley, Otago. wk Team: **Otago.** Umpired first-class cricket; Rugby: Otago.
CROY Martyn Gilbert 1994/95-2001/02 b 23.1.1974 Hamilton, Waikato. RHB wk Team: **Otago.** Played List A in NZ. Occ: Sports admin. NZ U19 Test; NZ U19 ODI. He played for New Zealand in a FC match.
CRUMP Charles 1864/65-1867/68 b 7.11.1837 Derby, England. d 22.2.1912 Palmerston North, Manawatu. Team: **Otago.** Occ: Comm agent.
CRUMP William Charles 1947/48 b 3.2.1928 Auckland. RHB wk Team: **Auckland.**
CUFF Charles Albert 1907/08 b 10.7.1877 Christchurch, Canterbury. d 30.6.1942 Christchurch, Canterbury. Team: **Canterbury.** Occ: Bank officer. Cousin: L.A.Cuff.
CUFF Leonard Albert 1886/87-1904/05 b 28.3.1866 Christchurch, Canterbury. d 9.10.1954 Launceston, Tasmania, Australia. Teams: **Canterbury, Auckland, New Zealand,** Tasmania. Sch: Melville House. Occ: Insurance agent. NZCA obit: 1955; Wisden obit: 1955. Athletics: New Zealand long jump champion 3 times (1889, 1896, 1897). In Paris, France in 1892 he won a silver medal for hurdles at an International Athletics Meeting. Secretary of the NZ Athletics Assn, he was elected one of the thirteen Founder Members of the International Olympic Committee (IOC). NZ selector. He played for New Zealand prior to being granted Test status. He holds the Canterbury 1st wicket partnership record of 306 with J.D.Lawrence against Auckland in 1893/94. Cousin: C.A.Cuff; son: A.G.Cuff (Tasmania).
CUMMING Craig Derek 1995/96-2009/10 b 31.8.1975 Timaru, South Canterbury. RHB RSM occ wk Teams: **Canterbury, Otago, New Zealand Test, New Zealand ODI.** Played List A in NZ; Played T20 in NZ. Sch: Timaru BHS.

CUMMINGS Edwin Moon 1909/10-1910/11 b 29.1.1885 Dunedin, Otago. d 22.11.1951 Christchurch, Canterbury. Team: **Otago.** Occ: Timber merchant. Brother: G.B.Cummings.
CUMMINGS George Buck 1902/03-1922/23 b 21.9.1882 Dunedin, Otago. d 30.12.1943 Auckland. Teams: **Otago, Auckland.** Occ: Warehouseman. Brother: E.M.Cummings.
CUMMINS Gerald Ian 1978/79 b 11.11.1958 Rangiora, North Canterbury. LHB RFM Team: **Canterbury.** Played List A in NZ. Sch: Christchurch BHS. Occ: Physiotherapist.
CUNIS Robert Smith 1960/61-1976/77 b 5.1.1941 Whangarei, Northland. d 9.8.2008 Whangarei, Northland. RHB RFM Teams: **Auckland, Northern Districts, New Zealand Test.** Played List A in NZ. Sch: Whangarei HS. Occ: School principal. Rugby: Auckland. NZCA obit: 2009; Wisden obit: 2009. NZCA COY: 1969. One of the highlights of his international career was his battling 96-run partnership with Mark Burgess for the ninth wicket in the second innings against Pakistan in the third Test in Dhaka in 1969. The partnership helped New Zealand save the match and sealed their first series win on foreign soil. NZ selector and coach. Son: S.J.Cunis.
CUNIS Stephen John 1998/99-2005/06 b 17.1.1978 Whakatane, Bay of Plenty. RHB RFM Team: **Canterbury.** Played List A in NZ; Played T20 in NZ. Sch: Whangarei HS. Occ: School teacher. NZ U19 Test; NZ U19 ODI. Father: R.S.Cunis.
CUNNINGHAM John 1882/83 b 18.11.1854 New Plymouth, Taranaki. d 20.8.1932 Toorak, Victoria, Australia. Team: **Taranaki.** Occ: Horse trainer.
CUNNINGHAM William Henry Ranger 1922/23-1930/31 b 23.1.1900 Christchurch, Canterbury. d 29.11.1984 Christchurch, Canterbury. RHB RMF Teams: **Canterbury, New Zealand.** Occ: New Zealand Railways employee. Rugby League: Canterbury. NZCA obit: 1985. He was regarded as one of the best bowlers in New Zealand. In England he suffered a case of what now would be called, in golfing terms, the yips, that delicate state where players can no longer sink their putts. Another factor in his decline was the problems suffered in his relationship with the captain of the side, Tom Lowry. He played for New Zealand prior to being granted Test status. Nephew: G.F.Anderson.
CURRIE Clive James 1976/77 b 25.12.1955 Wellington. LHB OB Team: **Wellington.** Played List A in NZ. Sch: Rongatai Coll. Occ: Schoolteacher. Rugby: All Black, Wellington and Wanganui. On the 1978 All Black rugby tour of the British Isles, his jaw was broken in the Test against Wales which ended both his tour and his rugby career.
CURRIE Donald Cameron 1959/60-1962/63 b 7.7.1934 Christchurch, Canterbury. RHB LB Teams: **Central Districts, Canterbury.**
CURRIE Ernest William 1893/94-1899/00 b 9.4.1873 Dunedin, Otago. d 23.10.1932 Randwick, Sydney, New South Wales, Australia. RHB wk Teams: **Otago,** Queensland. Occ: Clerk. Rugby: Australia, Queensland and Otago.
CURTIN Paul 1974/75-1980/81 b 10.5.1954 Rose Park, Adelaide, South Australia, Australia. LHB LB Teams: **Northern Districts,** South Australia. Sch: Angle Park Technical School, Australia. Occ: Sales manager. Brothers: B.G.Curtin (South Australia), P.D.Curtin (South Australia).
CURTIS William Michael 1955/56-1958/59 b 30.8.1933 Auckland. d 1.12.2009 Wellington. LHB wk Team: **Wellington.** Sch: Nelson Coll. Wellington selector.
CUSHEN John Arthur James 1967/68-1986/87 b 15.2.1950 Dunedin, Otago. RHB RFM Teams: **Otago, Auckland.** Played List A in NZ. Sch: Kings HS. Otago CA board member.
CUTLER Arthur Sydney Hamilton 1938/39-1946/47 b 17.1.1913 Palmerston North, Manawatu. d 27.8.1997 Invercargill, Southland. RHB LB Team: **Otago.** Occ: Schoolteacher. Umpired first-class cricket. NZCA obit: 1998.
DACRE Charles Christian Ralph 1914/15-1936 b 15.5.1899 Devonport, Auckland. d 2.11.1975 Devonport, Auckland. RHB SLA occ wk Teams: **Auckland, New Zealand,** Gloucestershire. Soccer: New Zealand and Auckland. NZCA obit: 1976; Wisden obit: 1977. He played for New Zealand prior to being granted Test status. He was the youngest NZ FC cricketer when he made his debut aged 15 years 224 days for Auckland v Wellington in 1914/15. Brother: L.M.Dacre; nephew: D.D.Coleman.
DACRE Life Marwell 1912/13-1913/14 b 6.10.1896 Devonport, Auckland. d 28.4.1972 Auckland. RHB Team: **Auckland.** Occ: Farm labourer. MM. NZCA obit: 1972. Brother: C.C.R.Dacre; nephew: D.D.Coleman.
DAKIN Albert Eddington 1905/06 b 1873 Melbourne, Victoria, Australia. d 1964 Melbourne, Victoria, Australia. Team: **Canterbury.**

DALEY Nathan Michael 2002/03-2003/04 b 2.6.1977 Sydney, New South Wales, Australia. RHB wk Team: **Northern Districts.** Played List A in NZ. Sch: Fraser HS.

DALGLEISH Richard William 1906/07-1907/08 b 1880 Galashiels, Selkirkshire, Scotland. d 16.9.1955 Napier, Hawke's Bay. M Team: **Hawke's Bay.** Occ: Wool clerk. He represented South Canterbury in the early 1900s taking 5/56 against Lord Hawke's 1902/03 team and 14 wickets in a non-first-class match against North Canterbury in 1904/05.

DALTON C J 1893/94 Team: **Wellington.** He arrived in Wellington from Melbourne in early 1893, but nothing else is known of him.

D'ARCY John William 1955/56-1961/62 b 23.4.1936 Christchurch, Canterbury. RHB Teams: **Canterbury, Wellington, Otago, New Zealand Test.** Sch: Christchurch BHS. Occ: Coy director.

D'ARCY William Alexander 1891/92 b 30.1.1863 Orongaronga, Wairarapa. d 23.10.1940 Wanganui. Team: **Taranaki.** Sch: Wanganui CS. Occ: Farmer.

DARRAGH James Francis 1919/20 b 2.4.1890 Invercargill, Southland. d 29.1.1952 Invercargill, Southland. Team: **Southland.** Occ: Gardener.

D'AUVERGNE Philip Godfrey 1969/70-1978/79 b 23.6.1950 Invercargill, Southland. LHB SLA Team: **Canterbury.** Played List A in NZ. Sch: Timaru BHS. Occ: School teacher.

DAVENPORT Robert Noel 1881/82-1883/84 b 26.11.1852 Adelaide, South Australia, Australia. d 22.12.1934 Port Elliott, South Australia, Australia. Team: **Otago.** Sch: Mill Hill, England.

DAVIDSON Michael Philip Forbes 2006/07-2008/09 b 24.9.1981 Christchurch, Canterbury. RHB LFM Team: **Canterbury.** Played List A in NZ; Played T20 in NZ. Sch: Christ Coll.

DAVIES Chris Andrew 1998/99 b 16.1.1980 Nelson. LHB LM Team: **Otago.**

DAVIS David Grant 1920/21 b 12.1.1902 Wanstead, Hawke's Bay. d 2.3.1995 Auckland. RHB RM wk Team: **Hawke's Bay.** Sch: Wanganui CS. Occ: Judge. NZCA obit: 1995; Wisden obit: 1996. At the time of his death he had been the oldest surviving New Zealand first-class cricketer and the last living player that had played a first-class match for Hawke's Bay.

DAVIS Harry 1938/39-1939/40 RHB RM Team: **Canterbury.**

DAVIS Heath Te-ihi-o-te-rangi 1991/92-2003/04 b 30.11.1971 Lower Hutt, Wellington. RHB RF Teams: **Wellington, Auckland, New Zealand Test, New Zealand ODI.** Played List A in NZ. NZ U19 ODI.

DAVIS Te Ahu Trevor 2004/05-2008/09 b 9.12.1985 Auckland. RHB RFM Team: **Northern Districts.** Played List A in NZ; Played T20 in NZ. Sch: St Pauls, Hamilton. NZ U19 ODI.

DAVIS Winston Walter 1979/80-1991/92 b 18.9.1958 Sion Hill, Kingstown, St Vincent. RHB RF Teams: **Wellington,** Glamorgan, Northamptonshire, Tasmania, West Indies Test, West Indies ODI, Windward Islands, Combined Leeward and Windward Islands. Played List A in NZ. Occ: Cricket pro. In 1998 he was left paralysed from the neck down after suffering spinal injuries when he fell from a tree. He was part of West Indies 1983 World Cup squad, taking a record 7/51 against Australia at Headingley.

DAWE James 1873/74 b 1844 New Zealand. d 6.8.1919 Christchurch, Canterbury. LHB Team: **Canterbury.** Occ: Schoolmaster. Umpired first-class cricket.

DAWE William Hill 1865/66 b 8.4.1835 Bath, Somerset, England. d 12.8.1912 Christchurch, Canterbury. He died as a result of senile decay. Team: **Canterbury.** Sch: Sherborne, England. Occ: Commission agent.

DAWES Alexander 1884/85-1894/95 b 20.11.1859 Inverness, Scotland. d 24.2.1939 Dunedin, Otago. Team: **Otago.** Occ: Coach builder.

DAWSON Frederick Francis 1950/51 b 19.6.1917 Timaru, South Canterbury. d 27.4.1986 Christchurch, Canterbury. RHB Team: **Canterbury.** Sch: Christchurch BHS. NZCA obit: 1986. Canterbury CA President and life member.

DAWSON Garth James 1980/81-1984/85 b 17.10.1959 Invercargill, Southland. LHB OB Team: **Otago.** Played List A in NZ.

DAWSON James Hurren Martin 1957/58-1962/63 b 28.10.1937 Christchurch, Canterbury. RFM Team: **Canterbury.** Sch: Christ Coll. Occ: Solicitor.

DAY George 1903/04 b 1.10.1879 Wellington. d 7.8.1953 Wellington. Team: **Wellington.** Sch: Mt Cook HS. Occ: Builder.

DEAN Kenrick Holt 1914/15 b 29.7.1895 Napier, Hawke's Bay. d 30.10.1987 Otaki, Horowhenua. Team: **Hawke's Bay.** Sch: Paeroa HS. Occ: Doctor.

DEANE Alan J 1947/48 RHB Team: **Auckland.**
DEAS Kenneth Robin 1947/48-1960/61 b 10.7.1927 Papatoetoe, Auckland. d 20.10.2000 Auckland. RHB SLA Teams: **Auckland,** Scotland. Occ: Pharmacist. NZCA obit: 2001. NZ and Auckland selector. He also served as chairman of Auckland Cricket, becoming a life member and president and at the time of his death he was vice-patron. He was Auckland delegate to the New Zealand Cricket Council and was a manager of international touring teams. He was also president of New Zealand Cricket.
DE BOORDER Andrew Philip 2007/08-2009/10 b 6.7.1988 Hastings, Hawke's Bay. RHB RM Team: **Auckland.** Played List A in NZ. Sch: Macleans Coll; Kings Coll. NZ U19 Test; NZ U19 ODI. Brother: D.C.de Boorder.
DE BOORDER Derek Charles 2007/08-2009/10 b 25.10.1985 Hastings, Hawke's Bay. RHB wk Team: **Otago.** Played List A in NZ; Played T20 in NZ. Sch: Macleans Coll. NZ U19 ODI. He took a NZ record of 8 catches in an innings and 10 in the match for Otago v Wellington in 2009/10. Brother: A.P.de Boorder.
DEES James Gibson 1873/74 b Q3 1845 Morpeth, Northumberland, England. d Q3 1911 Whitehaven, Cumberland, England. Team: **Wellington.** Sch: Ampleforth, England. Occ: Civil engineer. He was agent to the Earl of Lonsdale.
DE GRANDHOMME Colin 2005/06-2009/10 b 22.7.1986 Harare, Zimbabwe. RHB RFM Teams: **Auckland,** Zimbabwe A. Played List A in NZ; Played T20 in NZ. Sch: St Georges Coll, Zimbabwe. He played for Zimbabwe A before emigrating to New Zealand with the intention of becoming a resident. He holds the NZ domestic T20 7th wicket partnership record of 77 with A.K.Kitchen for Auckland against Otago in 2009/10. Father: L.L.de Grandhomme (Zimbabwe); grandfather: H.L.de Grandhomme (Rhodesia).
DE GROEN Richard Paul 1987/88-1995/96 b 5.8.1962 Otorohanga, Waikato. RHB RFM Teams: **Auckland, Northern Districts, New Zealand Test, New Zealand ODI.** Played List A in NZ. Sch: Mt Albert GS. Occ: Olympic games manager. New Zealand team manager for three Commonwealth Games (1998, 2002 and 2006) and three Olympic Games (2000, 2002 and 2004).
DELLOW Harold Noel 1954/55-1955/56 b 14.2.1929 Ashburton, Mid Canterbury. LHB RM Team: **Canterbury.** Sch: Timaru BHS. Occ: Manager.
DE MAUS Herbert Seton 1889/90-1896/97 b 15.9.1871 Levuka, Fiji. d 15.7.1932 Suva, Fiji. RHB S Team: **Canterbury, New Zealand.** Occ: Clerk. A leading cricketer of the 1890s, he scored 118 against the 1893/94 NSW team. He moved to Fiji shortly thereafter where he spent the rest of his life. He played for New Zealand prior to being granted Test status.
DEMPSEY David Angus 1979/80-1987/88 b 27.5.1955 Christchurch, Canterbury. RHB RM Team: **Canterbury.** Played List A in NZ. Sch: Christchurch BHS. Occ: Salesman.
DEMPSTER Charles Stewart 1921/22-1947/48 b 15.11.1903 Wellington. d 14.2.1974 Wellington. RHB RS occ wk Teams: **Wellington, New Zealand Test,** Scotland, Leicestershire, Warwickshire. Occ: Textile industry. Book: C.S.Dempster: His Record Innings by Innings by W.Harte. Commemorated in the C.S.Dempster gates at the Basin Reserve. NZCA obit: 1974; Wisden obit: 1975. WCOY: 1932. He was regarded as one of NZ best cricketers and has the second highest Test batting average (65.72) in history for completed careers of 10 or more innings.
DEMPSTER Eric William 1947/48-1960/61 b 25.1.1925 Wellington. LHB SLA Teams: **Wellington, New Zealand Test.** Occ: Orthopaedic technician. Umpired first-class cricket. Otago selector.
DENCKER Henry Frederick Christian 1886/87 b 13.3.1865 Upper Moutere, Nelson. d 6.9.1949 Hamilton, Waikato. Team: **Nelson.** Occ: Farmer.
DENHAM Hono Evan Horrell 1945/46 b 18.5.1913 Brisbane, Queensland, Australia. d 16.6.1991 Christchurch, Canterbury. RHB LB Team: **Canterbury.** Sch: Christ Coll. Occ: Doctor. NZCA obit: 1992; Wisden obit: 1992.
DENHAM James 1884/85 wk Team: **Canterbury.**
DENSHIRE William Bankes 1873/74 b 17.10.1853 Baston, Lincolnshire, England. d 29.4.1920 Ashburton, Mid Canterbury. Team: **Nelson.** Sch: Marlborough, England. Occ: Farmer.
DENT Thomas Henry 1900/01-1901/02 b 1879 Sydney, New South Wales, Australia. d 11.9.1929 Kyogle, New South Wales, Australia. LB Team: **Hawke's Bay.** Occ: Bank officer. He had the best bowling figures for Hawke's Bay when he took 9/47 against Wellington in 1900/01.

DE TERTE James William 2007/08-2009/10 b 16.1.1983 Sydney, New South Wales, Australia. RHB RM Team: **Central Districts.** Sch: Lindesfarne Coll. Occ: Cricket pro.

DEVCICH Anton Paul 2004/05-2009/10 b 28.9.1985 Hamilton, Waikato. LHB SLA Team: **Northern Districts.** Played List A in NZ; Played T20 in NZ. Sch: Hamilton BHS. NZ U19 ODI.

DEVLIN Alan John 1983/84 b 2.10.1959 Rangiora, North Canterbury. LHB RM Team: **Canterbury.** Played List A in NZ. Sch: Rangiora HS.

DEWES Albert Evelyn 1882/83-1883/84 b 4.1860 Blenheim, Marlborough. d 5.7.1892 Auckland. He died at the age of 32 from influenza. wk Team: **Auckland.** Occ: Solicitor.

DIAMANTI Brendon John 2003/04-2009/10 b 30.4.1981 Blenheim, Marlborough. RHB RM Teams: **Central Districts, New Zealand ODI, New Zealand T20.** Played List A in NZ; Played T20 in NZ. Sch: Marlborough Boys Coll.

DICK Arthur Edward 1956/57-1968/69 b 10.10.1936 Middlemarch, Otago. RHB wk Teams: **Otago, Wellington, New Zealand Test.** Played List A in NZ. SACOY 1962. Wellington and Otago selector.

DICKEL Carlson Richard Wellesley 1970/71-1982/83 b 2.7.1946 Dunedin, Otago. RHB LB Teams: **Otago, Canterbury.** Played List A in NZ. Sch: Otago BHS. Occ: Schoolteacher. Basketball: New Zealand coach; his son Mark played basketball for New Zealand.

DICKEL Thomas Henry Victor 1917/18 b 31.7.1897 Dunedin, Otago. d 18.2.1969 Dunedin, Otago. Team: **Otago.** Occ: Traffic inspector.

DICKESON Clifford Wayne 1973/74-1986/87 b 26.3.1955 Kawakawa, Northland. RHB SLA Team: **Northern Districts.** Played List A in NZ. Sch: Whangarei HS. Occ: Cricket coach. NZCA COY: 1980. ND selector.

DICKINSON George 1863/64-1873/74 b 1828 Sheffield, Yorkshire, England. d 15.6.1913 Christchurch, Canterbury. Team: **Canterbury.** Occ: Farmer. Umpired first-class cricket. Wisden obit: 1914.

DICKINSON George Ritchie 1921/22-1943/44 b 11.3.1903 Dunedin, Otago. d 17.3.1978 Lower Hutt, Wellington. RHB RF Teams: **Otago, Wellington, New Zealand Test.** Sch: Otago BHS. Occ: Store foreman. Rugby: All Blacks and Otago. NZCA obit: 1978; Wisden obit: 1979.

DICKSON James Fairfield Wills 1911/12-1914/15 b 1887 unknown. d 21.7.1970 Auckland. Team: **Wellington.** Occ: Solicitor.

DIND Melbourne Hall 1917/18-1919/20 b 1879 Queensland, Australia. d 30.1.1946 Wellington. LHB Team: **Wellington.** Occ: Council employee.

DINEEN Barry Michael Joseph 1956/57-1963/64 b 17.9.1936 Christchurch, Canterbury. RHB RM Teams: **Canterbury, Central Districts.** Sch: Christchurch BHS. Occ: Coy director. Rugby: Canterbury.

DITCHFIELD William George 1933/34 b 21.5.1903 Sydney, New South Wales, Australia. d 21.3.1991 Dunedin, Otago. RHB RM Team: **Otago.** Occ: Window dresser. NZCA obit: 1992; Wisden obit: 1993. A noted musician, he played bass, harmonica and banjo in a pioneering NZ jazz band 'The Tumbleweeds'.

DIVER Robert John 1998/99 b 19.9.1974 Auckland. RHB Team: **Northern Districts.** Played List A in NZ.

DIXON David Collins 1919/20 b 26.11.1890 Fylde, Lancashire, England. d 29.5.1974 Opotiki, Bay of Plenty. Team: **Southland.** Occ: Merchant.

DIXON Ernest Richter 1873/74 b 22.6.1854 Lee, Middlesex, England. d 9.1.1889 Porere, Hawke's Bay. He drowned in an unsuccessful attempt to save a farm employee. Team: **Auckland.** Sch: Winchester, England. Occ: Farm manager.

DIXON William Gordon 1875/76-1885/86 b 21.7.1856 Little Sutton, Cheshire, England. d 26.1.1938 Point Piper, Sydney, New South Wales, Australia. RF Team: **Otago.** Occ: Bank officer. Rugby: Otago.

DOBBS Peter Wayne 1988/89-1994/95 b 20.2.1968 Dunedin, Otago. RHB Team: **Otago.** Played List A in NZ. NZ U19 Test; NZ U19 ODI.

DOIG John Allen 1914/15-1920/21 b 24.3.1872 Beechworth, Victoria, Australia. d 24.11.1951 Invercargill, Southland. Team: **Southland.** Occ: Sports dealer. Rugby: Southland. Wisden obit: 1952. During his minor cricket career he was credited with no fewer than fifty hat-tricks. On five occasions he took all ten wickets in an innings. A member of the Invercargill Club for forty-six years, he represented Southland for twenty years, playing his last game for them at the age of 63. His interest was not confined to cricket, and he did much for rugby football, hockey, athletics, basketball, boxing and golf in Southland.

DOLLERY Horace Edgar 1933-1955 b 14.10.1914 Reading, Berkshire, England. d 20.1.1987 Edgbaston, Birmingham, Warwickshire, England. RHB occ wk Teams: **Wellington,** England Test, Warwickshire. Sch: Reading Sch, England. Occ: Cricket pro. Books: Professional captain; Tom Dollery by N.Rogers. Wisden obit: 1988. WCOY: 1952. An English pro played and coached in NZ.

DOLLERY Keith Robert 1947/48-1956 b 9.12.1924 Cooroy, Queensland, Australia. RHB RFM Teams: **Auckland,** Warwickshire, Queensland, Tasmania. Sch: Mackay HS, Australia. Occ: Sales manager.

DONALD David Lindsay 1957/58-1960/61 b 20.7.1933 Palmerston North, Manawatu. RHB RS Team: **Northern Districts.**

DONALDSON Grant Thomas 1998/99-2003/04 b 8.6.1976 Upper Hutt, Wellington. RHB RM Team: **Wellington.** Played List A in NZ. Sch: Heretaunga Coll. Occ: Insurance officer.

DONALDSON John Bruce 1949/50 b 3.10.1919 Masterton, Wairarapa. d 25.1.1984 Auckland. RHB RM Team: **Auckland.** Sch: Dannevirke HS. Rugby: Auckland. Rugby League: Auckland and New Zealand Māori. Swimming: Auckland. NZCA obit: 1984; Wisden obit: 1984.

DONEGHUE Arthur Edgar 1919/20-1927/28 b 31.5.1897 Sydney, New South Wales, Australia. d 8.12.1960 Wellington. RHB Team: **Wellington.** Sch: Petone Coll. Occ: Comm agent.

DONKERS Brendon Peter 2002/03-2003/04 b 25.7.1976 Hokitika, West Coast. RHB RM Team: **Canterbury.** Sch: Rangiora HS. Indoor cricket: New Zealand.

DONNELLY Ian Telford 1981/82 b 26.2.1946 Timaru, South Canterbury. RHB OB Team: **Auckland.** Played List A in NZ.

DONNELLY Jason Patrick 2009/10 b 24.4.1987 Auckland. LHB SLA Team: **Canterbury.** Sch: Te Awamatu Coll. NZ U19 ODI. He holds the New Zealand record for the most runs conceded in an innings, 4/257 for Canterbury v Northern Districts in 2009/10.

DONNELLY Martin Paterson 1936/37-1960/61 b 17.10.1917 Ngaruawahia, Waikato. d 22.10.1999 Sydney, New South Wales, Australia. LHB SLA Teams: **Wellington, Canterbury, New Zealand Test,** Oxford University, Middlesex, Warwickshire. Sch: New Plymouth BHS. Occ: Marketing manager. Rugby: Canterbury, Oxford University and England. Book: New Zealand cricket's master craftsman by R.Nye. NZCA obit: 2000; Wisden obit: 2000. WCOY: 1948.

DOODY Brad James Kelvin 1995/96-2001/02 b 17.8.1973 Rangiora, North Canterbury. LHB LB Team: **Canterbury.** Played List A in NZ.

DORMER Michael Edmund Francis 1961/62 b 22.4.1937 Lower Hutt, Wellington. RHB wk Team: **Auckland.**

DORREEN Neil 1927/28-1930/31 b 11.10.1901 Hampden, Otago. d 20.8.1984 Hastings, Hawke's Bay. RHB wk Team: **Canterbury.** Sch: West Christchurch BHS. Rugby: Canterbury. He holds the NZ 7th wicket partnership record of 265 with J.L.Powell for Canterbury v Otago in 1929/30.

DOUGLAS Graham William 1965/66-1967/68 b 13.5.1945 Nelson. RHB LM Team: **Central Districts.** Son: M.W.Douglas.

DOUGLAS Mark William 1987/88-2000/01 b 20.10.1968 Nelson. LHB occ wk Teams: **Central Districts, Wellington, New Zealand ODI.** Played List A in NZ. NZ U19 Test; NZ U19 ODI. Father: G.W.Douglas.

DOUGLAS William 1878/79 b 6.6.1848 Longford, Tasmania, Australia. d 7.9.1887 Gore, Southland. Team: **Otago.** Sch: Horton Coll, Australia. Occ: Manager. He scored a king pair on his first-class debut.

DOUGLAS William Mackie 1922/23-1928/29 b 6.6.1903 Dunedin, Otago. d 5.7.1981 Auckland. LHB SLA Team: **Otago.** Sch: Otago BHS. Occ: Grocer. Soccer: Otago.

DOULL Lincoln John 1990/91-1993/94 b 8.1.1964 Pukekohe, Franklin. RHB RM Team: **Wellington.** Played List A in NZ. Occ: Contractor. Brother: S.B.Doull.

DOULL Simon Blair 1989/90-2001/02 b 6.8.1969 Pukekohe, Franklin. RHB RM Teams: **Northern Districts, New Zealand Test, New Zealand ODI.** Played List A in NZ. Occ: Commentator. NZCA COY: 1997. Brother: L.J.Doull.

DOWKER Raymond Thomas 1949/50-1956/57 b 6.7.1919 New Brighton, Christchurch, Canterbury. d 17.12.2004 Christchurch, Canterbury. RHB Team: **Canterbury**. Sch: Christchurch BHS. Occ: Auctioneer. NZCA obit: 2005. NZCA COY: 1955. Grandson: B.M.Walker.
DOWLING Graham Thorne 1958/59-1971/72 b 4.3.1937 Christchurch, Canterbury. RHB RM Teams: **Canterbury, New Zealand Test**. Played List A in NZ. Sch: St Andrews Coll. Occ: Manager. OBE. NZCA COY: 1962. In 1969 he had to have half a finger amputated after an accident while keeping wicket. NZ selector. CEO NZ cricket. In his first Test as captain in 1967/68 he scored 239 to lead the NZ team to their first win over the Indians.
DOWNES Alexander Dalziel 1887/88-1913/14 b 2.2.1868 Emerald Hill, South Melbourne, Victoria, Australia. d 10.2.1950 Dunedin, Otago. RHB OB Teams: **Otago, New Zealand**. Occ: Brass finisher. Umpired first-class cricket. Rugby: Otago. NZCA obit: 1950; Wisden obit: 1951. NZ selector. He played for New Zealand prior to being granted Test status; taking four wickets in four consecutive balls against Auckland in January 1894.
DOWNES John 1884/85 b 1860 Te Tai Rawhiti, Hawke's Bay. d 2.7.1940 Hastings, Hawke's Bay. Team: **Hawke's Bay**. Sch: Te Aute Coll. Occ: Ploughman. He was the second known player of Maori heritage (after E.T.Broughton in 1883/84) to play FC cricket.
DOWNES Leslie William 1975/76 b 19.9.1945 Lower Hutt, Wellington. RHB wk Team: **Central Districts**. Played List A in NZ.
DOWNES Thomas Alan 1940/41-1946/47 b 12.1.1921 Palmerston North, Manawatu. d 24.6.1960 Wellington. LF Team: **Wellington**. Sch: Palmerston North BHS. NZCA obit: 1960.
DOWNES William Fowles 1865/66-1875/76 b 1843 Nantwich, Cheshire, England. d 1.1.1896 Wanganui. Team: **Otago**. Occ: Bank officer.
DRABBLE Arthur Brownell 1884/85-1891/92 b 12.2.1864 Llandudno, Caernarvonshire, Wales. d 28.7.1931 Warwick, England. wk Team: **Otago**. Sch: Otago BHS. Occ: Farmer.
DRAKE William Tasman 1920/21 b 2.12.1884 Hobart, Tasmania, Australia. d 15.4.1946 Hastings, Hawke's Bay. Team: **Minor Assoc**. Sch: Selwyn Coll. Occ: Anglican Reverend.
DRAVID Rahul Sharad 1990/91-2010 b 11.1.1973 Indore, Madhya Pradesh, India. RHB OB occ wk Teams: **Canterbury**, Kent, India Test, ICC World XI Test, India ODI, Asian Cricket Council XI ODI, ICC World XI ODI, Karnataka. Sch: St Joseph's BHS, Bangalore. India. Occ: Cricket pro. WCOY: 2000. ICOY 2000. Indian Test Player who played for Canterbury in order to get match practice.
DRAVITZKI Terence Michael 1962/63 b 11.2.1940 New Plymouth, Taranaki. RHB occ wk Team: **Central Districts**.
DREDGE Frank William P 1905/06 b Q1 1880 Alderbury, Wiltshire, England. d 22.8.1916 Somme, France. LHB Team: **Wellington**. Book: 1909 Football Annual.
DREW Duncan John 2000/01-2001/02 b 11.11.1976 Oamaru, North Otago. RHB wk Team: **Otago**. Occ: Physiotherapist.
DRISCOLL Alfred 1914/15-1918/19 b 30.9.1883 Christchurch, Canterbury. d 16.7.1944 Dunedin, Otago. Team: **Southland**. Occ: Tobacconist. Umpired first-class cricket.
DROWN Richard John 1991/92-1992/93 b 2.5.1966 Hastings, Hawke's Bay. RHB RM Team: **Auckland**. Played List A in NZ.
DRUM Christopher James 1996/97-2001/02 b 10.7.1974 Auckland. RHB RFM Teams: **Auckland, New Zealand Test, New Zealand ODI**. Played List A in NZ. Sch: Rosmini Coll.
DRUMMOND John 1903/04 b 1885 Napier, Hawke's Bay. d 25.1.1958 Elgin, Cape Province, South Africa. Team: **Hawke's Bay**. Sch: Napier BHS. Occ: Doctor. Rugby: Galasheils. Son-in-law: R.R.Yuill (Natal).
DRY Lance Richard 1994/95-1998/99 b 14.12.1975 Wellington. RHB LB Team: **Wellington**. Wellington selector.
DRYDEN Charles Henry 1884/85-1894/95 b 1860 Wellington. d 1.7.1943 Russell, Northland. LHB LB Team: **Wellington**. Occ: Builder. Wisden obit: 1944. He took 12 wickets for 93 against Canterbury, and in 1891 against the same side 11 for 56. Brother: W.E.Dryden.
DRYDEN Walter Edward 1885/86 b 1864 Wellington. d 11.7.1892 Wellington. He died aged 28. Team: **Wellington**. Sch: Mt Cook HS. Occ: Boilermaker. Brother: C.H.Dryden.

DU CHATEAU Victor Henry 1932/33-1939/40 b 1.8.1911 Wellington. d 26.9.2005 Auckland. LHB RFM Team: **Wellington.** Sch: Wellington Coll. Occ: Accountant. NZCA obit: 2006; Wisden obit: 2007. Grandfather: H.Roberts; uncle: E.J.Roberts.

DUCKMANTON Albert George 1951/52-1961/62 b 9.10.1933 Christchurch, Canterbury. RHB OB Team: **Canterbury.** Sch: Christchurch BHS. Occ: Purchasing officer. Member NZCC board.

DUDNEY William Hudson 1883/84-1893 b 8.1.1860 Portslade, Brighton, Sussex, England. d 16.6.1922 Aldrington, Hove, Sussex, England. RHB wk Teams: **Canterbury, Sussex.** Occ: Brewer.

DUFAUR Edmund Thomas 1873/74-1877/78 b Q4 1849 St Pancras, London, England. d 21.2.1901 Auckland. He died from spinal paralysis, the result of an accident. wk Team: **Auckland.** Occ: Solicitor. Brother: P.P.E.Dufaur.

DUFAUR Percy Parker Espie 1882/83 b Q1 1861 Marylebone, London, England. d 6.11.1944 Auckland. Team: **Auckland.** Sch: Parnell GS. Occ: Solicitor. Brother: E.T.Dufaur.

DUFF Stuart William 1985/86-1995/96 b 14.12.1962 Hastings, Hawke's Bay. RHB SLA Team: **Central Districts.** Played List A in NZ. Book: Duffy.

DUFFY Richard John 1940/41-1945/46 b 1911 New Zealand. d 21.6.1998 Otaki, Wellington. RHB SLA Team: **Wellington.** He took 10/80 in a Wellington club game in 1935/36.

DUMBLETON Douglas Philip 1947/48 b 27.4.1918 Wellington. d 4.3.2005 Mount Maunganui, Bay of Plenty. RHB RM Team: **Wellington.** Sch: Rongatai Coll. Occ: Soldier. Umpired Test and first-class cricket. NZCA obit: 2005.

DUNCAN Alfred William 1919/20 b 8.1.1895 Wellington. d 21.1.1975 Wellington. SLA Team: **Wellington.** Sch: Wellington Coll. Occ: Accountant. NZCA obit: 1975. NZ selector.

DUNCAN Arthur Alexander Keith 1879/80 b 11.1.1860 Christchurch, Canterbury. d 13.2.1911 Wellington. Team: **Wellington.** Sch: Christchurch BHS. Occ: Civil servant.

DUNCAN Arthur Donald Stewart 1893/94-1900/01 b 6.8.1875 Colombo, Ceylon. d 10.3.1951 Wellington. Team: **Wellington.** Sch: Wanganui CS. Occ: Coy secretary. Golf: New Zealand representative; won the New Zealand amateur golf championship 10 times between 1899 and 1926 and the New Zealand open championship in 1907, 1910 and 1911.

DUNCAN Graham Hugh Reid 1971/72 b 1.12.1947 New Plymouth, Taranaki. LHB Team: **Central Districts.**

DUNCAN Hugh 1921/22-1924/25 b 26.8.1898 Auckland. d 31.8.1964 Blenheim, Marlborough. RHB Team: **Otago.** Occ: Coy manager. NZCA obit: 1964; Wisden obit: 1965. Auckland and Wellington selector, life-member and president of the Auckland CA, Management Committee of the New Zealand Cricket Council.

DUNCAN Stuart Ferguslie 1925/26-1940/41 b 15.7.1906 Dunedin, Otago. d 2.7.1971 Dunedin, Otago. RHB Team: **Otago.** Sch: Otago BHS. Occ: Manager. Soccer: New Zealand and Otago. NZCA obit: 1971. Otago selector.

DUNCAN William Mackay 1957/58 b 29.12.1933 Christchurch, Canterbury. RHB LM Team: **Northern Districts.**

DUNLOP David Edward Logan 1883/84-1887/88 b 8.5.1855 New Zealand. d 7.1.1898 Nannine, Western Australia, Australia. He died in a mine accident. LB Team: **Canterbury.** Occ: Miner.

DUNN Eric Frederick 1955/56-1956/57 b 10.8.1929 Whangarei, Northland. RHB RM Team: **Auckland.** Sch: Whangarei HS.

DUNNE Robert Stephen 1965/66-1968/69 b 22.4.1943 Dunedin, Otago. RHB LM Team: **Otago.** Occ: Manufacturer. Umpired Test and first-class cricket. Book: Alone in the Middle: An Umpire's Story.

DUNNET Desmond Murray 1942/43-1950/51 b 20.8.1913 Christchurch, Canterbury. d 24.2.1980 Oxted, Surrey, England. RHB wk Teams: **Canterbury, Otago.** Sch: St Andrews Coll. NZCA obit: 1980.

DUNNING Brian 1961/62-1977/78 b 20.3.1940 Warkworth, Auckland. d 16.2.2008 Whangarei, Northland. LHB RM Teams: **Northern Districts, New Zealand.** Played List A in NZ. Hockey: Northland. NZCA obit: 2008; Wisden obit: 2009. ND selector. He played for New Zealand in a FC match.

DUNNING Edward James 1936/37 b 1913 Devonport, Auckland. d 14.3.1937 Leigh, Northland. He drowned when a dinghy capsized as he was returning from a farewell party for J.Cowie, the New Zealand fast bowler, who soon was to start on the tour to England. He was aged 22. RHB Team: **Auckland**. Wisden obit: 1938.

DUNNING John Angus 1923/24-1937/38 b 6.2.1903 Omaha, Northland. d 24.6.1971 Adelaide, South Australia, Australia. RHB RM,OB Teams: **Otago, Auckland, New Zealand Test,** Oxford University. Sch: Auckland GS. Occ: Headmaster. Rhodes scholar. NZCA obit: 1971; Wisden obit: 1972.

DUNSTER Lawrence Raymond 1932/33 b 11.10.1909 Christchurch, Canterbury. d 18.3.1968 Christchurch, Canterbury. RHB Team: **Canterbury**. Sch: Christ Coll. Occ: Coy manager.

DURET Ernest Francis De Montbrun 1886/87-1889/90 b 1856 Paris, France. d 19.9.1926 Manly, Sydney, New South Wales, Australia. Teams: **Wellington, Otago**. Occ: Agent.

DUSTIN William Henry 1927/28-1943/44 b 30.8.1909 Palmerston North, Manawatu. d 24.9.2001 Wanganui. RHB Team: **Wellington.**

DWYER Kevin Francis 1950/51-1953/54 b 12.2.1929 Wellington. RHB Team: **Auckland.**

DYHRBERG Percy William 1951/52 b 10.2.1918 Wellington. d 30.3.1990 New Zealand. LHB Team: **Central Districts.**

DYKES Ross Alexander 1967/68-1976/77 b 26.2.1945 Auckland. LHB wk Team: **Auckland.** Played List A in NZ. Sch: Auckland GS. NZ and Auckland selector, Otago cricket CEO.

EARNEY Herbert Douglas 1910/11 b 17.2.1887 Napier, Hawke's Bay. d 10.1.1963 Napier, Hawke's Bay. Team: **Hawke's Bay.** Occ: Wharfinger.

EASTMAN Lawrence Charles 1920-1939 b 3.6.1897 Enfield Wash, Middlesex, England. d 17.4.1941 Harefield, Middlesex, England. He died in Harefield Sanatorium, following an operation, at the age of 43. His end was hastened through a high-explosive bomb bursting close to him while he was performing his duties as a warden. This caused him severe shock. RHB RM, LB Teams: **Otago**, Essex. Sch: Leyton Technical Institute, England. Occ: Cricket pro. DCM, MM. An English pro, played and coached in NZ. Brother: G.F.Eastman (Essex).

EATHORNE Sean William 2004/05-2005/06 b 5.5.1986 Dunedin, Otago. RHB OB Team: **Otago.** Played List A in NZ; Played T20 in NZ. Sch: Kavanagh Coll. NZ U19 ODI.

ECKHOFF Albertus David 1899/00-1914/15 b 24.6.1875 Dunedin, Otago. d 1.4.1949 Wellington. Team: **Otago.** Occ: Blacksmith.

ECKHOFF Lawrence Raymond James 1975/76 b 19.5.1952 Dunedin, Otago. RHB RFM Team: **Otago.** Played List A in NZ.

ECKHOLD Alfred George 1906/07-1921/22 b 28.12.1885 Adelaide, South Australia, Australia. d 24.10.1931 Dunedin, Otago. Team: **Otago.** Occ: Maltster. Rugby: All Blacks and Otago. He holds the Otago 8th wicket partnership record of 165* with J.N.Crawford against Wellington in 1914/15.

EDDINGTON Warren Lex 1977/78-1984/85 b 14.10.1955 Methven, Mid Canterbury. RHB RM Team: **Canterbury.** Sch: Timaru BHS.

EDEN James 1887/88-1891/92 b 1864 Nelson. d 12.3.1929 Waimea, Nelson. Team: **Nelson.** Occ: Farmer. Brothers: T.G.Eden, W.Eden.

EDEN Thomas Gowland 1874/75-1891/92 b 9.5.1855 Nelson. d 19.11.1914 Waimea, Nelson. Team: **Nelson.** Occ: Farmer. He had the best bowling and match figures for Nelson when he took 9/43 and 14/63 against Wellington in 1875/76. Brothers: J.Eden, W.Eden.

EDEN William 1874/75-1881/82 d 14.6.1930 Waimea, Nelson. Team: **Nelson.** Occ: Farmer. Brothers: J.Eden, T.G.Eden.

EDGAR Arthur John 1955/56 b 22.5.1924 Auckland. d 21.4.1992 Wellington. RHB wk Team: **Wellington.** NZCA obit: 1992; Wisden obit: 1993. Son: B.A.Edgar.

EDGAR Bruce Adrian 1975/76-1989/90 b 23.11.1956 Wellington. LHB RSM occ wk Teams: **Wellington, New Zealand Test, New Zealand ODI.** Played List A in NZ. Sch: Rongatai Coll. Book: An opener's tale. NZCA COY: 1979. He holds the Wellington 1st wicket partnership record of 333 with A.H.Jones against Auckland in 1988/89. Father: A.J.Edgar.

EDMONDS David Baxter 1933/34-1946/47 b 10.11.1907 Auckland. d 6.1.1950 Auckland. wk Team: **Auckland.** Occ: Machinist.

EDMUNDS Ernest Edward 1875/76-1876/77 b 11.8.1846 Worthing, Sussex, England. d 8.9.1920 Wellington. wk Team: **Wellington.** Sch: Epsom Coll, England. Occ: Gentleman.

EDMUNDS Mervyn Ray 1958/59-1959/60 b 13.1.1932 Wellington. RHB wk Team: **Otago**.
EDSER Henry 1883/84 b Q2 1862 Islington, London, England. d 9.12.1938 Christchurch, Canterbury. Team: **Canterbury**. Occ: Civil servant.
EDWARD Stewart James 1964/65-1967/68 b 1.11.1943 Hamilton, Waikato. RHB RM Team: **Otago**.
EDWARDS Allan James 1940/41 b 12.4.1920 Dunedin, Otago. d 18.8.1942. He was killed in action, at sea, off Cherbourg, France, aged 22. Team: **Otago**. Sch: Otago BHS. Occ: RNZAF.
EDWARDS Charles Howard 1884/85-1887/88 b 1856 Kew, Victoria, Australia. d 20.3.1924 Napier, Hawke's Bay. RS Team: **Hawke's Bay**. Occ: Gas coy manager. Umpired first-class cricket.
EDWARDS Graham Neil 1973/74-1984/85 b 27.5.1955 Nelson. RHB wk Teams: **Central Districts, New Zealand Test, New Zealand ODI**. Played List A in NZ.
EDWARDS Lee Jonathan 1998/99-2009/10 b 21.4.1979 Wellington. RHB RFM Team: **Wellington**.
ELL James Anthony 1933/34-1945/46 b 15.9.1915 Lower Hutt, Wellington. d 8.7.2007 Waikanae, Wellington. RHB Team: **Wellington**. Sch: Johnsonville HS. Occ: Commercial artist. NZCA obit: 2008. He holds the record for the highest score in Wellington Senior club cricket of 291.
ELLIOTT Grant David 1996/97-2009/10 b 21.3.1979 Johannesburg, Transvaal, South Africa. RHB RFM Teams: **Wellington, New Zealand Test, New Zealand ODI, New Zealand T20, Surrey, Transvaal B, Griqualand West, Gauteng**. Played List A in NZ; Played T20 in NZ. Sch: St Stithian's Coll, Johannesburg, South Africa.
ELLIOTT Harry Sinclair 1891/92-1897/98 b 1870 Nelson. d 2.11.1941 Hawera, Taranaki. Team: **Taranaki**. Occ: Town clerk.
ELLIOTT Thomas 1894/95-1905/06 b 1867 Waikato. wk Team: **Auckland**.
ELLIOTT William Leonard Tenison 1924/25-1929/30 b 8.8.1900 Balclutha, Otago. d 8.4.1970 Auckland. RHB Team: **Auckland**. Occ: Coy manager.
ELLIS Andrew Malcolm 2002/03-2009/10 b 24.3.1982 Christchurch, Canterbury. RHB RFM Team: **Canterbury**. Played List A in NZ; Played T20 in NZ. Sch: Shirley BHS. NZ U19 Test; NZ U19 ODI.
ELLIS Harry 1904/05-1914/15 b 1878 Concord, New South Wales, Australia. d 6.7.1943 Napier, Hawke's Bay. wk Teams: **Canterbury, Hawke's Bay**. Occ: Farmer. An Australian, he coached at Christ College, Christchurch, before moving to Hawke's Bay.
ELLIS Norman 1941/42-1943/44 b 17.10.1913 Dunedin, Otago. d 27.10.2005 Oamaru, North Otago. RHB Team: **Auckland**. Umpired first-class cricket.
ELLIS Richard Hugh 1971/72-1976/77 b 22.5.1945 Nelson. RHB RM Team: **Central Districts**. Played List A in NZ.
ELLIS Samuel Howard (Sir) 1911/12 b 2.6.1889 Waipu, Northland. d 19.1.1949 Fiji. wk Team: **Auckland**. Sch: Auckland GS. Occ: Solicitor. During the First World War he became a pilot in the Royal Flying Corps and whilst he was a Flight Lieutenant he was shot down and captured. He subsequently became a successful businessman and between 1940 and 1942 he donated £15,500 to the RAF to purchase three fighter planes.
ELMES Cedric James 1927/28-1940/41 b 23.5.1909 Christchurch, Canterbury. d 9.3.1995 Dunedin, Otago. LHB SLA Teams: **Otago, New Zealand**. Sch: Christ Coll. Occ: Bank clerk. NZCA obit: 1995. Otago selector. He played for New Zealand in a FC match. He was the first New Zealander to be out for 99 in first-class cricket and he finished his career without scoring a hundred.
EMERY Raymond William George 1936/37-1953/54 b 28.3.1915 Auckland. d 18.12.1982 Auckland. RHB RM Teams: **Auckland, Canterbury, New Zealand Test**. Sch: Takapuna GS. Occ: Airport manager. Rugby: New Zealand Services. NZCA obit: 1983. NZCA COY: 1952.
ENGLAND 1879/80 Team: **Wellington**. Occ: Bank officer.
ENGLAND John Everest 1958/59-1961/62 b 1.6.1940 Christchurch, Canterbury. RHB wk Teams: **Canterbury**. Sch: Christ Coll. Occ: Solicitor.
ENGLEFIELD Jarrod Ian 1998/99-2005/06 b 18.12.1979 Blenheim, Marlborough. RHB Team: **Canterbury, Central Districts**. Played List A in NZ; Played T20 in NZ. Sch: Marlborough HS. NZ U19 Test; NZ U19 ODI. He holds the Central Districts 5th wicket partnership record of 301 with L.R.P.L.Taylor against Wellington in 2004/05.

ERASMUS Pieter Bernardus 2006/07-2009/10 b 19.3.1983 Ceres, Cape Province, South Africa. RHB LFM Team: **Auckland.** Played List A in NZ. Sch: Orewa Coll.
EVANS Alun Wyn 1996-2006/07 b 20.8.1975 Glanamman, Dyfed, Wales. RHB RM Teams: **Northern Districts,** Glamorgan. Played List A in NZ; Played T20 in NZ.
EVANS Cyril Edward 1919/20-1928/29 b 10.1.1896 Christchurch, Canterbury. d 13.5.1975 Christchurch, Canterbury. RHB LB Team: **Canterbury.** Sch: Christchurch BHS. Occ: Clerk. Rugby: All Blacks and Canterbury. NZCA obit: 1976.
EVANS Henry 1868/69-1875/76 b 6.8.1846 Launceston, Tasmania, Australia. Teams: **Wellington,** Tasmania. Occ: Architect. He played cricket for Tasmania before moving to Wellington where he played two FC matches. He lived in Timaru in the late 1870s and early 1880s and he designed the St Joseph Church in Timaru. He is believed to have moved to England. Uncle: N.G.Clayton (Tasmania); brother-in-law: H.S.Hickson.
EVEREST James Kerse 1954/55-1956/57 b 28.3.1918 Frankton, Hamilton, Waikato. d 28.9.1992 Hamilton, Waikato. LHB RM Teams: **Auckland, Northern Districts.** Sch: Hamilton Tech Coll. Occ: Linesman. NZCA obit: 1993; Wisden obit: 1993. NZCA COY: 1957. ND selector. He scored 264 for Waikato v Manawatu in 1956/57, the third highest score in Hawke Cup history.
EVERSON Olaf James Nigel 1943/44 b 6.2.1912 Auckland. d 27.11.1995 Hamilton, Waikato. RHB wk Team: **Otago.** Occ: Preacher. NZCA obit: 1996.
EWING George Proudfoot 1884/85 b 7.4.1851 Hillhead, Glasgow, Lanarkshire, Scotland. d 29.10.1930 Whangaroa, Northland. occ wk Team: **Auckland.** Occ: Farmer.
FACOORY Paul Richard 1976/77-1984/85 b 3.8.1951 Dunedin, Otago. RHB Team: **Otago.** Played List A in NZ. Sch: Kings HS. Occ: Managing director.
FAIRBAIRN Andrew 1884/85 b 18.12.1862 Mallow, Co Cork, Ireland. d 24.7.1925 Marylebone, London, England. LHB Team: **Otago.** Occ: Merchant.
FAIREY George Sumner 1911/12-1912/13 b 27.12.1884 Brightwater, Nelson. d 17.6.1956 Napier, Hawke's Bay. OB Team: **Hawke's Bay.** Occ: Farmer.
FAIRLEY Samuel Anthony 2001/02-2006/07 b 19.9.1980 Whakatane, Bay of Plenty. LHB RM Team: **Wellington.** Played List A in NZ; Played T20 in NZ. Sch: Aotea Coll.
FANNIN Henry Albert 1892/93-1899/00 b 1870 Napier, Hawke's Bay. d 20.1.1959 Hastings, Hawke's Bay. Team: **Hawke's Bay.** Occ: Clerk. He took a hat-trick for Hawke's Bay v Taranaki in 1897/98.
FARMAN Ray Newson 1957/58-1959/60 b 2.3.1927 Warkworth, Auckland. d 1.7.1996 Rarotonga, Cook Islands. LHB OB Team: **Auckland.** NZCA obit: 1997; Wisden obit: 1998. Auckland selector.
FARRANT Anthony John 1980/81-1982/83 b 20.6.1955 Fairlie, South Canterbury. RHB RM Team: **Canterbury.** Played List A in NZ. Sch: Burnside HS. Occ: Bank officer. Brother: D.G.Farrant.
FARRANT David Graeme 1981/82-1986/87 b 1.8.1960 Fairlie, South Canterbury. RHB RM Team: **Canterbury.** Played List A in NZ. Sch: Burnside HS. Occ: Sales manager. Brother: A.J.Farrant.
FAYEN Herman 1882/83 b 1858 Nelson. d 19.5.1943 Taradale, Napier, Hawke's Bay. Team: **Nelson.** Occ: Bush worker.
FEARON Charles Devey 1865/66 b 26.4.1846 Hunstanton, Norfolk, England. d 21.10.1876 Nelson. He died at the age of 30 from 'general debility and break up of the constitution'. Team: **Canterbury.** Sch: Christ Coll; Marlborough Coll, England. Occ: Farm manager.
FENTON Arthur 1895/96-1914/15 b 27.2.1870 Tarnagulla, Victoria, Australia. d 20.5.1950 Melbourne, Victoria, Australia. RHB OB Teams: **Hawke's Bay, Wellington,** Victoria. Occ: Groundsman; coach.
FENTON William Rex 1964/65-1971/72 b 8.5.1943 Auckland. RHB Team: **Auckland.** Played List A in NZ.
FENWICK Fairfax Frederick 1875/76 b 8.9.1852 Elsinore, Denmark. d 31.8.1920 Cobham, Kent, England. occ wk Team: **Otago.** Sch: Christ Coll; Otago BHS. Occ: Bank manager. Brother: H.S.Fenwick.
FENWICK Herbert Shakespeare 1891/92 b 1861 Copenhagen, Denmark. d 18.7.1934 Dunedin, Otago. wk Team: **Canterbury.** Sch: Christ Coll. Occ: Sharebroker. Rugby: Canterbury. Brother: F.F.Fenwick.

FERDINANDS Rene Edouard Denis 1998/99 b 3.5.1969 Colombo, Ceylon. RHB SLA Team: **Northern Districts.** Occ: University lecturer. He undertook a PhD study into bowling actions.
FERNLEY George Henry 1893/94 Team: **Hawke's Bay.** Occ: Labourer. He went to Coolgardie, Western Australia in 1898 with the gold rush but returned to New Zealand shortly thereafter. Nothing is known of him after 1899. He scored a king pair on his FC debut.
FERRIES Kenneth Ian 1961/62-1974/75 b 7.5.1936 Wyalkatchem, Western Australia, Australia. RHB RFM Teams: **Canterbury,** Western Australia. Occ: Clerk.
FERROW Desmond Joseph 1956/57-1957/58 b 29.10.1933 Wollongong, New South Wales, Australia. RHB OB Team: **Northern Districts.** Occ: Coy director.
FINCH Christopher John William 1993/94-1995/96 b 23.6.1975 Balclutha, Otago. RHB RM Team: **Otago.** Played List A in NZ. Sch: Otago BHS. NZ U19 ODI.
FINCH Walter Philip 1884/85 b 12.10.1860 Dunedin, Otago. d 6.7.1943 Napier, Hawke's Bay. Team: **Hawke's Bay.** Sch: Otago BHS. Occ: Architect.
FINDLAY Brent Robert 2005/06 b 16.10.1985 Christchurch, Canterbury. RHB RM Team: **Canterbury.** Played List A in NZ; Played T20 in NZ. Sch: Wellington Coll. NZ U19 ODI.
FINDLAY Craig Owen 1995/96-1996/97 b 17.8.1971 Waipukurau, Hawke's Bay. RHB RM Team: **Central Districts.** Played List A in NZ. Sch: Napier BHS. Occ: Cricket coach.
FINDLAY James Lloyd 1925/26 b 6.10.1895 Wellington. d 17.3.1983 Westminster, London, England. RHB SLA Team: **Canterbury.** Sch: Wellington Coll. Occ: Air Commodore. CBE, MC, Chevalier of the Legion d'Honneur and Commander of Legion of Merit, U.S.A. NZCA obit: 1983. Brother: J.W.Findlay.
FINDLAY John Wilfred 1910/11-1911/12 b 27.11.1891 Wellington. d 1.6.1951 Mount Kisco, New York, United States of America. He died of a heart ailment aged 59. RF Team: **Wellington.** Sch: Wellington Coll. Occ: Insurance coy director. Brother: J.L.Findlay.
FINLAY Dean John Howard 1988/89 b 7.5.1965 Palmerston North, Manawatu. RHB LFM Team: **Central Districts.**
FINLAYSON Charles Gordon 1909/10-1930/31 b 9.8.1889 Napier, Hawke's Bay. d 9.7.1943 Otahuhu, Auckland. LHB LM Teams: **Wellington, Auckland, New Zealand.** Occ: Carpenter. Rugby League: New Zealand and Wellington. He played for New Zealand prior to being granted Test status.
FIRTH Joseph Pentland 1880/81-1885/86 b 25.3.1859 Cobden, West Coast. d 13.4.1931 Wellington. RHB LF Teams: **Nelson, Wellington.** Sch: Nelson Coll. Occ: Schoolmaster, Wellington Coll. Rugby: Wellington and Nelson. Book: Firth of Wellington by J.Elliott. CMG.
FISHER Arthur Hadfield 1890/91-1909/10 b 11.2.1871 Nelson. d 23.3.1961 Dunedin, Otago. RHB LM Team: **Otago, New Zealand.** Sch: Otago BHS. Occ: Insurance manager. Golf: NZ Golf championship in 1904, Otago champion in 1903. NZCA obit: 1961; Wisden obit: 1962. He played for New Zealand prior to being granted Test status. He has the best bowling figures for Otago when he took 9/48 against Queensland in 1896/97. Brother: R.L.Fisher.
FISHER Frederick Eric 1951/52-1954/55 b 28.7.1924 Johnsonville, Wellington. d 19.6.1996 Palmerston North, Manawatu. RHB LM Teams: **Wellington, Central Districts, New Zealand Test.** Occ: Cricket coach. Rugby: Wanganui and Taranaki. NZCA obit: 1997; Wisden obit: 1997. NZCA COY: 1953.
FISHER Ian David 1982/83-1991/92 b 1.3.1961 Auckland. LHB RM Teams: **Auckland, Central Districts.** Played List A in NZ.
FISHER Ronald Lewellin 1904/05-1905/06 b 28.2.1880 Christchurch, Canterbury. d 26.3.1959 Chatswood, Sydney, New South Wales, Australia. Team: **Canterbury.** Sch: Otago BHS; Christs Coll. Occ: Commercial agent. Brother: A.H.Fisher.
FITZGERALD James 1883/84-1884/85 b 20.3.1862 Pigeon Bay, Canterbury. d 24.6.1943 Dunedin, Otago. Team: **Otago.** Occ: Doctor.
FITZHERBERT Henry Samuel 1879/80 b 11.9.1852 Wellington. d 5.2.1912 New Plymouth, Taranaki. Team: **West Coast (North Island).** Sch: Wanganui CS. Occ: Magistrate. Umpired first-class cricket. MP.
FITZSIMMONS Edward 1889/90-1895/96 b 1869 unknown. d 28.1.1942 Wanganui. RHB OB Team: **Wellington.** Occ: Clerk. Wisden obit: 1943.
FLAHERTY John Patrick 1964/65-1968/69 b 4.8.1942 Dunedin, Otago. RHB LM Team: **Otago.**

FLANAGAN Christopher Warren 1986/87-1994/95 b 7.5.1964 Christchurch, Canterbury. LHB LM Team: **Canterbury.** Played List A in NZ. Sch: Christchurch BHS. Occ: Real estate company employee.
FLANAGHAN James 1873/74 Team: **Wellington.** Occ: Plumber.
FLAWS Thomas 1952/53-1962/63 b 13.5.1932 Dunedin, Otago. LHB wk Team: **Otago.**
FLEMING Stephen Paul 1991/92-2007/08 b 1.4.1973 Christchurch, Canterbury. LHB RSM Teams: **Canterbury, Wellington, New Zealand Test, New Zealand ODI, New Zealand T20,** Middlesex, Yorkshire, Nottinghamshire, ICC World XI ODI. Played List A in NZ; Played T20 in NZ. Sch: Cashmere HS. Occ: Cricket pro. NZ U19 Test; NZ U19 ODI. Book: Balance of power. NZCA COY: 1998, 2003, 2004. He holds the NZ Test 8th wicket partnership record of 256 with J.E.C.Franklin against South Africa in 2005/06. He was the first New Zealander to pass 7,000 Test runs. He made a career-highest score of 274 not out against Sri Lanka in 2003.
FLYNN Daniel Raymond 2004/05-2009/10 b 16.4.1985 Rotorua, Bay of Plenty. LHB SLC Teams: **Northern Districts, New Zealand Test, New Zealand ODI, New Zealand T20.** Played List A in NZ; Played T20 in NZ. Sch: Tauranga BC. Occ: Cricket pro. NZ U19 ODI.
FOGO Robert Harwood Broughton 1914/15-1919/20 b 20.1.1896 Christchurch, Canterbury. d 22.8.1964 Invercargill, Southland. Team: **Southland.** Occ: Clerk.
FOLEY Henry 1927/28-1932/33 b 28.1.1906 Wellington. d 16.10.1948 Brisbane, Queensland, Australia. LHB Teams: **Wellington, New Zealand Test.** Sch: Wellington Coll. Occ: Bank accountant. NZCA obit: 1948; Wisden obit: 1950.
FOLEY Michael 1876/77-1882/83 b 1844 New Zealand. d 21.11.1904 Wellington. He died in hospital as the result of a fractured skull, and in connection with whose death John Kilmartin was charged with manslaughter. An inquest jury returned a verdict that the deceased came by his death from injuries from a fall, the effect of a blow administered by John Kilmartin. At his subsequent trial Kilmartin was acquitted, a verdict of not guilty being returned. It was found that Kilmartin and Foley had been drinking together and quarrelled. In a struggle, Foley fell and died from the effects. Teams: **Wellington, Taranaki.** Occ: Police officer. Umpired first-class cricket.
FORD Roger Murray 1988/89-1993/94 b 29.11.1965 Leeston, Canterbury. RHB RFM Team: **Canterbury.** Played List A in NZ. Sch: St Andrews Coll. Occ: Civil servant. He holds the Canterbury 9th wicket partnership record of 182* with L.K.Germon against Wellington in 1989/90. During this partnership he and Germon broke the world record for the most runs in a first-class over - 77 off R.H.Vance. The 22-ball over contained 17 no-balls - due to a miscount there were only five legitimate balls.
FORD William Justice 1873-1896 b 7.11.1853 Paddington, London, England. d 3.4.1904 Kensal Green, Kensington, London, England. He died of pneumonia. RHB RSr occ wk Teams: **Nelson,** Cambridge University, Middlesex. Sch: Repton, England. Occ: Schoolmaster, Nelson Coll. Wisden obit: 1905. He was a renowned big hitter, his longest measured hit was 143 yards 2 feet. He made many large scores in minor cricket, his best innings being 250 for M.C.C. v Uxbridge in 1881. Brothers: F.G.J.Ford (England, Middlesex, Cambridge University), A.F.J.Ford (Middlesex), L.G.B.J.Ford, W.A.J.Ford; father: W.A.Ford (Marylebone Cricket Club); nephews: N.M.Ford (Derbyshire, Oxford University, Middlesex), C.G.Ford; uncle: G.J.Ford (Oxford University).
FORDE Lindsay James 1976/77 b 27.7.1954 Dunedin, Otago. M Team: **Canterbury.** Played List A in NZ. Sch: Xavier Coll.
FORDE Simon Francis 1998/99-2000/01 b 25.1.1972 Tuatapere, Southland. RHB OB Team: **Otago.** Played List A in NZ. Occ: Policeman. He won a Royal Humane Society Bronze Medal with two other policemen - each put their own safety in jeopardy as, without protection of any kind, they attempted to extinguish the flames engulfing the adults in a situation of intense heat, thick smoke and potential explosion and, in dense smoke, continued to search the premises for others believed to be at risk. Otago selector.
FORDHAM Wolverley Attwood 1877/78 b 9.9.1859 Broxbourne, Hertfordshire, England. d 24.2.1921 Ashwell, Hertfordshire, England. Team: **Wellington.** Sch: Rugby, England. Occ: Brewer.
FORREST James Cameron 1996/97-1997/98 b 16.6.1974 Auckland. LHB RM Team: **Auckland.** Played List A in NZ.

FORSYTH Herbert 1917/18 b 8.7.1896 Christchurch, Canterbury. d 3.5.1969 Christchurch, Canterbury. wk Team: **Canterbury**. Occ: Railway employee.
FOSTER Philip Stanley 1909/10-1919/20 b 4.4.1885 Timaru, South Canterbury. d 20.3.1965 Christchurch, Canterbury. RHB OB Teams: **Wellington, Canterbury**. Sch: Wanganui CS; Otago BHS. Occ: Doctor.
FOUHY Roger James 2005/06 b 25.3.1972 Hamilton, Waikato. RHB RMF Team: **Wellington**. Occ: Police officer.
FOULDS Brian Graham 1969/70-1970/71 b 14.12.1944 Melbourne, Victoria, Australia. RHB LFM Team: **Northern Districts**.
FOWKE John Nicholls 1880/81-1906/07 b 23.10.1859 Tenby, Pembrokeshire, Wales. d 24.4.1938 Christchurch, Canterbury. RHB wk Teams: **Canterbury, Auckland, New Zealand**. Occ: Bootclicker. Wisden obit: 1939. Canterbury selector. He played for New Zealand prior to being granted Test status.
FOWLER Edwin 1865/66-1881/82 b Q4 1840 Islington, London, England. d 31.5.1909 Armadale, Melbourne, Victoria, Australia. RHB RS wk Teams: **Canterbury**, Victoria.
FOWLER George 1879/80-1887/88 Team: **Nelson**. Sch: Spring Grove. Occ: Farmer. Brothers: L.A.Fowler, S.Fowler, J.Fowler.
FOWLER John 1873/74-1881/82 LHB RF(u) Team: **Canterbury**. Occ: Farmer. In 1898 he returned from Canterbury district to reside in Nelson, but nothing is known after that time. Brothers: L.A.Fowler, S.Fowler, G.Fowler.
FOWLER Louis Arthur 1882/83-1897/98 b 25.8.1865 Waimea South, Nelson. d 22.10.1927 Stratford, Taranaki. Teams: **Nelson, Taranaki**. Sch: Spring Grove. Occ: Farmer. Brothers: G.Fowler, S.Fowler, J.Fowler.
FOWLER Samuel 1873/74-1883/84 b 10.8.1854 Waimea South, Nelson. d 13.7.1915 Riwaka, Nelson. LHB Team: **Nelson**. Occ: Farmer. Brothers: G.Fowler, L.A.Fowler, S.Fowler.
FOWLER William Peter 1979/80-1989/90 b 13.3.1959 St Helens, Lancashire, England. RHB SLA Teams: **Northern Districts, Auckland**, Derbyshire. Played List A in NZ. Sch: Kamo HS.
FOX George Henry 1888/89-1889/90 b 20.2.1867 Tredington, Gloucestershire, England. d 29.10.1920 Millbank, London, England. Team: **Otago**. Occ: Doctor. He later changed his name to George Henry Lane-Fox.
FOX Ronald Henry 1904-1927 b 23.1.1880 Caversham, Dunedin, Otago. d 27.8.1952 Firs Hill, Bloxham, Oxfordshire, England. RHB wk Teams: **New Zealand**. Sch: Haileybury, England. Occ: Soldier. NZCA obit: 1953; Wisden obit: 1953. A wicket-keeper, he was a member of the MCC team which toured New Zealand in 1906/07. He played one match for NZ on their 1927 tour of England. He played for New Zealand prior to being granted Test status.
FRAME William David 1955/56-1957/58 b 31.8.1932 Mosgiel, Otago. d 12.2.1965 Papanui, Christchurch, Canterbury. He murdered his girlfriend and her parents before turning the gun on himself. RHB RMF Team: **Otago**. Sch: Otago BHS. Occ: Fruiterer. NZCA obit: 1965.
FRANCIS John Patterson Emillius 1880/81 b Q2 1846 Epping, Essex, England. d 6.4.1891 Auckland. Team: **Wellington**. Sch: Merchant Taylor's, England. Occ: Schoolmaster.
FRANKISH Ernest Hay 1903/04-1905/06 b 4.7.1876 Christchurch, Canterbury. d 22.1.1962 Raumati Beach, Wellington. RHB Team: **Canterbury**. Sch: Christ Coll; Wanganui CS. Occ: Grain merchant. Brother: F.S.Frankish.
FRANKISH Frank Stanley 1894/95-1903/04 b 2.11.1872 Christchurch, Canterbury. d 30.5.1909 Wanganui. He died of consumption aged 36. LFM Teams: **Canterbury, New Zealand**. Sch: Christ Coll. Occ: Bank clerk. Wisden obit: 1910. He played for New Zealand prior to being granted Test status. Brother: E.H.Frankish.
FRANKLIN James Edward Charles 1998/99-2010 b 7.11.1980 Wellington. LHB LFM Teams: **Wellington, New Zealand Test, New Zealand ODI, New Zealand T20**, Gloucestershire, Glamorgan. Played List A in NZ; Played T20 in NZ. Sch: Wellington Coll. Occ: Cricket pro. NZ U19 Test; NZ U19 ODI. NZCA COY: 2006. He holds the NZ Test 8th wicket partnership record of 256 with S.P.Fleming against South Africa in 2005/06. He took a Test hat-trick for New Zealand v Bangladesh in 2004/05.
FRANKLIN Trevor John 1980/81-1992/93 b 15.3.1962 Mt Eden, Auckland. RHB RM Teams: **Auckland, New Zealand Test, New Zealand ODI**. Played List A in NZ. Sch: Mt Albert GS. Occ: Policeman. Book: New Zealand cricketer. He had his leg shattered when he was run over by

a luggage trailer at Gatwick Airport in 1986 and he didn't play a Test for nearly two years. He holds the Auckland 2nd wicket partnership record of 241 with J.J.Crowe against Wellington in 1988/89.

FRANKS Paul John 1996-2010 b 3.2.1979 Mansfield, Nottinghamshire, England. LHB RFM Teams: **Canterbury,** England ODI, Nottinghamshire. Sch: Minster School, Southwell, England. Occ: Cricket pro. An English pro, played and coached in NZ.

FRASER Ian Comyn 1918/19 b 25.8.1902 Inverness, Scotland. d 2.2.1990 Shrewsbury, Shropshire, England. Team: **Otago**. Sch: Otago BHS. Occ: Doctor. Soccer: Otago.

FRASER Thomas Campbell 1937/38-1952/53 b 29.10.1917 Dunedin, Otago. d 20.5.1998 Dunedin, Otago. RHB RSM Team: **Otago**. Occ: Managing director. NZCA obit: 1998; Wisden obit: 1999.

FRATER Robert Ernest 1918/19-1931/32 b 24.2.1902 Devonport, Auckland. d 17.8.1968 Nelson. RHB Team: **Auckland**. Occ: Sales manager. NZCA obit: 1968. Central Districts selector.

FREEMAN Alexander Abercrombie 1887/88 b 1868 Napier, Hawke's Bay. d 18.7.1918 Wellington. Team: **Hawke's Bay**. Occ: Compositor.

FREEMAN Barry Thomas 1969/70-1970/71 b 28.2.1948 Dunedin, Otago. RHB Team: **Otago**. Sch: Otago BHS. Father: T.A.Freeman.

FREEMAN Douglas Linford 1932/33-1933/34 b 8.9.1914 Randwick, Sydney, New South Wales, Australia. d 31.5.1994 Sydney, New South Wales, Australia. RHB LBG Teams: **Wellington, New Zealand Test**. Sch: Nelson Coll. Occ: Manager. NZCA obit: 1995; Wisden obit: 1995. He managed the Fijian team that toured New Zealand in 1953/54. He was the second youngest man ever to play a Test for New Zealand, making his debut after only one FC match.

FREEMAN Jeffrey 1972/73-1975/76 b 10.5.1950 Wellington. RHB LMF Team: **Northern Districts**. Played List A in NZ.

FREEMAN Thomas Alfred 1943/44-1949/50 b 16.4.1923 Balclutha, Otago. d 20.6.2003 Christchurch, Canterbury. RHB RM Team: **Otago**. Sch: Otago BHS. Occ: Schoolteacher. NZCA obit: 2004. Son: B.T.Freeman.

FREW Robert Mathew 1995/96-2002/03 b 28.12.1970 Darfield, Canterbury. RHB Team: **Canterbury**. Played List A in NZ. Sch: Darfield HS.

FRITH Charles 1877/78-1889/90 b 19.1.1854 Bodmin, Cornwall, England. d 3.4.1919 Dunedin, Otago. RHB OB Teams: **Canterbury, Otago**. Occ: Compositor. Umpired first-class cricket. Wisden obit: 1920. He took a hat-trick for Otago v Canterbury in 1884/85. Brother: W.Frith.

FRITH William 1877/78-1893/94 b 26.6.1856 Edmonton, Middlesex, England. d 19.11.1949 Ashburton, Mid Canterbury. LHB SLA Teams: **Canterbury, Otago, Wellington**. Occ: Printer. Brother: C.Frith.

FULLER Arthur Charles 1917/18-1923/24 b 9.8.1880 Christchurch, Canterbury. d 27.9.1947 Christchurch, Canterbury. RHB wk Team: **Canterbury**. Occ: Boarding-house keeper.

FULLER Donald McCormick 1889/90-1894/95 b 19.6.1869 Picton, Marlborough. d 10.5.1936 Picton, Marlborough. Team: **Wellington**. Occ: Accountant. Wisden obit: 1937.

FULLER Edwin Thomas Augustus 1872/73-1882/83 b 17.5.1850 Launceston, Tasmania, Australia. d 1.8.1917 St Leonards, Sydney, New South Wales, Australia. F Team: **Canterbury**. Occ: Clerk.

FULLER James Kerr 2009/10 b 20.1.1990 Cape Town, Cape Province, South Africa. RHB RFM Team: **Otago**. Sch: Westlake BHS.

FULTON Frederick 1868/69-1883/84 b 1.6.1850 Aligarh, Bengal Presidency (now Uttar Pradesh), India. d 3.8.1923 Napier, Hawke's Bay. occ wk Teams: **Otago, Hawke's Bay**. Occ: Accountant. Umpired first-class cricket. He had his arm mangled in a flax cutter in 1874; his arm was saved and though incapacitated, he played strenuous and successful cricket for many years. Brother: J.C.Fulton; uncle: J.Fulton; son: P.R.Fulton.

FULTON James 1863/64-1867/68 b 27.6.1830 Futtehgurh, Bengal Presidency (now Fatehgarh, Uttar Pradesh), India. d 20.11.1891 Taieri Mouth, Otago. He died of heart disease. Team: **Otago**. Sch: Blackheath Proprietory School, England. Occ: Sheep farmer. MP. In 1890 he was one of the Royal Commissioners appointed to make inquiries as to the prevalence of sweating in the colony. Nephews: F.Fulton, J.C.Fulton; great-nephew: G.R.Fulton.

FULTON John Charles 1867/68-1882/83 b 31.3.1849 Aligarh, Bengal Presidency (now Uttar Pradesh), India. d 28.10.1908 Marton, Rangitikei. He died of heart disease. Teams: **Otago, Taranaki**. Occ: Civil servant. Brother: F.Fulton; uncle: J.Fulton; nephew: P.R.Fulton.

FULTON Peter Gordon 2000/01-2009/10 b 1.2.1979 Christchurch, Canterbury. RHB RM Teams: **Canterbury, New Zealand Test, New Zealand ODI, New Zealand T20.** Played List A in NZ; Played T20 in NZ. Sch: Christ Coll. He scored the highest maiden century in NZ FC cricket - 301* for Canterbury v Auckland in 2002/03. Uncle: R.W.Fulton.
FULTON Peter Robertson 1900/01-1920/21 b 23.11.1880 Ahuriri, Napier, Hawke's Bay. d 21.8.1963 Waihi, Bay of Plenty. LB Team: **Hawke's Bay.** Occ: Comm traveller. Father: F.Fulton; uncle: J.C.Fulton; great-uncle: J.Fulton.
FULTON Roddy Woodhouse 1972/73-1984/85 b 5.8.1951 Christchurch, Canterbury. LHB RM Teams: **Canterbury, Northern Districts.** Played List A in NZ. Sch: Christ Coll. Occ: Breeder. Canterbury selector. Nephew: P.G.Fulton.
FURLONG Blair Donald Marie 1963/64-1972/73 b 10.3.1945 Dannevirke, Hawke's Bay. LHB OB Team: **Central Districts.** Played List A in NZ. Sch: Dannevirke HS. Occ: Cricket administrator. Rugby: All Blacks and Hawke's Bay. CD cricket CEO. He took a hat-trick for NZ Under-23 XI v Canterbury in 1964/65. Sons: C.J.M.Furlong, J.B.M.Furlong.
FURLONG Campbell James Marie 1994/95-2001/02 b 16.6.1974 Napier, Hawke's Bay. RHB OB Team: **Central Districts.** Played List A in NZ; Played T20 in NZ. Occ: Accountant. NZ U19 Test; NZ U19 ODI. Brother: J.B.M.Furlong; father: B.D.M.Furlong.
FURLONG John Bernard Marie 1990/91-1993/94 b 28.6.1972 Napier, Hawke's Bay. RHB RF Team: **Central Districts.** NZ U19 Test. Brother: C.J.M.Furlong; father: B.D.M.Furlong.
GADSDON Shane Robert 2008/09 b 8.4.1991 Auckland. RHB wk Team: **Northern Districts.** Sch: Howick Coll.
GAFFANEY Christopher Blair 1995/96-2004/05 b 30.11.1975 Dunedin, Otago. RHB Team: **Otago.** Played List A in NZ; Played T20 in NZ. Sch: Otago BHS. Occ: Policeman. Umpired first-class cricket. NZ U19 Test; NZ U19 ODI.
GALE Aaron James 1989/90-1997/98 b 8.4.1970 Balclutha, Otago. RHB RM Team: **Otago.** Played List A in NZ. Sch: Otago BHS. Occ: Accountant. NZ U19 Test; NZ U19 ODI. He took a hat-trick for Otago v Canterbury in 1992/93.
GALE Alexander Duncan Shanks 1929/30 b 17.12.1892 Glasgow, Lanarkshire, Scotland. d 31.3.1965 Dunedin, Otago. Team: **Otago.** Sch: Otago BHS. Occ: Clerk.
GALLAND Arthur 1914/15-1930/31 b 20.5.1891 Dunedin, Otago. d 26.8.1975 Dunedin, Otago. RHB wk Team: **Otago.** Occ: Plumber. NZCA obit: 1975.
GALLAUGHER Robert George 1945 b 8.1.1923 Epsom, Auckland. LHB SLA Team: **New Zealand Services.**
GALLAWAY Iain Watson 1946/47-1947/48 b 26.12.1922 Dunedin, Otago. RHB wk Team: **Otago.** Occ: Commentator. Book: Not a Cloud in the Sky. QSO, MBE. President of NZ cricket.
GALLICHAN Norman 1927/28-1938/39 b 3.6.1906 Palmerston North, Manawatu. d 25.3.1969 Taupo, Waikato. RHB SLA Teams: **Wellington, New Zealand Test.** Sch: Palmerston North BHS. NZCA obit: 1969; Wisden obit: 1970. He was called upon after the original fourteen players for the 1937 tour of England had been selected.
GALLOP David Langton 1956/57-1965/66 b 10.9.1937 Christchurch, Canterbury. RHB LB Team: **Canterbury.** Sch: Christchurch BHS. Occ: Accountant. QSM.
GARDINER William 1889/90-1895/96 b 1864 Auckland. d 27.1.1924 Wellington. Teams: **Auckland, Wellington.** Occ: Contractor. Rugby: Wellington.
GARDNER Cecil 1882/83 b Q4 1858 Hackney, London, England. d 21.1.1902 Natal, South Africa. In 1889 he left New Zealand for Sydney, he then went to America and entered into business as a fruit rancher at San Jose. He left America in 1901 to accept an appointment in the South African civil service but died of fever within a year of his arrival. Team: **Auckland.** Occ: Farmer.
GARNER Craig Douglas 1992/93-1996/97 b 12.7.1971 Porirua, Wellington. RHB OB Team: **Central Districts.** Played List A in NZ. Sch: Waimea Coll.
GARRARD Charles Wilson 1886/87-1904/05 b 9.10.1868 Nelson. d 21.2.1930 Auckland. Team: **Canterbury.** Sch: Christchurch BHS. Occ: School inspector. Umpired first-class cricket. Sons: W.R.Garrard, D.R.Garrard; son-in-law: W.J.Smeeton.
GARRARD Derwent Raoul 1917/18-1941/42 b 6.10.1897 Christchurch, Canterbury. d 14.6.1977 Auckland. RHB LB occ wk Teams: **Auckland, New Zealand.** Sch: Auckland GS. Occ: Civil servant. NZCA obit: 1977. Auckland selector. He played for New Zealand prior to being granted Test status. Brother: W.R.Garrard; father: C.W.Garrard; brother-in-law: W.J.Smeeton.

GARRARD Wilson Roziere 1918/19-1924/25 b 14.6.1899 Papanui, Christchurch, Canterbury. d 2.6.1956 Auckland. RHB wk Teams: **Auckland, New Zealand.** Sch: Auckland GS. Occ: Solicitor. NZCA obit: 1956; Wisden obit: 1958. He played for New Zealand prior to being granted Test status. Brother: D.R.Garrard; father: C.W.Garrard; brother-in-law: W.J.Smeeton.
GARROD C W 1917/18-1919/20 Team: **Wellington.**
GARROD Charles William 1966/67 b 6.4.1947 Blenheim, Marlborough. RHB Team: **Central Districts.**
GARTY John 1886/87 b 6.1.1864 Mt Grey, North Canterbury. d 28.1.1897 Sydney, New South Wales, Australia. Team: **Canterbury.** Occ: Clerk.
GARWOOD Walter John 1873/74-1876/77 b 30.4.1849 Tortington, Sussex, England. d 10.4.1885 Brisbane, Queensland, Australia. He died of tuberculosis aged 36. Team: **Otago, Wellington.** Occ: Miner. He was presented with a bat for making the highest score for Otago against Auckland in 1873/74.
GASSON Ernest Arthur 1924/25-1925/26 b 14.8.1887 Christchurch, Canterbury. d 3.3.1962 Christchurch, Canterbury. RHB Team: **Canterbury.** Sch: Makotuku Sch. Occ: Builder. Wisden obit: 1964. Canterbury selector. Son: E.A.Gasson.
GASSON Ernest Arthur 1937/38 b 11.11.1907 Christchurch, Canterbury. d 7.9.1942 El Alamein, Egypt. He was killed in action. RHB Team: **Canterbury.** Occ: Comm traveller. Father: E.A.Gasson.
GATENBY David John 1972/73-1978/79 b 12.2.1952 Launceston, Tasmania, Australia. RHB LBG Teams: **Canterbury, Tasmania.** Played List A in NZ. Sch: Scotch Coll, Launceston, Australia. Occ: Farmer. He played for Canterbury while doing a three-year agricultural course there. Brother: P.R.Gatenby (Tasmania).
GAUSSEN Herbert Ponsonby Loftus 1903/04-1910/11 b 21.2.1871 Edenfarm, Leitram, Ireland. d 28.6.1956 Vasey, Victoria, Australia. Teams: **Hawke's Bay.** Occ: Farmer. He was born Herbert Ponsonby Loftus **Tottenham,** the name he played under when he represented Hawke's Bay, but changed his name to Gaussen by Royal Licence on 21st September 1906 after his wife Emilia Gaussen inherited Brookman's Park from her father. He played for the M.C.C. on the 1911/12 tour of the West Indies.
GEAKE Samuel James 1913/14-1914/15 b 1888 Bendigo, Victoria, Australia. d 23.12.1961 Hastings, Hawke's Bay. LHB SLA Team: **Hawke's Bay.**
GEARRY George Neville 1953/54-1956/57 b 17.12.1923 Christchurch, Canterbury. d 4.1.1990 Christchurch, Canterbury. He died in a car accident. LHB RM Team: **Canterbury.** Sch: West Christchurch BHS. NZCA obit: 1990; Wisden obit: 1991. Son: R.M.Gearry.
GEARRY Roy Malcolm 1964/65-1973/74 b 18.12.1946 Christchurch, Canterbury. RHB RM Teams: **Canterbury, Central Districts.** Played List A in NZ. Sch: Christchurch BHS. Occ: Plumber. Father: G.N.Gearry.
GEARY Thomas Francis Clive 1940/41 b 6.5.1922 Dunedin, Otago. d 24.7.2004 Christchurch, Canterbury. LHB RM Team: **Otago.** Sch: Kings HS. Occ: Schoolteacher. Rugby: Otago. NZCA obit: 2004. Otago selector.
GEDDES Albert Edward 1899/00-1903/04 b 22.8.1871 Melbourne, Victoria, Australia. d 12.8.1935 Dunedin, Otago. LHB Team: **Otago.** Occ: Billiard manager.
GEDDIS Clifton Stewart 1914/15-1920/21 b 30.12.1894 Auckland. d 31.3.1953 Napier, Hawke's Bay. occ wk Team: **Hawke's Bay.** Occ: Newspaper proprietor.
GEDYE Arnold Ernest 1919/20 b 23.2.1897 Auckland. d 30.12.1976 Auckland. RHB Teams: **Wellington.** Occ: Civil servant. Son: S.G.Gedye.
GEDYE Sidney Graham 1956/57-1964/65 b 2.5.1929 Otahuhu, Auckland. RHB Teams: **Auckland, New Zealand Test.** Sch: Otahuhu Coll. NZCA COY: 1964. Auckland selector. Father: A.E.Gedye.
GELLATLY Stephen James 2007/08 b 25.3.1980 Palmerston North, Manawatu. LHB Team: **Wellington.** Played List A in NZ.
GEORGE Arthur Andrew 1913/14 b 28.7.1866 Wakefield, South Australia, Australia. d 2.5.1931 Wellington. Team: **Wellington.** Occ: Draper.
GERMON Lee Kenneth 1987/88-2001/02 b 4.11.1968 Christchurch, Canterbury. RHB LB wk Teams: **Canterbury, Otago, New Zealand Test, New Zealand ODI.** Played List A in NZ. Sch: Christchurch BHS. Occ: Sports admin. NZ U19 Test; NZ U19 ODI. He holds the Canterbury 9th

wicket partnership record of 182* with R.M.Ford against Wellington in 1989/90. During this partnership he and Ford broke the world record for the most runs in a first-class over - 77 off R.H.Vance. The 22-ball over contained 17 no-balls - due to a miscount there were only five legitimate balls. Germon also holds the Canterbury 10th wicket partnership record of 160 with W.A.Wisnicki against Northern Districts in 1997/98.

GERRARD James Porter 1924/25-1926/27 b 17.11.1904 Devonport, Auckland. d 7.7.1964 Devonport, Auckland. Team: **Auckland.** Sch: Auckland GS. Occ: Manager. Soccer: New Zealand. NZCA obit: 1964.

GIBBES William Richard Ladsey 1905/06-1914/15 b 1880 Cootamundra, New South Wales, Australia. d 21.11.1918 Wellington. He died of Spanish flu aged 38. LHB LFM Team: **Wellington.** Occ: Accountant. Wisden obit: 1919.

GIBBS Clifford Samuel 1929/30 b 19.2.1905 Rangiora, North Canterbury. d 2.7.1976 Christchurch, Canterbury. RHB SLA Team: **Canterbury.** Sch: St Andrews Coll. Occ: New Zealand Farmers wool department manager.

GIBBS Paul Bryan 1990/91 b 3.7.1965 Marton, Rangitikei. RHB RM Team: **Central Districts.** Played List A in NZ.

GIBSON John Grant 1968/69-1980/81 b 12.11.1948 Hamilton, Waikato. RHB OB Teams: **Northern Districts, Auckland.** Played List A in NZ. He holds the Northern Districts 2nd wicket partnership record of 237 with C.M.Kuggeleijn against Canterbury in 1980/81.

GIBSON William Alexander James 1895/96-1897/98 b 1872 New Zealand. d 26.11.1961 Auckland. Team: **Hawke's Bay.** Occ: Journalist. Originally from Southland, he lived in Gisborne and was an occasional Hawke's Bay player. In a senior game in Gisborne he took 9 wickets for 2 runs.

GIFFORD Joseph Jarvis 1919/20-1920/21 b 22.10.1899 Napier, Hawke's Bay. d 6.8.1930 Napier, Hawke's Bay. He died aged 30. M Team: **Hawke's Bay.** Occ: Journalist.

GILBERTSON Alan William 1951/52-1953/54 b 6.12.1927 Invercargill, Southland. d 7.5.2009 Invercargill, Southland. RHB RM Team: **Otago.** Occ: Builder. He holds the Otago 7th wicket partnership record of 182 with B.Sutcliffe against Canterbury in 1952/53. Father: J.Gilbertson; uncle: J.H.Gilbertson.

GILBERTSON James 1914/15-1920/21 b 15.1.1889 Invercargill, Southland. d 20.3.1974 Invercargill, Southland. RHB wk Team: **Southland.** Occ: Builder. Brother: J.H.Gilbertson; son: A.W.Gilbertson.

GILBERTSON John Henry 1914/15-1918/19 b 18.8.1883 Invercargill, Southland. d 6.8.1930 Invercargill, Southland. RHB Team: **Southland.** Occ: Land broker. Brother: J.Gilbertson; nephew: A.W.Gilbertson.

GILES Eric David 1960/61 b 15.3.1939 Auckland. d 2.10.1990 Auckland. LHB occ wk Team: **Auckland.** Sch: Auckland GS. NZCA obit: 1991.

GILES Gary Victor 1961/62-1975/76 b 12.1.1940 Hamilton, Waikato. LHB RM Team: **Northern Districts.** Played List A in NZ.

GILES Leslie Albert 1929/30 b 2.1.1906 Burwood, Christchurch, Canterbury. d 1.6.1981 Auckland. RHB Team: **Otago.** Sch: Otago BHS. Occ: Railway employee. Rugby: Otago. NZCA obit: 1981; Wisden obit: 1982.

GILES Maurice Edwin 1951/52-1953/54 b 27.2.1928 Wellington. d 6.7.2001 Wellington. LHB RM Team: **Wellington.**

GILHOOLY Richard John 2004/05 b 26.3.1979 Hastings, Hawke's Bay. LHB RFM Team: **Wellington.** Sch: St Johns Coll, Napier.

GILL Brian 1969/70 b 5.6.1948 Auckland. RHB LMF Team: **Northern Districts.**

GILL James Allan 1953/54-1963/64 b 11.4.1928 Invercargill, Southland. LHB wk Team: **Otago.** Otago selector.

GILL John George 1882/83-1884/85 b 1854 Durham, England. d 15.3.1888 Takapuna, Auckland. He died of apoplexy aged 34. F Team: **Auckland.** Occ: Farmer.

GILL Michael Frederick 1974/75-1981/82 b 19.3.1957 Wanganui. RHB RMF Team: **Central Districts.** Played List A in NZ.

GILL Stephen John 1981/82-1987/88 b 28.9.1957 Nelson. LHB LM Team: **Central Districts.** Played List A in NZ.

GILLESPIE Hector David 1920/21-1931/32 b 29.5.1901 Auckland. d 12.10.1954 Auckland. RHB Team: **Auckland.** Sch: Auckland GS. Occ: Law clerk. NZCA obit: 1954; Wisden obit: 1955. In Auckland club cricket in 1924/25 he and J.E.Mills shared an opening stand of 441.
GILLESPIE Mark Raymond 1999/00-2009/10 b 17.10.1979 Wanganui. RHB RFM Teams: **Wellington, New Zealand Test, New Zealand ODI, New Zealand T20.** Played List A in NZ; Played T20 in NZ. Sch: Tawa Coll. NZ U19 Test; NZ U19 ODI. He holds the record for the best NZ international T20 bowling figures of 4/7 against Kenya in 2007.
GILLESPIE Stuart Ross 1979/80-1988/89 b 2.3.1957 Wanganui. RHB RFM Teams: **Northern Districts, Auckland, New Zealand Test, New Zealand ODI.** Played List A in NZ.
GILLOTT Eric Kenneth 1971/72-1978/79 b 15.4.1951 Waiuku, Franklin. RHB SLA Team: **Northern Districts, New Zealand.** Played List A in NZ. He played for New Zealand in a first-class match.
GIVEN Andrew Moncrieff 1914/15 b 30.1.1886 Dunedin, Otago. d 19.7.1916 Pozieres, France. He was killed in action whilst serving as a private in the Australian Forces. He died on the same day and in the same battle as A.E.Pratt (Auckland). Team: **Otago.** Sch: Otago BHS. Occ: Stationery salesman.
GLASGOW James Mcclure 1866/67-1868/69 b 1850 India. d 12.8.1934 Wellington. wk Team: **Otago.** Sch: Otago BHS. Occ: Civil servant; accountant.
GLEESON Charles 1877/78 b 1845 Auckland. d 31.10.1931 Thames, Thames Valley. Team: **Auckland.**
GLEESON Horace Atwood 1917/18-1920/21 b 14.8.1878 Williamstown, Victoria, Australia. d 1959 Melbourne, Victoria, Australia. Team: **Southland.** Sch: Grenville Coll, Ballarat, Australia. Occ: Manager of paint store; musician.
GLEN Adam 1872/73-1886/87 b 1.3.1853 Dunedin, Otago. d 3.7.1937 Auckland. Team: **Otago.** Occ: Compositor. Umpired first-class cricket. Otago selector.
GLOVER Ross Lewis 1985/86-1990/91 b 5.5.1964 Masterton, Wairarapa. RHB OB Team: **Central Districts.** Played List A in NZ.
GODBY Harry Eden 1874/75-1875/76 b 2.7.1847 Ramsgate, Kent, England. d 1911 Newtown, New South Wales, Australia. wk Team: **Otago.** Sch: Marlborough, England. Brother: M.J.Godby.
GODBY Michael John 1875/76-1880/81 b 29.9.1850 Henley, Oxfordshire, England. d 14.12.1923 Marylebone, London, England. Teams: **Otago, Canterbury.** Sch: Winchester, England. Occ: Solicitor. Brother: H.E.Godby.
GODWIN AUSTEN Edmund 1877/78 b 15.11.1854 Chilworth, Surrey, England. Team: **Canterbury.** The second highest mountain in the world, the Karakoram peak K2 in the Himalayas was at one stage named Mount Godwin-Austen in honour of his brother Henry.
GOLDER Scott Bernard 1999/00 b 17.9.1976 Lower Hutt, Wellington. RHB occ wk Team: **Wellington.** Played List A in NZ; Played T20 in NZ.
GOLD-SMITH Harold Desmond 1905/06 b Q1 1888 Wandsworth, London, England. d 12.2.1919 Edinburgh, Midlothian. Scotland. He died of illness shortly after the end of the war; he had served as a gunner in the NZ Forces. Team: **Hawke's Bay.** Sch: Christ Coll; Napier BHS. Occ: Clerk.
GOLLAR William James 1890/91 b 11.3.1858 Hobart, Tasmania, Australia. d 31.8.1916 Dunedin, Otago. Team: **Otago.** Occ: Baker. Wisden obit: 1917.
GOODE Norman William 1909/10 b 24.7.1881 Millthorpe, New South Wales, Australia. d 15.10.1959 Hamilton, Waikato. wk Team: **Auckland.** Occ: Builder. He represented North Tasmania against the 1907/08 English team that toured Australia.
GOODER Frederick John 1884/85 b 17.1.1862 Wellington. d 13.4.1948 Wellington. Team: **Wellington.** Occ: Salesman.
GOODSON Matthew Charles 1989/90-1994/95 b 3.3.1970 Palmerston North, Manawatu. RHB LB Teams: **Central Districts, Wellington.** Sch: Palmerston North BHS. He holds the Wellington 8th wicket partnership record of 180 with R.G.Twose against Otago in 1994/95.
GOODSON Matthew John 1891/92 b 1863 Wanganui. d 3.6.1919 Hawera, Taranaki. Team: **Taranaki.** Sch: Wanganui CS. Occ: Farmer.
GORDON Leslie Albert Chester 1917/18 b 1882 Melbourne, Victoria, Australia. d 28.10.1946 Christchurch, Canterbury. Team: **Canterbury.** Occ: Insurance inspector.

GORDON Robert Wilfred 1912/13 b 22.10.1889 Auckland. d 29.1.1914 Auckland. He drowned, aged 24, whilst on a pleasure cruise with a group of friends; he tried unsuccessfully to save the life of his fiancée's sister, who had been swept overboard during heavy seas. His headstone poignantly reads - 'He went to succour those in need, he gave his life, his all.' Team: **Auckland**. Occ: Clerk.

GORE Arthur Hector 1885/86-1901/02 b 1866 Australia. d 29.9.1944 Vancouver, British Columbia, Canada. LB Teams: **Wellington, Hawke's Bay**. Sch: Wellington Coll. Occ: Insurance agent. Brothers: C.S.Gore, R.Gore.

GORE Charles St George 1891/92-1903/04 b 1.10.1871 Wellington. d 11.12.1913 Wellington. He acted as a special constable during the general strike and was on duty on the wharves a week before his death. He caught a chill a few days before his death and pneumonia supervened. RHB Teams: **Wellington, New Zealand**. Occ: Civil servant. Wisden obit: 1915. Tennis: Wellington. He played for New Zealand prior to being granted Test status. Brothers: A.H.Gore, R.Gore.

GORE Ross 1896/97 b 1869 Wellington. d 25.11.1925 Woollahra, Sydney, New South Wales, Australia. Team: **Wellington**. Sch: Wellington Coll. Occ: Insurance. Secretary Royal Sydney Golf Club. Tennis: Wellington. Brothers: A.H.Gore, C.S.Gore.

GOSSAGE Frederick Herbert 1893/94 b Q1 1866 Aigburth, Lancashire, England. d 25.2.1944 Guildford, Surrey, England. Team: **Hawke's Bay**. Occ: Civil servant.

GOUGE 1874/75-1875/76 Team: **Wellington**.

GOUGH William John 1953/54 b 20.10.1929 Dunedin, Otago. d 14.8.1978 Dunedin, Otago. RHB Team: **Otago**. Sch: Otago BHS. Occ: Clerk.

GOULD Ian James 1975-1996 b 19.8.1957 Taplow, Buckinghamshire, England. LHB wk Teams: **Auckland,** England ODI, Middlesex, Sussex. Played List A in NZ. Sch: Westgate Sch, England. Occ: Umpire. Umpired first-class cricket. An English pro, played and coached in NZ.

GRACE Thomas Marshall Percy 1911/12-1913/14 b 11.7.1890 Pukawa, Waikato. d 8.8.1915 Monash Valley, Gallipoli, Turkey. He was killed in action aged 25. Team: **Wellington**. Sch: Wellington Coll. Occ: Civil servant. Rugby: New Zealand Maori and Wellington. Wisden obit: 1917.

GRAHAM Archibald Clifford 1944/45 b 20.1.1917 Dunedin, Otago. d 10.6.2000 Auckland. RHB RM Team: **Otago**. Sch: Otago BHS. Occ: Journalist. NZCA obit: 2004. Brother: C.G.Graham.

GRAHAM Bernard Neylon 1953/54-1956/57 b 27.10.1922 Gisborne, Poverty Bay. d 14.6.1992 Gisborne, Poverty Bay. RHB Teams: **Auckland, Northern Districts**. Sch: Marist Bros, Gisborne. Occ: Schoolteacher. NZCA obit: 2004.

GRAHAM Colin Gordon 1954/55-1955/56 b 7.6.1929 Dunedin, Otago. RHB RAB Team: **Otago**. Sch: Otago BHS. Occ: Schoolteacher. Brother: A.C.Graham.

GRAHAM Henry 1892/93-1906/07 b 22.11.1870 Carlton, Melbourne, Victoria, Australia. d 7.2.1911 Seacliff, Dunedin, Otago. He died at the age of 40. RHB LB Teams: **Otago, New Zealand,** Australia Test, Victoria. Sch: Berwick Coll, Australia. Occ: Cricket pro. Wisden obit: 1912. Otago coach. He played for New Zealand prior to being granted Test status. He scored a Test century on debut for Australia in England in 1893 and also scored a Test century on his debut appearance in Australia in 1894/95.

GRAHAM Maurice 1934/35-1936/37 b 12.8.1902 Leeston, Canterbury. d 26.2.1993 Christchurch, Canterbury. LHB RM Team: **Canterbury**. Sch: Christchurch BHS. NZCA obit: 1997.

GRAHAM William Hay 1917/18-1918/19 b 25.12.1881 Auckland. d 28.7.1961 Auckland. RHB Team: **Auckland**. Sch: Auckland GS. Occ: Civil servant.

GRANT Milton Reid 1911/12 b 14.6.1880 Milton, Otago. d 7.12.1961 Napier, Hawke's Bay. Team: **Hawke's Bay**. Sch: Woodville. Occ: Schoolteacher.

GRANT Thomas Alexander Brandon 1920/21-1924/25 b 1894 Australia. d 9.6.1966 Lower Hutt, Wellington. LHB SLA Teams: **Canterbury, Wellington**. Sch: Nth Canterbury HS. Occ: Clerk. NZCA obit: 1966.

GRAY Douglas John 1956/57-1959/60 b 22.3.1936 Auckland. d 6.9.2004 Matamata, Waikato. LHB RM Team: **Northern Districts**. NZCA obit: 2005.

GRAY Evan John 1975/76-1991/92 b 18.11.1954 Wellington. RHB SLA Teams: **Wellington, New Zealand Test, New Zealand ODI**. Played List A in NZ. Sch: St Patricks Coll, Wellington. Occ: Coy director. Umpired first-class cricket. He holds the Wellington 6th wicket partnership record of 226 with R.W.Ormiston against Central Districts in 1981/82.

GRAY James 1917/18-1919/20 b 15.3.1885 Oamaru, Otago. d 17.11.1975 Christchurch, Canterbury. Team: **Canterbury**. Occ: Builder. He scored 343 in a Christchurch club cricket match in 1917/18.
GREATBATCH Mark John 1982/83-1999/00 b 11.12.1963 Auckland. LHB RM occ wk Teams: **Auckland, Central Districts, New Zealand Test, New Zealand ODI.** Played List A in NZ. Sch: Auckland GS. Occ: Cricket coach. Book: Boundary hunter. NZ selector and coach. On his Test debut he scored 107* against England at Auckland in 1987/88.
GREEN Arthur Richard Wenman Pennefather 1884/85-1886/87 b 1859 Buninyong, Victoria, Australia. d 3.8.1935 Tauranga, Bay of Plenty. Team: **Nelson**. Occ: Bank auditor.
GREEN L 1926/27 b Australia. wk Team: **Otago**. He was reported to have come from Australia in 1926.
GREEN Lindsay Athol 1959/60-1961/62 b 14.10.1938 Sydney, New South Wales, Australia. RHB OB Team: **Auckland**. Sch: Auckland GS.
GREENFIELD Alfred 1875/76 b 1829 England. d 31.5.1920 Nelson. Team: **Nelson**. Occ: Civil servant. Umpired first-class cricket. Son: F.E.Greenfield.
GREENFIELD Francis Edmund 1880/81-1891/92 b 13.4.1862 Nelson. d 24.1.1941 Christchurch, Canterbury. Team: **Nelson**. Sch: Nelson Coll. Occ: Surveyor. Father: A.Greenfield.
GREENSTREET Wayne Anthony 1969/70-1972/73 b 21.1.1949 Lower Hutt, Wellington. RHB RM Teams: **Wellington, Central Districts (not FC), New Zealand.** Played List A in NZ. Sch: Hutt Valley Memorial Coll. Occ: Manager. He played for New Zealand in a FC match.
GREGORY Cyril John 1883/84 b 29.5.1859 St Thomas, Devon, England. Team: **Hawke's Bay**. Sch: Weymouth GS, England. Occ: Farmer.
GREGORY George Richard 1922/23-1928/29 b Q1 1892 Madeley, Shropshire, England. d 17.8.1970 Christchurch, Canterbury. Team: **Canterbury**. Occ: Coy manager. Umpired first-class cricket. NZCA obit: 1970.
GRENIER D 1912/13 Team: **Auckland**.
GRIERSON Trevor James 1877/78 b 25.4.1849 Cardiff, Glamorgan, Wales. d 21.9.1913 Christchurch, Canterbury. He died of cirrhosis of the liver. Team: **Auckland**. Occ: Sharebroker; farmer.
GRIEVE Andrew John 1884/85-1887/88 b 24.10.1863 Dunedin, Otago. d 12.12.1941 Dunedin, Otago. Team: **Otago**. Occ: Tinsmith.
GRIFFITHS Adrian Alfred 1984/85-1985/86 b 23.5.1951 Blenheim, Marlborough. LHB OB Team: **Wellington**. Brother: R.J.Griffiths.
GRIFFITHS Bernard George 1931/32-1937/38 b 24.2.1910 Wellington. d 29.9.1982 Wellington. RHB LBG Team: **Wellington, New Zealand.** NZCA obit: 1982. He was a controversial omission from the 1937 touring side, when after having been informed of his selection, he was subsequently omitted from the team. He played for New Zealand in a first-class match. Nephew: S.J.Maguiness.
GRIFFITHS Roderick Joseph 1975/76-1980/81 b 20.4.1948 Blenheim, Marlborough. RHB LFM Team: **Northern Districts**. Brother: A.A.Griffiths.
GRIGGS Bevan Barry John 2000/01-2009/10 b 29.3.1978 Palmerston North, Manawatu. RHB wk Team: **Central Districts**. Played List A in NZ; Played T20 in NZ. Sch: Palmerston North BHS. He holds the Central Districts 6th wicket partnership record of 235 with M.S.Sinclair against Wellington in 2008/09.
GRIMMETT Clarence Victor 1911/12-1940/41 b 25.12.1891 Caversham, Dunedin, Otago. d 2.5.1980 Kensington Park, Adelaide, South Australia, Australia. RHB LBG Teams: **Wellington, Australia Test, Victoria, South Australia.** Sch: Mt Cook HS. Occ: Sign writer; insurance salesman. Books: Getting Wickets; Tricking the Batsman; Grimmett on Cricket; Clarrie Grimmett: the Bradman of spin by Ashley Mallett. NZCA obit: 1980; Wisden obit: 1981. WCOY: 1931. He moved to Australia in 1914 and played in 37 Tests for Australia, taking a then Test record of 216 wickets at 24 runs. He took 1424 first-class wickets at 22 runs apiece and was the first bowler of any country to capture 200 Test wickets.
GRINDROD George Arnold 1896/97 b Q4 1870 West Derby, Liverpool, Lancashire, England. d 7.1.1949 Hawera, Taranaki. Team: **Taranaki**. Occ: Carpenter.

GROVES Leslie Joseph 1929/30-1949/50 b 9.6.1911 Dunedin, Otago. d 4.9.1990 Dunedin, Otago. RHB LBG Team: **Otago.** Sch: Otago BHS. Occ: Assistant manager. Soccer: New Zealand and Otago. NZCA obit: 1991; Wisden obit: 1991.

GROVES Thomas George 1914/15-1920/21 b 22.2.1891 Invercargill, Southland. d 11.11.1940 Invercargill, Southland. Team: **Southland.** Sch: Invercargill Sth. Occ: Clerk.

GUDGEON George 1897/98 b 1876 England. d 18.10.1922 New Plymouth, Taranaki. SLA Team: **Taranaki.** Occ: Cycle importer.

GUILLEN Simpson Clairmonte 1947/48-1960/61 b 24.9.1924 Port of Spain, Trinidad. RHB wk Teams: **Canterbury, New Zealand Test,** West Indies Test, Trinidad. Occ: Insurance agent. Book: Calypso Kiwi. NZCA COY: 1956. Brother: N.N.Guillen (Trinidad); father: V.Guillen (Trinidad); grandson: L.V.van Beek; great-nephew J.C.Guillen (Trinidad and Tobago).

GUINEY Charles Edward 1918/19 b 29.4.1895 Christchurch, Canterbury. d 15.12.1972 Glendowie, Auckland. Team: **Canterbury.** Sch: Christchurch BHS. Occ: Journalist. Umpired first-class cricket.

GULLY John 1982/83 b 15.7.1957 Nelson. RHB RM Team: **Canterbury.** Sch: Nelson Coll. Occ: Outdoor adventure company employee.

GUNTHORP Henry 1895/96-1902/03 b 29.4.1871 Marylebone, London, England. d 7.10.1962 Balclutha, Otago. Teams: **Canterbury, Otago.** Occ: Dentist.

GUPTILL Martin James 2005/06-2009/10 b 30.9.1986 Auckland. RHB OB Teams: **Auckland, New Zealand Test, New Zealand ODI, New Zealand T20.** Played List A in NZ; Played T20 in NZ. Sch: Avondale Coll. Occ: Cricket pro. NZ U19 ODI. He holds the NZ Test 6th wicket partnership record of 339 with B.B.McCullum against Bangladesh in 2009/10. He is the only NZ player to score 99 on his first-class debut. He also holds the NZ domestic T20 1st wicket partnership record of 149 with L.Vincent for Auckland against Wellington in 2009/10.

GUTHARDT David John 1985/86-1988/89 b 24.10.1958 Nelson. RHB wk Team: **Central Districts.** Played List A in NZ.

GUY John William 1953/54-1972/73 b 29.8.1934 Nelson. LHB RSM Teams: **Central Districts, Canterbury, Otago, Wellington, Northern Districts, New Zealand Test,** Northamptonshire. Played List A in NZ. Sch: Nelson Coll. Occ: Sportsgoods dealer. NZ and ND selector.

HADDEN Alfred Ernest 1905/06-1910/11 b 1877 Sydney, New South Wales, Australia. d 23.12.1936 Auckland. RHB Teams: **Auckland, New Zealand.** Occ: Wharf labourer. He was a tally-clerk on the Auckland wharf and in 1911 he was arrested on a charge of cargo theft. His defence was that he was addicted to drink and was not aware of what he was doing. He was convicted and served two years in gaol. On his release he went to Sydney but only stayed a fortnight having lost his job at a timber mill because of his drinking habits. Later he returned to NZ where he was convicted of a breach of his prohibition order. He served in the NZ forces in WW1. He died in a Salvation Army hostel. He played for New Zealand prior to being granted Test status.

HADDON Gerald Peter 1969/70 b 31.5.1941 Palmerston North, Manawatu. RHB Team: **Central Districts.**

HADLEE Barry George 1961/62-1980/81 b 14.12.1941 Christchurch, Canterbury. RHB Teams: **Canterbury, New Zealand ODI.** Played List A in NZ. Sch: Christchurch BHS. Occ: Accountant. Brothers: D.R.Hadlee, R.J.Hadlee; father: W.A.Hadlee.

HADLEE Dayle Robert 1966/67-1983/84 b 6.1.1948 Riccarton, Christchurch, Canterbury. RHB RMF Teams: **Canterbury, New Zealand Test, New Zealand ODI.** Played List A in NZ. Sch: Christchurch BHS. Occ: Schoolteacher; coach. NZCA COY: 1975. Canterbury selector. NZ bowling coach before taking on a position with the ICC's Global Cricket Academy in Dubai. Brothers: R.J.Hadlee, B.G.Hadlee; father: W.A.Hadlee.

HADLEE Richard John (Sir) 1971/72-1990 b 3.7.1951 St Albans, Christchurch, Canterbury. LHB RF Teams: **Canterbury, New Zealand Test, New Zealand ODI,** Nottinghamshire, Tasmania. Played List A in NZ. Sch: Christchurch BHS. Occ: Cricket pro. Books: Changing Pace: a Memoir; Rhythm and Swing; Hadlee Hits Out; At the Double; Richard Hadlee: His Record Innings by Innings by W.Harte. Sir. NZCA COY: 1979, 1983, 1984, 1986, 1987. WCOY: 1982. ICOY 1989. He was the first player to reach 400 Test wickets. NZ selector and manager. He took a hat-trick for Canterbury v Central Districts in 1971/72. He has the best Test bowling figures for New Zealand when he took 9/52 against Australia in 1985/86 - in this game he had match figures of 15/123. He also took 9/55 for New Zealand against West Zone in 1988/89. He has taken the most first-class wickets by a New Zealander, 1,490. Brothers: D.R.Hadlee, B.G.Hadlee; father: W.A.Hadlee.

HADLEE Walter Arnold 1933/34-1951/52 b 4.6.1915 Lincoln, Christchurch, Canterbury. d 29.9.2006 Christchurch, Canterbury. RHB RM Teams: **Canterbury, Otago, New Zealand Test.** Sch: Christchurch BHS. Occ: Accountant. Rugby: Otago and Canterbury. Book: The innings of a lifetime. CBE, OBE. NZCA obit: 2007; Wisden obit: 2007. Chairman of NZCC board. NZ and Canterbury selector. Sons: D.R.Hadlee, R.J.Hadlee, B.G.Hadlee.

HAGGETT Herbert Edward 1894/95-1897/98 b 3.9.1868 Christchurch, Canterbury. d 18.8.1938 Lower Hutt, Wellington. Team: **Taranaki.** Sch: Gloucester St, Christchurch. Occ: Printer.

HAIG Frederick Hill 1919/20 b 23.4.1895 Wanganui. d 3.12.1948 Dunedin, Otago. Team: **Otago.** Occ: Saddler.

HAIG Shaun Barry 2005/06-2009/10 b 19.3.1982 Auckland. RHB RM occ wk Team: **Otago.** Played List A in NZ; Played T20 in NZ. He holds the Otago 3rd wicket partnership record of 306 with N.T.Broom against Central Districts in 2009/10.

HAIG William Smith 1949/50-1957/58 b 6.4.1921 Prestonpans, East Lothian, Scotland. d 21.8.1967 Dunedin, Otago. RHB OB Team: **Otago.** Occ: Accountant. NZCA obit: 1967. He holds the Otago 5th wicket partnership record of 266 with B.Sutcliffe against Auckland in 1949/50.

HAINSWORTH Stean Craig Wilby 1988/89 b 22.12.1965 Upper Hutt, Wellington. RHB RM Team: **Wellington.** Sch: Hutt Valley HS. Occ: Accountant.

HALDANE G 1885/86 Team: **Wellington.**

HALES Everett Olive 1896/97-1909/10 b 27.10.1876 Wellington. d 1.11.1947 Wellington. LF Team: **Wellington.** Sch: Wellington Coll. Occ: Public trustee.

HALIDAY Selwyn Gordon 1942/43 b 13.11.1922 Auckland. RHB Teams: **North Island Army, New Zealand Army.**

HALL Peter James 1948-1955/56 b 4.12.1927 The Peak, Hong Kong. RHB RM Teams: **Otago,** Cambridge University. Sch: Geelong GS, Australia.

HALL W K 1904/05-1905/06 Team: **Hawke's Bay.** He was a former Sydney player.

HALLAMORE Reginald Gerard 1898/99-1918/19 b 7.2.1871 Penryn, Cornwall, England. d 10.12.1941 Invercargill, Southland. OB wk Teams: **Hawke's Bay, Southland.** Occ: Land agent.

HALLEY Russell 1886/87-1890/91 b 1863 unknown. d 6.7.1909 Wellington. RHB LM Team: **Canterbury.** Occ: Warehouseman. Umpired first-class cricket.

HALLIDAY Charles John 1876/77-1886/87 b 30.12.1844 Calcutta (now Kolkata), Bengal, India. d 22.5.1906 Brompton, London, England. Team: **Nelson.** Sch: Rugby, England. Occ: Coy secretary.

HALLIDAY Henry Holden 1873/74-1880/81 b 30.3.1853 Nelson. d 19.7.1922 Hokitika, West Coast. occ wk Team: **Nelson.** Sch: Nelson Coll. Occ: Clerk.

HAMBROOK Thomas Stephen 1951/52-1958/59 b 6.6.1922 London, England. d 2.9.1987 Auckland. LHB LM Team: **Auckland.** NZCA obit: 1987.

HAMILTON Archibald James 1914/15-1920/21 b 1890 New Zealand. d 6.3.1957 Invercargill, Southland. Team: **Southland.** Occ: Clerk. Brother: D.C.Hamilton.

HAMILTON Bruce Glanville 1953/54 b 22.10.1932 Wanganui. RHB Team: **Central Districts.**

HAMILTON Donald Cameron 1919/20 b 19.1.1883 Invercargill, Southland. d 14.4.1925 Auckland. He died from an overdose of a drug taken to induce sleep. Team: **Southland.** Sch: Southland BHS. Occ: Chemist. Rugby: All Blacks and Southland. His rugby career ended when he was banned from playing rugby after playing a game of rugby league. Brother: A.J.Hamilton.

HAMILTON Ian Malone 1926/27-1932/33 b 13.12.1906 Christchurch, Canterbury. d 29.8.1992 Ashburton, Mid Canterbury. LHB Team: **Canterbury, New Zealand.** Sch: Christ Coll. Occ: Accountant. NZCA obit: 1995. He played for New Zealand prior to being granted Test status.

HAMILTON John James 1877/78-1879/80 b Q3 1855 Exeter, Devon. d Q2 1904 Salford, Lancashire, England. Team: **Wellington.**

HAMILTON Lance John 1996/97-2006/07 b 5.4.1973 Papakura, Auckland. RHB LFM Teams: **Central Districts, New Zealand ODI.** Played List A in NZ; Played T20 in NZ. Sch: Rosehill Coll. Occ: Real estate agent.

HAMMEL John Ernest 1962/63-1965/66 b 4.11.1940 Wellington. d 14.3.1983 Wellington. LHB Team: **Wellington.** NZCA obit: 1983.

HAMMOND George 1920/21 b 9.8.1887 Winton, Southland. d 20.11.1947 Invercargill, Southland. Team: **Southland.** Occ: Farmer.

HAMPTON Barry Leon 1961/62-1968/69 b 16.1.1941 Westport, West Coast. RHB RM Team: **Central Districts.** He holds the Central Districts 7th wicket partnership record of 219 with B.W.Yuile against Canterbury in 1967/68. Brother: I.R.Hampton.

HAMPTON George Samuel 1932/33 b 31.8.1905 Hoddesden, Hertfordshire, England. d 29.12.2000 Cambridge, Waikato. RHB wk Team: **Auckland.** Occ: Farmer. NZCA obit: 2002.

HAMPTON Ian Robert 1962/63-1965/66 b 30.7.1942 Motueka, Tasman. LHB RM Team: **Central Districts.** CD selector. Brother: B.L.Hampton.

HANCOCK Kim Bruce 1985/86-1986/87 b 22.7.1966 Matamata, Waikato. RHB RFM Team: **Northern Districts.** Sch: Matamata Coll. Occ: Accountant. NZ U19 Test; NZ U19 ODI.

HANDFORD Alick 1892-1914/15 b 3.5.1869 Wilford, Nottinghamshire, England. d 15.10.1935 Tavistock, Devon, England. RHB RM Teams: **Southland,** Nottinghamshire. Occ: Cricket pro. Umpired first-class cricket. Wisden obit: 1936. Southland coach. An English pro, played and coached in NZ. Brother: S.Handford (United States of America).

HARBRIDGE Brian Christopher 1939/40-1940/41 b 22.12.1917 Te Aroha, Thames Valley. d 19.3.1983 Napier, Hawke's Bay. RHB wk Team: **Canterbury.** Sch: Christchurch BHS. Occ: Surveying engineer. NZCA obit: 1983.

HARDEN George Wilfred 1894/95 b 1864 Mangawhai, Northland. d 30.1.1933 Wanganui. Team: **Taranaki.** Occ: Bank manager.

HARDEN Richard John 1985-2000 b 16.8.1965 Bridgwater, Somerset, England. RHB SLA Teams: **Central Districts,** Somerset, Yorkshire. Played List A in NZ. Sch: Kings Coll, Taunton, England. An English pro, played and coached in NZ.

HARDING Malcolm Garland 1986/87 b 28.5.1959 Hamilton, Waikato. RHB OB Team: **Northern Districts.**

HARDSTAFF Joseph 1930-1955 b 3.7.1911 Nuncargate, Nottinghamshire, England. d 1.1.1990 Worksop, Nottinghamshire, England. RHB RM Teams: **Auckland,** England Test, Nottinghamshire, Europeans (India). Sch: Kirkby Woodhouse, England. Occ: Cricket pro. Wisden obit: 1991. WCOY: 1938. An English pro, played and coached in NZ. Father: J.Hardstaff (England, Nottinghamshire); son: J.Hardstaff (Free Foresters).

HARFORD Noel Sherwin 1953/54-1966/67 b 30.8.1930 Winton, Southland. d 30.3.1981 Auckland. He committed suicide by monoxide poisoning. RHB RSM Teams: **Central Districts, Auckland, New Zealand Test.** Sch: Palmerston North BHS. Occ: Coy director. Basketball: New Zealand. NZCA obit: 1981; Wisden obit: 1981. NZCA COY: 1958. ND selector.

HARFORD Roy Ivan 1965/66-1967/68 b 30.5.1936 Fulham, London, England. LHB wk Teams: **Auckland, New Zealand Test.**

HARGREAVES James Percy 1886/87 b 13.8.1868 Christchurch, Canterbury. d 11.10.1924 Christchurch, Canterbury. Team: **Canterbury.** Sch: Christ Coll. Occ: Bank officer.

HARKNESS John Tinline 1892/93-1900/01 b 6.4.1867 Richmond, Nelson. d 15.12.1960 Christchurch, Canterbury. Teams: **Auckland, Otago.** Occ: Accountant.

HARLEY Edward Steane 1864/65-1868/69 c 9.10.1839 Leicester, England. d 9.6.1901 Ashley, Canterbury. RHB Team: **Canterbury.** Occ: Accountant. Umpired first-class cricket. He took the initial steps for founding the first freezing works in Canterbury.

HARLIWICH Jack Austin 1951/52 b 14.7.1930 Christchurch, Canterbury. RHB RM Team: **Canterbury.** Sch: Christchurch Technical Coll. Occ: Cabinet maker.

HARMAN Annesley Frederick George 1889/90-1893/94 b 10.11.1864 Christchurch, Canterbury. d 18.6.1895 Christchurch, Canterbury. He died of pneumonia aged 28. Team: **Canterbury.** Sch: Christ Coll. Occ: Clerk. Rugby: Canterbury. Brothers: R.D.Harman, T.D.Harman.

HARMAN Richard Dacre 1883/84-1896/97 b 3.6.1859 Christchurch, Canterbury. d 26.12.1927 Christchurch, Canterbury. Team: **Canterbury.** Sch: Christ Coll. Occ: Architect. Umpired first-class cricket. Tennis: NZ Singles Champion 1891, Doubles Champion five times with F.Wilding. Rugby: Canterbury. Brothers: A.F.G.Harman, T.D.Harman.

HARMAN Thomas De Renzy 1882/83-1901/02 b 3.2.1861 Christchurch, Canterbury. d 21.4.1950 Christchurch, Canterbury. Team: **Canterbury.** Sch: Christ Coll. Occ: Solicitor. Athletics: New Zealand Long Jump Champion in 1889. Rugby: Canterbury. Brothers: A.F.G.Harman, R.D.Harman.
HARPER Frederick 1886/87-1894/95 b 24.11.1863 Bolton, Lancashire, England. d 19.1.1937 Christchurch, Canterbury. Team: **Otago.**
HARPER Gordon Dentford 1958/59 b 1.4.1937 Te Waitere, Waikato. d 26.6.1997 Auckland. RHB RMF Team: **Northern Districts.** NZCA obit: 1998; Wisden obit: 1998.
HARPUR Thomas Arthur 1938/39 b 5.12.1915 Hunterville, Rangitikei. d 26.8.1986 Rotorua, Bay of Plenty. Team: **Wellington.**
HARRIS Anthony James 2005/06 b 26.6.1982 Dunedin, Otago. RHB occ wk Team: **Otago.** Sch: Kavanagh Coll.
HARRIS Ben Zinzan 1988/89-1994/95 b 20.2.1964 Christchurch, Canterbury. RHB RM Teams: **Canterbury, Otago.** Played List A in NZ. Sch: Waitaki BHS. Occ: Radio station manager. Canterbury selector. Brother: C.Z.Harris; father: P.G.Z.Harris.
HARRIS Chris Zinzan 1989/90-2009/10 b 20.11.1969 Christchurch, Canterbury. LHB RM,OB Teams: **Canterbury, New Zealand Test, New Zealand ODI.** Played List A in NZ; Played T20 in NZ. Sch: Christchurch BHS. Occ: Cricket pro. NZ U19 Test; NZ U19 ODI. Indoor cricket: New Zealand. Book: Harry - Chris Harris story. NZCA COY: 1997. He holds the Canterbury 5th wicket partnership record of 290 with G.W.Stead against Central Districts in 1996/97 and the NZ domestic T20 3rd wicket partnership record of 109* with J.G.Myburgh for Canterbury against Northern Districts in 2007/08. He took a hat-trick for New Zealand v Orange Free State in 1994/95. Brother: B.Z.Harris; father: P.G.Z.Harris.
HARRIS Clifford Morris 1928/29-1929/30 b 6.11.1907 Christchurch, Canterbury. d 15.2.1970 Christchurch, Canterbury. LHB RM Team: **Canterbury.** Sch: St Andrews Coll. Occ: Schoolmaster.
HARRIS John Hyde 1865/66 b 21.11.1825 Deddington, Oxfordshire, England. d 24.7.1886 Dunedin, Otago. Team: **Otago.** Sch: Deddington Sch, England. Occ: Barrister. MP. He became the first Superintendent of Otago in 1853. He was president of the successful 1865 Dunedin Exhibition. He gained a prominent position in national politics when he became the Solicitor-General from 1867 to 1868. He speculated on land on the Taieri and in North Dunedin. In the late 1860s his investments failed and he lost £28,000 and declared himself insolvent. Forced to resign from politics and return to being a lawyer, he never recovered his losses.
HARRIS Leonard Montague 1881/82-1893/94 b 21.12.1855 Swansea, Tasmania, Australia. LHB Teams: **Otago, Wellington.** Occ: Merchant. Bankrupted in 1899, living in Western Australia in 1926, nothing known of him since.
HARRIS Michael John 1964-1982 b 25.5.1944 St Just-in-Roseland, Cornwall, England. RHB LB wk Teams: **Wellington,** Middlesex, Nottinghamshire, Eastern Province. Played List A in NZ. Sch: Gerrans, England. Occ: Squash club proprietor. An English pro, played and coached in NZ.
HARRIS Parke Gerald Zinzan 1949/50-1964/65 b 18.7.1927 Christchurch, Canterbury. d 1.12.1991 Christchurch, Canterbury. RHB RM Teams: **Canterbury, New Zealand Test.** Sch: Waitaki BHS. Occ: Dentist. NZCA obit: 1992; Wisden obit: 1992. NZCA COY: 1961. Sons: C.Z.Harris, B.Z.Harris.
HARRIS Roger Meredith 1955/56-1973/74 b 27.7.1933 Otahuhu, Auckland. RHB RM Teams: **Auckland, New Zealand Test.** Played List A in NZ. Sch: Auckland GS.
HARRIS Stuart Joseph 1975/76 b 12.8.1943 New Plymouth, Taranaki. RHB RM Team: **Northern Districts.**
HARRIS Victor 1913/14 Team: **Wellington.**
HARRISON Hubert James Herbert 1940/41-1943/44 b 30.5.1917 Devonport, Auckland. d 26.2.1977 Otahuhu, Auckland. RHB RFM Team: **Auckland.** Occ: Grocer.
HART Ashley William 1981/82-1985/86 b 10.7.1956 Blenheim, Marlborough. LHB wk Team: **Canterbury.** Played List A in NZ. Occ: Coy director.
HART Benjamin Patrick 1997/98 b 4.5.1977 Hamilton, Waikato. RHB wk Team: **Otago.**
HART Gregory Richard James 1994/95 b 23.4.1971 Christchurch, Canterbury. RHB Team: **Central Districts.**

HART Matthew Norman 1990/91-2004/05 b 16.5.1972 Hamilton, Waikato. LHB SLA Teams: **Northern Districts, New Zealand Test, New Zealand ODI.** Played List A in NZ. NZ U19 Test; NZ U19 ODI. Brother: R.G.Hart.

HART Robert Garry 1992/93-2003/04 b 2.12.1974 Hamilton, Waikato. RHB wk Teams: **Northern Districts, New Zealand Test, New Zealand ODI.** Played List A in NZ. NZ U19 Test; NZ U19 ODI. Brother: M.N.Hart.

HART Ronald Terence 1980/81-1993/94 b 7.11.1961 Lower Hutt, Wellington. RHB OB occ wk Teams: **Central Districts, Wellington, New Zealand ODI.** Played List A in NZ. He holds the NZ 2nd wicket partnership record of 317 with P.S.Briasco for Central Districts v Canterbury in 1983/84.

HARTLAND Blair Robert 1986/87-1996/97 b 22.10.1966 Christchurch, Canterbury. RHB Teams: **Canterbury, New Zealand Test, New Zealand ODI.** Played List A in NZ. Sch: Christchurch BHS. Occ: Coy director. NZ U19 Test; NZ U19 ODI. Father: I.R.Hartland.

HARTLAND Ian Robert 1960/61-1965/66 b 12.8.1939 Christchurch, Canterbury. d 6.3.1992 Christchurch, Canterbury. RHB RM Team: **Canterbury.** Sch: Christchurch BHS. Occ: Insurance agent. NZCA obit: 1992; Wisden obit: 1993. Son: B.R.Hartland.

HARTLAND John Ford 1877/78-1890/91 b 2.1.1862 Lyttelton, Christchurch, Canterbury. d 8.2.1918 Remuera, Auckland. He died from blood poisoning. RHB Team: **Canterbury.** Sch: Christ Coll. Occ: Secretary, Auckland Racing Club. Rugby: Canterbury. He is the third youngest NZ cricketer.

HARTSHORN David John 1984/85-1993/94 b 17.5.1966 Christchurch, Canterbury. RHB LB Teams: **Canterbury, Central Districts.** Played List A in NZ. Sch: Christchurch BHS. Occ: Doctor. NZ U19 Test; NZ U19 ODI.

HARVIE Mathew James 2003/04-2009/10 b 6.12.1984 Dunedin, Otago. RHB RFM Team: **Otago.** Played List A in NZ; Played T20 in NZ. Sch: Otago BHS.

HARVIE Walter Leslie Douglas 1914/15 b 18.6.1891 Auckland. d 23.5.1969 Auckland. Team: **Auckland.**

HARWOOD Norman John 1959/60 b 29.12.1929 Palmerston North, Manawatu. RHB RM Team: **Northern Districts.**

HARWOOD Robert Crawford 1944/45-1945/46 b 20.11.1923 Dunedin, Otago. d 23.11.1992 Christchurch, Canterbury. LHB SLA Team: **Otago.** NZCA obit: 1995.

HASELL Alfred Spearpoint 1894/95-1895/96 b Q2 1872 Croydon, Surrey, England. d 13.1.1955 New Plymouth, Taranaki. Team: **Canterbury.** Sch: Christchurch Normal. Occ: Farmer; sports store.

HASKELL Oscar Hungerford 1877/78-1889/90 b 24.4.1857 Brighton, Tasmania, Australia. d 3.9.1943 Southport, Queensland, Australia. LHB Team: **Otago.**

HASKELL Wilfred John Raymond 1955/56-1968/69 b 12.12.1936 Karachi, Sind, India (now in Pakistan). RHB RMF Team: **Wellington.** Sch: Nelson Coll. Wellington selector.

HASLAM Mark James 1991/92-2001/02 b 26.9.1972 Bury, Lancashire, England. LHB SLA Teams: **Auckland, New Zealand Test, New Zealand ODI.** Played List A in NZ. Occ: Schoolmaster.

HASTINGS Brian Frederick 1957/58-1976/77 b 23.3.1940 Island Bay, Wellington. RHB LBG Teams: **Wellington, Central Districts, Canterbury, New Zealand Test, New Zealand ODI.** Played List A in NZ. Sch: Wellington Coll. Occ: Christchurch Press Company employee. NZCA COY: 1969. He holds the NZ and all nations Test 10th wicket partnership record of 151 with R.G.Collinge against Pakistan in 1972/73 (the all nations Test partnership has since been equalled by Azhar Mahmood and Mushtaq Ahmed in 1997/98). Son: M.A.Hastings.

HASTINGS Mark Andrew 1992/93-2000/01 b 8.5.1968 Christchurch, Canterbury. RHB RM Team: **Canterbury.** Played List A in NZ. Sch: Burnside HS. Occ: Astrograss layer. Father: B.F.Hastings.

HATCH Roland Keith 1945/46 b 2.7.1916 Marton, Rangitikei. d 30.10.2007 Wellington. M Team: **Wellington.** Sch: Palmerston North BHS. Occ: Coy director. Brother: R.J.Hatch.

HATCH Ronald J 1933/34 FM Team: **Wellington.** Sch: Palmerston North BHS. Brother: R.K.Hatch.

HATWELL Jaden Glenn 2003/04 b 1.12.1977 Hamilton, Waikato. RHB OB Team: **Northern Districts.** Played List A in NZ.

HAUGHTON Joseph Henry 1876/77 b 1833 Plymouth, Devon, England. d 27.5.1908 Roxburgh, Central Otago. Team: **Wellington.** Occ: Miner. Umpired first-class cricket.
HAVILL Philip John 1969/70 b 8.4.1937 Papatoetoe, Auckland. LHB RM Team: **Northern Districts.**
HAWKE George 1900/01-1910/11 b 1871 Greytown, Wairarapa. d 19.9.1950 Napier, Hawke's Bay. Team: **Hawke's Bay.** Occ: Postmaster.
HAWKINS William H 1886/87-1896/97 LFM occ wk Team: **Auckland.**
HAWKINS William Henry 1887/88-1894/95 b 1861 Patrick Plains, New South Wales, Australia. d 10.8.1930 New Plymouth, Taranaki. wk Team: **Hawke's Bay.** Occ: Schoolteacher; storekeeper; auctioneer. Rugby: Hawke's Bay. MP.
HAWKSWORTH William 1929/30-1933/34 b 3.3.1911 Nelson. d 14.7.1966 Oxford, England. wk Team: **Otago.** Sch: Nelson Coll; Wairapara HS. Occ: Obstetrician and gynaecologist. OBE. NZCA obit: 1966. He holds the NZ 10th wicket partnership record of 184 with R.Blunt for Otago v Canterbury in 1931/32.
HAWORTH Brian Ashley 1953/54-1958/59 b 3.2.1932 Christchurch, Canterbury. RHB Team: **Canterbury.** Sch: West Christchurch BHS. Occ: Coy director.
HAWTHORNE Arthur 1906/07-1909/10 b 1873 Mt Moriac, Victoria, Australia. Team: **Wellington.** Sch: Mt Cook HS.
HAY David 1913/14-1914/15 Team: **Wellington.** Sch: Wellington Coll.
HAY Gregory Robert 2006/07-2008/09 b 14.7.1984 Rotorua, Bay of Plenty. RHB OB Team: **Central Districts.** Played List A in NZ; Played T20 in NZ. Sch: Waimea Coll.
HAY James Campbell 1917/18-1918/19 b 28.12.1885 Akaroa, Canterbury. d 18.10.1936 Pigeon Bay, Akaroa, Canterbury. Team: **Canterbury.** Sch: Christchurch BHS. Occ: Sheep farmer.
HAY Stuart Carlton 1931/32 b 6.10.1909 Auckland. d 23.7.1987 Auckland. LHB Team: **Auckland.** Sch: Auckland GS. Occ: Stock exchange chairman. Rugby: Auckland. OBE. NZCA obit: 1987. Father: W.P.C.Hay; uncle: T.D.B.Hay.
HAY Thomas Douglas Baird 1893/94-1927 b 31.8.1876 Auckland. d 19.4.1967 Auckland. RHB Teams: **Auckland, New Zealand.** Sch: Auckland GS. Occ: Sharebroker. Rugby: Auckland. NZCA obit: 1967; Wisden obit: 1968. NZ manager. He played for New Zealand prior to being granted Test status. Brother: W.P.C.Hay; nephew: S.C.Hay.
HAY William Arthur 1917/18 b 6.12.1873 Peterhead, Aberdeenshire, Scotland. d 16.6.1945 Perth, Western Australia, Australia. SLA Team: **Otago.** Occ: Methodist minister.
HAY William Patrick Carlton 1893/94 b 17.3.1875 Auckland. d 15.4.1945 Auckland. Team: **Auckland.** Sch: Auckland GS. Occ: Sharebroker. Rugby: Auckland. Soccer: Auckland. Brothers: T.D.B.Hay; son: S.C.Hay.
HAYDEN Simon Christopher 1996/97 b 26.10.1970 Ashford, Kent, England. RHB Team: **Auckland.** Played List A in NZ.
HAYDON William Henry 1895/96-1897/98 b 30.7.1872 Dunedin, Otago. d 18.4.1904 Dunedin, Otago. wk Team: **Otago.** Occ: Hotelkeeper.
HAYES John Arthur 1946/47-1960/61 b 11.1.1927 Auckland. d 25.12.2007 Auckland. RHB RF Teams: **Auckland, Canterbury, New Zealand Test.** Sch: Mt Albert GS. Occ: Coy director. NZCA obit: 2008; Wisden obit: 2008. NZCA COY: 1958.
HAYES Roydon Leslie 1991/92-1995/96 b 9.5.1971 Paeroa, Thames Valley. RHB RF Teams: **Northern Districts, New Zealand ODI.** Played List A in NZ. He took a hat-trick for Northern Districts v Central Districts in 1995/96.
HAYES William Hugh James 1909/10-1927/28 b 26.4.1890 Halswell, Christchurch, Canterbury. d 30.6.1972 Christchurch, Canterbury. RHB RM occ wk Team: **Canterbury.** Occ: Shop assistant. NZCA obit: 1972.
HAYNE Gareth Peter 2006/07-2007/08 b 13.6.1981 Auckland. RHB OB Team: **Auckland.** Sch: Macleans Coll. NZ U19 ODI.
HAYWARD G 1910/11 wk Team: **Auckland.**
HAYWARD Richard Edward 1979-1985/86 b 15.2.1954 Ickenham, Middlesex, England. LHB LM occ wk Teams: **Central Districts,** Hampshire, Somerset. Played List A in NZ. Sch: Latymer Upper Sch, England. Occ: Cricket coach. Canterbury coaching director. An English pro, played and coached in NZ.
HAYWARD W 1885/86-1886/87 Team: **Hawke's Bay.**

HAYWARD William 1935/36 b 3.11.1909 Auckland. d 28.11.1982 Auckland. RHB wk Team: **Auckland.** NZCA obit: 1983.
HEENAN Donald 1928/29-1929/30 b 25.11.1908 Gore, Southland. d 14.6.1961 Invercargill, Southland. wk Team: **Otago.** Occ: Clerk.
HEENAN George Charles 1882/83-1897/98 b 13.9.1855 Bhaugulpore, Bengal, India. d 24.10.1912 Pauk, Burma. He moved to Burma to work as a surveyor in 1910. Teams: **Wellington, Taranaki.** Sch: Cheltenham, England. Occ: Geologist. Rugby: Wellington. His son Patrick was executed for treason whilst serving with the Allied forces in Singapore in 1942.
HEFFORD Brent Edward 1999/00-2008/09 b 8.5.1978 Blenheim, Marlborough. LHB RM Team: **Central Districts.** Played List A in NZ; Played T20 in NZ.
HEGGLUN Gregory James Tristran 2004/05-2007/08 b 7.8.1984 Blenheim, Marlborough. RHB RM Team: **Central Districts.** Played List A in NZ; Played T20 in NZ.
HELEY Gilbert Borland 1917/18 b 5.9.1892 Greymouth, West Coast. d 10.9.1966 Auckland. Team: **Southland.** Occ: Coy manager.
HELLABY Alan Thomas Ranken 1979/80-1987/88 b 11.11.1958 Auckland. RHB RM Team: **Auckland.** Played List A in NZ.
HELLICAR Ames 1872/73 b 2.3.1847 Bristol, England. d 27.12.1907 Melbourne, Victoria, Australia. Team: **Otago.** Occ: Bank officer.
HELMORE George Henry Noble 1883/84-1891/92 b 15.6.1862 Christchurch, Canterbury. d 28.6.1922 Maidenhead, Berkshire, England. wk Team: **Canterbury.** Sch: Christ Coll. Occ: Solicitor. Rugby: All Blacks and Canterbury.
HEMI Ronald Courtney 1950/51 b 15.5.1933 Whangarei, Northland. d 13.9.2000 Hamilton, Waikato. LHB Team: **Auckland.** Sch: Hamilton BHS. Occ: Accountant. Rugby: All Blacks and Auckland. NZCA obit: 2001. He was chosen for Auckland in the 1950/51 season, aged only 17.
HEMMINGSON Francis Edward 1945/46-1949/50 b 5.9.1912 Auckland. d 7.4.1963 Auckland. LHB SLA Team: **Auckland.** Occ: Builder. NZCA obit: 1964.
HEMUS Lancelot Gerald 1904/05-1921/22 b 13.11.1881 Auckland. d 27.10.1933 Auckland. RHB Team: **Auckland, New Zealand.** Occ: Accountant. NZ selector. He played for New Zealand prior to being granted Test status.
HENDERSON John Duncan 1960/61 b 8.8.1928 Hastings, Hawke's Bay. RHB RM Team: **Central Districts.**
HENDERSON Matthew 1921/22-1931/32 b 2.8.1895 Auckland. d 17.6.1970 Lower Hutt, Wellington. LHB LFM Teams: **Wellington, New Zealand Test.** Occ: Accountant. NZCA obit: 1970; Wisden obit: 1971.
HENDERSON Norman Douglas 1935/36 b 13.1.1913 Dunedin, Otago. d 30.10.2000 Auckland. RHB RFM Team: **Otago.** Sch: Otago BHS. Occ: Accountant. NZCA obit: 2002.
HENDLEY William 1864/65-1872/73 c 16.11.1834 Pirton, Hertfordshire, England. d 4.9.1895 Dunedin, Otago. He died of pneumonia. RM Team: **Otago.** Occ: Groundsman; Pro cricketer.
HENDRY Russell 1961/62-1973/74 b 2.3.1939 Dunedin, Otago. RHB Team: **Otago.** Played List A in NZ. Sch: Kings HS.
HENDY William James 1927/28 b 2.4.1900 Auckland. d 23.9.1992 Auckland. RHB OB Team: **Auckland.** NZCA obit: 1993; Wisden obit: 1994. At the time of his death he was New Zealand's oldest first-class cricketer. In 1925/26 he scored 300* for the Auckland Suburban Association against Christchurch High School Old Boys, who had two future Test bowlers, Cromb and Merritt, in their attack. Hendy was 200* at lunch.
HENRY David William 1980/81 b 13.6.1947 Nambour, Queensland, Australia. RHB RM Team: **Wellington.** Played List A in NZ.
HENRY Graham William 1965/66-1967/68 b 8.6.1946 Christchurch, Canterbury. RHB wk Teams: **Canterbury, Otago.** Sch: Christchurch BHS. Occ: Headmaster. Rugby: Coached Auckland, Wales and New Zealand; IRB coach of the year in 2005, 2006 and 2008.
HENRY Paul James 1996/97 b 16.10.1970 Mataura, Southland. RHB wk Team: **Otago.** Sch: St Peter's Coll. Gore. Occ: Real estate agent.
HEPBURN Wilfred Frederick Tenekaha 1931/32-1940/41 b 25.8.1910 Wellington. d 7.9.1973 Wellington. RHB Team: **Wellington.** NZCA obit: 1973.

HERMANSSON Gary Le Roy 1962/63 b 17.1.1941 Palmerston North, Manawatu. RHB wk Team: **NZ Under-23s**. Sch: Palmerston North BHS. Occ: Psychologist. Rugby: Manawatu. Sports psychologist with the 1998 and 2002 Commonwealth Games teams and the 2000 Olympic team.

HEWAT David Falconer 1887/88-1889/90 b 23.1.1866 Oamaru, North Otago. d 2.2.1959 Wellington. F Team: **Wellington**. Sch: Oamaru HS. Brother: R.Hewat.

HEWAT Robert 1889/90 b 18.10.1863 Oamaru, North Otago. d 17.11.1953 Oamaru, North Otago. Team: **Otago**. Occ: Accountant. Brother: D.F.Hewat.

HEWSON Allan Roy 1978/79 b 6.6.1954 Lower Hutt, Wellington. RHB wk Team: **Wellington**. Played List A in NZ. Sch: Hutt Valley HS. Occ: Manager. Rugby: All Blacks and Wellington.

HICK Graeme Ashley 1983/84-2008 b 23.5.1966 Salisbury (now Harare), Zimbabwe. RHB OB Teams: **Northern Districts, Auckland (not FC)**, England Test, England ODI, Worcestershire, Queensland, Zimbabwe. Played List A in NZ. Sch: Prince Edward BHS, Zimbabwe. Occ: Cricket pro. Books: My Early Life; Hick 'n' Dilley Circus. MBE. WCOY: 1987. An English pro, played and coached in NZ.

HICKEY Charles Ernest Henry 1902/03-1910/11 b 10.4.1880 Wellington. d 9.6.1919 Wellington. LB Team: **Wellington**. Occ: Estate agent.

HICKMOTT Rupert George 1911/12-1914/15 b 19.3.1894 Christchurch, Canterbury. d 16.9.1916 Somme, France. He was killed in action aged 22. RHB Teams: **Canterbury, New Zealand**. Sch: Christchurch BHS. Occ: Clerk. Wisden obit: 1917. He came to the fore in November 1911 by scoring 235 without a mistake for XV Colts v the Canterbury XI, and the same year was selected for Canterbury. He was then only 17 years of age and his form that season was so good that he had made 1,466 runs with an average of 81.44. He played for New Zealand prior to being granted Test status.

HICKSON Henry Claude 1898/99-1911/12 b 4.9.1878 Wellington. d 15.7.1948 Wellington. RHB Team: **Wellington, New Zealand**. Sch: St Patricks Coll, Wellington. Occ: Civil servant. NZCA obit: 1948. He played for New Zealand prior to being granted Test status. Brother: W.R.S.Hickson.

HICKSON Henry Samuel 1879/80-1881/82 b 19.4.1859 Wellington. d 29.4.1883 Wellington. He died of pneumonia. Team: **Wellington**. Occ: Clerk. Rugby: Wellington. Brother-in-law: H.Evans.

HICKSON William Richard Stanley 1896/97-1906/07 b 4.5.1877 Greymouth, West Coast. d 30.11.1930 Wellington. Team: **Wellington**. Sch: St Patricks Coll, Wellington. Occ: Accountant. Hockey: Wellington. Brother: H.C.Hickson.

HIDDLESTON John Sydney 1909/10-1928/29 b 10.12.1890 Invercargill, Southland. d 30.10.1940 Wellington. RHB RM Teams: **Otago, Wellington, New Zealand**. Occ: Merchant. Wisden obit: 1941. He played for New Zealand prior to being granted Test status.

HIGGINS Bryan Breton 1956/57 b 29.6.1927 Suva, Fiji. d 24.8.2003 Hastings, Hawke's Bay. RHB LB Team: **Northern Districts**. Occ: Exec director. NZCA obit: 2004. ND selector.

HIGGINS William Lawrence 1910/11-1920/21 b 15.11.1888 St Leonard's, Dunedin, Otago. d 3.7.1968 Ashburton, Mid Canterbury. Team: **Otago**. Occ: Storekeeper.

HIINI Brandon Christopher 2005/06-2009/10 b 11.12.1981 Invercargill, Southland. RHB RMF Team: **Canterbury**. Played List A in NZ; Played T20 in NZ. Sch: Christchurch BHS. Occ: Policeman. He holds the Canterbury 8th wicket partnership record of 220 with P.J.Wiseman against Northern Districts in 2005/06.

HILL Anthony John 1975/76-1976/77 b 13.3.1952 Auckland. RHB OB Team: **Central Districts**. Nephew: D.L.Vettori; son: J.V.Hill.

HILL Donald 1961/62-1967/68 b 6.1.1940 Christchurch, Canterbury. RHB occ wk Teams: **Canterbury, Auckland**. Sch: Christchurch BHS. Occ: Shop manager.

HILL George Henry Fitzroy 1891/92-1901/02 b 16.7.1868 Portsea, Portsmouth, Hampshire, England. d 23.11.1918 Waikari, North Canterbury. He took his own life. occ wk Team: **Hawke's Bay**. Sch: Epsom Coll, England. Occ: Farmer.

HILL Henry Philip 1873/74 b 13.7.1845 Newport, Shropshire, England. d 6.1.1924 Christchurch, Canterbury. LHB SLA Team: **Canterbury**. Sch: Marlborough, England. Occ: Runholder. A pioneering runholder, he introduced Romney sheep and Jersey cattle to Canterbury.

HILL John 1961/62-1962/63 b 22.9.1930 Gore, Southland. d 26.8.2002 Invercargill, Southland. RHB LM Team: **Otago**. Sch: Gore HS. NZCA obit: 2003. Son: R.J.Hill.

HILL Joseph Vettori 1999/00-2000/01 b 18.10.1976 Blenheim, Marlborough. RHB Team: **Central Districts.** Played List A in NZ. Cousin: D.L.Vettori; father: A.J.Hill.
HILL Robert John 1976/77-1979/80 b 1.2.1954 Gore, Southland. RHB RM Team: **Otago.** Played List A in NZ. Father: J.Hill.
HILLS Peter William 1978/79-1989/90 b 3.12.1958 Ranfurly, Central Otago. RHB LFM Team: **Otago.** Played List A in NZ. Sch: Aparima Coll. Occ: Coy director.
HINDMARSH Harris Smith Waghorn 1920/21 b 7.6.1900 Napier, Hawke's Bay. d 10.7.1958 Napier, Hawke's Bay. Team: **Hawke's Bay.** Sch: Christ Coll. Occ: Wine merchant. Brother: J.S.Hindmarsh.
HINDMARSH John St John 1907/08-1913/14 b 14.11.1883 Napier, Hawke's Bay. d 26.6.1961 Napier, Hawke's Bay. Team: **Hawke's Bay.** Brother: H.S.W.Hindmarsh.
HINTON Simon David 1994/95 b 21.3.1968 Clyde, Central Otago. RHB RM Team: **Otago.**
HINTZ Andrew John 1985/86-1987/88 b 8.12.1963 Christchurch, Canterbury. RHB RFM Team: **Canterbury.** Played List A in NZ. Sch: Burnside HS. Occ: Coy director.
HIPKISS Edwin 1966/67 b 6.2.1947 Wallasey, Cheshire, England. RHB RMF Team: **Northern Districts.** Sch: Tauranga Boys Coll.
HIRA Roneel Magan 2006/07-2007/08 b 23.1.1987 Auckland. LHB SLA Team: **Auckland.** Played List A in NZ; Played T20 in NZ. Sch: Kelston BHS. NZ U19 ODI.
HITCHCOCK Paul Anthony 1999/00-2008/09 b 23.1.1975 Whangarei, Northland. RHB RM Teams: **Wellington, Auckland, New Zealand ODI, New Zealand T20.** Played List A in NZ; Played T20 in NZ. Sch: Westlake BHS; Takapuna GS.
HITCHCOCK Raymond Edward 1947/48-1964 b 28.11.1929 Christchurch, Canterbury. LHB LBG occ wk Teams: **Canterbury,** Warwickshire. Sch: West Christchurch BHS. Rugby: North Midlands. Book: R.E.Hitchcock's benefit: Season 1963.
HITCHENS William Henry 1913/14 b 7.6.1878 Christchurch, Canterbury. d 9.8.1952 Christchurch, Canterbury. FM Team: **Hawke's Bay.** Occ: Farm hand.
HOAR Frank Rutter 1928/29 b 21.9.1896 Wellington. d 27.5.1972 Masterton, Wairapara. RHB LB Team: **Wellington.** Occ: Sculptor.
HOAR Newman Ronald 1942/43-1944/45 b 1920 Masterton, Wairarapa. RHB F Team: **Wellington.** CD selector.
HODDER Reginald William 1882/83-1886/87 b 1867 Nelson. d 21.1.1926 London, England. occ wk Team: **Nelson.** Sch: Nelson Coll. Occ: Writer.
HODGE George 1907/08 b 1878 Clunes, Victoria, Australia. d 1953 Parkville, Victoria, Australia. LHB wk Team: **Wellington.** Occ: Labourer. He was wicket-keeper for the Ballarat representative team against NSW on their 1906/07 Sheffield Shield tour.
HODGSON Wayne Gilbert 1979/80-1981/82 b 25.6.1959 Nelson. RHB LB Team: **Central Districts.** Played List A in NZ.
HOGG Kyle William 2001-2010 b 2.7.1983 Birmingham, Warwickshire, England. LHB RFM Teams: **Otago,** Lancashire, Worcestershire, Nottinghamshire. Sch: Saddleworth HS, England. Father: W.Hogg (Lancashire, Warwickshire); grandfather: S.Ramadhin (West Indies, Trinidad, Lancashire).
HOLDAWAY William Arthur 1918/19 b 18.3.1893 Dunedin, Otago. d 23.8.1967 Dunedin, Otago. Team: **Otago.** Occ: Tinsmith.
HOLDEN Allen Clyde 1937/38-1939/40 b 18.4.1911 Christchurch, Canterbury. d 12.12.1980 Dunedin, Otago. RHB Team: **Otago.** Sch: Otago BHS. Occ: Barrister.
HOLDEN William James 1917/18-1918/19 b 20.7.1883 Dunedin, Otago. d 2.8.1949 Invercargill, Southland. Team: **Otago.** Occ: Salesman.
HOLDERNESS Henry Victor Angel 1918/19 b 24.5.1889 Dunedin, Otago. d 17.7.1974 Dunedin, Otago. Team: **Otago.** Occ: Storeman.
HOLDING Michael Anthony 1972/73-1989 b 16.2.1954 Half Way Tree, Kingston, Jamaica. RHB RF Teams: **Canterbury,** Lancashire, Derbyshire, Tasmania, West Indies Test, West Indies ODI, Jamaica. Played List A in NZ. Sch: Kingston Coll, Jamaica. Occ: Commentator. Books: The Whispering Death; No Holding Back. WCOY: 1977.

HOLDSHIP Alfred Richardson 1893/94-1898/99 b 15.10.1867 Auckland. d 28.1.1923 Sydney, New South Wales, Australia. RHB Team: **Wellington, New Zealand**. Sch: Cheltenham, England. Occ: Solicitor. Wisden obit: 1924. NZ selector. He played for New Zealand prior to being granted Test status. Brother: W.E.J.Holdship (Middlesex).

HOLDSWORTH Frank 1891/92-1902/03 b 1871 Wellington. d 4.8.1941 Wellington. RHB RM Team: **Wellington**. Sch: Wanganui CS. Occ: Solicitor. Wisden obit: 1943.

HOLE Henry Whitworth 1874/75 b 1855 Woolsey, Devon, England. d 23.6.1942 Wanganui. Team: **Nelson**. Sch: Sherborne, England. Occ: Shipping agent.

HOLLAND Chester Arthur 1913/14-1924/25 b 26.8.1888 Bunnythorpe, Manawatu. d 10.11.1976 Wellington. RHB OB Team: **Wellington, New Zealand**. Sch: Palmerston North BHS. Occ: Salesman. NZCA obit: 1977. He played for New Zealand prior to being granted Test status.

HOLLAND Peter Jesse 1976/77-1983/84 b 5.5.1958 Nelson. RHB OB Teams: **Central Districts, Northern Districts, Wellington**. Played List A in NZ. Sch: St Joseph's, Masterton.

HOLLAND Robert George 1978/79-1987/88 b 19.10.1946 Camperdown, Sydney, New South Wales, Australia. RHB LBG Teams: **Wellington**, Australia Test, Australia ODI, New South Wales. Played List A in NZ. Sch: Boorugal HS, Australia. Occ: Maintenance engineer.

HOLLANDS Lewis Douglas 1969/70-1971/72 b 25.10.1940 Gore, Southland. RHB Team: **Otago**.

HOLLE Rowland Leatre 1883/84-1893/94 b 1859 Kyneton, Victoria, Australia. d 3.8.1929 Granville, Sydney, New South Wales, Australia. Teams: **Wellington, Auckland**. Occ: Tailor's cutter. Umpired first-class cricket.

HOLLINGS Alfred Maurice 1926/27-1929/30 b 13.5.1906 Billericay, Essex, England. d 5.3.1988 Wellington. RHB Team: **Wellington**.

HOLLOWAY Robert Alexander 1961/62-1964/65 b 15.11.1940 Invercargill, Southland. RHB Team: **Otago**.

HOLLYWOOD John Edgar 1947/48-1949/50 b 23.5.1926 Auckland. d 16.7.1952 Sydney, New South Wales, Australia. He went to Sydney to study veterinary science and whilst there committed suicide by throwing himself under a tram, aged 26. RHB RFM Team: **Auckland**. Sch: Auckland GS. Occ: Veterinary student. NZCA obit: 1952.

HOLMES Allan 1870/71-1873/74 b 25.1.1845 Geelong, Victoria, Australia. d 9.4.1909 Dunedin, Otago. Team: **Otago**. Occ: Barrister.

HOLMES William 1880/81-1883/84 b 1849 unknown. d 26.11.1885 Wellington. On the Saturday before his death he took part in a cricket match played on the Basin Reserve, but an attack of inflammation set in and he died aged 36. Teams: **Nelson, Wellington**. Sch: Nelson Coll. Occ: Civil servant.

HOLT William Roberts 1964/65 b 31.5.1935 Whangarei, Northland. RHB RM Team: **Northern Districts**. Sch: Whangarei HS.

HOOD Brett Lewis 2000/01 b 11.9.1973 Warkworth, Auckland. RHB wk Team: **Northern Districts**.

HOOK Glen Hall 1935/36-1942/43 b 1.4.1917 Auckland. d 8.11.1972 Auckland. RHB SLC Team: **Auckland**. Occ: Bank clerk.

HOOTON Rex Clive 1968/69-1979/80 b 14.2.1947 Auckland. RHB SLA Teams: **Northern Districts, Auckland**. Played List A in NZ. Sch: Auckland GS. Auckland selector.

HOPE John 1885/86-1899/00 b 28.5.1866 Dunedin, Otago. d 29.3.1950 Dunedin, Otago. LM Team: **Otago**. Occ: Funeral director. He is the only NZ cricketer located of Jewish heritage.

HOPE John Hayhurst 1863/64-1866/67 c 6.2.1841 Little Eaton, Derbyshire, England. d 12.11.1910 Buenos Aires, Argentina. RHB wk Team: **Otago**. Sch: Aldenham, England. Occ: Farmer.

HOPE Raymond William 1925/26-1933/34 b 19.1.1904 Wanganui. d 24.6.1978 Christchurch, Canterbury. RHB RFM Teams: **Wellington, Canterbury, New Zealand**. NZCA obit: 1978. He played for New Zealand prior to being granted Test status.

HOPKINS Brian Henry 1966/67 b 22.7.1941 Chippenham, Wiltshire, England. RHB RM Team: **Wellington**.

HOPKINS Cyril Cooper 1908/09-1912/13 b 4.5.1882 Yass, New South Wales, Australia. d 25.9.1968 Wahroonga, New South Wales, Australia. Team: **Otago**.

HOPKINS Gareth James 1997/98-2009/10 b 24.11.1976 Lower Hutt, Wellington. RHB wk Teams: **Northern Districts, Canterbury, Otago, Auckland, New Zealand ODI, New Zealand T20.** Played List A in NZ; Played T20 in NZ. Sch: Taupo Coll. NZ U19 Test; NZ U19 ODI. He holds the NZ domestic T20 6th wicket partnership record of 96 with S.L.Stewart for New Zealand A against English Lions in 2008/09.
HORE Andrew John 1996/97-2003/04 b 18.6.1969 Oamaru, North Otago. LHB RM Team: **Otago.** Played List A in NZ. Sch: Waitaki BHS.
HORNE Matthew Jeffery 1992/93-2005/06 b 5.12.1970 Takapuna, Auckland. RHB RM Teams: **Auckland, Otago, New Zealand Test, New Zealand ODI.** Played List A in NZ. He holds the NZ 5th wicket partnership record of 347* with A.C.Barnes for Auckland v Northern Districts in 2003/04. Brother: P.A.Horne.
HORNE Philip Andrew 1979/80-1990/91 b 21.1.1960 Upper Hutt, Wellington. LHB occ wk Teams: **Auckland, New Zealand Test, New Zealand ODI.** Played List A in NZ. Occ: Product promotions manager. Badminton: New Zealand in the 1990 Commonwealth Games. Brother: M.J.Horne.
HORNE Terry Bryce 1977/78-1979/80 b 2.10.1953 Nelson. RHB Team: **Central Districts.**
HORSLEY Nicholas Keith Woodward 2001/02-2007/08 b 22.9.1980 Hamilton, Waikato. LHB OB Teams: **Auckland, Northern Districts.** Played List A in NZ; Played T20 in NZ. Sch: Kings Coll. NZ U19 ODI. He holds the Northern Districts 5th wicket partnership record of 155 with J.A.H.Marshall against Canterbury in 2005/06.
HORSPOOL Ernest 1909/10-1928/29 b 23.8.1891 Dargaville, Northland. d 21.6.1957 Auckland. RHB Teams: **Auckland, New Zealand.** Occ: Milk vendor. NZCA obit: 1957; Wisden obit: 1959. He played for New Zealand prior to being granted Test status.
HORTIN Russell George 1963/64 b 10.10.1940 Ashburton, Mid Canterbury. RHB Team: **Canterbury.**
HORTON Martin John 1952-1970/71 b 21.4.1934 Worcester, England. RHB OB Teams: **Northern Districts,** England Test, Worcestershire. Sch: Sacred Heart, Droitwich, England. Occ: Cricket coach. NZ coach. Worcestershire chairman. An English pro, played and coached in NZ.
HOSKIN David Craig 1956/57-1964/65 b 16.10.1935 Christchurch, Canterbury. RHB RMF Team: **Northern Districts.** Sch: Hamilton BHS.
HOSKIN Richard Neville 1980/81-1992/93 b 18.10.1959 Invercargill, Southland. RHB LB occ wk Team: **Otago.** Played List A in NZ. Sch: Southland BHS. Otago selector. He holds the Otago 4th wicket partnership record of 235 with K.J.Burns against Northern Districts in 1987/88. Cousin: M.J.Lamont.
HOSKING David Robert 1967/68 b 20.1.1941 Auckland. RHB LB Team: **Wellington.**
HOTTER Stephen John 1988/89-1999/00 b 2.12.1969 New Plymouth, Taranaki. RHB LFM Team: **Wellington.** Played List A in NZ. Sch: Aotea Coll. Occ: Sports conditioner. NZ U19 ODI. He took a wicket with his first ball in first-class cricket and took a hat-trick for Wellington v Otago in 1996/97. Cousin: R.A.Verry.
HOUGH Kenneth William 1956/57-1959/60 b 24.10.1928 Auburn, Sydney, New South Wales, Australia. d 2.9.2009 Gladstone, Queensland, Australia. RHB RMF Teams: **Northern Districts, Auckland, New Zealand Test.** Soccer: New Zealand and Australia. Wisden obit: 2010. NZCA COY: 1959.
HOUGHTON Julian Hugh Playfair 1953/54 b 16.2.1931 Christchurch, Canterbury. d 6.10.2004 Masterton, Wairarapa. RHB occ wk Team: **Central Districts.** Sch: Nelson Coll. Occ: Stock agent. NZCA obit: 2005.
HOUGHTON Mark Vincent 2007/08-2008/09 b 3.11.1984 Upper Hutt, Wellington. RHB SLA Team: **Wellington.** Played List A in NZ; Played T20 in NZ. Sch: St Patricks Coll, Wellington.
HOUNSELL Alan Russell 1968/69-1976/77 b 8.2.1947 Christchurch, Canterbury. RHB RFM Teams: **Canterbury, Wellington, Auckland, Northern Districts.** Played List A in NZ. Sch: Christchurch BHS. Occ: Insurance officer. Wellington selector.
HOUNSELL Patrick James 1987/88-1988/89 b 7.6.1958 Blenheim, Marlborough. LHB SLA Team: **Auckland.** Sch: Mt Roskill GS. Occ: Computer programmer.
HOUPAPA David Wiremu 2006/07 b 14.11.1981 Newman, Western Australia, Australia. LHB RM Team: **Auckland.** Played List A in NZ; Played T20 in NZ.

HOW Jamie Michael 2000/01-2009/10 b 19.5.1981 New Plymouth, Taranaki. RHB OB Teams: **Central Districts, New Zealand Test, New Zealand ODI, New Zealand T20.** Played List A in NZ; Played T20 in NZ. Sch: Palmerston North BHS. NZ U19 ODI. He holds the NZ 1st wicket partnership record of 428 with P.Ingram for Central Districts v Wellington in 2009/10.

HOWARD Arthur Harold Spowers 1895/96-1905/06 b 1866 Auckland. d 26.3.1951 Parnell, Auckland. Teams: **Wellington, Hawke's Bay.** Occ: Civil servant.

HOWARTH Geoffrey Philip 1968/69-1985/86 b 29.3.1951 Auckland. RHB OB Teams: **Auckland, Northern Districts, New Zealand Test, New Zealand ODI,** Surrey. Played List A in NZ. Sch: Auckland GS. Book: Shaken but not stirred. CBE, OBE. NZCA COY: 1975. NZ coach. Brother: H.J.Howarth.

HOWARTH Hedley John 1962/63-1978/79 b 25.12.1943 Grey Lynn, Auckland. d 7.11.2008 Auckland. He died of cancer. LHB SLA Teams: **Auckland, New Zealand Test, New Zealand ODI.** Played List A in NZ. Sch: Auckland GS. Occ: Fisherman. NZCA obit: 2009; Wisden obit: 2009. NZCA COY: 1970. Brother: G.P.Howarth.

HOWDEN Alister Macdonald 1906/07-1914/15 b 20.8.1877 Rothesay, Bute, Scotland. d 25.11.1938 Takapuna, Auckland. RHB LB Teams: **Auckland, New Zealand.** Sch: Otago BHS. Occ: Produce broker. He played for New Zealand prior to being granted Test status. Brother: C.E.Howden; nephew: C.P.Howden.

HOWDEN Charles Ernest 1902/03-1908/09 b 22.10.1881 Dunedin, Otago. d 9.10.1963 Rotorua, Bay of Plenty. RHB Team: **Otago.** Sch: Otago BHS. Occ: Doctor. Brother: A.M.Howden; son: C.P.Howden.

HOWDEN Charles Peter 1937/38 b 21.10.1911 Auckland. d 6.7.2003 Auckland. RHB Team: **Otago.** Sch: Kings Coll. Occ: Doctor. NZCA obit: 2006. Father: C.E.Howden; uncle: A.M.Howden.

HOWE Arthur George 1886/87 b 1864 New Zealand. d 12.12.1927 Nelson. Team: **Hawke's Bay.** Occ: Bookkeeper.

HOWE Gilbert 1913/14 b 6.8.1891 Wellington. d 10.1.1917 Messines, Belgium. He was killed in action aged 26. LHB wk Team: **Wellington.** Sch: Kilbirnie. Occ: Clerk. Wisden obit: 1918. Brother-in-law: A.E.Birch.

HOWELL Glynn Alexander 1998/99-2001/02 b 11.10.1976 Napier, Hawke's Bay. RHB wk Teams: **Canterbury, Wellington.** Sch: Christchurch BHS. Occ: Insurance account manager. Brother: L.G.Howell; father: J.H.Howell.

HOWELL John Hollis 1966/67-1972/73 b 17.6.1943 Waipawa, Hawke's Bay. RHB RM Team: **Central Districts.** Played List A in NZ. Sons: L.G.Howell, G.A.Howell.

HOWELL Llorne Gregory 1990/91-2004/05 b 8.7.1972 Napier, Hawke's Bay. RHB RM Teams: **Canterbury, Central Districts, Auckland, Northern Districts, New Zealand ODI.** Played List A in NZ. Sch: Christchurch BHS. NZ U19 Test; NZ U19 ODI. Brother: G.A.Howell; father: J.H.Howell.

HOWELL William Boyne 1902/03-1918/19 b 13.7.1883 Christchurch, Canterbury. d 18.2.1960 Christchurch, Canterbury. RHB LM Team: **Canterbury.** Sch: Christchurch BHS.

HOWLETT John Thomas 1891/92-1903/04 b 8.4.1868 North Melbourne, Victoria, Australia. d 15.6.1931 East Melbourne, Victoria, Australia. Teams: **Auckland,** Victoria. Occ: Butcher. Vice-President of Victorian Cricket Association.

HUGHES William John 1891/92-1905/06 b 14.11.1858 Invercargill, Southland. d 4.12.1934 Napier, Hawke's Bay. RHB RM Team: **Hawke's Bay.** Occ: Clerk. Umpired first-class cricket.

HUME James Edward 1880/81 b 1858 Glasgow, Lanarkshire, Scotland. d 1.6.1909 Malaya. LHB Team: **Otago.** Sch: Otago BHS. Occ: Surveyor.

HUMPHREYS Edward 1899-1920 b 24.8.1881 Ditton, Kent, England. d 6.11.1949 Maidstone, Kent, England. RHB SLA Teams: **Canterbury,** Kent. Occ: Cricket pro. An English pro, played and coached in NZ.

HUMPHRIES Charles 1879/80-1888/89 Team: **Nelson.** Occ: Hotelkeeper.

HUNT Alan James 1980/81-1992/93 b 27.9.1959 Dunedin, Otago. RHB OB Team: **Auckland.** Played List A in NZ. Book: Alan Hunt - celebrating 10 years. CD coach.

HUNT Herbert Amos 1929/30-1930/31 b 16.9.1904 Swannanoa, North Canterbury. d 2.6.1972 Christchurch, Canterbury. RHB wk Team: **Auckland.** Occ: Freezer worker.

HUNT Raymond Thomas 1947/48-1959/60 b 17.9.1921 Dunedin, Otago. d 15.8.1994 Birmingham, Warwickshire, England. He died following a heart attack during a Golden Oldies rugby tournament. RHB Teams: **Otago, Canterbury.** Sch: Otago BHS. Occ: Schoolteacher. NZCA obit: 1995; Wisden obit: 1995. Otago selector and coach.
HUNTER Allan Arthur 1951/52-1955/56 b 6.3.1926 Nelson. d 31.8.1982 Nelson. RHB SLA Team: **Central Districts.** Occ: Butcher.
HUNTER David Jeremy 1989/90-1991/92 b 5.12.1968 Mosgiel, Otago. RHB RFM Team: **Otago.** Played List A in NZ.
HUNTER R J 1884/85 Team: **Wellington.**
HUNTER Raymond John 1975/76-1984/85 b 23.12.1947 Rotorua, Bay of Plenty. RHB OB Team: **Auckland.**
HUNTLEY Herbert John 1912/13 b 4.11.1883 Brighton, Melbourne, Victoria, Australia. d 28.3.1944 Tuapeka, Otago. Team: **Otago.** Occ: Farm manager.
HUSSEY James Michael 1901/02-1907/08 b 27.5.1880 Dunedin, Otago. d 24.8.1950 Wanganui. Teams: **Hawke's Bay, Otago, Auckland.** Sch: Dunedin Christian Bros. Occ: Solicitor.
HUTCHINGS John Henry 1903/04-1924/25 b 22.12.1882 Wellington. d 6.5.1966 Wellington. RHB S Team: **Wellington.** Occ: Insurance clerk. NZCA obit: 1966.
HUTCHISON Frank Copland 1917/18-1919/20 b 25.1.1897 Dunedin, Otago. d 17.12.1990 Wanganui. Team: **Otago.** Sch: Otago BHS. Occ: Doctor. Rugby: Wellington and Otago. Golf: Taranaki, Wanganui and Manawatu; NZ Veterans golf champion.
HUTCHISON Raymond William 1965/66-1975/76 b 21.7.1944 Dunedin, Otago. LHB SLA Teams: **Otago, Central Districts.** Played List A in NZ. Occ: Dentist. Umpired first-class cricket.
HUXFORD Neville Alfred 1964/65-1969/70 b 27.10.1937 Wellington. d 21.11.2006 Auckland. RHB RMF Teams: **Wellington, Canterbury.** Sch: Wellington Technical Coll. Occ: Salesman. NZCA obit: 2007.
IBADULLA Kassem Ben Khalid 1982/83-1990/91 b 13.10.1964 Birmingham, Warwickshire, England. RHB OB Teams: **Otago,** Gloucestershire. Played List A in NZ. Sch: Otago BHS. Occ: Insurance broker. Father: Khalid Ibadulla.
IBADULLA Khalid 1951/52-1972 b 20.12.1935 Lahore, Punjab, India (now in Pakistan). RHB RM,OB Teams: **Otago,** Warwickshire, Tasmania, Pakistan Test, Punjab. Sch: Manzang HS, Lahore, India. Occ: Cricket coach. NZOM. Otago selector. Son: K.B.K.Ibadulla.
ILES Peter Albert 1946/47-1951/52 b 23.12.1926 Palmerston North, Manawatu. LHB LB Team: **Auckland.**
INGHAM Craig Donald 1990/91-1994/95 b 26.7.1965 Nelson. LHB OB Team: **Central Districts.** Played List A in NZ.
INGLE William Shaw 1879/80 b Q2 1856 Pontefract, Yorkshire, England. d 14.4.1899 Wanganui. He was found dead in his bed from heart disease. Team: **Wellington.** Occ: Ironmonger.
INGRAM Peter John 2001/02-2009/10 b 25.10.1978 Hawera, Taranaki. RHB OB Teams: **Central Districts, New Zealand Test, New Zealand ODI, New Zealand T20.** Played List A in NZ; Played T20 in NZ. Sch: Freyburg HS. Occ: Schoolteacher. NZ U19 ODI. He holds the NZ 1st wicket partnership record of 428 with J.How for Central Districts v Wellington in 2009/10 and the Central Districts 3rd wicket partnership record of 264 with M.S.Sinclair against Northern Districts in 2008/09.
IRVING Alexander Edward 1917/18-1923/24 b 4.2.1900 Auckland. d 10.5.1951 Auckland. RHB Team: **Auckland.** Sch: Auckland GS. Occ: Accountant.
IRVING Bruce Carlyle 1962/63-1972/73 b 19.8.1932 Christchurch, Canterbury. RHB OB Team: **Canterbury.** Sch: West Christchurch BHS. Occ: Salesman.
IRVING Richard John Robert 1996/97-2000/01 b 19.9.1969 Christchurch, Canterbury. LHB wk Team: **Auckland.** Played List A in NZ. Occ: Schoolmaster AGS.
IRWIN Gareth Dudley 2002/03 b 6.3.1981 Hamilton, Waikato. LHB LFM Team: **Northern Districts.** NZ U19 ODI. Indoor cricket: New Zealand.
ISHERWOOD Brian Philip 1965/66-1972/73 b 18.6.1946 Christchurch, Canterbury. LHB wk Team: **Canterbury.** Played List A in NZ. Sch: Methven HS.
IZARD Ernest Battersbee 1890/91-1897/98 b 18.2.1868 Wellington. d 23.2.1948 Nelson. Teams: **Wellington, Taranaki.** Sch: Harrow, England.

JACK Murray William 1955/56-1957/58 b 21.7.1932 Timaru, South Canterbury. LHB SLA Team: **Canterbury.** Sch: Timaru BHS.
JACKMAN Charles Keith Quentin 1934/35-1941/42 b 4.2.1906 Christchurch, Canterbury. d 23.2.1988 Auckland. LHB wk Teams: **Canterbury, Auckland, New Zealand.** Sch: Christ Coll. Occ: Accountant. NZCA obit: 1988; Wisden obit: 1989. He played for New Zealand in a first-class match.
JACKSON H 1918/19 Team: **Southland.**
JACOBS Arthur Woolf 1893/94 b 1866 St Kilda, Victoria, Australia. d 1948 East Melbourne, Victoria, Australia. Team: **Auckland.** Sch: Wellington Coll. Occ: Merchant.
JACOBS Edwin Le Grand 1873/74 b 14.3.1853 Croydon, Surrey, England. d 26.4.1901 Palmerston North, Manawatu. Team: **Wellington.** Occ: Publican.
JACOBS Jack 1927/28-1945 b 16.4.1909 Dunedin, Otago. d 15.6.2003 Southport, Queensland, Australia. RHB occ wk Team: **Canterbury.** Sch: Christchurch BHS. NZCA obit: 2004.
JACOBS Sydney 1899/00 b Q2 1867 Alderbury, Wiltshire, England. d 17.10.1932 Christchurch, Canterbury. Team: **Wellington.** Sch: Wellington Coll. Occ: Warehouseman.
JACOBSEN Norman Reginald 1919/20-1920/21 b 3.1.1889 Wellington. d 6.5.1950 Wellington. M Team: **Hawke's Bay.** Sch: Auckland GS. Occ: Schoolteacher. Hockey: New Zealand.
JACOMB John Newton 1860/61-1863/64 b 3.10.1841 New Town, Tasmania, Australia. d 5.11.1891 Walhalla, Victoria, Australia. LHB Teams: **Otago,** Victoria. Sch: Scotch Coll, Melbourne, Australia. Occ: Hotelkeeper; gold miner.
JAMES Harley Thomas George 1997/98-2000/01 b 29.7.1978 Wellington. RHB Team: **Canterbury.** Sch: Rangiora HS. Occ: Pharmacist.
JAMES Kenneth Cecil 1923/24-1946/47 b 12.3.1904 Wellington. d 21.8.1976 Palmerston North, Manawatu. RHB wk Teams: **Wellington, New Zealand Test,** Northamptonshire. Sch: Wellington Coll. NZCA obit: 1976; Wisden obit: 1977. He holds the Wellington 10th wicket partnership record of 138 with A.W.S.Brice against Otago in 1926/27.
JAMES Kevan David 1980-1999 b 18.3.1961 Lambeth, London, England. LHB LMF Teams: **Wellington,** Middlesex, Hampshire. Played List A in NZ. Sch: Edmonton County School, England. An English pro, played and coached in NZ.
JAMES Robert Michael 1956-1964/65 b 2.10.1934 Wokingham, Berkshire, England. RHB RM Teams: **Wellington,** Cambridge University. Sch: St John's, Leatherhead, England. Occ: Cricket coach.
JAMES Stanley Neville 1953/54 b 3.1.1932 Wanganui. d 12.10.2002 Wanganui. RHB RM Team: **Otago.** Occ: Assistant superintendent. NZCA obit: 2003.
JAMES Vincent 1939/40-1944/45 b 24.8.1915 Napoleons, Victoria, Australia. RHB wk Team: **Canterbury.** Canterbury selector.
JAMIESON Murray Duncan 1980/81-1981/82 b 8.12.1952 Dunedin, Otago. RHB LM Team: **Central Districts.** Played List A in NZ.
JARVIS Terrence Wayne 1964/65-1976/77 b 29.7.1944 Auckland. RHB SLA Teams: **Auckland, Canterbury, New Zealand Test.** Played List A in NZ. Sch: Auckland GS. Occ: TV executive. He co-founded Sky TV New Zealand and became a leading breeder of racehorses. He holds the NZ Test 1st wicket partnership record of 387 with G.M.Turner against the West Indies in 1971/72.
JEFFERSON Mark Robin 1996/97-2006/07 b 28.6.1976 Oamaru, North Otago. RHB SLA Teams: **Wellington, Northern Districts.** Played List A in NZ. Sch: Gisborne BHS. Occ: Schoolteacher. NZ U19 Test; NZ U19 ODI. Rugby: Poverty Bay. Father: R.G.Jefferson.
JEFFERSON Robin Gerard 1965/66-1969/70 b 18.8.1941 Christchurch, Canterbury. LHB RM Teams: **Otago, Wellington.** Lawn Bowls: Won the NZ national pairs. Son: M.R.Jefferson.
JESTY Trevor Edward 1966-1991 b 2.6.1948 Gosport, Hampshire, England. RHB RM occ wk Teams: **Canterbury,** England ODI, Hampshire, Surrey, Lancashire, Border, Griqualand West. Played List A in NZ. Sch: Privet County Secondary Modern, Gosport, England. Occ: Cricket pro. WCOY: 1983. An English pro, played and coached in NZ.
JOEL Louis Joseph 1899/00 b 12.9.1864 Dunedin, Otago. d 6.5.1949 Dunedin, Otago. Team: **Otago.** Sch: Otago BHS. Occ: Accountant. Umpired first-class cricket.
JOHNSON J 1919/20 Team: **Hawke's Bay.**

JOHNSON Vaughn Francis 1984/85-1990/91 b 2.9.1960 Dunedin, Otago. RHB RM Team: **Otago.** Played List A in NZ. Wellington selector.
JOHNSTON Charles Edgar 1896/97 b 1869 New Zealand. d 4.3.1945 Feilding, Manawatu. Team: **Hawke's Bay.** Sch: Christ Coll. Occ: Farmer. Umpired first-class cricket.
JOHNSTON Robert J 1872/73-1873/74 b 1849 Scotland. d 17.12.1897 Earnscleugh, Otago. He was drowned off the Earnscleugh dredge in Central Otago. Team: **Otago.** Occ: Farmer.
JOHNSTON William 1889/90-1902/03 b 24.8.1867 Edinburgh, Midlothian, Scotland. d 14.9.1947 Dunedin, Otago. Team: **Otago.** Occ: Caretaker.
JOLLY John Logan 1933/34 b 7.7.1912 Cromwell, Central Otago. d 9.7.1995 Sydney, New South Wales, Australia. LHB RM Team: **Otago.** Sch: Otago BHS. Occ: Mining engineer. Rugby: Otago. NZCA obit: 2003.
JONAS Glenn Ralph 1993/94-1999/00 b 13.8.1970 Carterton, Wairapara. RHB RM Teams: **Wellington, Otago.** Played List A in NZ. Sch: Hutt Valley Memorial Coll.
JONES A O 1911/12 Team: **Auckland.**
JONES Andrew Howard 1979/80-1995/96 b 9.5.1959 Wellington. RHB OB Teams: **Central Districts, Otago, Wellington, New Zealand Test, New Zealand ODI.** Played List A in NZ. Book: What is it like to be an international cricketer? by K.Boon. NZCA COY: 1988, 1989, 1991, 1994. He holds the NZ 3rd wicket partnership record of 467 with M.J.Crowe v Sri Lanka in 1990/91, the NZ Test 2nd wicket partnership record of 241 with J.G.Wright against England in 1991/92 and the Wellington 1st wicket partnership record of 333 with B.A.Edgar against Auckland in 1988/89.
JONES Barrie Llewellyn 1954/55 b 7.8.1929 Wanganui. RHB RM Team: **Central Districts.**
JONES C 1944/45 Team: **Wellington.**
JONES Gregory John 1976/77 b 20.1.1956 Auckland. RHB Team: **Auckland.**
JONES James Frederick 1950/51-1956/57 b 18.12.1931 Wellington. RHB RFM Teams: **Wellington, Central Districts.** He took a hat-trick for Wellington v Central Districts in 1953/54.
JONES Noel Harrington Pryce 1918/19-1920/21 b 11.12.1891 Christchurch, Canterbury. d 11.5.1948 Christchurch, Canterbury. Team: **Canterbury.** Occ: Coy manager.
JONES Raymond Peter 1980/81-1984/85 b 12.10.1958 Christchurch, Canterbury. LHB OB Teams: **Canterbury, Otago.** Played List A in NZ. Sch: Shirley BHS.
JONES Richard Andrew 1993/94-2009/10 b 22.10.1973 Auckland. RHB Teams: **Auckland, Wellington, New Zealand Test, New Zealand ODI.** Played List A in NZ; Played T20 in NZ. Sch: Takapuna GS. NZ U19 Test; NZ U19 ODI. He took a wicket with his first (and only) ball in first-class cricket.
JONES Samuel Percy 1880/81-1908/09 b 1.8.1861 Sydney, New South Wales, Australia. d 14.7.1951 Auckland. RHB RFM Teams: **Auckland,** Australia Test, New South Wales, Queensland. Sch: Sydney GS, Australia. Occ: Caretaker; coach. Book: Currency Lads by Max Bonnell. NZCA obit: 1951; Wisden obit: 1952. When he died, aged 90, he was then the oldest Test cricketer and the last survivor of the side which beat England in the 'Ashes' Test Match at The Oval in 1882.
JONES Stewart Thornbury 1953/54 b 24.1.1929 Naseby, Central Otago. RHB RFM Team: **Otago.** Sch: Kings HS.
JOPLIN Frank 1913/14 b 27.2.1894 Wellington. d 1.3.1984 Wellington. RHB Team: **Wellington.** Sch: Wellington Coll. Occ: Schoolteacher.
JORDAN Alistar Bruce 1968/69-1979/80 b 5.9.1949 Inglewood, Taranaki. LHB RFM Teams: **Central Districts, New Zealand.** Played List A in NZ. Sch: New Plymouth BHS. He played for New Zealand in a first-class match.
JUDD William 1886/87 b 1.5.1864 Greytown, Wairarapa. d 25.12.1906 Masterton, Wairarapa. LHB Team: **Wellington.** Sch: Greytown. Occ: Sheep farmer.
KAIN Martin Owen 2008/09 b 16.5.1988 Nelson. LHB SLA Team: **Canterbury.** Sch: St Andrews Coll. Occ: Student.
KALLENDER Jocelyn Arthur 1893/94-1904/05 b Q1 1870 Brentford, Middlesex, England. d 7.10.1953 Auckland. F Team: **Auckland.** Occ: Bank officer.
KASPER Ronald John 1966/67-1978/79 b 22.3.1946 Auckland. RHB RM Teams: **Auckland,** Natal B, Natal. Played List A in NZ. Sch: Auckland GS.

KAVANAGH Edward James 1914/15-1920/21 b 3.7.1888 Invercargill, Southland. d 16.3.1960 Hastings, Hawke's Bay. LHB LBG Team: **Southland.** Occ: Hospital orderly.
KAVANAGH Vivian Claude 1912/13 b 2.6.1882 Mauku, Franklin. d 9.8.1917 Ypres, Belgium. He was killed in action aged 35. Team: **Auckland.** Occ: Builder. Hockey: Auckland.
KAY Dennis Jon 1974/75-1977/78 b 12.4.1948 Palmerston North, Manawatu. d 27.11.2007 Palmerston North, Manawatu. LHB RM Team: **Central Districts.** Played List A in NZ. Sch: Freyburg HS. Occ: Truck driver. NZCA obit: 2008.
KEAN Russell James 1976/77-1977/78 b 25.3.1951 Wellington. RHB Team: **Wellington.** Sch: Wellington Coll. Occ: Engineer.
KEAST Albert Victor Ernest Manley 1917/18-1922/23 b 2.7.1895 Dunedin, Otago. d 20.4.1969 Christchurch, Canterbury. Team: **Otago.** Occ: Fruit grower.
KELLETT Simon Andrew 1989-1995 b 16.10.1967 Mirfield, Yorkshire, England. RHB RM Teams: **Wellington,** Yorkshire. Sch: Whitcliffe Mount Sch, England. Occ: Schoolteacher. An English pro, played and coached in NZ.
KELLY David Patrick 1998/99-2002/03 b 29.3.1979 Dunedin, Otago. RHB RSM Teams: **Central Districts, Northern Districts.** Played List A in NZ. NZ U19 ODI. Sch: John McLashan Coll. Occ: Farmer.
KELLY Felix Vincent 1889/90-1897/98 b 26.9.1866 Alma Plains, South Australia, Australia. d 31.1.1945 Wellington. Team: **Auckland.** Sch: Auckland GS. Occ: Surveyor. He had a reputation of being one of the best rifle shots in Auckland, having won innumerable trophies. He was a successful surveyor and engineer but he was bankrupted in 1931 as a result of the great depression. His son Felix was a well known artist.
KELLY James William Henry 1950/51 b 9.12.1928 Stillwater, North Auckland. d 9.1.1995 Auckland. RHB wk Team: **Wellington.** Occ: Manager. NZCA obit: 1995. Son: P.J.Kelly.
KELLY Leigh Edwin 1998/99 b 27.8.1974 Palmerston North, Manawatu. RHB RM Team: **Wellington.** Indoor cricket: New Zealand.
KELLY Paul James 1980/81-1988/89 b 15.2.1960 Palmerston North, Manawatu. RHB wk Team: **Auckland.** Played List A in NZ. Sch: Westlake BHS. Occ: Bank manager. Father: J.W.H.Kelly.
KELLY Robert Arthur 1961/62 b 4.6.1936 Dannevirke, Hawke's Bay. RHB Team: **Central Districts.**
KEMBER Hamish John 1990/91-1994/95 b 29.2.1968 Timaru, South Canterbury. LHB SLA Team: **Canterbury.** Played List A in NZ. Sch: Burnside HS. Occ: Bank officer. NZ U19 Test; NZ U19 ODI.
KEMNITZ Ernest James 1914/15 b 27.8.1894 Dunedin, Otago. d 6.2.1929 Nelson. RHB wk Team: **Southland.** Sch: Otago BHS. Occ: Solicitor. Wisden obit: 1930.
KEMP John Gregory 1960/61-1969/70 b 21.3.1940 Auckland. d 28.12.1993 Sydney, New South Wales, Australia. He died in a Sydney hospital a week after a second liver transplant. LHB Team: **Auckland.** Soccer: New Zealand. NZCA obit: 1994; Wisden obit: 1995.
KEMP Raymond James 1945/46-1949/50 b 6.4.1918 Wellington. d 27.12.1994 Upper Hutt, Wellington. RHB Team: **Wellington.**
KENNEDY Kevin Dennis 1964/65-1974/75 b 21.1.1945 Gisborne, Poverty Bay. RHB SLA Team: **Northern Districts.** Played List A in NZ.
KENNEDY Peter Gerard 1985/86-1991/92 b 20.4.1965 Christchurch, Canterbury. RHB Team: **Canterbury.** Played List A in NZ. Sch: Christchurch BHS. He holds the Canterbury 3rd wicket partnership record of 394* with R.T.Latham against Northern Districts in 1990/91.
KENNEDY Robert John 1993/94-1999/00 b 3.6.1972 Dunedin, Otago. RHB RM Teams: **Otago, Wellington, New Zealand Test, New Zealand ODI.** Played List A in NZ. Sch: Otago BHS. Occ: Bartender.
KENNEDY Roland Ralph 1920/21 b 19.2.1896 Onehunga, Auckland. d 13.5.1952 Napier, Hawke's Bay. Team: **Hawke's Bay.** Sch: Napier BHS.
KENNEDY William Charles 1877/78-1883/84 b 1853 New Zealand. d 24.8.1889 Sydney, New South Wales, Australia. His body was found on the north shore of Sydney harbour under circumstances pointing to suicide by poison. The inquest found that he had been drinking heavily and the jury returned a verdict that death was due to the excessive use of alcohol. Team: **Wellington.** Occ: Bank officer.

KENNY John 1911/12 b 7.10.1883 Dunedin, Otago. d 15.4.1937 Dunedin, Otago. He was killed by a runaway tram, which left the tracks and mounted the kerb. Team: **Otago**. Occ: Brassfounder.
KENT Leonard Alfred Walter 1943/44-1951/52 b 26.12.1924 Auckland. LHB wk Team: **Auckland**.
KERR Alexander Charles 1906/07-1912/13 b 1876 New South Wales, Australia. d 30.4.1953 Auckland. RHB SLA Team: **Auckland**. Occ: Wharf labourer. Son: A.C.Kerr.
KERR Allen Charles 1941/42-1945/46 b 13.6.1906 Mudgee, New South Wales, Australia. d 28.11.1985 Auckland. LHB OB Team: **Auckland**. NZCA obit: 1986. The main stand at the Auckland Domain is named in his honour. He scored 122 on his first-class debut for Auckland v Wellington in 1941/42. Father: A.C.Kerr.
KERR Frank Bevan 1934/35-1936/37 b 28.10.1916 Perth, Western Australia, Australia. d 24.7.1943 Solomon Islands. He was killed in action aged 26. RHB Team: **Otago**. Occ: Manufacturing agent.
KERR John Lambert 1929/30-1942/43 b 28.12.1910 Dannevirke, Hawke's Bay. d 27.5.2007 Christchurch, Canterbury. RHB RM Teams: **Canterbury, New Zealand Test**. Sch: Wanganui Tech Coll. Occ: Accountant. OBE, CNZM. NZCA obit: 2007; Wisden obit: 2008. NZ and Canterbury selector and NZ manager.
KERR Robert James 1993/94-1997/98 b 6.4.1966 Wellington. RHB occ wk Team: **Wellington**. Played List A in NZ. Indoor cricket: New Zealand. Father-in-law: B.A.G.Murray.
KETTLE Charles Cargill 1868/69-1871/72 b 4.6.1850 Dunedin, Otago. d 17.12.1918 Auckland. Team: **Otago**. Sch: Otago BHS; Nelson Coll. Occ: Lawyer; stipendiary magistrate.
KIDDEY John William 1956/57-1964/65 b 5.7.1929 Christchurch, Canterbury. RHB LM Team: **Canterbury**. Sch: Christchurch BHS. Occ: Warehouse manager. Hockey: New Zealand. Canterbury selector.
KILGOUR William Alexander 1901/02-1907/08 b 2.2.1878 Dunedin, Otago. d 4.3.1935 Auckland. Team: **Otago**. Occ: Fruit grower.
KING Charles Barrett 1893/94 b 1847 unknown. d 10.11.1917 Auckland. He was killed by a fall from a tram car. wk Team: **Auckland**. Occ: Union secretary.
KING George Alfred 1873/74 b 1845 Fulham, London, England. d 26.2.1894 Wellington. Team: **Auckland**. Sch: St. John's, Hurstpierpoint, England. Occ: Journalist. He wrote under the nom de plume of "Vigilant" and was regarded as one of the best sporting writers in the colony. Book: The Auckland Cricketers' Tour to the South 1873/74.
KING Richard Terrence 1991/92-2002/03 b 23.4.1973 Wellington. RHB RSM Teams: **Otago, Auckland, Central Districts**. Played List A in NZ.
KING Robert Harvey 1977/78 b 19.10.1956 Gore, Southland. LHB RFM Team: **Canterbury**. Played List A in NZ. Sch: Timaru BHS. Occ: Petrol station manager.
KINGSLAND Thomas Daniel 1886/87 b 16.6.1862 Lower Huntley, Victoria, Australia. d 8.12.1933 Invercargill, Southland. Team: **Otago**. Occ: Fellmonger. Umpired first-class cricket. Chairman of the Southland CA.
KINGSTON George Richard 1917/18 b 8.3.1900 Invercargill, Southland. d 6.7.1979 Timaru, South Canterbury. Team: **Southland**. Sch: Christ Coll. Occ: Doctor.
KINGSTONE Charles Napoleon 1927/28 b 2.7.1895 Auckland. d 6.5.1960 New Plymouth, Taranaki. occ wk Team: **Rest of NZ**. Sch: Grafton Sch. Occ: Salesman. Rugby: All Blacks and Taranaki. Because of the World War I years of 1914-18 and then injuries from a motor accident on the way to a cricket match in 1922 his only rugby at top level was in the 1920-21 seasons.
KINSELLA David Arthur 1961/62-1965/66 b 23.2.1937 New Plymouth, Taranaki. RHB RFM Team: **Central Districts**. Sch: New Plymouth BHS. Umpired Test and first-class cricket.
KINVIG Alfred George 1893/94-1903/04 b 16.3.1874 Dunedin, Otago. d 15.2.1965 Christchurch, Canterbury. LHB Teams: **Otago, Canterbury**. Occ: Clerk.
KINVIG James Gordon 1909/10 b 19.6.1888 Christchurch, Canterbury. d 31.7.1917 Ploegsteert Wood, near Ypres, Belgium. He was killed in action aged 29. RHB Team: **Wellington**. Occ: Warehouseman. Rugby: Wellington.
KIRK Christopher Matthew 1969/70-1978/79 b 15.7.1947 Christchurch, Canterbury. LHB SLA Teams: **Canterbury, Otago**. Played List A in NZ. Sch: Xavier Coll. Occ: Lincoln College administrator.

KIRKCALDIE James Cullen 1903/04 b 18.4.1875 Enfield, Middlesex, England. d 16.8.1931 Dunedin, Otago. Team: **Wellington**. Sch: Wellington Coll. Occ: Chemist.

KIRKER William David Rea 1887/88-1893/94 b 1866 Christchurch, Canterbury. d 27.2.1942 Wellington. Team: **Wellington**. Occ: Warehouseman.

KISSLING John Herbert Percy 1885/86-1889/90 b 1868 Blenheim, Marlborough. d 11.5.1929 Auckland. RHB Teams: **Nelson, Auckland**. Sch: St John's, Auskland. Occ: Insurance manager.

KITCHEN Anaru Kyle 2008/09-2009/10 b 21.2.1984 Auckland. RHB SLA Team: **Auckland**. Played List A in NZ; Played T20 in NZ. Sch: Auckland GS. He holds the NZ domestic T20 5th wicket partnership record of 101 with L.Vincent for Auckland against Wellington in 2009/10 and the NZ domestic T20 7th wicket partnership record of 77 with C.de Grandhomme for Auckland against Otago in 2009/10.

KITT George Arthur 1886/87 b Q1 1853 Shoreditch, London, England. d 2.2.1940 Campbelltown, New South Wales, Australia. Team: **Otago**. Occ: Bookkeeper.

KITTO Ernest Victor Morland 1894/95 b 21.1.1871 Scotland. d 27.12.1897 at sea, between NZ and Montevideo on a voyage to England aged 26. Team: **Canterbury**. Sch: Loretto, Scotland.

KIVELL David Sydney 1952/53-1955/56 b 17.6.1932 Napier, Hawke's Bay. RHB Team: **Central Districts**.

KNAPP Charles Arthur 1873/74-1884/85 b 27.11.1845 Sleaford, Lincolnshire, England. d 8.9.1927 Wellington. occ wk Team: **Wellington**. Sch: Lancing Coll, England. Occ: Settler. Umpired first-class cricket. Rugby: Wellington. Wisden obit: 1928. Chairman of the Management Committee of the Wellington CA.

KNAPP Charles Henry 1873/74-1876/77 b 21.6.1845 Nelson. d 14.7.1929 Waimea South, Nelson. Team: **Nelson**. Occ: Police constable. Brothers: W.H.Knapp, K.J.Knapp.

KNAPP Edmund Courtenay 1943/44-1944/45 b 24.4.1917 Greymouth, West Coast. d 19.2.1989 Wanganui. OB Team: **Wellington**. Wisden obit: 1990.

KNAPP Kempster James 1873/74-1877/78 b 1850 Nelson. d 8.4.1879 Nelson. He died at the age of 28. Team: **Nelson**. Occ: Farmer. Brothers: C.H.Knapp, W.H.Knapp.

KNAPP William Harvey 1875/76-1876/77 b 1844 Nelson. d 24.8.1935 Nelson. Team: **Nelson**. Occ: Farmer. Brothers: C.H.Knapp, K.J.Knapp.

KNIGHT Alexander Rutherford 1918/19-1943/44 b 24.1.1899 Dunedin, Otago. d 8.4.1986 Auckland. RHB OB Team: **Otago**. Sch: Otago BHS. Occ: Civil servant. NZCA obit: 1986.

KNOWLES David John 1983/84 b 15.8.1948 Te Aroha, Thames Valley. RHB OB Team: **Auckland**. Played List A in NZ.

KOHLHASE Sebastian Winston 1963/64-1969/70 b 22.8.1942 Aleipata, Samoa. LHB RM Teams: **Northern Districts, Auckland**. Sch: St Pauls, Hamilton. Occ: Manager. President of Samoan CA and chef-de-mission for the Samoan team at the 2008 Beijing Olympics.

KORTLANG Harry Herbert Lorenz 1909/10-1926/27 b 12.3.1880 Carlton, Melbourne, Victoria, Australia. d 15.2.1961 Cottesloe, Western Australia, Australia. RHB Teams: **Wellington, New Zealand,** Victoria. Occ: Comm traveller. NZCA obit: 1961; Wisden obit: 1962. He played for New Zealand prior to being granted Test status.

KREEFT Charles Vaughan 1882/83 b 1859 Williamstown, Victoria, Australia. d 1.8.1924 Wellington. RHB RF Team: **Wellington**. Sch: Wellington Coll. Occ: Civil servant. Rugby: Wellington.

KRUSKOPF Ernest Alexander 1944/45 b 3.2.1918 Lawrence, Otago. d 21.1.1981 Invercargill, Southland. Team: **Otago**. Occ: Civil servant.

KUCHEN Gustave 1880/81 b 1856 Sweden. d 3.9.1897 Wellington. Team: **Wellington**. Occ: Tobacconist.

KUGGELEIJN Christopher Mary 1975/76-1990/91 b 10.5.1956 Auckland. RHB OB Teams: **Northern Districts, New Zealand Test, New Zealand ODI.** Played List A in NZ. Sch: Tokoroa HS. Occ: Schoolteacher. Book: Kuggs. ND coach and selector. He holds the Northern Districts 2nd wicket partnership record of 237 with J.G.Gibson against Canterbury in 1980/81.

KULKARNI Dhawal Sunil 2008/09-2010 b 10.12.1988 Bombay (now Mumbai), Maharashtra, India. RHB RM Teams: **Wellington,** Mumbai. Sch: IES New English, India. Occ: Cricket pro. Indian tourist who played for Wellington in order to get match practice whilst on the 2008/09 tour of NZ.

KURU Jeremy Newton 2009/10 b 17.2.1985 Napier, Hawke's Bay. RHB RMF Team: **Central Districts.** Sch: Hawke's Bay HS.

LABATT Andrew Brennan Mountjoye 1887/88-1897/98 b 1.3.1869 Lambeth, London, England. d 27.4.1922 Auckland. Teams: **Canterbury, Auckland, New Zealand.** Occ: Clerk. He played for New Zealand prior to being granted Test status.

LABATT Frederick Hubert De Burgh 1891/92 b 1861 Moneymore, Co Londonderry, Ireland. d 1.8.1947 Christchurch, Canterbury. Team: **Canterbury.** Sch: Otago BHS. Occ: Accountant.

LAKER James Charles 1946-1964/65 b 9.2.1922 Frizinghall, Bradford, Yorkshire, England. d 23.4.1986 Putney, London, England. RHB OB Teams: **Auckland,** England Test, Surrey, Essex. Sch: Salts High School, England. Occ: Cricket pro. Books: Over to Me; Spinning round the world; Cricket contrasts; J.C.Laker by G.Hudd. Wisden obit: 1987. NZCA COY: 1952; WCOY: 1952. An English pro, played and coached in NZ.

LAMASON David William 1990/91-1996/97 b 23.4.1971 Wanganui. LHB RFM Team: **Central Districts.** Played List A in NZ. Sch: Wanganui City Coll. Rugby: Wellington.

LAMASON John Rider 1927/28-1946/47 b 29.10.1905 Wellington. d 25.6.1961 Wellington. RHB OB Teams: **Wellington, New Zealand.** Sch: Mt Cook HS. Occ: Clerk. Rugby: Wellington. NZCA obit: 1961; Wisden obit: 1962. His wife, Ina, represented Wellington and New Zealand at cricket and hockey. He played for New Zealand in a first-class match.

LAMB Andrew Robert 2008/09-2009/10 b 1.1.1978 Bathurst, New South Wales, Australia. RHB RFM Team: **Wellington.** Played List A in NZ. Sch: Bathurst HS, Australia. Occ: Schoolteacher; Personal trainer.

LAMBERT Herbert Norman 1917/18-1932/33 b 29.1.1900 Wellington. d 19.7.1984 New Plymouth, Taranaki. RHB OB Teams: **Wellington, New Zealand.** Sch: Wellington Coll. NZCA obit: 1984; Wisden obit: 1984. He played for New Zealand prior to being granted Test status.

LAMBERT Sydney Chowne 1873/74-1874/75 b 11.10.1852 at sea. d 10.10.1916 Wellington. RF Team: **Otago.** Sch: Otago BHS; Christs Coll. Occ: Clerk. Umpired first-class cricket. Wisden obit: 1917.

LAMBLY Sean Owen 1993/94-1994/95 b 7.10.1970 Auckland. RHB Team: **Northern Districts.** Played List A in NZ. Occ: Site manager.

LAMONT Michael James 1990/91-1998/99 b 16.1.1967 Invercargill, Southland. LHB Team: **Otago.** Played List A in NZ. NZ U19 Test; NZ U19 ODI. Cousin: R.N.Hoskin.

LANCE Henry Porcher 1863/64-1864/65 b 1833 Somerset, England. d 19.5.1886 Riccarton, Christchurch, Canterbury. wk Team: **Canterbury.** Sch: Winchester, England. Occ: Runholder. MP. When an undergraduate at Oxford he was known as a very skilful steeplechase rider and afterwards under the name of "Mr Dart" was acknowledged as one of the boldest and most accomplished gentlemen riders in England. First president of the Canterbury Cricket Association. in 1877. Son-in-law: E.D.Tanner.

LANE Mark Edward Landon 1990/91-1996/97 b 31.1.1969 Blenheim, Marlborough. RHB wk Teams: **Wellington, Central Districts, Canterbury.** Played List A in NZ. Sch: Marlborough Boys Coll. Occ: NZC employee. NZ U19 Test; NZ U19 ODI.

LANGDON Maurice Charles 1957/58-1964/65 b 12.10.1934 Wanganui. RHB RM Team: **Northern Districts.** Occ: Architect.

LANGRIDGE Gary John 1976/77-1981/82 b 5.4.1952 Wellington. LHB Team: **Central Districts.** Played List A in NZ.

LANGRIDGE James 1924-1953 b 10.7.1906 Chailey, Sussex, England. d 10.9.1966 Withdean, Brighton, Sussex, England. LHB SLA Teams: **Auckland,** England Test, Sussex. Sch: Newick Sch, England. Occ: Cricket pro. NZCA obit: 1967; Wisden obit: 1967. WCOY: 1932. An English pro, played and coached in NZ. Brother: J.G.Langridge (Sussex); son: R.J.Langridge (Sussex).

LANKHAM George 1873/74 b 6.9.1830 Perth, Scotland. d 4.11.1908 Devonport, Auckland. RS Team: **Auckland.** Occ: Saddler. Son: W.Lankham.

LANKHAM William 1882/83-1883/84 b 4.12.1861 Auckland. d 2.12.1886 Devonport, Auckland. He died of consumption aged 24. RMF Team: **Auckland.** He took a hat-trick for Auckland v Taranaki in 1882/83. Father: G.Lankham.

LARSEN Gavin Rolf 1984/85-1998/99 b 27.9.1962 Wellington. RHB RM Teams: **Wellington, New Zealand Test, New Zealand ODI.** Played List A in NZ. Sch: Onslow Coll. Books: Grand Larseny; The cricket postman. He holds the Wellington 5th wicket partnership record of 341 with E.B.McSweeney against Central Districts in 1987/88.

LASH Edmund Goodridge 1897/98 b 19.8.1874 Ahaura, Nelson. d 11.5.1958 Auckland. Team: **Taranaki.** Sch: Fitzroy Sch. Occ: Coy secretary. Brother: F.W.Lash.

LASH Frederick William 1893/94-1896/97 b 7.4.1870 Cobden, West Coast. d 10.11.1965 Auckland. Team: **Wellington.** Occ: Labourer. Brother: E.G.Lash.

LATHAM J K 1903/04 Team: **Wellington.** An Englishman, he arrived in NZ in 1903.

LATHAM Rodney Terry 1980/81-1994/95 b 12.6.1961 Christchurch, Canterbury. RHB RM Teams: **Canterbury, New Zealand Test, New Zealand ODI.** Played List A in NZ. Sch: Linwood HS. Occ: Golf club manager. He holds the Canterbury 3rd wicket partnership record of 394* with P.G.Kennedy against Northern Districts in 1990/91.

LATHBURY William Henry 1875/76 b 29.9.1843 Horninglow, Staffordshire, England. d 7.3.1884 Charters Towers, Queensland, Australia. He died from natural causes aged 40. F Team: **Otago.** Occ: Brewer.

LAWRENCE Charles William Hughes 1987/88 b 19.9.1963 Christchurch, Canterbury. RHB RFM Team: **Canterbury.** Played List A in NZ. Sch: Christ Coll. Occ: Farmer.

LAWRENCE James 1873/74 b 1849 Surrey, England. d 2.10.1898 Wellington. A shock sustained in a collision with a steam-roller 18 months before his death ultimately led to his demise. Team: **Wellington.** Occ: Gas coy fireman.

LAWRENCE James Duncan 1891/92-1906/07 b 11.3.1867 Ferrymead, Christchurch, Canterbury. d 21.6.1946 Christchurch, Canterbury. RHB Teams: **Canterbury, New Zealand.** Sch: Cooks School. Occ: Chemist. He played for New Zealand prior to being granted Test status. He holds the Canterbury 1st wicket partnership record of 306 with L.A.Cuff against Auckland in 1893/94.

LAWS Frederick Arthur 1896/97-1909/10 b 21.7.1877 Birmingham, Warwickshire, England. d 1.4.1954 Wellington. Teams: **Wellington, Hawke's Bay.** Occ: Railway employee. Umpired first-class cricket.

LAWSON Alfred Noel 1944/45 b 25.12.1912 Dunedin, Otago. d 22.11.1974 Wellington. wk Team: **Otago.** Sch: Otago BHS. Occ: Coy secretary. NZCA obit: 1975. Otago selector.

LAWSON Henry Wallace 1883/84-1897/98 b 1862 Balmain, Sydney, New South Wales, Australia. d 8.7.1923 Auckland. M Teams: **Wellington, Auckland.** Sch: Wellington Coll. Occ: Bank manager.

LAWSON Robert Arthur 1992/93-2003/04 b 14.9.1974 Dunedin, Otago. RHB OB Team: **Otago.** Played List A in NZ. Sch: Otago BHS. NZ U19 Test; NZ U19 ODI.

LAWTON Joseph Clement 1890/91-1893/94 b 9.5.1857 Moseley, Birmingham, Warwickshire, England. d 20.1.1934 Blackpool, Lancashire, England. M Teams: **Otago, New Zealand.** Occ: Cricket pro. Wisden obit: 1935. On his 57th birthday, playing for Blackpool against Fylde, he took seven wickets for one run, five men falling to consecutive balls. He played for New Zealand prior to being granted Test status.

LAXMAN Vangipurappu Venkata Sai 1992/93-2010 b 1.11.1974 Hyderabad, Andhra Pradesh, India. RHB OB occ wk Teams: **Otago,** Lancashire, India Test, India ODI, Hyderabad (India). Sch: Little Flower HS, Hyderabad, India. WCOY: 2002. Indian Test player who played for Otago to obtain match practice whilst on the 2008/09 tour of NZ.

LEACH William Edmund 1876/77-1885 b 7.11.1851 Lower Fold, Rochdale, Lancashire, England. d 30.11.1932 Ivinghoe Town Farm, Buckinghamshire, England. RHB RABu Teams: **Canterbury,** Lancashire. Sch: Marlborough, England. Occ: Sugar plantation owner (Argentina). Wisden obit: 1933. Brothers: H.Leach (Lancashire), J.Leach (Lancashire), R.Leach (Lancashire), R.C.Leach (Lancashire).

LEADER John Vernon 1928/29-1940/41 b 14.5.1908 Christchurch, Canterbury. d 22.3.1995 Dunedin, Otago. LHB RM Team: **Otago.** Sch: Otago BHS. Occ: Coy secretary. NZCA obit: 1995; Wisden obit: 1996. Otago selector.

LEE Christopher David 1991/92-1996/97 b 9.9.1971 Wellington. RHB RFM Teams: **Wellington, Auckland.** Played List A in NZ.

LEE George Henry 1870/71-1875/76 b Q2 1851 Chelsea, Middlesex, England. d 22.5.1931 Christchurch, Canterbury. Team: **Canterbury.** Occ: Farmer. Rugby: Canterbury.

LEE Jamie Baden 2003/04 b 3.12.1971 Gisborne, Poverty Bay. RHB RM Team: **Northern Districts.** Played List A in NZ. Sch: Awatapu Coll.

LEES Warren Kenneth 1970/71-1987/88 b 19.3.1952 Dunedin, Otago. RHB RM wk Teams: **Otago, New Zealand Test, New Zealand ODI.** Played List A in NZ. Sch: Kings HS. Occ: Cricket admin; coach. Book: Wally: the Warren Lees story by B.Edwards. MBE. NZ selector and coach; Otago coach, CEO, selector. He holds the Otago 6th wicket partnership record of 165 with G.M.Turner against Wellington in 1975/76.

LEFEBVRE Roland Philippe 1990-1995 b 7.2.1963 Rotterdam, Netherlands. RHB RM Teams: **Canterbury,** Netherlands, Netherlands ODI, Somerset, Glamorgan. Played List A in NZ. Sch: Montessori Lyceum, Rotterdam, Netherlands. Occ: Physiotherapist; cricket pro. A Dutch pro, played and coached in NZ.

LEGGAT Ian Bruce 1950/51-1961/62 b 7.6.1930 Invercargill, Southland. RHB RM Teams: **Central Districts, New Zealand Test.** Occ: Survey draughtsman. Rugby: Nelson. ND selector. He holds the NZ 9th wicket partnership record of 239 with H.B.Cave for Central Districts v Otago in 1952/53. Cousin: J.G.Leggat.

LEGGAT John Gordon 1944/45-1955/56 b 27.5.1926 Wellington. d 9.3.1973 Christchurch, Canterbury. RHB Teams: **Canterbury, New Zealand Test.** Sch: Christchurch BHS. Occ: Solicitor. NZCA obit: 1973; Wisden obit: 1974. NZCA COY: 1954. NZ selector; Chairman of the Board of Control of the New Zealand Cricket Council. Cousin: I.B.Leggat.

LEGGAT Richard Ian 1979/80-1983/84 b 28.8.1960 Christchurch, Canterbury. RHB LB occ wk Team: **Canterbury.** Played List A in NZ. Sch: Christchurch BHS. Occ: Stockbroker.

LEIGH Jeffrey Allan 1977/78 b 26.10.1950 Stratford, Taranaki. LHB wk Team: **Northern Districts.** Sch: Stratford HS. Occ: Pastor.

LEITH John 1880/81 b 31.5.1857 Melbourne, Victoria, Australia. d 28.7.1928 Dunedin, Otago. Team: **Otago.** Sch: Middle Dist. Sch, Dunedin. Occ: Clerk.

LEMIN Thomas George Frederick 1929/30-1942/43 b 5.11.1905 Zeehan, Tasmania, Australia. d 29.11.1988 Dunedin, Otago. He died in a car accident. RHB RM Team: **Otago.** NZCA obit: 1990.

LEONARD Bradford John 2005/06 b 8.11.1979 Rotorua, Bay of Plenty. RHB RMF Team: **Northern Districts.** Played List A in NZ.

LEONARD David John 1989/90-1993/94 b 25.11.1965 Timaru, South Canterbury. RHB RFM Team: **Central Districts.** Played List A in NZ.

LESTER Stephen Garland 1929/30-1935/36 b 18.3.1906 Amberley, North Canterbury. d 24.10.1971 Christchurch, Canterbury. RHB RM Team: **Canterbury.** Sch: Christ Coll. Occ: Farmer. NZCA obit: 1972.

LEVERS Walter Charles Sidney 1895/96-1908/09 b 9.3.1864 Bingham, Nottinghamshire, England. d 10.11.1922 Auckland. He underwent a sudden and severe operation for an old internal trouble and was making a recovery when pneumonia supervened. RHB wk Teams: **Wellington, Hawke's Bay.** Occ: Wine merchant. Wisden obit: 1924.

LEWIS Max Lloyd 1949/50 b 13.7.1923 Auckland. d 5.6.1985 Auckland. LHB Team: **Auckland.** NZCA obit: 1986.

LEWIS Thomas William 1896/97-1898/99 b 1865 Wellington. d 22.9.1927 Napier, Hawke's Bay. Team: **Hawke's Bay.** Sch: Wellington Coll. Occ: Solicitor.

LIGGINS Frederick Collingwood 1896/97-1900/01 b 5.6.1873 Dunedin, Otago. d 28.5.1926 Perth, Western Australia, Australia. Team: **Otago.** Sch: Otago BHS. Occ: Insurance manager.

LINDSAY John Kenneth 1980/81-1991/92 b 2.4.1957 Winton, Southland. RHB OB Team: **Otago.** Played List A in NZ.

LINES Austin 1881/82-1891/92 b 22.2.1857 Nelson. d 21.11.1941 Nelson. Team: **Nelson.** Occ: Farmer.

LINN Warren Stuart 1980/81 b 10.9.1954 Hawera, Taranaki. RHB RM Teams: **Auckland, Central Districts.** Played List A in NZ.

LISSETTE Allen Fisher 1954/55-1962/63 b 6.11.1919 Morrinsville, Waikato. d 24.1.1973 Hamilton, Waikato. RHB SLA Teams: **Auckland, Northern Districts, New Zealand Test.** Occ: Bursar. MBE. NZCA obit: 1973; Wisden obit: 1974. CD selector.

LITTLE David Shane 1998/99 b 1.7.1974 Lower Hutt, Wellington. RHB RFM Team: **Wellington.** Played List A in NZ.

LITTLE Douglas 1911/12 Team: **Wellington**.
LITTLE John Clince 1947/48 b 11.2.1927 Wellington. d 28.9.2004 Tauranga, Bay of Plenty. RHB RM Team: **Wellington**.
LITTLEJOHN Alexander Ironside 1887/88-1889/90 b 1860 Scotland. d 25.5.1910 Wellington. Team: **Wellington**. Occ: Jeweller.
LITTLEJOHN William Still 1885/86-1886/87 b 19.9.1859 Turriff, Aberdeenshire, Scotland. d 7.10.1933 Hawthorn, Victoria, Australia. Team: **Nelson**. Sch: Aberdeen GS, Scotland. Occ: Schoolmaster. Book: Dr.W.S.Littlejohn: the story of a great headmaster by A.E.Pratt. NZRFU president in 1899. He was the headmaster of Scotch College, Melbourne from 1904 to 1933.
LIVINGSTON Thomas Oliver 1917/18 b 2.9.1889 Dunedin, Otago. d 1956 Balmain, Sydney, New South Wales, Australia. Team: **Otago**.
LLOYD Dennis Patrick 1968/69-1980/81 b 1.12.1948 Auckland. RHB OB Team: **Northern Districts**. Played List A in NZ.
LLOYD Nicholas Alloway 1990/91 b 29.9.1963 Maidstone, Kent, England. RHB wk Team: **Northern Districts**. Played List A in NZ.
LOBB Dion Victor 2006/07 b 3.12.1980 Dunedin, Otago. RHB RM Team: **Otago**.
LOCKETT John Barnett 1874/75-1879/80 b 8.9.1854 Muswellbrook, New South Wales, Australia. d 13.9.1929 Wanganui. Team: **Wellington**. Occ: Contractor. Rugby: Wellington.
LOGAN Gregory Ross 1986/87-1989/90 b 25.6.1963 Waikari, North Canterbury. RHB LM Team: **Central Districts**. Played List A in NZ.
LOHREY Malcolm Kent 1943/44 b 3.9.1913 Te Kinga, West Coast. d 18.4.1992 Christchurch, Canterbury. RHB RM Team: **Canterbury**.
LOMAS Arthur Leslie 1919/20 b 13.2.1895 Dunedin, Otago. d 11.2.1924 Wellington. He died aged 28 from respiratory problems caused by gas poisoning suffered during the First World War. Team: **Otago**. Occ: Draftsman.
LONDON Raymond Pearce 1920/21 b 26.9.1894 Pahiatua, Wairarapa. d 7.9.1946 Wanganui. Team: **Minor Assoc**. Occ: Mercer.
LONG Robert Inder 1953/54-1963/64 b 13.4.1932 Ranfurly, Central Otago. d 11.2.2010 Auckland. RHB RM Team: **Otago**. Sch: Otago BHS. Occ: Accountant.
LONGDEN Arthur 1883/84-1885/86 b 11.11.1856 Christchurch, Canterbury. d 1.7.1924 Christchurch, Canterbury. Team: **Canterbury**. Occ: Bank manager. Wisden obit: 1925.
LONSDALE William Meehan 2006/07-2007/08 b 16.9.1986 Lincoln, Christchurch, Canterbury. RHB LMF Team: **Canterbury**. Sch: Christ Coll.
LOUGHNAN Henry Hamilton 1870/71-1885/86 b 1849 Patna, Bihar, India. d 6.6.1939 Christchurch, Canterbury. Team: **Canterbury**. Sch: Stonyhurst Coll, England. Occ: Barrister.
LOVE W J 1920/21 wk Team: **Hawke's Bay**.
LOVERIDGE Greg Riaka 1994/95-2002/03 b 15.1.1975 Palmerston North, Manawatu. RHB LB Teams: **Central Districts, New Zealand Test,** Cambridge University. Played List A in NZ. Sch: Awatapu Coll. Occ: Coy director. NZ U19 Test; NZ U19 ODI.
LOWANS Graeme Edward 1959/60-1964/65 b 8.5.1934 Nelson. LHB RSM Team: **Central Districts**.
LOWE George Ellis 1873/74-1874/75 b 1.6.1847 Wellington. d 3.4.1922 Wellington. Team: **Wellington**. Occ: Foreman.
LOWES Paul Robert 1990/91 b 8.6.1966 Hastings, Hawke's Bay. LHB OB Team: **Central Districts**.
LOWRY Thomas Coleman 1917/18-1937/38 b 17.2.1898 Fernhill, Hawke's Bay. d 20.7.1976 Okawa, Hastings, Hawke's Bay. RHB RSM wk Teams: **Auckland, Wellington, New Zealand Test,** Somerset, Cambridge University. Sch: Christ Coll. Occ: Sheep farmer. Book: Tom Lowry: leader in a thousand by R.Francis. NZCA obit: 1976; Wisden obit: 1977. NZ selector. Brothers-in-law: A.P.F.Chapman (England, Cambridge University, Kent), R.H.B.Bettington (Oxford University, Middlesex, New South Wales); father: T.H.Lowry.
LOWRY Thomas Henry 1891/92 b 25.7.1865 Hastings, Hawke's Bay. d 23.9.1944 Okawa, Hastings, Hawke's Bay. Team: **Hawke's Bay**. Sch: Christ Coll. Occ: Sheep farmer. Horse Racing: He owned the champion racehorse "Desert Gold" winner of 19 consecutive races in 1919 which is still the Australasian record. Son: T.C.Lowry.

LOYE Malachy Bernard 1991-2010 b 27.9.1972 Northampton, England. RHB OB Teams: **Auckland,** England ODI, Northamptonshire, Lancashire. Played List A in NZ. Sch: Moulton Comp, England. Occ: Cricket pro. An English pro, played and coached in NZ.
LUCENA Roger Edward 1891/92 b 29.6.1868 Wellington. d 11.1.1943 Hawera, Taranaki. Team: **Taranaki.** Sch: Wellington Coll. Occ: Settler.
LUCKIE Martin Maxwell Fleming 1891/92-1919/20 b 1868 Nelson. d 3.7.1951 Wellington. Team: **Wellington.** Sch: Wellington Coll. Occ: Solicitor. Umpired first-class cricket. Wellington City Council named a park, with playing fields for cricket and football, in his honour. Wisden obit: 1952. President of the Wellington CA. Brother-in-law: T.S.Ronaldson.
LUDBROOK Edward Reginald 1891/92-1895/96 b 17.1.1872 Remuera, Auckland. d 3.12.1937 Kawakawa, Northland. Team: **Hawke's Bay.** Sch: Christ Coll. Occ: Accountant; sheep farmer. Umpired first-class cricket.
LUNDON John Raphael 1892/93-1893/94 b 26.11.1868 Auckland. d 6.10.1957 Devonport, Auckland. Team: **Auckland.** Sch: Auckland GS. Occ: Solicitor. Umpired first-class cricket.
LUSK Harold Butler 1899/00-1920/21 b 8.6.1877 Auckland. d 13.2.1961 Auckland. RHB Teams: **Auckland, Canterbury, Wellington, New Zealand.** Sch: Auckland GS. Occ: Schoolmaster. Golf: New Zealand champion in 1910. NZCA obit: 1961; Wisden obit: 1962. He played for New Zealand prior to being granted Test status. He scored 334* in a Christchurch club game in 1915/16. Cousins: Hugh B.Lusk, R.B.Lusk, W.N.B.Lusk.
LUSK Hugh Butler 1889/90-1908/09 b 12.1.1866 Mangonui, Northland. d 26.2.1944 Napier, Hawke's Bay. RHB Teams: **Auckland, Hawke's Bay, New Zealand.** Sch: Auckland GS; Christs Coll. Occ: Solicitor. Golf: New Zealand Amateur Champion 1910. Umpired first-class cricket. He played for New Zealand prior to being granted Test status. Brothers: R.B.Lusk, W.N.B.Lusk; cousin: Harold B.Lusk.
LUSK Robert Butler 1891/92-1894/95 b 1867 Auckland. d 28.5.1946 Auckland. Team: **Taranaki.** Sch: Auckland GS. Occ: Solicitor. Umpired first-class cricket. Rugby: Auckland, Taranaki and New South Wales. Brothers: Harold B.Lusk, W.N.B.Lusk; cousin: Hugh B.Lusk; father-in-law: W.L.Rees; brother-in-law: A.W.Rees.
LUSK William Newell Butler 1899/00-1903/04 b 15.1.1875 Auckland. d 23.7.1956 Te Kuiti, King Country. wk Team: **Auckland.** Sch: Auckland GS. Occ: Mining agent. Rugby: Taranaki. NZCA obit: 1956. Brothers: Harold B.Lusk, R.B.Lusk; cousin: Hugh B.Lusk.
LUXFORD Frank Hayes 1880/81-1883/84 b 3.5.1862 Wellington. d 1.11.1954 Wellington. Team: **Wellington.** Sch: Wellington Coll. Occ: Farmer.
LYNCH Daniel Joseph Francis 1877/78-1889/90 b 1854 Auckland. d 3.12.1920 Auckland. Team: **Auckland.** Occ: Surveyor. Brother: R.F.Lynch.
LYNCH G 1873/74 Team: **Otago.**
LYNCH Robert Francis 1873/74-1883/84 b 1856 Auckland. d 19.8.1938 Auckland. Team: **Wellington.** Occ: Civil servant. Rugby: Wellington. Brother: D.J.F.Lynch.
LYNCH Robert Kevin 2001/02-2002/03 b 25.5.1982 Auckland. LHB wk Team: **Auckland.** Sch: Auckland GS. NZ U19 Test; NZ U19 ODI. Brother: S.M.Lynch.
LYNCH Stephen Michael 1995/96-1999/00 b 18.2.1976 Auckland. RHB Team: **Auckland.** Played List A in NZ. Sch: Auckland GS. NZ U19 Test; NZ U19 ODI. Brother: R.K.Lynch.
LYON Brendan John 1997/98 b 5.4.1975 Auckland. RHB wk Team: **Auckland.** Played List A in NZ.
LYON Trevor De Jaques 1931/32 b 17.2.1909 Wellington. d 2.6.1984 Thames, Thames Valley. RHB RM Team: **Auckland.** NZCA obit: 1984. ND selector.
LYTHE Timothy Ignatius 2005/06-2007/08 b 19.4.1980 Auckland. RHB OB Teams: **Auckland, Central Districts.** Played List A in NZ; Played T20 in NZ. Sch: Mt Albert GS.
MCALEVEY Lynn George 1975/76 b 31.5.1953 Dunedin, Otago. RHB SLA Team: **Otago.** Sch: Kings HS. Occ: University lecturer.
MCARLEY Vernon Aubrey Clinton 1947/48-1957/58 b 29.9.1923 Dunedin, Otago. RHB RM Team: **Otago.** Sch: Otago BHS. Occ: Schoolteacher. Hockey: Otago.
MACARTNEY Charles George 1905/06-1935/36 b 27.6.1886 West Maitland, New South Wales, Australia. d 9.9.1958 Little Bay, Sydney, New South Wales, Australia. RHB SLA Teams: **Otago,** Australia Test, New South Wales. Sch: Fort Street, Australia. Occ: Clerk. Books: My cricketing days; Charlie Macartney: Cricket's 'Governor-General by P Sharpham. NZCA obit:

1958; Wisden obit: 1959. WCOY: 1922. An Australian pro, played and coached in NZ. Cousin: F.S.Cummins (New South Wales); grandfather: G.Moore (New South Wales); uncles: L.D.Moore (New South Wales), W.H.Moore (New South Wales, Western Australia).

MACASSEY James Ernest 1900/01-1912/13 b 14.3.1878 Dunedin, Otago. d 2.7.1941 Dunedin, Otago. LHB LFM Team: **Hawke's Bay.** Sch: Otago BHS. Occ: Coy manager. Rugby: Hawke's Bay.

MCBEATH Andrew John 1919/20 b 1882 unknown. d 13.9.1930 Invercargill, Southland. He died as the result of an accident. Team: **Southland.** Occ: Driver.

MCBEATH Daniel Jason 1917/18-1926/27 b 8.4.1897 Malvern, Canterbury. d 13.4.1963 Timaru, South Canterbury. LHB LM Teams: **Otago, Canterbury, Southland, New Zealand.** Occ: Coy director. NZCA obit: 1963; Wisden obit: 1964. He played for New Zealand prior to being granted Test status. He took 9/56 for Canterbury v Auckland in 1918/19 and had the best match figures for Canterbury of 15/169 in this game.

MCBEATH G 1919/20 Team: **Southland.**

MCCARTEN Vincent Dennehy Aloysius 1944/45 b 9.4.1913 Dunedin, Otago. d 28.7.1993 Christchurch, Canterbury. RHB occ wk Team: **Otago.** NZCA obit: 1995.

MCCARTHY Bernard 1894/95-1902/03 b 24.7.1874 Charleston, Buller. d 7.7.1948 Hawera, Taranaki. OB Team: **Taranaki, New Zealand.** Sch: St Patricks Coll, Wellington. Occ: Solicitor. NZCA obit: 1948. He played for New Zealand prior to being granted Test status.

MCCARTHY C 1941/42 Team: **Wellington.**

MCCAUSLAND Edward Elsmere Montgomery 1885/86 b 11.5.1865 Victoria, Australia. d 9.11.1936 Bondi, Sydney, New South Wales, Australia. Team: **Wellington.** Occ: Bank manager. Rugby: New Zealand 'Natives'.

MCCAW Peter Malcolm 1952/53 b 10.2.1930 Inglewood, Taranaki. RHB SLA Team: **Wellington.**

MCCLENAGHAN Mitchell John 2007/08-2008/09 b 11.6.1986 Hastings, Hawke's Bay. LHB LMF Team: **Central Districts.** Played List A in NZ; Played T20 in NZ. Sch: Howick Coll. He took a hat-trick for Central Districts v Canterbury in 2008/09.

MCCONE Ryan James 2008/09-2009/10 b 5.9.1987 Christchurch, Canterbury. LHB LM Team: **Canterbury.** Sch: St Andrews Coll. Occ: Student. He scored 102 on first-class debut for Canterbury v Otago in 2008/09 when batting at no.9.

MCCONNELL George Thomas 1960/61-1971/72 b 3.1.1944 Innisfail, Queensland, Australia. RHB OB Team: **Wellington.** Played List A in NZ.

MACCORMICK Arthur Delotte 1888/89 b 1864 Balmain, Sydney, New South Wales, Australia. d 14.1.1948 Sydney, New South Wales, Australia. Team: **Otago.** Brothers: C.E.MacCormick, E.MacCormick.

MACCORMICK Charles Edward 1884/85-1893/94 b 29.1.1862 Balmain, Sydney, New South Wales, Australia. d 30.7.1945 Auckland. Team: **Auckland.** Sch: Auckland GS. Occ: Judge. Umpired first-class cricket. In 1906 he was appointed a judge of the Native Land Court and in 1940 was appointed Chief Justice. He was heavily involved in the administration of Auckland cricket and rugby. Brothers: E.MacCormick, A.D.MacCormick.

MACCORMICK Evan 1900/01-1913/14 b 15.3.1882 Auckland. d 13.11.1918 Auckland. He died of Spanish flu aged 36. Team: **Auckland.** Sch: Auckland GS. Occ: Solicitor. Rugby: Auckland. Brothers: C.E.MacCormick, A.D.MacCormick.

MCCOY Alan Winston 1929/30-1936/37 b 13.1.1906 Geraldine, South Canterbury. d 1.1.1980 Auckland. LHB LB Team: **Auckland.** Sch: Auckland GS. Great-nephew: S.L.J.M.Hawk (Durham UCCE).

MCCULLOUGH Robert Bruce 1971/72 b 13.6.1943 Waipawa, Hawke's Bay. RHB LM Team: **Wellington.**

MCCULLUM Brendon Barrie 1999/00-2009/10 b 27.9.1981 Dunedin, Otago. RHB wk Teams: **Otago, Canterbury, New Zealand Test, New Zealand ODI, New Zealand T20,** Glamorgan. Played List A in NZ; Played T20 in NZ. Sch: Kings HS. Occ: Cricket pro. NZ U19 Test; NZ U19 ODI. NZCA COY: 2008. He holds the NZ Test 6th wicket partnership record of 339 with M.J.Guptill against Bangladesh in 2009/10, the world record for the highest T20 score 158* for Kolkata v Bangalore in 2007/08 and the NZ record for the highest T20 international score with 116* v Australia in 2009/10. Brother: N.L.McCullum; father: S.J.McCullum.

MCCULLUM Nathan Leslie 1999/00-2009/10 b 1.9.1980 Dunedin, Otago. RHB OB Teams: **Otago, New Zealand ODI, New Zealand T20.** Played List A in NZ; Played T20 in NZ. Sch: Kings HS. NZ U19 ODI. He holds the NZ domestic T20 4th wicket partnership record of 140* with A.C.Mascarenhas for Otago against Canterbury in 2008/09. Brother: B.B.McCullum; father: S.J.McCullum.

MCCULLUM Stuart James 1976/77-1990/91 b 6.12.1956 Eltham, Taranaki. LHB occ wk Team: **Otago.** Played List A in NZ. Sch: Kings HS. Otago selector. Sons: B.B.McCullum, N.L.McCullum.

MCDERMID E W 1906/07 b Melbourne, Victoria, Australia. Team: **Wellington.** An Australian known to be in NZ between 1906 and 1907.

MCDONALD Colin John 1968/69 b 8.2.1948 Dunedin, Otago. d 3.10.2005 Invercargill, Southland. RHB RFM Team: **Otago.** Sch: Kings HS. Occ: Journalist. NZCA obit: 2006.

MACDONALD F 1863/64 b Victoria, Australia. Team: **Otago.** He came from Australia where he had played club cricket in Melbourne but nothing is known of him after 1864. He had match figures of 10/31 in his only first-class match.

MACDONALD Farquhar A 1889/90-1896/97 b 30.9.1866 New Zealand. d 7.4.1919 Auckland. Team: **Canterbury.** Occ: Sheep farmer.

MACDONALD Garry Kevin 1984/85-1990/91 b 12.8.1956 Blenheim, Marlborough. LHB SLA Team: **Canterbury.** Sch: Marlborough Boys Coll. Occ: Cricket coach. Canterbury selector.

MCDONALD John William 1956/57-1957/58 b 7.4.1933 Hamilton, Waikato. RMF Team: **Auckland.**

MCDONNELL Randell Thomas 1864/65-1875/76 b 27.1.1843 St Pancras, London, England. d 12.4.1923 Dunedin, Otago. Teams: **Canterbury, Otago.** Occ: Saddler. Umpired first-class cricket.

MCDONOGH James John Murphy 1893/94-1908/09 b 13.4.1871 Killarney, Co Kerry, Ireland. d 26.1.1912 Philadelphia, Pennsylvania, United States of America. He died aged 40. Teams: **North Island,** Europeans (India), Gentlemen of Philadelphia. Occ: Soldier. Wisden obit: 1913. He was one of the participants in the Jameson Raid in South Africa in 1896, an event which precipitated the Anglo-Boer war. He subsequently served with distinction in the Anglo-Boer War and subsequently saw service in Egypt. He played cricket in NZ whilst living there in the early 1890s.

MCDOUGALL Angus William 1944/45-1946/47 b 2.4.1913 Port Chalmers, Dunedin, Otago. d 3.5.1983 Lower Hutt, Wellington. RHB RM Team: **Otago.** Occ: Policeman. NZCA obit: 1983.

MCDOWELL William 1883/84 b 1837 Scotland. d 14.6.1918 Christchurch, Canterbury. Team: **Canterbury.** Occ: Labourer.

MACE Christopher 1861/62-1863/64 b 24.12.1830 Bedale, Yorkshire, England. d 23.11.1907 Sydenham, Christchurch, Canterbury. He died of influenza brought on by bronchitis. Teams: **Otago,** Victoria. Occ: Miner. Brothers: J.Mace, H.Mace.

MACE Henry 1877/78 b 4.6.1837 Bedale, Yorkshire, England. d 19.7.1902 New Brighton, Christchurch, Canterbury. He died of rheumatic fever. wk Team: **Wellington.** Sch: Bedale Sch, England. Occ: Cordial manufacturer. Umpired first-class cricket. In 1861 he came to New Zealand. The township of Macetown was named after his family. Brothers: C.Mace, J.Mace.

MACE John 1860/61-1863/64 b 28.12.1828 Bedale, Yorkshire, England. d 30.4.1905 Te Aroha, Thames Valley. RHB LMr Teams: **Otago,** Victoria. Occ: Farmer. Brothers: C.Mace, H.Mace.

MCEWAN Murray Lawson 1957/58 b 20.9.1936 Dunedin, Otago. d 4.4.1984 Otaki, Horowhenua. LHB Team: **Otago.** Sch: Otago BHS. Occ: Bank officer. Basketball: Southland. NZCA obit: 1984.

MCEWAN Paul Ernest 1976/77-1990/91 b 19.12.1953 Christchurch, Canterbury. RHB RM Teams: **Canterbury, New Zealand Test, New Zealand ODI.** Played List A in NZ. Sch: St Andrews Coll. Occ: Finance advisor.

MCEWIN James Nankivell 1917/18-1927/28 b 11.9.1898 Wellington. d 13.6.1979 Christchurch, Canterbury. RHB LBG Team: **Canterbury.** Occ: Storeman.

MACFARLANE James 1887/88-1895/96 b 17.7.1866 Dunedin, Otago. d 11.12.1942 Dunedin, Otago. Teams: **Otago, Canterbury.** Occ: Bootmaker.

MCFARLANE John Hugh 1964/65 b 30.9.1933 Mount Gambier, South Australia, Australia. RHB RM Team: **Northern Districts.**

MACFARLANE Thomas 1870/71-1873/74 Team: **Otago**.
MCFARLANE Thomas Albert 1909/10-1919/20 b 9.7.1890 Dunedin, Otago. d 20.4.1967 Palmerston North, Manawatu. RHB Team: **Otago, New Zealand**. Occ: Foundry worker. Umpired first-class cricket. NZCA obit: 1967; Wisden obit: 1968. He played for New Zealand prior to being granted Test status.
MACGIBBON Anthony Roy 1947/48-1961/62 b 28.8.1924 Christchurch, Canterbury. d 6.4.2010 Christchurch, Canterbury. RHB RFM Teams: **Canterbury, New Zealand Test**. Sch: Christ Coll. Occ: Engineer. NZCA COY: 1954. Canterbury and Wellington selector.
MCGILL Rex 1969/70-1971/72 b 17.3.1949 Te Awamutu, Waikato. LHB OB Team: **Northern Districts**.
MCGIRR Herbert Mendelson 1913/14-1932/33 b 5.11.1891 Wellington. d 14.4.1964 Nelson. RHB RM Teams: **Wellington, New Zealand Test**. Occ: Cricket coach. NZCA obit: 1964; Wisden obit: 1965. He was aged 38 when he made his Test debut. Father: W.P.McGirr.
MCGIRR William Peter 1883/84-1889/90 b 12.12.1859 Melbourne, Victoria, Australia. d 6.5.1934 Wellington. M Team: **Wellington**. Sch: Model Sch, Melbourne, Australia. Occ: Printer. Umpired first-class cricket. Son: H.M.McGirr.
MCGLASHAN Peter Donald 2000/01-2009/10 b 22.6.1979 Napier, Hawke's Bay. RHB wk Teams: **Central Districts, Otago, Northern Districts, New Zealand ODI, New Zealand T20**. Played List A in NZ; Played T20 in NZ. Sch: Napier BHS. Occ: Cricket pro. NZ U19 Test; NZ U19 ODI. He took a NZ record of 12 catches in a FC match for Northern Districts v Central Districts in 2009/10. He holds the Northern Districts 8th wicket partnership record of 163 with G.W.Aldridge against Canterbury in 2008/09 and the Northern Districts 10th wicket partnership record of 113* with G.W.Aldridge against Wellington in 2005/06. Grandfather: R.M.Schofield.
MCGREGOR Gordon George 1935/36-1939/40 b 4.1.1915 Dunedin, Otago. d 24.10.1982 Dunedin, Otago. RHB RAB Team: **Otago**. Occ: Civil servant.
MCGREGOR J 1884/85 Team: **Otago**.
MCGREGOR Peter Brien 1960/61-1974/75 b 28.12.1941 Auckland. RHB RM Teams: **Auckland, Northern Districts, Wellington, Central Districts**. Played List A in NZ. Sch: Auckland GS. Auckland and Wellington selector.
MCGREGOR Spencer Noel 1947/48-1968/69 b 18.12.1931 Dunedin, Otago. d 21.11.2007 Christchurch, Canterbury. RHB occ wk Teams: **Otago, New Zealand Test**. Sch: King Edward Tech Coll. NZCA obit: 2008; Wisden obit: 2008. NZCA COY: 1968. NZ, Otago and Canterbury selector.
MCGREGOR Thomas 1879/80 LHB LM Team: **West Coast (North Island)**.
MCGUIRE Alexander James 1957/58 b 5.10.1932 Wellington. RHB Team: **Central Districts**.
MCHAFFIE James 1931/32 b 22.6.1910 Glasgow, Lanarkshire, Scotland. d 27.5.1994 Wellington. Team: **Otago**. Sch: Otago BHS. Occ: Doctor.
MCHARDY David Scott 1991/92-1997/98 b 21.11.1970 Blenheim, Marlborough. RHB LB occ wk Teams: **Otago, Wellington**. Played List A in NZ.
MCINNIS Evon Junior 2003/04-2007/08 b 2.1.1980 St Elizabeth, Jamaica. RHB RMF Teams: **Central Districts**, Jamaica. Played List A in NZ.
MCINTOSH Colin Fraser 1914/15 b 17.5.1892 Queensland, Australia. d 23.3.1977 Wellington. Team: **Wellington**.
MCINTOSH Timothy Gavin 1998/99-2009/10 b 4.12.1979 Auckland. LHB occ wk Teams: **Auckland, Canterbury, New Zealand Test**. Played List A in NZ. Sch: Auckland GS. NZ U19 Test; NZ U19 ODI.
MCINTYRE John Mclachlan 1961/62-1982/83 b 4.7.1944 Auckland. LHB SLA Teams: **Auckland, Canterbury, New Zealand**. Played List A in NZ. Sch: Auckland GS. Occ: Salesman. NZCA COY: 1981. He played for New Zealand in a FC match.
MCINTYRE Patrick J 1887/88 b 1844 New Zealand. d 23.11.1898 Wellington. He died from laryngitis. Team: **Wellington**. Occ: Civil servant. Umpired first-class cricket.
MCKAY Andrew John 2002/03-2009/10 b 17.4.1980 Auckland. RHB LFM Teams: **Auckland, Wellington, New Zealand ODI, New Zealand T20**. Played List A in NZ; Played T20 in NZ. Occ: Physiotherapist.

MCKECHNIE Brian John 1971/72-1985/86 b 6.11.1953 Gore, Southland. RHB RFM Teams: **Otago, New Zealand ODI.** Played List A in NZ. Sch: Southland BHS. Occ: Accountant. Rugby: All Blacks and Southland. Book: Double All Black. NZ and Canterbury selector.
MCKECHNIE Donald Ernest Cameron 1975/76-1980/81 b 23.3.1944 Dunedin, Otago. RHB SLA Team: **Otago.** Played List A in NZ. Sch: Kings HS. Umpired first-class cricket.
MCKELLAR Arnaud Henry 1919/20 b 17.11.1891 Auckland. d 28.4.1968 Nelson. Team: **Wellington.** Occ: Canister maker.
MCKENNA Terry Murray 1987/88-1989/90 b 30.4.1964 Lower Hutt, Wellington. RHB RM Team: **Central Districts.** Played List A in NZ. Occ: Sales manager.
MCKENZIE Grant William 1983/84-1990/91 b 11.5.1961 Napier, Hawke's Bay. RHB SLA Team: **Northern Districts.** Played List A in NZ. Sch: Nelson Coll.
MACKENZIE Gregory John 1990/91-1992/93 b 7.12.1967 Brisbane, Queensland, Australia. RHB RM Team: **Wellington.**
MCKENZIE Henry Alexander Willmore 1876/77 b 24.3.1851 Wellington. d 13.11.1918 Wellington. Team: **Wellington.** Sch: Wellington Coll. Occ: Journalist.
MCKENZIE John 1893/94-1894/95 Team: **Otago.**
MCKENZIE Marcel Norman 1998/99-2007/08 b 13.5.1978 Oamaru, North Otago. RHB LB Teams: **Canterbury, Otago.** Played List A in NZ. Sch: Shirley BHS. Father: N.W.McKenzie.
MACKENZIE Michael Curran 1992/93 b 18.9.1974 Ranfurly, Central Otago. RHB LB Team: **Otago.**
MCKENZIE Norman Wills 1972/73 b 7.5.1946 Kurow, North Otago. RHB SLA Team: **Otago.** Son: M.N.McKenzie.
MACKENZIE Robert Henry Craig 1929/30 b 17.2.1904 Wellington. d 19.7.1993 Wellington. RHB Team: **Wellington.** Sch: Wellington Coll. Occ: Schoolteacher. Rugby: All Blacks and Wellington. Books: Walter Nash: Pioneer and Prophet; History of the Hutt Hospital. NZCA obit: 1996.
MCKEOWN James Arthur 1938/39-1954/55 b 2.3.1916 Wellington. d 9.4.1976 Wellington. LBG Team: **Wellington.**
MACKERSY William Wallace 1906/07-1907/08 b 6.5.1875 Alexandra, Central Otago. d 27.2.1959 Dunedin, Otago. LB Team: **Otago.** Occ: Coy manager. Umpired first-class cricket.
MACKINLAY Robb Ian James 1986/87 b 20.12.1966 Auckland. RHB Team: **Auckland.** Sch: Auckland GS. Occ: Accountant. NZ U19 Test.
MCKINNON Mark Robert 1983/84-1988/89 b 10.4.1960 Auckland. RHB OB Team: **Northern Districts.**
MACKLE John McGregor 1980/81-1981/82 b 15.8.1953 Temuka, South Canterbury. d 27.6.2010 Christchurch, Canterbury. RHB wk Team: **Canterbury.** Played List A in NZ. Sch: St Bedes Coll.
MCKNIGHT Kenneth James 1987/88-1991/92 b 8.4.1964 Ranfurly, Central Otago. LHB wk Team: **Otago.** Sch: Otago BHS. Father: S.G.McKnight.
MCKNIGHT Stewart Gemmell 1958/59-1966/67 b 9.1.1935 Ranfurly, Central Otago. RHB Team: **Otago.** Sch: Otago BHS. Occ: Farmer. Curling: New Zealand. Otago selector. Life member of Otago Cricket and Otago Rugby. Son: K.J.McKnight.
MCLACHLAN Duncan Bell 1912/13-1921/22 b 30.10.1893 Dunedin, Otago. d 15.9.1958 Chatswood, Sydney, New South Wales, Australia. Teams: **Otago, Canterbury.** Occ: Piano tuner.
MCLEAN Alan 1947/48 RHB RM Team: **Wellington.**
MCLEAN Nixon Alexei Mcnamara 1992/93-2005/06 b 20.7.1973 Stubbs, St Vincent. LHB RF Teams: **Canterbury,** Hampshire, Somerset, Kwazulu-Natal, West Indies Test, West Indies ODI, Windward Islands, St Vincent and the Grenadines. Played List A in NZ. Occ: Cricket pro. Cousin: R.J.J.McLean (Windward Islands).
MCLELLAN George William 1965/66-1967/68 b 6.9.1940 Wellington. RHB Team: **Wellington.**
MCLENNAN William 1879/80 F Team: **Otago.** Occ: Baker.
MACLEOD Donald Norman 1956/57-1967/68 b 17.11.1932 Wellington. d 29.5.2008 Auckland. RHB OB Teams: **Central Districts, Wellington, Canterbury.** Sch: Wellington Coll. Rugby: Wellington. NZCA obit: 2008. He scored 117 on his first-class debut for Central Districts v Wellington in 1956/57.

MCLEOD Edwin George 1920/21-1940/41 b 14.10.1900 Auckland. d 14.9.1989 Auckland. LHB LB Teams: **Auckland, Wellington, New Zealand Test.** Sch: Auckland GS. Occ: Railway employee. Hockey: New Zealand; national selector. NZCA obit: 1990; Wisden obit: 1990. At the time of his death he was the oldest surviving Test cricketer.

MCLEOD John Colin 1970/71-1971/72 b 30.9.1947 Whangarei, Northland. RHB LB Team: **Northern Districts.**

MCLEOD Richard James 1990/91 b 13.10.1965 Nelson. RHB RFM Team: **Central Districts.**

MCMAHON Francis Leonard 1908/09-1913/14 b 9.10.1887 North Sydney, New South Wales, Australia. d 5.7.1968 Porirua, Wellington. RHB Team: **Auckland, New Zealand.** Occ: Hotel employee. NZCA obit: 1971. He played for New Zealand prior to being granted Test status. He shared a 518-run partnership with A.Young in a Gisborne club game in 1910/11 - this is the highest partnership in any grade of cricket in NZ.

MCMAHON Noel Albert 1936/37-1949/50 b 24.5.1916 Auckland. RHB LB Teams: **Auckland, New Zealand.** He played for New Zealand in a FC match.

MCMAHON Trevor George 1953/54-1964/65 b 8.11.1929 Wellington. RHB wk Teams: **Wellington, New Zealand Test.** Wellington selector. Son: P.J.S.McMahon.

MCMASTER George Henry 1891/92 b 1862 unknown. d 14.9.1944 Wellington. Team: **Wellington.** Occ: Civil servant.

MCMATH William 1917/18-1918/19 b 1881 Amherst, Victoria, Australia. d 5.12.1920 Auckland. He died in hospital as a result of injuries received through being run over by a tram when both his legs were severed. RHB RM Team: **Auckland.** Occ: Grocer.

MCMILLAN Craig Douglas 1994/95-2007 b 13.9.1976 Christchurch, Canterbury. RHB RM Teams: **Canterbury, New Zealand Test, New Zealand ODI, New Zealand T20,** Hampshire. Played List A in NZ; Played T20 in NZ. Sch: Shirley BHS. NZ U19 Test; NZ U19 ODI. Book: Out of the park. NZCA COY: 2001. He holds the NZ Test 5th wicket partnership record of 222 with N.J.Astle against Zimbabwe in 2000/01. In 2000/01 he took 26 runs off an over by Younis Khan which was a record at the time. He holds the New Zealand record for the fastest ODI century (off 67 balls) against Australia in 2006/07. Cousin: J.M.McMillan.

MCMILLAN James Michael 2000/01-2009/10 b 14.6.1978 Christchurch, Canterbury. RHB RFM Team: **Otago.** Played List A in NZ; Played T20 in NZ. Cousin: C.D.McMillan.

MCMILLAN Norman Henry 1931/32 b 2.9.1906 Timaru, South Canterbury. d 16.7.1942 El Alemain, Egypt. He was killed in action aged 33. Team: **Auckland.** Sch: Kings Coll. Occ: Bank officer. Wisden obit: 1943.

MCMULLAN John James Morrell 1917/18-1929/30 b 23.4.1893 Dunedin, Otago. d 28.4.1967 Dunedin, Otago. LHB occ wk Team: **Otago.** NZCA obit: 1967. NZ selector. He scored 157* on his first-class debut for Otago v Southland in 1917/18.

MCMURRAY Samuel 1884/85-1896/97 b 1863 Ireland. d 24.8.1937 Christchurch, Canterbury. Team: **Canterbury.** Sch: West Christchurch BHS. Occ: Timber merchant.

MCNALLY Stephen Ray 1978/79-1985/86 b 28.9.1958 Christchurch, Canterbury. RHB LM Team: **Canterbury.** Played List A in NZ. Occ: Coy director.

MCNEIL Frank Anderson 1905/06 b 1877 New Zealand. d 21.10.1930 Wellington. Team: **Auckland.**

MACNEIL Hugh 1877/78-1893/94 b 26.10.1860 Glasgow, Lanarkshire, Scotland. d 14.9.1924 Townsville, Queensland, Australia. RHB Team: **Otago.** Sch: Christ Coll; Otago BHS. Occ: Tobacconist. Golf: New Zealand Amateur Champion 1894; Australian Amateur Champion 1902. Umpired first-class cricket.

MCNICHOLL Kenneth James 1952/53-1956/57 b 27.11.1930 Prebbleton, Christchurch, Canterbury. d 23.11.1997 Christchurch, Canterbury. LHB RM Team: **Canterbury.** NZCA obit: 1998.

MCPHERSON Robert 1889/90 b 1864 Christchurch, Canterbury. d 13.10.1904 Auckland. Team: **Auckland.** Occ: Schoolteacher.

MCPHERSON Ross James 1959/60-1970/71 b 24.10.1938 Whangarei, Northland. LHB LB Team: **Northern Districts.** Sch: Whangarei HS.

MCRAE Donald Alexander Noel 1937/38-1945/46 b 25.12.1912 Christchurch, Canterbury. d 10.8.1986 Christchurch, Canterbury. LHB LM Teams: **Canterbury, New Zealand Test.** Soccer: New Zealand. NZCA obit: 1994; Wisden obit: 1995.

MCRAE Gavin Peter 1993/94 b 24.3.1965 Blenheim, Marlborough. RHB wk Team: **Central Districts.** Played List A in NZ.
MCSKIMMING Warren Charles 1999/00-2009/10 b 21.6.1979 Ranfurly, Central Otago. RHB RM Team: **Otago.** Played List A in NZ; Played T20 in NZ. Sch: Waitaki BHS. NZ U19 ODI. He holds the Otago 9th wicket partnership record of 208 with B.E.Scott against Auckland in 2004/05 and the NZ domestic T20 10th wicket partnership record of 29 with I.G.Butler for Otago against Central Districts in 2009/10.
MCSWEENEY Ervin Bruce 1979/80-1993/94 b 8.3.1957 Wellington. RHB wk Teams: **Central Districts, Wellington, New Zealand ODI.** Played List A in NZ. Sch: Colenso HS. Occ: Cricket administrator. He holds the Wellington 5th wicket partnership record of 341 with G.R.Larsen against Central Districts in 1987/88.
MCVICAR Alexander Cameron 1920/21 b 15.4.1885 Wellington. d 21.7.1964 Palmerston North, Manawatu. Team: **Minor Associations.** Sch: Mt Cook HS. Occ: Train driver. NZCA obit: 1964. Sons: C.C.McVicar, S.A.McVicar.
MCVICAR Colin Cameron 1950/51-1951/52 b 3.6.1916 Palmerston North, Manawatu. d 17.2.1987 Palmerston North, Manawatu. RHB SLA Team: **Central Districts.** Sch: Palmerston North BHS. Occ: Clerk. NZCA obit: 1987. Brother: S.A.McVicar; father: A.C.McVicar.
MCVICAR Stuart Alexander 1943/44-1950/51 b 15.7.1918 Palmerston North, Manawatu. d 13.1.1990 Kenepuru, Porirua, Wellington. RHB Team: **Wellington.** Brother: C.C.McVicar; father: A.C.McVicar.
MADDOCK Henry Dyer 1863/64-1869/70 b 1836 New Zealand. d 30.9.1888 Woollahra, Sydney, New South Wales, Australia. u Team: **Otago.** Occ: Solicitor. MP.
MAGUINESS Stephen James 1981/82-1987/88 b 27.1.1959 Palmerston North, Manawatu. RHB RM Team: **Wellington.** Played List A in NZ. He took a hat-trick for Wellington v Northern Districts in 1983/84. Uncle: B.G.Griffiths.
MAHONEY Jeremiah John 1902/03-1911/12 b 26.7.1880 Sydney, New South Wales, Australia. d 1.8.1966 Sydney, New South Wales, Australia. RHB wk Teams: **Wellington, New Zealand.** Occ: Tailor's presser. He played for New Zealand prior to being granted Test status.
MAHONEY Lawrence Albert 1948/49 b 14.9.1911 Christchurch, Canterbury. d 30.1.2008 Christchurch, Canterbury. RHB RM Team: **Canterbury.** Sch: Rangiora HS. Occ: Branch manager. MBE. NZCA obit: 2008.
MAINGAY Cameron Tenison 1970/71 b 27.10.1937 Paparoa, Northland. RHB RM Team: **Auckland.** Played List A in NZ. Occ: Real estate agent. Auckland selector.
MAINWARING Randolph 1866/67-1870/71 c 26.7.1840 Whitmoor, Staffordshire, England. d 12.1902 Edmonton, Middlesex, England. Team: **Canterbury.** Sch: Rugby, England. Occ: Civil servant; journalist. He was also well known as a journalist, writer, and artist.
MALCOLM Robert John 1882/83-1883/84 b 14.11.1864 Waimea West, Nelson. d 4.11.1922 Masterton, Wairarapa. Team: **Nelson.** Sch: Nelson Coll. Occ: Bank clerk.
MALCOLM Thomas James 1885/86 b 1861 Ballarat, Victoria, Australia. d 29.10.1897 Wellington. Team: **Wellington.** Occ: Warehouseman.
MALCOLM Walter 1914/15 b 25.12.1893 Blenheim, Marlborough. d 23.12.1917 Poeleapelle, Belgium. He was killed in action aged 22. Team: **Otago.** Occ: Maltster.
MALCON Patrick John 1972/73 b 2.4.1947 Gisborne, Poverty Bay. RHB Team: **Wellington.** Played List A in NZ. Occ: Cricket admin. ND selector.
MALET Francis Blundell Warre 1883/84 b 26.3.1855 Bengal, India. wk Team: **Canterbury.** Occ: Accountant. He patented a wire strainer in 1882, was bankrupt in UK 1887, discharged 1901, and nothing is known of him after that.
MALLARD John James Jaffray 1882/83-1884/85 b 18.12.1860 West Melbourne, Victoria, Australia. d 26.3.1935 Dunedin, Otago. Team: **Otago.** Sch: Otago BHS. Occ: Insurance manager. Rugby: Otago.
MALLENDER Neil Alan 1980-1996 b 13.8.1961 Kirk Sandall, Yorkshire, England. RHB RFM Teams: **Otago,** England Test, Northamptonshire, Somerset. Played List A in NZ. Sch: Beverley GS, England. Occ: Umpire. Umpired first-class cricket. An English pro, played and coached in NZ.
MALLOCH Trevor Stuart 1953/54 b 2.12.1928 Wellington. RHB RFM Team: **Wellington.**

MALONE Thomas Joseph 1895/96-1908/09 b 17.5.1876 Christchurch, Canterbury. d 5.6.1933 Christchurch, Canterbury. RHB RS Team: **Canterbury, New Zealand**. Occ: Grinder. He played for NZ in a non-first-class match prior to being granted Test status. In this match against Melbourne Cricket Club he captured 7/64.

MANSILL Charles Henry 1882/83 b 1861 Wellington. d 16.8.1945 Auckland. Team: **Wellington**. Sch: Te Aroha Coll. Occ: Builder.

MAPLES Edward 1868/69-1873/74 b 1840 Liverpool, Lancashire, England. d 8.6.1878 Christchurch, Canterbury. Team: **Canterbury**. Occ: Farmer. Umpired first-class cricket.

MAPPLEBECK Walter Oliver 1936/37-1940/41 b 19.7.1914 Christchurch, Canterbury. d 27.4.1992 Lower Hutt, Wellington. RHB RFM Team: **Canterbury**. Sch: Christchurch BHS. Occ: Schoolmaster. NZCA obit: 1992; Wisden obit: 1993.

MARC Kervin 1994-1999/00 b 9.1.1975 Mon Repos, St Lucia. RHB RF Teams: **Central Districts**, Middlesex. Sch: London Oratory, England. Occ: Fashion designer. An English pro, played and coached in NZ.

MARCHANT John William Allman 1873/74-1881/82 b 9.10.1841 Belgaum, Mysore, India. d 22.12.1920 Wellington. Team: **Wellington**. Sch: Queens Coll, Hampshire, England. Occ: Surveyor. Chief Surveyor for Canterbury and in 1902 became Surveyor General of New Zealand.

MARCROFT Walter Henry 1894/95 b 2.1.1868 Kaipara, Northland. d 10.11.1963 Auckland. Team: **Taranaki**. Sch: Whangarei HS. Occ: Carpenter.

MARRIS Brian Alfred 1917/18-1919/20 LB Team: **Wellington**. Sch: Wellington Coll.

MARSDON John Pascoe 1948/49-1959/60 b 5.2.1928 Auckland. LHB LM Team: **Auckland**. Sch: Auckland GS.

MARSHALL Evan James 1990/91-2001/02 b 29.1.1970 Invercargill, Southland. LHB RM Team: **Otago**. Played List A in NZ. Sch: James Hargest HS.

MARSHALL George 1888/89-1901/02 b 1863 Scotland. d 1.7.1907 Christchurch, Canterbury. He died of nephritis aged 44. RHB occ wk Teams: **Canterbury, Hawke's Bay**. Occ: Insurance manager.

MARSHALL Hamish John Hamilton 1998/99-2010 b 15.2.1979 Warkworth, Rodney. RHB RM occ wk Teams: **Northern Districts, New Zealand Test, New Zealand ODI, New Zealand T20**, Gloucestershire. Played List A in NZ; Played T20 in NZ. Sch: Kings Coll. NZ U19 ODI. NZCA COY: 2005. Twin brother: J.A.H.Marshall.

MARSHALL James Andrew Hamilton 1997/98-2009/10 b 15.2.1979 Warkworth, Rodney. RHB RM Teams: **Northern Districts, New Zealand Test, New Zealand ODI, New Zealand T20**. Played List A in NZ; Played T20 in NZ. Sch: Kings Coll. NZ U19 ODI. He holds the Northern Districts 5th wicket partnership record of 155 with N.K.W.Horsley against Canterbury in 2005/06. Twin brother: H.J.H.Marshall.

MARSHALL Joy Marriott 1891/92 b 23.1.1867 Isleworth, Middlesex, England. d 2.9.1903 Heathcote River, Christchurch, Canterbury. He was found drowned in the Heathcote river, an inquest returning an open verdict. wk Team: **Taranaki**. Sch: Haileybury, England; Wanganui CS. Occ: Anglican Reverend. Rugby: Canterbury and Wanganui. Tennis: New Zealand singles champion in 1890 and 1896, New Zealand doubles champion with brother Patrick in 1893. Wisden obit: 1905. In a fill-up exhibition match against Lord Hawke's team at Wanganui in 1902/03 he scored 109*. Brother: P.Marshall.

MARSHALL Kevin Brian 1983/84 b 25.4.1958 Wellington. RHB RM Team: **Wellington**. Played List A in NZ.

MARSHALL Patrick 1900/01 b 22.12.1869 Sapiston, Suffolk, England. d 10.11.1950 Wellington. Team: **Auckland**. Sch: Wanganui CS. Occ: Professor. Rugby: Canterbury. Tennis: NZ doubles champion with brother J.M. in 1893. Books: He wrote 22 books and textbooks on the geography and geology of New Zealand. Brother: J.M.Marshall.

MARSHALL Peter Gordon 1991/92 b 4.4.1963 Gore, Southland. LHB LM Team: **Otago**.

MARSHALL Robert Alexander 1936/37 b Q1 1913 Taumarunui, King Country. d 23.8.1956 Hamilton, Waikato. wk Team: **Auckland**. Occ: Veterinary assistant.

MARTIN A 1896/97-1897/98 wk Team: **Hawke's Bay**.

MARTIN Bruce Philip 1999/00-2009/10 b 25.4.1980 Whangarei, Northland. RHB SLA Team: **Northern Districts**. Played List A in NZ; Played T20 in NZ. Sch: Kerikeri HS. NZ U19 Test; NZ U19 ODI.

MARTIN Christopher Stewart 1997/98-2010 b 10.12.1974 Christchurch, Canterbury. RHB RFM Teams: **Canterbury, Auckland, New Zealand Test, New Zealand ODI, New Zealand T20,** Warwickshire, Essex. Played List A in NZ; Played T20 in NZ. Sch: Christchurch BHS. Occ: Cricket pro. NZCA COY: 2005.
MARTIN George Alexander 1908/09 b 3.5.1869 Napier, Hawke's Bay. d 24.2.1961 Dunedin, Otago. Team: **Otago.** Occ: Tailor.
MARTIN Harry 1883/84-1897/98 Team: **Hawke's Bay.** Brother: J.H.Martin.
MARTIN James Henry 1883/84-1896/97 b 1861 New Zealand. d 31.7.1933 Napier, Hawke's Bay. Team: **Hawke's Bay.** Occ: Tailor. Umpired first-class cricket. Brother: H.Martin.
MARTIN Kenneth Wayne 1984/85-1987/88 b 28.4.1953 New Plymouth, Taranaki. RHB RM Team: **Central Districts.** Played List A in NZ.
MARTIN Wayne Stuart 1976/77 b 23.12.1955 Mosgiel, Otago. RHB RMF Teams: **New Zealand Under-23s, Otago (not FC).** Played List A in NZ.
MASEFIELD Robert Valentine 1984/85 b 19.8.1955 Akaroa, Canterbury. RHB LB Team: **Canterbury.** Sch: Christ Coll. Occ: Farmer.
MASON Frederick Richard 1902/03-1914/15 b 4.2.1881 Onekawa, Napier, Hawke's Bay. d 11.5.1936 Ponsonby, Auckland. RHB Teams: **Auckland, New Zealand.** Occ: Accountant. Wisden obit: 1937. He played for New Zealand prior to being granted Test status.
MASON Ian Robert 1960/61-1965/66 b 14.4.1942 Wellington. RHB Team: **Wellington.**
MASON Michael James 1997/98-2009/10 b 27.8.1974 Carterton, Wairarapa. RHB RFM Teams: **Central Districts, New Zealand Test, New Zealand ODI, New Zealand T20.** Played List A in NZ; Played T20 in NZ. Sch: Kuranui Coll. Occ: Cricket pro.
MASON Walter Finch 1873/74-1875/76 b 27.12.1847 Yateley, Hampshire, England. d 18.10.1924 Onerahi, Whangarei, Northland. Team: **Wellington.** Sch: Wellington Coll, England. Occ: Sheep farmer. He came to New Zealand in the late 1860s supposedly to embark on sheep farming but apparently thought that the pioneering farming lifestyle required was beneath him and lived by independent means.
MASSEY Harold Bruce 1926/27-1932/33 b 13.4.1906 Gisborne, Poverty Bay. d 9.7.1994 Queensland, Australia. RHB RM Team: **Wellington.** Sch: Mt Cook HS.
MASTERS Terence Cooper 1969/70 b 28.3.1945 Dunedin, Otago. RHB RMF Team: **Northern Districts.**
MATATUMUA Ata Mamea 1966/67-1967/68 b 28.9.1940 Apia, Upolu, Samoa. RHB RM Team: **Otago.** Sch: Samoa Coll. Occ: Doctor.
MATHER Stephen Robert 1993/94-2000/01 b 13.8.1973 Napier, Hawke's Bay. RHB RM Teams: **Wellington, Otago.** Played List A in NZ. NZ U19 Test; NZ U19 ODI.
MATHESON Alexander Malcolm 1926/27-1946/47 b 27.2.1906 Omaha, North Auckland. d 31.12.1985 Auckland. RHB RM Teams: **Auckland, Wellington, New Zealand Test.** Sch: Auckland GS. Occ: Headmaster. Rugby: Otago and Auckland, Test referee. NZCA obit: 1986; Wisden obit: 1987. Wellington selector. He holds the Auckland 7th wicket partnership record of 224 with V.J.Scott against Canterbury in 1937/38 and the Auckland 8th wicket partnership record of 189 with W.N.Carson against Wellington in 1938/39.
MATHIAS Harold Rolleston 1883/84-1886/87 b 1864 Christchurch, Canterbury. d 8.4.1954 Lawrence, Otago. Team: **Canterbury.** Sch: Christ Coll. Occ: Sheep farmer. Rugby: Canterbury. Brother: R.B.Mathias.
MATHIAS Rodolph Blofield 1888/89-1893/94 b 5.6.1861 Christchurch, Canterbury. d 22.10.1907 Napier, Hawke's Bay. He died from a paralytic seizure. Team: **Canterbury.** Sch: Christ Coll. Occ: Deputy court registrar. Brother: H.R.Mathias.
MATHIESON John 1882/83 OB Team: **Taranaki.** Occ: Bush worker. He married Rhoda Lewis in NZ on 7 March 1884 and was last heard of when he divorced her in 1904 and was reported to be working in the bush in Taranaki province.
MATHIESON Peter Robert 1970/71 b 10.12.1948 Invercargill, Southland. RHB Team: **NZ Under-23s.**
MATTHEWS Dennis Neal 1963/64-1964/65 b 16.7.1943 Paeroa, Thames Valley. LHB LB Team: **Northern Districts.**
MATTHEWS Richard Charles 1969/70-1975/76 b 17.5.1950 Auckland. RHB RFM Team: **Auckland.**

MATTHEWS Samuel James 1942/43 b 3.5.1923 Auckland. d 14.5.1992, Northcote, Auckland. RHB RM Team: **North Island Army.**
MAUNDER Paul Alan 1961/62 b 8.2.1945 Palmerston North, Manawatu. RHB Team: **Central Districts.** Sch: Palmerston North BHS. Occ: Film director. He studied at the National Institute of Dramatic Art in Sydney and the London Film School. Returning to New Zealand he directed three drama productions which were screened on television, before shifting stage to concentrate on theatre. He made his first-class debut aged 16.
MAWHINNEY Russell Eric Wilson 1983/84-1990/91 b 28.3.1960 Ranfurly, Central Otago. LHB LM Teams: **Otago, Northern Districts,** Griqualand West. Played List A in NZ. Sch: Ranfurly HS. Occ: Lawyer.
MAYALL David 1913/14 b 4.6.1891 Auckland. d 18.11.1972 Auckland. wk Team: **Auckland.** Sch: Northcote. Occ: Orchardist.
MAYNARD Matthew Peter 1985-2005 b 21.3.1966 Oldham, Lancashire, England. RHB RM occ wk Teams: **Northern Districts, Otago,** England Test, England ODI, Glamorgan. Played List A in NZ. Sch: Ysgol David Hughes Sch, Wales. Occ: Cricket pro. Book: On the attack - a batsman's story. WCOY: 1998. An English pro, played and coached in NZ. He holds the Northern Districts 3rd wicket partnership record of 261 with S.A.Thomson against Auckland in 1990/91. Son: T.L.Maynard (Glamorgan).
MEADOWS Nicholas Andrew Peter 1980/81 b 1.1.1962 Morecambe, Lancashire, England. RHB RFM Team: **Wellington.** Played List A in NZ.
MEALE Trevor 1951/52-1958 b 11.11.1928 Papatoetoe, Auckland. d 21.5.2010 Orewa, Auckland. LHB RM Teams: **Wellington, New Zealand Test.**
MEARES William Edward Devenish 1873/74-1876/77 b 14.12.1848 Kiama, New South Wales, Australia. d 17.10.1923 Christchurch, Canterbury. wk Team: **Otago.** Occ: Insurance manager. Umpired first-class cricket. Son: F.Devenish-Meares (New South Wales, Western Australia).
MEDLOW John Thomas 1894/95 b Q3 1852 Chesterton, Cambridgeshire, England. LFM Team: **Canterbury.** Occ: Cricket coach. He left England in 1882 and had coaching engagements in Queensland, New South Wales and Victoria prior to the United and Midland Clubs in Christchurch engaging him to coach between 1894/95 and 1898. Nothing else known of him.
MEECH Maxon Dennis 1946/47 b 25.10.1914 Wellington. d 27.6.1977 Wellington. RHB RM Team: **Wellington.** Occ: Warehouse manager.
MELDRUM Alexander Lewis 1886/87-1889/90 b 1863 Kamo, Whangarei, Northland. d 5.11.1893 Auckland. Team: **Auckland.** Sch: Auckland GS. Occ: Clerk. Brothers: D.Meldrum, W.Meldrum.
MELDRUM David 1892/93 b 1867 Kamo, Whangarei, Northland. d 14.8.1957 Wanganui. Team: **Auckland.** Sch: Auckland GS. Occ: Warehouse manager. Brothers: A.L.Meldrum, W.Meldrum.
MELDRUM William 1884/85-1886/87 b 28.7.1865 Kamo, Whangarei, Northland. d 13.2.1964 Burnham, Canterbury. F Team: **Auckland.** Sch: Auckland GS. Occ: Solicitor. Rugby: Auckland. Chess: New Zealand champion in 1896. CB, CMG, DSO, Serbian Order of the White Eagle and Colonial Auxiliary Forces Officers' Decoration. NZCA obit: 1964. Brothers: A.L.Meldrum, D.Meldrum.
MENDELSON Wallingford 1893/94 b 29.12.1872 Geraldine, South Canterbury. d 19.8.1902 Durban, Natal, South Africa. He died of myelitis. Team: **Canterbury.** Sch: Christ Coll. Occ: Solicitor. Rugby: Canterbury, Cambridge University. Athletics: Cambridge University where he was the champion athlete of 1895. The long jump was his best performance. Against Oxford University in 1895, each side had won four events, and the final result depended on the long jump. On this occasion Mendelson carried Cambridge to victory with a jump of 22 feet 5½ inches, defeating C.B.Fry, the famous cricketer.
MENZIES Robert Edward James 1936/37-1946/47 b 17.4.1916 Melbourne, Victoria, Australia. d 11.9.1983, Palmerston North, Manawatu. RHB RM Teams: **Canterbury, Wellington, New Zealand.** Sch: Christchurch BHS. He played for New Zealand in a first-class match.
MERCHANT Cameron James 2007/08-2009/10 b 4.1.1984 Darlinghurst, Sydney, New South Wales, Australia. LHB OB Teams: **Northern Districts, Wellington.** Played List A in NZ; Played T20 in NZ. Sch: St Michaels, Carrara, Austrlaia. Occ: Computer programmer.
MERRIN Russell Conway 1967/68-1974/75 b 11.5.1945 Kaiapoi, North Canterbury. LHB RFM Team: **Canterbury.** Played List A in NZ. Sch: Rangiora HS.

MERRITT William Edward 1926/27-1946 b 18.8.1908 Sumner, Christchurch, Canterbury. d 9.6.1977 Christchurch, Canterbury. RHB LBG Teams: **Canterbury, New Zealand Test,** Northamptonshire. Sch: Christchurch BHS. Occ: Sports dealer. Rugby League: Canterbury, Wigan and Halifax. NZCA obit: 1977; Wisden obit: 1978. He was 18 when picked for the first New Zealand team to tour England in 1927 and had played only four first-class matches.

METGE Cedric Leslie 1923/24-1924/25 b 9.12.1900 Auckland. d 8.10.1985 Christchurch, Canterbury. LHB Team: **Auckland.** Sch: Auckland GS. Occ: Schoolteacher.

MEULI Edgar Milton 1945/46-1959/60 b 20.2.1926 Hawera, Taranaki. d 15.4.2007 Auckland. RHB LB Teams: **Auckland, Central Districts, New Zealand Test.** Sch: New Plymouth BHS. Occ: Schoolteacher. NZCA obit: 2007.

MIDDLETON Brent James 1973/74 b 18.2.1954 Lower Hutt, Wellington. LHB Team: **Wellington.** Played List A in NZ. Sch: Parkway Coll. Occ: Horticulturist.

MIDDLETON Frederick Stewart 1905/06-1921/22 b 28.5.1883 Boorowa, New South Wales, Australia. d 21.7.1956 Auckland. RHB RM Teams: **Auckland, Wellington, New Zealand,** New South Wales. Occ: Labourer. NZCA obit: 1956. He played for New Zealand prior to being granted Test status. He took a hat-trick for Wellington v Hawke's Bay in 1919/20.

MIDLANE Frederick Alexander 1898/99-1918/19 b 28.3.1883 Wellington. d 18.10.1976 Wigan, Lancashire, England. RHB Teams: **Wellington, Auckland, New Zealand.** Sch: Mt Cook HS. Occ: Carpet salesman. NZCA obit: 1977. He played for New Zealand prior to being granted Test status.

MILBURN Barry Douglas 1963/64-1982/83 b 24.11.1943 Maori Hill, Dunedin, Otago. RHB wk Teams: **Otago, New Zealand Test.** Played List A in NZ. Sch: Kings HS.

MILES Christopher <u>Charles</u> 1883/84 b Q2 1850 Durrington, Wiltshire, England. d 13.11.1936 Palmerston North, Manawatu. occ wk Team: **Wellington.** Sch: Marlborough, England. Occ: Publican; sharebroker.

MILLENER David <u>John</u> 1964/65-1970 b 2.5.1944 Epsom, Auckland. RHB RMF Teams: **Auckland,** Oxford University. Sch: Auckland GS. Occ: Professor. Rhodes scholar.

MILLER Bert 1914/15 Team: **Hawke's Bay.**

MILLER David Lawson 1892/93-1905/06 b 30.1.1870 Holytown, Lanarkshire, Scotland. d 12.4.1943 Clayfield, Queensland, Australia. LHB LF Teams: **Auckland,** New South Wales, Queensland. Umpired first-class cricket.

MILLER Lawrence Somerville Martin 1950/51-1959/60 b 31.3.1923 New Plymouth, Taranaki. d 17.12.1996 Kapiti, Wellington. LHB LSM Teams: **Central Districts, Wellington, New Zealand Test.** Sch: New Plymouth BHS. Occ: Railway employee. NZCA obit: 1997; Wisden obit: 1997. NZCA COY: 1953.

MILLER Robert Michael 2002/03 b 30.12.1979 Christchurch, Canterbury. LHB Team: **Canterbury.** Sch: Christchurch BHS. OCc: School teacher.

MILLINGTON Gordon Innes 1876/77-1880/81 b 4.5.1848 Rugby, Warwickshire, England. d 27.4.1923 Oamaru, North Otago. Team: **Otago.** Sch: Rugby, England. Occ: Farmer.

MILLMOW Jonathan Paul 1986/87-1991/92 b 22.9.1967 Wellington. RHB RFM Teams: **Wellington, New Zealand ODI.** Played List A in NZ. Occ: Journalist. NZ U19 Test; NZ U19 ODI.

MILLS Arthur Stewart 1947/48 b 20.12.1923 Invercargill, Southland. d 28.12.2001 Auckland. RHB wk Team: **Otago.** Occ: Pilot. NZCA obit: 2005.

MILLS Charles 1919/20 wk Team: **Hawke's Bay.**

MILLS Edward 1884/85-1886/87 b 7.3.1863 Ashford, Kent, England. d 9.7.1956 Forster, New South Wales, Australia. Team: **Auckland.** Brothers: G.Mills, I.Mills, W.Mills; nephew: J.E.Mills.

MILLS George 1886/87-1902/03 b 23.3.1867 Dartford, Kent, England. d 13.3.1942 Auckland. RHB RS Teams: **Auckland, Hawke's Bay, Otago, New Zealand.** Occ: Groundsman. Wisden obit: 1943. He played for New Zealand prior to being granted Test status. Brothers: I.Mills, E.Mills, W.Mills; son: J.E.Mills.

MILLS George Henry 1935/36-1957/58 b 1.8.1916 Dunedin, Otago. d 17.12.1979 Dunedin, Otago. RHB wk Team: **Otago.** Sch: Otago BHS. Occ: Fitter. NZCA obit: 1980. Otago selector.

MILLS Isaac 1889/90-1903/04 b 5.4.1869 Medway, Kent, England. d 16.8.1956 Auckland. RHB Team: **Auckland, New Zealand.** Occ: Presser. NZCA obit: 1956; Wisden obit: 1958. He played for New Zealand prior to being granted Test status. Brothers: G.Mills, E.Mills, W.Mills; nephew: J.E.Mills.

MILLS Jason Martin 1991/92-1998/99 b 12.8.1969 Auckland. RHB wk Team: **Auckland.** Played List A in NZ.

MILLS John Ernest 1924/25-1937/38 b 3.9.1905 Carisbrook, Dunedin, Otago. d 11.12.1972 Hamilton, Waikato. LHB Teams: **Auckland, New Zealand Test.** Occ: Insurance agent. NZCA obit: 1973; Wisden obit: 1973. On his Test debut, he hit 117 against England at Wellington in 1929/30 and with C.S.Dempster added 276 for the first wicket. In Auckland club cricket in 1924/25 he and H.D.Gillespie shared in an opening stand of 441. Father: G.Mills; uncles: I.Mills, E.Mills, W.Mills.

MILLS Kyle David 1998/99-2008/09 b 15.3.1979 Auckland. RHB RM Teams: **Auckland, New Zealand Test, New Zealand ODI, New Zealand T20.** Played List A in NZ; Played T20 in NZ. Sch: Macleans Coll. NZ U19 ODI.

MILLS Stuart Michael 2003/04-2006/07 b 22.6.1982 Wellington. RHB wk Team: **Wellington.** Played List A in NZ; Played T20 in NZ. Sch: Wellington Coll.

MILLS William 1894/95-1903/04 b 19.3.1875 Auckland. d 8.4.1962 Birkdale, Auckland. RM Teams: **Taranaki, Auckland.** NZCA obit: 1979. Brothers: G.Mills, I.Mills, E.Mills; nephew: J.E.Mills.

MILLTON William Varnham 1877/78-1886/87 b 10.2.1858 Christchurch, Canterbury. d 22.6.1887 Christchurch, Canterbury. He died of typhoid aged 29. Team: **Canterbury.** Sch: Christ Coll. Occ: Solicitor. Rugby: All Blacks and Canterbury. In 1878 he had been a hero of a passenger rescue from the 'Melrose' which was wrecked off Timaru. Secretary of the Canterbury RFU.

MILNE Adam Fraser 2009/10 b 13.4.1992 Palmerston North, Manawatu. RHB RMF Team: **Central Districts.** Sch: Palmerston North BHS.

MILNE James Damian 1985/86-1987/88 b 2.12.1961 Wellington. RHB wk Team: **Wellington.**

MILNES Glenn Stefan 1997/98-1999/00 b 15.10.1974 Motueka, Tasman. RHB Team: **Central Districts.** Played List A in NZ. Sch: Hornby HS. Occ: Investment manager. Grandfather: L.A.Milnes.

MILNES Leslie Albert 1942/43-1948/49 b 3.7.1922 Dunedin, Otago. RHB Team: **Otago.** Sch: Otago BHS; Kings HS. Occ: Accountant. Grandson: G.S.Milnes.

MISHRA Amit 2001/02-2010 b 24.11.1982 Delhi, India. RHB LB Teams: **Central Districts,** India Test, India ODI, India T20, Haryana. Indian Test Player who played for Central Districts in order to get match practice whilst on the 2008/09 tour of NZ.

MITCHELL D 1881/82-1882/83 b Southend-on-Sea, Essex, England. wk Team: **Otago.** He went to Victoria in 1883. In 1885 it was reported that he had joined the Carlton Club, Melbourne, where he played with the second eleven. While in Invercargill he played for Banks and Civil Service in 1881 and both Unmarried and Under-25s in 1882.

MITCHELL Errol William 1926/27 b 10.9.1897 Tikokino, Hawke's Bay. d 25.3.1948 Hastings, Hawke's Bay. LBG Team: **Wellington.** Occ: Civil servant.

MITCHELL William John 1964/65-1968/69 b 1.12.1947 Auckland. RHB RM Teams: **Northern Districts, Otago.** Sch: Hamilton BHS. He scored 127 on first-class debut for Northern Districts v Pakistan in 1964/65.

MOHAMMAD WASIM 1994/95-2009/10 b 8.8.1977 Rawalpindi, Punjab, Pakistan. RHB LBG occ wk Teams: **Otago,** Pakistan Test, Pakistan ODI, Rawalpindi, Agriculture Development Bank of Pakistan, Rawalpindi B, Khan Research Laboratories, Rawalpindi Rams. Played List A in NZ.

MOIR Alexander Mckenzie 1949/50-1961/62 b 17.7.1919 Dunedin, Otago. d 17.6.2000 Dunedin, Otago. RHB LBG Teams: **Otago, New Zealand Test.** Sch: King Edward Tech Coll. Occ: Schoolteacher. Soccer: Otago. NZCA obit: 2000. NZCA COY: 1951. He took a hat-trick for Otago v Canterbury in 1950/51.

MOLONEY Denis Andrew Robert 1929/30-1940/41 b 11.8.1910 Dunedin, Otago. d 15.7.1942 Ruweisat Ridge, El Alamein, Egypt. He died of wounds while a prisoner of war aged 32. RHB LB Teams: **Otago, Wellington, Canterbury, New Zealand Test.** Sch: Otago BHS. Occ: Insurance clerk. Wisden obit: 1945.

MOLONY David Matthew 1985/86-1987/88 b 30.5.1966 Wellington. RHB RFM Team: **Wellington**. Played List A in NZ. He had match figures of 15/203 for Otago v Central Districts in 1953/54.
MONAGHAN David Wyatt 1942/43 b 13.7.1922 Pahiatua, Wairarapa. d 27.1.1944 Caserta, Italy. He was killed in action aged 21, the youngest known NZ first-class cricketer to die. Team: **South Island Army**. Sch: Christ Coll. Occ: Civil servant. Father: H.W.Monaghan.
MONAGHAN Harold Wyatt 1905/06-1913/14 b 7.10.1886 Karori, Wellington. d 15.10.1958 Levin, Horowhenua. LHB RM Teams: **Wellington, Canterbury, New Zealand**. Sch: Christ Coll; Wellington Coll. Occ: Anglican Reverend. Book: From Age to Age, the story of the Church of England in the Diocese of Wellington 1858-1958. NZCA obit: 1958; Wisden obit: 1960. He had been Archdeacon of Timaru and of Rangitiki. He played for New Zealand in a non-first-class match prior to being granted Test status. Son: D.W.Monaghan.
MONCK John Stanley 1873/74 b 28.2.1845 Coley Park, Reading, Berkshire, England. d 3.9.1929 Sumner, Christchurch, Canterbury. Team: **Canterbury**. Sch: Bradfield Coll, England. Occ: Farmer. Athletics: New Zealand Champion long distance runner in 1872.
MONK Leonard Stanley 1901/02 b 14.11.1873 Dunedin, Otago. d 21.7.1948 Edgecliff, Sydney, New South Wales, Australia. Team: **Otago**. Occ: Actor.
MONK Philip George 1928/29-1929/30 b 23.8.1907 Auckland. d 17.10.1993 Christchurch, Canterbury. RHB RM Team: **Otago**. NZCA obit: 1995.
MONTEATH Alastair Patrick Johnstone 1939/40 b 12.9.1913 Christchurch, Canterbury. d 27.6.1942 Western Desert, Libya. He was killed in action aged 28. occ wk Team: **Otago**. Sch: Christ Coll. Occ: Salesman. Wisden obit: 1943.
MONTEITH Leslie Thomas James 1924/25 b 26.1.1905 Auckland. d 17.11.1993 Auckland. RHB OB Team: **Auckland**. Sch: Auckland GS. Hockey: New Zealand. NZCA obit: 1994.
MOONEY Francis Leonard Hugh 1941/42-1954/55 b 26.5.1921 Wellington. d 8.3.2004 Wellington. RHB RAB wk Teams: **Wellington, New Zealand Test.** Sch: St Patricks Coll, Wellington. Occ: Coy manager. NZCA obit: 2004; Wisden obit: 2005. NZ and Wellington selector.
MOORE Francis Edward 1894/95-1897/98 b 4.1.1874 Kaiapoi, North Canterbury. d 10.10.1908 Hawera, Taranaki. Team: **Taranaki**. Occ: Farmer.
MOORE Henry Walter 1876/77-1894/95 b Q1 1849 Cranbrook, Kent, England. d 20.8.1916 Upper Norwood, London, England. RHB Teams: **Canterbury, Taranaki**. Occ: Farmer. Rugby: Canterbury.
MOORE James Gerald Harle 1905/06 b 18.9.1877 Kaihiku, Otago. d 6.4.1933 St Peters, Sydney, New South Wales, Australia. Team: **Otago**. Occ: Wool classer. Book: With the Fourth New Zealand Rough Riders.
MOORE Percival Claude Evelyn 1919/20 b 19.11.1894 Wellington. d 2.12.1952 New Plymouth, Taranaki. Team: **Wellington**. Occ: Civil servant.
MOORE Thomas Richard 1866/67-1874/75 b 1844 England. d 23.7.1935 Palmerston North, Manawatu. Team: **Canterbury**. Sch: Christ Coll. Occ: Gentleman.
MOORE William Shaw 1879/80 b 1862 New Plymouth, Taranaki. d 26.8.1894 Wellington. Team: **West Coast (North Island).** Occ: Printer.
MOORHOUSE Malcolm 1883/84-1907/08 b Q4 1866 Hackney, London, England. RHB wk Teams: **Canterbury, Wellington**. Occ: Comm traveller. An Englishman, he came to NZ in the 1880s and then returned to England for almost 20 years before coming to NZ in the mid 1900s. He is thought to have returned to England.
MORESBY Tracey Archer 1889/90-1893/94 b Q2 1867 Stoke Damerel, Plymouth, Devon, England. Team: **Auckland**. Occ: Solicitor. He was divorced from his wife in 1921 and left New Zealand. Nothing more is known of him.
MOREY Henry Andrew Thomas 1888/89 b 1.7.1854 Charlton, Kent, England. d 30.7.1926 Parua Bay, Whangerei, Northland. Team: **Wellington**.
MORGAN Greg Jan 2007/08-2009/10 b 6.2.1989 East London, Border, South Africa. RHB RM Team: **Auckland**. Played List A in NZ; Played T20 in NZ. Sch: Howick Coll. NZ U19 Test; NZ U19 ODI. He holds the Auckland 9th wicket partnership record of 151 with R.A.Young against Northern Districts in 2007/08.

MORGAN Harold Rhys 2000/01-2001/02 b 3.11.1978 Wellington. RHB RM Team: **Wellington**. Sch: Wellington Coll. Occ: Bank officer.
MORGAN Haydn John 2000/01 b 5.7.1973 Torquay, Devon, England. RHB OB Team: **Central Districts**. Played List A in NZ.
MORGAN Henry Alan 1963/64-1977/78 b 5.6.1938 Wellington. LHB RM Team: **Wellington**. Played List A in NZ. Son: R.G.Morgan.
MORGAN Leighton James 2001/02-2009/10 b 16.2.1981 Wellington. RHB SLA Teams: **Wellington, Otago**. Played List A in NZ. Sch: St Patricks Coll, Wellington. NZ U19 ODI.
MORGAN Richard Glen 1993/94-2001/02 b 24.6.1972 Wellington. RHB LM Teams: **Northern Districts, Auckland**. Played List A in NZ. Father: H.A.Morgan.
MORGAN Ross Winston 1957/58-1976/77 b 12.2.1941 Auckland. RHB OB occ wk Teams: **Auckland, New Zealand Test**. Played List A in NZ. Sch: Auckland GS. NZCA COY: 1965.
MORGAN Rurie Tranton 1932/33-1945 b 30.7.1912 Wellington. d 4.1.1980 Wellington. RHB RSM Team: **Wellington**. Occ: Carpenter. NZCA obit: 1980; Wisden obit: 1981.
MORICE Francis Henry 1886/87-1889/90 b 1851 La Colle, Quebec, Canada East. d 19.6.1912 Dunedin, Otago. He died of heart failure. Team: **Wellington**. Sch: Grange Court, Chigwell, England. Occ: Public trustee. Wisden obit: 1913. He was a sergeant-major of the New Zealand Contingent which went to Sydney in January 1901 to represent the colony at the swearing in of the Governor-General.
MORLAND Douglas Michael 1965/66-1973/74 b 8.2.1944 Palmerston North, Manawatu. RHB RM Team: **Central Districts**. Played List A in NZ.
MORLAND Nathan Douglas 1996/97-2003/04 b 20.12.1976 Dunedin, Otago. RHB OB Team: **Otago**. Played List A in NZ. Sch: Otago BHS. Occ: Schoolteacher. NZ U19 Test; NZ U19 ODI.
MORRIS Alexander 1884/85 b 14.11.1858 Dunedin, Otago. d 1.4.1918 Dunedin, Otago. Team: **Otago**. Sch: Otago BHS. Occ: Bank inspector.
MORRIS Charles 1863/64 b 1840 unknown. Team: **Otago**. He came from Australia where he had played club cricket in Melbourne. He played club cricket in Dunedin but nothing is known of him after 1865.
MORRIS John Bentham 1951/52-1956/57 b 9.1.1933 Paddington, London, England. d 9.1.1970 Auckland. RHB Team: **Auckland**. Sch: Kings Coll. Occ: Doctor. NZCA obit: 1970. Brother: P.P.W.Morris.
MORRIS Peter Philip Woodward 1961/62-1962/63 b 3.12.1937 Auckland. RHB Team: **Auckland**. Sch: Kings Coll. Brother: J.B.Morris.
MORRIS Philip Robert 1975/76-1976/77 b 15.5.1952 Dunedin, Otago. LHB RM Team: **Otago**. Played List A in NZ. Sch: Kings HS.
MORRISON Alexander Ross 1965/66-1966/67 b 23.9.1937 Auckland. RHB Team: **Auckland**.
MORRISON Bruce Donald 1953/54-1964/65 b 17.12.1933 Lower Hutt, Wellington. LHB RM Teams: **Wellington, New Zealand Test**. Wellington selector.
MORRISON Daniel Kyle 1985/86-1996/97 b 3.2.1966 Auckland. RHB RFM Teams: **Auckland, New Zealand Test, New Zealand ODI**, Lancashire. Played List A in NZ. Sch: Takapuna GS. NZ U19 Test; NZ U19 ODI. Book: Mad as I wanna be. NZCA COY: 1990, 1993. At one time he held the world record of 24 Test ducks. His final heroics for New Zealand came with the bat, scoring 14 in an unbeaten 10th-wicket stand of 106 with Nathan Astle which saved a Test v England in 1996/97 - he was dropped from the team and it turned out to be his final appearance. He took a hat-trick in a ODI for New Zealand v India in 1993/94.
MORRISON Henry Bannerman 1880/81 b 20.9.1850 Barony, Glasgow, Lanarkshire, Scotland. d 10.11.1913 Burgess Hill, Sussex, England. Team: **Otago**. Occ: Farmer.
MORRISON James Barrie 1958/59-1959/60 b 24.3.1936 Wellington. RHB Team: **Wellington**.
MORRISON John Francis Maclean 1965/66-1983/84 b 27.8.1947 Wellington. RHB SLA Teams: **Central Districts, Wellington, New Zealand Test, New Zealand ODI**. Played List A in NZ. Sch: New Plymouth BHS. Wellington selector.
MORRISON William 1876/77-1880/81 b 21.5.1850 Alva, Clackmannan, Scotland. d 31.10.1910 Dunedin, Otago. Team: **Otago**.

MORRISON Wilson Edward William 1877/78 b 1851 Dublin, Ireland. d 28.10.1882 Auckland. He died aged 31. Team: **Canterbury.** Sch: St Peters, York, England. Occ: Schoolteacher. Whilst at Oxford University he was the co-editor of a satirical student magazine: The Shotover Papers or Echoes from Oxford.

MOSS Albert Edward 1889/90 b 3.10.1863 Hugglescote, Leicestershire, England. d 12.12.1945 Hadleigh, Essex, England. RF Team: **Canterbury.** Occ: Salvation Army. Umpired first-class cricket. Books: Well played by F.Coutts; 10 for 28 by Mike Batty. He is the only man to take 10 wickets in an innings on first-class debut and remains the only New Zealander to have taken 10 wickets in an innings when he took 10/28 for Canterbury v Wellington in 1889/90. He was presented with the ball as a trophy. However, he had a rather bizarre personal life. He was tried in the Supreme Court, Christchurch in August 1891 for wounding his wife with intent to murder. He was found not guilty on the grounds of insanity and remanded to Lyttelton Prison, "till the pleasure of the Colonial Secretary is known". He was released in early 1896 on condition that he did not contact his wife again and was deported to Rio de Janeiro. Hoping to redeem himself, he went first to South America and then to South Africa, working for the Salvation Army in Pretoria. By chance, his wife read an article about his work in the Salvation Army magazine, The War Cry, and, after returning the ball to him, herself went to South Africa and re-married him. Moss died at the age of 82 after which the ball was given to Lancaster Park the home of the Canterbury club. It is now looked after by the Salvation Army, but an agreement has been made for it to be displayed at Lancaster Park on special occasions such as the 125th anniversary of the Canterbury CA in 2002.

MOSS James Robert 1965/66-1969/70 b 5.12.1945 Invercargill, Southland. RHB LMF Team: **Wellington.**

MOSS Robert Mortimer 1903/04 b 13.11.1884 Wellington. d 21.5.1932 Masterton, Wairarapa. RHB Team: **Wellington.** Sch: Mt Cook HS. Occ: Insurance agent.

MOTLEY Arthur 1879-1888/89 b 5.2.1858 Osmondthorpe Hall, Yorkshire, England. d 28.9.1897 Canning Town, Essex, England. RHB RF Teams: **Wellington,** Yorkshire. Sch: Rugby, England. Occ: Clerk. Umpired first-class cricket.

MOTZ Richard Charles 1957/58-1969 b 12.1.1940 Christchurch, Canterbury. d 29.4.2007 Christchurch, Canterbury. RHB RF Teams: **Canterbury, New Zealand Test.** Sch: Linwood HS. Occ: Publican. He was inducted into the New Zealand Sports Hall of Fame. NZCA obit: 2007; Wisden obit: 2008. NZCA COY: 1961. WCOY: 1966. SACOY 1962. He was the first New Zealander to take 100 Test wickets.

MOUNTAIN Lance Sydney 1967/68-1973/74 b 7.9.1940 Kawakawa, Northland. RHB wk Team: **Northern Districts.** Played List A in NZ.

MOWATT William 1903/04 b 30.7.1884 Wellington. d 30.6.1943 Dunedin, Otago. Team: **Wellington.** Sch: Te Aro. Occ: Ship surveyor.

MOYLE Herbert 1950/51-1956/57 b 4.8.1922 Auckland. d 3.10.2000 Auckland. RHB RFM Team: **Auckland.**

MOYNIHAN Thomas Desmond 1940/41-1952/53 b 27.2.1921 Kaikoura, North Canterbury. d 12.12.1988 Christchurch, Canterbury. RHB RM Team: **Canterbury.** Sch: West Christchurch BHS.

MUIR Cedric Alfred 1943/44 b 13.11.1912 Patea, Taranaki. d 2.6.1975 Whangarei, Northland. Team: **Wellington.** Occ: Builder. NZCA obit: 1975.

MUIR Frederick Joseph 1872/73 b 1849 Mintaro, South Australia, Australia. d 25.4.1921 Woollahra, Sydney, New South Wales, Australia. Team: **Otago.** Sch: Otago BHS. Occ: Accountant. He was bankrupted in 1891, arrested for false pretences in Victoria in 1892 and jailed for a year for publishing an obscene poem in WA in 1897.

MUIR Glenn Andrew 1995/96-1997/98 b 17.11.1971 Dunedin, Otago. LHB RM Team: **Canterbury.** Played List A in NZ. Sch: St Thomas Coll.

MUIR Murray Fergus 1949/50 b 16.2.1928 Dunedin, Otago. d 5.10.2004 Andersons Bay, Dunedin, Otago. OB Team: **Otago.**

MULCOCK Edward 1936/37-1943/44 b 6.7.1909 Christchurch, Canterbury. d 15.7.1994 Christchurch, Canterbury. RHB RM Teams: **Canterbury, Otago.** Sch: Christchurch BHS. Occ: Headmaster. NZCA obit: 1994; Wisden obit: 1995. He took a hat-trick for Canterbury v Otago in 1937/38.

MUMFORD Jonathan Butler 1873/74-1877/78 b 1842 Ealing, Middlesex, England. d 14.12.1892 Auckland. He was batting (non-striker) in a cricket match on the Auckland Domain when he collapsed and died of heart apoplexy aged 50. Team: **Auckland.** Umpired first-class cricket.
MUMMERY Ernest Lee 1961/62 b 26.11.1935 Wanganui. RHB SLA Team: **Central Districts.**
MUNRO Colin 2006/07-2007/08 b 11.3.1987 Durban, Natal, South Africa. LHB RM Team: **Auckland.** Played List A in NZ. Sch: Pakuranga Coll. NZ U19 ODI.
MURDOCH Donald Howden 1943/44-1944/45 b 27.3.1923 Lawrence, Otago. LHB LB Team: **Otago.** Sch: Kings HS. Son: G.H.Murdoch.
MURDOCH Geoffrey Howden 1974/75 b 3.5.1954 Dunedin, Otago. RHB LB Team: **Otago.** Father: D.H.Murdoch.
MURDOCH Ronald Lindsay 1964/65 b 28.12.1945 Dunedin, Otago. RHB Team: **Otago.** Sch: Otago BHS.
MURDOCH Stephen Joseph 2009/10 b 6.8.1983 Wellington. RHB RM Team: **Wellington.** Played List A in NZ. Sch: St Patricks Coll, Wellington. NZ U19 ODI.
MURDOCH Timothy John 1977/78 b 27.7.1955 Christchurch, Canterbury. RHB Team: **NZ Under-23s.** Occ: Cricket administrator.
MURDOCK Warren Thomas 1962/63-1974/75 b 12.1.1944 New Plymouth, Taranaki. RHB Team: **Central Districts.** Played List A in NZ. Sch: New Plymouth BHS.
MURISON William Dick 1864/65-1866/67 b 24.2.1837 Alyth, Perthshire, Scotland. d 28.12.1877 Dunedin, Otago. Team: **Otago.** Sch: Edinburgh HS. Occ: Journalist. MP.
MURPHY Anthony John 1985-1994 b 6.8.1962 Withington, Manchester, Lancashire, England. RHB RMF Teams: **Central Districts,** Lancashire, Surrey. Played List A in NZ. Sch: Xaverian Coll, Manchester, England.
MURRAY Bruce Alexander Grenfell 1958/59-1972/73 b 18.9.1940 Johnsonville, Wellington. RHB LB Teams: **Wellington, New Zealand Test.** Played List A in NZ. Sch: Hutt Valley HS. NZCA COY: 1970. Wellington selector.
MURRAY Darrin James 1990/91-1997/98 b 4.9.1967 Christchurch, Canterbury. RHB RM Teams: **Canterbury, New Zealand Test, New Zealand ODI.** Played List A in NZ. Sch: Shirley BHS. Occ: Manager. NZ U19 Test; NZ U19 ODI.
MURRAY Graham Bryan 2004/05 b 3.10.1976 Wellington. RHB RM Team: **Wellington.** Played List A in NZ; Played T20 in NZ.
MURRAY Ronald Mckenzie 1946/47-1950/51 b 15.6.1927 Wellington. d 8.4.1951 Christchurch, Canterbury. He died, aged 23, from injuries received when he fell accidentally while visiting a sick friend at Hanmer Springs, Canterbury. RHB RM Team: **Wellington.** Occ: Journalist. NZCA obit: 1951; Wisden obit: 1952. He took a hat-trick for Wellington v Otago in 1949/50.
MURTAGH John Richard 1988/89-1991/92 b 21.7.1967 Geraldine, South Canterbury. RHB RM Teams: **Otago, Wellington.** Played List A in NZ. NZ U19 Test; NZ U19 ODI.
MYBURGH Johannes Gerhardus 1997/98-2009/10 b 22.10.1980 Pretoria, Transvaal, South Africa. RHB OB Teams: **Canterbury,** Northerns B, Northerns, Titans. Played List A in NZ; Played T20 in NZ. Sch: Pretoria BHS, South Africa. Occ: Cricket pro. He holds the Canterbury 2nd wicket partnership record of 254* with M.H.W.Papps against Central Districts in 2007/08 and the NZ domestic T20 3rd wicket partnership record of 109* with C.Z.Harris for Canterbury against Northern Districts in 2007/08. He is the youngest scorer of a double century in South African first-class cricket as a 17-year-old in 1997/98. Brother S.J.Myburgh (Northerns).
MYTTON Henry Whitehead 1863/64-1866/67 b 16.9.1840 Garth, Glamorgan, Wales. d 6.7.1890 Rugby, Tennessee, United States of America. Team: **Canterbury.** Sch: Cheltenham, England. Occ: Civil servant.
NAPIER Eric John 1913/14-1920/21 b 6.9.1888 Taradale, Hawke's Bay. d 26.7.1959 Lower Hutt, Wellington. SLA Team: **Hawke's Bay.**
NAPIER Graham Richard 1997-2010 b 6.1.1980 Colchester, Essex, England. RHB RM Teams: **Wellington, Central Districts,** Essex. Played List A in NZ; Played T20 in NZ. Sch: Gilberd School, Colchester, England. An English pro, played and coached in NZ.

NASH Dion Joseph 1990/91-2001/02 b 20.11.1971 Auckland. RHB RFM Teams: **Northern Districts, Otago, Auckland, New Zealand Test, New Zealand ODI,** Middlesex. Played List A in NZ. Sch: Auckland GS. NZ U19 Test; NZ U19 ODI. NZCA COY: 1999. NZ selector. He holds the Northern Districts 7th wicket partnership record of 136 with A.R.Tait against Central Districts in 1997/98.
NASH J A 1919/20 Team: **Wellington.**
NASH Richard George 1886/87 b 1852 New Zealand. d 12.5.1937 Invercargill, Southland. Team: **Hawke's Bay.** Occ: Sign writer.
NATHU Anup 1980/81-1991/92 b 8.10.1960 Wellington. RHB RFM Team: **Canterbury.** Played List A in NZ. Sch: Rongatai Coll. Occ: Restauranteur.
NAUGHTON Dominic Hugh 1908/09-1911/12 b 11.9.1879 Nelson. d 1960 Chatswood, Sydney, New South Wales, Australia. LHB Team: **Wellington.** Sch: St Patricks Coll, Wellington. Occ: Civil servant. Brother: M.P.Naughton.
NAUGHTON Michael Patrick 1897/98 b 1873 unknown. d 16.8.1959 Lower Hutt, Wellington. RHB Team: **Wellington.** Sch: St Patricks Coll, Wellington. Occ: Railway employee. Brother: D.H.Naughton.
NAYLOR John 1879/80-1880/81 b 1846 Leeds, Yorkshire, England. d 28.5.1905 Stoke, Nelson. Team: **Nelson.** Occ: Schoolmaster.
NEAL David William 1971/72-1976/77 b 4.9.1951 Blenheim, Marlborough. RHB RM Team: **Central Districts.** Played List A in NZ.
NEALE Edgar Rollo 1920/21-1921/22 b 24.10.1889 Nelson. d 25.7.1960 Nelson. RHB Team: **Minor Assoc, South Island.** Sch: Nelson Coll. Occ: Accountant. OBE, MP. NZCA obit: 1960. Secretary of the Nelson Jockey Club and Nelson Trotting Club. He served on the Nelson City Council from 1925 to 1960, being mayor 1941-1947.
NEELY Donald Owen 1964/65-1970/71 b 21.12.1935 Wellington. RHB Teams: **Wellington, Auckland.** Sch: Rongatai Coll. Books: A prolific writer of books on cricket including Men in White, the definitive history of NZ cricket, and the Summer Game, a photographical history of cricket in NZ. He also edited the NZ cricket annual 1973-1993. NZ and Wellington selector. MBE.
NEESHAM James Douglas Sheehan 2009/10 b 17.9.1990 Auckland. LHB RM Team: **Auckland.** Played List A in NZ; Played T20 in NZ. NZ U19 Test. Sch: Auckland GS. NZ U19 ODI.
NEILL Robert 1889/90-1905/06 b 20.1.1864 Greenock, Renfrewshire, Scotland. d 27.8.1930 Auckland. RHB LB Teams: **Auckland, New Zealand.** Sch: Auckland GS. Occ: Merchant. Wisden obit: 1931. He played for New Zealand prior to being granted Test status. He took 9/75 for Auckland v Wellington in 1891/92 and 9/86 for Auckland v Wellington in 1897/98. Brother: T.Neill.
NEILL Thomas 1892/93-1897/98 b 18.9.1867 Greenock, Renfrewshire, Scotland. d 1949 Auckland. Team: **Auckland.** Sch: Auckland GS. Occ: Clerk. Umpired first-class cricket. Brother: R.Neill.
NEILSON William Francis 1874/75-1878/79 b 24.9.1848 Liverpool, Lancashire, England. d 2.5.1880 Christchurch, Canterbury. He died as a result of rheumatic fever aged 31. RHB Team: **Canterbury.** Sch: Rugby, England. Occ: Farmer. Umpired first-class cricket. NZCA obit: 1980.
NELSON Francis Arthur 1908/09-1909/10 b 31.5.1889 Wellington. d 16.7.1965 Auckland. Team: **Hawke's Bay.** Sch: St Patricks Coll, Wellington. Occ: Clerk.
NELSON Frederick Montague 1892/93-1897/98 b 1869 Napier, Hawke's Bay. d 29.10.1928 Hastings, Hawke's Bay. Team: **Hawke's Bay.** Sch: Christ Coll. Occ: Sheep farmer.
NELSON James 1912/13 LM Team: **Hawke's Bay.**
NELSON James Archibald 1914/15 b 27.8.1873 Christchurch, Canterbury. d 1.6.1950 Christchurch, Canterbury. Team: **Otago.** Occ: Policeman.
NETHULA Tarun Sai 2008/09-2009/10 b 8.5.1983 Kurnool, Andhra Pradesh, India. RHB LBG Team: **Auckland.** Sch: Mt Roskill GS.
NEUTZE Peter Stephen 1984/85-1989/90 b 5.9.1963 Auckland. RHB LB Teams: **Otago, Auckland, Northern Districts.** Played List A in NZ. Occ: Lawyer.

NEVIN Christopher John 1995/96-2009/10 b 3.8.1975 Dunedin, Otago. RHB wk Teams: **Wellington, New Zealand ODI.** Played List A in NZ; Played T20 in NZ. Sch: Hutt Valley HS. NZ U19 Test; NZ U19 ODI. He holds the Wellington 7th wicket partnership record of 250 with M.D.J.Walker against Otago in 2003/04.

NEWBIGIN Edward James Dudley 1953/54 b 15.10.1931 Hastings, Hawke's Bay. RHB RF Team: **Wellington.**

NEWDICK Graham Anthony 1970/71-1980/81 b 11.1.1949 Lower Hutt, Wellington. RHB OB Teams: **Wellington, New Zealand.** Played List A in NZ. He played for New Zealand in a FC match.

NEWMAN Alex 1930/31 b 24.3.1909 Brightwater, Nelson. d 2.6.1992 Nelson. RHB RM Team: **Wellington.** Sch: Nelson Coll. NZCA obit: 1996. Brothers: J.Newman, S.Newman; son: P.A.Newman.

NEWMAN Jack (Sir) 1922/23-1935/36 b 3.7.1902 Brightwater, Nelson. d 23.9.1996 Nelson. RHB LM Teams: **Canterbury, Wellington, New Zealand Test.** Sch: Nelson Coll. Occ: Coy director. Sir, KB, CBE. NZCA obit: 1997; Wisden obit: 1997. NZ selector and president of the New Zealand Cricket Council. He was the world's senior Test player when he died aged 94. Brothers: A.Newman, S.Newman; nephew: P.A.Newman.

NEWMAN John Alfred 1906-1930 b 12.11.1884 Southsea, Hampshire, England. d 21.12.1973 Groote Schuur, Cape Town, Cape Province, South Africa. RHB RFM Teams: **Canterbury,** Hampshire. Occ: Cricket pro. NZCA obit: 1974; Wisden obit: 1974. An English pro, played and coached in NZ.

NEWMAN Philip Alfred 1958/59 b 24.8.1937 Nelson. RHB Team: **Central Districts.** Sch: Nelson Coll. Father: A.Newman; uncles: J.Newman, S.Newman.

NEWMAN Stanley 1929/30 b 28.8.1907 Brightwater, Nelson. d 20.8.1956 Palmerston North, Manawatu. RHB RFM Team: **Wellington.** Sch: Nelson Coll. Occ: Coy director. Brothers: J.Newman, A.Newman; nephew: P.A.Newman.

NEWTON Frank William 1938/39 b 2.1.1909 unknown. d 17.9.1973 Auckland. LHB SLA Team: **Canterbury.**

NEWTON Gollan Mclean 1883/84-1886/87 b 1866 Napier, Hawke's Bay. d 18.12.1920 Cambridge, Waikato. RFM Team: **Hawke's Bay.** Sch: Napier BHS. Occ: Solicitor.

NEWTON Robert Walker 1973/74-1974/75 b 30.5.1952 Lincoln, Canterbury. LHB wk Teams: **Canterbury, Wellington.** Played List A in NZ.

NIBLETT Andrew Dylan 2006/07 b 25.4.1977 Vanderbijlpark, Transvaal, South Africa. RHB RMF Team: **Central Districts.**

NICHOLLS Joseph Cowie 1876/77 b 14.4.1859 Launceston, Tasmania, Australia. d 27.7.1954 Maheno, North Otago. Team: **Otago.** Sch: Christ Coll; Otago BHS. Occ: Farmer. In 1901 he became Major-Commanding No.1 Regiment Otago Mounted Rifles and Lieutenant-Colonel in 1902. During World War 1 he was the Commander of the Otago Mounted Rifle Brigade and Otago Military District.

NICHOLLS Sydney 1882/83-1893/94 b 3.1864 London, England. d 29.4.1929 Wellington. RHB wk Team: **Wellington.** Sch: Mt Cook HS. Occ: Hotelkeeper. Rugby: Wellington. Wisden obit: 1930. His three sons were Rugby All Blacks.

NICHOLSON Colin Ross 1959/60-1963/64 b 9.9.1939 Oamaru, North Otago. LFM Teams: **Canterbury, Otago.** Sch: Southland BHS. Brother: K.A.Nicholson.

NICHOLSON J A 1893/94 Team: **Auckland.**

NICHOLSON Kenneth Alan 1971/72 b 7.8.1945 Otautau, Southland. RHB RM Team: **Otago.** Played List A in NZ. Brother: C.R.Nicholson.

NICHOLSON Victor Rylands 1914/15 b 25.8.1892 Melbourne, Victoria, Australia. d 11.4.1946 Maungaturoto, Northland. He died as the result of an accident. Team: **Otago.** Sch: Otago BHS. Occ: Doctor.

NICOL Robert James 2001/02-2009/10 b 28.5.1983 Auckland. RHB OB,RM Teams: **Auckland, Canterbury, New Zealand T20.** Played List A in NZ; Played T20 in NZ. Sch: Kings Coll. NZ U19 Test; NZ U19 ODI.

NIELSEN Bradley John 2001/02-2002/03 b 26.10.1979 Auckland. RHB RM Team: **Auckland.** Played List A in NZ.

NIGHTINGALE Alan Francis 1950/51-1958/59 b 1.11.1928 Greymouth, West Coast. RHB RM Team: **Wellington.**
NIMMO John Robert 1933/34-1936/37 b 12.6.1910 Dunedin, Otago. d 2.11.1994 Dunedin, Otago. RHB RM Team: **Otago.** Occ: Clerk. NZCA obit: 1995.
NIVEN Robert Campbell 1887/88-1901/02 b 11.12.1859 Emerald Hill, South Melbourne, Victoria, Australia. d 14.4.1919 Wellington. wk Teams: **Otago, Wellington, New Zealand.** Occ: Clerk. Umpired in first-class cricket. He played for New Zealand in a non-first-class match prior to being granted Test status.
NIXON Douglas Charles 1926/27-1927/28 b 10.9.1898 Fairlie, South Canterbury. d 3.10.1980 Christchurch, Canterbury. LHB RFM Team: **Canterbury.** Sch: Christchurch BHS. Occ: Land agent.
NOEMA-BARNETT Kieran 2008/09-2009/10 b 4.6.1987 Dunedin, Otago. LHB RM Team: **Otago (not FC), Central Districts.** Played List A in NZ; Played T20 in NZ. Sch: Kavanagh Coll. NZ U19 ODI.
NOON Wayne Michael 1989-2003 b 5.2.1971 Grimsby, Lincolnshire, England. RHB wk Teams: **Canterbury,** Northamptonshire, Nottinghamshire. Played List A in NZ. Sch: Caistor GS, England. Occ: Cricket pro. An English pro, played and coached in NZ.
NORMAN Alfred David 1907/08-1912/13 b 5.3.1885 Christchurch, Canterbury. d 1.2.1963 Christchurch, Canterbury. RHB Team: **Canterbury.** Sch: West Christchurch BHS. Occ: Pattern maker.
NORMAN William Bruce 1959/60-1962/63 b 4.3.1932 Auckland. RHB RM Team: **Auckland.**
NORRIS William Edward 1940/41-1942/43 b 7.4.1908 Palmerston North, Manawatu. d 17.10.1988 Palmerston North, Manawatu. LHB wk Team: **Wellington.**
NORTH Robert Henry 1917/18 b 21.9.1883 Dunedin, Otago. d 8.6.1952 Christchurch, Canterbury. RHB Team: **Canterbury.** Occ: Schoolmaster. Father: T.H.North.
NORTH Thomas Henry 1893/94-1896/97 b Q4 1858 Crickhowell, Monmouthshire, England. d 11.9.1942 Christchurch, Canterbury. RHB RFM Team: **Canterbury.** Occ: Comm traveller. Umpired first-class cricket. Wisden obit: 1943. Son: R.H.North.
NOTMAN John 1879/80 b Q4 1850 West Ham, London, England. d 20.5.1909 Wanganui. Team: **West Coast (North Island).** Occ: Comm agent.
NOTTMAN Harold Cooper 1941/42 b 18.2.1917 Rochdale, Lancashire, England. d 2.8.2008 Hampstead, London, England. RHB RM Team: **Auckland.**
NUTTALL Andrew John 1977/78-1988/89 b 7.9.1957 Darfield, Canterbury. RHB SLA Team: **Canterbury.** Played List A in NZ. Occ: Finance advisor.
OAKLEY David Frederick 1980/81-1984/85 b 21.11.1960 Wellington. RHB Team: **Wellington.** Played List A in NZ. Sch: St Patricks Coll, Wellington. Father: J.H.Oakley.
OAKLEY John Hayward 1946/47 b 7.2.1925 Palmerston North, Manawatu. RHB Team: **Wellington.** Son: D.F.Oakley.
O'BRIEN Adolphus B 1882/83-1889/90 Team: **Auckland.** Sch: Oscott Coll, England. Occ: Schoolteacher. He lived in Auckland into the 1900s.
O'BRIEN Francis Patrick 1932/33-1945/46 b 11.2.1911 Christchurch, Canterbury. d 22.10.1991 Christchurch, Canterbury. RHB RM Teams: **Canterbury,** Northamptonshire. Sch: St Bedes Coll. NZCA obit: 1992; Wisden obit: 1992. Canterbury selector.
O'BRIEN Iain Edward 2000/01-2010 b 10.7.1976 Lower Hutt, Wellington. RHB RM Teams: **Wellington, New Zealand Test, New Zealand ODI, New Zealand T20,** Leicestershire, Middlesex. Played List A in NZ; Played T20 in NZ. Sch: Petone Coll. Indoor cricket: New Zealand.
O'BRIEN John Joseph 1905/06-1920/21 b 1886 unknown. d 20.12.1939 Napier, Hawke's Bay. RHB RMF Team: **Hawke's Bay.** Occ: Carter. Son: M.A.O'Brien.
O'BRIEN Matthew Alexander 1932/33-1943/44 b 26.7.1910 Napier, Hawke's Bay. d 12.11.1974 Lower Hutt, Wellington. RHB M Team: **Wellington.** Rugby: Wellington, Hawke's Bay. NZCA obit: 1975. Father: J.J.O'Brien.
O'CONNELL William James 1919/20-1920/21 b 9.9.1897 Napier, Hawke's Bay. d 6.4.1973 Napier, Hawke's Bay. OB Team: **Hawke's Bay.** Occ: Clerk.
O'CONNOR Kevin James 1969/70-1970/71 b 20.6.1940 Dunedin, Otago. LHB Team: **Otago.**

O'CONNOR Luke 1876/77 b 1844 New Zealand. d 29.5.1927 Wellington. Team: **Wellington**. Occ: Dairyman.

O'CONNOR Shayne Barry 1994/95-2002/03 b 15.11.1973 Hastings, Hawke's Bay. LHB LFM Teams: **Otago, New Zealand Test, New Zealand ODI.** Played List A in NZ. Occ: Farmer. NZ U19 Test; NZ U19 ODI.

ODELL Charles Shead 1869/70-1870/71 b 1821 Cambridge, England. d 11.10.1875 Motueka, Tasman. Team: **Canterbury.** Occ: Doorman.

O'DOWD Alexander Patrick 1991/92-1996/97 b 25.2.1967 Auckland. RHB OB Teams: **Auckland, Northern Districts.** Played List A in NZ. Sch: Westlake BHS. Occ: Manager.

O'DOWDA Karl Robert 1988/89-2000/01 b 8.5.1970 New Plymouth, Taranaki. RHB RFM Teams: **Central Districts, Otago.** Played List A in NZ. Sch: New Plymouth BHS. Occ: Policeman. NZ U19 Test; NZ U19 ODI.

OGIER Henry John 1889/90-1891/92 b 1865 unknown. d 29.11.1954 Wanganui. wk Team: **Canterbury.** Occ: Upholsterer. Brother: P.H.W.Ogier.

OGIER Phillippe Herbert William 1889/90-1891/92 b 30.9.1863 Christchurch, Canterbury. d 27.11.1941 Wellington. LB wk Team: **Wellington.** Occ: Printer. Brother: H.J.Ogier.

OGILVIE John Edward 1953/54-1963/64 b 12.9.1931 Petone, Lower Hutt, Wellington. RHB Team: **Wellington.**

OHLSON Frederick John 1894/95-1902/03 b 1865 Auckland. d 20.5.1942 Auckland. Team: **Auckland.** Sch: Auckland GS. Occ: Schoolteacher. Rugby: Auckland. Wisden obit: 1943. He was a prominent figure in Auckland cricket and rugby football circles, especially on the administrative side of these games.

OLIVER Charles Joshua 1923/24-1942/43 b 1.11.1905 Wanganui. d 25.9.1977 Brisbane, Queensland, Australia. RHB Teams: **Canterbury, New Zealand.** Sch: Waltham. Occ: Carpenter. Rugby: All Blacks and Canterbury. NZCA obit: 1977; Wisden obit: 1978. He played for New Zealand prior to being granted Test status.

OLLIFF Caleb 1903/04-1912/13 b 9.2.1883 Auckland. d 21.5.1961 Auckland. RHB LB Teams: **Auckland, New Zealand.** NZCA obit: 1961; Wisden obit: 1962. He played for New Zealand prior to being granted Test status. He took a hat-trick for Auckland v Wellington in 1912/13.

OLLIVIER Arthur Morton 1866/67-1882/83 b 23.3.1851 Kensington, London, England. d 21.10.1897 Christchurch, Canterbury. RHB occ wk Team: **Canterbury.** Sch: Christ Coll. Occ: Accountant. Umpired first-class cricket. Rugby: Canterbury. Chess: New Zealand champion in 1888. NZ and Canterbury selector. He was the youngest cricketer to represented Canterbury. Brother: F.M.Ollivier; son: K.M.Ollivier.

OLLIVIER Frank Morton 1867/68 b 1845 Hammersmith, London, England. d 19.5.1918 Parramatta, Sydney, New South Wales, Australia. Team: **Canterbury.** Sch: Christ Coll. Occ: Barrister. Later in life he lost a leg in an accident. Brother: A.M.Ollivier; nephew: K.M.Ollivier.

OLLIVIER Keith Morton 1900/01-1911/12 b 2.8.1880 Christchurch, Canterbury. d 12.9.1951 Christchurch, Canterbury. RHB LB Teams: **Canterbury, New Zealand.** Sch: Christ Coll. Occ: Bank manager. Rugby: Canterbury. NZCA obit: 1951. He played for New Zealand prior to being granted Test status. Father: A.M.Ollivier; uncle: F.M.Ollivier.

O'MALLEY Peter William 1947/48-1954/55 b 24.3.1927 Christchurch, Canterbury. d 9.10.1997 Christchurch, Canterbury. RHB LBG Team: **Canterbury.** Sch: Christchurch BHS. Soccer: New Zealand. NZCA obit: 1998.

O'NEIL Thomas Patrick 1965/66 b 24.7.1936 Wellington. RHB RM Team: **Wellington.**

O'NEILL Samuel Raymond 1944/45-1951/52 b 1.8.1911 Waihi, Bay of Plenty. d 18.7.1983 Wellington. LHB RM Team: **Wellington.** NZCA obit: 1983.

ONGLEY Arthur Montague 1901/02-1903/04 b 21.6.1882 Oamaru, North Otago. d 17.10.1974 Palmerston North, Manawatu. LB Team: **Hawke's Bay.** Sch: St Patricks Coll, Wellington. Occ: Solicitor. Rugby: Manawatu and Hawke's Bay. CBE. NZCA obit: 1974; Wisden obit: 1976. CD selector, president of the CD association, President of both New Zealand rugby and cricket associations. Son: J.A.Ongley.

ONGLEY Joseph Augustine (Sir) 1938/39-1951/52 b 5.2.1918 Feilding, Manawatu. d 22.10.2000 Wellington. RHB Teams: **Wellington, Central Districts, New Zealand.** Sch: St Patricks Coll, Wellington. Occ: Judge. KBE, MC. NZCA obit: 2001. NZ manager, CD selector, life member and patron. He played for New Zealand in a FC match. He scored 110 on FC debut for Wellington v Otago in 1938/39. Father: A.M.Ongley.

ORAM Jacob David Philip 1997/98-2009 b 28.7.1978 Palmerston North, Manawatu. LHB RM Teams: **Central Districts, New Zealand Test, New Zealand ODI, New Zealand T20.** Played List A in NZ; Played T20 in NZ. Sch: Palmerston North BHS. Occ: Cricket pro. NZ U19 Test. NZCA COY: 2003. He holds the NZ Test 7th wicket partnership record of 225 with C.L.Cairns against South Africa in 2003/04.

ORCHARD Mark Geoffrey 2001/02-2007/08 b 8.11.1978 Hamilton, Waikato. RHB RM Team: **Northern Districts.** Played List A in NZ; Played T20 in NZ. Sch: Fraser HS. Occ: Bank officer. Indoor cricket: New Zealand. He holds the Northern Districts 6th wicket partnership record of 322 with J.A.F.Yovich against Central Districts in 2005/06. He took a hat-trick for Northern Districts v Canterbury in 2003/04. Great-grandfather: S.A.Orchard.

ORCHARD Sydney Arthur 1894/95-1912/13 b 12.12.1875 Elmore, Victoria, Australia. d 19.4.1947 Christchurch, Canterbury. LHB Team: **Canterbury.** Sch: West Christchurch BHS. Occ: Comm agent. Rugby: All Blacks, Manuwatu and Canterbury. Wisden obit: 1949. NZ selector and manager. He took a hat-trick for Canterbury v Auckland in 1909/10. Great-grandson: M.G.Orchard.

ORMISTON Ian Walter 1987/88 b 15.6.1963 New Plymouth, Taranaki. RHB OB Team: **Wellington.** Played List A in NZ. Sch: Spotswood Coll. Brother: R.W.Ormiston.

ORMISTON Ross William 1975/76-1985/86 b 19.10.1955 New Plymouth, Taranaki. RHB Teams: **Central Districts, Wellington.** Played List A in NZ. Sch: Spotswood Coll. He holds the Wellington 6th wicket partnership record of 226 with E.J.Gray against Central Districts in 1981/82. Brother: I.W.Ormiston.

O'ROURKE Matthew Harvey 1991/92 b 25.2.1967 Masterton, Wairarapa. RHB RM Team: **Auckland.** NZ U19 ODI. Brother: P.W.O'Rourke.

O'ROURKE Patrick William 1989/90-1992/93 b 12.1.1965 Masterton, Wairarapa. RHB RFM Team: **Wellington.** Played List A in NZ. Brother: M.H.O'Rourke.

ORR George 1923/24-1926/27 b 20.7.1896 St Leonards, Sydney, New South Wales, Australia. d 2.10.1972 Wanganui. RHB Team: **Wellington.** Occ: Coy manager.

OSBORN Harold Walter 1940/41-1941/42 b 14.6.1909 Wellington. d 11.12.1986 Wellington. RHB Team: **Wellington.** NZCA obit: 1987.

OSBORNE Geoffrey Colin 1977/78-1981/82 b 24.2.1956 Dunedin, Otago. LHB M Team: **Otago.** Played List A in NZ.

OSMOND Charles Henry 1884/85 b Q3 1859 St David's, Devon, England. d 20.10.1937 Auckland. Team: **Auckland.** Sch: Mansion House Sch, London, England. Occ: Land agent. Tennis: Taranaki. He had several gold-saving patents, the chief of which is an improvement in dredge tables and he was the patentee of an artificial minnow which was used by anglers throughout the world.

O'SULLIVAN David Robert 1971-1984/85 b 16.11.1944 Palmerston North, Manawatu. RHB SLA Teams: **Central Districts, New Zealand Test, New Zealand ODI,** Hampshire. Played List A in NZ. Sch: Palmerston North BHS. Occ: Insurance rep; sports store.

O'SULLIVAN John Michael 1946/47-1947/48 b 11.5.1918 Dunedin, Otago. d 17.7.1991 Dunedin, Otago. RHB RM Team: **Otago.**

OVERTON Guy William Fitzroy 1945/46-1955/56 b 8.6.1919 Dunedin, Otago. d 7.9.1993 Winton, Southland. LHB RF Teams: **Otago, New Zealand Test.** Sch: Otago BHS. Occ: Farmer. Umpired Test and first-class cricket. NZCA obit: 1994; Wisden obit: 1994. He took 169 first-class wickets but scored only 137 runs. Otago selector. He took a hat-trick for Otago v Canterbury in 1946/47.

OWENS Michael Barry 1991/92-1995/96 b 11.11.1969 Christchurch, Canterbury. RHB RFM Teams: **Canterbury, New Zealand Test, New Zealand ODI.** Played List A in NZ. Sch: Shirley BHS. Occ: Travel agent.

OWLES Horace Edward 1917/18 b 5.3.1900 New Brighton, Christchurch, Canterbury. d 10.12.1968 Gonville, Wanganui. Team: **Southland.** Sch: Wanganui Tech Coll. Occ: Engineer.

OXENHAM Brendon Scott 1990/91-1993/94 b 12.9.1971 Hamilton, Waikato. RHB OB Teams: **Northern Districts, Auckland.** Played List A in NZ.

PABST Joseph Charles 1894/95-1897/98 b 1870 Eaglehawk, Victoria, Australia. d 19.5.1924 Wellington. RHB occ wk Team: **Auckland.** Occ: Doctor. Wisden obit: 1925.

PAETZ David Laurence 1966/67 b 1.5.1940 Wellington. RHB OB Team: **Wellington.** Sch: Wellington Coll. Occ: Accountant.

PAGE Augustus Henry Chambers 1884/85 b Q4 1855 Stroud, Gloucestershire, England. d 13.8.1898 Melbourne, Victoria, Australia. Team: **Canterbury.** Occ: Asylum warder. He was a warder at the Sunnyside Asylum. In 1888 he moved to Melbourne and until his death was employed at the Kew Lunatic Asylum.

PAGE H 1895/96 wk Team: **Wellington.**

PAGE Joseph Elliot 1879/80-1880/81 b 9.1.1841 Sudbury, Suffolk, England. d 17.9.1907 Wellington. Team: **Wellington.** Sch: Suffolk GS, Englansd. Occ: Town clerk.

PAGE Milford Laurenson 1920/21-1942/43 b 8.5.1902 Lyttelton, Christchurch, Canterbury. d 13.2.1987 Christchurch, Canterbury. RHB RS Teams: **Canterbury, New Zealand Test.** Sch: Christchurch BHS. Occ: Salesman. Rugby: All Blacks and Canterbury. Book: The tour of the third All Blacks. NZCA obit: 1987; Wisden obit: 1988. He holds the Canterbury 4th wicket partnership record of 280 with A.W.Roberts against Wellington in 1931/32.

PAIRAUDEAU Bruce Hamilton 1946/47-1966/67 b 14.4.1931 Georgetown, Demerara, British Guiana. RHB LBG Team: **Northern Districts,** West Indies Test, British Guiana. Occ: Insurance agent. NZCA COY: 1959. ND selector. He was picked for his first first-class match for British Guiana before his 16th birthday. He scored a century in his third match aged 16 years and five months. Uncle: J.S.Dare (British Guiana).

PALETHORPE Arthur Lissant 1879/80 b Q2 1854 West Derby, Liverpool, Lancashire, England. d 23.7.1916 Sydney, New South Wales, Australia. Team: **Wellington.** Occ: Artist; singer. Known as Arthur Lissant, he came to NZ from England in the 1870s before moving to Australia. He appeared in the early productions of most of the Gilbert and Sullivan pieces and operas. He never reached the topmost rung in his profession, but he was a capable, reliable, and versatile actor, the possessor of a good baritone voice.

PALMER Edwin Vidal 1892/93-1893/94 b 23.5.1869 Christchurch, Canterbury. d 28.4.1917 Dunedin, Otago. LFM Team: **Canterbury, New Zealand.** Sch: Christ Coll. Occ: Clerk. He played for New Zealand prior to being granted Test status.

PAMMENT James Ian 1993/94-1995/96 b 24.9.1968 Huddersfield, Yorkshire, England. RHB RM Team: **Auckland.** Played List A in NZ. Occ: Cricket coach.

PAPPS Michael Hugh William 1998/99-2009/10 b 2.7.1979 Christchurch, Canterbury. RHB wk Teams: **Canterbury, New Zealand Test, New Zealand ODI.** Played List A in NZ; Played T20 in NZ. Sch: Shirley BHS. Occ: Cricket pro. NZ U19 Test; NZ U19 ODI. NZCA COY: 2007. He holds the Canterbury 2nd wicket partnership record of 254* with J.G.Myburgh against Central Districts in 2007/08. Brother: T.J.T.Papps

PAPPS Timothy James Terence 2003/04-2004/05 b 22.4.1981 Christchurch, Canterbury. LHB wk Team: **Canterbury.** Sch: Shirley BHS. Brother: M.H.W.Papps.

PARAMOR George Henry 1873/74-1880/81 b 19.6.1846 Margate, Kent, England. d 2.8.1925 Liverpool, Sydney, New South Wales, Australia. MF Team: **Otago.** Occ: Cricket pro.

PARK Desmond 1957/58 b 1.4.1936 Inglewood, Taranaki. RHB LB Team: **Central Districts.**

PARKER John Morton 1971-1983/84 b 21.2.1951 Dannevirke, Hawke's Bay. RHB LBG occ wk Teams: **Northern Districts, New Zealand Test, New Zealand ODI,** Worcestershire. Played List A in NZ. Sch: Mahurangi Coll. Occ: Sports mangement; commentator. Brothers: N.M.Parker, K.J.Parker; nephew: M.M.Parker.

PARKER Kenneth John 1970/71 b 12.4.1945 Dannevirke, Hawke's Bay. RHB OB Team: **Auckland.** Sch: Mahurangi Coll. Brothers: J.M.Parker, N.M.Parker; nephew: M.M.Parker.

PARKER Mark Morton 1996/97 b 2.10.1975 Timaru, South Canterbury. d 12.10.2002 Kuta, Bali. Indonesia. He died as a result of injuries received in a terrorist bomb blast, aged 27. RHB Team: **Otago.** Sch: Timaru BHS. Occ: Salesman. NZCA obit: 2003; Wisden obit: 2003. Father: N.M.Parker; uncles: J.M.Parker, K.J.Parker.

PARKER Norman Murray 1967/68-1978/79 b 28.8.1948 Dannevirke, Hawke's Bay. RHB Teams: **Otago, Canterbury, New Zealand Test, New Zealand ODI.** Played List A in NZ. Sch: Mahurangi Coll. Occ: Schoolteacher. Brothers: J.M.Parker, K.J.Parker; son: M.M.Parker.
PARKER Thomas Speight 1864/65-1866/67 b 29.8.1845 Bradford, Yorkshire, England. d 22.9.1880 Dunedin, Otago. Team: **Otago.** Occ: Wool broker.
PARKER William Henry 1880/81-1896/97 b 13.10.1862 East Collingwood, Melbourne, Victoria, Australia. d 11.9.1930 Dunedin, Otago. LB Team: **Otago.** Occ: Tanner. Umpired first-class cricket.
PARKIN Kenneth 1942/43-1945/46 b 20.2.1921 Wellington. d 2.7.1973 Wellington. RHB SLA Team: **Wellington.** Sch: Rongatai Coll. Occ: Coy director. NZCA obit: 1973.
PARKS James Horace 1924-1952 b 12.5.1903 Haywards Heath, Sussex, England. d 21.11.1980 Cuckfield, Sussex, England. RHB RSM Teams: **Canterbury,** England Test, Sussex. Occ: Cricket pro. An English pro, played and coached in NZ. Brother: H.W.Parks (Sussex); grandson: R.J.Parks (Hampshire, Kent); son: J.M.Parks (England, Sussex, Somerset).
PARLANE Michael Edward 1992/93-2009/10 b 22.7.1972 Pukekohe, Franklin. RHB occ wk Teams: **Northern Districts, Wellington.** Played List A in NZ; Played T20 in NZ. Sch: Bream Bay Coll. He holds the Northern Districts 1st wicket partnership record of 167 with M.D.Bell against Central Districts in 1994/95 and also the Northern Districts 4th wicket partnership record of 259 with G.E.Bradburn against Canterbury in 1996/97. Brother: N.R.Parlane.
PARLANE Neal Ronald 1996/97-2009/10 b 9.8.1978 Whangarei, Northland. RHB Teams: **Northern Districts, Wellington.** Played List A in NZ; Played T20 in NZ. Sch: Whangarei HS. NZ U19 Test; NZ U19 ODI. He holds the Wellington 4th wicket partnership record of 310 with J.D.Ryder against Central Districts in 2004/05 also the Northern Districts 9th wicket partnership record of 189 with D.R.Tuffey against Wellington in 1999/00. Brother: M.E.Parlane.
PARORE Adam Craig 1988/89-2001/02 b 23.1.1971 Auckland. RHB wk Teams: **Auckland, Northern Districts (not FC), New Zealand Test, New Zealand ODI.** Played List A in NZ. Sch: St Kentigern Coll. NZ U19 Test; NZ U19 ODI. Book: The wicked keeper. NZCA COY: 1995. He holds the Auckland 6th wicket partnership record of 209* with A.P.O'Dowd against Otago in 1991/92. Whilst sharing a Test 9th wicket partnership of 246 with Nathan Astle v Australia in 2001/02 he scored 103 batting at no.9.
PARRINGTON Henry Roberts 1875/76-1882/83 b Q4 1848 Thetford, Norfolk, England. d 1926 Brunswick, Melbourne, Victoria, Australia. Teams: **Wellington, Taranaki.** Occ: Solicitor.
PARSLOE Cyril Keith 1932/33-1940/41 b 27.9.1908 Wellington. d 13.9.1989 Wellington. LHB RFM Teams: **Wellington, New Zealand.** NZCA obit: 1990; Wisden obit: 1990. He played for New Zealand in a FC match.
PARSON Jonathan St John 1960/61-1963/64 b 12.4.1942 Napier, Hawke's Bay. RHB RFM Teams: **Canterbury, Wellington.** Sch: Christ Coll. Occ: Managing director.
PARSONS Austin Edward Werring 1971/72-1982/83 b 9.1.1949 Glasgow, Lanarkshire, Scotland. RHB LB Teams: **Auckland,** Sussex. Played List A in NZ. Sch: Avondale Coll.
PARTRIDGE Leonard Ernest 1942/43-1950/51 b 22.6.1922 Auckland. d 24.11.1977 Auckland. RHB RM Team: **Auckland.**
PASUPATI Mayu Yoga 1997/98-2006/07 b 5.12.1976 Jaffna, Sri Lanka. RHB RFM Teams: **Wellington, Auckland.** Played List A in NZ; Played T20 in NZ.
PATEL Dhiraj Ukabhai 1966/67-1971/72 b 29.4.1943 Navsari, Gujarat, India. RHB OB Teams: **Northern Districts,** Gujarat. Played List A in NZ.
PATEL Dipak Narshibhai 1976-1996/97 b 25.10.1958 Nairobi. Kenya. RHB OB Teams: **Auckland, New Zealand Test, New Zealand ODI,** Worcestershire. Played List A in NZ. Sch: George Salter Comp Sch, England. Occ: Cricket coach. Book: Dipak Patel benefit year 1995/96. NZCA COY: 1992. He was run out for 99 in what would have been his only Test century. He holds the Auckland 4th wicket partnership record of 280 with J.J.Crowe against Northern Districts in 1991/92. Auckland selector. Cousin: H.V.Patel (Worcestershire).
PATEL Jeetan Shashi 1999/00-2009/10 b 7.5.1980 Wellington. RHB OB Teams: **Wellington, New Zealand Test, New Zealand ODI, New Zealand T20,** Warwickshire. Played List A in NZ; Played T20 in NZ. Sch: Rongatai Coll. Occ: Cricket pro.

PATEL Minal Mahesh 1989-2007 b 7.7.1970 Bombay (now Mumbai), Maharashtra, India. RHB SLA Teams: **Central Districts,** England Test, Kent. Sch: Dartford GS. Occ: Cricket pro. An English pro, played and coached in NZ.
PATERSON A 1914/15 wk Team: **Wellington.**
PATERSON Andrew Timothy 1973/74 b 21.10.1947 Wellington. RHB RM Team: **Central Districts.**
PATERSON James Logan 1912/13-1922/23 b 25.1.1889 Southbridge, Canterbury. d 21.8.1966 Te Awanga, Hawke's Bay. M Teams: **Canterbury, Hawke's Bay, Auckland.** Sch: West Christchurch BHS. Occ: Clerk.
PATERSON Logan 1886/87-1887/88 b 1866 Christchurch, Canterbury. d 4.1.1927 Christchurch, Canterbury. Team: **Hawke's Bay.** Occ: Railway inspector.
PATRICK David Mcintosh 1907/08-1921/22 b 1886 Melbourne, Victoria, Australia. d 5.7.1968 Wellington. Team: **Wellington.** Occ: Builder. NZCA obit: 1968.
PATRICK Gordon Marlborough 1918/19 b 9.11.1897 Christchurch, Canterbury. d 14.1.1964 Wellington. Team: **Otago.** Occ: Dental mechanic.
PATRICK William Robert 1905/06-1926/27 b 17.6.1885 Lyttelton, Christchurch, Canterbury. d 14.8.1946 Christchurch, Canterbury. RHB OB Teams: **Otago, Canterbury, New Zealand.** Occ: Sports dealer. Wisden obit: 1949. NZ selector, coach to the Southland CA. He played for New Zealand prior to being granted Test status.
PATTIE Leslie 1884/85 b 1864 Riwaka, Nelson. d 26.11.1939 Te Awamutu, Waikato. Team: **Nelson.** Sch: Motukea HS. Occ: Farmer.
PATTON Bradley Michael King 2006/07-2009/10 b 9.11.1979 Hastings, Hawke's Bay. LHB RMF Team: **Central Districts.** Played List A in NZ. Sch: Lindesfarne Coll. NZ U19 Test; NZ U19 ODI.
PAUL Justin Mathew 1992/93-1994/95 b 17.11.1972 Dunedin, Otago. RHB OB Team: **Otago.** Played List A in NZ. NZ U19 Test; NZ U19 ODI. Uncle: R.S.Wilson.
PAWLEY Jason Glenn 1994/95 b 11.7.1972 Houston, Texas, United States of America. RHB RM Team: **Central Districts.** Played List A in NZ. Sch: Lindesfarne Coll.
PAWSON Michael John 1990/91-1994/95 b 13.1.1969 Masterton, Wairarapa. RHB RFM Team: **Central Districts.** Played List A in NZ.
PAWSON Scott James 1995/96-1998/99 b 21.12.1974 Christchurch, Canterbury. LHB RM Team: **Canterbury.** Played List A in NZ. Sch: Shirley BHS.
PAYNE Eustace Stanley John 1908/09 b 16.1.1887 Kensington, Melbourne, Victoria, Australia. d 12.11.1954 Berowra, Sydney, New South Wales, Australia. Team: **Wellington.**
PAYNE Ian Wallace 1947/48-1951/52 b 18.7.1921 Dunedin, Otago. RHB OB Team: **Otago.**
PAYTON Dermot Hurlston 1964/65-1976/77 b 19.2.1945 Carterton, Wairarapa. RHB Team: **Central Districts.** Played List A in NZ. Sch: Wanganui CS. Occ: Farmer. He was awarded an International Cricket Council centenary medal. CD selector.
PEACOCK Gavin Graham 1891/92 b 22.11.1866 Napier, Hawke's Bay. d 17.12.1918 Bartholomew's Siding, Putaruru, Waikato. Team: **Hawke's Bay.** Sch: Christ Coll. Occ: Tally clerk.
PEARCE Walter Charles 1893/94-1902/03 b 29.4.1870 Christchurch, Canterbury. d 20.3.1951 Christchurch, Canterbury. RHB RFM Teams: **Canterbury, New Zealand.** Occ: Warehouseman. NZCA obit: 1951. He played for New Zealand prior to being granted Test status.
PEARLESS Walter Hugh 1904/05 b 28.3.1879 Gippsland, Victoria, Australia. d 29.12.1940 Richmond, Nelson. Team: **Otago.** Sch: Nelson Coll. Occ: Doctor.
PEARSON Frederick Albert 1900-1926 b 23.9.1880 Brixton, London, England. d 10.11.1963 Newland, Droitwich, Worcestershire, England. RHB OB Teams: **Auckland,** Worcestershire. Occ: Cricket pro. NZCA obit: 1964; Wisden obit: 1964. An English pro, played and coached in NZ.
PEARSON Herbert Taylor 1932/33-1947/48 b 5.8.1910 Palmerston North, Manawatu. d 15.6.2006 Auckland. RHB RAB Team: **Auckland.** Sch: Kings Coll. Occ: Draper. Rugby: Auckland. NZCA obit: 2007; Wisden obit: 2007. Auckland selector.
PEARSON Lance Robert 1961/62-1970/71 b 1.1.1937 Dunedin, Otago. RHB Team: **Otago.** Sch: Kings HS. Occ: Businessman.

PENHEAROW Robin Anthony 1963/64-1975/76 b 5.10.1941 Simla, Punjab, India. d 8.8.2001 Gisborne, Poverty Bay. RHB LB Team: **Northern Districts.** Sch: Gisborne BHS. Occ: School principal. NZCA obit: 2006.

PENN Andrew Jonathan 1994/95-2003/04 b 27.7.1974 Wanganui. RHB RFM Teams: **Central Districts, Wellington, New Zealand ODI.** Played List A in NZ. Sch: Wanganui CS. NZ U19 Test; NZ U19 ODI.

PERCY Richard William 1884/85-1892/93 b 1862 unknown. d 15.12.1945 Levin, Horowhenua. Team: **Hawke's Bay.** Occ: Postal worker.

PERKINS William Robert 1952/53-1953/54 b 23.3.1934 Wellington. RHB OB Team: **Wellington.**

PERRIN Everard George 1917/18-1918/19 b 8.9.1890 Bulls, Rangitikei. d 25.12.1945 Christchurch, Canterbury. LHB Team: **Canterbury.**

PERRY Arthur 1877/78 b 11.2.1840 Battery Point, Hobart, Tasmania, Australia. d 21.4.1898 Timaru, South Canterbury. He died of mouth cancer. Team: **Canterbury.** Sch: Hobart HS, Australia. Occ: Solicitor. Brother: C.T.H.Perry.

PERRY Cecil Thomas Henry 1868/69-1870/71 b 3.3.1846 Battery Point, Hobart, Tasmania, Australia. d 4.8.1917 Timaru, South Canterbury. RHB Teams: **Canterbury,** Tasmania. Sch: Hobart HS, Australia. Occ: Solicitor. Brother: A.Perry.

PERRY David Leighton 1949/50-1958/59 b 30.6.1929 Auckland. RHB Team: **Auckland.**

PETERSON Simon James 1989/90-1996/97 b 17.11.1968 Auckland. RHB RM Team: **Auckland.** Played List A in NZ. NZ U19 Test; NZ U19 ODI.

PETHERICK Peter James 1975/76-1980/81 b 25.9.1942 Ranfurly, Central Otago. RHB OB Teams: **Otago, Wellington, New Zealand Test.** Played List A in NZ. Sch: Maniototo HS. NZCA COY: 1976. Wellington selector. He took a hat-trick on his Test debut v Pakistan in 1976/77. He took 9/93 for Otago v Northern Districts in 1975/76.

PETRIE Eric Charlton 1950/51-1966/67 b 22.5.1927 Ngaruawahia, Waikato. d 14.8.2004 Omokoroa, Bay of Plenty. RHB LB wk Teams: **Auckland, Northern Districts, New Zealand Test.** Occ: Manager. NZCA obit: 2005; Wisden obit: 2005. NZCA COY: 1963. The competition for club sides in Northern Districts is named after him. ND selector.

PETRIE Francis Roberts Salisbury 1920/21 b 19.11.1900 Invercargill, Southland. d 20.10.1970 Invercargill, Southland. Team: **Southland.** Occ: Valuer; land agent.

PETRIE Richard George 1988/89-1999/00 b 23.8.1967 Christchurch, Canterbury. RHB RFM Teams: **Canterbury, Wellington, New Zealand ODI.** Played List A in NZ. Sch: Shirley BHS. Occ: Coy manager.

PHILLIPS Edgar Morgan 1911/12-1920/21 b 28.7.1891 Wellington. d 13.8.1956 Gisborne, Poverty Bay. Team: **Wellington.** Occ: Postal worker.

PHILLIPS James 1885/86-1898/99 b 1.9.1860 Pleasant Creek (now Stawell), Victoria, Australia. d 21.4.1930 Burnaby, Vancouver, British Columbia, Canada. RHB RM Teams: **Canterbury,** Victoria, Middlesex. Occ: Cricket pro. Wisden obit: 1931. He is known more for his work as an umpire than for anything he accomplished as a player, when he stamped out throwing in first-class cricket in England in 1900.

PHILLIPS John Gregory 1977/78 b 18.9.1949 Christchurch, Canterbury. RHB Team: **Canterbury.** Sch: Linwood HS. Occ: Farmer.

PHILLIPS Ronald 1947/48 Team: **Wellington.**

PHILPOTT Philip Scott 1881/82 b 5.7.1859 Christchurch, Canterbury. d 27.7.1934 Morrinsville, Waikato. Team: **Canterbury.** Occ: Farmer.

PICK Robert Andrew 1983-1997 b 19.11.1963 Nottingham, England. LHB RFM Teams: **Wellington,** Nottinghamshire. Sch: Alderman Derbyshire Comp Sch, England. Occ: Cricket coach. An English pro, played and coached in NZ. Brother-in-law: D.J.Millns (Nottinghamshire, Leicestershire, Tasmania, Boland).

PICKETT Christopher John 1983/84 b 15.9.1955 Christchurch, Canterbury. RHB RSM Team: **Wellington.** Played List A in NZ.

PIERCE Roger Alen 1971/72-1984/85 b 24.5.1952 Motueka, Tasman. RHB RM Team: **Central Districts.** Played List A in NZ.

PIERCE W 1869/70-1872/73 LAB Team: **Canterbury.** Occ: Billiard room manager. Nothing is known of him after 1875.

PIGOTT Anthony Charles Shackleton 1978-1995 b 4.6.1958 Fulham, London, England. RHB RFM Teams: **Wellington,** England Test, Sussex, Surrey. Played List A in NZ. Sch: Harrow, England. Occ: Cricket administrator. An English pro, played and coached in NZ.

PITHER Richard John 1976/77-1984/85 b 23.2.1954 Christchurch, Canterbury. LHB SLA Team: **Wellington.** Played List A in NZ.

PLAYER Allen Shrewsbury 1919/20-1928/29 b 5.9.1893 Auckland. d 17.11.1962 Auckland. LHB RM Team: **Auckland.** Sch: Auckland GS. Occ: Solicitor. NZCA obit: 1963; Wisden obit: 1964.

PLAYLE William Rodger 1956/57-1967/68 b 1.12.1938 Palmerston North, Manawatu. RHB OB Teams: **Auckland, New Zealand Test,** Western Australia. Sch: Gisborne BHS; Auckland GS. Uncle: C.G.Crawford.

POCOCK Blair Andrew 1990/91-2000/01 b 18.6.1971 Papakura, Franklin. RHB RS Teams: **Auckland, Northern Districts, New Zealand Test.** Played List A in NZ. Sch: Auckland GS. NZ U19 Test; NZ U19 ODI. Uncle: M.G.Pocock.

POCOCK Michael Graeme 1965/66 b 18.12.1945 Te Kuiti, King Country. RHB RMF Team: **Northern Districts.** Nephew: B.A.Pocock.

POCOCK William Johnstone 1872/73-1883/84 b 1848 Clifton, Bristol, England. d 27.9.1928 East Brighton, Victoria, Australia. RHB OB Teams: **Canterbury,** New South Wales. Occ: Insurance agent. Umpired first-class cricket. Cousins: G.H.B.Gilbert (Middlesex, New South Wales), W.G.Grace (England, Gloucestershire, Kent, London County), G.F.Grace (England, Gloucestershire), E.M.Grace (England, Gloucestershire), H.Grace (Gloucestershire), W.R.Gilbert (Middlesex, Gloucestershire).

POLLARD Michael Alan 2009/10 b 2.11.1989 Wellington. RHB Team: **Wellington.** Played List A in NZ. Sch: Wellington Coll.

POLLARD Victor 1964/65-1974/75 b 7.9.1945 Burnley, Lancashire, England. RHB OB Teams: **Central Districts, Canterbury, New Zealand Test, New Zealand ODI.** Played List A in New Zealand. Sch: Palmerston North BHS. Occ: School teacher. Soccer: New Zealand. NZCA COY: 1967. He was a Baptist lay preacher who was opposed to playing cricket on Sundays.

POLLITT William 1946/47-1947/48 b 22.6.1918 unknown. d 9.8.1978 Palmerston North, Manawatu. LHB Team: **Canterbury.** Sch: Palmerston North BHS. Occ: Schoolteacher.

POLLOCK Neil David 1981/82-1986/87 b 25.8.1955 Pukekohe, Franklin. RHB RM Team: **Northern Districts.** Played List A in NZ.

POOLE Arthur Valentine 1914/15-1920/21 b 28.4.1878 Aston, Warwickshire, England. d 11.4.1955 Invercargill, Southland. Team: **Southland.** Occ: Coy director.

POORE Matt Beresford 1950/51-1961/62 b 1.6.1930 Christchurch, Canterbury. RHB OB Teams: **Canterbury, New Zealand Test.** Sch: Christchurch BHS. Occ: Regional manager.

POPE Thomas Roberts Warnock 1920/21 b 10.2.1900 Gore, Southland. d 1.12.1947 Otahuhu, Auckland. Team: **Southland.** Occ: Bank clerk.

POSA Mark Walter 1994/95 b 22.6.1966 Auckland. LHB OB Team: **Auckland.** Played List A in NZ. Sch: Kelston BHS.

POSTLES Alfred John 1924/25-1942/43 b 16.6.1903 Devonport, Auckland. d 11.8.1976 Auckland. RHB OB Team: **Auckland.** Sch: Auckland GS. Occ: Accountant. NZCA obit: 1976; Wisden obit: 1977. Auckland selector, President Auckland CA and of the New Zealand Cricket Council. Son: B.J.Postles.

POSTLES Bryce John 1952/53-1956/57 b 22.2.1931 Auckland. RHB Team: **Auckland.** Sch: Auckland GS. Auckland selector. Father: A.J.Postles.

POTTER Dean Frank 1991/92-1992/93 b 2.5.1970 Waiuku, Franklin. RHB LM Team: **Northern Districts.** Played List A in NZ.

POULTNEY Michael Glenn 1972/73 b 10.7.1950 Hamilton, Waikato. LHB RM Team: **Northern Districts.**

POWELL Graeme Arthur 1969/70-1977/78 b 2.1.1947 Dunedin, Otago. RHB RMF Team: **Otago.** Played List A in NZ.

POWELL John Llewellyn 1928/29-1932/33 b 21.3.1904 Islington, Christchurch, Canterbury. d 30.11.1959 Prebbleton, Christchurch, Canterbury. RHB RM Team: **Canterbury.** Sch: Christchurch BHS. Occ: Farmer. NZCA obit: 1960. He holds the NZ 7th wicket partnership record of 265 with N.Doreen for Canterbury v Otago in 1929/30. Brother: R.F.J.Powell.

POWELL Michael James 1996-2008 b 5.4.1975 Bolton, Lancashire, England. RHB RM occ wk Teams: **Otago**, Warwickshire, Griqualand West. Sch: Lawrence Sheriff Sch, England. An English pro, played and coached in NZ.

POWELL Robert Frederick James 1922/23 b 27.4.1902 Auburn, Sydney, New South Wales, Australia. d 25.2.1976 Christchurch, Canterbury. RHB RM occ wk Team: **Canterbury.** Sch: Christchurch BHS. Occ: Auctioneer. Umpired first-class cricket. Brother: J.L.Powell.

POWELL Samuel 1874/75-1876/77 b 1850 Victoria, Australia. d 22.10.1893 Wanganui. wk Team: **Nelson.** Occ: Farmer; horse trainer. He commenced horse training on his own account in Christchurch but owing to his health he sought a change and purchased Flemington Lodge, Wanganui. Nearly all of the principal race clubs in the colony secured his services as a starter.

POWELL Tyrone Lyndon 1971/72-1976 b 17.6.1953 Bargoed, Glamorgan, Wales. RHB OB Teams: **New Zealand Under-23s**, Glamorgan. Sch: Heretaunga Coll. Occ: Printer.

POWYS Arthur Littleton 1863/64-1867/68 b 17.10.1842 Thrapston, Northamptonshire, England. d 8.8.1875 Alexandra Colony, Argentina. He went to Argentina where he became director of a European colony called the Alexandra Colony. He was killed there by local Indians, aged 32. wk Team: **Canterbury.** Sch: Marlborough, England. Occ: Farmer. Brothers: W.N.Powys (Cambridge University, Hampshire), R.A.N.Powys.

POWYS Richard Atherton Norman 1865/66-1866/67 b 19.9.1844 Thrapston, Northamptonshire, England. d 10.6.1913 East Sheen, Surrey, England. Team: **Canterbury.** Sch: Marlborough, England. Occ: Secretary, Royal Veterinary College. Brothers: W.N.Powys (Cambridge University, Hampshire), A.L.Powys.

PRAIN George 1887/88 b 1857 Scotland. d 27.10.1914 Dunedin, Otago. He was killed in a Dunedin hotel bar. Newspapers reported that he was apparently wrestling with another man and fell on his head. Earnest Dallas was arrested on a charge of manslaughter but the coroner found that no blame was attachable to anybody and that Prain died from a meningeal haemorrhage. Evidence disclosed nothing in the nature of a scuffle. Team: **Hawke's Bay.** Sch: Otago BHS. Occ: Customs clerk. Umpired first-class cricket.

PRATT Albert Ernest 1912/13 b 16.4.1893 Auckland. d 19.7.1916 Pozieres, France. He was killed in action whilst serving as a lieutenant in the Australian Forces, aged 23. He died on the same day and in the same battle as A.M.Given (Otago). Team: **Auckland.** Sch: Auckland GS. Occ: Clerk.

PRATT Percy Mackenzie 1894/95-1897/98 b 12.1.1874 Bareilly, Bengal Presidency (now Uttar Pradesh), India. d 20.7.1961 Denmark, Western Australia, Australia. Team: **Taranaki.** Occ: Groundsman.

PRENTICE Eddy Shannon 1945/46 b 24.9.1920 Reefton, Buller. d 20.9.2009, Auckland. RHB RFM Team: **Auckland.**

PRESLAND Craig Miller 1982/83-1984/85 b 22.5.1960 Whangarei, Northland. RHB RM Team: **Northern Districts.** Played List A in NZ. Sch: Kamo HS. Occ: Coy director. Rugby: North Auckland.

PRESTON Alan Herbert 1955/56-1962/63 b 29.10.1932 Wellington. d 2.9.2004 Wellington. RHB OB Team: **Wellington.** Sch: Wellington Coll. Occ: Bookkeeper. Soccer: New Zealand. NZCA obit: 2005.

PRIDEAUX Edward William 1885/86 b 23.3.1864 Wellington. d 3.4.1948 Canterbury, Sydney, New South Wales, Australia. Team: **Wellington.**

PRIEST Mark Wellings 1984/85-1998/99 b 12.8.1961 Greymouth, West Coast. LHB SLA Teams: **Canterbury, New Zealand Test, New Zealand ODI.** Played List A in NZ. Sch: Papanui HS. Occ: Electrician. He took 9/95 for Canterbury v Otago in 1989/90.

PRIEST William Alexander 1931/32-1932/33 b 18.3.1909 Dunedin, Otago. d 8.12.1972 Wanganui. RHB Team: **Otago.** Sch: Otago BHS. Occ: Doctor.

PRIME Frederick Leopold 1907/08 b 19.11.1884 Auckland. d 21.5.1923 Devonport, Auckland. Team: **Auckland.** Sch: Wanganui CS. Occ: Ironmonger.

PRINCE Horace William 1923/24-1924/25 b 21.10.1900 Napier, Hawke's Bay. d 5.5.1977 Wellington. S Team: **Wellington.** NZCA obit: 1977.

PRINGLE Christopher 1989/90-1995/96 b 26.1.1968 Auckland. RHB RFM Teams: **Auckland, New Zealand Test, New Zealand ODI.** Played List A in NZ. Sch: Rosmini Coll. NZ U19 Test; NZ U19 ODI. Book: Save the last ball for me. He started his Test career on a high, with 11/152 in his third match (including 7/52 in the first innings) against Pakistan at Faisalabad, although he later admitted that he had tampered with the ball because he was sure Pakistan were doing it.

PRINGLE Martin Roy 1984/85-1991/92 b 18.8.1964 Auckland. RHB RM Team: **Auckland.** Played List A in NZ. Cousin: P.N.Webb.

PRITCHARD Thomas Leslie 1937/38-1956 b 10.3.1917 Kaupokonui, Taranaki. RHB RFM Teams: **Wellington, New Zealand,** Warwickshire, Kent. Sch: Hawera Tech Coll. He played for New Zealand in a FC match. He took three hat-tricks for Warwickshire.

PROCTER Raymond Albert 1960/61 b 9.3.1938 Dunedin, Otago. LHB Team: **Otago.** Sch: Kings HS.

PROUTING Robert Henry 1969/70 b 2.10.1938 Christchurch, Canterbury. RHB RM Team: **Otago.**

PRYOR Craig Robert 1997/98-2003/04 b 15.10.1973 Auckland. LHB RM Teams: **Auckland, Otago.** Played List A in NZ. Sch: Auckland GS. NZ U19 Test; NZ U19 ODI.

PUDNEY Richard Alan 2000/01 b 6.6.1978 Auckland. RHB Team: **Auckland.** Played List A in NZ.

PUNA Ashok 1971/72-1972/73 b 19.2.1953 Hamilton, Waikato. LHB OB Team: **Northern Districts.** Played List A in NZ. Sch: Hamilton BHS. Brother: K.N.Puna; father: N.Puna.

PUNA Kirti Narotam 1971/72-1978/79 b 10.9.1955 Hamilton, Waikato. RHB LB Team: **Northern Districts.** Played List A in NZ. Sch: Hamilton BHS. Brother: A.Puna; father: N.Puna.

PUNA Narotam 1956/57-1968/69 b 28.10.1929 Surat, Gujarat, India. d 7.6.1996 Hamilton, Waikato. RHB OB Teams: **Northern Districts, New Zealand Test.** Sch: Hamilton Tech Coll. Occ: Grocer. NZCA obit: 1997; Wisden obit: 1997. NZCA COY: 1966. Sons: A.Puna, K.N.Puna.

PURDUE John William 1938/39 b 13.6.1910 Invercargill, Southland. d 25.1.1985 Invercargill, Southland. Team: **Otago.** Occ: Cabinetmaker.

PUTT Albert Glanville 1947/48-1950/51 b 13.3.1927 Auckland. RHB Team: **Auckland.** Auckland selector.

QUARTERMAN Fraser James 2007/08 b 27.6.1983 Wellington. RHB LMF Team: **Wellington.** Sch: St Patricks Coll, Wellington. Occ: Fitness instructor.

QUEE Robert William 1899/00-1904/05 b 2.9.1877 Wellington. d 25.2.1920 Hawera, Taranaki. Team: **Wellington.** Sch: Mt Cook HS. Occ: Sign writer.

QUENTERY William George Lloyd 1893/94 b Q4 1861 Camberwell, London, England. d 9.6.1940 Auckland. Team: **Auckland.** Occ: Bank officer.

QUINN John Joseph 1913/14 b 1889 Ireland. d 3.12.1967 Wellington. Team: **Wellington.** Occ: Clerk.

RABONE Geoffrey Osborne 1940/41-1960/61 b 6.11.1921 Gore, Southland. d 19.1.2006 Auckland. RHB OB,LB Teams: **Wellington, Auckland, New Zealand Test.** Sch: Palmerston North BHS. Occ: Oil coy rep. NZCA obit: 2006; Wisden obit: 2007. SACOY 1954. NZ and Auckland selector.

RAE Benjamin Joseph 2006/07-2007/08 b 22.10.1986 Christchurch, Canterbury. RHB wk Team: **Canterbury.** Sch: Ashburton Coll.

RAINBIRD William Gerald 1934/35-1946/47 b 9.4.1916 Wellington. d 27.9.1997 Kenepuru, Porirua, Wellington. RHB Team: **Wellington.**

RAINES Stanley Victor 1919/20 b 18.1.1895 Invercargill, Southland. d 24.8.1948 Christchurch, Canterbury. Team: **Southland.** Occ: Licensing authority.

RAINS Albert George 1894/95-1896/97 b 7.2.1865 Melbourne, Victoria, Australia. d 17.7.1947 Perth, Western Australia, Australia. wk Team: **Otago, New Zealand.** He played for New Zealand prior to being granted Test status.

RAMSDEN John 1909/10-1914/15 b 29.9.1878 Melbourne, Victoria, Australia. d 12.8.1973 Christchurch, Canterbury. Team: **Otago.** Occ: Tea importer. NZCA obit: 1973.

RANCE Seth Hayden Arnold 2008/09-2009/10 b 23.8.1987 Wellington. RHB RM Team: **Central Districts.** Played List A in NZ; Played T20 in NZ. Sch: Wairarapa Coll.

RANDALL Clement Lindsay William 1948/49-1950/51 b 8.8.1913 Napier, Hawke's Bay. d 23.12.2007 Nelson. LHB RM Team: **Wellington.** NZCA obit: 2008. President Wellington CA.
RAPLEY Arthur Frank 1957/58-1959/60 b 2.9.1937 Kaiapoi, North Canterbury. RHB OB Team: **Canterbury.** Sch: Christchurch BHS. Occ: County clerk.
RASMUSSEN Scott 2005/06-2006/07 b 18.11.1978 Wellington. RHB RMF Team: **Wellington.** Played List A in NZ. Sch: Westlake BHS.
RATHIE David Stewart 1970/71-1980/81 b 29.5.1951 Roma, Queensland, Australia. RHB OB Teams: **Canterbury,** Queensland. Sch: Brisbane GS, Australia. Occ: Solicitor. Rugby: Australia, Queensland and NSW.
RATTRAY Charles William 1883/84-1896/97 b 9.7.1863 Dunedin, Otago. d 8.6.1939 Dunedin, Otago. Team: **Otago.** Sch: Otago BHS; Christs Coll. Occ: Merchant. Rugby: Otago. He was appointed Vice-Consul for Portugal in 1900.
RATTRAY Peter John 1980/81-1984/85 b 14.9.1958 Christchurch, Canterbury. RHB OB Team: **Canterbury.** Played List A in NZ. Sch: Christchurch BHS. Occ: Clerk.
RAVAL Jeet Ashokbhai 2008/09-2009/10 b 22.5.1988 Ahmedabad, Gujarat, India. LHB LB Team: **Auckland.** Sch: Avondale Coll. NZ U19 Test; NZ U19 ODI. In his second FC match he scored 256 for Auckland v Central Districts in 2008/09.
RAYNER Dominic Leo 2006/07 b 26.8.1983 Marton, Rangitikei. RHB RM Team: **Central Districts.** Sch: Rangitikei Coll. Occ: Builder.
RAYNER George Lucas 1884/85-1889/90 b 15.10.1863 Northampton, England. d 20.2.1915 Christchurch, Canterbury. He died as a result of pulmonary tuberculosis. Teams: **Canterbury, Otago.** Occ: Bootmaker.
READ James 1882/83 Team: **Taranaki.** Occ: Painter.
READ Reginald John 1904/05-1937/38 b 8.6.1886 Auckland. d 1.3.1974 Christchurch, Canterbury. RHB RM Team: **Canterbury, New Zealand.** Sch: Christchurch East. Occ: Foundry worker. NZCA obit: 1974; Wisden obit: 1976. He played for New Zealand prior to being granted Test status. he had the longest FC career in NZ FC history - 33 years from 1904/05 to 1937/38. His best match performance was 7/35 and 7/24 for Canterbury against Southland, then a first-class side, in 1920/21.
READ Robert 1899/00-1900/01 b 1870 London, England. d 15.2.1945 Wellington. Team: **Wellington.** Sch: Mt Cook HS. Occ: Coy secretary.
READE Lawrence Burnard 1958/59-1962/63 b 21.10.1930 Nelson. RHB RM Team: **Central Districts.**
READE Lawrence Edward 1869/70-1876/77 b 8.11.1846 Goruckpore, Bengal Presidency (now Uttar Pradesh), India. d 17.8.1910 Wellington. He fell from a tramcar on 2 July 1910 and suffered an injury to his head. He was subsequently operated upon, apparently recovered, and was discharged from the hospital on 29th July. He was admitted to hospital again on 15th August suffering from fits. Another operation was performed, but he died two days later. Teams: **Canterbury, Otago.** Sch: Tonbridge, England. Occ: Solicitor. He was a nephew of Charles Reade, the novelist and dramatist.
REANEY Henry Eaton Ivan 1932/33 b 18.9.1912 Napier, Hawke's Bay. d 1.7.1990 Hastings, Hawke's Bay. M Team: **Wellington.** CD selector. Brother: T.P.L.Reaney; father: P.S.Reaney.
REANEY Philip Stanley 1905/06 b Q3 1862 Bradford, Yorkshire, England. d 19.4.1927 Napier, Hawke's Bay. Team: **Hawke's Bay.** Occ: Sharebroker. Sons: H.E.I.Reaney, T.P.L.Reaney.
REANEY Thomas Philip Lewis 1927/28-1950/51 b 11.8.1909 Napier, Hawke's Bay. d 4.12.1994 Napier, Hawke's Bay. LHB RM Teams: **Wellington, Central Districts.** NZCA obit: 1995. He scored 299 in a Hawke's Cup game for Hawke's Bay v Wairapara in 1946/47. Brother: H.E.I.Reaney; father: P.S.Reaney.
REARDON George 1903/04 b 24.5.1880 Melbourne, Victoria, Australia. d 11.6.1932 Melbourne, Victoria, Australia. Team: **Otago.**
REDDINGTON Daryll John 2002/03 b 17.10.1972 Queenstown, Central Otago. RHB RM Team: **Otago.** Occ: Schoolteacher.
REDFEARN James 1862/63-1863/64 b 1836 Yorkshire, England. d 10.3.1916 Glenhuntly, Victoria, Australia. RHB Teams: **Otago,** Victoria. Occ: Horse trainer. Horse Racing: owned Malvolio, the winner of the Melbourne Cup in 1891. Wisden obit: 1917.

REDGRAVE William Patrick 1903/04-1908/09 b 23.1.1881 St Leonards, Sydney, New South Wales, Australia. d 28.11.1931 Crows Nest, Sydney, New South Wales, Australia. RHB Teams: **Wellington, Hawke's Bay, New Zealand.** Sch: Newington Coll, Australia. Occ: Groundsman. He played for New Zealand in a non-first-class match prior to being granted Test status.

REDMAYNE Arthur Tunstal 1880/81 b 25.4.1857 Hendon, Middlesex, England. d 27.12.1933 Ambleside, Westmorland, England. SLA Team: **Canterbury.** Sch: Rugby, England.

REDMOND Aaron James 1999/00-2009/10 b 23.9.1979 Auckland. RHB LB Teams: **Canterbury, Otago, New Zealand Test, New Zealand ODI, New Zealand T20.** Played List A in NZ; Played T20 in NZ. Sch: Kent Street HS, Australia. Father: R.E.Redmond.

REDMOND Rodney Ernest 1963/64-1975/76 b 29.12.1944 Whangarei, Northland. LHB SLA Teams: **Wellington, Auckland, New Zealand Test, New Zealand ODI.** Played List A in NZ. Sch: Whangarei HS. NZCA COY: 1973. On his Test debut he scored 107 and 56 against Pakistan at Christchurch in 1972/73. This match was his only Test. Son: A.J.Redmond.

REECE Albert Jack 1947/48 b Q1 1927 Christchurch, Canterbury. d 10.9.1966 Christchurch, Canterbury. RHB Team: **Canterbury.** Occ: Process worker. Hockey: New Zealand.

REEDER Francis James 1873/74 b Q4 1850 Wath-upon-Dearne, Yorkshire, England. d 28.7.1908 Brisbane, Queensland, Australia. LHB Team: **Canterbury.** Occ: Chemist.

REEKERS Darron John 1997/98-2005/06 b 26.5.1973 Christchurch, Canterbury. RHB RM occ wk Teams: **Canterbury (not FC), Otago,** Netherlands ODI, Netherlands T20. Played List A in NZ. Sch: St Thomas Coll. Occ: Cricket pro.

REES Arthur Westland 1889/90-1896/97 b 9.9.1866 Hokitika, West Coast. d 1.1.1921 Gisborne, Poverty Bay. SLA Teams: **Auckland, Hawke's Bay.** Sch: Auckland GS. Occ: Solicitor. On FC debut he had the best match figures for Auckland of 14/63 against Otago in 1889/90 - all 14 wickets were taken on one day which is a record for all NZ FC cricket. Father: W.L.Rees; brother-in-law: H.B.Lusk.

REES William Lee 1856/57-1877/78 b 16.12.1836 Bristol, England. d 18.5.1912 Gisborne, Poverty Bay. Teams: **Auckland,** Victoria. Sch: Private tutor. Occ: Solicitor. Books: In collaboration with his eldest daughter he wrote "A Life", a biography of George Grey; a novel, 'Gilbert Leigh'; an economic treatise; and a theological work. MP. Wisden obit: 1914. W.G.Grace's mother was the sister of W.L.Rees's father. He was called to the Bar at Melbourne in 1865, and migrated to Dunedin, Hokitika, Auckland, and Gisborne successively. He was prominent in the political world, and a great supporter of Sir George Grey. He was a Member of Parliament and once made a stone-walling speech of about twenty hours. Cousins: H.Grace (Gloucestershire), W.R.Gilbert (Middlesex, Gloucestershire), G.H.B.Gilbert (Middlesex, New South Wales), W.G.Grace (England, Gloucestershire, Kent, London County), G.F.Grace (England, Gloucestershire), E.M.Grace (England, Gloucestershire); son: A.W.Rees; son-in-law: H.B.Lusk.

REESE Daniel 1895/96-1920/21 b 27.1.1879 Christchurch, Canterbury. d 12.6.1953 Christchurch, Canterbury. LHB LSM Teams: **Canterbury, New Zealand,** London County, Essex. Sch: West Christchurch BHS. Occ: Coy director. Rugby: Canterbury. Book: Was it all cricket?. NZCA obit: 1953; Wisden obit: 1954. NZ and Canterbury selector, member of the Management Committee and President of the New Zealand Cricket Council. He played for New Zealand prior to being granted Test status. Brothers: J.B.Reese, T.W.Reese; nephew: D.W.Reese.

REESE Daniel Whitelaw 1917/18-1920/21 b 19.10.1898 Christchurch, Canterbury. d 11.1.1954 Elwood, Melbourne, Victoria, Australia. Team: **Canterbury.** Sch: Christchurch BHS. Occ: Salesman. Father: T.W.Reese; uncles: D.Reese, J.B.Reese.

REESE John Baillie 1900/01 b 23.4.1877 Christchurch, Canterbury. d 26.1.1971 Christchurch, Canterbury. Team: **Canterbury.** Sch: Christchurch BHS. Occ: Wool merchant. Brothers: D.Reese, T.W.Reese; nephew: D.W.Reese.

REESE Thomas Wilson 1887/88-1917/18 b 29.9.1867 Christchurch, Canterbury. d 13.4.1949 Christchurch, Canterbury. Team: **Canterbury.** Sch: Christchurch BHS. Occ: Clerk. Books: He wrote the history of New Zealand cricket in two volumes 1841-1914 and 1914-1933. Wisden obit: 1950. Cricket administrator. Brothers: D.Reese, J.B.Reese; son: D.W.Reese.

REEVES William Pember 1879/80-1887/88 b 10.2.1857 Lyttelton, Christchurch, Canterbury. d 16.5.1932 Kensington, London, England. Team: **Canterbury.** Sch: Christ Coll. Occ: Statesman. Umpired first-class cricket. Rugby: Canterbury. Books: State Experiments in Australia and New Zealand; The Long White Cloud. Knight of the Redeemer (Greece), Knight of St. George of

Greece. MP. He served as Minister of Labour (1891-1896). As Minister he introduced the Immigrants Exclusion Bill which barred immigrants from the country. His anti-foreigner stance earned him the nickname 'Undesirable Bill' Reeves. In 1896 he left New Zealand for London where he was Agent-General (1896-1905) and High Commissioner (1905-1908).

REID Douglas James 1953/54-1956/57 b 17.10.1928 Christchurch, Canterbury. RHB LM Team: **Canterbury.** Sch: Christchurch BHS. Occ: Quantity surveyor.

REID John Fulton 1975/76-1987/88 b 3.3.1956 Auckland. LHB LB wk Teams: **Auckland, New Zealand Test, New Zealand ODI.** Played List A in NZ. Sch: Lynfield Coll. Occ: Schoolteacher; NZC operations director. NZCA COY: 1981, 1985. Cousin: B.A.Reid (Australia, Western Australia).

REID John Richard 1947/48-1965 b 3.6.1928 Auckland. RHB RFM,OB occ wk Teams: **Wellington, Otago, New Zealand Test.** Sch: Hutt Valley HS. Occ: Cricket coach. Books: Million miles of cricket; Sword of the willow; John Reid : a cricketing life by J.Romanos. OBE. Inducted into the New Zealand Sports Hall of Fame in 1990. NZCA COY: 1951; WCOY: 1959, SACOY 1954, ICOY 1955/56. NZ and Otago selector. ICC match referee. He holds the NZ 4th wicket partnership record of 324 with W.M.Wallace v Cambridge University in 1949. In 1963 he set a then world record for the most sixes in an innings - 15 - while scoring 296 for Wellington against Northern Districts. Son: R.B.Reid.

REID Richard Bruce 1979/80-1991/92 b 3.12.1958 Lower Hutt, Wellington. RHB Teams: **Wellington, Auckland, New Zealand ODI,** Transvaal B. Played List A in NZ. Occ: CEO Otago Rugby; CEO Canterbury CA. Father: J.R.Reid.

REID Rodney Ernest 1958/59-1960/61 b 30.7.1939 Apia, Upolu, Samoa. RHB RM Team: **Wellington.** Sch: Rongatai Coll. Soccer: New Zealand and Wellington. He took a hat-trick for Wellington v Otago in 1958/59.

REINHOLDS Andrew Terence 1993/94-1995/96 b 11.11.1967 Wellington. RHB LM Team: **Auckland.** Played List A in NZ. Sch: Westlake BHS. Occ: Media manager.

RELF Albert Edward 1900-1921 b 26.6.1874 Burwash, Sussex, England. d 26.3.1937 Wellington College, Crowthorne, Berkshire, England. He shot himself, this was attributed to poor health and depression due to the serious illness of his wife. RHB RM,OB Teams: **Auckland,** England Test, Sussex, London County. Occ: Cricket pro. Wisden obit: 1938. WCOY: 1914. An English pro, played and coached in NZ. Brothers: R.R.Relf (Sussex), E.H.Relf (Sussex).

RENNER Joseph Ralph 1882/83 b 1857 New Zealand. d 10.12.1916 Wellington. Team: **Wellington.** Occ: Cabinetmaker.

RENWICK Cecil 1959/60 b 26.7.1924 Auckland. RHB SLA Team: **Auckland.** NZOM. Awarded an International Cricket Council centenary medal.

RESTIEAUX Charles 1900/01 b 19.2.1865 Christchurch, Canterbury. d 24.12.1918 Auckland. RM Team: **Auckland.** Occ: Bootmaker.

REWCASTLE Lindsay John 1979/80 b 5.2.1955 Invercargill, Southland. LHB OB Team: **Auckland.** Sch: Manurewa HS. Occ: Coy director.

RHODES David Kirk 1874/75 b 25.3.1847 Huddersfield, Yorkshire, England. d 22.12.1937 Caulfield, Victoria, Australia. Team: **Otago.** Occ: Postmaster.

RHODES Hiram 1872/73-1876/77 b 11.12.1850 Lockwood, Huddersfield, Yorkshire, England. d 1.1.1891 Huddersfield, Yorkshire, England. wk Team: **Otago.** Occ: Warehouseman.

RHODES Stewart John 2009/10 b 1.12.1986 Orange, New South Wales, Australia. LHB RFM Team: **Wellington.** Played List A in NZ. Sch: Blue Mountains GS, Australia. He scored 142* on FC debut for Wellington v Otago in 2009/10.

RICE Herbert Fergus 1937/38-1950/51 b 5.9.1918 Wellington. d 13.7.1982 Otaki, Horowhenua. RHB RM Teams: **Wellington, Central Districts.** NZCA obit: 1982.

RICHARDS Geoffrey Alan 1955/56 b 9.5.1922 Auckland. RHB OB Team: **Auckland.**

RICHARDS Henry Malcolm Rutherford 1987/88 b 14.9.1967 Darfield, Canterbury. RHB RM Team: **Canterbury.** Sch: Christ Coll. Occ: Landscape architect. NZ U19 Test; NZ U19 ODI.

RICHARDS Isaac 1889/90-1893/94 b 11.2.1859 Tavistock, Devon, England. d 10.5.1936 Christchurch, Canterbury. occ wk Team: **Auckland.** Sch: Wesleyan Coll, Taunton, England. Occ: Anglican Reverend. Wisden obit: 1937.

RICHARDS Kurt Daniel 2007/08 b 15.9.1987 Napier, Hawke's Bay. RHB RMF Team: **Central Districts.** Sch: Napier BHS.

RICHARDS Simon John 1983/84-1984/85 b 28.1.1964 Dunedin, Otago. RHB Team: **Otago**. Played List A in NZ.
RICHARDSON Charles Augustus 1886/87-1906/07 b 22.2.1864 Sydney, New South Wales, Australia. d 17.8.1949 Waipara, North Canterbury. RHB Teams: **Wellington, New Zealand,** New South Wales. Sch: Sydney GS, Australia. Occ: Insurance manager. He scored the first hundred for New Zealand in a representative match. He played for New Zealand prior to being granted Test status. Brother: W.A.Richardson (New South Wales).
RICHARDSON George Richard 1884/85-1891/92 b 1853 New Zealand. d 27.7.1934 Nelson. Team: **Nelson**.
RICHARDSON H 1865/66 Team: **Otago**. Sch: Blackheath Proprietory School, England.
RICHARDSON Mark Hunter 1989/90-2004/05 b 11.6.1971 Hastings, Hawke's Bay. LHB SLA Teams: **Auckland, Otago, New Zealand Test, New Zealand ODI,** Marylebone Cricket Club. Played List A in NZ. Sch: St Kentigern Coll. NZ U19 Test; NZ U19 ODI. Book: Thinking Negatively. NZCA COY: 2001. He scored 306 for New Zealand v Zimbabwe A in 2000/01, batting for 741 minutes which is the longest innings by a New Zealander.
RIDDIFORD Frederick 1882/83-1891/92 b 1850 Wellington. d 27.2.1901 Hawera, Taranaki. He was thrown from a horse which trod on him causing a bowel abscess from which he succumbed a year later. Team: **Taranaki**. Sch: Christ Coll. Occ: Sheep farmer. Umpired first-class cricket.
RIDDOLLS Alec Wilson 1941/42 b 26.10.1908 Burnley, Lancashire, England. d 18.5.1963 Christchurch, Canterbury. Team: **Wellington**. Occ: Schoolteacher.
RIDLAND James David 1945 b 17.1.1923 New Plymouth, Taranaki. d 4.2.1978 New Plymouth, Taranaki. LHB occ wk Team: **New Zealand Services**. Sch: New Plymouth BHS. Occ: Coy manager.
RIDLEY Archibald Ernest 1889/90-1909/10 b 22.9.1869 Chepstow, Monmouthshire, England. d 1.2.1950 Christchurch, Canterbury. RHB Teams: **Canterbury, New Zealand**. Occ: Insurance agent. NZCA obit: 1952. He played for New Zealand prior to being granted Test status. Brothers: H.C.Ridley, R.A.Ridley.
RIDLEY Harry Clifford 1891/92-1904/05 b Q3 1868 Chepstow, Monmouthshire, England. d 11.1.1949 Christchurch, Canterbury. occ wk Team: **Canterbury**. Occ: Gas coy officer. Brothers: A.E.Ridley, R.A.Ridley.
RIDLEY Reginald Arthur 1905/06-1906/07 b 23.3.1883 Christchurch, Canterbury. d 27.10.1971 Hastings, Hawke's Bay. Team: **Canterbury**. Brothers: A.E.Ridley, H.C.Ridley.
RIGG Archibald Anthony 1884/85 b 18.4.1865 Wellington. d 2.9.1918 Wellington. Team: **Wellington**. Sch: Mt Cook HS. Occ: Ironmonger.
RILEY James Denis 1968/69-1976/77 b 26.1.1948 Christchurch, Canterbury. LHB Teams: **Canterbury, Wellington, Auckland**. Played List A in NZ. Sch: Christ Coll. Occ: Vice-President of Reebok Corporation.
RILEY Joseph P 1885/86 b Australia. d 30.12.1891 San Francisco, California, United States of America. After leaving NZ he went to California and for some time kept an hotel at Butte City, Montana. He proceeded to San Francisco with the intention of starting as a saloon-keeper, however he died from a severe cold. Team: **Hawke's Bay**. Occ: Publican.
RILEY Leslie Ernest 1933/34-1934/35 b 21.3.1908 St Pancras, London, England. d 9.8.1999 Auckland. LHB SLA Teams: **Canterbury, Wellington**. Occ: Groundsman.
RITCHIE Aubrey Wallis 1951/52-1959/60 b 9.3.1925 Auckland. d 26.12.1995 Auckland. RHB wk Team: **Auckland**. NZCA obit: 1997. Brother: D.C.Ritchie.
RITCHIE Bryan Donald 1979/80-1981/82 b 6.12.1954 Christchurch, Canterbury. LHB wk Team: **Canterbury**. Played List A in NZ. Sch: Christchurch BHS. Occ: Manager.
RITCHIE Dawson Charles 1943/44 b 10.5.1920 Auckland. d 3.7.1994 Auckland. RHB Team: **Auckland**. Brother: A.W.Ritchie.
RITCHIE Tim David 1982/83-1990/91 b 10.1.1964 Christchurch, Canterbury. RHB SLA Team: **Wellington**. Played List A in NZ.
RIX Charles Theodore 1922/23 b 15.6.1891 Akaroa, Canterbury. d 21.11.1958 Temuka, South Canterbury. LHB SLA Team: **Canterbury**. Occ: Draper.

ROBERTS Albert William 1927/28-1950/51 b 20.8.1909 Christchurch, Canterbury. d 13.5.1978 Clyde, Central Otago. RHB RM Teams: **Canterbury, Otago, New Zealand Test.** Sch: West Christchurch BHS. Occ: Civil servant. Rugby: Canterbury. NZCA obit: 1978; Wisden obit: 1979. He holds the Canterbury 4th wicket partnership record of 280 with M.L.Page against Wellington in 1931/32.

ROBERTS Alexander 1959/60-1963/64 b 1.10.1939 Napier, Hawke's Bay. RHB Team: **Wellington.** Auckland selector. Son: S.A.Roberts.

ROBERTS Allen Christian 1945-1947/48 b 16.12.1922 Sandringham, Auckland. RHB RM Team: **Auckland.**

ROBERTS Andrew Duncan Glenn 1967/68-1983/84 b 6.5.1947 Te Aroha, Thames Valley. d 26.10.1989 Wellington. He died suddenly of a heart attack aged 42. RHB RM Teams: **Northern Districts, New Zealand Test, New Zealand ODI.** Played List A in NZ. Sch: St Pauls Hamilton. Occ: Cricket coach. NZCA obit: 1990; Wisden obit: 1990. NZCA COY: 1980. Wellington coaching director.

ROBERTS Andrew Richard 1989-1996 b 16.4.1971 Kettering, Northamptonshire, England. RHB LB Teams: **Wellington,** Northamptonshire. Sch: Bishop Stopford Comp Sch, England. An English pro, played and coached in NZ. Brother: T.W.Roberts (Lancashire, Northamptonshire).

ROBERTS Barry Leonard 1977/78 b 15.6.1946 Suva, Fiji. RHB Team: **Northern Districts.** Played List A in NZ. CD selector. Brother-in-law: B.L.Cairns; nephew: C.L.Cairns.

ROBERTS Edward James 1909/10 b 10.5.1891 Wellington. d 27.2.1972 Wellington. wk Team: **Wellington.** Sch: Brooklyn. Occ: Manufacturing agent. Rugby: All Blacks and Wellington. Father: H.Roberts; nephew: V.H.du Chateau.

ROBERTS Henry 1882/83-1889/90 b 8.7.1863 Wellington. d 1.1.1949 Wellington. Team: **Wellington.** Occ: Printer. Rugby: All Blacks and Wellington. He was the first try-scorer in All Black rugby and was followed into the New Zealand side by his son, E.J. 'Teddy', also a halfback, when he was chosen for the All Blacks to tour North America in 1913. They were the first All Black father-son representatives. Grandson: V.H.du Chateau; son: E.J.Roberts.

ROBERTS Sean Alexander 1994/95 b 21.12.1968 Napier, Hawke's Bay. RHB Team: **Auckland.** NZ U19 Test; NZ U19 ODI. Father: A.Roberts.

ROBERTS Stuart James 1985/86-1995/96 b 22.3.1965 Christchurch, Canterbury. RHB RFM Teams: **Canterbury, New Zealand ODI.** Played List A in NZ. Sch: Christchurch BHS. Occ: Bank manager.

ROBERTSON Frederick Humphrey 1897/98-1901/02 b 1878 unknown. d 17.9.1966 Auckland. wk Teams: **Taranaki, Wellington.** Occ: Insurance agent. Rugby: Wellington.

ROBERTSON Gary Keith 1979/80-1989/90 b 15.7.1960 New Plymouth, Taranaki. RHB RFM Teams: **Central Districts, New Zealand Test, New Zealand ODI.** Played List A in NZ. Sch: New Plymouth BHS. He holds the Central Districts 8th wicket partnership record of 173 with I.D.S.Smith against Northern Districts in 1982/83. Brother: S.P.Robertson.

ROBERTSON Gordon John 1937/38-1940/41 b 15.2.1909 Gisborne, Poverty Bay. d 4.9.1983 Lower Hutt, Wellington. RHB RM Team: **Otago.**

ROBERTSON Iain Anthony 2005/06-2008/09 b 9.11.1982 Christchurch, Canterbury. RHB OB Team: **Canterbury.** Played List A in NZ; Played T20 in NZ. Sch: St Bedes Coll. Occ: Cricket pro. NZ U19 Test; NZ U19 ODI.

ROBERTSON Stephen Paul 1985/86-1987/88 b 21.10.1963 New Plymouth, Taranaki. RHB RM Team: **Central Districts.** Played List A in NZ. Sch: New Plymouth BHS. Brother: G.K.Robertson.

ROBERTSON William 1893/94-1900/01 b 4.3.1864 Invercargill, Southland. d 5.4.1912 Auckland. OB Team: **Canterbury, New Zealand.** Occ: Cricket pro; coach. Wisden obit: 1913. He played for New Zealand prior to being granted Test status. He took 9/98 for Canterbury v Wellington in 1894/95.

ROBERTSON William Alexander 1960/61 b 22.9.1940 Ranfurly, Central Otago. RHB Team: **Otago.**

ROBIN Taraia Pere 1999/00-2000/01 b 30.8.1982 Hastings, Hawke's Bay. RHB RFM Team: **Central Districts.** Played List A in NZ. Sch: Lindesfarne Coll. NZ U19 Test; NZ U19 ODI.

ROBINSON Charles Walter 1911/12-1914/15 b 28.3.1892 Wellington. d 22.5.1947 Lower Hutt, Wellington. RHB RFM Teams: **Wellington, New Zealand.** Occ: Clerk. Wisden obit: 1949. He played for New Zealand prior to being granted Test status.
ROBINSON Grant Geoffrey 2001/02-2007/08 b 24.7.1979 Gisborne, Poverty Bay. LHB SLA Team: **Northern Districts.** Played List A in NZ. Sch: Gisborne BHS. Occ: Cricket administrator.
ROBINSON M 1877/78 Team: **Wellington.**
ROBINSON Mark Andrew 1987-2002 b 23.11.1966 Hull, Yorkshire, England. RHB RFM Teams: **Canterbury,** Northamptonshire, Yorkshire, Sussex. Sch: Hull GS, England. Occ: Cricket coach. An English pro, played and coached in NZ.
ROBINSON Rayford Harold 1934/35-1948/49 b 26.5.1914 Stockton, New South Wales, Australia. d 10.8.1965 Stockton, New South Wales, Australia. RHB LBG Teams: **Otago,** Australia Test, New South Wales, South Australia. Occ: Labourer. NZCA obit: 1967; Wisden obit: 1994.
ROBINSON Shane Andrew 1984/85-1996/97 b 24.8.1967 Dunedin, Otago. RHB wk Team: **Otago.** Played List A in NZ. NZ U19 Test; NZ U19 ODI.
ROBINSON William 1902/03-1912/13 b 1864 Cambridge, Waikato. d 21.3.1928 Wellington. RHB wk Team: **Auckland.** Occ: Carpenter. Wisden obit: 1929.
ROBINSON William Wills 1873/74-1884/85 b 17.6.1847 Birmingham, Warwickshire, England. d 14.9.1929 Wellingborough, Northamptonshire, England. LSM Team: **Auckland.** Sch: Epsom Coll, England.
RODGERS John Joseph 1908/09-1914/15 b 1877 Hokitika, West Coast. d 3.10.1941 Wellington. Team: **Wellington.** Occ: Schoolteacher. Umpired first-class cricket.
ROGERS Frederick Benjamin 1941/42 b 10.7.1918 New Plymouth, Taranaki. d 7.8.1998 Lower Hutt, Wellington. Team: **Wellington.** Nephew: K.F.H.Smith.
ROHRS Anthony John 1987/88 b 5.8.1961 Lower Hutt, Wellington. d 24.6.1988 Wellington. He died in a car accident, aged 26. LHB LM Team: **Wellington.** Played List A in NZ. Sch: Hastings BHS. NZCA obit: 1988; Wisden obit: 1989.
ROLLESTON Arthur Cecil 1889/90-1890/91 b 1867 Wellington. d 28.9.1918 Wellington. He died from a fractured skull a day after falling backwards on a pavement. Team: **Canterbury.** Sch: Christ Coll. Occ: Solicitor. He was a barrister and solicitor, and at one time was in partnership with F.Wilding.
ROMANOS Richard Francis 1951/52 b 28.10.1929 Wellington. RHB Team: **Wellington.**
RONALDSON Alan 1922/23 b 12.9.1896 Wellington. d 9.1.1965 Dunedin, Otago. RHB Team: **Wellington.** Occ: Civil servant. NZCA obit: 1965.
RONALDSON Thomas Sherriff 1883/84 b 1855 Cork, Ireland. d 4.12.1931 Wellington. Team: **Wellington.** Occ: Civil servant. Umpired first-class cricket. Rugby: Wellington. OBE. Brother-in-law: M.M.F.Luckie.
ROSE Gerald Alan 1958/59-1967/68 b 11.4.1941 Palmerston North, Manawatu. d 12.6.2007 Sydney, New South Wales, Australia. LHB Teams: **Central Districts, Northern Districts.** Sch: Palmerston North BHS. Occ: Vet. Rugby: NSW. Horse Racing: co-owned Belle du Jour, winner of the Golden Slipper in 2000. NZCA obit: 2007.
ROSE Henry 1876/77-1883/84 b 3.9.1853 Hampstead, London, England. d 9.6.1895 Dunedin, Otago. He died from influenza. Team: **Otago.** Sch: Repton, England. Occ: Merchant. Umpired first-class cricket. Rugby: Cambridge University and Otago. Soccer: Cambridge University.
ROSE W 1885/86 Team: **Wellington.**
ROSS Bertie Raymond 1929/30-1935/36 b 23.8.1909 Lower Hutt, Wellington. d 17.11.1987 Lower Hutt, Wellington. RHB Team: **Wellington.**
ROSS Christopher Jonathan 1975/76-1980 b 24.6.1954 Warri, Nigeria. RHB RM Teams: **Wellington,** Oxford University. Played List A in NZ. Sch: Wanganui CS. Occ: Solicitor. Rhodes scholar.
ROSS Craig Eric 2005/06 b 18.9.1980 Lincoln, Christchurch, Canterbury. RHB LMF Team: **Canterbury.** Sch: Riccarton HS.
ROSS Craig William 1989/90-1996/97 b 18.10.1970 Papakura, Franklin. RHB RM Team: **Northern Districts.** Played List A in NZ. NZ U19 Test; NZ U19 ODI.
ROSS Edward James 1883/84 b 29.1.1860 Christchurch, Canterbury. d 14.4.1937 Christchurch, Canterbury. Team: **Canterbury.** Sch: Christ Coll. Occ: Solicitor.

ROTCH Ricky Robert 1993/94 b 8.9.1966 Dunedin, Otago. RHB RFM Team: **Wellington.**
ROTHERHAM Gerard Alexander 1919-1928/29 b 28.5.1899 Allesley, Coventry, Warwickshire, England. d 31.1.1985 Bakewell, Derbyshire, England. RHB RM Teams: **Wellington, Cambridge University, Warwickshire.** Sch: Rugby, England. NZCA obit: 1985; Wisden obit: 1986. WCOY: 1918. Uncle: H.Rotherham (Warwickshire).
ROTHWELL James 1883/84 b 1844 Chester, Cheshire, England. d 29.12.1927 Timaru, South Canterbury. wk Team: **Canterbury.** Sch: Hollingworth Coll. Occ: Overseer.
ROWE Charles Gordon 1944/45-1952/53 b 30.6.1915 Glasgow, Lanarkshire, Scotland. d 9.6.1995 Palmerston North, Manawatu. RHB Teams: **Wellington, Central Districts, New Zealand Test.** Occ: Policeman. Hockey: New Zealand. NZCA obit: 1995; Wisden obit: 1996. CD selector.
ROWNTREE Richard William 1914/15-1931/32 b 6.4.1884 Leyburn, Yorkshire, England. d 16.6.1968 Auckland. RHB wk Teams: **Auckland, New Zealand.** Occ: Warehouseman. NZCA obit: 1968; Wisden obit: 1970. He appeared for the Yorkshire second eleven in 1904. After a serious illness he emigrated to New Zealand. He played for New Zealand prior to being granted Test status.
ROY Robert Alexander 1970/71-1971/72 b 7.10.1948 Gore, Southland. LHB SLA Team: **Otago.**
ROYFEE Gavin Ernest 1952/53 b 20.2.1929 Christchurch, Canterbury. RHB Team: **Canterbury.** Sch: Christchurch BHS. Occ: Shell Oil Company clerk.
RUGG Paul James 2003/04 b 20.6.1978 Christchurch, Canterbury. RHB wk Team: **Canterbury.** Sch: St Andrews Coll.
RULE Bernard Julian 1982/83 b 29.6.1957 Christchurch, Canterbury. RHB RM Team: **Wellington.** Played List A in NZ.
RUSHTON Neil William 2001/02-2003/04 b 3.10.1976 Oamaru, North Otago. RHB LM Team: **Otago.** Played List A in NZ. Sch: Waitaki BHS.
RUSS Thornton Stirling 1940/41-1945/46 b 3.1.1922 Auckland. d 9.2.1976 Wellington. RHB Team: **Wellington.** Occ: Manager. NZCA obit: 1976.
RUSTON John Michael 1962/63 b 4.3.1941 Wellington. d 30.4.2006 Brisbane, Queensland, Australia. RHB Team: **Canterbury.** Sch: Papanui HS. NZCA obit: 2008. Wellington selector.
RUTHERFORD Hamish Duncan 2008/09-2009/10 b 27.4.1989 Dunedin, Otago. LHB Team: **Otago.** Played List A in NZ; Played T20 in NZ. Sch: Otago BHS. Father: K.R.Rutherford; uncle: I.A.Rutherford.
RUTHERFORD Ian Alexander 1974/75-1983/84 b 30.6.1957 Dunedin, Otago. RHB RM,OB occ wk Teams: **Otago, Central Districts,** Worcestershire. Played List A in NZ. Sch: Kings HS. Occ: Accountant. Otago selector. Brother: K.R.Rutherford; nephew: H.D.Rutherford.
RUTHERFORD Kenneth Robert 1982/83-1999/00 b 26.10.1965 Dunedin, Otago. RHB RM Teams: **Otago, New Zealand Test, New Zealand ODI,** Transvaal, Gauteng. Played List A in NZ. Sch: Kings HS. Occ: Cricket pro. Books: Hell of a way to make a living; Ken Rutherford's book of cricket by M.Crean. NZCA COY: 1993. He holds the Otago 2th wicket partnership record of 254 with K.J.Burns against Wellington in 1987/88. In 1986 he scored 317 for NZ v Brian Close's XI - the innings included 199 between lunch and tea, his third hundred coming in 35 minutes off 33 balls. He hit 53 boundaries (8 sixes and 45 fours) which is the most boundaries by a New Zealander in an innings. Brother: I.A.Rutherford; son: H.D.Rutherford.
RUTHERFORD Robert Malcolm 1908/09-1913/14 b 4.10.1886 Dunedin, Otago. d 17.8.1960 Dunedin, Otago. Team: **Otago.** Occ: Solicitor.
RUTLEDGE Paul Donald 1982/83 b 30.7.1962 Christchurch, Canterbury. LHB wk Team: **Canterbury.** Played List A in NZ. Sch: Linwood HS. Occ: Communication specialist.
RYAN B 1903/04-1910/11 Team: **Hawke's Bay.** An Australian, in between playing for Hawke's Bay, he played club cricket in Wellington.
RYAN Maurice Lloyd 1965/66-1978/79 b 7.6.1943 Christchurch, Canterbury. RHB OB wk Teams: **Canterbury, Central Districts, New Zealand.** Played List A in NZ. Sch: Christchurch BHS. Occ: Coy manager. He played for New Zealand in a FC match.
RYDER Jesse Daniel 2002/03-2009/10 b 6.8.1984 Masterson, Wairarapa. LHB RM Teams: **Central Districts, Wellington, New Zealand Test, New Zealand ODI, New Zealand T20.** Played List A in NZ; Played T20 in NZ. Sch: Napier BHS. Occ: Cricket pro. NZ U19 ODI. NZCA

COY: 2009. He holds the NZ Test 4th wicket partnership record of 271 with L.R.P.L.Taylor against India in 2008/09 and the Wellington 4th wicket partnership record of 310 with N.R.Parlane against Central Districts in 2004/05.

SAINSBURY Edward Ashfield Popham 1893/94-1894/95 b 19.5.1875 Napier, Hawke's Bay. d 27.6.1938 Takapuna, Auckland. Team: **Hawke's Bay.** Sch: Marlborough, England. Occ: Settler. Umpired first-class cricket. Uncle: E.Sainsbury (Somerset, Gloucestershire).

ST JOHN Douglas Stuart 1946/47-1955/56 b 26.2.1928 Nelson. d 11.7.1992 Otane, Hawke's Bay. RHB Teams: **Otago, Wellington.** Sch: Otago BHS. Occ: Accountant. Hockey: New Zealand and Otago. NZCA obit: 1996.

SALE Edmund Vernon 1904/05-1914/15 b 6.7.1883 Taunton, Somerset, England. d 16.11.1918 Auckland. He died of Spanish flu at the age of 35. RHB occ wk Teams: **Auckland, New Zealand.** Occ: Journalist; dentist. Soccer: New Zealand and Auckland. Wisden obit: 1919. He played for New Zealand prior to being granted Test status. In 1905/06 he scored 284 in Auckland club cricket. Son: V.S.Sale.

SALE George Samuel 1863/64-1864/65 b 11.5.1831 Rugby, Warwickshire, England. d 25.12.1922 Kensington, London, England. RHB Team: **Canterbury.** Sch: Rugby, England. Occ: Professor. Umpired first-class cricket. He held the chair of Classics at Otago University from 1871 to 1908. He was a keen sportsman and played a major role in the development of both cricket and rugby at the University of Otago.

SALE Matthew James 1997/98 b 2.2.1975 Auckland. LHB wk Team: **Otago.**

SALE Vernon Scott 1934/35-1939/40 b 13.6.1915 Auckland. d 4.1.1991 Auckland. RHB RM occ wk Team: **Auckland.** Sch: Takapuna GS. Umpired first-class cricket. NZCA obit: 1991. Father: E.V.Sale.

SALES David John Grimwood 1996-2010 b 3.12.1977 Carshalton, Surrey, England. RHB RM occ wk Teams: **Wellington,** Northamptonshire. Played List A in NZ. Sch: Caterham School, England. Occ: Cricket pro. An English pro, played and coached in NZ.

SALMON Isaac John 1873/74-1881/82 b 16.11.1851 Sydney, New South Wales, Australia. d 26.11.1932 Palmerston North, Manawatu. Team: **Wellington.** Occ: Cabinetmaker. He took a hat-trick for Wellington v Nelson in 1873/74. Brothers: J.A.N.Salmon, W.J.Salmon.

SALMON James Alexander Nathaniel 1873/74-1880/81 b 8.1.1849 Sydney, New South Wales, Australia. d 28.11.1903 Wellington. He died of heart failure. Team: **Wellington.** Occ: Accountant. Brothers: I.J.Salmon, W.J.Salmon.

SALMON William Joseph 1873/74-1891/92 b 29.5.1846 Sydney, New South Wales, Australia. d 25.10.1907 Palmerston North, Manawatu. occ wk Teams: **Wellington, Hawke's Bay, Taranaki.** Occ: Comm traveller. Umpired first-class cricket. Brothers: J.A.N.Salmon, I.J.Salmon.

SAMPSON Brian Victor 1969/70 b 30.7.1945 Ashburton, Mid Canterbury. RHB Team: **Canterbury.**

SAMPSON George Hurfitt 1874/75 b 7.7.1845 Bell Block, Taranaki. d 17.3.1911 New Plymouth, Taranaki. Team: **Otago.** Occ: Farmer. Father: H.Sampson (Yorkshire).

SAMPSON Henry Charles 1970/71-1976/77 b 1.4.1947 New Plymouth, Taranaki. d 19.7.1999 Gold Coast, Queensland, Australia. He died from cancer aged 52. LHB occ wk Teams: **Central Districts, Otago, Canterbury.** Played List A in NZ. Sch: New Plymouth BHS. NZCA obit: 1999; Wisden obit: 2000. He scored 119 on FC debut for Central Districts v Wellington in 1970/71.

SAMUELS B 1919/20 Team: **Wellington.**

SANDBROOK Ian Patrick 2002/03 b 22.3.1983 Palmerston North, Manawatu. RHB SLA wk Team: **Central Districts.** Played List A in NZ. Sch: Palmerston North BHS. Occ: Cricket management. NZ U19 ODI.

SANDMAN Donald Mckay 1909/10-1926/27 b 3.11.1889 Christchurch, Canterbury. d 29.1.1973 Christchurch, Canterbury. RHB LBG Team: **Canterbury, New Zealand.** Occ: Plumber. Rugby: New Zealand Army and Canterbury. NZCA obit: 1973; Wisden obit: 1974. He played for New Zealand prior to being granted Test status.

SANDRI Mervin Francis 1956/57 b 20.1.1932 Roxburgh, Central Otago. RHB RM Team: **Otago.**

SANDS R 1905/06 b New South Wales, Australia. Team: **Auckland.** Occ: Cricket coach. He came from Australia in 1905 as a coach for the Auckland CA.

SATCHELL Robert Evan 1884/85 b Q4 1859 Tunbridge Wells, Kent, England. d 8.6.1909 Granity, West Coast. wk Team: **Nelson.** Sch: Epsom Coll, England. Occ: Schoolmaster.

SATHERLEY Clifton Robert 1959/60-1960/61 b 18.3.1939 Auckland. d 14.9.1961 Paeroa, Thames Valley. He died in a rail crossing accident aged 22. RHB RM Team: **Northern Districts.** Occ: Stock buyer. NZCA obit: 1962.

SAUNDERS John Victor 1899/00-1913/14 b 21.3.1876 Melbourne, Victoria, Australia. d 21.12.1927 Toorak, Melbourne, Victoria, Australia. He died whilst undergoing an operation aged 52. LHB LM,SLA Teams: **Wellington, New Zealand,** Australia Test, Victoria. Occ: Groundsman. He played for New Zealand prior to being granted Test status.

SAUNDERS Lloyd Havelock 1925/26 b 23.9.1897 Waihi, Bay of Plenty. d 8.3.1984 Devonport, Auckland. RHB RSM Team: **Auckland.**

SAVILE George 1867-1874 b 26.4.1847 Methley, Yorkshire, England. d 4.9.1904 Tetbury, Gloucestershire, England. RHB occ wk Teams: **Canterbury,** Cambridge University, Yorkshire. Sch: Rossall, England. Occ: Gentleman. Wisden obit: 1905. In a match in Hertfordshire, in 1874, he hit a ball a distance of 135 yards. Uncle: A.Savile (Cambridge University).

SAXON Kendall Reginald James von Tunzelmann 1923/24 b 1.9.1894 Nelson. d 1.6.1976 Pinner, Middlesex, England. wk Team: **Canterbury.** Sch: Nelson Coll. Occ: Schoolteacher. MC and bar. He won his MC for conspicuous gallantry in action. He assumed command and led his company with great courage and determination. Later, although wounded, he organised and consolidated the position won.

SAXTON Charles Kesteven 1934/35-1938/39 b 23.5.1913 Kurow, North Otago. d 4.7.2001 Dunedin, Otago. RHB occ wk Team: **Otago.** Sch: Otago BHS. Occ: Men's outfitter. Rugby: All Blacks and Otago. Books: The A.B.C. of rugby; Between Overs. MBE. NZCA obit: 2001. He selected and assisted with the coaching of the Otago team 1948-57, served on the NZRFU council 1956-71 and was manager of the 1967 All Blacks in Britain and France. He was president of the NZRFU in 1974 and elected a life member in 1976.

SCANDRETT John Carruthers 1935/36-1943/44 b 22.2.1915 Invercargill, Southland. d 29.8.2006 Nelson. LHB OB Team: **Otago.** Sch: Southland BHS. Occ: Branch manager. NZCA obit: 2007.

SCHAW Robert James 2006/07-2009/10 b 12.5.1984 Waipukurau, Hawke's Bay. LHB LB Teams: **Central Districts, Wellington.** Played List A in NZ; Played T20 in NZ. Sch: Napier BHS.

SCHMOLL Gustav Ernest 1903/04-1912/13 b 1869 Oamaru, North Otago. d 20.10.1942 Wellington. wk Teams: **Auckland, Wellington.** Occ: Upholsterer.

SCHOFER Jeffrey William James 1969/70 b 26.3.1943 Petone, Lower Hutt, Wellington. RHB Team: **Wellington.** Sch: Naenae Coll. Brother: P.J.Schofer.

SCHOFER Philip John 1983/84 b 22.4.1948 Lower Hutt, Wellington. RHB RM Team: **Wellington.** Played List A in NZ. Sch: Naenae Coll. Brother: J.W.J.Schofer.

SCHOFIELD Robin Matthew 1959/60-1974/75 b 6.11.1939 Hokitika, West Coast. d 6.1.1990 Taradale, Hawke's Bay. He was killed, aged 50, when a tree he was cutting fell on him. RHB SLA wk Team: **Central Districts.** Played List A in NZ. Occ: Schoolteacher. NZCA obit: 1990; Wisden obit: 1991. He was the first New Zealander to take seven dismissals behind the wicket in an innings in a first-class match. He performed this feat for Central Districts against Wellington at Wellington in 1964/65, all his victims being caught. In the same match he was also the first New Zealand wicket-keeper to make nine dismissals. Grandson: P.D.McGlashan.

SCHOLLUM William John 1920/21 b 21.3.1880 Puhoi, Auckland. d 13.10.1970 Puhoi, Auckland. Team: **Minor Associations.** Occ: Farmer.

SCHRADER Eric Augustine Alexander 1919/20 b 12.4.1898 Wellington. d 1976 Pukekohe, Franklin. Team: **Wellington.** Occ: Labourer.

SCHUSTER Hector Thomas 1963/64-1971/72 b 15.1.1942 Fiji. d 26.11.2007 Brisbane, Queensland, Australia. RHB OB Teams: **Auckland, Northern Districts.** Played List A in NZ. Sch: St Pauls, Hamilton. Rugby: Waikato. NZCA obit: 2008.

SCHWASS Andrew Mark 1998/99-2004/05 b 11.4.1974 Nelson. RHB RFM Team: **Central Districts.** Played List A in NZ.

SCOTT Alfred Henry 1925/26-1927/28 b 28.10.1901 Auckland. d 5.1.1984 Auckland. RHB wk Team: **Auckland.** Brother: V.J.Scott.

SCOTT Bradley Esmond 2000/01-2009/10 b 16.9.1979 Ashburton, Mid Canterbury. LHB LFM Teams: **Otago, Northern Districts.** Played List A in NZ; Played T20 in NZ. Sch: Kings HS. Occ: Schoolteacher. He holds the Otago 9th wicket partnership record of 208 with W.C.McSkimming against Auckland in 2004/05 and the NZ domestic T20 9th wicket partnership record of 47* with T.G.Southee for Northern Districts against Otago in 2009/10.

SCOTT Derek Grant 1985/86-1986/87 b 4.8.1964 Auckland. RHB RM Team: **Auckland.** Played List A in NZ.

SCOTT Nigel Alexander 1980/81-1984/85 b 19.12.1961 Bristol, England. RHB wk Team: **Auckland.** Played List A in NZ.

SCOTT Peter William 1962/63 b 17.10.1940 Matamata, Waikato. LHB SLA Team: **New Zealand Under-23s.**

SCOTT Roy Hamilton 1940/41-1954/55 b 6.3.1917 Clyde, Central Otago. d 5.8.2005 Christchurch, Canterbury. RHB RM Teams: **Canterbury, New Zealand Test.** Sch: West Christchurch BHS. Occ: Furniture manufacturer. NZCA obit: 2006; Wisden obit: 2007.

SCOTT Stephen James 1978/79-1985/86 b 2.4.1955 Matamata, Waikato. RHB RM Team: **Northern Districts.** Played List A in NZ.

SCOTT Verdun John 1937/38-1952/53 b 31.7.1916 Devonport, Auckland. d 2.8.1980 Devonport, Auckland. RHB RAB Teams: **Auckland, New Zealand Test.** Sch: Stanley Bay Sch. Rugby League: New Zealand. NZCA obit: 1980; Wisden obit: 1981. NZCA COY: 1950. He scored 122 on FC debut for Auckland v Canterbury in 1937/38 and holds the Auckland 7th wicket partnership record of 224 with A.M.Matheson against Canterbury in 1937/38. Brother: A.H.Scott.

SCRAGG Richard Steven 1996/97-2001/02 b 5.4.1978 Auckland. RHB LB Teams: **Auckland, Central Districts.**

SEARS Michael John 1990/91-1993/94 b 28.2.1967 Auckland. RHB RFM Team: **Wellington.** Played List A in NZ.

SECRETAN Henry Howell 1876/77-1886/87 b 25.2.1855 Blackheath, Kent, England. d 16.6.1911 Christchurch, Canterbury. He died of stomach cancer. RHB Team: **Canterbury.** Sch: Marlborough, England. Occ: Accountant. Wisden obit: 1912. Canterbury CA secretary.

SEED Henry Edsforth 1913/14 b 10.7.1893 Hastings, Hawke's Bay. d 3.2.1953 Napier, Hawke's Bay. Team: **Hawke's Bay.** Occ: Accountant.

SELLON Melville 1873/74-1875/76 b 20.5.1846 Grosmont, Monmouthshire, England. d 21.4.1880 Waimea, Nelson. Whilst riding to his home he died by the roadside from apoplexy. wk Team: **Nelson.** Sch: Bradfield Coll, England. Occ: Farmer.

SELWOOD Timothy 1966-1973 b 1.9.1944 Prestatyn, Flintshire, Wales. RHB RM Teams: **Central Districts,** Middlesex. Played List A in NZ. Sch: William Ellis Sch, England. Son: S.A.Selwood (Derbyshire).

SEMPLE Peter Charles 1961/62-1971/72 b 29.4.1941 Dunedin, Otago. RHB OB Team: **Otago.** Played List A in NZ. Sch: Otago BHS.

SERGENT Brian Walter Harold 1951/52-1952/53 b 27.11.1926 Wellington. d 1.8.1998 New Zealand. RHB RM Team: **Wellington.** Soccer: New Zealand.

SEWELL David Graham 1995/96-2005/06 b 20.10.1977 Christchurch, Canterbury. RHB LFM Teams: **Otago, New Zealand Test.** Played List A in NZ. Sch: Waitaki BHS. NZ U19 Test; NZ U19 ODI.

SHACKLOCK Francis Joseph 1883-1904/05 b 22.9.1861 Crich, Derbyshire, England. d 1.5.1937 Christchurch, Canterbury. RHB RF Teams: **Otago,** Nottinghamshire, Derbyshire. Occ: Cricket coach. Wisden obit: 1938. An English pro, played and coached in NZ.

SHAND Richard Cecil Stevens Alison 1937/38-1946/47 b 11.5.1916 Christchurch, Canterbury. d 23.12.1965 Christchurch, Canterbury. RHB Team: **Canterbury.** Sch: Christchurch BHS. NZCA obit: 1966.

SHARP Herbert Hastings 1904/05 b Q3 1881 Blackheath, Kent, England. d 1.9.1918 France. Team: **Hawke's Bay.** Sch: South Eastern Coll, Ramsgate, England. Occ: Farm manager.

SHARP Peter Andrew 1964/65-1965/66 b 11.8.1939 Invercargill, Southland. RHB OB Team: **Canterbury.** Sch: Southland BHS. Occ: School teacher. Basketball: Southland. Canterbury selector.

SHARP Thomas Murray 1934/35-1945/46 b 23.1.1916 Gisborne, Poverty Bay. d 11.5.1999 Gisborne, Poverty Bay. RHB LB Team: **Canterbury.** Sch: Gisborne BHS. Occ: Schoolteacher. NZCA obit: 2004. CD and ND selector.

SHARPE Michael Frank 1990/91-1996/97 b 8.10.1966 Dannevirke, Hawke's Bay. RHB RM Team: **Canterbury.** Played List A in NZ. Sch: Rangiora HS. Occ: Manager of indoor cricket school.

SHAW Gareth Simon 2001/02-2009/10 b 14.2.1982 Auckland. RHB RMF Teams: **Auckland, Otago.** Played List A in NZ. Sch: St Kentigern Coll. NZ U19 ODI. Brother: L.J.Shaw.

SHAW Hayden Jonathan 1999/00-2004/05 b 31.8.1980 Christchurch, Canterbury. RHB RFM Team: **Canterbury.** Played List A in NZ; Played T20 in NZ. Sch: Shirley BHS. Occ: Schoolteacher. NZ U19 Test; NZ U19 ODI. Hockey: New Zealand.

SHAW Lance Joseph 2005/06-2009/10 b 24.8.1983 Auckland. RHB RMF Team: **Auckland.** Played List A in NZ; Played T20 in NZ. Brother: G.S.Shaw.

SHAW Terence Edward 1956/57-1963/64 b 4.5.1937 Paeroa, Thames Valley. RHB RM Team: **Northern Districts.**

SHEATH Alfred George 1879/80 b 15.6.1859 Aston, Warwickshire, England. d Q2 1939 Hackney, London, England. Team: **Canterbury.** Sch: Christ Coll. Occ: Mining engineer.

SHEED Jordan William 2001/02-2008/09 b 24.9.1982 Timaru, South Canterbury. RHB LB,RMF Team: **Otago.** Played List A in NZ; Played T20 in NZ. Sch: Otago BHS. NZ U19 ODI.

SHEFFIELD James Roy 1929-1938/39 b 19.11.1906 Barking, Essex, England. d 16.11.1997 Auckland. RHB wk Teams: **Wellington,** Essex. Sch: Coopers Company Sch, England. Occ: Mountain guide; field officer. Book: Bolivian spy. NZCA obit: 1998; Wisden obit: 1998. In 1932-33, he was working as a cowboy in South America and trying to canoe down the River Paraguay. There was a war going on between Paraguay and Bolivia and the Paraguayans arrested Sheffield and locked him up until a British businessman intervened. He later wrote a novel based on the incident. An English pro, played and coached in NZ.

SHEPHERD James Stevens Fraser 1912/13-1930/31 b 29.2.1892 Reefton, Buller. d 11.7.1970 Dunedin, Otago. RHB Team: **Otago, New Zealand.** Occ: Warehouse manager. NZCA obit: 1970. He played for New Zealand prior to being granted Test status. In 1923/24 he shared with R.W.D.Worker in partnerships of 154 and 155 in the match v Wellington.

SHERLOCK Richard Roland 2003/04-2009/10 b 15.9.1983 Palmerston North, Manawatu. RHB RF Teams: **Central Districts, Canterbury, Auckland.** Played List A in NZ. Sch: Waimea Coll. NZ U19 ODI.

SHIRLEY Clifford Vernon 1945/46 b 22.3.1917 Invercargill, Southland. d 25.12.2001 Oamaru, North Otago. RHB RM Team: **Otago.** Occ: Law clerk. NZCA obit: 2002.

SHORT Anthony Warren 1978/79-1979/80 b 2.1.1953 Whangarei, Northland. RHB RM Team: **Central Districts.** Played List A in NZ.

SHOVE Ernest 1891/92 b Q3 1860 Lewisham, Kent, England. d 5.1.1928 Devonport, Auckland. Team: **Taranaki.** Occ: Farmer.

SHRECK Charles Edward 2003-2010 b 6.1.1978 Truro, Cornwall, England. RHB RFM Teams: **Wellington,** Nottinghamshire. Played List A in NZ; Played T20 in NZ. Sch: Truro, England. An English pro, played and coached in NZ.

SHRIMPTON Michael John Froud 1961/62-1979/80 b 23.6.1940 Feilding, Manawatu. RHB LB Teams: **Central Districts, Northern Districts, New Zealand Test.** Played List A in NZ. Occ: Schoolteacher.

SHUTTE Ryan Robert 2004/05 b 9.7.1982 Queenstown, Cape Province, South Africa. LHB RFM Team: **Northern Districts.** Played List A in NZ; Played T20 in NZ. Sch: Queens Coll, South Africa.

SIEDEBERG Henry George 1898/99-1921/22 b 13.7.1877 Dunedin, Otago. d 21.5.1945 Dunedin, Otago. RHB Teams: **Otago, New Zealand.** Sch: Otago BHS. Occ: Insurance agent. Billiards: Four times NZ Amateur champion. Soccer: Otago. Hockey: Otago. He played for New Zealand prior to being granted Test status.

SIGLEY Ernest John 1959/60-1960/61 b 9.12.1931 Christchurch, Canterbury. RHB RM Team: **Wellington.**

SIGLEY Martyn Andrew 1994/95-2002/03 b 16.11.1972 Hamilton, Waikato. RHB wk Team: **Central Districts.** Played List A in NZ. NZ U19 Test; NZ U19 ODI.

SILCOCK George Johnson 1877/78-1885/86 b 27.2.1850 Nelson. d 5.5.1915 Nelson. Team: **Nelson.** Occ: Fruit grower.

SILVA Wickrama Arachchige Sanjeewa 1990/91-2001/02 b 9.1.1970 Colombo, Ceylon (now Sri Lanka). RHB RM Teams: **Central Districts, Auckland,** Moors Sports Club.

SILVER Ronald Clifford Douglas 1935/36-1945/46 b 25.2.1910 Dunedin, Otago. d 22.6.1984 Dunedin, Otago. RHB RM Team: **Otago.** Occ: Storeman. Rugby: Otago and Canterbury. NZCA obit: 1984; Wisden obit: 1984.

SIMMONDS Geoffrey Wainhouse 1929/30 b 25.4.1909 Auckland. d 27.11.1976 Whangarei, Northland. RHB RM Team: **Canterbury.** Occ: Clerk.

SIMPSON Herbert 1917/18 b 4.8.1886 Auckland. d 8.3.1950 Auckland. RFM Team: **Auckland.**

SIMPSON John Brodie 1925/26-1937/38 b 11.1.1907 Auckland. d 16.6.1980 Birkenhead, Auckland. RHB RFM Team: **Auckland.** Sch: Kings Coll.

SIMPSON Rex 1955/56-1957/58 b 18.11.1925 New Plymouth, Taranaki. RHB LB Team: **Central Districts.** Sch: New Plymouth BHS.

SIMS Arthur (Sir) 1896/97-1913/14 b 27.7.1877 Spridlington, Lincolnshire, England. d 27.4.1969 East Hoathly, Sussex, England. RHB Team: **Canterbury, New Zealand.** Sch: Christchurch BHS. Occ: Coy director. Book: 84 Not Out: The Story of Sir Arthur Sims. Sir, KB. NZCA obit: 1969; Wisden obit: 1970. He played for New Zealand prior to being granted Test status. He holds the world 8th wicket partnership record of 433 with V.T.Trumper for Australians v Canterbury in 1913/14.

SINCLAIR Barry Whitley 1955/56-1970/71 b 23.10.1936 Wellington. RHB RAB Teams: **Wellington, New Zealand Test.** Played List A in NZ. Sch: Rongatai Coll. NZCA COY: 1964. Auckland selector.

SINCLAIR Ian Mckay 1953/54-1956/57 b 1.6.1933 Rangiora, North Canterbury. LHB OB Teams: **Canterbury, New Zealand Test.** Sch: Rangiora HS.

SINCLAIR Mathew Stuart 1995/96-2009/10 b 9.11.1975 Katherine, Northern Territory, Australia. RHB RM occ wk Teams: **Central Districts, New Zealand Test, New Zealand ODI, New Zealand T20.** Played List A in NZ; Played T20 in NZ. Sch: Palmerston North BHS. NZ U19 Test; NZ U19 ODI. On his Test debut he scored 214 against West Indies at Wellington in 1999/00. He holds the Central Districts 3rd wicket partnership record of 264 with P.J.Ingram against Northern Districts in 2008/09 and the Central Districts 6th wicket partnership record of 235 with B.B.J.Griggs against Wellington in 2008/09.

SINGE Shane Patrick Laurence 2003/04 b 13.3.1980 North Shore, Auckland. LHB occ wk Team: **Auckland.** Occ: Schoolteacher.

SKEET William Reginald 1938/39 b 28.7.1906 Greytown, Wairarapa. d 9.7.1989 Auckland. wk Team: **Auckland.**

SKELTON Peter Jeffrey 1953/54-1957/58 b 25.7.1934 Wanganui. d 1.8.2009 Christchurch, Canterbury. RHB Teams: **Otago, Northern Districts.** Sch: Kings HS.

SKITCH William Henry 1883/84 b 31.8.1860 Bendigo, Victoria, Australia. d 13.7.1944 Kawakawa, Northland. Team: **Otago.** Sch: Bendigo Sch, Australia. Occ: Farmer. Umpired first-class cricket. Member of the committee of the Otago CA.

SLOMAN John Alfred 1903/04 b 15.8.1874 Auckland. d 27.8.1938 Auckland. Team: **Auckland.** Sch: Auckland GS. Umpired first-class cricket.

SLOMAN Rupert Geoffrey 1913/14-1918/19 b 23.6.1890 Auckland. d 2.8.1951 Takapuna, Auckland. Team: **Auckland.** Sch: Auckland GS. Occ: Clerk.

SMALL Anthony Graham 1955/56 b 19.4.1936 Dannevirke, Hawke's Bay. LHB RFM Team: **Central Districts.**

SMALL Christopher Arran 2006/07 b 30.11.1986 Christchurch, Canterbury. LHB RM Team: **Canterbury.** Played List A in NZ; Played T20 in NZ. Sch: Christchurch BHS. Occ: Rugby pro. Rugby: Canterbury and Otago.

SMALL Peter Anthony Thomas 1946/47-1958/59 b 20.1.1925 Christchurch, Canterbury. d 21.4.2003 Christchurch, Canterbury. RHB RM Team: **Canterbury.** Sch: Christchurch BHS. Occ: Watchmaker. NZCA obit: 2004.

SMALL Richard Gordon 1958/59-1962/63 b 22.3.1938 Hastings, Hawke's Bay. LHB Team: **Central Districts.**

SMALLEY Howard Alfred Kendall 1964/65-1965/66 b 12.8.1942 Waiuku, Franklin. LHB Team: **Auckland.**

SMEETON Warwick James 1913/14-1929/30 b 29.9.1895 Auckland. d 1.11.1970 Hamilton, Waikato. RHB wk Team: **Auckland.** Sch: Auckland GS. Occ: Clerk. He was chosen for Auckland while at school. He went to England and played club cricket with W.G.Grace in 1914. Father-in-law: C.W.Garrard; brothers-in-law: W.R.Garrard, D.R.Garrard.

SMITH Benjamin Francis 1990-2010 b 3.4.1972 Corby, Northamptonshire, England. RHB RM Teams: **Central Districts,** Leicestershire, Worcestershire. Played List A in NZ. Sch: Kibworth HS. Occ: Cricket pro. An English pro, played and coached in NZ.

SMITH Bruce David 1965/66-1976/77 b 8.10.1946 Wellington. RHB OB Team: **Wellington.** Played List A in NZ.

SMITH Campbell John Poore 1983/84-1990/91 b 21.3.1960 Nelson. RHB RSM Team: **Central Districts.** Played List A in NZ.

SMITH Charles Robert 1891/92-1892/93 b 18.4.1864 Sydney, New South Wales, Australia. d 25.5.1920 Auckland. SLA Team: **Hawke's Bay.** Occ: Manager. Umpired first-class cricket. Wisden obit: 1921. He was one of the founders of the New Zealand Cricket Council and its first Honorary Secretary and also Treasurer of the Canterbury CA.

SMITH Craig Murray 2004/05-2007/08 b 9.1.1985 Oamaru, North Otago. RHB LM Team: **Otago.** Played List A in NZ. Sch: St Kevins Coll. NZ U19 ODI.

SMITH Edward Haining 1917/18 b 1.9.1899 Bannockburn, Otago. d 9.7.1976 Alexandra, Central Otago. Team: **Southland.** Occ: Architect.

SMITH Frank Aston 1922/23 b 21.3.1893 Kaiapoi, North Canterbury. d 18.10.1975 Christchurch, Canterbury. RHB Team: **Canterbury.** Occ: Builder. Grandson: G.B.Smith; son: F.B.Smith.

SMITH Frank Brunton 1942/43-1952/53 b 13.3.1922 Rangiora, North Canterbury. d 6.7.1997 Christchurch, Canterbury. RHB OB Teams: **Canterbury, New Zealand Test.** Sch: Christchurch BHS. Occ: School principal. NZCA obit: 1998. Son: G.B.Smith; father: F.A.Smith.

SMITH Geoffrey Brunton 1977/78-1978/79 b 22.11.1953 Christchurch, Canterbury. RHB Team: **Canterbury.** Played List A in NZ. Sch: Christchurch BHS. Occ: Schoolteacher. Father: F.B.Smith; grandfather: F.A.Smith

SMITH Horace Dennis 1931/32-1933/34 b 8.1.1913 Toowoomba, Queensland, Australia. d 25.1.1986 Christchurch, Canterbury. RHB RF Teams: **Otago, Canterbury, New Zealand Test.** NZCA obit: 1986; Wisden obit: 1987. He took a wicket with his first ball in Test cricket.

SMITH Ian David Stockley 1977/78-1991/92 b 28.2.1957 Nelson. RHB RAB wk Teams: **Central Districts, Auckland, New Zealand Test, New Zealand ODI.** Played List A in NZ. Sch: Palmerston North BHS. Occ: Commentator. Book: Smithy - just a drummer in the band. NZCA COY: 1989. He holds the NZ Test 9th wicket partnership record of 136 with M.C.Snedden against India in 1989/90. He scored 173 off 136 balls including 24 off one over from Atul Wassan. It was the highest score by a Test no. 9. In 1991/92 he held seven catches in a Test innings against Sri Lanka. He also holds the Central Districts 8th wicket partnership record of 173 with G.K.Robertson against Northern Districts in 1982/83. He holds the record for the most dismissals by a New Zealander - 426.

SMITH James Douglas 1967/68-1971/72 b 26.6.1940 Epsom, Auckland. RHB RF Team: **Northern Districts.** Played List A in NZ.

SMITH James Mowat 1914/15-1921/22 b 28.1.1891 Dunedin, Otago. d 7.9.1971 Auckland. Team: **Otago.** Sch: Otago BHS. Occ: Merchant.

SMITH John 1943/44-1945/46 b 1.7.1919 Christchurch, Canterbury. d 25.6.1999 Christchurch, Canterbury. LHB SLA Team: **Canterbury.** Sch: Christchurch Technical Coll. NZCA obit: 2004.

SMITH John Roseby 1962/63 b 30.11.1944 New Plymouth, Taranaki. RFM Team: **New Zealand Under-23s.**

SMITH Keith Frederick Henry 1953/54-1960/61 b 30.4.1929 Masterton, Wairarapa. RHB SLA Teams: **Wellington, Central Districts.** Wellington selector. He scored 141* on FC debut for Wellington v Central Districts in 1953/54. Uncle: F.B.Rogers.

SMITH Kingsley Paul 1993/94 b 15.9.1969 Rotorua, Bay of Plenty. LHB RM Team: **Northern Districts.** Played List A in NZ.

SMITH Lankford Daniel 1934/35-1956/57 b 23.12.1914 Ngaio, Wellington. d 1.11.1978 Dunedin, Otago. LHB SLA Team: **Otago.** Sch: Otago BHS. Occ: Schoolteacher. Soccer: New Zealand. NZCA obit: 1979; Wisden obit: 1980. NZ and Otago selector.
SMITH Nicholas George Stanley 1969/70-1971/72 b 6.8.1946 Dunedin, Otago. RHB RMF Teams: **Otago, Auckland.** Played List A in NZ.
SMITH Percival Herrick 1909/10 b 1883 Wellington. d 1932 Wanganui. RHB RMF Team: **Wellington.** Occ: Secretary and manager Wanganui Electricity Board.
SMITH Peter Horton 1956/57 b 8.3.1935 Wellington. RHB LBG occ wk Team: **Northern Districts.**
SMITH Rhiane Andrew 1993/94-1995/96 b 17.5.1974 Owaka, Otago. RHB RM Team: **Otago.** Played List A in NZ. Sch: Otago BHS. Occ: Retail veterinary sales. NZ U19 Test; NZ U19 ODI.
SMITH Robert Gary Thomas 2001/02 b 24.10.1974 Sutherland, Sydney, New South Wales, Australia. RHB LBG Team: **Otago.** Played List A in NZ. Occ: Schoolteacher.
SMITH Robert Wayne 1968/69-1976/77 b 14.5.1946 Wellington. LHB occ wk Team: **Wellington.** Played List A in NZ. Wellington selector.
SMITH Sydney Gordon 1899/00-1925/26 b 15.1.1881 San Fernando, Trinidad. d 25.10.1963 Auckland. LHB SLA Teams: **Auckland, New Zealand,** Northamptonshire, Trinidad. Occ: Cricket pro. NZCA obit: 1964; Wisden obit: 1964. He played for New Zealand prior to being granted Test status. Uncles: A.E.Smith (Barbados), F.B.Smith (Barbados).
SMYRK Edward William 1909/10-1919/20 b 1.5.1882 Reefton, Buller. d 14.8.1962 Wairoa, Hawke's Bay. OB Teams: **Hawke's Bay, Wellington.**
SNEDDEN Andrew Nesbitt Colin 1909/10-1927/28 b 3.4.1892 Auckland. d 27.9.1968 Auckland. RHB RM Teams: **Auckland, New Zealand.** Occ: Warehouseman. NZCA obit: 1969; Wisden obit: 1970. NZ selector. He played for New Zealand prior to being granted Test status. Brother: Cyril A.Snedden; grandson: M.C.Snedden; sons: Colin A.Snedden, W.N.Snedden.
SNEDDEN Colin Alexander 1938/39-1948/49 b 7.1.1918 Auckland. RHB OB Teams: **Auckland, New Zealand Test.** Occ: Journalist. Brother: W.N.Snedden; father: A.N.C.Snedden; nephew: M.C.Snedden; uncle: Cyril A Snedden.
SNEDDEN Cyril Alexander 1920/21 b 7.9.1893 Auckland. d 16.1.1985 Auckland. RHB LBG Team: **Auckland.** Sch: Sacred Heart Coll. Rugby League: President NZRL. NZCA obit: 1985. He scored 119 on FC debut for Auckland v Hawke's Bay in 1920/21 and also took 4 wickets for 1 run in the same game. Brother: A.N.C.Snedden; great-nephew: M.C.Snedden; nephews: Colin A Snedden, W.N.Snedden.
SNEDDEN Martin Colin 1977/78-1990 b 23.11.1958 Mt Eden, Auckland. LHB RMF Teams: **Auckland, New Zealand Test, New Zealand ODI.** Played List A in NZ. Sch: Rosmini Coll. Occ: Manager. Book: Martin Snedden benefit magazine. NZCA COY: 1982. NZ cricket CEO. He holds the NZ Test 9th wicket partnership record of 136 with I.D.S.Smith against India in 1989/90. Father: W.N.Snedden; grandfather: A.N.C.Snedden; great-uncle: Cyril A Snedden; uncle: Colin A Snedden.
SNEDDEN Warwick Nesbit 1946/47 b 10.7.1920 Auckland. d 25.12.1990 Auckland. RHB RM Team: **Auckland.** NZCA obit: 1991. Brother: Colin A.Snedden; father: A.N.C.Snedden; son: M.C.Snedden; uncle: Cyril A.Snedden.
SNOOK Clifford George 1947/48-1949/50 b 24.9.1924 Christchurch, Canterbury. LHB RM Team: **Canterbury.** Sch: Christchurch BHS. Occ: Accountant.
SNOOK Ian Robert 1971/72-1987/88 b 7.5.1950 Dunedin, Otago. RHB OB occ wk Team: **Central Districts.** Played List A in NZ. Sch: Kings HS. Occ: Cricket coach. Rugby: Taranaki and Wairarapa.
SNOWDEN Gary Albert 1968/69 b 29.10.1940 Nelson. d 1981 Nelson. RHB RM Team: **Wellington.**
SOLOMON Gary 1966/67 b 26.6.1944 Lower Hutt, Wellington. RHB RM Team: **Wellington.**
SOMANI Addil 1987-1993/94 b 22.10.1967 Kampala, Uganda. RHB LB Teams: **Northern Districts,** Nottinghamshire. Played List A in NZ. Sch: Melville HS. Occ: Bank clerk. NZ U19 Test; NZ U19 ODI.
SOMERVELL Robert Cooke 1911/12-1921/22 b 18.5.1892 Auckland. d 8.6.1967 Auckland. RHB Team: **Auckland, New Zealand.** Sch: Auckland GS. NZCA obit: 1967; Wisden obit: 1968. He played for New Zealand prior to being granted Test status.

SOMERVILLE William Edgar Richard 2004/05-2007/08 b 9.8.1984 Wadestown, Wellington. RHB OB Team: **Otago.**
SONNTAG Thomas Ryan 1883/84 b 28.8.1858 Eumemmering, Victoria, Australia. d 9.10.1938 Dunedin, Otago. Team: **Otago.** Occ: Nurseryman.
SORENSON Brian Joseph 1955/56-1957/58 b 13.11.1929 Auckland. d 7.5.2009 Auckland. LHB wk Team: **Auckland.** He had a club foot which did not affect his wicket-keeping ability. Brother: R.G.Sorenson.
SORENSON Robert Gordon 1943/44 b 19.9.1923 Auckland. RHB SLA Team: **Auckland.** Brother: B.J.Sorenson.
SOUTER John 1871/72-1873/74 b 1844 New Zealand. d 13.7.1905 Christchurch, Canterbury. Team: **Canterbury.** Occ: Nurseryman.
SOUTHALL Thomas Richard 1912/13-1914/15 b Q1 1878 Stourbridge, Worcestershire, England. d 28.4.1949 Wellington. LF Team: **Wellington.** Sch: Christ Coll. Occ: Civil servant.
SOUTHEE Timothy Grant 2006/07-2009/10 b 11.12.1988 Whangarei, Northland. RHB RFM Teams: **Northern Districts, New Zealand Test, New Zealand ODI, New Zealand T20.** Played List A in NZ; Played T20 in NZ. Sch: Kings Coll; Whangarei HS. NZ U19 Test; NZ U19 ODI. NZCA COY: 2008. He holds the NZ domestic T20 9th wicket partnership record of 47* with B.E.Scott for Northern Districts against Otago in 2009/10.
SOWDEN Roger James 1972/73 b 27.10.1949 Ashburton, Mid Canterbury. LHB LM Team: **Canterbury.**
SPACKMAN Clement Roy 1913/14-1919/20 b 10.6.1887 Napier, Hawke's Bay. d 5.1961 New York, United States of America. He was killed when hit by a taxi whilst crossing the road when on holiday in New York. LB Team: **Hawke's Bay.** Sch: Wanganui CS. Occ: Musician; schoolteacher.
SPARKS Lindsay Charles 1967/68-1970/71 b 5.12.1944 Waikari, North Canterbury. RHB RM Teams: **Central Districts, Auckland (not FC).** Played List A in NZ. Canterbury selector.
SPARLING John Trevor 1956/57-1970/71 b 24.7.1938 Mt Eden, Auckland. RHB OB Teams: **Auckland, New Zealand Test.** Sch: Auckland GS. Auckland selector.
SPEARMAN Craig Murray 1993/94-2009 b 4.7.1972 Auckland. RHB Teams: **Auckland, Central Districts, New Zealand Test, New Zealand ODI,** Gloucestershire. Played List A in NZ. Sch: Kelston BHS. Occ: Cricket pro. He scored 341 for Gloucestershire v Middlesex in 2004, eclipsing a 128-year-old record previously held by W.G.Grace for the highest score by a Gloucestershire player.
SPEED James Montgomery 1874/75-1879/80 b 10.8.1856 Wanganui. d 9.7.1925 Paris, France. Teams: **Nelson, Wellington.** Sch: Nelson Coll. Occ: Solicitor. Rugby: Wellington. Western Australian MP.
SPEED Stewart Raymond 1962/63-1970/71 b 13.12.1942 Auckland. RHB wk Team: **Auckland.**
SPEIGHT Martin Peter 1986-2001 b 24.10.1967 Walsall, Staffordshire, England. RHB wk Teams: **Wellington,** Sussex, Durham. Played List A in NZ. Sch: Hurstpierpoint, England. Occ: Cricket coach. An English pro, played and coached in NZ.
SPENCE David Victor 1955/56-1961/62 b 8.1.1930 Hastings, Hawke's Bay. LHB LB Team: **Central Districts.**
SPICE Jason Edward 1993/94-1996/97 b 7.12.1974 Matamata, Waikato. RHB SLA Team: **Northern Districts.** Played List A in NZ. Sch: Matamata Coll. Occ: Rugby player. NZ U19 Test; NZ U19 ODI. Rugby: Waikato, Auckland, Wellington and Cardiff.
SPIVEY John 1884/85-1885/86 wk Team: **Hawke's Bay.** Occ: Sawyer.
SPRAGG Brian Thomas 1987/88-1988/89 b 7.11.1965 Papakura, Franklin. RHB Team: **Northern Districts.** Played List A in NZ. Occ: Accountant. NZ U19 Test; NZ U19 ODI.
SPRAGGON Ralph Dew 1894/95-1896/97 b 13.8.1872 Dunedin, Otago. d 11.9.1939 Palmerston North, Manawatu. Team: **Otago.** Occ: Civil servant.
SPRING John Patrick 1877/78-1884/85 b 1833 Ireland. RHB wk Team: **Otago.** Occ: Accountant. Umpired first-class cricket. He was a British army officer who was bankrupted in Wales in 1872 and made his way to NZ where he was last heard of in 1887.
SPRING Leicester Russell 1936/37 b 2.9.1908 Waipawa, Hawke's Bay. d 31.5.1997 Auckland. RHB RM Team: **Auckland.** Sch: Palmerston North BHS. Occ: Newspaper proprietor. Horse Racing: owned Rising Fast which in 1953 won nine races out of 11 including the Caulfield and

Melbourne Cups. In 1954 Rising Fast won the Caulfield Cup and was controversially second in the Melbourne Cup. Rising Fast is recognised in both Australia and New Zealand as an all time champion. Book: Racing with Rising Fast, Whakatane Beacon and Leicester Spring. NZCA obit: 1997; Wisden obit: 1998.

STAFFORD Charles S 1884/85 Team: **Auckland**. Occ: Settler.

STAITE George 1895/96-1897/98 b 1855 Victoria, Australia. d 30.8.1948 Claremont, Western Australia, Australia. Team: **Hawke's Bay.**

STANDIDGE Jack Allen 1940/41 b 6.5.1907 Wellington. d 31.3.1958 Wellington. Team: **Wellington.** NZCA obit: 1958. Son: P.H.Standidge.

STANDIDGE Paul Henry 1957/58 b 1.4.1934 Wellington. LHB Team: **Wellington.** Father: J.A.Standidge.

STANLEY Frederick William 1950/51-1953/54 b 5.11.1923 Dunedin, Otago. d 22.10.1993 Dunedin, Otago. RHB RM Team: **Otago.** Occ: Upholsterer. NZCA obit: 1994.

STAPLES Arthur 1901/02-1903/04 b 8.1.1878 Wellington. d 13.8.1954 Wellington. Team: **Wellington.** Sch: Wellington Coll. Occ: Bootmaker.

STARK Donald William 1953/54 b 2.5.1930 Christchurch, Canterbury. RHB OB Team: **Canterbury.** Sch: Christchurch BHS. Occ: Grain and seed manager.

STEAD David William 1968/69-1985/86 b 26.5.1947 Christchurch, Canterbury. LHB LB,RM Team: **Canterbury.** Played List A in NZ. Sch: Rangiora HS. Occ: Groundsman for golf club. Sons: G.R.Stead, W.W.Stead.

STEAD Gary Raymond 1991/92-2005/06 b 9.1.1972 Christchurch, Canterbury. RHB LB Teams: **Canterbury, New Zealand Test.** Played List A in NZ. Sch: Shirley BHS. Occ: Cricket coach. NZ U19 Test; NZ U19 ODI. NZ women's team coach. He holds the Canterbury 5th wicket partnership record of 290 with C.Z.Harris against Central Districts in 1996/97. Brother: W.W.Stead; father: D.W.Stead.

STEELE Howard Keith Chillingworth 1970-1974/75 b 6.4.1951 Epsom, Auckland. d 7.6.2009 Berrima, New South Wales, Australia. RHB RM Teams: **Auckland,** Cambridge University. Played List A in NZ. Sch: Kings Coll. Occ: Lawyer. Rugby: Cambridge University (Blue). Wisden obit: 2010.

STEMSON William Isaac 1889/90-1908/09 b 30.6.1867 Christchurch, Canterbury. d 13.6.1951 Torbay, Western Australia, Australia. RHB RM Teams: **Auckland, New Zealand.** Occ: House furnisher. NZCA obit: 1953. He played for New Zealand in a non-first-class match prior to being granted Test status.

STEPHENS Michael James 1990/91-1993/94 b 1.11.1967 Auckland. RHB LFM Teams: **Auckland, Northern Districts.** Played List A in NZ. Indoor cricket: New Zealand.

STEPHENS William Bowden 1899/00-1900/01 b 1870 Christchurch, Canterbury. d 14.7.1954 Auckland. LB Team: **Auckland.** Occ: Railway employee.

STEPHEN-SMITH Leslie 1931/32 b 13.10.1904 Marlow, Buckinghamshire, England. d 22.5.1988 Auckland. wk Team: **Auckland.**

STEPHENSON Frederick Charles 1890/91-1904/05 b 1871 Dunedin, Otago. d 21.4.1944 Wellington. OB Teams: **Otago, Wellington, Canterbury.** Occ: Warehouseman.

STEVENS Colin James 1966/67-1967/68 b 17.10.1943 Christchurch, Canterbury. RHB Team: **Canterbury.** Sch: Christchurch BHS. Occ: Schoolteacher. ND selector.

STEVENS Edward Cephas John 1863/64-1883/84 b 18.10.1837 Salford, Lancashire, England. d 6.6.1915 Christchurch, Canterbury. RHB Team: **Canterbury.** Sch: Marlborough, England. Occ: Land agent. Umpired first-class cricket. MP.

STEVENS George Robert 1911/12-1920/21 b 5.10.1888 Napier, Hawke's Bay. d 1.7.1946 Napier, Hawke's Bay. Team: **Hawke's Bay.** Occ: Engineer. Brother: J.A.M.Stevens.

STEVENS John Ascot Mozart 1919/20 b 12.2.1894 Napier, Hawke's Bay. d 16.9.1967 Palmerston North, Manawatu. Team: **Hawke's Bay.** Occ: Brewer. Brother: G.R.Stevens.

STEVENS John Wise 1863/64-1865/66 Team: **Canterbury.**

STEWART Bruce Alexander 1972/73 b 10.9.1949 Masterton, Wairarapa. RHB RM Team: **Central Districts.** Played List A in NZ.

STEWART Gerald William 1968/69 b 10.2.1936 Dunedin, Otago. RHB RM Team: **Northern Districts.**

STEWART Raymond Darrell 1963/64-1974/75 b 15.11.1944 Dunedin, Otago. RHB Teams: **Otago, Central Districts.**
STEWART Russell Norman 1973/74-1977/78 b 25.1.1946 Dunedin, Otago. RHB Team: **Otago.** Played List A in NZ. Sch: Otago BHS.
STEWART Shanan Luke 2001/02-2009/10 b 21.6.1982 Christchurch, Canterbury. RHB RM Team: **Canterbury, New Zealand ODI.** Played List A in NZ; Played T20 in NZ. Sch: St Bedes Coll. NZ U19 Test; NZ U19 ODI. He holds the NZ 6th wicket partnership record of 379* with C.F.K.van Wyk for Canterbury v Central Districts in 2009/10 and the NZ domestic T20 6th wicket partnership record of 96 with G.J.Hopkins for New Zealand A against English Lions in 2008/09.
STIMPSON Alan James Peter 1974/75-1978/79 b 9.7.1951 Auckland. d 22.8.1994 Auckland. He was drowned in Manakua Harbour, Auckland in 1994, aged 43. RHB RFM Team: **Northern Districts.** Played List A in NZ. Sch: Takapuna GS. NZCA obit: 1995; Wisden obit: 1995.
STIRLING Derek Alexander 1981/82-1991/92 b 5.10.1961 Upper Hutt, Wellington. RHB RFM Teams: **Central Districts, Wellington, New Zealand Test, New Zealand ODI.** Played List A in NZ. Sch: Palmerston North BHS.
STOKES David Norman 1937/38-1938/39 b 16.11.1909 Christchurch, Canterbury. d 31.10.2004 Christchurch, Canterbury. RHB OB Team: **Canterbury.** NZCA obit: 2005. Canterbury selector.
STONE Charles Edward 1894/95-1895/96 b 1866 Ballarat, Victoria, Australia. d 9.1.1903 Auckland. He died aged 36. Team: **Auckland.** Sch: Mr Hamill's Sch. Occ: Hotelkeeper. Rugby: Auckland.
STONE Peter Desmond 1961/62-1968/69 b 5.5.1938 Kaitaia, Northland. RHB LB Team: **Northern Districts.**
STOTT Leslie Warren 1969/70-1983/84 b 8.12.1946 Rochdale, Lancashire, England. RHB RM Teams: **Auckland, New Zealand ODI.** Played List A in NZ. Sch: Auckland GS. Auckland selector.
STOYANOFF Philip Andrew 1980/81 b 19.3.1960 Upper Hutt, Wellington. LHB RFM Team: **NZ Under-23s.** Sch: Upper Hutt Coll. Occ: Turf manager.
STRANG Walter Wilson 1929/30 b 15.4.1888 Wellington. d 28.2.1944 Dunedin, Otago. RHB Team: **Otago.** Sch: Otago BHS. Occ: Sports dealer.
STRANGE C 1884/85 Team: **Canterbury.** Occ: Bank manager. An Englishman who played for MCC before coming to NZ.
STRANGE Raymond Brackley 1901/02-1903/04 b 27.10.1878 Christchurch, Canterbury. d 17.9.1962 Homebush, Sydney, New South Wales, Australia. Team: **Canterbury.** Occ: Accountant. He took a wicket with his first ball in FC cricket.
STRINGER Gilbert Henry 1933/34-1943/44 b 18.3.1910 Christchurch, Canterbury. d 20.5.1991 Wellington. LHB LSM Teams: **Canterbury, Wellington.** Sch: Christchurch BHS. Occ: Director-general NZ Broadcasting Commission. CBE. NZCA obit: 1992.
STRONACH Henry Donald 1892/93-1894/95 b 27.1.1865 Deepdale Station, Canterbury. d 5.4.1932 Dunedin, Otago. Team: **Otago.** Sch: Otago BHS. Occ: Insurance manager. Umpired first-class cricket.
STUBBS Arthur 1887/88 b 1862 unknown. d 1.9.1929 Auckland. Team: **Hawke's Bay.** Occ: Supreme Court deputy registrar.
STUDHOLME Edgar Channon 1891/92 b 29.7.1866 Waimate, South Canterbury. d 1.6.1949 Waimate, South Canterbury. Team: **Canterbury.** Sch: Christ Coll. Occ: Farmer. Book: Edgar Channon Studholme by C Hennessy. Cousin: W.P.Studholme.
STUDHOLME William Paul 1887/88-1888/89 b 23.4.1864 Waimate, South Canterbury. d 23.2.1941 Exeter, Devon, England. Team: **Canterbury.** Sch: Christ Coll. Occ: Farmer. Cousin: E.C.Studholme.
STYRIS Scott Bernard 1994/95-2009/10 b 10.7.1975 Brisbane, Queensland, Australia. RHB RFM Teams: **Northern Districts, Auckland, New Zealand Test, New Zealand ODI, New Zealand T20,** Middlesex, Durham. Played List A in NZ; Played T20 in NZ. Sch: Hamilton BHS. Occ: Cricket pro. NZ U19 Test; NZ U19 ODI. Indoor cricket: New Zealand. On his Test debut he scored 107 against West Indies at St George's, Grenada in 2002.

SU'A Murphy Logo 1988/89-1994/95 b 7.11.1966 Wanganui. LHB LFM Teams: **Northern Districts, Auckland, New Zealand Test, New Zealand ODI.** Played List A in NZ. Occ: Marketing manager.
SULZBERGER Glen Paul 1995/96-2004/05 b 14.3.1973 Kaponga, Taranaki. LHB OB Teams: **Central Districts, New Zealand ODI.** Played List A in NZ. NZ U19 Test; NZ U19 ODI.
SUNDERLAND Kelly John 1990/91 b 17.7.1970 Auckland. RHB RFM Team: **Auckland.** Played List A in NZ. Sch: Mt Roskill GS. Occ: Sales rep.
SUTCLIFFE Bert 1941/42-1965/66 b 17.11.1923 Ponsonby, Auckland. d 20.4.2001 Auckland. LHB SLA occ wk Teams: **Auckland, Otago, Northern Districts, New Zealand Test.** Sch: Takapuna GS. Occ: Cricket coach. Books: Between overs; Bert Sutcliffe: His Record Innings by Innings by W.Harte. MBE. New Zealand Sports Hall of Fame. Bert Sutcliffe Oval at Lincoln named in his honour. NZCA obit: 2001; Wisden obit: 2002. NZCA COY: 1948. WCOY: 1950. ICOY 1955/56. Sutcliffe was posthumously inducted into the ICC Hall of Fame. NZ, Otago and ND selector. He hit two triple centuries in FC cricket with a highest of 385 for Otago against Canterbury at Christchurch in 1952/53 - at the time the sixth-highest score ever and, until the advent of Brian Lara, the highest by a left-hander in first-class cricket. He had previously made 355 for Otago against Auckland in 1949/50. Six more scores over 200 included 243, followed by 100 not out in the second innings, against Essex in 1949. He holds the Auckland 1st wicket partnership record of 286 with D.D.Taylor against Canterbury in 1948/49. His opening partnerships of 220 and 286 with Taylor in this game is the only instance of two players putting on 200 in each innings of a first-class match. Sutcliffe's share was 141 and 135. He holds the Otago 1st wicket partnership record of 373 with L.Watt against Auckland in 1950/51, the Otago 5th wicket partnership record of 266 with W.S.Haig against Auckland in 1949/50 and the Otago 7th wicket partnership record of 182 with A.W.Gilbertson against Canterbury in 1952/53.
SUTCLIFFE H 1875/76 b Lancashire, England. LHB MF Team: **Otago.**
SUTHERLAND Trevor Donald 1979/80 b 4.7.1954 Dunedin, Otago. RHB Team: **Otago.**
SUTTON Robert Edwin 1958/59-1973/74 b 30.5.1940 Romford, Essex, England. RHB LFM Team: **Auckland.** Played List A in NZ.
SWEET Thomas Shardalow (changed name to Alfred Shardalow Simpson) 1873/74-1876/77 b 1.8.1851 Hackney, London, England. d 17.3.1905 Auburn, Melbourne, Victoria, Australia. F Teams: **Auckland, Canterbury.** Sch: Charterhouse, England. Occ: Publican. He was a noted fast bowler, and big hitter. In 1877 he was secretary and treasurer of the Midland CC. At a club meeting on 4 February 1878 it was found that Sweet had disappeared and there was a deficit of £62 in the account. He was also found to have embezzled money from his employer, The Press Company, as well as being in debt all over Christchurch. One amount was said to be £600. He also embezzled £100 from the Canterbury CA and accounts against him were still being requested in July. He abandoned his wife and children and a warrant was issued for his arrest. He had absconded from NZ to Victoria, remarried and changed his name to Alfred Shardalow Simpson. He died without having been brought to justice.
SYME George 1891/92-1897/98 b 1863 Glasgow, Lanarkshire, Scotland. d 21.3.1949 Hawera, Taranaki. Team: **Taranaki.** Occ: Timber merchant. Rugby: Taranaki.
SYME John Randal 1965/66-1966/67 b 30.9.1947 Auckland. LHB OB Team: **NZ Under-23s.** Occ: Engineer.
SYMES Ivo Alfred Hillis 1934/35-1935/36 b 10.12.1909 Wanganui. d 11.6.2002 Wellington. RHB RFM Team: **Wellington.** Sch: Wanganui CS. Occ: Stockbroker. NZCA obit: 2002.
SYMONDS Arthur Edmund 1926/27 b 8.5.1890 Dunedin, Otago. d 20.4.1946 Lower Hutt, Wellington. wk Team: **Otago.** Occ: Railway employee.
TAIAROA John Grey 1891/92-1898/99 b 16.9.1862 Otakou, Dunedin, Otago. d 31.12.1907 Dunedin, Otago. He was drowned when he tripped over a launch painter whilst getting out of a boat, fell into the water and was quickly carried under the wharf by the strong flood tide to his death. Team: **Hawke's Bay.** Sch: Otago BHS. Occ: Solicitor. Rugby: All Blacks and Otago.
TAIAROA Michael Patrick 2007/08 b 3.7.1988 Hastings, Hawke's Bay. RHB RM occ wk Team: **Central Districts.** Sch: St Johns Coll, Napier. NZ U19 Test; NZ U19 ODI.

TAIT Alex Ross 1994/95-2000/01 b 13.6.1972 Paparoa, Northland. RHB RM Teams: **Northern Districts, New Zealand ODI.** Played List A in NZ. Occ: Golf pro. He has the best bowling figures for Northern Districts - he took 9/48 against Auckland in 1996/97 and had match figures of 16/130. These are the best match bowling figures in NZ FC cricket.
TAIT William C 1872/73-1874/75 Team: **Otago.**
TALBOT George Logan 1929/30 b 2.4.1907 Christchurch, Canterbury. d 15.12.1943 Orsogna, Italy. He was killed in action. RHB RM Team: **Canterbury.** Sch: Christ Coll. Occ: Storeman. Cousin: R.O.Talbot.
TALBOT Ronald Osmond 1922/23-1935/36 b 26.11.1903 Christchurch, Canterbury. d 5.1.1983 Auckland. RHB RM Teams: **Canterbury, Otago, New Zealand.** Sch: Christ Coll. Occ: Manager. Rugby: Canterbury. NZCA obit: 1983. He played for New Zealand in a FC match. He scored 105 on FC debut for Canterbury v Otago in 1922/23. Cousin: G.L.Talbot.
TANNER Ernest Denton 1883/84-1885/86 b 17.2.1860 Napier, Hawke's Bay. d 14.4.1936 Newmarket, Suffolk, England. Team: **Hawke's Bay.** Occ: Horse exporter. Father-in-law: H.P.Lance.
TAPLEY Cecil Brock 1914/15-1918/19 b 25.12.1879 Stepney, South Australia, Australia. d 14.10.1965 Invercargill, Southland. Team: **Southland.**
TAPPING Harry Edward 1950/51-1952/53 b 27.3.1926 Gisborne, Poverty Bay. d 9.2.2008 Gisborne, Poverty Bay. RHB SLA Team: **Auckland.** NZCA obit: 2008; Wisden obit: 2009.
TARLETON John Walter 1884/85 b 29.6.1852 New Norfolk, Tasmania, Australia. d 31.12.1929 Sandy Bay, Hobart, Tasmania, Australia. Team: **Wellington.** Sch: Marlborough, England.
TARR Graeme Maxwell 1957/58-1958/59 b 20.11.1936 Hamilton, Waikato. RHB SLA Team: **Northern Districts.**
TARRANT David Richard 1954/55-1957/58 b 31.1.1937 Palmerston North, Manawatu. RHB RFM Team: **Central Districts.**
TATTERSALL Henry James 1912/13-1927/28 b 21.12.1892 Christchurch, Canterbury. d 5.11.1971 Palmerston North, Manawatu. RHB wk Teams: **Auckland, Wellington, New Zealand.** Sch: Christchurch BHS. NZCA obit: 1972. He played for New Zealand in a non-first-class match prior to being granted Test status.
TAYLOR Archibald Robert 1962/63-1965/66 b 26.11.1941 Westport, Buller. LHB RFM Teams: **Wellington, Auckland (not FC).** Played List A in NZ.
TAYLOR Bruce Richard 1963/64-1979/80 b 12.7.1943 Timaru, South Canterbury. LHB RFM Teams: **Canterbury, Wellington, New Zealand Test, New Zealand ODI.** Played List A in NZ. Sch: Timaru BHS. Occ: Bursar. NZCA COY: 1967. ICOY 1965. NZ, Wellington and Otago selector. On his Test debut he scored 105 and took 5/86 for New Zealand v India in 1964/65, the only man to have accopmplished this feat.
TAYLOR Donald Dougald 1946/47-1960/61 b 2.3.1923 Auckland. d 5.12.1980 Epsom, Auckland. RHB OB Teams: **Auckland, New Zealand Test,** Warwickshire. Sch: Mt Albert GS. NZCA obit: 1981. NZCA COY: 1949. Auckland selector. He holds the Auckland 1st wicket partnership record of 286 with B.Sutcliffe against Canterbury in 1948/49. His opening partnerships of 220 and 286 with Bert Sutcliffe in this game is the only instance of two players putting on 200 in each innings of a first-class match. Taylor's share was 99 and 143.
TAYLOR Francis James 1889/90-1890/91 b Q3 1859 Hull, Yorkshire, England. d 2.5.1937 Lower Hutt, Wellington. RM Team: **Wellington.** Occ: Storekeeper.
TAYLOR Frank Alwyn 1909/10-1913/14 b 1.3.1890 Auckland. d 25.6.1960 Elsfield, Oxfordshire, England. Team: **Auckland.** Sch: Auckland GS. Occ: Librarian, Oxford University.
TAYLOR Geoffrey William 1973/74-1974/75 b 22.7.1949 Waipawa, Hawke's Bay. RHB Team: **Northern Districts.** Played List A in NZ.
TAYLOR Henry Morgan 1919/20-1920/21 b 5.2.1889 Christchurch, Canterbury. d 20.6.1955 Christchurch, Canterbury. wk Team: **Canterbury.** Sch: Christ Coll; Christchurch BHS. Occ: Coy manager. Rugby: All Blacks and Canterbury.
TAYLOR Joseph Stanley 1911/12-1927/28 b 7.9.1886 Leichhardt, Sydney, New South Wales, Australia. d 3.9.1954 Newcastle, New South Wales, Australia. RHB Teams: **Wellington,** New South Wales. Sch: Newington Coll, Australia. Occ: Monumental mason.

TAYLOR Kenneth 1953-1968 b 21.8.1935 Primrose Hill, Huddersfield, Yorkshire, England. RHB RM,LB Teams: **Auckland,** England Test, Yorkshire. Sch: Stile Common Sch, England. Occ: Art teacher. An English pro, played and coached in NZ. Son: N.S.Taylor.

TAYLOR Kenneth George William 1983/84 b 10.11.1953 Lincoln, Canterbury. RHB RM Team: **Canterbury.** Played List A in NZ. Sch: Lincoln HS.

TAYLOR Leslie George 1910/11-1917/18 b 26.6.1894 Auckland. d 17.1.1977 Auckland. RHB Teams: **Auckland, New Zealand.** Sch: Mt Eden HS. Occ: Clerk. He played for New Zealand prior to being granted Test status.

TAYLOR Luteru Ross Poutoa Lote 2002/03-2009/10 b 8.3.1984 Lower Hutt, Wellington. RHB OB Teams: **Central Districts, New Zealand Test, New Zealand ODI, New Zealand T20.** Played List A in NZ; Played T20 in NZ. Sch: Palmerston North BHS. Occ: Cricket pro. NZ U19 Test; NZ U19 ODI. NZCA COY: 2009. He holds the NZ Test 4th wicket partnership record of 271 with J.D.Ryder against India in 2008/09 and the highest NZ domestic T20 score of 111* for Central Districts against Northern Districts in 2007/08. He also holds the Central Districts 5th wicket partnership record of 301 with J.I.Englefield against Wellington in 2004/05.

TAYLOR Robert 1863/64-1868/69 b 1835. d 30.10.1901 Sefton, Canterbury. Team: **Canterbury.**

TENNANT Augustus Eatwell 1863/64-1865/66 b 19.11.1841 Simla, Punjab, India. d 28.11.1892 Hokitika, West Coast. He died of Bright's disease. RHB wk Team: **Canterbury.** Sch: Rugby, England. Occ: Civil servant. In 1882 whilst working as a clerk in the stamp office he was gaoled for 9 months for embezzling £15.

TENNENT Robert Collings 1873/74 b 5.7.1849 Rio de Janeiro, Brazil. d 14.4.1939 Woodville, Tararua. He died from bronchopneumonia. Team: **Nelson.** Sch: Elizabeth Coll, Guernsey. Occ: Bank manager. He was prominent in the administration of Nelson rugby.

TESTRO James Charles 1882/83-1886/87 b 6.8.1851 Lambeth, London, England. d 30.4.1934 North Carlton, Melbourne, Victoria, Australia. occ wk Team: **Auckland.**

THERKLESON Ian James 1966/67-1973/74 b 11.10.1938 Wellington. RHB wk Team: **Wellington.** Played List A in NZ.

THIELE Craig Harvey 1980/81-1985/86 b 14.11.1953 Nelson. RHB RMF Team: **Canterbury.** Played List A in NZ. Sch: Timaru BHS. Occ: Real estate company employee. Canterbury selector.

THOMAS Arthur Ward 1911/12-1922/23 b 25.1.1881 Christchurch, Canterbury. d 7.5.1965 Christchurch, Canterbury. RHB RM Team: **Canterbury.** Sch: Christchurch BHS. Occ: Farmer. NZCA obit: 1965.

THOMAS Barry David 1980/81 b 20.11.1956 Wellington. RHB RSM Team: **Canterbury.** Sch: Burnside HS. Occ: School teacher.

THOMAS M 1937/38 Team: **Wellington.**

THOMAS Roderick Ian 1975/76-1977/78 b 14.2.1954 Picton, Marlborough. LHB RFM Team: **Central Districts.** Played List A in NZ.

THOMAS William Earle 1966/67 b 19.12.1947 Wanganui. LHB Team: **New Zealand Under-23s.**

THOMPSON Ewen Paul 2000/01-2009/10 b 17.12.1979 Warkworth, Rodney. LHB LFM Teams: **Central Districts, New Zealand ODI, New Zealand T20.** Played List A in NZ; Played T20 in NZ.

THOMPSON George Joseph 1897-1922 b 27.10.1877 Cogenhoe, Northampton, England. d 3.3.1943 Clifton, Bristol, England. RHB RFM Teams: **Auckland,** England Test, Northamptonshire. Sch: Wellingborough, England. Occ: Cricket coach. Wisden obit: 1944. WCOY: 1906. An English pro, played and coached in NZ.

THOMPSON Harry Fleetwood 1885/86 b Q4 1858 West Derby, Liverpool, Lancashire, England. d 6.8.1949 Wellington. Team: **Hawke's Bay.** Occ: Bank accountant; brewer; miner.

THOMPSON Neale Robert 1956/57-1962/63 b 2.2.1937 Invercargill, Southland. LHB occ wk Team: **Otago.**

THOMSON Graeme Bruce 1973/74-1980/81 b 31.7.1951 Invercargill, Southland. LHB LM Teams: **Otago, New Zealand.** Played List A in NZ. He played for New Zealand in a FC match.

THOMSON James Campbell 1873/74 b 20.2.1852 Edinburgh, Midlothian, Scotland. d 2.5.1890 Waratah, New South Wales, Australia. Team: **Otago.**

THOMSON James Cecil Alexander 1953/54 b 17.4.1933 Napier, Hawke's Bay. RHB SLA Team: **Wellington.**

THOMSON Keith 1959/60-1973/74 b 26.2.1941 Methven, Mid Canterbury. RHB RAB Teams: **Canterbury, New Zealand Test.** Played List A in NZ. Sch: West Christchurch BHS. Occ: School teacher. Umpired first-class cricket. Hockey: New Zealand. Brother: W.A.Thomson.
THOMSON Shane Alexander 1987/88-1996/97 b 27.1.1969 Hamilton, Waikato. RHB RFM,OB Teams: **Northern Districts, New Zealand Test, New Zealand ODI.** Played List A in NZ. NZ U19 Test; NZ U19 ODI. NZCA COY: 1994. His finest hour was the thrilling unbeaten 120 in a memorable run-chase against Pakistan at Christchurch in 1993/94. He holds the Northern Districts 3rd wicket partnership record of 261 with M.P.Maynard against Auckland in 1990/91.
THOMSON William Allen 1964/65-1973/74 b 4.8.1943 Methven, Mid Canterbury. LHB LB Team: **Canterbury.** Sch: West Christchurch BHS. Occ: Customs clerk. Brother: K.Thomson.
THORN Lindsay David Alexander 1978/79-1979/80 b 1.3.1952 Motueka, Tasman. RHB OB Team: **Canterbury.** Played List A in NZ. Sch: St Bedes Coll. Occ: School te acher.
TIDMARSH David Jason 1992/93 b 2.5.1971 Hay, New South Wales, Australia. RHB RM Team: **Northern Districts.** Occ: Policeman.
TILYARD James Thomas 1907/08 b 27.8.1889 Waratah, New South Wales, Australia. d 1.11.1966 Dannevirke, Hawke's Bay. LHB Team: **Wellington.** Occ: Mercer. Rugby: All Blacks and Wellington. NZCA obit: 1967.
TINDILL Eric William Thomas 1932/33-1949/50 b 18.12.1910 Nelson. d 1.8.2010 Wellington. LHB wk Teams: **Wellington, New Zealand Test.** Sch: Wellington Tech Coll. Occ: Accountant. Umpired Test and first-class cricket. Rugby: All Blacks and Wellington. Books: Famous New Zealanders; Eric Tindill by K.Boon; The tour of the third All Blacks. OBE. President, treasurer and secretary of the Wellington CA as well as a selector for both Wellington and New Zealand. He scored 106 on FC debut for Wellington v Auckland in 1932/33. When he died, aged 99, he was the oldest Test cricketer. Son: P.Tindill.
TINDILL Paul 1965/66 b 6.11.1939 Wellington. LHB wk Team: **Wellington.** Father: E.W.T.Tindill.
TODD Gregory Rex 2000/01-2009/10 b 17.6.1982 Masterton, Wairapara. LHB RM Teams: **Central Districts, Otago.** Played List A in NZ; Played T20 in NZ. Sch: Rathkeale Coll. NZ U19 Test; NZ U19 ODI.
TODD Keeley William Martin 2004/05-2007/08 b 31.7.1982 Auckland. LHB RM Team: **Auckland.** Played List A in NZ; Played T20 in NZ. Sch: Auckland GS.
TONKS Arthur Sidney 1891/92 b 1862 Auckland. d 3.9.1918 New Plymouth, Taranaki. Team: **Taranaki.** Sch: Auckland GS. Occ: Auctioneer.
TOOMEY Cecil Dominic Gerard 1939/40-1945/46 b 4.10.1915 Dunedin, Otago. d 11.8.1981 Dunedin, Otago. RHB Team: **Otago.** Occ: Dentist. NZCA obit: 1992. Brother: F.J.Toomey.
TOOMEY Francis Joachim 1934/35-1935/36 b 8.2.1904 Dunedin, Otago. d 14.3.1992 Dunedin, Otago. RHB wk Team: **Otago.** Occ: Manager. NZCA obit: 1992. Wisden obit: 1993. Brother: C.D.G.Toomey.
TOPP John Patrick 1978/79 b 7.3.1952 Lower Hutt, Wellington. RHB Team: **Wellington.** Occ: Management consultant.
TORKINGTON W 1904/05 b Australia. Team: **Hawke's Bay.** An Australian, he played for Hawke's Bay whilst living in Gisborne and was known to be in NZ between 1904 and 1907.
TORRANCE Richard Cameron 1905/06-1927/28 b 14.8.1884 Dunedin, Otago. d 28.9.1972 Dunedin, Otago. LM Team: **Otago.** Occ: Carpenter. Umpired Test and first-class cricket.
TOTMAN Basil 1897/98 b Q3 1874 Finchingfield, Essex, England. d 2.3.1953 Auckland. Team: **Auckland.** Occ: Orchardist.
TOTTENHAM Herbert Ponsonby Loftus - *see* GAUSSEN H.P.L.
TOVEY Edward Richard 1957/58-1963/64 b 25.12.1930 Kings Cross, Sydney, New South Wales, Australia. d 31.5.2002 St Leonards, Sydney, New South Wales, Australia. RHB wk Teams: **Auckland,** Queensland. Sch: Newington Coll, Australia. Occ: Manager. NZCA obit: 2003; Wisden obit: 2003.
TOWNSEND Leslie Fletcher 1922-1939 b 8.6.1903 Long Eaton, Derbyshire, England. d 17.2.1993 Richmond, Nelson. RHB RM,OB Teams: **Auckland,** England Test, Derbyshire. Sch: Long Eaton Sch, England. Occ: Cricket pro. NZCA obit: 1993; Wisden obit: 1994. An English pro, played and coached in NZ. Brother: A.F.Townsend (Derbyshire).

TOYNBEE Matthew Hall 1977/78-1984/85 b 29.11.1956 Nelson. RHB OB Team: **Central Districts.** Played List A in NZ. He took a hat-trick for Central Districts v Northern Districts in 1979/80.

TRACY Sean Robert 1982/83-1990/91 b 7.6.1963 Auckland. RHB RFM Teams: **Auckland, Canterbury, Otago, New Zealand,** Gloucestershire. Played List A in NZ. Sch: Auckland GS. Occ: School teacher. He played for New Zealand in a FC match.

TREIBER Karl 1979/80-1987/88 b 4.12.1955 Lendava, Slovenia, Yugoslavia. LHB LFM,SLA Team: **Northern Districts.** Played List A in NZ. Occ: Cricket coach.

TREMLETT Maurice Fletcher 1947-1960 b 5.7.1923 Stockport, Cheshire, England. d 30.7.1984 Southampton, Hampshire, England. RHB RFM Teams: **Central Districts,** England Test, Somerset. Sch: Taunton Priory, England. Occ: Cricket pro. Wisden obit: 1985. An English pro, played and coached in NZ. Grandson: C.T.Tremlett (England, Hampshire, Surrey); son: T.M.Tremlett (Hampshire).

TREWEEK Charles 1889/90-1894/95 b 12.5.1859 Wanganui. d 17.2.1942 New Plymouth, Taranaki. Team: **Canterbury.** Occ: Civil servant.

TRICKLEBANK William 1934/35-1936/37 b 30.12.1915 Wellington. d 15.5.1986 Hataitai, Wellington. RHB RFM Team: **Wellington.** Occ: Policeman. NZCA obit: 1987.

TRIST David George 1968/69-1977/78 b 22.9.1947 Christchurch, Canterbury. LHB RFM Teams: **Canterbury, New Zealand.** Played List A in NZ. Sch: Christchurch BHS. Occ: Cricket coach. NZ coach; Auckland and Canterbury selector. He played for New Zealand in a FC match.

TROTT Albert Edwin 1892/93-1911 b 6.2.1873 Abbotsford, Melbourne, Victoria, Australia. d 30.7.1914 Harlesden, Willesden, Middlesex, England. He committed suicide by shooting himself. RHB RFM,RM,OB Teams: **Hawke's Bay,** England Test, Middlesex, London County, Australia Test, Victoria. Occ: Cricket pro. WCOY: 1899. An Australian pro, played and coached in NZ. He took 4 wickets in 4 balls and a hat-trick in the same innings of his benefit match for Middlesex v Somerset in 1907. He is the only man to have hit a ball over the pavilion at Lord's. Brother: G.H.S.Trott (Australia, Victoria).

TROTT Ian Jonathan Leonard 2000/01-2010 b 22.4.1981 Cape Town, Cape Province, South Africa. RHB RM Teams: **Otago,** England Test, England ODI, England T20, Warwickshire, Boland, Western Province. Played List A in NZ; Played T20 in NZ. Sch: Rondebosch BHS, South Africa. Occ: Cricket pro. An English pro, played and coached in NZ. Half-brother: K.C.Jackson (Western Province, Boland).

TROUP Gary Bertram 1974/75-1986/87 b 3.10.1952 Taumarunui, King Country. RHB LFM Teams: **Auckland, New Zealand Test, New Zealand ODI.** Played List A in NZ. Occ: Sports management. Book: Troupy. Auckland selector.

TRUSCOTT Peter Bennetts 1961/62-1965/66 b 14.8.1941 Pahiatua, Wairarapa. RHB Teams: **Canterbury, Wellington, New Zealand Test.**

TUCKER Kinder Houghton 1895/96-1919/20 b 23.8.1875 Nelson. d 24.11.1939 Wellington. RHB LB Teams: **Wellington, New Zealand.** Sch: Wellington Coll. Occ: Engraver. Wisden obit: 1940. NZ and Wellington selector. He played for New Zealand prior to being granted Test status. In Wellington club cricket he took 9 wickets in each innings of a match in 1915 - 9/46 in the first innings and had exactly the same figures in the second. Brothers: W.C.Tucker, S.J.Tucker.

TUCKER Spencer Jacob 1892/93-1896/97 b 1865 Christchurch, Canterbury. d 6.7.1948 Wellington. Team: **Wellington.** Occ: Civil servant. Brothers: W.C.Tucker, K.H.Tucker. His daughter married R.M.Virtue's son.

TUCKER William Crawley 1891/92 b 1864 Christchurch, Canterbury. d 23.10.1939 Wanganui. Team: **Taranaki.** Occ: Telegraphist. Brothers: K.H.Tucker, S.J.Tucker.

TUCKWELL Bertie Joseph 1902/03-1917/18 b 6.10.1882 Carlton, Melbourne, Victoria, Australia. d 2.1.1943 Wellington. RHB Teams: **Otago, Wellington, New Zealand,** Victoria. Sch: University Coll, Armadale, Australia. He played for New Zealand prior to being granted Test status.

TUFFEY Daryl Raymond 1996/97-2009/10 b 11.6.1978 Milton, Otago. RHB RFM Teams: **Northern Districts, Auckland, New Zealand Test, New Zealand ODI, New Zealand T20.** Played List A in NZ; Played T20 in NZ. Sch: Manurewa HS. He holds the Northern Districts 9th wicket partnership record of 189 with N.R.Parlane against Wellington in 1999/00.

TUGAGA Malaesaili Julian 2008/09-2009/10 b 16.2.1990 Wellington. LHB RFM Team: **Wellington.** Played List A in NZ. Sch: Wellington Coll. He holds the Wellington 9th wicket partnership record of 225 with L.J.Woodcock against Central Districts in 2009/10. During this innings he scored his maiden FC century (103*) batting at no.10.
TUKE Charles Lawrence 1884/85 b 3.8.1858 Sittingbourne, Kent, England. d 30.12.1929 Remuera, Auckland. Team: **Hawke's Bay.** Sch: Haileybury, England; St Johns, Auckland. Occ: Anglican Reverend. Son: H.L.Tuke.
TUKE Hugh Latimer 1904/05 b 6.4.1885 Taradale, Hawke's Bay. d 7.6.1915 at sea, off Gallipoli, Turkey. He died on *HMHS Sicilia*, aged 29, of wounds received at Quinn's Post, Gallipoli. Team: **Hawke's Bay.** Occ: Farmer. Rugby: Hawke's Bay. Father: C.L.Tuke.
TURNBULL Albert John 1896/97 b 29.10.1866 Dunedin, Otago. d 29.11.1929 Dunedin, Otago. Team: **Otago.** Brother: P.J.Turnbull.
TURNBULL John Ashley 1955/56-1962/63 b 30.6.1935 Gisborne, Poverty Bay. RHB OB Teams: **Auckland, Northern Districts.**
TURNBULL Percival James 1884/85 b 25.10.1862 Hobart, Tasmania, Australia. d 12.3.1937 Christchurch, Canterbury. Team: **Otago.** Occ: Leather dresser. Brother: A.J.Turnbull.
TURNER Ashley Dean 2001/02-2004/05 b 13.6.1975 Lower Hutt, Wellington. RHB RMF Team: **Wellington.** Played List A in NZ.
TURNER Bruce Alexander 1951/52-1955/56 b 5.8.1930 Palmerston North, Manawatu. d 30.3.2010 Palmerston North, Manawatu. RHB Team: **Central Districts.** Sch: Palmerston North BHS. Occ: Coy director. Hockey: New Zealand and Manawatu.
TURNER George Addington 1878/79-1879/80 b 22.2.1858 Christchurch, Canterbury. d 2.7.1927 Dunedin, Otago. Team: **Canterbury.** Occ: Railway inspector. Umpired first-class cricket.
TURNER Glenn Maitland 1964/65-1982/83 b 26.5.1947 Dunedin, Otago. RHB OB Teams: **Otago, Northern Districts, New Zealand Test, New Zealand ODI,** Worcestershire. Played List A in NZ. Sch: Otago BHS. Occ: Cricket coach. Books: My way; Opening up; Lifting the covers; Glen Turner's century of centuries. NZCA COY: 1972. WCOY: 1971. ICOY 1977. NZ coach, selector and manager; Otago coach. He holds the NZ Test 1st wicket partnership record of 387 with T.W.Jarvis against the West Indies in 1971/72. He twice carried his bat through a completed Test innings, and in the West Indies in 1971/72 hit four double-centuries in all matches, including successive innings of 259 at Georgetown. He scored 100 FC centuries, the only NZ player to do so. His 100th century was 311* for Worcestershire v Warwickshire in 1983. He has scored the most first-class runs by a New Zealander - 34,346. He was the youngest player to bat through a Test innings (in 1969, in the Lord's Test, when he scored 43 not out). He made 1,000 runs before the end of May in the 1973 English season. He made a score of 141 not out against Gloucestershire when Worcester totalled 169 in 1977. He holds the Otago 6th wicket partnership record of 165 with W.K.Lees against Wellington in 1975/76.
TURNER Nicholas Mirek 2006/07-2009/10 b 3.8.1983 Invercargill, Southland. LHB RFM Teams: **Otago, Auckland.** Played List A in NZ; Played T20 in NZ.
TURTON Gibson Kirke 1863/64-1871/72 b 29.7.1841 Raglan, Waikato. d 3.7.1891 Wellington. At one time he was a partner in a law firm doing extensive business in Dunedin and was for a time provincial solicitor. Unfortunately he took to drink and gradually sank until he picked up a precarious living in Wellington, residing in a shed where he died of lung disease. Team: **Otago.** Occ: Barrister. MP. Umpired first-class cricket.
TWIST Charles Henry 1882/83-1883/84 b 1855 New Zealand. d 9.3.1935 Wellington. Team: **Wellington.** Occ: Groundsman. Umpired first-class cricket.
TWOSE Roger Graham 1989-2000/01 b 17.4.1968 Torquay, Devon, England. LHB RM Teams: **Northern Districts, Central Districts, Wellington, New Zealand Test, New Zealand ODI,** Warwickshire. Played List A in NZ. Sch: Kings Coll, Taunton, England. Occ: Bank officer. He holds the Wellington 8th wicket partnership record of 180 with M.J.Goodson against Otago in 1994/95. Uncles: R.W.Tolchard (England, Leicestershire), J.G.Tolchard (Leicestershire).
TYNAN John Christopher 1951/52-1953/54 b 5.12.1925 Wellington. RHB OB Team: **Wellington.** Sch: Wellington Coll. Hockey: New Zealand.
ULUIVITI Nacanieli Mataika 1953/54-1954/55 b 19.5.1932 Suva, Fiji. d 6.5.2004 Suva, Fiji. RHB RM Teams: **Auckland, Fiji.** Sch: Wanganui Tech Coll. Occ: Civil servant. Rugby: Fiji. NZCA obit: 2004; Wisden obit: 2005.

UNKA Hira 1968/69-1975/76 b 1.6.1943 Karadi, Mysore (now Karnataka), India. RHB RMF Team: **Northern Districts.** Played List A in NZ.

UNWIN Paul David 1986/87-1993/94 b 9.6.1967 Waipawa, Hawke's Bay. RHB OB Teams: **Central Districts, Canterbury,** Somerset. Played List A in NZ. Sch: Lindesfarne Coll. Occ: Schoolteacher.

UPHAM Ernest Frederick 1892/93-1909/10 b 24.3.1873 Wellington. d 23.10.1935 Paekakariki, Wellington. RHB RM Teams: **Wellington, New Zealand.** Sch: Thorndon Sch. Occ: Law clerk. Wisden obit: 1936. He took over a thousand wickets in club and representative cricket. He played for New Zealand prior to being granted Test status.

URU John Hope Wharukiti 1893/94-1894/95 b 26.3.1868 Kaiapoi, North Canterbury. d 29.11.1921 Wellington. F Team: **Canterbury.** Sch: Te Aute Coll. Occ: Farmer. Rugby: Canterbury. MP. He was the leader, with the rank of Captain, of the Maori contingent to Queen Victoria's Diamond Jubilee in 1897, and of the contingent to the celebrations of the inauguration of the Commonwealth of Australia in 1901.

UTTLEY Kenneth Frank Mcneill 1933/34-1951/52 b 21.8.1913 Oamaru, North Otago. d 15.6.1973 Palmerston North, Manawatu. RHB Teams: **Otago, Canterbury, Wellington.** Sch: Wairarapa Coll; Southland BHS. Occ: Doctor. Rugby: Otago. NZCA obit: 1973. NZ selector.

VAIKVEE Toivo 1973/74-1975/76 b 7.6.1947 Esbjerg. Denmark. RHB LB Team: **Wellington.** Sch: Palmerston North BHS.

VALLANGE William Henry Tracey Campbell Penney 1886/87 b 15.8.1864 Kensington, London, England. d Q1 1924 Southwark, London, England. Team: **Otago.** Occ: Doctor. Rugby: Otago.

VAN BEEK Logan Verjus 2009/10 b 7.9.1990 Christchurch, Canterbury. RHB RFM Team: **Canterbury.** Played List A in NZ. Sch: St Andrews Coll. NZ U19 ODI. Basketball: New Zealand Under-19s. Grandfather: S.C.Guillen; great-grandfather: V.Guillen (Trinidad); great-uncle: N.N.Guillen (Trinidad).

VANCE Robert Alan 1947/48-1961/62 b 29.12.1924 Wellington. d 7.11.1994 Wellington. RHB Team: **Wellington.** Sch: Wellington Coll. NZCA obit: 1995; Wisden obit: 1995. Wellington selector; chairman of the New Zealand Cricket Council; NZ manager. Son: R.H.Vance.

VANCE Robert Howard 1976/77-1990/91 b 31.3.1955 Wellington. RHB OB occ wk Teams: **Wellington, New Zealand Test, New Zealand ODI.** Played List A in NZ. Sch: Wellington Coll. He holds the world record for the most runs conceded in a first-class over - 77 against Canterbury in 1990. The 22-ball over contained 17 no-balls (due to a miscount there were only 5 legitimate balls). Father: R.A.Vance.

VAN WYK Cornelius Francoius Kruger 2000/01-2009/10 b 7.2.1980 Wolmaransstad, North-West Province, South Africa. RHB wk Teams: **Canterbury,** Northerns, Titans. Played List A in NZ; Played T20 in NZ. Sch: Afrikaanse Hoer Seunskool, South Africa. Occ: Cricket pro. He holds the NZ 6th wicket partnership record of 379* with S.L.Stewart for Canterbury v Central Districts in 2009/10.

VAUGHAN Justin Thomas Caldwell 1989/90-1996/97 b 30.8.1967 Hereford, England. LHB RM Teams: **Auckland, New Zealand Test, New Zealand ODI,** Gloucestershire. Played List A in NZ. Sch: Westlake BHS. Occ: Doctor. NZ U19 Test. NZCA COY: 1996. CEO NZ cricket. He scored 106* on FC debut for Auckland v Wellington in 1989/90.

VEAR Dennis John 1959/60-1960/61 b 5.4.1938 Auckland. RHB RM Team: **Otago.**

VEITCH John Robert 1957/58-1964/65 b 26.8.1937 Dunedin, Otago. d 22.12.2009 Tauranga, South Auckland. LHB Teams: **Otago, Canterbury.** Sch: Otago BHS. Occ: Storeman.

VEITCH Stuart William 1960/61-1966/67 b 22.4.1940 Gisborne, Poverty Bay. RHB Team: **Northern Districts.** Sch: Gisborne BHS.

VERHOEK Peter John 1978/79-1980/81 b 16.9.1955 Auckland. RHB OB Team: **Central Districts.** Played List A in NZ. Sch: Auckland GS. Occ: Vet.

VERMEULEN Michael John 2009/10 b 30.12.1982 Christchurch, Canterbury. RHB RMF Team: **Canterbury.**

VERNON Edward Saunderson 1878/79-1879/80 b 6.3.1851 Dublin, Ireland. d 27.6.1902 Fortrose, Southland. RHB Team: **Otago.** Sch: Christ Coll. Occ: Merchant.

VERNON John Wallace 1961/62 b 13.6.1940 Wanganui. RHB wk Team: **Central Districts.**

VERRY Ross Alexander 1985/86-1992/93 b 25.10.1964 Wellington. RHB OB Team: **Wellington.** Played List A in NZ. Occ: Bank manager. He holds the Wellington 3rd wicket partnership record of 346 with G.P.Burnett against Northern Districts in 1991/92. Cousin: S.J.Hotter.

VETTORI Daniel Luca 1996/97-2009/10 b 27.1.1979 Auckland. LHB SLA Teams: **Northern Districts, New Zealand Test, New Zealand ODI, New Zealand T20,** Nottinghamshire, Warwickshire, ICC World XI Test. ICC World XI ODI. Played List A in NZ; Played T20 in NZ. Sch: St Pauls, Hamilton. NZ U19 Test; NZ U19 ODI. Book: Turning point. NZCA COY: 2000, 2005. He was the youngest man to play Test cricket for New Zealand, at the age of 18 years 10 days. He holds the NZ domestic T20 2nd wicket partnership record of 115 with T.M.Dilshan for Northern Districts against Wellington in 2009/10. Cousin: J.V.Hill; uncle: A.J.Hill.

VIJAY Murali 2006/07-2010 b 1.4.1984 Madras (now Chennai), Tamil Nadu, India. RHB OB Team: **Central Districts,** India Test, India ODI, India T20, Tamil Nadu. Indian Test player who played for Central Districts in order to get match practice whilst on the 2008/09 tour of NZ.

VINCENT Lou 1997/98-2008 b 11.11.1978 Warkworth, Rodney. RHB RM occ wk Teams: **Auckland, New Zealand Test, New Zealand ODI, New Zealand T20,** Worcestershire, Lancashire. Played List A in NZ; Played T20 in NZ. Sch: Westlake BHS; Adelaide HS, Australia. Occ: Cricket pro. NZ U19 ODI. On his Test debut he scored 112 against Australia at Perth in 2001/02. He holds the record for the highest ODI score for NZ - 172 v Zimbabwe in 2005/06. He holds the NZ domestic T20 1st wicket partnership record of 149 with M.J.Guptill for Auckland against Wellington in 2009/10 and the NZ domestic T20 5th wicket partnership record of 101 with A.K.Kitchen for Auckland against Wellington in 2009/10.

VINCENT Richard Barrett 1886/87 b Q4 1846 Stepney, London, England. d 17.9.1924 Wellington. Team: **Wellington.** Occ: Assistant Secretary of the Treasury.

VIRTUE Robert Macintyre 1891/92 b 1865 Hokitika, West Coast. d 6.11.1930 Wellington. Team: **Wellington.** Sch: Hokitika HS. Occ: Merchant. His son married S.J.Tucker's daughter.

VISSER Peter John 1983/84-1986/87 b 10.5.1960 Waikari, North Canterbury. RHB RFM Team: **Central Districts.** Played List A in NZ. Sch: Middleton Grange. Occ: Sales rep. He took a hat-trick for Central Districts v Auckland in 1983/84.

VIVIAN Graham Ellery 1964/65-1978/79 b 28.2.1946 Auckland. LHB LB Teams: **Auckland, New Zealand Test, New Zealand ODI.** Played List A in NZ. Sch: Mt Albert GS. Occ: Turf supplier. NZCA COY: 1977. He made his Test debut against India at Calcutta in 1964/65 - it was also his first-class debut, his selection following an impressive pre-tour net session. Father: H.G.Vivian.

VIVIAN Henry Gifford 1930/31-1938/39 b 4.11.1912 Auckland. d 12.8.1983 Auckland. LHB SLA Teams: **Auckland, New Zealand Test.** Sch: Mt Albert GS. NZCA obit: 1983. Wisden obit: 1983. NZ and Auckland selector. Son: G.E.Vivian.

VIVIAN Leslie George 1912/13 b 1882 Richmond, Victoria, Australia. d 22.1.1931 Ohakune, Manawatu. He accidently drowned. Team: **Hawke's Bay.** Occ: Sawmill hand.

VOGEL Timothy Grant 1980/81-1983/84 b 11.7.1960 Upper Hutt, Wellington. RHB LFM Team: **Wellington.** Played List A in NZ. Occ: Barrister.

VORRATH William Nelson 1927/28-1929/30 b 21.10.1904 Dunedin, Otago. d 7.6.1934 Dunedin, Otago. He died aged 29. LHB Team: **Otago.** Occ: Plasterer. Rugby League: Otago. Wisden obit: 1935.

WADDINGHAM John Seaton 1953/54-1959/60 b 24.8.1934 Auckland. RHB Team: **Auckland.**

WADSWORTH Kenneth John 1968/69-1975/76 b 30.11.1946 Nelson. d 19.8.1976 Nelson. He died of cancer, aged 29. RHB RSM wk Teams: **Central Districts, Canterbury, New Zealand Test, New Zealand ODI.** Played List A in NZ. Sch: Waimea Coll. Occ: Orchardist; cricket pro. NZCA obit: 1976; Wisden obit: 1977. NZCA COY: 1973.

WAGNER Neil 2005/06-2009/10 b 13.3.1986 Pretoria, Transvaal, South Africa. LHB LMF Teams: **Otago,** Northerns, Titans. Played List A in NZ; Played T20 in NZ. Sch: Afrikaans BHS, Pretoria, South Africa.

WAGSTAFFE W G 1913/14-1919/20 wk Team: **Wellington.**

WAIDE Scott James 2001/02 b 11.7.1977 Dunedin, Otago. RHB OB Team: **Otago.** Sch: Kings HS.

WAINE Henry Colin 1944/45 b 19.1.1913 Christchurch, Canterbury. d 3.9.1995 New Zealand. RHB LBG Team: **Canterbury.**

WALKER Alexander Johnston 1866/67-1869/70 b 10.7.1842 Bowland, Selkirkshire, Scotland. d 15.6.1903 West Kensington, London, England. Team: **Canterbury.** Sch: Trinity Coll, England. Occ: Farmer.
WALKER Brooke Graeme Keith 1997/98-2004/05 b 25.3.1977 Auckland. RHB LB Teams: **Auckland, New Zealand Test, New Zealand ODI.** Played List A in NZ. Sch: Macleans Coll.
WALKER Derek John 1980/81-1987/88 b 23.11.1959 Dunedin, Otago. LHB RM Team: **Otago.** Played List A in NZ.
WALKER Matthew David John 1995/96-2003/04 b 17.1.1977 Opunake, Taranaki. RHB RM Teams: **Central Districts, Wellington, New Zealand ODI.** Played List A in NZ. NZ U19 Test; NZ U19 ODI. He holds the Wellington 7th wicket partnership record of 250 with C.J.Nevin against Otago in 2003/04.
WALLACE Alan 1910/11-1911/12 b 1.4.1891 Devonport, Auckland. d 10.5.1915 at sea, off Gallipoli, Turkey. He died of wounds aged 24. Team: **Auckland.** Sch: Auckland GS. Occ: Student. Soccer: Auckland. Rhodes scholar. Wisden obit: 1918.
WALLACE Colin Leslie 1978/79 b 2.10.1953 Auckland. RHB wk Team: **Auckland.**
WALLACE George Frederick 1936/37-1945/46 b 31.7.1913 Auckland. d 19.9.1997 Auckland. RHB OB Team: **Auckland.** Sch: Mt Albert GS. NZCA obit: 2006. Brother: W.M.Wallace; nephew: G.M.Wallace.
WALLACE Gregory Mervyn 1976/77 b 21.9.1950 Auckland. RHB Team: **Auckland.** Played List A in NZ. Father: W.M.Wallace; uncle: G.F.Wallace.
WALLACE Peter Eldred 1973/74 b 23.10.1946 Christchurch, Canterbury. LHB Team: **Canterbury.** Sch: West Christchurch BHS. Occ: Bank officer.
WALLACE Walter Mervyn 1933/34-1960/61 b 19.12.1916 Grey Lynn, Auckland. d 21.3.2008 Auckland. RHB OB Teams: **Auckland, New Zealand Test.** Sch: Mt Albert GS. Occ: Sports dealer. Book: A cricket master by J.Romanos. NZOM. NZCA obit: 2008; Wisden obit: 2009. NZ and Auckland selector and coach. He holds the NZ 4th wicket partnership record of 324 with J.R.Reid for New Zealand v Cambridge University in 1949. Brother: G.F.Wallace; son: G.M.Wallace.
WALLS John 1886/87 b 25.10.1856 Melbourne, Victoria, Australia. d 13.3.1945 Dunedin, Otago. Team: **Otago.**
WALMSLEY John William 1889/90 b 1859 Blackburn, Lancashire, England. d 16.7.1938 Cheviot, North Canterbury. RHB wk Team: **Canterbury.** Occ: Farmer.
WALMSLEY Kerry Peter 1994/95-2005/06 b 23.8.1973 Dunedin, Otago. RHB RFM Teams: **Auckland, Otago, New Zealand Test, New Zealand ODI.** Played List A in NZ. He took a wicket with his seventh ball in Test cricket.
WALMSLEY Walter Thomas 1945/46-1959/60 b 16.3.1916 Homebush, Sydney, New South Wales, Australia. d 25.2.1978 Hamilton, Waikato. RHB LBG Teams: **Northern Districts,** New South Wales, Tasmania, Queensland. Occ: Schoolteacher. NZCA obit: 1978; Wisden obit: 1979.
WALSH Ivan Alexander 1948/49-1949/50 b 29.12.1924 Dunedin, Otago. d 12.5.2005 Dunedin, Otago. RHB RM Team: **Otago.** Sch: Dunedin Christian Bros. Occ: Schoolteacher. Soccer: New Zealand. NZCA obit: 2005; Wisden obit: 2006.
WALTER Cyril Vincent 1945/46 b 4.12.1912 Nelson. d 23.5.1988 Christchurch, Canterbury. RHB Team: **Canterbury.** Sch: Christ Coll. Occ: Bookkeeper. Hockey: New Zealand. Books: Hockey: from bully to goal (1948); The theory and practice of hockey (1966); Hockey the gold medal way (published posthumously in 1989). Wisden obit: 1989.
WALTERS Henry George 1941/42 b 6.11.1917 Auckland. d 25.8.1944 at sea, in the English Channel. He was killed in action aged 26. LHB Team: **Auckland.**
WALTON Gary William 1985/86-1987/88 b 17.4.1959 Nelson. RHB OB Team: **Central Districts.**
WALTON Harold 1897/98 b 1874 New Zealand. d 9.12.1960 Auckland. Team: **Auckland.**
WARD Barry John 1986/87 b 28.9.1961 Timaru, South Canterbury. RHB wk Team: **Canterbury.** Played List A in NZ. Sch: Timaru BHS. Father: J.T.Ward.
WARD Brendan Peter 1986/87-1987/88 b 14.1.1957 Invercargill, Southland. RHB RM Team: **Northern Districts.** Played List A in NZ.
WARD James Sinclair 2000/01-2004/05 b 7.6.1974 Christchurch, Canterbury. LHB SLA Team: **Canterbury.** Sch: Christchurch BHS. Occ: Horticultural worker.

WARD John Thomas 1957/58-1970/71 b 11.3.1937 Timaru, South Canterbury. RHB wk Teams: **Canterbury, New Zealand Test**. Sch: Timaru West HS. Occ: Court bailiff. NZCA COY: 1968. Son: B.J.Ward.
WARD Sydney William 1929/30-1937/38 b 5.8.1907 Surry Hills, Sydney, New South Wales, Australia. RHB RM Team: **Wellington**. Occ: Jeweller. Rugby: Wellington, Nelson and East Coast. He is the oldest known NZ FC cricketer and the second after J.Wheatley to live beyond 100 years of age.
WAREHAM Clement Patrick Stephen 1934/35 b 23.3.1911 Wellington. d 30.9.1940 Hollingbourne, Kent, England. He was killed in a hit and run car accident while serving with the NZ forces, aged 29. Team: **Wellington**. Wisden obit: 1943.
WARNE William 1919/20-1920/21 wk Team: **Wellington**. Sch: Mt Cook HS. Occ: Driver.
WARNER Brian Henry 1944/45 b 1919 Auckland. d 24.1.1968 Auckland. RHB Team: **Auckland**. Occ: Bank clerk.
WARREN Walter Frederick 1894/95-1897/98 b 1871 Wellington. d 14.8.1944 Auckland. Teams: **Wellington, Auckland**. Occ: Soldier.
WARRINGTON John William 1973/74-1975/76 b 2.11.1948 Coventry, Warwickshire, England. LHB Teams: **Northern Districts, Auckland**. Played List A in NZ.
WASHER Alfred John 1919/20 b 1890 North Carlton, Melbourne, Victoria, Australia. d 3.11.1941 Invercargill, Southland. SLA Team: **Southland**. Occ: Plasterer.
WASHER Arthur Theobald 1884/85 b Q4 1855 Brighton, Sussex, England. d 19.11.1910 Christchurch, Canterbury. On the day of his death he had umpired in a local match. His death was caused by a blood clot blocking an artery. LHB SLA Team: **Canterbury**. Sch: Christ Coll. Occ: Accountant. Wisden obit: 1912.
WATERS Victor Herbert 1895/96-1905/06 b 31.5.1876 Wellington. d 15.11.1951 Wellington. Team: **Wellington**. Sch: Mt Cook HS. Occ: Shipping clerk.
WATLING Bradley-John 2004/05-2009/10 b 9.7.1985 Durban, Natal, South Africa. RHB wk Teams: **Northern Districts, New Zealand Test, New Zealand ODI, New Zealand T20**. Played List A in NZ; Played T20 in NZ. Sch: Hamilton BHS. NZ U19 ODI. He scored 378 in a Hamilton club game in 1997/98.
WATSON Eric Alexander 1947/48-1959/60 b 20.7.1925 Dunedin, Otago. RHB RM Team: **Otago**. Rugby: Otago; All Black coach 1979-80. Brother: L.F.Watson.
WATSON Francis Edward 1879/80 b 9.8.1860 St Helena. d 27.10.1930 Te Puke, Bay of Plenty. Team: **West Coast (North Island)**. Occ: Schoolmaster. He was born on the island of St. Helena while his parents were going to England on furlough from India. Brother: G.Watson.
WATSON George 1880/81-1883/84 b 1855 Bombay (now Mumbai), Maharashtra, India. d 23.11.1884 Christchurch, Canterbury. He died aged 29. LHB Team: **Canterbury**. Sch: High Wycombe Royal GS. Occ: Schoolmaster. He scored a century on FC debut - it was the first century in NZ FC cricket, 175 for Canterbury v Otago in 1880/81. Brother: F.E.Watson.
WATSON H 1909/10-1920/21 RM Team: **Canterbury**.
WATSON Harold Cooper 1907/08-1923/24 b 24.12.1879 Calverton, Nottinghamshire, England. d 2.7.1958 Auckland. RHB Teams: **Otago, Canterbury, Wellington**. Occ: Groundsman. Umpired first-class cricket. NZCA obit: 1958. Brother: L.C.Watson.
WATSON Leo Cooper 1911/12 b 30.7.1885 St Helens, Lancashire, England. d 21.11.1961 Christchurch, Canterbury. Team: **Otago**. Occ: Tomato grower. Brother: H.C.Watson.
WATSON Leonard Frank 1953/54 b 11.10.1927 Dunedin, Otago. RHB Team: **Otago**. Brother: E.A.Watson.
WATSON Leslie Thomas 1978/79 b 17.8.1956 Christchurch, Canterbury. RHB RM Team: **Canterbury**. Played List A in NZ. Sch: Papanui HS.
WATSON Thomas Melvin 1964/65 b 10.5.1943 Lower Hutt, Wellington. RHB RMF Team: **NZ Under-23s**.
WATSON William 1984/85-1994/95 b 31.8.1965 Auckland. RHB RFM Teams: **Auckland, New Zealand Test, New Zealand ODI**. Played List A in NZ. Sch: Westlake BHS. Book: Willie's Tail: Bouncers, bottle tops and bombs.
WATT David Glendenning 1943/44 b 21.7.1920 Ashburton, Mid Canterbury. d 29.8.1996 Wellington. RHB Team: **Otago**. Occ: Dentist. NZCA obit: 2002. He scored 105 on FC debut for Otago v Canterbury in 1942/43 - it was his only FC match.

WATT Leslie 1942/43-1962/63 b 17.9.1924 Waitati, Otago. d 15.11.1996 Dunedin, Otago. RHB Teams: **Otago, New Zealand Test**. Occ: Carton maker. NZCA obit: 1997; Wisden obit: 1997. He holds the Otago 1st wicket partnership record of 373 with B.Sutcliffe against Auckland in 1950/51.
WEALLEANS Kyle Andrew 1988/89-1994/95 b 2.3.1969 Matamata, Waikato. RHB LB Teams: **Northern Districts, New Zealand**. Played List A in NZ. Sch: Otumoetai Coll. Occ: NZ Air Force. He played for New Zealand in a FC match.
WEBB Christopher Allan 1981/82 b 8.6.1950 Otorohanga, Waikato. RHB SLA Team: **Central Districts**. Played List A in NZ.
WEBB George 1879/80-1896/97 b 1856 Co Galway, Ireland. d 7.6.1934 Levin, Horowhenua. RFM Team: **Wellington**. Occ: Clerk.
WEBB Murray George 1969/70-1973/74 b 22.6.1947 Invercargill, Southland. RHB RF Teams: **Otago, Canterbury, New Zealand Test**. Played List A in NZ. Sch: Timaru BHS. Occ: Caricaturist. NZCA COY: 1974. Brother: R.J.Webb.
WEBB Peter Neil 1976/77-1986/87 b 14.7.1957 Auckland. RHB occ wk Teams: **Auckland, New Zealand Test, New Zealand ODI**. Played List A in NZ. Cousin: M.R.Pringle.
WEBB Richard John 1975/76-1983/84 b 15.9.1952 Invercargill, Southland. RHB RFM Teams: **Otago, New Zealand ODI**. Played List A in NZ. Brother: M.G.Webb.
WEBB Robert Courtney 1937/38-1949/50 b 13.9.1917 Christchurch, Canterbury. d 8.5.1989 Christchurch, Canterbury. RHB wk Team: **Canterbury**. Sch: Christ Coll. Occ: Farmer. NZCA obit: 2005.
WEBB William Arthur Alexander 1897/98-1900/01 b 1872 Mosgiel, Otago. d 29.1.1913 Dunedin, Otago. Team: **Otago**.
WEBSTER Rudi Valentine 1961-1967/68 b 10.6.1939 Marchfield, St Philip, Barbados. RHB RFM Teams: **Otago**, Scotland, Warwickshire. Sch: Harrison Coll, Barbados. Occ: Doctor.
WEENINK Scott William 1995/96-2000 b 1.1.1973 Christchurch, Canterbury. RHB OB Teams: **Wellington**, Oxford University. Played List A in NZ. Sch: Rongatai Coll. Occ: Solicitor.
WEIR Alison Francis 1927/28 b 21.1.1903 Auckland. d 17.6.1969 Auckland. RHB Team: **Auckland**. Sch: Mt Albert GS. Occ: Solicitor. Brother: G.L.Weir.
WEIR Gordon Lindsay 1927/28-1946/47 b 2.6.1908 Auckland. d 31.10.2003 Auckland. RHB RM Teams: **Auckland, New Zealand Test**. Sch: Mt Albert GS. Occ: Schoolteacher. Rugby: Auckland. NZCA obit: 2004; Wisden obit: 2004. NZ and Auckland selector. He was the world's senior Test player when he died aged 95. Brother: A.F.Weir.
WELLS Frank Liddiard 1895/96-1896/97 b 21.10.1871 Dunedin, Otago. d 14.1.1932 Wellington. Team: **Otago**.
WELLS Jason Douglas 1989/90-2000/01 b 25.3.1970 Wellington. RHB OB Team: **Wellington**. Played List A in NZ. Sch: Rongatai Coll. He holds the Wellington 2nd wicket partnership record of 287 with M.D.Bell against Auckland in 1997/98.
WELLS Samuel Raymond 2007/08-2009/10 b 13.7.1984 Dunedin, Otago. LHB RM Team: **Otago**. Played List A in NZ. Occ: Student.
WENSLEY Albert Frederick 1922-1947/48 b 24.5.1898 Brighton, Sussex, England. d 17.6.1970 Ware, Hertfordshire, England. RHB RMF occ wk Teams: **Auckland**, Sussex, Nawanagar, Europeans (India). Occ: Cricket pro. NZCA obit: 1970; Wisden obit: 1971. An English pro, played and coached in NZ. He has the best bowling figures for Auckland, 9/36 against Otago in 1929/30.
WERRY Nathaniel William 1873/74-1883/84 b 1847 Smyoria, Anatolia, Turkey. d 26.5.1907 Kashmir, India. He died from cholera, aged 60. occ wk Team: **Wellington**. Sch: Eton, England. Occ: Manager, Wellington club. Rugby: Wellington.
WEST Gareth Lawrence 2000/01-2003/04 b 26.7.1976 New Plymouth, Taranaki. LHB LFM Teams: **Central Districts, Northern Districts**. Played List A in NZ. Sch: New Plymouth BHS. Brother: R.M.West.
WEST Regan Morris 1996/97-2009 b 27.4.1979 New Plymouth, Taranaki. LHB LFM,SLA Teams: **Central Districts, Wellington**, Ireland ODI, Ireland T20. Sch: New Plymouth BHS. Occ: Cricket pro. NZ U19 ODI. Brother: G.L.West.

WESTBROOK Roy Austin 1910/11-1921/22 b 3.1.1889 Scottsdale, Tasmania, Australia. d 7.8.1961 Wellington. RHB Teams: **Otago,** Tasmania. Sch: Launceston GS, Australia. Brother: K.R.Westbrook (Tasmania); uncle: N.R.Westbrook (Tasmania).
WESTON David Lynley 1950/51 b 30.7.1930 Whangarei, Northland. d 25.1.1977 Rotorua, Bay of Plenty. RHB Team: **Auckland.** Rugby: Auckland.
WESTON George Thorngate 1903/04-1904/05 b 21.10.1876 Hokitika, West Coast. d 19.9.1957 Christchurch, Canterbury. RHB wk Team: **Canterbury.** Sch: Christ Coll. Occ: Solicitor.
WESTON Timothy Ian 2005/06-2009/10 b 6.6.1982 Stratford, Taranaki. RHB wk Team: **Central Districts.** Played List A in NZ; Played T20 in NZ. Sch: New Plymouth BHS. Occ: Schoolteacher.
WESTWOOD Reginald James 1940/41 b 19.10.1907 Foxton, Horowhenua. d 4.5.1980 Palmerston North, Manawatu. RHB RM Team: **Canterbury.** Sch: Foxton HS. Occ: Caretaker.
WEYBURNE Bernard Augustine 1896/97-1905/06 b 15.10.1877 Lyttelton, Christchurch, Canterbury. d 18.12.1970 Wellington. Team: **Wellington.** Occ: Clerk.
WHEATLEY John 1882/83-1903/04 b 8.1.1860 Singleton, New South Wales, Australia. d 19.4.1962 Waimate, South Canterbury. He died aged 102 and was the oldest Canterbury cricketer. He and S.W.Ward are the only known New Zealand cricketers to live beyond 100 years. occ wk Team: **Canterbury.** Occ: Printer. NZCA obit: 1962; Wisden obit: 1963. New Zealand selector.
WHEELER Ben Matthew 2009/10 b 10.11.1991 Blenheim, Marlborough. RHB LM Team: **Central Districts.** Sch: Marlborough Boys Coll. NZ U19 ODI. Grandfather: R.T.Dowker.
WHEELER Graeme Paul 1981/82 b 30.10.1951 Hamilton, Waikato. RHB RM Team: **Wellington.** Played List A in NZ.
WHEELER William J 1944/45 LHB RM Team: **Auckland.**
WHELAN Reginald Francis William 1922/23 b 26.8.1900 Auckland. d 10.7.1970 Auckland. RHB Team: **Auckland.** Sch: Auckland GS. Occ: Insurance clerk.
WHITE B H 1876/77-1879/80 Team: **Nelson.**
WHITE David John 1979/80-1993/94 b 26.6.1961 Gisborne, Poverty Bay. RHB OB Teams: **Northern Districts, New Zealand Test, New Zealand ODI.** Played List A in NZ. Sch: Gisborne BHS. His maiden FC century was 209 for Northern Districts v Central Districts in 1985/86.
WHITE George Mason 1884/85-1905/06 b 12.10.1862 West Derby, Liverpool, Lancashire, England. d 26.5.1949 Auckland. RM Team: **Hawke's Bay.** Occ: Accountant.
WHITE Harold Reginald 1923/24 b 1.9.1896 East Brunswick, Victoria, Australia. d 10.9.1977 Wellington. Team: **Wellington.** Sch: Otago BHS. Occ: Customs clerk.
WHITE Jeremy Stuart Somes 1972/73-1973/74 b 15.10.1947 Ongaonga, Hawke's Bay. LHB RFM Team: **Northern Districts.** Played List A in NZ.
WHITE Kevin John 1978/79-1979/80 b 2.6.1958 Dannevirke, Hawke's Bay. RHB RM Teams: **Northern Districts, Central Districts.**
WHITE Norman Moore 1907/08 b 16.7.1887 Napier, Hawke's Bay. d 11.11.1918 Dannevirke, Hawke's Bay. He died aged 30. Team: **Hawke's Bay.** Sch: Christ Coll. Occ: Farmer. Brother: P.C.White.
WHITE Percy Claude 1906/07-1907/08 b 1868 Wharehine, Rodney. d 19.10.1946 Auckland. Team: **Auckland.** Occ: Contractor. Brother: N.M.White.
WHITE Peter 1910/11 Team: **Hawke's Bay.**
WHITELAW Paul Erskine 1928/29-1946/47 b 10.2.1910 Auckland. d 28.8.1988 Auckland. RHB Teams: **Auckland, New Zealand Test.** Sch: Auckland GS. Occ: Bank officer. NZCA obit: 1988; Wisden obit: 1989. He holds the Auckland 3rd wicket partnership record of 445 with W.N.Carson against Otago in 1936/37at Dunedin. This partnership stood as a world record for the third wicket until 1976/77.
WHITEMAN Samuel James George 2003/04 b 5.8.1982 Auckland. RHB RM Team: **Auckland.** Played List A in NZ. Sch: St Kentigern Coll. NZ U19 Test; NZ U19 ODI.
WHITFORD Onslow Rowan Davey 1947/48 b 26.8.1923 Christchurch, Canterbury. d 11.3.1986 Christchurch, Canterbury. RHB wk Team: **Canterbury.** Hockey: Canterbury. NZCA obit: 1986.

WHITTA Henry Beckett 1903/04-1919/20 b 2.3.1883 Christchurch, Canterbury. d 11.7.1944 Christchurch, Canterbury. RHB SLA Teams: **Canterbury, New Zealand.** Sch: West Christchurch BHS. Occ: Warehouseman. NZ and Canterbury selector. He played for New Zealand prior to being granted Test status.
WHYTE Gordon Lindsay 1939/40 b 13.8.1915 Wellington. d 24.6.2007 Wellington. LHB LB Team: **Wellington.** Sch: Wellington Coll. Occ: Commentator; airline industry. Book: It's not all cricket. BEM. NZCA obit: 2007.
WHYTE Robert Archibald 1934/35 b 10.12.1907 Wellington. d 15.1.1983 Porirua, Wellington. RHB occ wk Team: **Wellington.** Sch: Christ Coll. Occ: Manager. CBE. NZCA obit: 1983; Wisden obit: 1982.
WIGHT Peter Bernard 1950/51-1965 b 25.6.1930 Georgetown, Demerara, British Guiana. RHB OB occ wk Teams: **Canterbury,** Somerset, British Guiana. Sch: St Stanislaus Coll, Barbados. Occ: Umpire. An English pro, played and coached in NZ. Brothers: G.L.Wight (West Indies, British Guiana), H.A.Wight (British Guiana), N.D.Wight (British Guiana); cousins: C.V.Wight (West Indies, British Guiana), O.S.Wight (British Guiana).
WIGLEY William Cranston Henry 1893/94-1903/04 b 1871 Christchurch, Canterbury. d 4.12.1937 Christchurch, Canterbury. RHB Team: **Canterbury.** Sch: Christ Coll. Occ: Solicitor.
WIGZELL James 1877/78-1883/84 b 1860 Nelson. d 20.12.1947 Nelson. Team: **Nelson.** Sch: Bridge St, Nelson. Occ: Accountant.
WILDE Richard Gerard 1951/52 b 28.10.1926 Otaki, Horowhenua. d 11.8.2000 Feilding, Manawatu. NZ RHB Team: **Central Districts.**
WILDING Anthony Frederick 1900/01-1901/02 b 31.10.1883 Opawa, Christchurch, Canterbury. d 9.5.1915 Neuve Chappelle, France. He was killed in action. Team: **Canterbury.** Sch: Christ Coll. Occ: Solicitor. Tennis: When aged 16 he won the handicap singles at the New Zealand Championship meeting; he won the doubles championship (with Norman Brookes) at Wimbledon in 1907 and (with M.J.G.Ritchie) in 1908; the doubles championship of Europe at Hamburg in 1908; represented Australasia (with Norman Brookes) in the challenge round of the Davis Cup v America (1908), and won it in 1914; represented Australasia in the Davis Cup matches 1905-09; won the championship of New Zealand in 1906, 1908 and 1909; won the championship of South Africa in 1910 won the British' singles championship and doubles championship (with M.J.G.Ritchie) in 1910; he retained the singles championship at Wimbledon in 1911; he retained the singles championship at Wimbledon in 1912; represented Australasia at the Olympic contest in Stockholm and won the bronze medal in 1912; retained the singles championship at Wimbledon in 1913. Books: On and off the court; A sporting life by J.Davidson; Captain Anthony Wilding by A.Myers; A true champion by L.Richardson. Father: F.Wilding.
WILDING Frederick 1881/82-1899/00 b 20.11.1852 Montgomery, Wales. d 5.7.1945 Christchurch, Canterbury. RHB SLA Team: **Canterbury, New Zealand.** Sch: Shrewsbury School, England. Occ: Solicitor. Athletics: Held the English public school long-jump record of 20 feet 6 inches. Rugby: West England. Tennis: New Zealand doubles champion five times with R.Harman, mixed doubles champion once. President of the New Zealand Cricket Council and Canterbury CA. He played for New Zealand prior to being granted Test status. Son: A.F.Wilding.
WILES Allan Victor 1946/47 b 29.9.1920 Auckland. d 31.5.2008, North Shore, Auckland. RHB RM Team: **Auckland.** Rugby League: New Zealand.
WILKIE John Lamb 1901/02 b 29.1.1877 New Cumnock, Ayr, Scotland. d 19.6.1963 Mosgiel, Otago. Team: **Otago.** Occ: Flour miller. Brother: R.A.Wilkie.
WILKIE Robert Alexander 1899/00 b 23.11.1878 New Cumnock, Ayr, Scotland. d 7.11.1966 Bexley, Sydney, New South Wales, Australia. Team: **Otago.** Occ: Farmer. Tennis: Otago. He took up tennis when a dislocated shoulder put him out of cricket. Brother: J.L.Wilkie.
WILKINSON Anthony Mark 2002/03 b 15.8.1981 Dunedin, Otago. LHB LM Team: **Otago.** Played List A in NZ.
WILKINSON Glenn John 1996/97 b 23.4.1970 Wellington. RHB RM Team: **Wellington.** NZ U19 Test; NZ U19 ODI.
WILLIAMS Allen Marsh 1883/84 b 1852 Waimate North, Northland. d 11.11.1945 Te Aute, Hawke's Bay. Team: **Hawke's Bay.** Occ: Sheep farmer. Brothers: G.C.Williams, N.T.Williams.

WILLIAMS Arnold Butler 1886/87-1909/10 b 6.1.1870 Swansea, Glamorgan, Wales. d 20.8.1929 Wellington. RHB wk Teams: **Otago, Wellington, New Zealand**. Sch: Otago BHS. Occ: Warehouseman. Rugby: Wellington. Wisden obit: 1930. He played for New Zealand prior to being granted Test status.

WILLIAMS Arthur G 1927/28 RHB RM Team: **Auckland**. Wellington selector.

WILLIAMS Brett Russell 1987/88-1992/93 b 10.10.1965 Wellington. RHB SLA Team: **Wellington**. Played List A in NZ. Occ: Manager.

WILLIAMS Edward Heathcote 1891/92 b 23.3.1853 Pakaraka, Northland. d 28.11.1931 Hastings, Hawke's Bay. Team: **Hawke's Bay**. Sch: Auckland GS. Occ: Solicitor. He was the driving force behind Hawke's Bay cricket and president of the Hawke's Bay CA.

WILLIAMS Frank 1898/99-1908/09 b 1876 Bath, Somerset, England. d 16.7.1946 Dunedin, Otago. wk Team: **Otago**. Occ: Tailor. NZ and Otago selector.

WILLIAMS Garry John 1975/76-1977/78 b 11.3.1953 Dunedin, Otago. RHB occ wk Team: **Otago**.

WILLIAMS George Coldham 1883/84 b 1858 Waimate North, Northland. d 8.5.1944 Rangitapu, Hawke's Bay. Team: **Hawke's Bay**. Occ: Sheep farmer. Brothers: A.M.Williams, N.T.Williams.

WILLIAMS Heathcote Beetham 1891/92-1894/95 b 2.12.1868 Napier, Hawke's Bay. d 3.5.1961 Turihaua Station, Pouawa, Poverty Bay. Team: **Hawke's Bay**. Sch: Christ Coll. Occ: Sheep farmer. The H.B.Williams Memorial Library is named in memory of him. The library was opened in 1967 after the family of the late Heathcote Beetham Williams gave $70,000 to commemorate his many years of close relationship to Gisborne and the surrounding district.

WILLIAMS John Churchill 1970/71-1973/74 b 9.5.1941 Gisborne, Poverty Bay. d 17.3.2007 Auckland. RHB RM Team: **Auckland**. Played List A in NZ. Sch: Gisborne BHS. NZCA obit: 2007. Auckland selector.

WILLIAMS John Lloyd 1952/53 b 23.4.1931 Ashburton, Mid Canterbury. RHB Team: **Canterbury**. Occ: Quantity surveyor.

WILLIAMS John Nathaniel 1903/04-1908 b 24.1.1878 Kensington, London, England. d 25.4.1915 Gaba Tepe, Gallipoli Peninsula, Turkey. He was killed in action during the landing on Gallipoli. RHB Teams: **Hawke's Bay**, Gloucestershire. Sch: Eton, England. Occ: Metallurgist. Wisden obit: 1917. During 1902/3, having settled in New Zealand, he played a few times for Lord Hawke's team, his best score being 48 v XVIII of Manawatu. Brother: P.F.C.Williams (Gloucestershire).

WILLIAMS Junior Alfred 1974/75-1982/83 b 1.6.1950 Trelawny, Jamaica. RHB RFM Teams: **Wellington**, Jamaica. Played List A in NZ.

WILLIAMS Kenneth Struthers 1906/07-1913/14 b 4.1.1882 Christchurch, Canterbury. d 25.3.1920 Seacliff, Otago. He died at the Seacliff Mental Hospital. RHB Team: **Canterbury**. Sch: Christ Coll. Occ: Solicitor.

WILLIAMS Lindsay George 1951/52-1953/54 b 12.7.1933 Auckland. d 18.4.2008 Christchurch, Canterbury. RHB Team: **Wellington**. Sch: Hutt Valley HS. Occ: Soldier. OBE, MC. NZCA obit: 2008.

WILLIAMS Norman Theodore 1893/94-1894/95 b 13.9.1864 Waimate North, Northland. d 4.4.1928 Auckland. Team: **Auckland**. Occ: Insurance manager. Brothers: A.M.Williams, G.C.Williams.

WILLIAMS Owen Charles 1870/71-1884/85 b 20.6.1847 Impression Bay, Tasmania, Australia. d 18.11.1917 Kandy, Ceylon. RHB Teams: **Wellington**, Victoria. Occ: Bank officer. He was on a visit to his daughter in Ceylon when he died.

WILLIAMSON Kane Stuart 2007/08-2009/10 b 8.8.1990 Tauranga, Bay of Plenty. RHB OB Team: **Northern Districts, New Zealand ODI**. Played List A in NZ; Played T20 in NZ. Sch: Tauranga BC. NZ U19 Test; NZ U19 ODI.

WILLIS A 1946/47 Team: **Wellington**.

WILLS J W 1869/70 Team: **Otago**. Umpired first-class cricket.

WILSON Alexander Cracroft 1877/78 b 5.3.1840 Cawnpore, Bengal Presidency (now Kanpur, Uttar Pradesh), India. d 15.1.1911 Christchurch, Canterbury. Team: **Canterbury**. Sch: Rugby, England. Occ: Registrar of Canterbury Coll. Brother: W.C.Wilson.

WILSON Andrew Marsh 1979/80 b 16.5.1954 Wellington. LHB Team: **Wellington**. Played List A in NZ.

WILSON Benjamin Marcus 1892/93 b 11.11.1870 Thames, Thames Valley. d 22.9.1929 Wellington. Team: **Wellington**. Sch: Wellington Coll. Occ: Civil servant. Private Secretary to the Minister of Railways.

WILSON Bradley Svend 2004/05-2009/10 b 10.4.1985 Auckland. RHB OB Team: **Northern Districts**. Played List A in NZ; Played T20 in NZ. NZ U19 ODI.

WILSON Charles Geldart 1894/95-1919/20 b 9.1.1869 Carngham, Victoria, Australia. d 28.6.1952 Wellington. RHB Teams: **Otago, Wellington,** Victoria. Occ: Draper. NZCA obit: 1952; Wisden obit: 1953. Otago and Wellington selector; chairman of the Southland CA and President of the Southland Rugby Union and held similar roles in Dunedin and Wellington.

WILSON David Stuart 1935/36-1948/49 b 13.10.1914 Wellington. d 6.4.1989 Wellington. RHB LFM Team: **Wellington**. Sch: Rongatai Coll.

WILSON Ernest Summers 1927/28 b 31.3.1877 Dunedin, Otago. d 13.7.1959 Dunedin, Otago. Team: **Otago**. Occ: Coy secretary. Secretary for the Otago Rugby Football Union and Otago CA. He was the manager of the Otago team when he played his only first-class match at the ago of 50. He was allowed to bat in place of L.C.Eastman who was injured.

WILSON F E 1893/94 Team: **Hawke's Bay**. Sch: Cheltenham, England. Occ: Farmer.

WILSON George Charles Lee 1913/14 b 1.5.1887 Christchurch, Canterbury. d 14.12.1917 Belgium. He was killed in action aged 30. LB Teams: **Canterbury, New Zealand**. Occ: Carpenter. He played for New Zealand prior to being granted Test status.

WILSON Harold 1923/24-1926/27 RHB RFM Team: **Auckland**.

WILSON Henry Clarke 1896/97-1900/01 b 2.2.1868 Rangiora, North Canterbury. d 16.12.1945 Christchurch, Canterbury. RM Team: **Hawke's Bay**. Occ: Accountant. Rugby: All Blacks, Canterbury, Hawke's Bay and Wellington.

WILSON Ian David 1977/78-1979/80 b 8.8.1952 Christchurch, Canterbury. LHB LM Team: **Canterbury**. Sch: Cashmere HS.

WILSON J H 1883/84-1885/86 Team: **Wellington**.

WILSON Jeffrey William 1991/92-2004/05 b 24.10.1973 Invercargill, Southland. RHB RFM Teams: **Otago, New Zealand ODI, New Zealand T20**. Played List A in NZ. Sch: Cargill HS. Occ: Rugby player. NZ U19 Test; NZ U19 ODI. Rugby: All Blacks and Otago; Test referee. Books: Seasons of gold; The natural by P.Booth. Uncle: T.J.Wilson.

WILSON Michael 1959/60 b 7.3.1940 Blenheim, Marlborough. RHB RFM Team: **Central Districts**.

WILSON Norman Rowley 1957/58-1960/61 b 14.1.1935 Auckland. LHB Team: **Northern Districts**. ND selector.

WILSON Peter Drummond 1940/41 b 10.3.1907 Wellington. d 2.6.1986 Wellington. RHB LB Team: **Wellington**. Occ: Schoolteacher.

WILSON Robert Stanley 1971/72-1978/79 b 1.10.1948 Balclutha, Otago. RHB Team: **Otago**. Nephew: J.M.Paul.

WILSON S 1917/18-1918/19 Team: **Southland**.

WILSON Simon Wilfred James 1990/91-1994/95 b 3.9.1970 Blenheim, Marlborough. RHB Teams: **Central Districts, Canterbury**. Played List A in NZ. Sch: Marlborough Boys Coll. NZ U19 Test.

WILSON Thomas Henry 1891/92 b 1869 New Zealand. d 13.11.1918 Whakatane, Auckland. He died of influenza, aged 49 years. Team: **Auckland**. Sch: Waitaki BHS. Occ: Judge.

WILSON Thomas John 1984/85-1988/89 b 7.7.1957 Invercargill, Southland. LHB RM Team: **Otago**. Played List A in NZ. Nephew: J.W.Wilson.

WILSON Walter Cracroft 1863/64-1864/65 b 5.5.1843 Moradabad, Bengal Presidency (now Uttar Pradesh), India. d 9.6.1865 Rakaia River, Canterbury. He drowned at the age of 22 whilst crossing the Rakaia River. He was the first NZ FC cricketer to die. Team: **Canterbury**. Sch: Rugby, England. Occ: Farmer. Brother: A.C.Wilson.

WILTSHIRE John Robert 1974/75-1983/84 b 20.1.1952 Christchurch, Canterbury. RHB Teams: **Auckland, Central Districts**. Played List A in NZ. Occ: Lawyer; sports management. Hockey: Auckland.

WIREN Anders Galbraith 1945/46 b 14.11.1911 Wellington. d 18.9.1998 Wellington. LHB Team: **Wellington.** Sch: Wellington Coll. Occ: Insurance clerk. NZCA obit: 2008.
WISEMAN Paul John 1991/92-2008 b 4.5.1970 Takapuna, Auckland. RHB OB Teams: **Auckland, Otago, Canterbury, New Zealand Test, New Zealand ODI,** Durham. Played List A in NZ; Played T20 in NZ. Sch: Longbay Coll. Occ: Cricket coach. He took 9/13 for Canterbury v Central Districts in 2004/05. He holds the Canterbury 8th wicket partnership record of 220 with B.C.Hiini against Northern Districts in 2005/06.
WISNESKI Warren Anthony 1992/93-2003/04 b 19.2.1969 New Plymouth, Taranaki. RHB RM Teams: **Central Districts, Canterbury, New Zealand ODI.** Played List A in NZ. Sch: New Plymouth BHS. He holds the Canterbury 10th wicket partnership record of 160 with L.K.Germon against Northern Districts in 1997/98.
WIX Arthur Mckellar 1873/74-1874/75 b 4.7.1846 Wandsworth, London, England. d 26.3.1918 Windsor, Berkshire, England. Team: **Nelson.** Sch: Royal Military Coll, England. Occ: Farmer; soldier.
WIXON Richard Pahi 1991/92-1994/95 b 19.2.1957 Bluff, Southland. RHB SLA Teams: **Central Districts, Otago.** Played List A in NZ. Sch: James Hargest HS.
WOLSTENHOLME John 1886/87-1898/99 b 1851 Rishton, Lancashire, England. d 1.2.1914 Napier, Hawke's Bay. Team: **Hawke's Bay.** Occ: Schoolteacher. Umpired first-class cricket.
WONTNER Gerald 1872/73 b 17.12.1848 Shoreditch, London, England. d 6.10.1885 Upton Manor, Berkshire, England. Team: **Canterbury.** Occ: Soldier.
WOOD Bernard Bedingfield 1907/08-1918/19 b 25.2.1886 Christchurch, Canterbury. d 8.7.1974 Christchurch, Canterbury. RHB Team: **Canterbury.** Sch: Christ Coll. Occ: Merchant. Golf: New Zealand Amateur Champion in 1912 and 1913. He scored 108* on FC debut for Canterbury v Wellington in 1907/08.
WOOD James William Harrington 1882/83-1888/89 b 19.1.1854 Calcutta (now Kolkata), Bengal, India. d 17.9.1937 Nelson. Teams: **Wellington, Hawke's Bay, Nelson.** Occ: Insurance officer. Rugby: Wellington. Nelson representative on the inaugural NZ cricket council in 1894.
WOOD John 1868/69-1877/78 b 1839 England. d 26.1.1909 Christchurch, Canterbury. Team: **Canterbury, Wellington.** Occ: Painter.
WOODCOCK Luke James 2001/02-2009/10 b 19.3.1982 Wellington. LHB SLA occ wk Team: **Wellington.** Played List A in NZ; Played T20 in NZ. Sch: Newlands Coll. NZ U19 Test; NZ U19 ODI. He holds the Wellington 9th wicket partnership record of 225 with M.J.Tugaga against Central Districts in 2009/10 and the NZ domestic T20 8th wicket partnership record of 68* with M.D.Bell for Wellington against Auckland in 2008/09.
WOODS E R 1913/14 Team: **Auckland.**
WOODS Francis 1913/14-1926/27 b 28.1.1889 Christchurch, Canterbury. d 5.1.1951 Christchurch, Canterbury. RHB RM occ wk Team: **Canterbury.**
WOODS Norman Thomas 1958/59-1965/66 b 19.8.1936 Dunedin, Otago. LHB LM Team: **Otago.**
WORDSWORTH Charles William 1907/08-1909/10 b 9.9.1877 Rotherham, Yorkshire, England. d 10.6.1960 Redfern, Sydney, New South Wales, Australia. RM Teams: **Otago,** New South Wales. Occ: Baker; coach; He was engaged by the Otago CA as cricketer and coach.
WORKER George Herrick 2007/08-2009/10 b 23.8.1989 Palmerston North, Manawatu. LHB SLA Team: **Central Districts.** Played List A in NZ; Played T20 in NZ. Sch: Palmerston North BHS. NZ U19 Test; NZ U19 ODI.
WORKER Rupert Vivian De Renzy 1914/15-1929/30 b 15.4.1896 Auckland. d 23.4.1989 Napier, Hawke's Bay. LHB Teams: **Auckland, Canterbury, Otago, Wellington, New Zealand.** Sch: Auckland GS. Occ: Schoolteacher. NZCA obit: 1989; Wisden obit: 1990. He played for New Zealand prior to being granted Test status.
WORRALL John Henry 1951/52-1954/55 b 26.5.1927 Stanley Bay, Auckland. RHB occ wk Team: **Auckland.**
WORTHINGTON Calvert 1864/65-1865/66 b 29.8.1830 Burton-on-Trent, Staffordshire, England. d 17.11.1871 Burton-on-Trent, Staffordshire, England. Team: **Otago.** Sch: Repton, England.
WRATT William John 1882/83-1883/84 b 1864 Waimea South, Nelson. d 12.6.1941 Christchurch, Canterbury. Team: **Nelson.** Sch: Nelson Coll. Occ: Civil servant.

WRIGHT Ernest Llewellyn 1894/95-1900/01 b 10.11.1867 Panmure, Auckland. d 10.8.1940 Paddington, Sydney, New South Wales, Australia. LHB wk Teams: **Auckland, Wellington, Canterbury, New Zealand.** He played for New Zealand prior to being granted Test status.

WRIGHT Geoffrey Thomas 1955/56 b 25.3.1929 Darfield, Canterbury. d 2.4.2003 Christchurch, Canterbury. RHB Team: **Canterbury.** Sch: Christ Coll. Occ: Farmer. NZCA obit: 2003. Son: J.G.Wright.

WRIGHT H 1912/13-1913/14 Team: **Auckland.**

WRIGHT James Linton 1958/59 b 2.6.1936 Queensland, Australia. RHB LMF Team: **Northern Districts.**

WRIGHT John Geoffrey 1975/76-1992/93 b 5.7.1954 Darfield, Canterbury. LHB RM Teams: **Northern District, Canterbury, Auckland, New Zealand Test, New Zealand ODI,** Derbyshire. Played List A in NZ. Sch: Christ Coll. Occ: Cricket coach; Sales manager. Books: Christmas in Rarotonga; Indian Summers. MBE. NZCA COY: 1982, 1990. ICOY 1989. NZ selector and Indian coach. He holds the NZ Test 2nd wicket partnership record of 241 with A.H.Jones against England in 1991/92. In all first-class cricket he scored 25,073 runs with 59 centuries. Father: G.T.Wright.

WRIGHT Michael John Edward 1972/73-1983/84 b 17.1.1950 Whangarei, Northland. LHB RM wk Team: **Northern Districts.** Played List A in NZ.

WRIGLEY Oscar Llewellyn 1939/40-1942/43 b 6.8.1913 Wellington. d 26.11.1987 Wellington. RHB Team: **Wellington.** Sch: Rongatai Coll. Rugby: Otago. Wisden obit: 1989.

WYATT Ivan Edgar 1947/48 b 5.1.1924 Warkworth, Auckland. d 26.3.2009 Northcote, Auckland. RHB occ wk Team: **Auckland.** Sch: Auckland GS. Brother: J.L.Wyatt.

WYATT John Leonard 1956/57 b 7.3.1919 Leigh, Rodney. RHB Team: **Northern Districts.** Brother: I.E.Wyatt.

WYINKS William 1882/83-1885/86 b 11.9.1854 Elgin, Morayshire, Scotland. d 14.9.1921 Wellington. Team: **Otago.** Sch: Devonport HS. Occ: Registrar General of Lands. Umpired first-class cricket. Rugby: Otago.

WYLIE Robert Norman 1973/74 b 27.4.1948 Lower Hutt, Wellington. LHB RFM Team: **Central Districts.** Played List A in NZ.

WYNYARD William Thomas 1882/83-1907/08 b 1864 Devonport, Auckland. d 15.3.1938 Wellington. RHB occ wk Teams: **Auckland, Wellington.** Sch: Devonport Sch. Occ: Warehouseman. Rugby: All Blacks, Auckland and Wellington. Athletics: Auckland and Wellington. Wisden obit: 1939.

YATES Robert John 1873/74-1893/94 b 1845 Auckland. d 6.10.1931 Auckland. Team: **Auckland.** Occ: Groundsman. He played FC cricket for 20 years and was the groundsman at the Auckland Domain. He scored only one 50 in his FC career though he scored a number of centuries in club cricket.

YATES William Charles 1883/84 b 1859 Ahuriri, Napier, Hawke's Bay. d 19.9.1928 Napier, Hawke's Bay. wk Team: **Hawke's Bay.** Occ: Telegraphist.

YOCK Benjamin Arthur 1996/97-1997/98 b 8.2.1975 Christchurch, Canterbury. RHB wk Team: **Canterbury.** Played List A in NZ. Sch: St Andrews Coll.

YOUNG Bryan Andrew 1983/84-1998/99 b 3.11.1964 Whangarei, Northland. RHB wk Teams: **Northern Districts, Auckland, New Zealand Test, New Zealand ODI.** Played List A in NZ. His highest Test score was 267* in the innings victory over Sri Lanka in 1996/97.

YOUNG George Angus 1866/67-1867/68 b 1847 Ghazipur, Bengal Presidency (now Uttar Pradesh), India. d 20.4.1935 St Kilda, Melbourne, Victoria, Australia. Team: **Canterbury.** Occ: Deputy Chairman of the State Savings Bank of Australia.

YOUNG John Gordon 1921/22-1923/24 b 19.2.1901 Christchurch, Canterbury. d 20.3.1949 Dunedin, Otago. RHB Team: **Canterbury.** Occ: Fitter. Umpired first-class cricket.

YOUNG Reece Alan 1998/99-2009/10 b 15.9.1979 Auckland. RHB wk Team: **Auckland.** Played List A in NZ; Played T20 in NZ. Sch: Kelston BHS. He holds the Auckland 9th wicket partnership record of 151 with G.J.Morgan against Northern Districts in 2007/08.

YOUNG William H 1896/97-1905/06 wk Team: **Hawke's Bay.**

YOVICH Joseph Adam Frank 1996/97-2009/10 b 15.12.1976 Whangarei, Northland. LHB RFM Team: **Northern Districts.** Played List A in NZ; Played T20 in NZ. Sch: Whangarei HS. Occ: Draftsman. NZ U19 Test; NZ U19 ODI. He holds the Northern Districts 6th wicket partnership record of 322 with M.G.Orchard against Central Districts in 2005/06.

YUILE Bryan William 1959/60-1971/72 b 29.10.1941 Palmerston North, Manawatu. RHB SLA Teams: **Central Districts, Canterbury, New Zealand Test.** Played List A in NZ. Sch: Palmerston North BHS. NZCA COY: 1965. Due to his religious convictions he did not play cricket on Sundays. He holds the Central Districts 7th wicket partnership record of 219 with B.L.Hampton against Canterbury in 1967/68. He has the best bowling figures for Central Districts - 9/100 against Canterbury in 1965/66.

ZAVOS Spiro Bernard 1958/59 b 13.7.1937 Wellington. RHB SLA Team: **Wellington.** Sch: St Patricks Coll, Wellington. Occ: Writer. Books: he has written a number of rugby books.

ZIMMERMAN Carl 1925/26-1929/30 b 24.7.1898 Auckland. d 10.5.1969 Oamaru, North Otago. LHB LFM Team: **Otago.** Occ: Solicitor. In the non-first-class match between North Otago and the 1927/28 Australian team he scored 117 not out in less than fifty minutes.

NEW ZEALAND ONE-DAY CRICKETERS

Many of the cricketers in the first-class section above have played in List A or T20 cricket in New Zealand. It is noted in their entry where this is so. There are a number of cricketers who have not played first-class cricket but have taken part in List A and T20 cricket. Their details are given in this section.

AITKEN R A 1980/81 b 1959 unknown. Team: **Auckland.** Played List A in NZ. He played for Auckland Under-22s in 1980/81.
ALLEN Simon Rodney 2007/08-2008/09 b 5.9.1983 Wellington. RHB OB wk Team: **Wellington.** Played List A in NZ. Sch: Wellington Coll. NZ U19 ODI.
ANDERSON Lon 1973/74 Team: **Otago.** Played List A in NZ. Occ: Finance manager. He played for Central Otago and Otago Under-23s in 1966/67.
ANDREWS Gene Peter Glenn 2005/06 b 10.5.1982 Auckland. RHB Team: **Auckland.** Played List A in NZ; Played T20 in NZ. Sch: Auckland GS.
BALDWIN Bruce Cameron 1973/74 b 17.5.1950 Wanganui. Team: **Central Districts.** Played List A in NZ. Son: S.B.C.Baldwin.
BLIGH Allan William 1989/90 b 26.4.1961 Akaroa, Canterbury. RHB RM Team: **Otago.** Played List A in NZ. Sch: Timaru BHS. Occ: Civil servant.
BROOKE M T 1971/72 Team: **Central Districts.** Played List A in NZ. He played for Manuwatu and Thames Valley.
CALKIN Marc John Edward 2008/09 b 29.11.1979 Masterton, Wairarapa. RHB RM occ wk Team: **Central Districts.** Played T20 in NZ. Indoor cricket: New Zealand.
COLEMAN Guy Sebastian 2001/02 b 26.6.1974 Henderson, Auckland. RHB RFM Team: **Auckland.** Played List A in NZ. Sch: Glenfield Coll.
CRAIG Mark D C 2008/09 b 13.2.1989 Dunedin, Otago. RHB OB Team: **Otago.** Played T20 in NZ.
CRUIKSHANK Christopher Paul 2006/07 b 12.5.1985 Hawera, Taranaki. LHB LMF Team: **Central Districts.** Played List A in NZ; Played T20 in NZ. Sch: New Plymouth BHS.
DEAN Jeremy James Barton 2008/09 b 5.9.1985 Wellington. LHB wk Team: **Wellington.** Played List A in NZ; Played T20 in NZ. Sch: St Patricks Coll, Wellington.
DERRICK John 1983-1991 b 15.1.1963 Cwmaman, Glamorgan, Wales. RHB RM Teams: **Northern Districts,** Glamorgan. Played List A in NZ. Occ: Cricket coach. An English pro, played and coached in NZ.
DE SILVA Pinnaduwage Aravinda 1983/84-2001/02 b 17.10.1965 Colombo, Ceylon (now Sri Lanka). RHB OB Teams: **Auckland,** Kent, Sri Lanka Test, Sri Lanka ODI, Nondescripts Cricket Club. Played List A in NZ. Sch: Royal Coll, Colombo, Sri Lanka. Occ: Cricket pro. Book: Aravinda My Autobiography. WCOY: 1996.
DILSHAN Tillakaratne Mudiyanselage 1996/97-2009/10 b 14.10.1976 Kalutara, Sri Lanka. RHB OB occ wk Teams: **Northern Districts,** Sri Lanka Test, Sri Lanka ODI, Sri Lanka T20, Kalutara Town, Singha, Sebastianites, Bloomfield. Played T20 in NZ. Occ: Cricket pro. He holds the NZ domestic T20 2nd wicket partnership record of 115 with D.L.Vettori for Northern Districts against Wellington in 2009/10. Brother: T.M.N.Sampath (Bloomfield, Singha, Badureliya, Ruhuna).
ENOKA Wayne Steven 1997/98 b 30.1.1970 Wellsford, Auckland. RHB RM Team: **Auckland.** Played List A in NZ. Sch: Birkinhead Coll. Occ: Innkeeper. Indoor cricket: New Zealand.
FORD Brian Stuart 1994/95 b 28.8.1970 Kaiapoi, North Canterbury. RHB RM Team: **Canterbury.** Played List A in NZ.
FORDE Kevin Alexander 2006/07 b 22.11.1985 Invercargill, Southland. LHB RF Team: **Wellington.** Played List A in NZ; Played T20 in NZ.
FRANCIS Scott William Sanders 1994/95 b 17.9.1974 Hamilton, Waikato. RHB wk Team: **Auckland.** Played List A in NZ.

FRASER Angus Robert Charles 1984-2002 b 8.8.1965 Billinge, Lancashire, England. RHB RFM Teams: **Wellington,** England Test, England ODI, Middlesex. Played List A in NZ. Sch: Orange HS, England. Occ: Cricket pro. Book: My Tour Diaries: the Real Story of Life on Tour With England. WCOY: 1996. An English pro, played and coached in NZ. Brother: A.G.J.Fraser (Middlesex, Essex).

FRAUENSTEIN Carl 2006/07-2009/10 b 23.10.1985 Stutterheim, Cape Province, South Africa. RHB RMF Team: **Canterbury.** Played List A in NZ; Played T20 in NZ. Sch: Kings Coll. NZ U19 ODI.

FULTON John David 1993/94 b 7.12.1965 Lower Hutt, Wellington. RHB occ wk Team: **Central Districts.** Played List A in NZ.

GIDMAN Alexander Peter Richard 2007/08 b 22.6.1981 High Wycombe, Buckinghamshire, England. RHB RM Team: **Otago,** Gloucestershire. Played List A in NZ; Played T20 in NZ. Sch: Wycliffe Sch, England. Occ: Cricket pro. Brother: W.R.S.Gidman (Durham).

HABIB Aftab 1992-2006 b 7.2.1972 Reading, Berkshire, England. RHB RMF Teams: **Canterbury,** England Test, Middlesex, Leicestershire, Essex. Played List A in NZ. Sch: Taunton Sch, England. Occ: Cricket coach. An English pro, played and coached in NZ. Cousin: Z.A.Sadiq (Surrey, Derbyshire).

HALEY Ronald W 1970/71 Team: **Otago.** Played List A in NZ. He played for Otago Under-23s in 1964/65.

HODDER Paul S 1986/87 Team: **Northern Districts.** Played List A in NZ. Occ: Waikato rugby conditioner.

JANSEN Benjamin Robert 1999/00 b 24.2.1980 Wellington. RHB OB Team: **NZ Academy.** Played List A in NZ. Sch: Aotea Coll. NZ U19 Test; NZ U19 ODI.

JARVIS Paul William 1981-2000 b 29.6.1965 Redcar, Yorkshire, England. RHB RFM Teams: **Wellington,** England Test, England ODI, Yorkshire, Sussex, Somerset. Played List A in NZ. Occ: Cricket management. An English pro, played and coached in NZ.

KARAITIANA Ronald Punaoteaoranga Christopher 2008/09 b 3.12.1987 Masterton, Wairarapa. RHB RM Team: **Wellington.** Played List A in NZ. Sch: St Patricks Coll, Wellington. Occ: Social worker. NZ U19 ODI. Winner of the McDonald's Young Entertainers television contest in 1997, aged nine.

KEMP Graham 1987/88 b 6.11.1962 Dunedin, Otago. Team: **Otago.** Played List A in NZ.

KENCH Graeme Laurence 1982/83 b 23.2.1959 Christchurch, Canterbury. RHB wk Team: **Canterbury.** Played List A in NZ. Occ: Manager.

KNEEBONE Ross Francis 1992/93 b 1.8.1956 Hamilton, Waikato. LHB OB Team: **Northern Districts.** Played List A in NZ.

LARKINS Warwick Norwood 1978 b 31.3.1947 New Zealand. Team: **New Zealand.** He played for New Zealand in a non-first-class match.

LINTOTT Johnathan Richard 1997/98-1998/99 b 31.5.1973 Auckland. RHB RM Team: **Auckland.** Played List A in NZ.

MCLAGGAN Donald Stuart 1973/74 b 8.7.1945 Lower Hutt, Wellington. Team: **Northern Districts.** Played List A in NZ.

MCMAHON Philip James Sinclair 1994/95 b 11.11.1960 Wellington. LHB RM Team: **Wellington.** Played List A in NZ. Wellington selector. Father: T.G.McMahon.

MASCARENHAS Adrian Dimitri 1996-2009 b 30.10.1977 Chiswick, Middlesex, England. RHB RMF Teams: **Otago,** England ODI, England T20, Hampshire. Played List A in NZ; Played T20 in NZ. Sch: Trinity Coll, Perth, Australia. Occ: Cricket pro. An English pro, played and coached in NZ. He holds the NZ domestic T20 4th wicket partnership record of 140* with N.L.McCullum for Otago against Canterbury in 2008/09.

MAXWELL Neil Donald 1991/92-1995/96 b 12.6.1967 Lautoka, Fiji. RHB RFM Teams: **Canterbury,** Victoria, New South Wales. Played List A in NZ. Occ: Cricket administrator.

MAXWELL Robert James 1970/71 b 10.2.1945 Dunedin, Otago. Team: **Otago.** Played List A in NZ. Sch: Bayfield HS. He played for Central Otago.

MURPHY G 1973/74 Team: **Northern Districts.** Played List A in NZ. He played for Waikato.

MURRAY Luke 2007/08 b 2.5.1980 Palmerston North, Manawatu. RHB OB Team: **Central Districts.** Played List A in NZ. Sch: Freyburg HS.

NELSON John Charles 2001/02 b 3.5.1975 Blenheim, Marlborough. LHB Team: **Central Districts.** Played List A in NZ. Sch: Marlborough Boys Coll.

OGILVIE John David 1994/95-1995/96 b 3.12.1969 Motueka, Tasman. RHB Team: **Central Districts.** Played List A in NZ.

PATEL Brijesh Pursuram 1969/70-1987/88 b 24.11.1952 Baroda, Gujarat, India. RHB OB Teams: **Wellington,** India Test, India ODI, Mysore, Karnataka. Played List A in NZ. An Indian pro, played and coached in NZ. Cousin: Y.B.Patel; son: U.B.Patel; uncles: B.R.Patel, K.R.Patel, M.R.Patel.

QUINN John Lewis 1994/95 b 15.9.1970 Chertsey, Surrey, England. RHB LFM Team: **Canterbury.** Played List A in NZ. Occ: Sports psychologist.

RADLEY Clive Thornton 1964-1987 b 13.5.1944 Hertford, England. RHB LB Teams: **Auckland,** England Test, England ODI, Middlesex. Played List A in NZ. Sch: King Edward VI GS, England. Occ: Cricket coach. An English pro, played and coached in NZ.

RICHARDSON David John 1984/85 b 8.5.1958 Upper Hutt, Wellington. RHB RMF Team: **Central Districts.** Played List A in NZ.

SEWELL L J 1974/75-1976/77 Team: **Auckland.** Played List A in NZ. He played for Auckland Under-23s from 1968 to 1971.

SEYMOUR Adam Charles Hilton 1988-1994 b 7.12.1967 Royston, Hertfordshire, England. LHB RM Teams: **Northern Districts,** Essex, Worcestershire. Played List A in NZ. An English pro, played and coached in NZ.

SHACKEL Dayle Francis 1993/94 b 29.1.1970 Christchurch, Canterbury. RHB wk Team: **Otago.** Played List A in NZ. Sch: Kings HS. Occ: Physiotherapist. NZ cricket team physio. He suffered slight wounds from a terrorist bomb while on the 2002 tour of Pakistan.

SHAH Owais Alam 1996-2009 b 22.10.1978 Karachi, Sind, Pakistan. RHB OB Teams: **Wellington,** England Test, England ODI, England T20, Middlesex. Played List A in NZ; Played T20 in NZ. Sch: Isleworth & Syon Sch, England. Occ: Cricket pro. An English pro, played and coached in NZ.

SMIDT Glen S 1986/87 wk Team: **Central Districts.** Played List A in NZ. He played for Hawke's Bay.

STEAD Wayne William 1997/98 b 13.4.1973 Christchurch, Canterbury. LHB RM Team: **Canterbury.** Played List A in NZ. Sch: Shirley BHS. Occ: Management consultant. Brother: G.R.Stead; father: D.W.Stead.

STORKEY Ian Howard 1975/76 b 14.9.1950 Napier, Hawke's Bay. RHB wk Team: **Wellington.** Played List A in NZ. Sch: Colenso HS. Occ: Debt management consultant.

STRAUSS Andrew John 1998-2009/10 b 2.3.1977 Johannesburg, Transvaal, South Africa. LHB LM occ wk Teams: **Northern Districts,** England Test, England ODI, England T20, Middlesex. Played List A in NZ; Played T20 in NZ. Sch: Radley Coll, England. Occ: Cricket pro. Books: Coming into play; Testing Times. WCOY: 2005. An English pro, played and coached in NZ.

TOPIA Tane Henry 2000/01 b 18.11.1976 Auckland. RHB OB Team: **Auckland.** Played List A in NZ.

TRASK Carl Jeffery 1999/00 b 10.2.1974 Levin, Horowhenua. RHB RM Team: **Central Districts.** Played List A in NZ. Sch: Rotorua Lakes HS.

VIVIAN Luke John 2005/06-2008/09 b 12.6.1981 Launceston, Tasmania, Australia. RHB RM Teams: **Canterbury, Auckland.** Played List A in NZ; Played T20 in NZ. Sch: Macleans Coll. Occ: Personal trainer.

VOGTHERR John Russell 1971/72 b 30.1.1946 Lower Hutt, Wellington. RHB Team: **New Zealand.** Played List A in NZ. Sch: Hutt Valley HS. Occ: Civil servant.

WALKIN Gary John 1973/74 b 2.2.1944 Christchurch, Canterbury. RHB RFM Team: **Canterbury.** Played List A in NZ. Occ: Groundsman. He played for Hawke's Bay.

WALTON Timothy Charles 1994-1999 b 8.11.1972 Low Lead, York, England. RHB RM occ wk Teams: **Canterbury,** Northamptonshire, Essex. Played List A in NZ.

WELCH Graeme 1994-2006 b 21.3.1972 Durham, England. RHB RM Teams: **Wellington,** Warwickshire, Derbyshire. Played List A in NZ. Sch: Hetton Comp Sch, England. Occ: Cricket coach.

WHEELER Ian R 1974/75 b New Zealand. Team: **Central Districts.** Played List A in NZ. Occ: Manager. He played for Hutt Valley.

WHITAKER Paul Robert 1994-1998 b 28.6.1973 Keighley, Yorkshire, England. LHB OB Teams: **Central Districts,** Hampshire. Played List A in NZ.

WHITE Craig 1990-2007 b 16.12.1969 Morley Hall, Yorkshire, England. RHB OB,RFM Teams: **Central Districts,** England Test, England ODI, Yorkshire, Victoria. Played List A in NZ. Sch: Bendigo HS, Australia. Occ: Cricket coach. An English pro, played and coached in NZ.

WHITE Glen Aidan 1998/99 b 12.2.1970 Melbourne, Victoria, Australia. RHB SLA Team: **Wellington.** Played List A in NZ. Occ: Accountant.

WILLIAMS B R 1996/97 Team: **Central Districts.** Played List A in NZ. He played for Nelson.

YASIR ARAFAT Satti 1999/00-2009/10 b 12.3.1982 Rawalpindi, Punjab, Pakistan. RHB RFM Teams: **Otago,** Sussex, Kent, Pakistan Test, Pakistan ODI, Pakistan T20, Rawalpindi, Pakistan Reserves, Khan Research Laboratories, National Bank of Pakistan, Federal Areas. Played List A in NZ; Played T20 in NZ. A Pakistani pro, played and coached in NZ.

FIJIAN CRICKETERS

This section gives details of the Fijian cricketers who toured New Zealand in 1894/95, 1947/48 and 1953/54 and who played in first-class matches.

APTED Harry Joseph 1947/48-1953/54 b 30.4.1925 Suva, Fiji. LHB OB occ wk Team: **Fiji**. Sch: St Felix Coll, Fiji. Occ: Civil servant. Hockey: Fiji; Lawn bowls: Fiji. Fijian Sports Hall of Fame Inductee. Brother: W.W.Apted.
APTED William Walsh 1953/54 b 15.10.1930 Suva, Fiji. RHB OB wk Team: **Fiji**. Sch: St Felix Coll, Fiji. Brother: H.J.Apted.
ARIA Kaminieli Tako 1947/48 b 1921 Nadi, Fiji. d 1967 Fiji. RHB Team: **Fiji**. Occ: Policeman.
BOGISA Mosese 1947/48-1953/54 b 27.4.1922 Nadi, Fiji. RHB Team: **Fiji**. Occ: Labourer.
BULA Ilikena Lasarusa 1947/48-1953/54 b 15.11.1921 Tobou, Fiji. RHB Team: **Fiji**. Sch: Lau Provincial, Fiji. Fijian Sports Hall of Fame Inductee.
CAKOBAU Etuate Tuivanuavou Tugi 1930/31-1947/48 - *see the New Zealand First-Class Cricketers section.*
CAKOBAU George Kadavulevu (Sir) 1947/48 b 6.11.1912 Bau, Fiji. d 25.11.1989 Suva, Fiji. RHB Team: **Fiji**. Sch: Newington Coll, Australia. Occ: Statesman. Rugby: Fiji. Sir, GCMG, GCVO, OBE. Member of Fijian Parliament from 1952 to 1972; Governor General of Fiji from 1972 to 1982.
CALDWELL Reginald 1894/95 b 16.8.1860 Richmond, Victoria, Australia. d 4.10.1918 Woollahra, Sydney, New South Wales, Australia. RHB RM Team: **Fiji**. Sch: Private tutor. Occ: Solicitor.
COLLINS John Cyril 1894/95 RHB LB Team: **Fiji**. He played for Suva in 1924 but nothing is known of him after this.
DRIU Asaeli 1953/54 b 1.1.1930 Nadi, Fiji. LFM Team: **Fiji**.
EPELI Vacaracara 1894/95 b Fiji. d 23.6.1898 Fiji. RHB Team: **Fiji**. Occ: Policeman.
FENN Maurice Joseph 1947/48-1953/54 b 5.5.1911 Lau, Fiji. d 11.4.1995 Samoa. RHB LBG Team: **Fiji**. Sch: St Felix Coll, Fiji. Occ: Hospital orderly. Lawn Bowls: Samoa at Commonwealth Games.
GOSLING John William 1947/48 b 1921 Suva, Fiji. d 1994 unknown. RHB RM Team: **Fiji**. Sch: Suva GS, Fiji. Occ: Coy director.
GROOM Warner Ottley 1894/95 b 26.4.1847 Cullenswood, Tasmania, Australia. d 19.11.1926 Canterbury, Victoria, Australia. RHB Team: **Fiji**. Occ: Colonial administrator.
JOSKE Alexander Brewster 1894/95 b 25.3.1861 Croydon, Surrey, England. d 26.3.1922 unknown. LHB Team: **Fiji**. Occ: Commission agent.
KADAVULEVU Penaia 1894/95 b Fiji. d 13.12.1914 Fiji. RHB RFM Team: **Fiji**. From 1901 until his death, he was the paramount chief in Fiji. Half brother: F.L.Temesia.
KAVURU Nemani 1953/54 b 8.4.1928 Tailevau, Fiji. RHB RM Team: **Fiji**.
KUBUNAVANUA Petero 1947/48 b 1922 Ovalau, Fiji. d 20.11.1997 Fiji. LHB occ wk Team: **Fiji**. Occ: Policeman.
LOGANIMOCE Eroni 1953/54 b 6.10.1930 Tabout, Fiji. RM Team: **Fiji**.
LOGAVATU Isoa Tuinaceva 1947/48 b 1925 Nadi, Fiji. d 1991 Fiji. RHB RM,OB Team: **Fiji**. Occ: Clerk. NZCA obit: 2004; Wisden obit: 2004.
MARA Kamisese Kapaiwai Tuimacilai (Sir) 1953/54 b 13.5.1920 Lomaloma, Lau, Fiji. d 18.4.2004 Suva, Fiji. RHB RFM Team: **Fiji**. Sch: Sacred Heart Coll. Occ: Statesman. Book: The Pacific way. Sir, GCMG, KBE, CF.
MCOWAN Islay 1894/95 b 4.4.1871 Melbourne, Victoria, Australia. d 4.4.1948 Sydney, New South Wales, Australia. RHB wk Team: **Fiji**. Sch: Melbourne CEGS, Australia. Occ: Colonial administrator. Australian Rules: Carlton. CMG. British Counsel, High Commissioner for the Western Pacific and Secretary for Native Affairs.
NAILOVOLOVO Radelanimate 1894/95 b Fiji. RHB Team: **Fiji**.

RADDOCK Patrick Tasman 1947/48-1953/54 b 31.10.1920 Suva, Fiji. d 23.5.1977 Suva, Fiji. RHB wk Team: **Fiji.** Sch: Suva GS, Fiji. Occ: Civil servant. Hockey: Fiji, national selector, coach of the Fijian national teams. Rugby; coach of the Fijian national team and International referee. MBE. Fijian Olympic Order inductee. Fijian selector.

RAVOUVOU Semi Ravouvou 1947/48 b 1909 Saunaka, Nadi, Fiji. d 1967 Saunaka, Nadi, Fiji. RHB RM Team: **Fiji.** Occ: Civil servant.

SCOTT Henry Milne (Sir) 1894/95 b 10.4.1876 Levuka, Fiji. d 20.5.1956 Suva, Fiji. RHB RFM Team: **Fiji.** Sch: Sydney GS, Australia. Occ: Barrister. Sir, KC. Fijian Attorney-General, Member of the Legislative Council and mayor of Suva.

SIMMONS Morgan Fleet 1953/54 b 21.5.1924 Labasa, Fiji. d 18.11.1983 Labasa, Fiji. RMF Team: **Fiji.** Occ: Labourer. OBE. Mayor of Labasa; President of the Sugar Tradesman Union.

SNOW Philip Albert 1947/48 b 7.8.1915 Leicester, England. RHB Team: **Fiji.** Occ: Colonial administrator. Books: A Time of renewal; Years of Hope; Cricket in the Fijian Islands. OBE.

TEMESIA Feretareki Lagamu 1894/95 b Fiji. RHB Team: **Fiji.** Occ: Doctor. Half-brother: P.Kadevulevu.

TUIDRAKI Aisea Turuva 1947/48 b 3.2.1916 Nakava, Nadi, Fiji. d 1966 Nanukulau, Fiji. RHB Team: **Fiji.** Sch: Queen Victoria, Fiji. Occ: Policeman.

TUISAVAU Lutunauga Batinivuaiga 1894/95 b Fiji. d 16.12.1921 Fiji. RHB Team: **Fiji.**

TUIVANUAVOU Wilikonisoni 1894/95 b Fiji. RHB RF Team: **Fiji.**

TUIYAU Naitini N 1953/54 b 16.6.1915 Navatau, Fiji. d 1.3.2002 Fiji. RHB OB Team: **Fiji.** Rugby: Fiji.

UDAL John Symonds 1871-1894/95 b 10.11.1848 West Bromwich, Staffordshire, England. d 13.3.1925 St John's Wood, London, England. RHB RM Team: **Fiji.** Sch: Bromsgrove, England. Occ: Judge. Wisden obit: 1926. Fijian Attorney-General and Chief Justice of the Leeward Islands. Son: N.R.Udal (Oxford University); grandson: G.F.U.Udal (Middlesex, Leicestershire); great-great-grandson: S.D.Udal (England, Hampshire, Middlesex).

ULUIVITI Nacanieli Mataika 1953/54-1954/55 - *see the New Zealand First-Class Cricketers section.*

VILIAME Savu Mataika 1947/48 b 1906 Lau, Fiji. d 1986 Ono-i-lau, Fiji. RHB RFM Team: **Fiji.** Occ: Policeman.

WENDT Alfred John 1947/48 b 1913 Levuka, Fiji. d 1996 Fiji. RHB LM Team: **Fiji.** Occ: Clerk.

NEW ZEALAND FIRST-CLASS CAREER RECORDS 1863/64-2009/10

		First	Last	M	I	NO	Runs	HS	Avg	100	50	Runs	Wkts	OW	Avg	Best	5i	10m	ct	st
T.R.Abercrombie	Sland	1920/21		1	1	0	1	1	1.00	-	-									
D.C.Aberhart	CD	1976/77	1982/83	37	57	15	581	40*	13.83	-	1	2268	100		22.68	6-55	5	-	23	-
	Cant	1983/84		1	1	0	6	6	6.00	-	-	72	1		72.00	1-53	-	-	1	
	All	1976/77	1983/84	38	58	15	587	40*	13.65	-	1	2340	101		23.16	6-55	5	-	24	
W.M.Aberhart	Well	1985/86		2	3	1	28	24	14.00	-	-	119	1		119.00	1-50	-	-	-	
B.Abernethy	Otago	1981/82	1982/83	13	21	5	256	57*	16.00	-	1	626	17		36.82	4-85	-	-	6	
R.J.Ackland	Auck	1980/81	1983/84	5	2	1	5	5	5.00	-	-	246	9		27.33	5-44	1	-	1	
	All	1976/77	1983/84	6	4	1	9	5	3.00	-	-	305	10		30.50	5-44	1	-	5	
A.E.Ackroyd	Otago	1906/07		3	6	0	113	42	18.83	-	-								1	
	Cant	1907/08		1	2	0	0	0	0.00	-	-								6	
	All	1906/07	1907/08	4	8	0	113	42	14.12	-	-								6	
A.A.Adams	Otago	1905/06	1907/08	2	4	0	41	21	10.25	-	-								4	
A.R.Adams	Auck	1997/98	2007/08	50	72	5	1564	117*	23.34	1	9	4549	221		20.58	6-25	11	2	27	
	All	1997/98	2010	115	153	16	3158	124	23.05	3	12	11090	463		23.95	6-25	17	2	81	
S.D.Adams	Auck	1982/83	1984/85	2	3	1	13	7*	6.50	-	-	11	0						3	
T.D.Adams	Otago	1907/08		3	6	0	32	18	5.33	-	-								1	
J.M.Adcock	Nel	1891/92		1	2	0	23	20	11.50	-	-	10	0							
A.H.Addison	Cant	1909/10		2	4	0	15	10	3.75	-	-	26	2		13.00	2-11	-	-	1	
J.R.B.A'Deane	HB	1893/94		3	6	0	33	17	5.50	-	-	70	3		23.33	2-31	-	-	2	
D.T.Ager	All	1944/45		1	2	0	0	0	0.00	-	-									
J.M.Aiken	Well	1989/90	1998/99	28	50	5	1595	170*	35.44	4	6								19	
	Auck	1999/00	2000/01	14	24	0	435	85	18.12	-	2								8	
	All	1989/90	2000/01	46	81	6	2170	170*	28.93	4	9								33	
G.M.Aim	Otago	1955/56		4	8	1	74	41	10.57	-	-								2	
	Well	1960/61	1962/63	5	8	1	116	31	16.57	-	-								3	
	All	1955/56	1962/63	9	16	2	190	41	13.57	-	-								5	
D.M.L.Airey	Well	1977/78		6	11	3	111	33	13.87	-	-	6	0						2	
W.F.Airey	Well	1927/28	1939/40	7	14	0	213	47	15.21	-	-	6	0						2	
G.D.Alabaster	Otago	1955/56	1975/76	69	108	16	2340	108	25.43	3	12	4777	205		23.30	7-74	13	1	29	
	Cant	1957/58	1959/60	5	8	0	75	43	9.37	-	-	205	8		25.62	2-9	-	-	2	
	ND	1960/61	1962/63	16	31	1	622	58	20.73	-	2	778	43		18.09	8-30	2	-	19	
	All	1955/56	1975/76	96	154	20	3200	108	23.88	3	14	6391	275		23.24	8-30	15	2	54	
J.C.Alabaster	Otago	1956/57	1971/72	65	100	6	1306	67*	13.89	-	3	5738	264		21.73	6-39	14	3	49	
	All	1955/56	1971/72	143	212	30	2427	82	13.33	-	5	12687	500		25.37	7-41	25	4	94	
A.J.Alcock	CD	1992/93	1994/95	9	14	7	66	29*	9.42	-	-	488	14		34.85	3-43	-	-	5	
W.A.Aldersley	Well	1909/10	1922/23	6	10	2	133	48	16.62	-	-	196	8		24.50	4-47	-	-	-	
J.D.Alderson	Cant	1949/50	1950/51	7	12	5	29	7*	4.14	-	-	412	17		24.23	5-66	1	-	6	
C.W.Aldridge	Cant	1973/74		4	4	1	45	28	15.00	-	-	293	9		32.55	4-45	-	-	3	
G.W.Aldridge	ND	1998/99	2009/10	77	102	33	1534	75	22.23	-	4	6387	214		29.84	6-49	8	1	34	
	All	1998/99	2009/10	79	103	33	1542	75	22.02	-	4	6416	218		29.43	6-49	8	1	35	
R.E.Alexander	Cant	1933/34		1	1	0	7	7	7.00	-	-	88	3		29.33	2-33	-	-	1	
W.H.Alington	Cant	1868/69	1869/70	2	4	1	45	26*	15.00	-	-								-	
B.C.Allan	Otago	1956/57		3	4	0	33	15	8.25	-	-	89	3		29.66	1-5	-	-	-	

151

		First	Last	M	I	NO	Runs	HS	Avg	100	50	Runs	Wkts	OW	Avg	Best 1-4	5i	10m	ct	st
J.M.Allan	Otago	1993/94	1997/98	16	29	0	537	56	18.51	-	1	4	1		4.00		-	-	21	-
C.W.Allard	Cant	1920/21		1	2	0	0	0	0.00	-	-						-	-	-	-
I.D.Allardyce	Cant	1917/18		3	5	0	174	60	34.80	-	1						-	-	-	-
	Well	1918/19		1	2	0	9	5	4.50	-	-						-	-	-	-
C.F.W.Allcott	All	1917/18	1918/19	4	7	0	183	60	26.14	-	1						-	-	1	-
	HB	1920/21		1	2	1	35	24*	35.00	-	-	142	5		28.40	5-142	1	-	1	-
	Auck	1921/22	1931/32	27	45	9	1044	114*	29.00	1	4	2796	115		24.31	7-75	7	2	24	-
	Otago	1945/46		1	1	0	19	19	19.00	-	-	91	3		30.33	3-91	-	-	1	-
	All	1920/21	1945/46	82	116	26	2514	131	27.93	5	5	5892	220		26.78	7-75	13	2	61	-
G.S.Allen	Well	1977/78		3	4	0	94	42	23.50	-	-	21	0		-	-	-	-	1	-
J.Allen	Otago	1869/70	1874/75	7	12	1	65	22	5.90	-	-						-	-	7	-
J.H.Allen	Otago	1944/45		1	2	1	1	1	1.00	-	-						-	-	-	-
P.F.Allen	Cant	1928/29	1934/35	7	10	2	278	103	34.75	1	1	57	0		-	-	-	-	2	3
R.Allen	Cant	1941/42	1953/54	11	19	12	128	31*	18.28	-	-	944	41		23.02	5-58	3	-	7	-
	All	1941/42	1953/54	12	21	13	136	31*	17.00	-	-	1005	41		24.51	5-58	3	-	7	-
A.P.Alloo	Otago	1914/15		1	2	0	4	4	2.00	-	-	91	0		-	-	-	-	2	-
A.W.Alloo	Otago	1913/14	1930/31	43	80	3	1806	101	23.45	2	9	3254	125		26.03	6-20	10	3	23	-
	All	1913/14	1930/31	51	94	6	2043	101	23.21	2	11	3615	131		27.59	6-20	10	3	24	-
H.C.Alloo	Otago	1919/20	1928/29	22	41	2	744	62	19.07	-	2	174	3		58.00	2-59	-	-	14	-
G.I.Allott	Cant	1994/95	1996/97	9	10	6	49	11*	12.25	-	-	881	43		20.48	6-60	3	-	-	-
	All	1994/95	1999	31	40	18	107	13*	4.86	-	-	3097	102		30.36	6-60	4	1	6	-
P.J.W.Allott	Well	1985/86	1986/87	13	12	5	177	66*	25.28	-	1	1064	46		23.13	5-40	3	-	6	-
	All	1978	1991	245	262	64	3360	88	16.96	-	10	16665	652		25.55	8-48	30	-	136	-
F.G.Alpe	Well	1908/09		1	2	0	6	4	3.00	-	-	60	0		-	-	-	-	2	-
S.Alpe	Auck	1873/74	1879/80	3	5	0	42	17	8.40	-	-						-	-	2	-
	Cant	1875/76	1884/85	3	6	1	37	23	7.40	-	-						-	-	2	-
	Well	1882/83		7	13	2	163	29*	14.81	-	-						-	-	2	-
	All	1873/74	1884/85	13	24	3	242	29*	11.52	-	-						-	-	6	-
Amandeep Singh	ND	2005/06		1	1	0	0	0	0.00	-	-	38	2		19.00	2-38	-	-	-	-
	Cant	2006/07	2007/08	3	3	1	13	6	6.50	-	-	243	5		48.60	2-65	-	-	2	-
	All	2005/06	2007/08	4	4	1	13	6	4.33	-	-	281	7		40.14	2-38	-	-	2	-
L.D.Andersen	Auck	1960/61		3	4	3	28	15	28.00	-	-	280	7		40.00	2-41	-	-	2	-
	ND	1967/68		2	4	1	8	5	2.00	-	-	172	3		57.33	2-81	-	-	-	-
	All	1960/61	1967/68	5	8	3	36	15	7.20	-	-	452	10		45.20	2-41	-	-	2	-
C.J.Anderson	Cant	1997/98	2000/01	17	30	5	618	65	24.72	-	5	1126	26		43.30	4-97	-	-	8	-
C.J.Anderson	Cant	2006/07	2009/10	15	26	5	590	88*	28.09	-	2	508	13		39.07	5-22	1	-	10	-
G.F.Anderson	Cant	1949/50	1950/51	6	10	0	67	33	6.70	-	-						-	-	10	5
H.T.Anderson	Otago	1999/00		2	4	0	75	36	18.75	-	-						-	-	2	-
I.P.Anderson	Cant	1964/65		1	1	0	0	0	0.00	-	-						-	-	4	1
J.M.Anderson	Auck	2007/08		1	2	0	5	5	2.50	-	-	95	2		47.50	2-95	-	-	-	-
	All	2002	2010	111	132	54	792	37*	10.15	-	-	11342	409		27.73	7-43	22	3	44	-
L.G.Anderson	Otago	1923/24		1	2	1	5	4	5.00	-	-	23	1		23.00	1-23	-	-	1	-
N.J.C.Anderson	HB	1909/10		1	1	0	2	2	2.00	-	-						-	-	-	-
P.S.Anderson	ND	1977/78	1978/79	7	6	0	20	10*	10.00	-	-	675	20		33.75	5-38	2	1	6	-
R.G.Anderson	Otago	1961/62	1964/65	15	27	5	265	48	12.04	-	-	1069	43		24.86	3-29	-	-	6	-
	All	1961/62	1964/65	16	29	6	307	48	13.34	-	-	1143	43		26.58	3-29	-	-	6	-

		First	Last	M	I	NO	Runs	HS	Avg	100	50	Runs	Wkts	OW	Avg	Best	5i	10m	ct	st
R.W.Anderson	Cant	1967/68	1976/77	4	4	0	35	24	8.75	-	-	107	5		21.40	4-49	-	-	5	
	ND	1969/70		6	10	1	223	37	24.77	-	-								5	
	Otago	1971/72	1981/82	35	67	3	1762	105*	27.53	1	12								22	
	CD	1977/78	1981/82	30	55	3	1959	127	37.67	4	10	35	0		-	-	-	-	26	
	All	1967/68	1981/82	111	197	14	5609	155	30.65	8	28	154	5		30.80	4-49	-	-	79	
R.G.Anderson	HB	1919/20		1	2	0	11	14	5.50	-	-								-	
T.R.Anderson	CD	1998/99	2002/03	14	14	4	56	14	5.60	-	-	1414	41		34.48	6-37	1	-	3	
	All	1997/98	2002/03	16	15	4	56	14	5.09	-	-	1520	42		36.19	6-37	1	-	4	
W.M.Anderson	Cant	1938/39	1949/50	32	51	4	1728	137	36.76	2	11	608	14		43.42	5-90	1	-	20	
	All	1938/39	1949/50	37	61	4	1973	137	34.61	2	13	687	18		38.16	5-90	1	-	24	
T.Andrew	Otago	1872/73		1	2	0	7	6	3.50	-	-								-	
B.Andrews	Cant	1963/64	1966/67	15	21	9	144	21	12.00	-	-	1045	46		22.71	6-27	2	-	5	
	CD	1966/67	1969/70	19	24	7	158	19*	9.29	-	-	1525	78		19.55	7-37	5	-	8	
	Otago	1970/71	1973/74	16	20	3	110	21	6.47	-	-	1390	56		24.82	5-19	3	-	12	
	All	1963/64	1973/74	57	74	22	474	21	9.11	-	-	4601	198		23.23	7-37	11	-	26	
E.H.Andrews	HB	1898/99		1	1	1	0	0	0.00	-	-	16	0		-	-	-	-	2	
F.M.Andrews	Auck	1935/36	1940/41	3	3	1	21	17*	21.00	-	-	232	14		16.57	4-45	-	-	2	
	Well	1941/42		1	2	0	46	26	23.00	-	-	138	3		46.00	3-108	-	-	2	
	All	1935/36	1942/43	5	7	1	67	26	16.75	-	-	465	22		21.13	4-45	-	-	3	
S.L.Andrews	ND	2000/01	2006/07	6	6	0	76	59*	19.00	-	1	471	10		47.10	2-22	-	-	5	
S.Andrews	Cant	1933/34	1935/36	5	6	1	17	7	3.40	-	-	342	13		26.30	6-59	1	-	2	
	All	1933/34	1935/36	6	7	1	23	7	3.83	-	-	445	17		26.17	6-59	1	-	6	
J.Ansenne	Auck	1893/94		1	2	0	10	6	5.00	-	-								-	
G.E.Anson	All	1879/80		1	1	0	2	2	2.00	-	-								-	
A.Anthony	Cant	1905/06	1908/09	12	23	2	519	104	24.71	1	1	38	6		6.33	3-2	-	-	5	
	Auck	1909/10	1930/31	40	70	4	1867	116	28.28	3	11	1773	69		25.69	6-43	2	-	17	
	All	1905/06	1930/31	52	93	6	2386	116	27.42	4	12	1811	75		24.14	6-43	2	-	22	
R.G.Arblaster	Auck	1977/78	1979/80	10	18	3	274	61*	18.26	-	1	14	1		14.00	1-14	-	-	7	
J.Aris	Otago	1870/71		1	2	0	3	2	1.50	-	-								-	
H.F.Arkwright	All	1920/21		1	2	0	2	1	1.00	-	-								-	
J.T.B.Armitage	Well	1874/75	1881/82	8	15	3	76	20	6.33	-	-	243	34	1	7.15	5-18	2	-	3	
D.W.Armstrong	CD	1958/59		2	3	1	9	8*	4.50	-	-	123	1		123.00	1-47	-	-	2	
J.Arneil	Auck	1882/83	1893/94	9	16	2	248	59*	17.71	-	1	60	2		30.00	2-9	-	-	3	
B.J.Arnel	ND	2005/06	2009/10	29	33	13	147	32	7.35	-	-	2284	95		24.04	6-18	4	-	6	
	All	2005/06	2009/10	34	42	13	164	32	5.65	-	-	2800	111		25.22	6-18	4	-	8	
A.P.Arnold	Cant	1953/54		5	8	2	412	118	68.66	2	1	6	0		-	-	-	-	3	
	All	1951	1960	174	306	15	8013	122	27.53	7	45	85	3		28.33	1-5	-	-	79	
J.Arnold	Nel	1877/78	1879/80	2	4	0	14	10	3.50	-	-								-	
W.Arnold	Nel	1891/92		1	2	0	1	1	0.50	-	-								1	
F.L.Ashbolt	Well	1893/94	1900/01	18	29	9	275	37*	13.75	-	-	1551	105		14.77	8-58	11	3	21	
	All	1893/94	1900/01	21	35	11	330	37*	13.75	-	-	1682	105		16.01	8-58	11	3	23	
D.A.Ashby	Cant	1875/76	1889/90	15	27	4	468	59	20.34	-	2	568	52		10.92	6-27	4	1	12	
	All	1873	1889/90	17	31	4	468	59	17.33	-	2	586	53		11.05	6-27	4	1	12	
P.Ashcroft	HB	1905/06	1911/12	7	12	5	92	27*	13.14	-	-								5	
J.G.Ashenden	Well	1935/36	1944/45	15	25	4	160	27	7.61	-	-	1453	51		28.49	6-44	1	-	10	
	All	1935/36	1944/45	16	25	4	160	27	7.61	-	-	1498	53		28.26	6-44	1	-	10	1

		First	Last	M	I	NO	Runs	HS	Avg	100	50	Runs	Wkts	OW	Avg	Best	5i	10m	ct	st
W.M.Ashton	HB	1883/84		1	2	0	0	0	0.00	-	-	2	0		-	-	-	-	-	-
D.N.Askew	CD	1991/92	1994/95	19	24	8	187	31	11.68	-	-	1207	53		22.77	4-40	-	-	6	-
	Auck	1997/98		2	3	0	50	32	16.66	-	-	173	1		173.00	1-52	-	-	1	-
	All	1991/92	1997/98	21	27	8	237	32	12.47	-	-	1380	54		25.55	4-40	-	-	7	-
J.W.Askew	Nel	1881/82		1	1	0	0	0	0.00	-	-								-	-
A.M.Astle	CD	1978/79		1	2	1	4	4*	-	-	-								1	-
N.J.Astle	Cant	1991/92	2006/07	32	45	7	1409	191	37.07	3	6	75	0		-	-	-	-	19	-
	All	1991/92	2006/07	171	272	24	9321	223	37.58	19	50	1340	52		25.76	6-22	2	-	134	-
T.D.Astle	CD	2005/06	2009/10	36	65	4	1407	101	23.06	1	7	4897	150		32.64	6-22	2	-	28	-
C.M.H.Atkinson	CD	1975/76	1976/77	10	18	1	341	50*	20.05	-	1	2154	59		36.50	6-103	3	-	6	-
F.A.Atkinson	Nel	1888/89	1891/92	2	4	0	26	10	6.50	-	-	58	0		-	-	-	-	-	-
C.L.Auckram	CD	1989/90	1991/92	16	13	9	30	14*	7.50	-	-	1163	33		35.24	7-61	2	-	2	-
H.O.Audinwood	HB	1906/07		1	2	1	13	8	13.00	-	-	69	1		69.00	1-69	-	-	-	-
M.H.Austen	Otago	1989/90	1996/97	25	47	3	1253	100*	28.47	1	9	1225	26		47.11	5-71	1	-	15	-
	Well	1992/93	1995/96	26	45	3	1453	202	34.59	3	5	435	24		18.12	4-43	1	-	16	-
	All	1982/83	1996/97	66	120	8	3619	202*	32.31	6	16	1813	55		32.96	5-71	1	-	48	-
E.G.Austin	see E. Goodwin Austen																			
E.Austin	CD	1996/97																			2
G.G.Austin	Otago	1896/97	1912/13	7	9	3	59	24*	9.83	-	-	960	40		24.00	5-156	1	-	20	-
T.T.L.Austin	Otago	1877/78	1888/89	29	54	1	771	64	14.54	-	5	303	17		17.82	6-63	1	-	22	-
J.Austin-Smellie	Well	2009/10		9	17	2	186	36	12.40	-	-								5	-
F.Ayles	Otago	1908/09		3	5	1	162	97	40.50	-	1								5	-
H.Azhar Abbas	Well	2004/05		3	5	1	81	47	20.25	-	-	2	1		2.00	1-1	-	-	4	-
	Auck	2007/08	2008/09	3	4	2	36	22*	18.00	-	-	275	7		39.28	3-60	-	-	-	-
	All	1995/96	2008/09	5	7	2	33	15	6.60	-	-	394	12		32.83	3-52	-	-	2	-
F.T.Badcock	Well	1924/25	1929/30	45	66	23	321	44*	7.46	-	-	3879	154		25.18	6-38	6	2	12	-
	Otago	1930/31	1936/37	19	37	1	1107	155	30.75	2	7	2079	115		18.07	7-50	9	5	25	-
	All	1924/25	1945	21	40	0	1068	136	26.70	2	4	1977	79		25.02	6-72	4	-	11	-
R.A.Baddeley	Auck	1969/70	1971/72	53	96	3	2383	155	25.62	4	13	5211	221		23.57	7-50	14	5	38	-
S.A.R.Baddeley	Auck	1929/30		13	13	4	66	25	7.33	-	-	770	30		25.66	6-79	-	-	4	-
B.Bailey	HB	1905/06	1910/11	4	4	1	82	32	27.33	-	1	7	0		-	-	-	-	1	-
J.F.Bailey	ND	1965/66		8	15	0	163	33	10.86	-	1	31	1		31.00	1-14	-	-	5	-
M.D.Bailey	ND	1989/90	2001/02	4	7	1	90	30*	15.00	-	-	209	3		69.66	2-46	-	-	6	-
	All	1989/90	2001/02	78	122	8	3468	180*	30.42	6	13	267	8		33.37	2-27	-	-	75	-
K.B.Bain	Cant	1906/07		89	138	9	3882	180*	30.09	8	14	286	9		31.77	2-27	-	-	86	-
W.G.C.Bain	Well	1937/38	1913/14	2	3	0	26	25	8.66	-	-	9	0		-	-	-	-	1	-
C.K.Bain	Cant	1971/72	1944/45	3	5	0	26	25	5.20	-	-	34	1		34.00	1-9	-	-	3	-
E.G.H.Baker	Well	1919/20	1920/21	8	15	2	259	104*	19.92	-	1								-	-
G.R.Baker	Well	1991/92	1994/95	1	2	1	8	7*	8.00	-	-								-	-
	Otago	1993/94		4	7	0	99	57	14.14	-	1								4	-
	All	1991/92	1994/95	11	13	2	224	47	20.36	-	1								31	1
H.S.Baker	Otago	1925/26		6	10	1	170	53	18.88	-	1								18	4
J.Baker	Otago	1889/90	1906/07	17	23	3	394	53	19.70	-	1	72	5		14.40	2-11	-	-	49	5
	All	1889/90	1906/07	1	2	0	2	2	1.00	-	-	88	5		17.60	2-11	-	-	17	-
L.C.Baker	Otago	1944/45	1945/46	37	69	5	1279	103	19.98	1	5								20	-
				41	77	5	1476	103	20.50	1	6									
				2	4	0	35	17	8.75	-	-								-	-

		First	Last	M	I	NO	Runs	HS	Avg	100	50	Runs	Wkts	OW	Avg	Best	5i	10m	ct	st
M.P.Baker	CD	1966/67	1971/72	16	24	2	473	142	21.50	1	1	357	11		32.45	4-62			9	
	ND	1974/75		1	2	2	49	31*	-			40	1		40.00	1-23			-	
	All	1966/67	1974/75	17	26	4	522	142	23.72	1	1	397	12		33.08	4-62			9	
P.J.M.Baker	Cant	1988/89		1	1	0	6	6	6.00			134	1		134.00	1-73			1	
T.S.Baker	CD	1874/75	1879/80	3	4	0	39	33	9.75										-	
W.A.Baker	Well	1911/12	1929/30	33	61	4	1778	143	31.19	3	9	106	8		13.25	5-50	1		22	
	All	1911/12	1929/30	36	67	4	1874	143	29.74	3	9	106	8		13.25	5-50	1		22	
L.Balaji	Well	2008/09		1	1	0	12	12	12.00			94	3		31.33	2-55			-	
	All	2001/02	2009/10	69	75	13	807	47	13.01			6495	259		25.07	7-42	16	4	23	
S.B.C.Baldwin	CD	2006/07		1	2	0	0	0	0.00			81	1		81.00	1-33			-	
T.D.Ball	Auck	1894/95	1896/97	3	5	0	42	30	8.40										-	
L.H.F.Balmain	Nel	1880/81		1	2	0	90	50	45.00										1	
J.E.Banks	Well	1923/24	1925/26	7	12	3	217	76*	24.11										1	
J.W.H.Bannerman	Sland	1914/15		1	2	0	11	10	5.50			84	3		28.00	3-84			-	
W.E.Bannerman	Otago	1911/12	1914/15	3	5	1	24	10	6.00			130	4		32.50	3-75			3	
R.T.Barber	Well	1945/46	1958/59	42	75	3	1708	117	23.39		11	8	0		-	-			49	
	CD	1959/60		2	5	2	208	78	20.80		2								10	
	All	1945/46	1959/60	49	89	6	2002	117	23.01		14								61	
M.R.H.Barbour	ND	1959/60		3	5	1	38	14*	9.50			8	0		-	-			3	
C.W.Barclay	CD	1955/56		1	1	0	6	6	6.00			193	1		193.00	1-115			1	
F.Barclay	Auck	1902/03	1903/04	2	4	1	13	6	4.33			21	1		21.00				-	
W.S.Barclay	Well	1920/21	1925/26	9	15	6	137	34	15.22			160	8		20.00	4-57			1	2
	All	1920/21	1925/26	10	16	7	204	67*	22.66			287	17		16.88	6-65	1		2	2
C.F.Barker	Cant	1873/74		2	4	0	74	30	18.50			314	18		17.44	6-65	1		2	
A.C.Barnes	Auck	1993/94	2004/05	73	113	10	2879	134*	27.95	4	12	2719	83		32.75	5-24	1		38	
	All	1993/94	2004/05	78	121	10	3006	134*	27.08	4	12	2823	89		31.71	5-24	1		39	
W.E.P.Barnes	Cant	1882/83	1893/94	16	28	4	290	49*	12.08			211	9		23.44	2-43			23	
D.Barnett	Nel	1873/74	1877/78	2	4	0	9	5	2.25			7	1		7.00	1-7			-	
G.E.F.Barnett	CD	2004/05	2007/08	20	37	0	837	118	23.25	1	5	90	1		90.00	1-10			17	
	All	2004/05	2009	29	53	1	1190	136	22.88	2	5	115	1		115.00	1-10			28	
B.J.Barrett	Auck	1985/86		3	1	1	0	0*	-			210	10		21.00	4-51			3	
	ND	1986/87	1989/90	18	22	10	116	25*	9.66			1361	43		31.65	4-32			3	
	All	1985	1989/90	31	28	14	124	25*	8.85			2355	73		32.26	4-32			4	
J.S.Barrett	All	1913/14		1	2	1	5	4*	5.00										-	
A.Barron	Cant	1904/05		1	2	1	30	30	15.00										1	
	Well	1905/06		1	1	0	18	18	18.00										-	
	All	1904/05	1905/06	2	3	1	48	30	16.00										1	
J.R.Barron	Otago	1917/18	1929/30	12	13	0	140	34	11.66			209	13		16.07	3-13			3	
R.D.W.Barry	Cant	1891/92	1904/05	12	21	2	251	35	13.21			42	1		42.00	1-21			11	
R.W.Barry	Cant	1901/02		1	2	1	17	13*	17.00			75	0		-	-			-	
C.E.Bartlett	CD	1996/97		1	2	2	0	0*	-			207	6		34.50	3-70			-	
D.J.Bartlett	Auck	2009/10		2	2	1	12	10*	12.00			1528	60		25.46	5-72			1	
G.A.Bartlett	CD	1958/59	1969/70	25	43	5	537	99*	14.13		2	494	24		20.58	4-39			14	
	Cant	1963/64	1965/66	7	13	3	303	72	30.30		2	4249	150		28.32	6-38	3		3	
	All	1958/59	1969/70	61	104	14	1504	99*	16.71		4								39	
A.E.Barton	Well	1904/05		1	2	0	17	14	8.50			20	0		-	-			-	

		First	Last	M	I	NO	Runs	HS	Avg	100	50	Runs	Wkts	OW	Avg	Best	5i	10m	ct	st
H.D.Barton	Auck	1995/96	1997/98	13	24	5	366	76*	19.26	-	3	716	14		51.14	3-60	-	-	6	
	Cant	1998/99	2000/01	3	4	0	153	62	38.25	-	1	107	0				-	-		
	All	1995/96	2000/01	17	29	5	572	76*	23.83	-	5	888	16		55.50	3-60	-	-	6	
P.T.Barton	Well	1954/55	1967/68	46	77	4	1825	118	25.00	2	5	187	7		26.71	3-33	-	-	35	
	All	1954/55	1967/68	71	122	4	2820	118	23.89	3	8	187	7		26.71	3-33	-	-	54	
P.H.Barton	ND	1962/63	1974/75	5	9	4	98	29*	16.33	-	-	336	11		30.54	4-48	-	-	8	
	Otago	1964/65		3	6	3	54	20	9.00	-	-	237	9		26.33	3-55	-	-	1	
	All	1962/63	1974/75	8	15	3	152	29*	12.66	-	-	573	20		28.65	4-48	-	-	9	
R.H.Barton	ND	1957/58		2	3	2	15	9*	15.00	-	-	43	0				-	-	2	
W.E.Barton	Auck	1882/83	1886/87	9	16	1	388	83	25.86	-	2	97	6		16.16	3-25	-	-	4	
	All	1879/80	1886/87	10	18	3	464	83	30.93	-	3	97	6		16.16	3-25	-	-	4	
J.R.M.Bassett-Graham																				
	Auck	2009/10		1	2	0	22	15	11.00	-	-						-	-		
G.C.Bateman	Cant	1979/80	1984/85	23	25	6	183	30	9.63	-	-	1681	63		26.68	6-66	2	-	5	
S.N.Bateman	Cant	1977/78	1984/85	19	29	6	181	25	7.86	-	-	1194	31		38.51	3-23	-	-	9	
A.E.Bates	Cant	1891/92	1897/98	8	11	2	59	29*	6.55	-	-	441	28		15.75	6-71	1	1	9	
M.D.Bates	Auck	2003/04	2009/10	17	19	9	191	57	19.10	-	1	1495	52		28.75	6-55	3	-	8	
T.Battersby	Sland	1914/15	1918/19	2	4	0	8	6	2.00	-	-	15	0				-	-	3	
B.J.Bayley	Cant	1957/58		4	5	0	88	46	17.60	-	-	6	1		6.00	1-6	-	-	1	
	ND	1961/62	1964/65	8	15	1	169	30	12.07	-	-	10	0				-	-	2	
	All	1957/58	1964/65	12	20	1	257	46	13.52	-	-	16	1		16.00	1-6	-	-	5	
A.Bayly	Tara	1891/92		6	7	1	39	20*	6.50	-	-	205	9		22.77	6-54	1	-	7	
F.Bayly	Tara	1882/83		1	2	1	4	4	2.00	-	-	83	3		27.66	3-83	-	-	-	
G.T.Bayly	Tara	1882/83	1897/98	8	13	2	36	12	3.27	-	-	319	17		18.76	3-19	3	-	3	
H.Bayly	Tara	1891/92		2	4	1	13	6*	4.33	-	-	30	2		15.00	2-11	-	-	-	
C.E.Beal	Otago	1906/07	1908/09	9	15	2	62	29*	20.66	-	-	25	0				-	-	2	
	Cant	1913/14	1914/15	9	21	1	333	105	25.61	1	1	57	3		19.00	2-16	-	-	4	
	All	1906/07	1914/15	12	21	2	436	105	24.22	1	1	111	3		37.00	2-16	-	-	7	
W.M.Beal	Otago	1909/10		1	2	1	1	1*	1.00	-	-						-	-	-	
A.M.Beale	HB	1893/94	1895/96	6	9	2	17	5	2.42	-	-	272	16		17.00	6-53	1	-	1	
D.A.Beard	ND	1987/88	1990/91	8	10	3	99	28	14.14	-	-	614	23		26.69	6-18	1	-	3	
D.D.Beard	Well	1945/46		1	2	0	35	27	17.50	-	-	63	2		31.50	2-63	-	-	-	
	CD	1950/51	1960/61	49	85	14	1791	81*	25.22	-	9	4531	213		21.27	7-56	8	2	41	
	ND	1961/62	1964/65	8	14	1	125	34	9.61	-	-	792	42		18.85	6-71	3	1	7	
	All	1945/46	1964/65	66	115	17	2166	81*	22.10	-	9	6000	278		21.58	7-56	12	3	50	
L.A.D.Beard	Well	1927/28		2	2	1	76	60*	76.00	-	1	82	1		82.00	1-44	-	-	1	
N.B.Beard	Otago	2008/09	2009/10	12	16	9	180	42	25.71	-	-	1222	28		43.64	6-107	1	-	3	
W.S.Beard	Cant	1878/79		1	1	0	5	5	5.00	-	-	12	0				-	-	1	
	Auck	1886/87		1	1	1	0	0	0.00	-	-						-	-	-	
	All	1878/79	1886/87	2	2	1	5	5	2.50	-	-	12	0				-	-	1	
S.P.Beare	Otago	2001/02	2004/05	6	11	0	137	60	12.45	-	1	106	8		13.25	2-5	-	-	9	
T.G.Beatson	ND	1971/72		2	2	0	1	1*	0.50	-	-	58	2		29.00	2-34	-	-	1	
	All	1970/71	1971/72	3	4	2	3	1*	1.50	-	-	217	5		43.40	2-34	-	-	1	
M.A.Beban	Well	1969/70		4	5	0	28	17	5.60	-	-						-	-	3	
C.H.Beck	Otago	1884/85	1890/91	7	14	1	215	48	16.53	-	-	261	7		37.28	3-96	-	-	2	

		First	Last	M	I	NO	Runs	HS	Avg	100	50	Runs	Wkts	OW	Avg	Best	5i	10m	ct	st
J.E.F.Beck	Well	1954/55	1961/62	18	27	1	713	149	27.42	2	2	10	0		18.00				12	
V.S.Beeby	All	1953/54	1961/62	41	68	5	1508	149	23.93	2	8	21	0		37.00				19	
E.M.Beechey	Otago	1919/20		2	3	2	37	29*	37.00			72	4		18.00	3-16			1	
G.D.Beer	Well	1906/07	1918/19	2	3	2	37	29*	37.00			72	4		18.00	3-16			1	
	CD	1963/64	1964/65	15	26	0	576	180	22.15	1	2	148	4		37.00	2-25			9	
	Otago	1965/66	1967/68	6	10	0	168	35	16.80			7	1		7.00	1-7			4	
N.C.Begg	All	1962/63	1967/68	12	24	2	397	57	18.04										5	
J.D.Behrent	Otago	1939/40	1940/41	19	36	2	572	57	16.82		1								10	
	Otago	1959/60		3	4	1	30	16	10.00			7	1		7.00	1-7				
A.G.Q.Bell	Auck	1963/64	1967/68	12	19	0	292	74	15.33		2	238	5		47.60	2-43			1	
F.Bell	All	1959/60	1967/68	14	22	1	308	74	15.40		2	493	17		29.00	3-35			15	
F.H.D.Bell	Otago	1888/89	1893/94	12	21	1	184	37	9.20		2	611	17		35.94	3-35			16	
M.D.Bell	HB	1886/87		1	2	0	7	4	3.50										9	
	Well	1873/74	1876/77	2	3	0	2	2	0.66			40	2		20.00	2-40			1	
R.C.Bell	ND	1993/94	1996/97	20	34	0	1017	78	32.80		8								17	
W.Bell	Well	1997/98	2009/10	93	162	11	6495	265	43.01	20	31	11	0						79	
F.W.J.Bellamy	All	1993/94	2009/10	168	287	18	9811	265	36.47	24	53	23	0						137	
R.G.Bellars	Otago	1914/15	1920/21	4	7	0	71	26	10.14			22	0						1	
S.E.Belsham	Cant	1949/50	1958/59	8	11	5	42	11*	7.00			655	17		38.52	3-61			7	
C.A.Benbow	Auck	1952/53		2	4	2	35	22	5.83			310	11		28.18	4-86			7	
A.P.Bennett	All	1949/50	1958/59	21	33	16	170	22	10.00			1783	44		40.52	4-31			4	
A.C.Bennett	Cant	1931/32	1938/39	21	39	2	1119	132	30.24	3	3	488	10		48.80	5-31			15	
D.R.T.Bennett	Otago	1944/45	1945/46	4	7	1	71	24	11.83										25	
E.A.Bennett	All	1931/32	1945/46	26	48	3	1226	132	27.24	3	3	525	11		47.72	5-31	1		33	
H.K.Bennett	Auck	1873/74		3	6	0	28	13*	5.60										1	
J.H.Bennett	Auck	1953/54	1958/59	6	9	0	105	41	11.66			188	17		11.05	4-9			13	
	Well	1891/92	1896/97	6	8	2	54	30	9.00		1	119	19		6.26	6-5	3	1	2	
	Nel	1885/86	1886/87	6	3	0	55	52	18.33										3	
	HB	1892/93	1896/97	3	6	0	58	31	9.66										2	
	ND	1996/97		3	6	4	25	15*	25.00			189	4		47.25	2-55			3	
	Well	1913/14	1917/18	3	6	4	57	45*				54	0						1	
	Cant	2005/06	2009/10	32	31	13	105	27	5.83			3309	89		37.17	7-50	1		7	
	All	2005/06	2009/10	33	33	14	108	27	5.68			3395	91		37.30	7-50	1		8	
	Cant	1898/99	1919/20	40	69	15	757	58	14.01		2	3367	205		16.42	7-35	17	4	11	
	All	1898/99	1919/20	52	91	16	880	58	11.73		2	4471	241		18.55	7-35	20	4	15	
J.H.Bennett	Cant	1863/64		1	2	0	10	5	5.00										2	
N.Bennett	Cant	1950/51	1951/52	6	10	0	58	25	5.80			81	3		27.00	1-8			2	
R.D.Bennett	Auck	1975/76		1	2	0	1	1	0.50			89	2		44.50	1-31				
W.Bent	Cant	1867/68		1	2	0	1	1	0.50										1	
C.A.Berendsen	Well	1911/12		4	7	1	19	8*	3.16										7	
C.H.Beresford	Tara	1882/83		1	2	0	8	8	4.00											
E.H.L.Bernau	HB	1914/15		4	10	0	39	31	19.50			88	4		22.00	4-88			2	
	Well	1922/23	1927/28	6	10	2	276	117	27.60	1	1	518	13		39.84	3-69			4	
A.E.Berry	All	1914/15	1927/28	28	39	6	651	117	17.59	1	2	1672	58		28.82	6-35	1		10	4
F.M.Betts	Otago	1955/56		4	8	3	100	43	20.00			112	5		22.40	3-49			5	
	Well	1873/74		1	2	0	4	2	2.00											

		First	Last	M	I	NO	Runs	HS	Avg	100	50	Runs	Wkts	OW	Avg	Best	5i	10m	ct	st
J.A.Betts	HB	1908/09		1	2	0	22	14	11.00	-	-	129	3		43.00	2-45	-	-	1	
D.Beuth	CD	1968/69		3	2	1	4	4	4.00	-	-	698	25		27.92	5-35	1	-	-	
J.A.Beuth	ND	1962/63	1969/70	12	16	4	62	36	5.16	-	-								2	
P.Beveridge	Auck	1918/19		2	4	1	136	93*	45.33	-	1								1	
F.Beyeridge	Well	1985/86	1989/90	17	18	3	224	43*	14.93	-	-	1125	34		33.08	4-64	-	-	8	
	All	1985/86	1989/90	18	19	3	224	43*	14.93	-	-	1210	34		35.58	4-64	-	-	8	
E.F.Bezzant	Well	1943/44	1943/44	2	4	0	65	36	16.25	-	-								-	
	All	1942/43	1943/44	4	8	0	218	78	27.25	-	2								2	
Bhupinder Singh	Auck	2009/10		4	3	1	27	14*	13.50	-	-	571	17		33.58	4-93	-	-	2	
A.Bigg-Wither	Nel	1886/87	1887/88	2	3	0	9	5	3.00	-	-								2	1
J.Bigg-Wither	Nel	1885/86	1886/87	2	3	0	14	10	4.66	-	-								-	
G.P.Bilby	Well	1962/63	1976/77	54	95	11	2852	161	33.95	3	15	34	1		34.00	1-2	-	-	52	
	All	1962/63	1976/77	57	101	11	2936	161	32.62	3	15	34	1		34.00	1-2	-	-	55	
I.S.Billcliff	Otago	1990/91	1994/95	29	53	3	1073	121	21.46	1	4	61	1		61.00	1-7	-	-	13	
	Well	1995/96		5	9	0	224	86	24.88	-	2								2	
	Auck	1997/98	1998/99	7	12	0	278	94	23.16	-	1								4	
	All	1990/91	2008	46	84	4	1964	126	24.55	2	9	61	1		61.00	1-7	-	-	28	
M.R.Billcliff	Otago	1998/99		2	3	1	11	8	3.66	-	-	61	1		61.00	1-17	-	-	1	
N.D.Binnie	Well	1921/22		1	1	0	4	4	4.00	-	-								-	
A.E.Birch	Well	1909/10	1910/11	2	4	0	91	62	22.75	-	1								2	
W.G.Bird	All	1942/43		1	2	1	14	14	14.00	-	-	96	4		24.00	4-58	-	-	-	
H.A.Bishop	HB	1903/04		2	4	0	133	98	33.25	-	1								4	
	Cant	1905/06		12	19	0	460	90	24.21	-	3	10	1		10.00	1-10	-	-	10	
	All	1903/04	1914/15	15	25	0	599	98	23.96	-	4	10	1		10.00	1-10	-	-	10	
R.E.Bishop	HB	1914/15	1914/15	5	10	0	212	61	21.20	-	2								2	
W.Bishop	Well	1920/21		1	2	0	0	0	0.00	-	-								-	
J.Black	Otago	1874/75		1	2	1	5	3*	5.00	-	-								-	
P.M.Blackbourn	CD	1895/96		3	4	2	154	58	77.00	-	2								6	4
A.Blacklock	Well	1983/84		15	27	1	569	69	21.88	-	3								8	
C.P.Blacklock	Well	1884/85	1895/96	2	3	0	22	12	7.33	-	-								1	
J.P.Blacklock	Well	1905/06	1913/14	18	35	0	821	124	24.14	1	6								11	2
	All	1904/05	1913/14	20	39	1	864	124	22.73	1	6								11	
J.W.Blacklock	Well	1877/78	1883/84	7	14	1	75	27	5.76	-	-	22	0		-	-	-	-	4	
R.V.Blacklock	Well	1883/84	1895/96	29	52	4	718	84*	14.95	-	6			2					10	
	All	1883/84	1895/96	31	56	4	771	84*	14.82	-	6								11	1
I.A.Blackmore	ND	1964/65		1	2	0	8	8	5.50	-	-								-	
J.H.Blackmore	ND	1968/69	1972/73	12	23	3	314	54	15.70	-	2	22	0		-	-	-	-	4	
	All	1968/69	1972/73	14	27	3	360	54	15.00	-	2	22	0		-	-	-	-	5	
S.J.Blackmore	Well	1991/92	2001/02	29	50	3	1396	107*	29.70	2	7	2	0		-	-	-	-	21	
T.E.Blain	CD	1982/83	1994/95	83	145	15	4547	161	34.97	7	28	120	2		60.00	1-12	-	-	139	19
	Cant	1983/84		3	5	3	122	53*	61.00	-	1	8	0		-	-	-	-	5	
	All	1982/83	1994/95	118	199	30	5749	161	34.01	8	32	128	2		64.00	1-12	-	-	210	26
B.R.Blair	Otago	1977/78	1989/90	90	154	5	5055	143	33.92	7	34	1266	37		34.21	4-44	-	-	65	
	ND	1984/85	1985/86	10	19	1	510	66	28.33	-	4	321	11		29.18	3-10	-	-	10	
	All	1977/78	1989/90	110	190	6	5995	143	32.58	7	40	1750	55		31.81	4-26	-	-	81	
J.R.Blair	Otago	1926/27		1	2	0	10	10	5.00	-	-								1	

		First	Last	M	I	NO	Runs	HS	Avg	100	50	Runs	Wkts	OW	Avg	Best	5i	10m	ct	st
R.Blair	Auck	1882/83	1883/84	2	4	0	54	21	13.50	-	-	31	0		31.00	1-12			16	
R.W.Blair	Well	1951/52	1964/65	59	84	19	887	59	13.64	-	1	5004	330		15.16	9-72	30	10	16	
	CD	1955/56		5	9	0	105	40	11.66	-	-	726	42		17.28	7-100	5	1	4	
	All	1951/52	1964/65	119	172	36	1672	79	12.29	-	3	9961	537		18.54	9-72	41	12	46	
R.A.J.Blair	Otago	1953/54		1	2	0	2	2	1.00	-	-								2	
W.L.Blair	Otago	1967/68	1990/91	81	149	9	3654	140	26.10	2	15	42	0						66	
	All	1967/68	1990/91	82	151	9	3698	140	26.04	2	15	42	0						66	
W.A.Blair	ND	1920/21		1	2	0	17	15	8.50	-	-									
D.C.Blake	CD	1992/93		1	0	0															
	CD	1993/94	1998/99	18	17	5	81	14	6.75	-	-	21	0						6	
	All	1992/93	1998/99	19	17	5	81	14	6.75	-	-	1274	42		30.33	5-63	1	-	6	
T.W.Blake	ND	1964/65		1	2	0	1	1	0.50	-	-	1295	42		30.83	5-63	1	-	5	
D.J.Blakely	Otago	1940/41	1950/51	4	6	0	87	28	14.50	-	-								5	
G.A.W.Blakely	Otago	1980/81	1984/85	9	18	0	325	74	18.05	-	1	32	1		32.00	1-32	-	-	4	
J.W.Blakely	Otago	1940/41	1946/47	2	4	1	6	5*	2.00	-	-	26	1		26.00	1-13	-	-	1	
E.O.Blamires	Well	1911/12	1912/13	5	9	0	174	65	19.33	-	2	701	14		50.07	4-56	-	-	8	
	Otago	1923/24	1926/27	14	28	1	841	133	31.14	2	4	743	15		49.53	4-56	-	-	11	
	All	1911/12	1926/27	20	39	1	1015	133	26.71	2	5	16	0						20	
H.L.Blamires	HB	1911/12	1913/14	3	6	1	112	55*	22.40	-	1								2	
J.A.R.Blandford	Well	1932/33	1936/37	8	15	1	199	62	13.26	-	1								5	7
	Auck	1939/40	1940/41	4	5	0	127	58*	42.33	-	1								9	4
	All	1932/33	1940/41	15	24	1	430	62	20.47	-	2								17	12
J.P.Blane	Auck	1949/50		2	4	0	64	32	16.00	-	-	82	3		27.33	2-8	-	-	1	
R.G.Blinko	HB	1913/14		1	2	0	31	21	15.50	-	-								3	
P.J.Bloomfield	CD	1957/58	1958/59	6	9	2	10	5	1.42	-	-	467	17		27.47	4-30	1	-	1	
A.R.Bloxham	Cant	1864/65		1	2	0	28	18	14.00	-	-									
E.D.Blundell	Well	1930/31	1937/38	19	32	11	236	27*	11.23	-	-	2219	78		28.44	6-82	5	1	6	
	All	1927	1937/38	48	68	22	400	27*	8.69	-	-	4924	195		25.25	6-25	12	1	16	
R.C.Blunt	Cant	1917/18	1924/25	27	53	3	1886	174	37.72	4	8	780	28		27.85	4-60	-	-	27	
	Otago	1926/27	1931/32	16	31	2	1510	338*	52.06	4	4	1400	45		31.11	8-99	3	-	14	
	All	1917/18	1935	123	209	15	7953	338*	40.99	15	40	6638	213		31.16	8-99	5	-	88	
H.K.P.Boam	Well	2008/09	2009/10	6	10	3	142	49*	20.28	-	3	175	5		35.00	3-56	-	-	4	
J.H.Board	HB	1910/11	1914/15	6	12	0	514	134	42.83	1	3								5	2
	All	1891	1914/15	525	906	97	15674	214	19.37	9	64								848	359
E.R.Boddington	Nel	1880/81	1885/86	4	6	1	47	36	9.40	-	-	46	0						1	
	Well	1887/88		2	3	1	51	47*	25.50	-	-	4	1		4.00	1-4	-	-	1	
	All	1880/81	1887/88	6	9	2	98	47*	14.00	-	-	17	1		17.00	1-17	-	-	2	
H.A.Boddington	Nel	1880/81	1895/96	5	9	1	90	35	11.25	-	-	21	2		10.50	1-4	-	-	4	
	Otago	1883/84		7	14	1	167	46	12.84	-	-	6	0						4	
	All	1880/81	1895/96	12	23	2	257	46	12.23	-	-	34	0						2	
B.E.Bodle	Auck	1958/59		1	2	1	3	3	3.00	-	-	40	0						6	
T.P.Bogue	Sland	1919/20	1920/21	2	3	1	5	5	2.50	-	-	22	0						-	
E.H.Bold	Well	1919/20		1	2	0	10	10	5.00	-	-								2	1
B.A.Bolton	Cant	1955/56	1964/65	34	60	2	1336	138	23.03	1	5	1205	57		21.14	7-23	1	-	13	
	Well	1966/67	1970/71	21	36	2	620	74*	18.23	-	1	882	38		23.21	6-46	1	-	8	
	All	1955/56	1970/71	61	107	4	2092	138	20.31	1	6	2144	96		22.33	7-23	3	-	24	

		First	Last	M	I	NO	Runs	HS	Avg	100	50	Runs	Wkts	OW	Avg	Best	5i	10m	ct	st
S.F.Bolton	Nel	1888/89		1	2	0	2	2	1.00	-	-	28	1		28.00	5-37	4	-	-	-
K.Bond	Well	1876/77		1	2	1	4	4*	4.00	-	-								-	-
S.E.Bond	Cant	1996/97	2009/10	25	29	10	474	100	24.94	1	2	2103	87		24.17	5-37	4	-	6	
	All	1996/97	2009/10	60	70	20	830	100	16.60	1	2	5478	225		24.34	7-66	12	1	24	
S.L.Boock	Otago	1973/74	1989/90	88	109	43	653	35*	9.89	-	-	8235	399		20.63	8-57	28	5	50	
	Cant	1975/76	1977/78	22	26	7	154	21*	8.10	-	-	1830	102		17.94	7-57	7		10	
	All	1973/74	1989/90	164	195	67	1092	37	8.53	-	-	14314	640		22.36	8-57	40	5	83	
J.F.Booker	Cant	1947/48		1	2	0	25	25	25.00	-	-	84	4		21.00	3-41	-	-		
M.K.Boon	Cant	1922/23	1926/27	11	20	0	352	72	17.60	-	2								9	4
	All	1922/23	1927/28	13	24	0	376	72	15.66	-	2								10	5
R.H.Booth	Cant	1917/18		4	8	2	106	49*	17.66	-	-								-	
R.S.Booth	Nel	1881/82		1	1	0	19	19	19.00	-	-								1	
R.S.Bopara	Auck	2009/10		5	9	0	294	90	32.66	-	2	369	6		61.50	3-109	-	-	3	
	All	2002	2010	103	172	22	6332	229	42.21	17	25	4585	107		42.85	5-75	1	-	67	
J.B.Borton	Otago	1864/65	1865/66	2	4	0	5	5	1.25	-	-	54	5		10.80	3-22	1	-	2	
G.S.Botting	CD	1950/51	1952/53	12	18	2	106	27*	6.62	-	-								14	
	Otago	1953/54		3	6	0	55	16	18.33	-	-								4	
	All	1948/49	1953/54	16	25	3	164	27*	8.20	-	-								9	
G.R.Bottomley	Otago	1889/90		2	3	0	14	10	4.66	-	-								24	
F.A.A.J.W.Bottrell	HB	1912/13		1	1	0	13	11*	13.00	-	-								-	
A.Bouch	Otago	1876/77		1	2	0	13	13	6.50	-	-	12	0		-	-	-	-	1	
W.W.Boulnois	HB	1912/13		1	2	0	31	16	15.50	-	-									
J.J.Boult	ND	2008/09	2009/10	3	4	0	157	76	39.25	-	1	260	9		28.88	4-78	-	-	1	
T.A.Boult	ND	2008/09	2009/10	6	7	3	43	35	10.75	-	-	453	18		25.16	5-58	1	-	5	
	All	2008/09	2009/10	9	11	4	64	35	9.14	-	-	639	22		29.04	5-58	1	-	8	
C.S.Bowden	Auck	1883/84		1	1	0	0	0	0.00	-	-	15	0		-	-	-	-	-	
D.J.Bowden	Well	2005/06	2009/10	31	45	9	1071	106*	29.75	1	4	2305	68		33.89	4-48	-	-	9	
D.W.Bowden	CD	1950/51	1957/58	16	28	0	475	60	16.96	-	1								9	
F.Bowles	Well	1911/12		1	2	0	39	39	19.50	-	-									
E.H.Bowley	Auck	1926/27	1928/29	11	21	2	879	120	46.26	1	6	878	40		21.95	4-27	-	-	14	
	All	1912	1934	510	859	47	28378	283	34.94	52	149	19257	741		25.98	9-114	28	2	374	
C.Boxshall	Cant	1897/98	1914/15	50	83	17	798	46	12.09	-	-								69	38
	All	1897/98	1914/15	65	110	26	1027	46	12.22	-	-								80	45
T.A.Boyer	Well	1997/98	1999/00	13	19	1	631	104	35.05	1	4	91	0		-	-	-	-	2	
D.J.Boyle	Cant	1980/81	1994/95	69	121	12	3216	149	29.50	3	19	500	9		55.55	3-38	-	-	56	
J.G.Boyle	Well	1982/83	1985/86	29	51	1	1237	89	24.74	-	9	24	0						10	
	Cant	1986/87	1990/91	6	11	1	238	50	23.80	-	1									
	All	1982/83	1990/91	35	62	2	1475	89	24.58	-	10								11	
T.J.Boyle	ND	1986/87		3	5	0	18	13	3.60	-	-	24	0		-	-	-	-	-	
B.P.Bracewell	CD	1977/78	1979/80	9	9	4	66	27	13.20	-	-	252	2		126.00	1-71	-	-	4	
	Otago	1981/82	1982/83	15	22	4	232	36*	12.88	-	-	637	20		31.85	3-55	-	-	5	
	ND	1983/84	1989/90	34	48	10	551	57*	14.50	-	1	880	35		25.14	4-41	-	-	15	
	All	1977/78	1989/90	77	106	24	965	57*	11.76	-	1	2659	96		27.69	6-49	2	-	32	
D.A.J.Bracewell	CD	2008/09	2009/10	12	17	1	274	60*	17.12	-	1	1235	26		47.50	5-47	1	-	4	

		First	Last	M	I	NO	Runs	HS	Avg	100	50	Runs	Wkts	OW	Avg	Best	5i	10m	ct	st
D.W.Bracewell	Cant	1974/75	1975/76	4	3	3	23	20*	-	-	-	286	7		40.85	2-32	-	-	-	-
	CD	1976/77	1979/80	21	36	5	507	56	16.35	-	2	1185	32		37.03	4-44	-	-	12	-
J.G.Bracewell	All	1974/75	1979/80	26	41	9	553	56	17.28	-	2	1558	43		36.23	4-44	-	-	14	-
	Otago	1978/79	1981/82	23	37	4	651	51	19.72	-	2	1923	102		18.85	7-9	10	3	20	-
	Auck	1982/83	1989/90	42	60	10	1598	104*	31.96	2	11	4189	168		24.93	7-65	8	2	51	-
	All	1978/79	1990	149	208	40	4354	110	25.91	4	21	13919	522		26.66	8-81	33	9	125	-
M.A.Bracewell	Otago	1977/78		1	2	2	8	7*	-	-	-	65	0		-	-	-	-	-	-
G.E.Bradburn	ND	1985/86	2001/02	115	188	23	4614	148*	27.96	4	28	7272	231		31.48	6-56	3	-	108	-
	All	1985/86	2001/02	127	206	27	4978	148*	27.81	4	30	8174	250		32.69	6-56	4	-	122	-
J.C.Bradburn	HB	1919/20	1920/21	4	8	0	117	35	14.62	-	-								2	-
W.P.Bradburn	ND	1957/58	1968/69	55	103	5	2015	107	20.56	1	7	804	19		42.31	2-13	-	-	64	-
	All	1957/58	1968/69	57	107	5	2077	107	20.36	1	7	804	19		42.31	2-13	-	-	66	-
A.J.Bradley	ND	1993/94	1994/95	6	10	1	145	57	16.11	-	1	102	5		20.40	3-18	-	-	4	-
M.J.Bradley	Auck	1987/88		3	6	4	21	13	3.50	-	-								3	-
M.J.Bradley	Auck	1985/86	1987/88	6	6	0	70	37*	35.00	-	-	309	13		23.76	3-37	-	-	3	-
R.R.A.F.Bradley	ND	1990/91		1	1	0	0	0	0.00	-	-	31	1		31.00	1-31	-	-	-	-
D.J.Brady	Otago	1971/72		1	1	0	47	47	47.00	-	-								2	-
	All	1970/71	1971/72	2	3	0	86	47	28.66	-	-								3	-
R.Braithwaite	HB	1885/86		1	2	0	4	4	2.00	-	-	41	2		20.50	2-41	-	-	-	-
J.H.Bray	Well	1958/59	1966/67	5	8	1	43	13	7.16	-	-	290	12		24.16	4-99	-	-	3	-
W.T.Bray	Well	1914/15	1920/21	5	8	0	177	82	25.28	-	1	27	1		27.00	1-11	-	-	3	-
R.P.Brazendale	Auck	1983/84		1	2	0	1	1	0.50	-	-	59	3		19.66	3-59	-	-	-	-
L.C.Breen	Otago	1993/94	1994/95	8	15	0	282	100	18.80	1	1	2	0		-	-	-	-	1	-
M.C.Bremner	Cant	1987/88		4	7	0	94	35	13.42	-	-								3	-
I.N.Brennan	Well	1958/59		3	6	0	102	40	17.00	-	-	2	0		-	-	-	-	1	-
D.E.Brian	Well	1946/47		1	2	0	53	27	26.50	-	-	87	1		87.00	1-87	-	-	-	-
	CD	1953/54	1955/56	6	12	2	175	81	15.90	-	1	368	13		28.30	3-32	-	-	3	-
	All	1946/47	1955/56	7	14	2	228	81	17.53	-	1	455	14		32.50	3-32	-	-	4	-
P.S.Briasco	CD	1982/83	1991/92	81	146	16	4301	157	33.08	6	25	1206	34		35.47	3-28	-	-	63	-
	All	1982/83	1991/92	83	148	16	4390	157	33.25	6	26	1206	34		35.47	3-28	-	-	64	-
A.W.S.Brice	Well	1902/03	1927/28	56	96	13	1426	87	17.18	-	8	4684	229		20.45	9-67	17	7	41	-
	All	1902/03	1927/28	61	105	13	1575	87	17.11	-	8	5260	247		21.29	9-67	19	7	43	-
W.B.Bridgman	Cant	1954/55		2	4	2	4	4*	2.00	-	-	144	3		48.00	2-63	-	-	-	-
K.D.Briggs	Otago	1959/60		2	4	0	14	9	3.50	-	-								4	-
W.R.Brinsley	Otago	1917/18		1	3	0	10	10	3.33	-	-								1	-
A.E.L.Britton	Cant	1945/46	1952/53	18	30	9	331	46	15.76	-	1								28	12
C.H.Broad	Nel	1888/89	1891/92	2	4	0	13	12	3.25	-	-	39	2		19.50	2-13	-	-	4	-
	Otago	1897/98	1899/00	2	11	1	138	60	12.54	-	1	25	0		-	-	-	-	1	-
	All	1888/89	1899/00	8	15	1	151	60	10.06	-	1	64	2		32.00	2-13	-	-	4	-
C.L.Broad	Cant	1966/67		3	5	0	102	43	20.40	-	1	147	8		18.37	5-61	1	-	4	-
E.W.Broad	Nel	1891/92		1	2	1	13	13	13.00	-	-								-	-
J.M.Brodie	Well	2007/08	2009/10	14	22	2	770	110	35.00	2	5								4	-
J.F.Brook	Auck	1913/14		3	6	0	117	35	19.50	-	-	127	1		127.00	1-52	-	-	16	-
E.W.Brooke	Well	1889/90		2	3	0	29	11	9.66	-	-								7	-
V.G.Brooker	Auck	1947/48	1948/49	2	3	1	50	19*	25.00	-	-	186	3		62.00	3-74	-	-	1	-

		First	Last	M	I	NO	Runs	HS	Avg	100	50	Runs	Wkts	OW	Avg	Best	5i	10m	ct	st
W.Brook-Smith	Auck	1904/05	1922/23	29	51	6	1215	112*	27.00	2	4	619	24		25.79	4-63	-	-	16	-
	All	1904/05	1922/23	30	53	6	1279	112*	27.21	2	4	624	24		26.00	4-63	-	-	16	-
D.J.Broom	Otago	2009/10		2	3	0	119	119	39.66	1	-	29	0		-	-	-	-	-	-
N.T.Broom	Cant	2002/03	2004/05	16	26	2	821	109*	34.20	1	3	79	2		39.50	1-8	-	-	17	-
	Otago	2005/06	2009/10	38	59	6	2478	196	46.75	7	12	262	3		87.33	1-9	-	-	26	-
	All	2002/03	2009/10	55	87	8	3301	196	41.78	8	15	371	5		74.20	1-8	-	-	43	-
R.F.Broom	Well	1954/55		3	4	0	47	21	11.75	-	-	114	6		19.00	3-18	-	-	1	-
E.J.Brosnahan	Cant	1919/20	1928/29	8	15	1	281	73*	20.07	-	1	4	0		-	-	-	-	1	-
E.T.Broughton	HB	1883/84		1	2	0	0	0	-	-	-								-	-
R.D.Broughton	ND	1980/81	1986/87	21	39	0	880	122	22.56	1	3	32	0		-	-	-	-	12	-
C.M.Brown	Auck	1993/94	1996/97	15	21	5	81	16*	5.06	-	-	1118	57		19.61	6-50	3	1	2	-
	All	1993/94	1997	19	27	8	132	19	6.94	-	-	1335	63		21.19	6-50	3	1	2	-
D.R.Brown	Well	1995/96		6	10	0	257	47	25.70	-	-	440	28		15.71	5-39	2	-	2	-
	All	1989	2006/07	209	319	41	8511	203	30.61	10	44	16177	567		28.53	8-89	21	4	130	-
J.W.Brown	Well	1879/80	1884/85	6	11	3	90	21*	11.25	-	-								-	-
K.V.Brown	Auck	1992/93		1	1	0	0	0	0.00	-	-	45	1		45.00	1-45	-	-	-	-
M.T.Brown	CD	1973/74	1974/75	5	9	4	36	10	7.20	-	-	236	2		118.00	1-27	-	-	2	-
R.W.Brown	Otago	1870/71		1	2	1	2	1*	2.00	-	-								-	-
R.K.Brown	CD	1988/89	1993/94	22	32	6	536	90	20.61	-	3	319	3		106.33	2-40	-	-	10	-
R.E.Brown	CD	1952/53	1957/58	14	20	1	236	48*	18.15	-	-	784	28		28.00	5-29	1	-	10	-
S.E.V.Brown	Sland	1917/18		1	2	1	12	8	12.00	-	-	46	1		46.00	1-46	-	-	-	-
S.W.Brown	Auck	1987/88	1994/95	51	78	13	1920	209*	29.53	2	11	2218	72		30.80	5-39	4	-	38	-
	All	1987/88	1994/95	53	81	13	1975	209*	29.04	2	11	2377	72		33.01	5-39	4	-	40	-
V.R.Brown	Cant	1978/79	1986/87	65	111	11	2872	161*	28.72	5	15	4393	159		27.62	7-28	4	2	38	-
	Auck	1987/88	1989/90	4	6	0	132	60	22.00	-	1	76	2		38.00	1-20	-	-	3	-
	All	1978/79	1989/90	83	136	17	3485	161*	29.28	6	19	5506	190		28.97	7-28	4	2	49	-
W.J.Brown	Auck	1944/45	1954/55	9	12	1	35	10	3.18	-	-	825	27		30.55	4-84	1	-	1	-
L.V.Browne	Well	1928/29	1930/31	2	3	0	3	3	1.00	-	-	3	0		-	-	-	-	-	-
M.G.Browne	Well	1937/38	1951/52	9	15	4	177	58	16.09	-	1	723	22		32.86	6-89	1	-	2	-
S.C.Brownette	HB	1910/11	1912/13	2	4	1	14	10	4.66	-	-								-	-
D.G.Brownlie	Cant	2009/10		5	9	2	364	112*	52.00	1	2	82	0		-	-	-	-	9	-
J.A.Bruce	Well	1907/08	1922/23	8	13	3	325	107	32.50	1	-	12	0		-	-	-	-	9	-
R.W.Bruce	HB	1891/92	1896/97	6	11	1	117	30	11.70	-	-	158	9		17.55	4-29	-	-	3	-
J.S.B.Bruges	Cant	1908/09		1	2	0	2	2	1.00	-	-								1	-
L.R.Brunton	Otago	1913/14	1914/15	5	10	2	233	67	29.12	-	1								-	-
	All	1908/09	1914/15	6	12	3	235	67	23.50	-	1								1	-
W.Bryars	Cant	1913/14	1925/26	15	27	3	343	49	14.29	-	-								25	15
J.Bryce	Cant	1887/88		1	2	0	2	1	1.00	-	-								-	-
T.J.Bryden	Well	1876/77		1	2	0	8	6	4.00	-	-	49	7		7.00	5-20	1	-	-	-
R.Buchan	Otago	1912/13	1913/14	2	4	0	29	15	7.25	-	-								-	-
J.T.Buchanan	Well	1943/44	1945/46	6	12	3	136	37	15.11	-	-	533	22		24.22	7-66	1	-	2	-
W.B.Buchanan	Cant	1883/84	1884/85	5	9	0	174	64	19.33	-	-								8	-
J.Buck	HB	1884/85		1	1	0	6	6	6.00	-	-								1	-
	HB	1886/87	1887/88	2	4	0	26	14	6.50	-	-	48	2		24.00	2-48	-	-	-	-
W.F.Buckland	Auck	1873/74	1882/83	7	11	5	48	11*	8.00	-	-	303	23		13.17	4-19	-	-	4	-
G.T.Buist	CD	1956/57	1957/58	8	13	0	168	51	12.92	-	1	30	0		-	-	-	-	2	-

Name	Team	First	Last	M	I	NO	Runs	HS	Avg	100	50	Runs	Wkts	OW	Avg	Best	5i	10m	ct	st
C.E.Bulfin	CD	1996/97	1997/98	10	14	2	106	37	8.83	-	-	707	29		24.37	5-53	3	1	4	
	Well	1998/99	2000/01	7	9	2	155	47	22.14	-	-	477	11		43.36	2-31	-	-	1	
C.L.Bull	All	1996/97	2000/01	22	31	5	338	47	13.00	-	-	1626	50		32.52	5-53	3	1	5	
	Cant	1965/66	1983/84	58	97	5	1743	115*	19.36	1	6	34	0		-	-	-	-	30	
A.D.Bullick	All	1965/66	1983/84	60	101	7	1841	115*	19.58	1	6	34	0		-	-	-	-	30	
A.T.Burgess	Otago	2007/08	2009/10	6	9	2	130	42	18.57	-	-	538	12		44.83	3-51	-	-	2	
	Cant	1940/41	1951/52	13	21	1	403	61*	20.15	-	1	491	16		30.68	6-52	1	-	12	
G.C.Burgess	All	1940/41	1951/52	14	23	1	466	61*	22.19	-	2	491	16		30.68	6-52	1	-	12	
M.G.Burgess	Auck	1940/41	1954/55	7	13	0	219	35	18.25	-	-								1	
	Auck	1966/67	1979/80	68	116	13	4228	146	41.04	10	26	319	8		39.87	2-26	-	-	75	
C.Burke	All	1963/64	1980/81	192	322	35	10281	146	35.82	20	62	1148	30		38.26	3-23	-	-	152	
	Auck	1937/38	1953/54	39	50	13	739	51*	19.97	-	2	3490	140		24.92	6-47	6	1	23	
D.Burn	All	1937/38	1953/54	60	73	18	959	51*	17.43	-	2	5199	200		25.99	6-23	7	1	31	
G.G.Burnes	Nel	1880/81	1881/82	2	4	1	19	8*	6.33	-	-	42	5		8.40	3-26	-	-	-	
G.P.Burnett	Well	1883/84	1886/87	2	4	-	11	8*	9.00	-	-								2	
	Well	1987/88	1992/93	44	80	13	2029	32	30.28	-	12	46	1		46.00	1-46	-	-	30	
N.S.H.Burnette	ND	1993/94	1994/95	12	22	1	766	203*	36.47	1	4								11	
J.C.Burns	Well	1987/88	1994/95	60	109	15	2960	131	31.48	2	18	46	1		46.00	1-46	-	-	45	
K.J.Burns	Well	1940/41	1945/46	5	10	0	231	55	23.10	-	1								2	
	Well	1914/15		1	4	-	15	7*	5.00	-	-								3	
M.Burns	Otago	1980/81	1991/92	57	98	6	2699	136	29.33	3	16	50	0		-	-	-	-	30	
R.C.Burns	All	1980/81	1991/92	58	100	6	2729	136	29.03	3	16	50	0		-	-	-	-	30	
T.A.Burns	Well	2006/07	2009/10	13	16	5	48	8	4.36	-	-	894	32		27.93	4-41	-	-	4	
J.T.Burrows	Cant	1928/29	1933/34	15	23	5	176	27	9.77	-	-								14	17
R.D.Burson	ND	1964/65		2	2	0	9	7	4.50	-	-								-	
	Cant	1926/27	1932/33	9	12	0	36	14*	-	-	-	136	5		27.20	3-16	-	-	4	
D.T.A.Burt	Cant	1997/98	2007/08	17	27	12	263	41*	15.47	-	-	684	31		22.06	4-24	-	-	4	
J.R.Burt	All	1997/98	2007/08	18	29	11	292	41*	16.22	-	-	1600	42		38.09	6-35	1	-	7	
H.E.L.Burton	Otago	1924/25			3	2	7	7	3.50	-	-	1670	47		35.53	6-35	1	-	7	
	Otago	1901/02	1908/09	3	4	0	72	27	18.00	-	-								2	
	Well	1909/10	1921/22	22	39	3	825	79	22.91	-	6	2	0		-	-	-	-	2	
H.G.E.L.Burton	Auck	1922/23	1923/24	5	9	0	299	65	33.22	-	1	4	0		-	-	-	-	4	
J.E.L.Burton	All	1909/10	1923/24	27	48	3	1124	79	24.97	-	7	6	0		-	-	-	-	6	
	All	1893/94	1897/98	7	10	1	200	63	22.22	-	1								6	
W.Burton	Well	1946/47		2	2	0	37	36	18.50	-	-								4	
J.W.Burtt	All	1946/47	1949/50	4	7	0	73	36	10.42	-	-	22	0		-	-	-	-	1	
	All	1940/41		1	2	0	10	7	5.00	-	-								-	
L.M.Burtt	Cant	1965/66	1972/73	40	66	6	1785	130*	29.75	1	8	1135	24		47.29	4-49	-	-	17	
N.V.Burtt	CD	1973/74	1974/75	10	19	1	363	77	20.16	-	2	82	2		41.00	2-21	-	-	2	
	All	1964/65	1974/75	54	91	8	2378	130*	28.65	1	11	1398	27		51.77	4-49	-	-	23	
T.B.Burtt	Cant	2006/07	2009/10	24	28	9	212	29*	11.15	-	-	2509	76		33.01	6-108	5	-	6	
	Cant	1937/38	1947/48	7	10	2	44	18	5.50	-	-	682	16		42.62	4-69	-	-	2	
B.J.Bush	All	1937/38	1948/49	9	14	4	59	18	5.90	-	-	827	22		37.59	4-69	-	-	3	
	Cant	1943/44	1954/55	46	75	20	1038	55	18.87	-	3	4991	241		20.70	8-35	16	3	34	
	All	1943/44	1954/55	84	124	29	1644	68*	17.30	-	4	9054	408		22.19	8-35	29	5	53	
	Cant	1887/88		1	2	1	10	6*	10.00	-	-	59	8		7.37	6-40	1	-	1	

		First	Last	M	I	NO	Runs	HS	Avg	100	50	Runs	Wkts	OW	Avg	Best	5i	10m	ct	st
R.G.Bush	Auck	1932/33	1934/35	9	15	1	317	55	22.64	-	1	588	22		26.72	4-35	-	-	5	-
W.E.Bush	All	1932/33	1936/37	10	17	1	319	55	19.93	-	1	641	25		25.64	4-35	-	-	5	-
	Auck	1910/11		1	1	0	4	4	4.00	-	-	5	0		-	-	-	-	-	-
F.Butler	Cant	1914/15		1	1	0	4	4	4.00	-	-								-	-
	All	1914/15	1923/24	4	7	0	183	54	26.14	-	1								3	-
I.G.Butler	ND	2001/02	2004/05	16	19	11	159	52*	19.87	-	-	1415	49		28.87	5-44	1	-	3	-
	Otago	2008/09	2009/10	6	10	2	159	45	19.87	-	-	484	13		37.23	2-18	-	-	2	-
	All	2001/02	2009/10	43	56	18	648	68	17.05	-	2	3989	126		31.65	6-46	2	-	11	-
K.O.Butler	Auck	1953/54		1	1	1	24	24	-	-	-	35	0		-	-	-	-	-	-
L.C.Butler	Well	1951/52	1967/68	50	80	12	1324	101*	19.47	1	6	2827	117		24.16	8-50	2	1	47	-
	All	1951/52	1967/68	53	85	12	1396	101*	19.12	1	6	2914	120		24.28	8-50	2	1	47	-
W.P.Butler	Otago	1901/02		1	1	0	2	2	2.00	-	-								-	-
G.L.Butlin	Otago	1889/90		1	2	1	4	2	2.00	-	-	33	3		11.00	3-23	-	-	12	-
L.A.Butterfield	Cant	1934/35	1945/46	15	24	3	475	82	22.61	-	2	645	29		22.24	5-24	3	-	12	-
	All	1934/35	1945/46	18	29	3	589	82	22.65	-	3	747	38		19.65	5-9	3	-	13	-
T.Butterworth	Otago	1866/67		1	1	0	2	5*	-	-	-								-	-
	All	1857/58	1866/67	3	4	1	35	24	11.66	-	-								1	-
F.W.A.Byerley	Auck	1931/32		1	2	0	85	77	42.50	-	1								-	-
C.Cachopa	Auck	2004/05	2006/07	9	12	1	240	69	20.00	-	1	5	0		-	-	-	-	4	-
J.B.Cain	Auck	1994/95		8	10	1	116	30	12.88	-	-								23	-
A.E.Cairns	Otago	1867/68	1870/71	3	5	0	39	13*	9.75	-	-	120	8		15.00	3-68	-	-	1	-
B.L.Cairns	CD	1972/73	1975/76	17	31	5	711	92	27.34	-	6	1513	58		26.08	5-54	3	-	4	-
	Otago	1976/77	1979/80	33	51	4	996	110	21.19	-	6	2925	119		24.57	8-46	8	3	26	-
	ND	1981/82	1984/85	17	31	2	769	89	26.51	-	6	1252	63		19.87	6-19	3	-	8	-
	All	1971/72	1988	148	226	25	4165	110	20.72	1	23	12544	473		26.52	8-46	24	5	89	-
C.L.Cairns	ND	1988/89	2005/06	8	10	2	206	79	25.75	-	-	730	20		36.50	3-20	-	-	6	-
	Cant	1990/91	2005/06	29	37	5	948	158	29.62	1	10	2240	100		22.40	7-34	3	-	8	-
	All	1988		217	341	38	10702		35.32	13	71	18322	647		28.31	8-47	30	6	78	2
H.W.Cairns	Otago	1864/65	1869/70	4	7	0	50	25	7.14	-	-	0	1		0.00	1-0	-	-	4	-
M.G.Cairns	Auck	2001/02		1	1	0	1	1	1.00	-	-								-	-
E.T.T.Cakobau	Auck	1930/31		1	1	0	7	7	7.00	-	-								1	-
	All	1930/31	1947/48	3	5	1	89	47*	22.25	-	-	205	11		18.63	5-72	1	-	2	-
J.W.Calder	All	1971/72		2	2	0	40	26	20.00	-	-	31	0		-	-	-	-	-	-
D.J.Calkin	CD	1969/70		4	5	0	24	15	4.80	-	-								5	-
R.J.Calland	ND	1977/78		1	2	1	13	8*	13.00	-	-	41	0		-	-	-	-	1	-
S.T.Callaway	Cant	1900/01	1906/07	17	32	1	563	65	18.16	-	3	1912	145		13.18	8-33	17	8	17	-
	All	1888/89	1906/07	62	112	8	1747	86	16.79	-	10	5465	320		17.07	8-33	33	12	48	-
W.Calvert	Cant	1865/66	1867/68	2	4	0	4	3	1.00	-	-								1	-
D.S.Cameron	Otago	1930/31		1	2	1	6	6	6.00	-	-	31	1		31.00	1-20	-	-	-	-
D.A.Cameron	Well	1929/30	1932/33	4	8	0	158	71	19.75	-	1								2	-
E.H.J.Cameron	Otago	1953/54	1954/55	5	8	4	82	21	20.50	-	-	204	10		20.40	3-30	-	-	2	-
F.J.Cameron	Otago	1952/53	1966/67	68	105	43	716	43	11.54	-	-	5204	258		20.17	6-21	9	-	17	-
	All	1952/53	1966/67	119	176	92	993	43	11.82	-	-	9658	447		21.60	7-27	21	-	26	-
H.R.Cameron	Otago	1939/40		1	2	1	44	26	22.00	-	-								-	-
J.N.A.Cameron	Otago	1917/18		1	1	0	3	3	3.00	-	-								1	-
S.M.Cameron	Cant	1940/41	1955/56	5	6	2	56	29*	14.00	-	-	376	14		26.85	4-47	-	-	-	-

		First	Last	M	I	NO	Runs	HS	Avg	100	50	Runs	Wkts	OW	Avg	Best	5i	10m	ct	st
R.H.J.Camm	Sland	1919/20	1920/21	2	4	0	23	12	5.75	-	-	626	22		28.45	6-93	2	-	8	
J.W.Cammish	Auck	1950/51		5	9	3	31	7*	5.16	-	-	781	25		31.24	6-93	2	-	8	
C.Campbell	All	1950/51	1954	7	10	3	31	7*	4.42	-	-								8	
	HB	1920/21		2	1	0	0	0*	-	-	-								2	
	All	1920/21	1921/22	2	2	1	1	1	1.00	-	-								2	
J.Campbell	Otago	1868/69		1	2	0	17	11	8.50	-	-									
K.O.Campbell	Otago	1963/64	1978/79	61	107	14	2613	111	28.09	3	17	871	30		29.03	5-27	1	-	52	2
	All	1963/64	1978/79	73	128	18	2857	111	25.97	3	17	1071	30		35.70	5-27	1	-	70	2
P.A.Campbell	Otago	1989/90	1994/95	3	6	1	89	37	17.80	-	-	9	1		9.00	1-9	-	-	2	
T.T.Campbell	Tara	1894/95		1	2	0	2	2	1.00	-	-								1	
F.F.Cane	HB	1920/21		2	4	0	62	33	15.50	-	-									
R.B.Canney	Nel	1877/78		1	2	0	22	15	11.00	-	-								1	
D.Canning	HB	1893/94	1899/00	8	15	2	77	21	5.92	-	-								4	3
T.K.Canning	Auck	1999/00	2006/07	56	82	10	2067	115	28.70	3	7	4822	196		24.60	6-44	6	-	27	
	All	1998/99	2006/07	61	88	10	2155	115	27.62	3	8	5042	206		24.47	6-44	6	-	29	
A.Cant	Cant	1890/91	1900/01	2	4	1	41	30*	13.66	-	-								-	
J.R.Capstick	Well	1946/47		2	6	0	104	44	17.33	-	-	5	0		-	-	-	-	-	
A.Cargill	Otago	1876/77	1883/84	4	7	0	51	20	7.28	-	-	6	2		3.00	2-6	-	-	-	
T.A.Carlton	Cant	1909/10	1914/15	18	31	0	436	63	18.16	-	2	1099	60		18.31	6-42	3	1	11	
	Otago	1920/21	1921/22	5	10	0	139	33	13.90	-	-	544	27		20.14	5-39	2	-	5	
	All	1909/10	1931/32	60	103	28	1153	63	15.37	-	2	4553	185		24.61	6-42	3	2	48	
W.Carlton	Auck	1899/00		1	2	0	10	9	5.00	-	-	15	2		7.50	2-7	-	-	1	
	Cant	1909/10	1911/12	11	22	3	429	88*	22.57	-	3	356	17		20.94	3-17	-	-	4	
	All	1898/99	1913/14	19	38	7	727	88*	23.45	-	6	557	27		20.62	3-17	-	-	11	
R.M.Carrington	Cant	1953/54		5	7	0	45	31	9.00	-	-	192	7		27.42	4-9	-	-	2	
S.M.Carrington	ND	1981/82	1986/87	38	51	16	379	53	10.82	-	1	2859	96		29.78	5-69	1	-	15	
	All	1981/82	1986/87	41	54	16	395	53	10.39	-	1	3109	102		30.48	5-69	1	-	16	
J.R.Carson	Auck	1963/64	1973/74	14	24	2	475	62	21.59	-	3	152	3		50.66	1-15	-	-	10	
	ND	1967/68	1968/69	10	19	0	406	77	21.36	-	3	253	4		63.25	2-39	-	-	11	
	All	1963/64	1973/74	24	43	2	881	77	21.48	-	6	405	7		57.85	2-39	-	-	21	
W.Carson	Otago	1884/85	1887/88	4	8	1	73	34	10.42	-	-	148	15		9.86	6-51	2	-	4	
W.N.Carson	Auck	1936/37	1939/40	9	11	1	821	290	82.10	4	-	390	18		21.66	3-22	-	-	10	
	All	1936/37	1939/40	31	51	0	1535	290	34.88	4	3	752	35		21.48	4-20	-	-	27	
E.C.Carston	Cant	1946/47		2	3	2	4	4*	4.00	-	-	80	0		-	-	-	-	-	
R.D.Carswell	ND	1957/58		1	1	0	8	8	8.00	-	-								1	
R.M.Carter	Cant	1982/83	1984/85	9	18	1	254	45	14.94	-	1	74	1		74.00	1-12	-	-	6	
	All	1978	1984/85	60	85	16	1112	79	16.11	-	1	1566	39		40.15	4-27	-	-	35	
A.G.Cartwright	Otago	1961/62	1963/64	6	10	1	48	15	5.33	-	-	388	11		35.27	3-27	-	-	2	
L.F.Casey	Otago	1920/21	1922/23	6	12	3	91	25*	10.11	-	-	450	16		28.12	4-51	-	-	2	
W.A.Cate	Well	1908/09	1922/23	4	7	2	41	11	8.20	-	-								6	
	All	1908/09	1922/23	5	9	2	43	11	6.14	-	-								4	
S.B.Cater	Well	1974/75	1982/83	30	38	4	318	40	9.35	-	-	1791	68		26.33	6-32	2	-	13	
C.H.Cato	HB	1891/92	1907/08	26	46	2	667	56	15.15	-	1	145	4		36.25	2-18	-	-	8	
V.G.Cavanagh	Otago	1927/28	1938/39	27	52	0	1271	89	24.44	-	9	35	0		-	-	-	-	9	

165

		First	Last	M	I	NO	Runs	HS	Avg	100	50	Runs	Wkts	OW	Avg	Best	5i	10m	ct	st
H.B.Cave	Well	1945/46	1949/50	11	21	2	133	17	7.00			1016	40		25.40	6-44	5	1	4	
	CD	1950/51	1958/59	37	61	12	1210	118	24.69	2	3	2962	150		19.74	7-31	7	1	27	
	All	1945/46	1958/59	117	175	39	2187	118	16.08	2	3	8664	362		23.93	7-31	13	1	70	
E.R.Caygill	Cant	1910/11	1913/14	11	21	0	468	87	22.28		1								8	
D.R.Cederman	CD	2004/05		1	2	0	5	4	2.50											
B.W.Cederwall	Well	1973/74	1983/84	52	76	15	1158	94	18.98		7	2578	107		24.09	6-42	3		41	
G.N.Cederwall	Well	1978/79	1990/91	35	52	11	794	68	19.36		2	2488	73		34.08	7-97	1		14	
C.S.Chadwick	Otago	1912/13	1924/25	16	30	6	235	71*	9.79		1								17	
L.N.Chadwick	Otago	1919/20		2	3	0	42	28	14.00										1	
R.J.M.Chadwick	HB	1904/05		1	2	0	3	3	1.50											
	All	1913/14		1	2	2	0	0	0.00			42	0							
R.S.Challies	Well	1904/05	1913/14	2	4	0	3	3	0.75			35	1		35.00	1-26			2	
	CD	1946/47	1955/56	9	15	7	40	11*	5.00			77	1		77.00	1-26			2	
	All	1951/52	1954/55	7	9	3	58	15	9.66			836	21		39.80	6-112	1		4	
M.C.Chamberlain	Cant	1946/47	1955/56	17	25	10	98	15	6.53			630	22		28.63	5-52	2		4	
K.S.Chambers	Cant	1988/89		1	1	0	20	20*				1669	45		37.08	6-112	2		6	
S.P.Chan	Cant	1973/74		1	2	1	0	0	0.00			89	3		29.66	3-65				
	Well	2006/07	2009/10	2	2	0	35	35	17.50			52	1		52.00	1-33			1	
	All	2009/10		1	1	0	17	11	8.50			215	6		35.83	3-58			1	
P.J.B.Chandler	All	2006/07	2009/10	3	4	0	52	35	13.00			74	0							
	Cant	1994/95	2001/02	26	45	6	1075	177	27.56	2	2	289	6		48.16	3-58			9	
A.T.Chapman	Cant	1994/95	2001/02	31	53	7	1296	177	28.17	2	3								20	
H.Chapman	Well	1881/82	1891/92	6	12	4	41	12	5.12			315	19		16.57	6-49	1		3	
J.E.Chapman	Well	1943/44	1944/45	5	10	2	191	49	23.87		1	188	4		47.00	1-16			2	
M.Chapman	Otago	1885/86	1886/87	3	5	1	44	36	11.00										3	
M.E.Chapple	Cant	1864/65	1867/68	3	5	1	21	12	5.25										1	
	Cant	1949/50	1960/61	44	79	9	2364	165	33.77	3	14	1562	66		23.66	5-24	3		23	
	CD	1950/51	1965/66	29	44	3	1181	92	28.80	2	8	1398	59		23.69	5-34	1		14	
	All	1949/50	1971/72	119	201	16	5344	165	28.88	4	31	3559	142		25.06	5-24	4		67	
L.A.Charles	HB	1919/20		1	1	0	24	23	12.00										2	
E.J.Chatfield	Well	1973/74	1989/90	84	67	32	354	24*	10.11		1	7531	403		18.68	8-24	23	7	36	
	All	1973/74	1989/90	157	135	71	582	24*	9.09			13429	587		22.87	8-24	27	8	51	
R.W.H.Cherry	Otago	1919/20	1931/32	23	43	3	792	123*	19.80	1	2								3	
V.J.T.Chettleburgh	Otago	1932/33	1940/41	19	34	6	733	84	26.17	1	2	414	11		37.63	2-41			12	
E.L.Child	Auck	1953/54		5	9	1	155	41	19.37			458	18		25.44	5-37	2		3	
	ND	1958/59		3	4	0	75	41	18.75			117	3		39.00	2-23			2	
	All	1953/54	1958/59	8	13	1	230	41	19.16			575	21		27.38	5-37	2		5	
M.J.Child	ND	1977/78	1986/87	22	36	9	527	66*	19.51		1	1538	57		26.98	7-59	1		14	
I.H.Ching	CD	1950/51		1	1	0	173	47	13.30										7	
W.E.Chisholm	Well	1885/86	1955/56	8	14	1	0	0	0.00											
W.J.R.Christopherson	Well	1926/27		1	2	1	51	46	51.00		1									
B.Church	Otago	1871/72		1	2	0	3	2*	3.00										1	
		First	Last	M	I	NO	Runs	HS	Avg	100	50	Runs	Wkts	OW	Avg	Best	5i	10m	ct	st
G.A.Churchill	All	1942/43		1	1	0	2	2	1.00											
D.P.Claffey	Otago	1888/89	1889/90	2	4	1	31	19*	10.33			89	1		89.00	1-79			1	
C.G.Clark	Auck	1913/14		3	6	2	60	15*	15.00			341	11		31.00	5-108	1		1	

Name	Team	Years														
C.R.Clark	Cant	1895/96	9	14	3	195	61*	17.72	-	121	3	40.33	1-16	-	-	6
G.H.Clark	Otago	1872/73	8	15	2	125	30	9.61	-						-	3
J.B.Clark	Otago	1933/34	3	5	1	63	25	15.75	-						-	5
L.A.Clark	Well	1955/56	14	21	6	291	68*	19.40	-	948	40	23.70	5-52	2	-	7
	Otago	1958/59	10	17	2	201	38*	13.40	-	431	18	23.94	3-71	-	-	10
	Auck	1959/60	12	19	4	215	36	14.33	-	704	32	22.00	6-29	1	-	4
	All	1955/56 1961/62	37	58	12	720	68*	15.65	-	2125	91	23.35	6-29	3	-	22
L.G.Clark	Otago	1929/30	2	4	3	5	2*	5.00	-						-	2
M.J.Clark	Auck	1992/93 1996/97	5	8	0	133	64	16.62	-	12	1	12.00	1-5	-	-	2
	Auck	1990/91	6	10	0	158	64	15.80	-	12	1	12.00	1-5	-	-	2
	All	1996/97		2	0	14	10	7.00	-						-	4
T.L.Clark	Auck	1931/32	1	2	0	14	10	7.00	-							
A.E.Clarke	Otago	1893/94 1898/99	13	24	1	493	64	21.43	-	117	5	23.40	2-15	-	-	6
	Well	1900/01 1901/02	3	5	0	132	76	26.40	-	67	7	9.57	4-25	-	-	1
	All	1889/90 1901/02	25	44	1	808	76	18.79	-	223	14	15.92	4-25	-	-	12
D.B.Clarke	Auck	1950/51 1954/55	14	27	4	152	25*	8.44	-	1452	66	22.00	5-47	2	-	4
	ND	1956/57 1962/63	11	19	0	212	47	13.25	-	950	49	19.38	8-37	2	-	5
	All	1950/51 1962/63	27	48	9	369	47	10.54	-	2474	117	21.14	8-37	4	1	9
D.S.Clarke	ND	1957/58 1960/61	6	11	3	107	28	13.37	-						-	3
W.V.Clarke	HB	1913/14	1	2	0	25	23	12.50	-	48	1	48.00	1-29	-	-	-
C.Clayforth	Auck	1873/74	2	4	0	34	19	8.50	-							
D.L.J.Clayton	Auck	1894/95 1902/03	8	14	2	170	21*	14.16	-	248	14	17.71	6-37	1	-	4
F.Clayton	Cant	1893/94	2	3	0	7	4	2.33	-						-	1
F.D.Clayton	Otago	1892/93 1896/97	6	6	0	69	28	13.80	-	10	0	-	-	-	-	3
O.C.Cleal	Auck	1940/41 1951/52	26	46	4	1599	98	38.07	-	675	19	35.52	3-32	-	-	24
	All	1940/41 1951/52	27	48	4	1603	98	36.43	11	675	19	35.52	3-32	-	-	26
R.H.Cleave	Auck	1933/34 1944/45	4	7	1	152	77*	25.33	11						-	1
D.C.Cleverley	Auck	1930/31	27	38	9	133	16*	4.58	1	2700	98	27.55	8-75	3	-	14
	CD	1952/53	1	1	1	7	7*	-	-	49	1	49.00	1-14	-	-	-
	All	1930/31 1952/53	30	43	13	159	16*	5.30	1	2879	99	29.08	8-75	3	-	14
R.J.Coates	Auck	1917/18 1923/24	10	16	4	60	12	5.00	-	816	25	32.64	5-56	1	-	4
L.T.Cobcroft	Cant	1897/98 1899/00	8	14	0	371	75	26.50	3	148	12	12.33	6-23	-	-	10
	Well	1906/07 1909/10	14	14	0	256	47	18.28	-	448	22	20.36	5-87	-	-	8
	All	1895/96 1909/10	23	42	2	868	85*	21.70	5	702	37	18.97	6-23	2	-	18
A.P.Cobden	Cant	1935/36	3	6	0	184	79	30.66	1	61	2	30.50	2-40	-	-	3
C.Cockburn	Well	1887/88	1	2	0	12	10	6.00	-							
W.E.Cockcroft	Sland	1914/15	2	4	1	41	18*	13.66	-						-	3
L.Cohen	Cant	1890/91	1	2	0	26	20	13.00	-						-	1
N.Cohen	HB	1919/20	1	2	1	11	11*	11.00	-						-	-
E.C.Cole	Tara	1896/97	1	1	0	20	20	20.00	-	48	6	8.00	4-27	-	-	1
D.D.Coleman	Auck	1948/49 1957/58	30	54	1	1173	87	22.13	7	20	0	-	-	-	-	14
	All	1948/49 1957/58	31	56	1	1212	87	22.03	7	20	0	-	-	-	-	14
A.W.Coles	Nel	1873/74 1875/76	2	4	2	23	12*	11.50	-	18	4	4.50	3-5	-	-	1
M.J.Coles	Well	1966/67 1975/76	29	32	11	127	31	6.04	-	2324	76	30.57	5-22	2	-	3
	All	1965/66 1975/76	32	37	12	168	31	6.72	-	2414	79	30.55	5-22	2	-	3
B.D.Coley	Well	1971/72	3	5	1	47	27	11.75	-						-	2
A.R.Collier	ND	1976/77	3	3	0	25	17	8.33	-	163	3	54.33	1-8	-	-	2

		First	Last	M	I	NO	Runs	HS	Avg	100	50	Runs	Wkts	OW	Avg	Best	5i	10m	ct	st
R.O.Collinge	CD	1963/64	1969/70	21	26	12	208	57	14.85	-	1	1376	61		22.55	7-56	2	-	11	
	Well	1967/68	1974/75	28	29	5	355	45	14.79	-	-	2099	120		17.49	8-64	9	3	9	
	ND	1975/76	1977/78	19	18	4	141	39	10.07	-	-	1665	77		21.62	6-32	5	1	4	
	All	1963/64	1978	163	178	50	1848	68*	14.43	-	4	12793	524		24.41	8-64	22	4	57	
A.E.Collins	Cant	1977/78		1	2	0	34	18	17.00	-	-								-	
D.C.Collins	Well	1905/06	1926/27	20	35	1	1184	172	34.82	4	3	559	16		34.93	4-47	-	-	13	
	All	1905/06	1926/27	53	96	8	2604	172	29.59	6	9	870	32		27.18	4-10	-	-	33	
J.U.Collins	Nel	1884/85		1	2	0	19	19	9.50	-	-								-	
K.I.Collins	Cant	1892/93	1895/96	5	9	1	58	26	9.66	-	-	43	1		43.00	1-10	-	-	1	
W.E.Collins	All	1884/85	1895/96	6	9	1	77	26	9.62	-	-	43	1		43.00	1-10	-	-	1	
E.T.Collinson	Cant	1978/79		1	1	1	0	0	0.00	-	-								3	
I.A.Colquhoun	Well	1887/88	1888/89	2	2	0	52	42	26.00	-	-								-	2
	Otago	1868/69	1885/86	16	29	3	359	59	13.80	-	1	108	8		13.50	5-69	1	-	7	2
	CD	1953/54	1963/64	53	79	31	730	44*	15.20	-	-								102	28
	All	1953/54	1963/64	57	85	33	768	44*	14.76	-	-								108	28
H.F.W.Colson	Auck	1877/78		1	2	0	0	0	0.00	-	-								-	1
P.G.Coman	Cant	1968/69	1977/78	44	78	4	2603	104	35.17	2	18	83	1		83.00	1-3	-	-	18	
	All	1962/63	1977/78	46	82	4	2635	104	33.78	2	18	83	1		83.00	1-3	-	-	20	
J.W.Condliffe	Otago	1909/10	1913/14	8	15	2	103	34	7.92	-	-								12	4
	Well	1917/18	1922/23	17	28	1	422	62	15.62	-	1								14	14
	All	1909/10	1924/25	30	52	3	610	62	12.44	-	1								32	20
C.J.Coney	Well	1966/67		1	2	0	4	4	2.00	-	-	29	2		14.50	2-29	-	-	-	
J.V.Coney	All	1965/66	1966/67	2	4	0	19	13	4.75	-	-	61	3		20.33	2-29	-	-	2	
	Well	1971/72	1986/87	74	126	21	3251	120*	30.96	4	16	1707	62		27.53	6-17	1	-	95	
	All	1970/71	1986/87	165	272	48	7872	174*	35.14	8	47	3460	111		31.17	6-17	1	-	192	
B.E.Congdon	CD	1960/61	1970/71	55	93	8	2807	202*	33.02	3	13	304	9		33.77	3-37	-	-	58	
	Well	1971/72		5	9	0	272	89	30.22	-	2	66	4		16.50	2-44	-	-	5	
	Otago	1972/73	1973/74	6	10	1	531	173*	59.00	2	3	201	6		33.50	1-5	-	-	4	
	All	1974/75	1977/78	26	48	1	1354	110*	31.48	2	8	1113	41		27.14	6-42	2	-	19	
	All	1960/61	1978	241	416	40	13101	202*	34.84	23	68	6125	204		30.02	6-42	4	1	201	
T.W.C.Connell	Well	1901/02		2	3	1	7	4	3.50	-	-	109	5		21.80	4-65	-	-	1	
P.Connelly	All	1896/97		3	4	0	9	4	3.00	-	-	133	5		26.60	4-65	-	-	1	
N.Conradi	Well	1908/09		2	3	0	31	16	10.33	-	-	222	14		15.85	6-103	2	-	5	
J.Conway	Otago	1917/18	1925/26	10	18	0	233	39	12.94	-	-	231	6		38.50	2-21	-	-	1	
	Otago	1879/80		1	2	0	63	49	31.50	-	1	44	0		-	-	-	-	5	
A.J.Cook	All	1861/62	1879/80	10	17	3	156	49	11.14	-	-	424	32		13.25	6-42	3	-	9	
	Well	1955/56	1956/57	3	5	2	45	31*	22.50	-	-	30	0		-	-	-	-	2	
R.F.Cook	Cant	1947/48	1948/49	3	2	1	9	9	9.00	-	-	318	8		39.75	4-41	-	-	2	
	All	1942/43	1948/49	4	4	2	12	9	6.00	-	-	376	9		41.77	4-41	-	-	2	
F.H.Cooke	Otago	1879/80	1884/85	7	13	2	48	16*	4.36	-	-	567	61		9.29	9-73	6	3	4	
	Nel	1885/86	1888/89	4	6	0	58	34	9.66	-	-	216	22		9.81	5-27	1	-	4	
	All	1879/80	1888/89	11	19	2	106	34	6.23	-	-	783	83		9.43	9-73	7	3	8	
W.A.Cooke	Cant	1891/92		2	4	1	22	12*	7.33	-	-	4	0		-	-	-	-	-	
B.G.Cooper	ND	1980/81	1994/95	62	110	4	2982	116*	28.13	4	18	793	26		30.50	5-40	1	-	38	
D.M.Cooper	CD	1993/94	1996/97	4	7	1	148	48	24.66	-	-	65	1		65.00	1-34	-	-	-	
I.W.Cooper	Auck	1924/25	1927/28	13	24	5	580	80	30.52	-	4	583	6		97.16	1-18	-	-	3	

		First	Last	M	I	NO	Runs	HS	Avg	100	50	Runs	Wkts	OW	Avg	Best	5i	10m	ct	st
W.H.Cooper	Auck	1941/42	1943/44	3	5	1	99	52	24.75	-	1	56	1	-	56.00	1-3	-	-	1	-
C.C.Corfe	Cant	1871/72	1883/84	8	12	0	235	88	19.58	-	1	47	5	-	9.40	5-22	1	-	2	-
C.J.Cornelius	Cant	2001/02	2004/05	3	6	0	36	19*	7.20	-	-	210	3	-	70.00	3-67	-	-	1	-
W.A.Cornelius	Cant	2000/01	2004/05	14	19	8	58	14*	5.27	-	-	1137	40	-	28.42	7-53	3	1	6	-
C.A.Cornish	Well	1874/75		1	2	1	5	5*	5.00	-	-									
A.J.Cotterill	Cant	1865/66	1873/74	10	17	0	258	72	15.17	-	1								4	
A.K.Cotterill	HB	1901/02		3	5	1	25	17*	6.25	-	-									
B.W.Cotterill	HB	1901/02	1908/09	6	11	1	78	20	7.80	-	-	237	11	-	21.54	4-23	-	-	1	-
C.N.Cotterill	HB	1893/94		1	1	0	4	4	4.00	-	-									
E.J.Cotterill	Cant	1880/81	1889/90	6	8	2	211	75*	35.16	-	1								3	
	Auck	1895/96		1	2	0	15	8	7.50	-	-									
	All	1880/81	1895/96	7	10	2	226	75*	28.25	-	1								3	
G.R.Cotterill	HB	1899/00		2	2	0	11	8	5.50	-	-	41	2	-	20.50	2-41	-	-	1	-
H.Cotterill	Cant	1873/74	1884/85	3	6	0	13	6	2.16	-	-								-	
W.J.Cotterill	Cant	1881/82	1893/94	13	23	1	336	74*	15.27	-	1								6	
H.E.Cotton	Auck	1873/74	1877/78	3	6	2	38	14*	19.00	-	-	7	0	-	-	-	-	-	1	-
G.G.Coull	Cant	1954/55	1961/62	8	15	0	162	45	10.80	-	-	148	7	-	21.14	4-58	-	-	4	-
R.Coulstock	Otago	1863/64		1	2	0	2	2	1.00	-	-								-	
R.N.Couper	Otago	1855/56	1863/64	3	6	0	24	16	4.00	-	-	30	3	-	10.00	3-30	-	-	1	-
R.J.M.Coupland	All	1951/52		3	6	1	89	36	17.80	-	-	130	4	-	32.50	3-66	-	-	2	-
R.W.Coupland	Otago	1942/43		1	2	0	17	10	8.50	-	-								1	
H.D.Coutts	Tara	1930/31	1932/33	7	12	1	165	32*	15.00	-	-	282	14	-	20.14	4-41	-	-	5	-
P.J.C.Coutts	CD	1882/83	1891/92	3	6	0	22	10	3.66	-	-	3	1	-	3.00	1-3	-	-	1	-
	Well	1958/59	1972/73	24	42	0	1092	152	28.00	3	3	5	0	-	-	-	-	-	14	-
	All	1969/70		5	10	0	287	102	28.70	1	1	14	0	-	-	-	-	-	7	-
J.Cowie	Auck	1958/59	1972/73	29	52	3	1379	152	28.14	4	4	19	0	-	-	-	-	-	21	-
	All	1932/33	1949/50	34	43	11	349	54	10.90	-	1	3378	154	-	21.93	6-44	7	1	15	-
W.P.Cowlishaw	All	1932/33	1949/50	86	104	29	762	54	10.16	-	1	8001	359	-	22.28	6-3	20	-	35	-
A.Cox	Cant	1864/65		1	2	1	16	12*	16.00	-	-	6	3	-	2.00	3-3	-	-	1	-
K.F.S.Cox	Cant	1924/25	1926/27	5	8	0	396	204	49.50	1	2								2	
R.D.Cox	Otago	1933/34		1	2	0	14	8	7.00	-	-								-	
T.A.Cox	All	1971/72		4	2	2	0	0	0.00	-	-	65	3	-	21.66	3-65	0	0	1	-
S.W.G.Coxon	Well	1883/84	1886/87	4	7	0	38	19	5.42	-	-	45	6	-	7.50	4-12	-	-	2	-
T.C.Crabb	Auck	1884/85		3	6	0	105	30	17.50	-	-								4	
C.A.Crafar	CD	1997/98		2	4	1	49	24	16.33	-	-								4	
E.D.Craik	CD	1986/87		1	0	0						76	0	-	-	-	-	-	1	-
A.A.Cramond	Otago	1999/00		1	2	1	20	18	20.00	-	-	51	5	-	10.20	4-25	-	-	-	-
C.G.Crawford	Cant	1904/05		1	2	0	11	9	5.50	-	-								1	
	All	1920/21	1931/32	13	24	0	513	70	21.37	-	2								4	
F.R.Crawford	Well	1920/21	1931/32	15	28	2	551	70	21.19	-	2	231	5	-	46.20	2-37	-	-	5	-
	All	1937/38	1947/48	10	19	0	380	55	20.00	-	3	284	6	-	47.33	2-37	-	-	5	-
J.N.Crawford	Otago	1937/38	1947/48	12	23	1	459	55	20.86	-	3	388	30	-	12.93	6-37	4	-	8	-
	Well	1914/15		4	7	2	337	178*	67.40	1	2	242	16	-	15.12	5-47	3	-	-	-
	All	1917/18	1921	2	3	2	156	110	78.00	1	-								2	
	All	1904	1921	210	325	34	9488	232	32.60	15	43	16842	815	-	20.66	8-24	57	12	162	-

169

Name	Team	First	Last	M	I	NO	Runs	HS	Avg	100	50	Runs	Wkts	OW	Avg	Best	5i	10m	ct	st
E.E.Crawshaw	Cant	1907/08	1910/11	7	14	3	56	26	5.09	-	-	355	12		29.58	2-20	-	-	11	
W.J.Crawshaw	All	1907/08	1913/14	8	16	3	73	26	5.61	-	-	382	13		29.38	2-20	-	-	11	
	Otago	1877/78	1883/84	6	12	0	97	39	8.08	-	-								4	
	Cant	1885/86	1886/87	2	3	0	65	25	21.66	-	-								3	
	Well	1891/92		2	4	1	87	40	29.00	-	-								2	
	Tara	1896/97	1897/98	3	5	0	144	106	28.80	1	-								1	
	All	1877/78	1897/98	13	24	1	393	106	17.08	1	1								10	
M.C.Creagh	Otago	1866/67		1	1	0	1	1	1.00	-	-								-	
T.M.Creed	HB	1910/11	1913/14	5	10	0	224	82	22.40	-	1	204	11		18.54	3-37	-	-	1	
T.E.Creeks	Well	1886/87		1	2	0	0	0	0.00	-	-	37	4		9.25	3-18	-	-	-	
D.B.Crene	ND	1966/67		2	4	3	8	5*	8.00	-	-	135	5		27.00	4-67	-	-	1	
A.E.Cresswell	Well	1948/49	1949/50	3	10	5	30	15	6.00	-	-	466	25		18.64	5-32	2	-	5	
	CD	1950/51	1951/52	5	9	3	64	18	10.66	-	-	319	10		31.90	4-42	-	-	1	
	All	1948/49	1951/52	13	21	9	96	18	8.00	-	-	857	38		22.55	5-32	2	-	7	
G.F.Cresswell	Well	1949/50		3	4	2	7	5	3.50	-	-	204	12		17.00	3-32	-	-	2	
	CD	1950/51	1954/55	8	10	3	18	6	2.57	-	-	642	32		20.06	5-31	3	-	11	
	All	1948/49	1954/55	33	36	19	89	12*	5.23	-	-	2794	124		22.53	8-100	8	1	11	
L.M.Crocker	ND	1982/83	1988/89	54	100	3	2663	126	27.45	2	14	12	0		-	-	-	-	40	
S.J.Croft	Auck	2008/09		8	10	1	330	59	36.66	-	2	248	4		62.00	2-31	-	-	10	
	All	2005	2010	59	90	9	2509	122	30.97	1	17	1375	31		44.35	4-51	-	-	48	
I.B.Cromb	Cant	1929/30	1946/47	54	96	5	2986	171	32.81	3	18	3791	131		28.93	5-52	4	-	67	
	All	1929/30	1946/47	88	148	12	3950	171	29.04	3	24	6152	222		27.71	8-70	10	2	103	
M.J.Crombie	Well	1900/01	1911/12	3	5	0	106	63	21.20	-	1								2	
B-J.Crook	Well	2007/08	2008/09	9	13	1	333	101*	27.75	1	1	2	1		2.00	1-2	-	-	5	
R.C.Crook	Well	1930/31	1933/34	9	17	2	253	32*	16.86	-	-	464	15		30.93	4-43	-	-	10	
C.S.Cross	Nel	1873/74	1888/89	6	10	1	81	27*	9.00	-	-	147	15		9.80	4-19	-	-	4	
	All	1884/85	1895/96	14	25	1	411	67	17.12	-	2	15	0		-	-	-	-	7	2
W.H.Cross	Nel	1875/76	1895/96	22	39	2	538	67	14.54	-	2	189	20		9.45	4-19	-	-	11	2
H.E.Crosse	HB	1919/20		2	3	0	35	16	11.66	-	-	6	0		-	-	-	-	2	
D.W.Crowe	Well	1953/54	1876/77	1	2	0	20	28*	10.00	-	-								4	1
	Cant	1957/58		2	3	0	35	17	10.00	-	-	3	0		-	-	-	-	-	
	All	1953/54	1957/58	3	5	0	55	19	11.00	-	-	3	0		-	-	-	-	-	
J.J.Crowe	Auck	1982/83	1991/92	59	95	9	4245	156	49.36	11	24	27	1		55.00	1-10	-	-	71	
	All	1977/78	1991/92	180	304	34	10233	159	37.90	22	56	55	14		21.71	5-69	1	-	199	
M.D.Crowe	Auck	1979/80	1982/83	25	45	7	1632	150	42.94	4	10	304	14		21.71	5-69	1	-	28	
	CD	1983/84	1989/90	32	55	7	3299	242	68.72	13	10	832	29		28.68	5-18	2	-	31	
	Well	1990/91	1994/95	9	16	2	865	193*	66.53	4	2	81	0		-	-	-	-	3	
	All	1979/80	1995/96	247	412	62	19608	299	56.02	71	80	4010	119		33.69	5-18	4	-	226	
J.Crowther	Well	1873/74	1881/82	2	4	1	15	7	5.00	-	-								3	
W.R.J.Croxford	Otago	1890/91	1893/94	6	10	1	118	24	13.11	-	-								7	
M.G.Croy	Otago	1994/95	2001/02	42	74	8	1351	104	20.46	1	4								127	5
	All	1994/95	2001/02	65	106	15	1664	104	18.28	1	4								183	14
C.Crump	Otago	1864/65		3	3	0	8	5	4.00	-	-								1	
W.C.Crump	Auck	1947/48		1	2	1	2	2	1.00	-	-								1	
C.A.Cuff	Cant	1907/08	1867/68	2	4	1	32	19*	10.66	-	-	15	0		-	-	-	-	-	1

		First	Last	M	I	NO	Runs	HS	Avg	100	50	Runs	Wkts	OW	Avg	Best	5i	10m	ct	st
L.A.Cuff	Cant	1886/87	1895/96	16	28	4	674	176	24.96	1	4	387	28		13.82	4-14	-	-	6	
	Auck	1896/97		2	4	0	133	80	33.25	-	1	15	1		15.00	1-15	-	-	3	
	All	1886/87	1904/05	24	43	1	964	176	22.95	1	5	431	29		14.86	4-14	-	-	17	
C.D.Cumming	Cant	1995/96	1999/00	25	45	3	1444	187	34.38	1	7	104	1		104.00	1-29	-	-	13	
	Otago	2000/01	2009/10	75	133	12	5237	173	43.28	17	25	1551	30		51.70	3-31	-	-	42	
	All	1995/96	2009/10	127	226	18	7790	187	37.45	19	36	1704	32		53.25	3-31	-	-	62	
E.M.Cummings	Otago	1909/10	1910/11	2	4	1	14	12	4.66	-	-	145	2		72.50	2-69	-	-	-	
G.B.Cummings	Otago	1902/03	1904/05	4	7	1	72	26*	12.00	-	-								3	
	Auck	1907/08	1922/23	10	17	1	423	90	26.43	-	2	303	8		37.87	2-25	-	-	10	
	All	1902/03	1922/23	14	24	2	495	90	22.50	-	2	303	8		37.87	2-25	-	-	13	
G.I.Cummins	Cant	1978/79		3	4	2	16	10	8.00	-	-	157	3		52.33	2-37	-	-	2	
R.S.Cunis	Auck	1960/61	1973/74	62	75	21	1084	111	20.07	1	5	4603	229		20.10	7-29	14	2	15	
	ND	1975/76	1976/77	14	13	5	98	29	12.25	-	-	1199	29		41.34	4-58	-	-	6	
	All	1960/61	1976/77	132	157	45	1849	111	16.50	1	6	10287	386		26.65	7-29	18	2	30	
S.J.Cunis	Cant	1998/99	2005/06	32	46	9	583	64*	15.75	-	2	2266	79		28.68	5-59	3	-	9	
J.Cunningham	Tara	1882/83		1	2	0	10	9	5.00	-	-									
W.H.R.Cunningham	Cant	1922/23	1930/31	19	34	10	280	33*	11.66	-	-	2108	72		29.27	6-33	3	-	5	
	All	1922/23	1930/31	32	50	16	396	33*	11.64	-	-	3122	91		34.30	6-33	4	-	8	
C.J.Currie	Well	1976/77		3	5	1	59	36*	14.75	-	-								1	
D.C.Currie	CD	1959/60	1962/63	9	14	4	68	15	6.80	-	-	686	28		24.50	6-50	2	-	3	
	Cant	1960/61		2	3	1	28	28	14.00	-	-	88	3		29.33	2-42	-	-	1	
	All	1959/60	1962/63	11	17	5	96	28	8.00	-	-	774	31		24.96	6-50	2	-	4	
E.W.Currie	Otago	1893/94	1894/95	6	10	2	83	42	10.37	-	-								3	
	All	1893/94	1899/00	7	12	2	97	42	9.70	-	-								3	
P.Curtin	ND	1980/81		4	8	3	66	17	13.20	-	-	251	5		50.20	2-36	-	-	3	
	All	1974/75	1980/81	5	10	4	76	17	12.66	-	-	306	6		51.00	2-36	-	-	4	
W.M.Curtis	Well	1955/56	1958/59	17	25	3	118	15	5.36	-	-								31	4
	All	1955/56	1958/59	18	27	4	167	27	7.26	-	-								39	4
J.A.J.Cushen	Otago	1967/68	1986/87	30	43	9	287	44	8.44	-	-	2591	84		30.84	6-34	3	-	9	
	Auck	1976/77	1982/83	38	27	16	156	30*	14.18	-	-	2891	107		27.01	6-27	3	1	9	
	All	1967/68	1986/87	69	72	25	466	44	9.91	-	-	5582	194		28.77	6-27	4	1	19	
A.S.H.Cutler	Otago	1938/39	1946/47	7	13	0	211	51	16.23	-	1	4	0		-	-	-	-	2	
C.C.R.Dacre	Auck	1914/15	1932/33	31	55	3	1714	145	32.96	5	8	680	23		29.56	4-38	-	-	25	
	All	1914/15	1936	268	439	20	12223	223*	29.17	24	59	1219	39		31.25	5-35	-	-	166	6
L.M.Dakin	Auck	1912/13	1913/14	2	4	1	36	23*	12.00	-	-	100	0		-	-	-	-	1	
A.E.Dakin	Cant	1905/06		2	4	2	8	4	4.00	-	-									
N.M.Daley	ND	2002/03	2003/04	4	4	0	5	4	5.00	-	-									
R.W.Dalgleish	HB	1906/07	1907/08	2	4	0	45	26	11.25	-	-	119	10		11.90	5-49	1	-	11	3
C.J.Dalton	Well	1893/94		1	2	0	0	0	0.00	-	-	8	0		-	-	-	-	1	
J.W.D'Arcy	Cant	1955/56	1958/59	20	36	1	1126	85	32.17	-	7	5	1		5.00	1-0	-	-	14	
	Well	1959/60		1	2	1	9	8	4.50	-	-								2	
	Otago	1960/61	1961/62	8	15	1	279	62	19.92	-	1								3	
	All	1955/56	1961/62	53	90	3	2009	89	23.09	5	12	12	1		12.00	1-0	-	-	26	
W.A.D'Arcy	Tara	1891/92		1	2	1	14	12*	14.00	-	-								-	
J.F.Darragh	Sland	1919/20		1	2	1	4	3*	4.00	-	-									
P.G.D'Auvergne	Cant	1969/70	1978/79	5	9	2	158	87	22.57	-	1	219	1		219.00	1-42	-	-	6	

		First	Last	M	I	NO	Runs	HS	Avg	100	50	Runs	Wkts	OW	Avg	Best	5i	10m	ct	st
R.N.Davenport	Otago	1881/82	1883/84	2	3	1	54	38*	27.00	-	-	923	31		29.77	5-39	1	-	2	-
M.P.F.Davidson	Cant	2006/07	2008/09	11	15	1	234	56	16.71	-	1								4	-
C.A.Davies	Otago	1998/99		2	3	0	27	18	9.00	-	-								-	-
D.G.Davis	HB	1920/21		3	5	0	88	61	17.60	-	1								-	-
H.Davis	Cant	1938/39	1939/40	6	9	3	117	33	19.50	-	-	538	17		31.64	3-25	-	-	6	-
H.T.Davis	Well	1991/92	1998/99	41	47	22	347	38*	13.88	-	-	4243	141		30.09	5-32	3	-	17	-
	Auck	2002/03	2003/04	7	6	2	62	29	15.50	-	-	469	15		31.26	4-93	-	-	2	-
	All	1991/92	2003/04	71	81	34	538	38*	11.44	-	-	6693	215		31.13	5-32	6	-	26	-
T.T.Davis	ND	2004/05	2008/09	7	8	1	43	30	6.14	-	-	559	13		43.00	3-61	-	-	4	-
W.W.Davis	Well	1990/91		6	9	2	67	27*	9.57	-	-	544	25		21.76	4-43	-	-	-	-
	All	1979/80	1991/92	181	227	61	2346	77	14.13	-	5	17316	608		28.48	7-52	28	7	56	-
J.Dawe	Cant	1873/74		1	2	0	2	2	1.00	-	-								-	-
W.H.Dawe	Cant	1865/66		1	2	0	14	14	7.00	-	-	22	1		22.00	1-16	-	-	-	-
A.Dawes	Otago	1884/85	1894/95	2	3	0	4	2	1.33	-	-	5	0		-	-	-	-	1	-
F.F.Dawson	Cant	1950/51		3	6	1	116	54	23.20	-	1								3	-
G.J.Dawson	Otago	1980/81	1984/85	36	63	8	1561	79	28.38	-	9	58	0		-	-	-	-	29	-
J.H.M.Dawson	Cant	1957/58	1962/63	11	17	8	107	41*	11.88	-	-	769	31		24.80	6-72	1	-	6	-
G.Day	Well	1903/04		1	2	0	12	11	6.00	-	-								-	-
K.H.Dean	HB	1914/15		2	4	1	11	6*	3.66	-	-	89	3		29.66	2-39	-	-	1	-
A.J.Deane	Auck	1947/48		2	4	0	39	22	9.75	-	-								-	-
K.R.Deas	Auck	1947/48	1960/61	16	31	4	491	73	18.18	-	1	313	9		34.77	4-81	-	-	7	-
	All	1947/48	1960/61	18	34	4	522	73	17.40	-	1	313	9		34.77	4-81	-	-	7	-
A.P.de Boorder	Auck	2007/08	2009/10	15	22	2	689	125*	34.45	1	3	263	5		52.60	2-56	-	-	8	-
D.C.de Boorder	Otago	2007/08	2009/10	22	32	6	843	74	32.42	-	6								64	10
J.G.Dees	Well	1873/74		2	4	0	17	10	4.25	-	-	8	1		8.00	1-8	-	-	-	-
C.de Grandhomme	Auck	2006/07	2009/10	26	37	0	1121	106*	37.36	3	4	1057	37		28.56	4-65	-	-	20	-
	All	2005/06	2009/10	32	49	7	1418	109	33.76	4	5	1283	42		30.54	4-65	-	-	24	-
R.P.de Groen	Auck	1987/88	1989/90	12	16	8	46	25*	5.75	-	-	963	27		35.66	5-47	2	-	2	-
	ND	1990/91	1995/96	38	38	13	220	35	8.80	-	-	3320	157		21.14	7-50	8	2	7	-
	All	1987/88	1995/96	60	64	25	311	35	7.97	-	-	5266	210		25.07	7-50	10	2	10	-
H.N.Dellow	Cant	1954/55	1955/56	5	8	1	37	15*	5.28	-	-	367	11		33.36	3-84	-	-	1	-
H.S.De Maus	Cant	1889/90	1896/97	20	38	4	938	113	27.58	1	6	627	36		17.41	7-48	2	-	8	-
	All	1889/90	1896/97	23	44	4	1071	113	26.77	1	6	668	41		16.29	7-48	2	-	9	-
D.A.Dempsey	Cant	1979/80	1987/88	32	63	3	1517	131	25.28	4	4	286	5		57.20	3-67	-	-	18	-
C.S.Dempster	Well	1921/22	1947/48	40	76	3	2602	154	35.64	4	18	73	0		-	-	-	-	24	-
	All	1921/22	1947/48	184	306	36	12145	212	44.98	35	55	300	8		37.50	2-4	-	-	94	-
E.W.Dempster	Well	1947/48	1947/48	35	61	10	1194	105	23.41	1	6	2150	70		30.71	5-93	1	-	22	-
	All	1947/48	1960/61	52	88	15	1593	105	21.82	1	7	3142	102		30.80	5-46	3	-	25	2
H.F.C.Dencker	Nel	1886/87		1	2	1	8	7*	8.00	-	-								-	-
H.E.H.Denham	Cant	1945/46		1	1	0	2	2	2.00	-	-								3	-
J.Denham	Cant	1884/85		1	2	1	15	10*	15.00	-	-								3	-
W.B.Denshire	Nel	1873/74		2	2	0	13	10	6.50	-	-	28	1		28.00	1-28	-	-	2	-
T.H.Dent	HB	1900/01	1901/02	5	8	1	122	56	17.42	-	1	542	35		15.48	9-47	3	1	4	-
J.W.de Terte	CD	2007/08	2009/10	3	6	1	153	77*	30.60	-	1								-	-
A.P.Devcich	ND	2004/05	2009/10	10	17	2	282	94*	18.80	-	1	214	5		42.80	2-20	-	-	9	-
A.J.Devlin	Cant	1983/84		3	4	0	25	20	6.25	-	-	16	0		-	-	-	-	1	-

		First	Last	M	I	NO	Runs	HS	Avg	100	50	Runs	Wkts	OW	Avg	Best	5i	10m	ct	st
A.E.Dewes	Auck	1882/83	1883/84	2	4	1	18	15*	6.00	-	-	1982	57		34.77	6-73	3	1	5	
B.J.Diamanti	CD	2003/04	2009/10	27	42	5	952	136	25.72	2	3								7	
A.E.Dick	Otago	1956/57	1960/61	16	27	0	514	86	19.03	-	2								10	2
	Well	1962/63	1968/69	20	28	4	517	60	21.54	-	2								38	21
	All	1956/57	1968/69	78	126	12	2315	127	20.30	1	10	4	0		-	-	-	-	148	
C.R.W.Dickel	Otago	1970/71	1982/83	13	19	3	208	56	13.00	-	1	20	0		-	-	-	-	5	
	Cant	1973/74	1974/75	8	12	4	116	31*	14.50	-	-	609	27		22.55	5-22	1	-	3	
	All	1970/71	1982/83	21	31	7	324	56	13.50	-	1	758	26		29.15	6-89	1	-	8	
												1367	53		25.79	6-89	2	-		
T.H.V.Dickel	Otago	1917/18		1	1	0	28	28	28.00	-	-	38	0		-	-	-	-	-	
C.W.Dickeson	ND	1973/74	1986/87	90	134	27	1289	59	12.04	-	3	8242	282		29.22	7-79	9	2	59	
G.Dickinson	Cant	1863/64	1873/74	9	17	3	88	30	6.28	-	-	256	20		12.80	4-43	-	-	6	
G.R.Dickinson	Otago	1921/22	1937/38	31	55	12	894	104	20.79	1	4	3315	127		26.10	7-90	11	2	16	
	Well	1943/44		2	2	0	49	39	24.50	-	-	113	2		56.50	2-91	-	-	-	
	All	1921/22	1943/44	39	69	15	1013	104	18.75	1	4	4045	150		26.96	7-90	11	2	19	
J.F.W.Dickson	Well	1911/12	1914/15	3	5	1	46	18*	11.50	-	-	70	1		70.00	1-20	-	-	-	
M.H.Dind	Well	1917/18	1919/20	11	20	1	384	63*	20.21	-	2	103	3		34.33	1-1	-	-	4	
B.M.J.Dineen	Cant	1956/57		4	6	0	59	27*	11.80	-	-	117	1		117.00	1-17	-	-	3	
	CD	1962/63	1963/64	7	13	0	239	67	18.38	-	2								1	
	All	1956/57	1963/64	11	19	0	298	67	16.55	-	2	117	1		117.00	1-17	-	-	4	
W.G.Ditchfield	Otago	1933/34		1	2	0	66	55	33.00	-	1								4	
R.J.Diver	ND	1998/99		2	2	0	9	6	4.50	-	-								-	
D.C.Dixon	Sland	1919/20		1	2	0	13	13	6.50	-	-	20	1		20.00	1-20	-	-	-	
E.R.Dixon	Auck	1873/74		1	1	0	0	0	0.00	-	-								-	
W.G.Dixon	Otago	1875/76	1885/86	9	18	2	156	30	9.75	-	-	189	7		27.00	3-23	-	-	3	
P.W.Dobbs	Otago	1988/89	1994/95	54	99	6	2606	144*	28.02	3	14	101	2		50.50	2-44	-	-	25	
	All	1988/89	1994/95	55	101	6	2641	144*	27.80	3	14	101	2		50.50	2-44	-	-	25	
J.A.Doig	Sland	1914/15	1920/21	7	13	0	118	29	9.07	-	-	600	38		15.78	7-46	5	1	3	
H.E.Dollery	Well	1950/51		4	7	0	94	47	13.42	-	-								-	
K.R.Dollery	All	1933	1955	436	717	66	24414	212	37.50	50	127	32	0		-	-	-	-	292	14
	Auck	1949/50		2	3	1	6	4*	3.00	-	-	131	0		-	-	-	-	-	
	All	1947/48	1956	80	107	27	958	41	11.97	-	-	6018	227		26.51	8-42	9	2	24	
D.L.Donald	ND	1957/58	1960/61	19	37	0	827	106	22.35	1	5	4	0		-	-	-	-	14	
	All	1957/58	1960/61	21	40	0	930	106	23.25	1	6	4	0		-	-	-	-	14	
G.T.Donaldson	Well	1998/99	2003/04	48	80	7	1824	96	24.98	1	13	154	3		51.33	2-15	-	-	32	
J.B.Donaldson	Auck	1949/50		3	5	0	85	50	17.00	-	1	257	7		36.71	3-56	-	-	1	
A.E.Doneghue	Well	1919/20	1927/28	6	10	3	37	13	5.28	-	-								3	
B.P.Donkers	Cant	2002/03	2003/04	8	10	5	109	38	21.80	-	-	574	12		47.83	3-37	-	-	2	
I.T.Donnelly	Auck	1981/82		2	2	1	1	1*	1.00	-	-	106	4		26.50	4-70	-	-	1	
J.P.Donnelly	Cant	2009/10		5	5	0	20	13	5.00	-	-	704	14		50.28	4-150	-	-	-	
M.P.Donnelly	Well	1936/37	1940/41	5	10	1	458	138*	50.88	1	4	56	3		18.66	2-12	-	-	3	
	Cant	1938/39	1939/40	6	11	1	381	104	38.10	1	2	420	9		46.66	2-43	-	-	3	
B.J.K.Doody	All	1936/37	1960/61	131	221	26	9250	208*	47.43	23	46	1683	43		39.13	4-32	-	-	74	
	Cant	1995/96	2001/02	24	44	1	968	93	22.51	-	7	18	0		-	-	-	-	23	
	All	1995/96	2001/02	25	46	1	1123	137	24.95	1	7	18	0		-	-	-	-	23	
M.E.F.Dormer	Auck	1961/62		4	5	1	48	22	12.00	-	-								5	3
N.Dorreen	Cant	1927/28	1930/31	5	8	3	192	105*	38.40	1	-								11	6

173

Name	Team	First	Last	M	I	NO	Runs	HS	Avg	100	50	Runs	Wkts	OW	Avg	Best	5i	10m	ct	st
G.W.Douglas	CD	1965/66	1967/68	10	14	2	287	63*	23.91	-	-	232	9		25.77	4-30	-	-	5	
M.W.Douglas	CD	1987/88	2000/01	76	132	19	3838	144	33.96	7	21	120	4		30.00	2-29	-	-	71	
	Well	1993/94	1994/95	12	18	3	708	106	47.20	2	5								7	
	All	1987/88	2000/01	94	160	23	4808	144	35.09	9	29	120	4		30.00	2-29	-	-	82	
W.Douglas	Otago	1878/79		1	2	0	0	0	0.00	-	-								-	
W.M.Douglas	Otago	1922/23	1928/29	12	21	6	83	20	5.53	-	-	1134	30		37.80	5-88	1	-	7	
L.J.Doull	Well	1990/91	1993/94	16	25	5	436	79	21.80	-	1	798	21		38.00	4-45	-	-	10	
S.B.Doull	ND	1989/90	2001/02	47	56	12	1099	108	24.97	1	4	3026	111		27.26	6-38	4	2	7	
	All	1989/90	2001/02	99	126	27	1938	108	19.57	1	4	7233	250		28.93	7-65	12	1	28	
R.T.Dowker	Cant	1949/50	1956/57	24	43	5	1147	122	28.93	1	7	47	3		15.66	2-25	-	-	16	
G.T.Dowling	Cant	1958/59	1971/72	59	102	7	3720	206	39.15	8	17	122	3		40.66	1-4	-	-	53	
	All	1958/59	1971/72	158	282	13	9399	239	34.94	16	44	378	9		42.00	3-100	-	-	111	
A.D.Downes	Otago	1887/88	1913/14	44	77	7	809	63	11.55	-	1	3902	287		13.59	8-35	33	13	26	2
	All	1887/88	1913/14	51	91	8	882	63	10.62	-	1	4564	311		14.67	8-35	33	13	31	2
J.Downes	HB	1884/85		1	1	0	1	1	1.00	-	-	37	2		18.50	2-37	-	-	1	
L.W.Downes	CD	1975/76		8	15	7	287	89*	35.87	-	2								24	
T.A.Downes	Well	1940/41	1946/47	5	10	7	47	22*	15.66	-	-	404	8		50.50	3-74	-	-	1	
W.F.Downes	Otago	1865/66	1875/76	9	16	2	102	22	7.28	-	-	420	60		7.00	7-38	5	2	8	1
A.B.Drabble	Otago	1884/85	1891/92	4	8	1	47	22	6.71	-	-								2	
W.T.Drake	All	1920/21		1	2	0	26	15	13.00	-	-	20	1		20.00	1-20	-	-	-	
R.S.Dravid	Cant	2008/09		1	1	0	102	102	102.00	1	-								-	
T.M.Dravitzki	All	1990/91	2010	274	453	63	21873	270	56.08	60	112	273	5		54.60	2-16	-	-	337	1
F.W.P.Dredge	CD	1962/63		1	2	0	8	8	4.00	-	-								-	
D.J.Drew	Well	1905/06		1	1	0	16	16	16.00	-	-								-	
A.Driscoll	Otago	2000/01	2001/02	4	5	0	52	28	13.00	-	-								16	
R.J.Drown	Sland	1914/15	1918/19	3	6	1	48	36	8.00	-	-								-	
	Auck	1991/92	1992/93	9	10	3	58	17*	8.28	-	-	591	27		21.88	4-6	-	-	3	
C.J.Drum	Auck	1996/97	2001/02	31	42	17	313	60*	12.52	-	1	2216	130		17.04	6-34	6	2	10	
	All	1996/97	2001/02	50	64	26	377	60*	9.92	-	1	3669	199		18.43	6-34	7	2	21	
J.Drummond	HB	1903/04		1	2	0	3	3	1.50	-	-	80	4		20.00	4-80	-	-	-	
L.R.Dry	Well	1994/95	1998/99	5	5	0	56	30	18.66	-	-	183	4		45.75	4-90	-	-	2	
C.H.Dryden	Cant	1884/85	1894/95	21	33	2	177	23	5.70	-	-	868	76		11.42	7-24	7	2	12	
W.E.Dryden	Well	1885/86		1	2	0	8	6*	8.00	-	-	23	1		23.00	1-23	-	-	2	
V.H.du Chateau	Well	1932/33	1939/40	6	12	0	156	32	13.00	-	-								2	
A.G.Duckmanton	Cant	1951/52	1961/62	17	28	2	387	69	14.88	-	1	760	32		23.75	5-29	1	-	3	
W.H.Dudney	Cant	1883/84		6	11	0	208	40	18.90	-	-								14	
	All	1883/84	1893	36	67	4	912	97	14.47	-	1								5	6
E.T.Dufaur	Auck	1873/74	1877/78	4	8	0	71	27	8.87	-	-								38	1
P.P.E.Dufaur	Auck	1882/83		2	3	0	10	7	3.33	-	-	7	0		-	-	-	-	1	
S.W.Duff	CD	1985/86	1995/96	85	129	29	3079	164*	30.79	1	17	6856	208		32.96	6-36	4	2	54	
	All	1985/86	1995/96	88	134	29	3167	164*	30.16	1	17	7051	217		32.49	6-36	5	2	54	
R.J.Duffy	Well	1940/41	1945/46	9	18	1	458	71	26.94	-	4	206	5		41.20	2-31	-	-	1	
D.P.Dumbleton	Well	1947/48		1	1	0	1	1*		-	-	133	2		66.50	2-86	-	-	-	
A.W.Duncan	Well	1919/20		2	3	1	35	16	17.50	-	-	121	1		121.00	1-62	-	-	4	
A.A.K.Duncan	Well	1879/80		2	4	0	16	8	4.00	-	-								-	
A.D.S.Duncan	Well	1893/94	1900/01	3	5	0	52	19	10.40	-	-	41	5		8.20	2-12	-	-	4	

		First	Last	M	I	NO	Runs	HS	Avg	100	50	Runs	Wkts	OW	Avg	Best	5i	10m	ct	st
G.H.R.Duncan	CD	1971/72		1	2	0	47	47	23.50	-	-	24	0		-	-	-	-	5	
H.Duncan	Otago	1921/22	1924/25	9	16	0	247	67	15.43	-	1	186	6		31.00	3-70	-	-	5	
S.F.Duncan	Otago	1925/26	1940/41	5	10	0	142	52	14.20	-	1	715	74		9.66	6-7	8	2	3	
W.M.Duncan	ND	1957/58		5	8	3	21	6	4.20	-	-	776	29		26.75	7-66	8	-	5	
D.E.I.Dunlop	Cant	1883/84	1887/88	10	17	1	132	23	9.42	-	-	321	6		53.50	3-47	-	-	8	
E.F.Dunn	Auck	1955/56	1956/57	10	15	1	190	75*	13.57	-	1	411	10		41.10	3-47	-	-	3	
R.S.Dunne	Otago	1968/69		5	7	1	22	7	4.40	-	-								4	
	All	1965/66	1968/69	6	9	2	30	7	4.28	-	-								7	
D.M.Dunnet	Cant	1943/44	1944/45	6	7	2	90	32	18.00	-	-								11	8
	Otago	1950/51		5	7	2	18	18	18.00	-	-									
	All	1942/43	1950/51	11	12	3	128	32	14.22	-	-								11	8
B.Dunning	ND	1961/62	1977/78	82	148	10	3898	142	28.24	3	22	1804	51		35.37	5-37	1	-	57	10
	All	1961/62	1977/78	83	150	10	3929	142	28.06	3	22	1804	51		35.37	5-37	1	-	58	10
E.J.Dunning	Auck	1936/37		2	2	0	0	0	0.00	-	-								2	
J.A.Dunning	Otago	1923/24	1937/38	29	54	5	681	45	13.89	-	-	3002	121		24.80	6-51	8	1	20	
	Auck	1928/29		3	3	1	69	34	34.50	-	-	326	14		23.28	6-71	2	-	3	
	All	1923/24	1937/38	60	95	14	1057	45	13.04	-	-	6290	228		27.58	6-42	15	2	34	
L.R.Dunster	Cant	1932/33		2	3	0	39	32	13.00	-	-								2	
E.F.D.Duret	Well	1886/87	1887/88	3	5	0	44	21	8.80	-	-								2	
	Otago	1889/90		1	2	0	28	15	14.00	-	-								-	
	All	1886/87	1889/90	4	7	0	72	21	10.28	-	-								2	
W.H.Dustin	Well	1927/28	1943/44	10	20	2	422	92	23.44	-	3	12	0		-	-	-	-	1	
	Auck	1943/44		11	22	2	435	92	21.75	-	3	27	1		27.00	1-11	-	-	1	
K.F.Dwyer	CD	1950/51	1953/54	7	14	0	361	56	25.78	-	2								4	
P.W.Dyhrberg	Well	1951/52		1	2	0	7	5	3.50	-	-								-	
R.A.Dykes	Auck	1967/68	1976/77	31	50	0	723	82	20.08	-	2								57	24
H.D.Earney	HB	1910/11		1	2	1	1	1*	1.00	-	-								-	
L.C.Eastman	Otago	1927/28	1928/29	6	9	1	404	91	50.50	-	4	637	21		30.33	5-78	1	-	4	
	All	1920	1939	451	693	50	13385	161	20.81	7	61	26939	1006		26.77	7-28	30	3	260	
S.W.Eathorne	Otago	2004/05	2005/06	5	10	0	72	28	7.20	-	-								4	
A.D.Eckhoff	Otago	1899/00	1914/15	15	26	9	112	19	6.58	-	-	836	21		39.80	6-27	1	-	13	
L.R.J.Eckhoff	Otago	1975/76		1	1	1	0	0*	0.00	-	-	104	1		104.00	1-82	-	-	-	
A.G.Eckhold	Otago	1906/07	1921/22	19	35	3	702	60*	21.93	-	3	75	3		25.00	1-5	-	-	8	
W.L.Eddington	Cant	1977/78	1984/85	7	11	4	129	49*	18.42	-	-	272	6		45.33	1-20	-	-	3	
J.Eden	Nel	1887/88	1891/92	2	3	1	33	31	16.50	-	-	51	7		7.28	5-26	1	-	-	
T.G.Eden	Nel	1874/75	1891/92	11	22	4	144	25	8.00	-	-	312	49		6.37	9-43	6	2	5	1
W.Eden	Nel	1874/75	1881/82	5	9	1	34	8	4.25	-	-	41	9		4.55	5-17	1	-	5	1
A.J.Edgar	Well	1955/56		5	5	0	35	16	7.00	-	-								6	1
B.A.Edgar	Well	1975/76	1989/90	87	160	13	6494	162	44.17	15	32	70	1		70.00	1-0	-	-	47	
	All	1975/76	1989/90	175	307	26	11304	203	40.22	24	61	92	2		46.00	1-0	-	-	93	7
D.B.Edmonds	Auck	1933/34	1946/47	11	14	1	109	28	8.38	-	-								22	1
E.E.Edmunds	Well	1875/76	1876/77	2	4	0	14	7	3.50	-	-								2	
M.R.Edmunds	Otago	1958/59	1959/60	9	14	2	45	11	3.75	-	-								14	2
H.Edser	Cant	1883/84		2	4	0	28	13	14.00	-	-	168	14		12.00	8-75	2	1	-	
S.J.Edward	Otago	1966/67	1967/68	2	4	0	42	13	10.50	-	-	122	2		61.00	2-49	-	-	2	
	All	1964/65	1967/68	3	6	0	54	13	9.00	-	-	202	2		101.00	2-49	-	-	3	

175

		First	Last	M	I	NO	Runs	HS	Avg	100	50	Runs	Wkts	OW	Avg	Best	5i	10m	ct	st
A.J.Edwards	Otago	1940/41	1887/88	1	2	0	16	16	8.00	-	-	102	9		11.33	4-17	-	-	3	-
C.H.Edwards	HB	1884/85	1984/85	2	3	1	22	22	11.00	-	-	20	0		-	-	-	-	3	-
G.N.Edwards	CD	1973/74	1984/85	67	122	5	3709	177*	31.70	5	19	32	0		-	-	-	-	99	15
L.J.Edwards	All	1973/74	1984/85	92	164	8	4589	177*	29.41	5	25								126	16
J.A.Ell	Well	1998/99	2009/10	4	4	0	34	27	8.50	-	-	355	8		44.37	3-71	-	-	3	-
G.D.Elliott	Well	1933/34	1945/46	26	50	1	1176	89*	24.00	-	9	35	1		35.00	1-21	-	-	16	-
	All	1933/34	1945/46	28	54	1	1185	89*	22.35	-	9	35	1		35.00	1-21	-	-	17	-
	All	2005/06	2009/10	26	39	3	1312	196*	36.44	4	7	1403	39		35.97	3-44	-	-	11	-
	Tara	1996/97	2009/10	52	82	3	2288	196*	29.33	5	12	2424	65		37.29	4-56	-	-	31	-
H.S.Elliott	Tara	1891/92	1897/98	3	5	1	16	7	4.00	-	-	54	4		13.50	3-8	-	-	3	-
T.Elliott	Auck	1894/95	1905/06	12	20	1	141	47	7.42	-	-	86	7		12.28	3-10	-	-	3	5
W.L.T.Elliott	Auck	1924/25	1929/30	6	9	1	85	30	10.62	-	-	282	10		28.20	2-25	-	-	4	
A.M.Ellis	Cant	2002/03	2009/10	42	66	9	1545	78	27.10	-	10	2437	73		33.38	5-63	1	-	22	
H.Ellis	All	1904/05	1908/09	3	6	0	57	19*	14.25	-	-	82	3		27.33	2-50	-	-	-	
	HB	1913/14	1914/15	3	6	1	71	40	11.83	-	-	92	6		15.33	5-50	1	-	2	1
	All	1904/05	1914/15	6	12	1	128	40	12.80	-	-	174	9		19.33	5-50	1	-	2	1
N.Ellis	Auck	1941/42	1943/44	6	6	0	222	69	37.00	-	3								2	
R.H.Ellis	CD	1971/72	1976/77	24	24	1	392	68	17.81	-	2	802	32		25.06	4-19	-	-	9	
S.H.Ellis	Auck	1911/12		3	6	2	75	49	18.75	-	-								3	3
C.J.Elmes	Otago	1927/28	1940/41	39	75	6	1568	94	22.72	-	5	2454	67		36.62	5-40	3	-	30	
	All	1927/28	1940/41	45	82	6	1707	99	22.46	-	6	2797	72		38.84	5-40	3	-	35	
R.W.G.Emery	Auck	1936/37	1946/47	9	12	0	358	123	29.83	2	1	391	10		39.10	4-41	-	-	6	
	Cant	1947/48	1953/54	13	26	2	773	110	29.83	1	5	311	10		31.10	2-24	-	-	4	
	All	1936/37	1953/54	24	42	2	1177	123	29.42	3	5	754	22		34.27	4-41	-	-	10	
England	Well	1879/80		2	3	0	37	29	12.33	-	-								-	
J.E.England	Cant	1958/59	1961/62	6	10	1	79	18	8.77	-	-	4	0		-	-	-	-	10	4
J.I.Englefield	CD	1998/99	2005/06	25	40	6	1549	127	45.55	2	15	44	1		44.00	1-22	-	-	17	
	Cant	1999/00	2001/02	21	40	0	1151	172	28.77	2	8	48	1		48.00	1-22	-	-	6	
	All	1998/99	2005/06	55	97	7	3113	172	34.58	3	25	120	4		30.00	2-15	-	-	28	
P.B.Erasmus	Auck	2006/07	2009/10	4	4	0	89	60	22.25	-	1								-	
A.W.Evans	ND	2004/05	2005/06	18	33	4	1128	104*	38.89	2	6	86	0		-	-	-	-	10	
	All	1996	2006/07	56	96	11	2631	125	30.95	2	12	91	0		-	-	-	-	34	
C.E.Evans	Cant	1919/20	1928/29	13	26	1	388	62	15.52	-	1	207	10		20.70	2-10	-	-	5	
H.Evans	Well	1873/74	1875/76	2	4	0	24	17	6.00	-	-	82	7		11.71	5-22	1	-	3	
	All	1868/69	1875/76	3	6	0	37	17	6.16	-	-	169	12		14.08	5-22	2	-	5	
J.K.Everest	Auck	1954/55	1955/56	8	15	0	433	103	33.30	1	1	0	0		-	-	-	-	1	
	ND	1956/57		5	10	1	376	104	41.77	1	3	14	0		-	-	-	-	1	
	All	1954/55	1956/57	13	25	1	809	104	36.77	2	4	14	0		-	-	-	-	2	
O.J.N.Everson	Otago	1943/44		1	2	1	54	28	54.00	-	-								-	
G.P.Ewing	Auck	1884/85		3	5	0	56	36	11.20	-	-								2	
P.R.Facoory	Otago	1976/77	1984/85	28	50	4	843	57	17.20	-	3								20	
A.Fairbairn	Otago	1884/85		5	4	0	19	13	4.75	-	-								1	
G.S.Fairey	HB	1911/12	1912/13	2	3	0	27	24	9.00	-	-	45	3		15.00	3-33	-	-	-	
S.A.Fairey	Well	2001/02	2006/07	16	25	3	443	59*	20.13	-	2								7	
H.A.Fannin	HB	1892/93	1899/00	11	20	1	116	25	6.10	-	-	635	43		14.76	8-19	4	2	8	
R.N.Farman	Auck	1957/58	1959/60	11	20	3	309	96*	18.17	-	1	1	0		-	-	-	-	4	

		First	Last	M	I	NO	Runs	HS	Avg	100	50	Runs	Wkts	OW	Avg	Best	5i	10m	ct	st
A.J.Farrant	Cant	1980/81	1982/83	4	7	1	41	18	6.83	-	-	182	2		91.00	1-26	-	-	1	-
D.G.Farrant	Cant	1981/82	1986/87	4	7	1	84	33	14.00	-	-	221	4		55.25	1-7	-	-	1	-
H.Fayen	Nel	1882/83		1	2	0	4	4	2.00	-	-								-	-
C.D.Fearon	Cant	1865/66		1	2	0	6	5*	6.00	-	-								-	-
A.Fenton	HB	1903/04	1910/11	11	21	3	170	39	9.44	-	-	1117	45		24.82	6-41	2	-	5	-
	Well	1911/12	1914/15	2	4	0	22	11	5.50	-	-	101	4		25.25	2-30	-	-	1	-
	All	1895/96	1914/15	14	27	3	195	39	8.12	-	-	1254	50		25.08	6-41	2	-	6	-
W.R.Fenton	Auck	1971/72		2	4	0	28	18	7.00	-	-								-	-
	All	1964/65	1971/72	3	6	0	64	33	10.66	-	-								1	-
F.F.Fenwick	Otago	1875/76		1	2	0	1	1	0.50	-	-								1	-
H.S.Fenwick	Cant	1891/92		1	2	1	47	30*	47.00	-	-								2	-
R.E.D.Ferdinands	ND	1998/99		1	2	1	8	5	8.00	-	-	81	0		-	-	-	-	-	-
G.H.Fernley	HB	1893/94		1	2	2	0	0	0.00	-	-								-	-
K.I.Ferries	Cant	1966/67	1974/75	21	25	11	149	44	10.64	-	-	1671	78		21.42	5-67	3	-	3	-
	All	1961/62	1974/75	22	26	11	158	44	10.53	-	-	1732	79		21.92	5-67	3	-	3	-
D.J.Ferrow	ND	1956/57	1957/58	4	5	0	16	14	3.20	-	-	220	9		24.44	4-50	-	-	1	-
C.J.W.Finch	Otago	1993/94	1995/96	3	5	0	23	7	4.60	-	-	165	1		165.00	1-89	-	-	2	-
W.P.Finch	HB	1884/85		1	2	0	0	0	0.00	-	-								2	-
B.R.Findlay	Cant	2005/06		1	2	0	23	19	11.50	-	-	88	3		29.33	2-57	-	-	3	-
C.O.Findlay	CD	1995/96	1996/97	8	11	3	224	52	28.00	-	1	520	17		30.58	2-19	-	-	6	-
J.L.Findlay	Cant	1925/26		3	5	4	30	9*	30.00	-	-	329	9		36.55	4-54	-	-	-	-
J.W.Findlay	Well	1910/11	1911/12	4	7	1	51	22*	8.50	-	-	199	13		15.30	4-42	-	-	4	-
D.J.H.Finlay	CD	1988/89		1	1	0	39	39	39.00	-	-	101	1		101.00	1-76	-	-	-	-
C.G.Finlayson	Well	1909/10	1920/21	4	8	1	142	51	20.28	-	1	213	8		26.62	4-121	-	-	1	-
	Auck	1929/30	1930/31	2	4	0	83	40	20.75	-	-	83	0		-	-	-	-	1	-
	All	1909/10	1930/31	7	13	1	225	51	18.75	-	1	388	9		43.11	4-121	-	-	2	-
J.P.Firth	Nel	1880/81		1	2	0	40	27	20.00	-	-	2	0		-	-	-	-	2	-
	Well	1882/83	1885/86	5	8	0	159	54	19.87	-	1	256	32		8.00	8-13	1	-	8	-
	All	1880/81	1885/86	6	10	0	199	54	19.90	-	1	258	32		8.06	8-13	1	-	10	-
A.H.Fisher	Otago	1890/91	1909/10	40	71	0	953	76	15.37	-	3	2766	176		15.71	9-50	9	1	23	-
	All	1890/91	1909/10	46	83	11	1079	76	14.98	-	4	3228	197		16.38	9-50	11	1	26	-
F.E.Fisher	Well	1951/52	1953/54	11	21	5	429	68	26.81	-	2	936	41		22.82	8-34	1	2	7	-
	CD	1954/55		3	5	0	33	14	6.60	-	-	218	11		19.81	4-55	-	-	2	-
	All	1951/52	1954/55	15	28	5	485	68	21.08	-	2	1232	53		23.24	8-34	2	2	9	-
I.D.Fisher	Auck	1982/83	1991/92	9	13	1	152	41	15.20	-	1	380	13		29.23	4-37	-	-	5	-
	CD	1989/90	1990/91	12	20	6	293	71	20.92	-	1	807	28		28.82	5-43	2	-	4	-
	All	1982/83	1991/92	21	33	7	445	71	18.54	-	2	1187	41		28.95	5-43	2	-	9	-
R.L.Fisher	Cant	1904/05	1905/06	3	4	1	26	20*	8.66	-	-	158	7		22.57	3-40	-	-	2	-
J.Fitzgerald	Otago	1883/84	1884/85	2	3	0	7	4	2.33	-	-	83	7		11.85	5-30	1	-	-	-
H.S.Fitzherbert	All	1879/80		1	2	2	0	0	0.00	-	-								-	-
E.Fitzsimmons	Well	1889/90	1895/96	15	24	4	134	19	6.70	-	-	683	33		20.69	5-39	1	-	12	-
J.P.Flaherty	Otago	1964/65	1968/69	9	11	4	40	15*	5.71	-	-	481	13		37.00	4-52	-	-	5	-
C.W.Flanagan	Cant	1986/87	1994/95	21	28	4	487	69*	20.29	-	2	1421	52		27.32	6-30	2	1	8	-
J.Flanaghan	Well	1873/74		1	2	0	1	1	0.50	-	-	13	4		3.25	4-13	-	-	-	-
T.Flaws	Otago	1952/53	1962/63	27	47	4	438	35	10.18	-	-								44	29

		First	Last	M	I	NO	Runs	HS	Avg	100	50	Runs	Wkts	OW	Avg	Best	5i	10m	ct	st
S.P.Fleming	Cant	1991/92	1999/00	25	37	4	1336	118	40.48	2	8	110	0		-	-	-	-	28	
	Well	2001/02	2006/07	10	16	2	588	115	42.00	1	5								9	
	All	1991/92	2007/08	247	406	32	16409	274*	43.87	35	93								340	
D.R.Flynn	ND	2004/05	2009/10	30	49	4	1524	110	33.86	5	6	129	1		140.00	1-37	-	-	9	
	All	2004/05	2009/10	54	91	10	2528	110	31.20	5	12	143	1		143.00	1-37	-	-	20	
R.H.B.Fogo	Sland	1914/15	1919/20	3	6	3	21	9	7.00	-	-	132	6		22.00	3-26	-	-	2	
H.Foley	Well	1927/28	1932/33	10	18	3	446	136	29.73	1	1	125	3		41.66	2-16	-	-	10	
	All	1927/28	1932/33	15	26	6	670	136	33.50	1	2	138	4		34.50	2-16	-	-	13	
M.Foley	Well	1876/77		1	2	0	0	0	0.00	-	-								-	
	Tara	1882/83		1	2	0	21	17	10.50	-	-								1	
	All	1876/77	1882/83	2	4	0	21	17	5.25	-	-								1	
R.M.Ford	Cant	1988/89	1993/94	32	24	13	148	23*	13.45	-	-	2315	86		26.91	6-35	2	-	9	
	All	1988/89	1993/94	33	24	13	148	23*	13.45	-	-	2366	87		27.19	6-35	2	-	9	
W.J.Ford	Nel	1886/87	1888/89	3	2	0	48	30	12.00	-	-	25	0		-	-	-	-	2	
	All	1873	1896	25	42	2	711	75	17.77	-	4	213	13		16.38	6-56	1	-	19	
L.J.Forde	Cant	1976/77		4	2	1	1	1*	1.00	-	-	199	3		66.33	1-14	-	-	3	
S.F.Forde	Otago	1998/99	2000/01	10	19	1	299	48	16.61	-	-	148	4		37.00	2-31	-	-	8	
W.A.Fordham	Well	1877/78		1	2	0	14	13*	14.00	-	-			1		1-?	-	-	-	
J.C.Forrest	Auck	1996/97	1997/98	9	18	1	232	48	13.64	-	-								3	
H.Forsyth	Cant	1917/18		2	2	1	4	3	2.00	-	-								-	
P.S.Foster	Well	1909/10		1	2	0	7	7	3.50	-	-								-	
	Cant	1918/19	1919/20	2	2	0	44	31	22.00	-	-								-	
	All	1909/10	1919/20	3	4	0	51	31	12.75	-	-								-	
R.J.Fouhy	Well	2005/06		2	2	2	-	1*	-	-	-	103	3		34.33	2-35	-	-	1	
B.G.Foulds	ND	1969/70	1970/71	5	7	4	36	16*	12.00	-	-	323	7		46.14	2-29	-	-	34	14
J.N.Fowke	Cant	1880/81	1906/07	27	44	9	341	36	9.74	-	-								9	11
	Auck	1889/90	1893/94	12	21	3	209	30*	11.61	-	-								45	28
	All	1880/81	1906/07	40	67	12	561	36	10.20	-	-								45	
E.Fowler	Cant	1868/69	1881/82	16	24	0	408	40	17.00	-	-	262	23		11.39	7-66	1	-	13	4
	All	1865/66	1881/82	17	25	0	445	40	17.80	-	-	262	23		11.39	7-66	1	-	14	4
G.Fowler	Nel	1879/80	1887/88	7	13	1	97	28	8.08	-	-	313	45		6.96	6-9	2	-	4	
J.Fowler	Cant	1873/74	1881/82	7	12	3	196	65	21.77	-	1	38	2		19.00	2-30	-	-	2	
L.A.Fowler	Nel	1882/83	1891/92	7	14	1	72	17	5.53	-	-	122	11		11.09	5-55	1	-	1	
	Tara	1897/98		1	2	0	6	4	3.00	-	-								-	
	All	1882/83	1897/98	8	16	1	78	17	5.20	-	-	122	11		11.09	5-55	1	-	3	
S.Fowler	Nel	1873/74	1883/84	10	19	2	186	28*	10.94	-	-	72	13		5.53	5-14	1	-	3	
W.P.Fowler	ND	1979/80	1984/85	15	27	3	418	51	17.41	-	1	535	10		53.50	2-4	-	-	15	
	Auck	1981/82	1989/90	13	20	3	354	56	20.82	-	2	628	27		23.25	6-41	1	-	6	
	All	1979/80	1989/90	77	125	17	2577	116	23.86	2	17	1775	44		40.34	6-41	1	-	49	
G.H.Fox	Otago	1888/89	1889/90	2	4	0	17	11	4.25	-	-	2	1		2.00	1-2	-	-	-	
R.H.Fox	All	1904	1927	19	32	6	407	54	15.65	-	1	51	2		25.50	1-17	-	-	26	8
W.D.Frame	Otago	1955/56	1957/58	7	9	2	52	16	7.42	-	-	414	26		15.92	5-49	2	-	3	
J.P.E.Francis	Well	1880/81		1	2	0	11	11	5.50	-	-	105	8		13.12	6-53	1	-	1	
E.H.Frankish	Cant	1903/04	1905/06	5	8	0	46	13	7.66	-	-	156	8		19.50	3-42	-	-	2	
F.S.Frankish	Cant	1894/95	1903/04	14	26	6	209	56	9.50	-	1	1282	80		16.02	7-26	6	3	14	
	All	1894/95	1903/04	18	34	5	278	56	9.58	-	1	1719	94		18.28	7-26	7	3	16	

		First	Last	M	I	NO	Runs	HS	Avg	100	50	Runs	Wkts	OW	Avg	Best	5i	10m	ct	st
J.E.C.Franklin	Well	1998/99	2009/10	55	80	10	2775	219	39.64	6	11	4234	181		23.39	7-30	6	1	19	
T.J.Franklin	All	1998/99	2010	132	201	28	5949	219	34.38	11	26	10871	411		26.45	7-14	13	1	50	
	Auck	1980/81	1992/93	88	157	14	5041	181	35.25	11	26	40	1		40.00	1-21			52	
P.J.Franks	All	1980/81	1992/93	148	254	20	7794	181	33.30	12	40	51	1		51.00	1-21			79	
	Cant	2002/03		1	2	0	51	41	25.50				0							
	All	1996	2010	175	249	44	5643	123*	27.52	4	30	14685	460		31.92	7-56	11	1	56	
I.C.Fraser	Otago	1918/19		1	2	0	1	1	0.50											
T.C.Fraser	Otago	1937/38	1952/53	14	27	4	587	118	25.52	1	3	10	0						10	
R.E.Frater	Auck	1918/19	1931/32	15	29	3	580	88	22.30		3								10	
A.A.Freeman	HB	1887/88		1	2	0	6	6	3.00											
B.T.Freeman	Otago	1969/70	1970/71	8	15	0	199	57	13.26		1	52	3		17.33	3-52			6	
D.L.Freeman	Well	1932/33	1933/34	3	4	0	26	8	6.50			326	13		25.07	5-102	1		3	
	All	1932/33	1933/34	5	6	0	28	8	4.66			495	14		35.35	5-102	1		3	
J.Freeman	ND	1972/73	1975/76	5	9	0	128	35	14.22			261	5		52.20	2-49			1	
T.A.Freeman	Otago	1943/44	1949/50	16	27	4	393	64*	17.08		2	1340	26		51.53	4-34			13	
	All	1943/44	1949/50	17	29	4	417	64*	16.68		2	1377	27		51.00	4-34			14	
R.M.Frew	Cant	1995/96	2002/03	35	65	3	1809	125	29.17	3	10	4	0						22	
C.Frith	Cant	1877/78	1880/81	4	5	0	17	8	3.40			170	20		8.50	7-25	1		4	
	Otago	1881/82	1889/90	10	17	6	49	9	4.45			435	43		10.11	5-8	2		8	
W.Frith	All	1877/78	1889/90	14	22	6	66	9	4.12			605	63		9.60	7-25	6	1	12	
	Cant	1877/78	1888/89	7	10	0	131	51	13.10		1	302	34		8.88	8-18	2		9	
	Otago	1881/82		1	2	1	1	1	1.00			70	8		8.75	4-27				
	Well	1889/90	1893/94	7	9	0	111	46	12.33			433	37		11.70	6-51	2		8	
	All	1877/78	1893/94	15	21	1	243	51	12.15			805	79		10.18	8-18	4	2	17	
A.C.Fuller	Cant	1917/18	1923/24	9	17	5	132	31*	11.00										7	
D.M.Fuller	Well	1889/90	1894/95	12	21	3	296	56	16.44		1	33	1		33.00	1-24			7	
E.T.A.Fuller	Cant	1872/73	1882/83	9	13	2	51	14	4.63			568	59	6	9.62	7-47	8	3	3	
J.K.Fuller	Otago	2009/10		2	3	0	31	24	10.33			231	2		115.50	1-33			6	
F.Fulton	Otago	1868/69	1878/79	4	8	1	67	22	9.57										1	
	HB	1883/84		1	2	0	3	3	1.50										2	
	All	1868/69	1883/84	5	10	1	70	22	7.77										3	
J.Fulton	Otago	1863/64	1867/68	5	8	1	97	26	13.85			4	1		4.00	1-4			6	
J.C.Fulton	Otago	1867/68	1874/75	5	9	1	53	16	6.62			126	4		31.50	4-60			2	
	Tara	1882/83		1	2	1	0	0*	0.00											
	All	1867/68	1882/83	7	13	2	54	16	4.90			131	7		18.71	4-60			2	
P.G.Fulton	Cant	2000/01	2009/10	58	105	11	4486	301*	47.72	8	24	376	11		34.18	4-49			44	
	All	2000/01	2009/10	84	143	12	5652	301*	43.14	9	31	402	11		36.54	4-49			66	
P.R.Fulton	HB	1900/01	1920/21	18	34	2	435	60	13.59		1	1027	36		28.52	5-71	2		8	
R.W.Fulton	Cant	1972/73	1984/85	20	35	6	764	68	26.34		3								10	
	ND	1973/74	1976/77	25	44	2	1036	106	25.26	1	6	100	2		50.00	2-34			10	
	All	1972/73	1984/85	45	79	8	1800	106	25.71	1	9	100	2		50.00	2-34			20	
B.D.M.Furlong	CD	1963/64	1972/73	14	20	3	245	49	14.41			806	20		40.30	4-27			10	
	All	1963/64	1974/75	15	22	3	246	49	12.94			921	26		35.42	6-115	1		10	
C.J.M.Furlong	CD	1994/95	2001/02	40	58	9	900	88	18.36		3	3877	80		48.46	7-72	1		51	
	All	1994/95	2001/02	42	61	9	933	88	17.94		3	4104	92		44.60	7-72	1		53	

		First	Last	M	I	NO	Runs	HS	Avg	100	50	Runs	Wkts	OW	Avg	Best	5i	10m	ct	st
J.B.M.Furlong	CD	1990/91	1993/94	4	3	0	82	51*	-	-	1	105	2		52.50	2-30			3	
	All	1990/91	1993/94	4	5	2	140	51*	-	-	2	195	2		97.50	2-30			3	
S.R.Gadsdon	ND	2008/09		2	3	2	13	9	6.50										7	1
C.B.Gaffaney	Otago	1995/96	2004/05	75	138	11	4326	194	34.06	7	23	47	2		23.50	1-3			63	
	All	1995/96	2004/05	83	152	11	4711	194	33.41	8	24	47	2		23.50	1-3			73	
A.J.Gale	Otago	1989/90	1997/98	47	77	23	751	60	13.90		1	3251	124		26.21	6-42	3		13	
	All	1989/90	1997/98	52	81	24	844	60	14.80		2	3576	131		27.29	6-42	3		14	
A.D.S.Gale	Otago	1929/30		1	2	0	31	28	15.50											
A.Galland	Otago	1914/15	1930/31	44	79	4	1643	115	21.90	1	7	430	15		28.66	4-54			48	9
	All	1914/15	1930/31	45	81	4	1681	115	21.83	1	7	430	15		28.66	4-54			48	9
R.G.Gallaugher		1945		1	1	0	2	2	2.00			27	0						-	
I.W.Gallaway	Otago	1946/47	1947/48	3	3	0	26	22	8.66										-	1
N.Gallichan	Well	1929/30	1938/39	11	19	3	337	62	21.06		2	778	27		28.81	5-90	1		7	
	All	1927/28	1938/39	31	43	8	636	62	18.17		3	2244	86		26.09	6-46	4	1	22	
D.L.Gallop	Cant	1956/57	1965/66	24	41	2	803	124	20.58	1	5	963	27		35.66	3-27			16	
W.Gardiner	Auck	1889/90	1893/94	7	13	1	167	61	13.91		1								5	
	Well	1895/96		2	4	0	142	59	35.50		1									
	All	1889/90	1895/96	9	17	1	309	61	19.31		2								5	
C.Gardner	Auck	1882/83		4	6	0	74	21	12.33										5	
C.D.Garner	CD	1992/93	1996/97	10	17	1	150	37	9.37			4	0		-	-			1	
C.W.Garrard	Cant	1886/87	1904/05	13	21	1	326	50*	17.15			163	2		81.50	1-20			9	
D.R.Garrard	Auck	1917/18	1941/42	28	42	9	816	62	24.72		5	2121	85		24.95	8-51	6	2	4	
	All	1917/18	1941/42	32	50	11	960	67*	24.61		5	2358	92		25.63	8-51	6	2	16	
W.R.Garrard	Auck	1918/19	1924/25	11	20	3	209	44	12.29										18	
	All	1918/19	1924/25	12	22	4	215	44	11.94										18	
C.W.Garrod	Well	1917/18	1919/20	4	6	2	25	14	6.25			219	11		19.90	7-59	1		1	
C.W.Garrod	CD	1966/67		4	6	1	38	16	7.60										4	
J.Garty	Cant	1886/87		1	1	0	10	10	10.00			70	7		10.00	6-41	1		1	
W.J.Garwood	Otago	1873/74		2	2	0	33	31	16.50			28	6		4.66	3-5			1	
	Well	1876/77		1	2	0	22	13	11.00			22	0		-	-			1	
	All	1873/74	1876/77	3	4	0	55	31	13.75			50	6		8.33	3-5			2	
E.A.Gasson	Cant	1924/25	1925/26	6	11	0	162	27	14.72			12	0		-	-			5	
E.A.Gasson	Cant	1937/38		3	6	0	100	34	16.66										2	
D.J.Gatenby	Cant	1972/73	1978/79	5	6	0	34	12	11.33			343	8		42.87	3-23			5	
	All	1972/73	1978/79	9	12	3	83	17*	10.37			627	12		52.25	3-23			6	
H.P.L.Gaussen	HB	1903/04		1	2	2	0	0*	-			26	1		26.00	1-26			1	
S.J.Geake	All	1903/04	1910/11	11	20	0	260	77	13.00		1	26	1		26.00	1-26			2	
G.N.Geary	HB	1913/14	1914/15	3	6	1	44	13*	8.80			91	2		45.50	1-14			1	
R.M.Geary	Cant	1953/54	1956/57	14	21	2	337	79	17.73		2	832	32		26.00	6-32	1		11	
	CD	1964/65	1973/74	7	10	1	156	59	17.33		1	48	0		-	-			2	
	All	1964/65	1973/74	4	7	3	78	21*	19.50										2	
T.F.C.Geary	Otago	1940/41		11	17	4	234	59	18.00		1	48	0		-	-			4	
A.E.Geddes	Otago	1899/00	1903/04	9	2	1	13	12	6.50			60	0		-	-			-	
C.S.Geddis	HB	1914/15	1920/21	3	15	1	266	77	19.00		1	131	7		18.71	3-5			12	
A.E.Gedye	Well	1919/20		2	5	0	41	15	8.20			10	1		10.00	1-10			1	1
					4	0	29	17	7.25										-	

		First	Last	M	I	NO	Runs	HS	Avg	100	50	Runs	Wkts	OW	Avg	Best	5i	10m	ct	st
S.G.Gedye	Auck	1956/57	1964/65	40	73	4	2169	104	31.43	3	11	5	0						19	
S.J.Gellatly	All	1956/57	1964/65	45	83	4	2387	104	30.21	3	13	5	0						19	
A.A.George	Well	2007/08		5	8	2	200	67*	33.33	-	2								4	
L.K.Germon	Well	1913/14		1	2	0	16	9	8.00	-	-								-	-
	Cant	1987/88	1997/98	76	101	25	2336	160*	30.73	3	8								217	21
	Otago	2001/02		4	7	1	93	23	13.28	-	-								1	
	All	1987/88	2001/02	103	142	35	3123	160*	29.18	4	10	12	1		12.00	1-12			258	26
J.P.Gerrard	Auck	1924/25	1926/27	3	5	1	117	75	29.25	-	1								-	
W.R.L.Gibbes	Well	1905/06	1914/15	14	25	3	557	81	25.31	-	5	12	1		12.00	1-12			9	
C.S.Gibbs	Cant	1929/30		1	0	0						15	0							
P.B.Gibbs	CD	1990/91		3	3	2	12	9	12.00	-	-	669	25		26.76	5-35	1		9	
J.G.Gibson	ND	1968/69	1980/81	49	92	5	2580	128	29.65	4	11	63	1		63.00	1-23			23	
	Auck	1972/73		3	5	1	136	48*	34.00	-	-	223	4		55.75	2-41			3	
W.A.J.Gibson	All	1968/69	1980/81	53	99	6	2786	128	29.95	4	12	19	0						26	
J.J.Gifford	HB	1895/96	1897/98	3	5	0	21	15	4.20	-	-	43	1		43.00	1-27			-	
A.W.Gilbertson	HB	1919/20	1920/21	2	3	0	11	7*	11.00	-	-	47	0						-	
J.Gilbertson	Otago	1951/52	1953/54	8	14	3	187	38*	17.00	-	-								4	
J.H.Gilbertson	Sland	1914/15	1920/21	7	12	2	133	26*	13.30	-	-	18	2		9.00	2-18			5	
E.D.Giles	Sland	1914/15	1918/19	2	4	0	28	10	7.00	-	-	66	3		22.00	2-6			2	
G.V.Giles	Auck	1960/61		3	5	0	79	23	15.80	-	-								1	
L.A.Giles	ND	1961/62	1975/76	25	46	0	907	81	19.71	-	5	76	4		19.00	1-9			13	
M.E.Giles	Otago	1929/30		1	2	0	23	18	11.50	-	-								-	
R.J.Gilhooly	Well	1951/52	1953/54	3	6	0	77	23	12.83	-	-	126	1		126.00	1-21			-	
B.Gill	Well	2004/05		1	2	1	17	13	17.00	-	-	55	1		55.00	1-46			-	
J.A.Gill	ND	1969/70		1	1	1	0	0*		-	-	52	1		52.00	1-27			-	
J.G.Gill	Otago	1953/54	1963/64	16	29	2	458	91	16.96	-	2	258	14		18.42	4-56			18	5
M.F.Gill	Auck	1882/83	1884/85	6	8	4	24	14	6.00	-	-	1397	44		31.75	6-53	4		1	
S.J.Gill	CD	1974/75	1981/82	19	23	11	71	16	5.91	-	-	1204	30		40.13	4-28	1		4	
H.D.Gillespie	CD	1981/82	1987/88	20	32	3	736	107	29.44	1	4	71	2		35.50	2-43	-		8	
	Auck	1920/21	1931/32	27	48	1	1171	183	24.91	2	6	71	2		35.50	2-43	-		20	
	All	1920/21	1931/32	30	53	1	1208	183	23.23	2	6								20	
M.R.Gillespie	Well	1999/00	2009/10	48	59	10	884	81*	18.04	-	3	4622	194	9	23.82	6-42	9	-	8	
	All	1999/00	2009/10	53	66	11	915	81*	16.63	-	3	5200	213	10	24.41	6-42	10	2	8	
S.R.Gillespie	ND	1979/80	1982/83	23	32	4	309	59	11.03	-	1	1851	73		25.35	5-30	2		6	
	Auck	1984/85	1988/89	9	11	3	229	73	28.62	-	2	459	13		35.30	3-15	-		9	
	All	1979/80	1988/89	36	48	8	599	73	14.97	-	3	2689	99		27.16	5-30	3		18	
E.K.Gillott	ND	1971/72	1978/79	20	33	14	170	22	8.94	-	-	1987	68		29.22	6-79	2		7	
	All	1971/72	1978/79	31	37	17	172	22	8.60	-	-	2493	81		30.77	6-79	2		9	
A.M.Given	Otago	1914/15		1	1	1	4	4*		-	-	59	3		19.66	3-32	-		-	
J.M.Glasgow	Otago	1866/67	1868/69	3	5	1	61	25	15.25	-	-	1	0						-	
C.Gleeson	Auck	1877/78		1	2	0	27	26	13.50	-	-								-	
H.A.Gleeson	Sland	1917/18	1920/21	5	9	0	121	55	13.44	-	1								1	
A.Glen	Otago	1872/73	1886/87	6	11	2	29	13	3.22	-	-	267	13		20.53	4-55	-		4	
R.L.Glover	CD	1985/86	1990/91	11	18	2	351	113	21.93	1	1	24	0						6	
H.E.Godby	Otago	1874/75	1875/76	2	4	0	73	24	18.25	-	1	22	0						6	1

181

		First	Last	M	I	NO	Runs	HS	Avg	100	50	Runs	Wkts	OW	Avg	Best	5i	10m	ct	st
M.J.Godby	Otago	1875/76	1880/81	1	2	1	45	25	22.50	-	-	109	3		36.33	2-64	-	-	1	-
	Cant	1877/78		3	5	1	78	26*	19.50	-	-	8	0		-	-	-	-	-	-
	All	1875/76	1880/81	4	7	2	123	26*	20.50	-	-	117	3		39.00	2-64	-	-	1	-
E.Godwin Austen	Cant	1877/78		1	2	0	23	23*	12.00	-	-								-	-
S.B.Golder	Well	1999/00		1	2	0	8	4	4.00	-	-								1	-
H.D.Gold-Smith	HB	1905/06		1	2	0	13	13	6.50	-	-	57	1		57.00	1-57	-	-	2	-
W.J.Gollar	Otago	1890/91		1	2	1	32	32	32.00	-	-								-	-
N.W.Goode	Auck	1909/10		1	2	1	10	5*	10.00	-	-								-	-
F.J.Gooder	Well	1884/85		2	3	2	10	9*	10.00	-	-								2	2
M.C.Goodson	CD	1989/90		12	16	5	165	61	12.69	-	1	26	1		27.00	1-26	-	-	5	-
	Well	1991/92	1994/95	17	21	5	194	61	12.12	-	1	121	6		20.16	5-51	1	-	5	-
	All	1989/90	1994/95									589	29		20.31	6-48	2	-	6	-
												874	37		23.62	6-48	3	-	6	-
M.J.Goodson	Tara	1891/92		1	2	0	1	1	0.50	-	-								1	-
L.Gordon	Cant	1917/18		1	2	0	30	19	15.00	-	-	14	0		-	-	-	-	-	-
R.W.Gordon	Auck	1912/13		1	2	0	34	19	17.00	-	-								-	-
A.H.Gore	Well	1885/86	1888/89	6	8	0	86	33	10.75	-	-	316	32	1	9.87	7-53	2	-	3	-
	HB	1891/92	1901/02	20	35	1	357	42	10.50	-	-	1021	57		17.91	6-26	4	1	15	-
	All	1885/86	1901/02	26	43	1	443	42	10.54	-	-	1337	89	1	15.02	7-53	6	1	18	-
C.S.Gore	Well	1891/92	1903/04	23	42	5	662	57	17.89	-	2								14	-
	All	1891/92	1903/04	25	46	6	677	57	16.92	-	2								14	-
R.Gore	Well	1896/97		1	2	0	19	17	9.50	-	-								-	-
F.H.Gossage	HB	1893/94		3	6	0	52	28	8.66	-	-	15	0		-	-	-	-	3	-
Gouge	Well	1874/75	1875/76	2	4	0	25	17	6.25	-	-	20	0		-	-	-	-	3	-
W.J.Gough	Otago	1953/54		1	2	0	31	27	15.50	-	-								-	-
I.J.Gould	Auck	1979/80		3	6	0	101	54	16.83	-	1								3	2
T.M.P.Grace	All	1975	1996	298	399	63	8756	128	26.05	4	47	365	7		52.14	3-10	-	-	536	67
A.C.Graham	Well	1911/12	1913/14	2	3	1	48	28	24.00	-	-	58	5		11.60	4-6	-	-	1	-
B.N.Graham	Otago	1944/45		1	2	0	10	8	5.00	-	-	71	4		17.75	4-22	-	-	-	-
	Auck	1953/54		2	4	0	45	22	11.25	-	-								-	-
	ND	1956/57		4	8	1	106	56	15.14	-	1								1	-
	All	1953/54	1956/57	6	12	1	151	56	13.72	-	1								2	-
C.G.Graham	Otago	1954/55	1955/56	5	8	0	133	46	16.62	-	-	39	0		-	-	-	-	3	-
H.Graham	Otago	1903/04	1906/07	9	17	0	338	60	19.88	-	1	128	5		25.60	4-39	-	-	7	-
	All	1892/93		114	201	9	5054	124	26.32	7	24	258	6		43.00	4-39	-	-	85	-
M.Graham	Cant	1934/35	1936/37	9	13	4	68	30*	7.55	-	-	588	26		22.61	5-76	1	-	3	-
W.H.Graham	Auck	1917/18	1918/19	3	6	0	76	30	12.66	-	-	108	3		36.00	2-42	-	-	3	-
M.R.Grant	HB	1911/12		1	1	0	1	1	1.00	-	-								-	-
T.A.B.Grant	Cant	1920/21	1921/22	4	8	2	233	78	38.83	-	3	90	3		30.00	2-19	-	-	3	-
	Well	1922/23	1924/25	4	8	0	61	21	7.62	-	-	169	4		42.25	2-33	-	-	1	-
	All	1920/21	1924/25	9	18	2	305	78	19.06	-	3	285	8		35.62	2-19	-	-	4	-
D.J.Gray	ND	1956/57	1959/60	14	26	4	403	74*	18.31	-	2								7	-
	All	1956/57	1959/60	16	29	4	441	74*	17.64	-	2								9	-
E.J.Gray	Well	1975/76	1991/92	120	181	38	4228	128*	29.56	5	21	9778	357		27.38	8-37	13	3	109	-
	All	1975/76	1991/92	162	241	51	5472	128*	28.80	6	28	12522	444		28.20	8-37	16	3	138	-
J.Gray	Cant	1917/18	1919/20	10	18	1	404	100	23.76	1	1	140	9		15.55	7-44	1	-	4	-

		First	Last	M	I	NO	Runs	HS	Avg	100	50	Runs	Wkts	OW	Avg	Best	5i	10m	ct	st
M.J.Greatbatch	Auck	1982/83	1985/86	24	42	7	884	119*	25.25	1	4	2	0		144.00	1-23	-	-	16	-
	CD	1986/87	1999/00	61	107	8	4363	202*	44.07	14	15	144	1		144.00	1-23	-	-	73	-
	All	1982/83	1999/00	170	292	31	9890	202*	37.89	24	43	149	1		149.00	1-23	-	-	144	2
A.R.W.P.Green	Nel	1884/85	1886/87	3	5	1	16	4	4.00	-	-	5	0		-	-	-	-	-	-
L.Green	Otago	1926/27		2	4	1	50	30	16.66	-	-								1	-
L.A.Green	Auck	1959/60	1961/62	6	9	1	52	18	6.50	-	-	474	12		39.50	3-52	-	-	1	-
A.Greenfield	Nel	1875/76		1	2	1	3	3*	3.00	-	-								-	-
F.E.Greenfield	Nel	1880/81	1891/92	4	7	0	93	27	13.28	-	-								5	-
W.A.Greenstreet	Well	1969/70	1972/73	21	27	9	327	33	18.16	-	-	1534	61		25.14	5-34	3	-	7	-
	All	1969/70	1972/73	24	32	10	397	37	18.04	-	-	1742	71		24.53	5-34	3	-	10	-
C.J.Gregory	HB	1883/84		1	1	0	2	2	1.00	-	-								-	-
G.R.Gregory	Cant	1922/23	1928/29	16	28	0	631	67	22.53	-	5	52	1		52.00	1-0	-	-	5	-
D.Grenier	Auck	1912/13		1	2	0	23	14	11.50	-	-								-	-
T.J.Grierson	Auck	1877/78		1	2	0	10	10	5.00	-	-								-	-
A.J.Grieve	Otago	1884/85	1887/88	3	6	0	51	31	8.50	-	-	6	0		-	-	-	-	2	-
A.A.Griffiths	Well	1984/85	1985/86	3	2	2	19	15*	-	-	-	270	5		54.00	3-49	-	-	2	-
B.G.Griffiths	Well	1931/32	1937/38	12	19	5	129	28	9.21	-	-	1138	43		26.46	6-55	3	-	3	-
	All	1931/32	1937/38	14	21	5	155	28	9.68	-	-	1344	50		26.88	6-55	3	-	3	-
R.J.Griffiths	ND	1975/76	1980/81	7	7	6	26	12*	26.00	-	-	477	13		36.69	2-20	-	-	2	-
B.B.J.Griggs	CD	2000/01	2009/10	82	129	16	3144	143	27.82	2	19								230	7
	All	2000/01	2009/10	83	130	16	3155	143	27.67	2	19								236	7
C.V.Grimmett	Well	1911/12	1913/14	9	17	2	241	33*	15.06	-	-	679	22		30.86	4-48	-	-	7	-
	All	1911/12	1940/41	248	321	54	4720	71*	17.67	-	12	31737	1424		22.28	10-37	127	33	140	-
G.A.Grindrod	Tara	1896/97		1	1	0	0	0	0.00	-	-								1	-
L.J.Groves	Otago	1929/30	1949/50	16	30	4	297	35	11.42	-	-	1305	31		42.09	6-88	1	-	8	-
T.G.Groves	Sland	1914/15	1920/21	4	7	0	14	10	2.00	-	-	114	6		19.00	4-25	-	-	3	-
G.Gudgeon	Tara	1897/98		2	4	1	15	8*	5.00	-	-	66	3		22.00	3-36	-	-	1	-
S.C.Guillen	Cant	1952/53	1960/61	42	73	5	2186	197	32.14	3	12	49	1		49.00	1-1	-	-	69	18
	All	1947/48	1960/61	66	109	10	2672	197	26.98	3	14	49	1		49.00	1-1	-	-	111	34
C.E.Guiney	Cant	1918/19		2	3	0	12	11	4.00	-	-								1	-
J.Gully	Cant	1982/83		2	6	0	53	22	8.83	-	-	106	4		26.50	4-91	-	-	3	-
H.Gunthorp	Cant	1895/96		1	2	1	1	1	1.00	-	-	13	0		-	-	-	-	-	-
	Otago	1902/03		1	2	0	12	6	6.00	-	-	119	4		29.75	4-91	-	-	1	-
	All	1895/96	1902/03	2	4	1	13	6	4.33	-	-	67	1		67.00	1-8	-	-	-	-
M.J.Guptill	Auck	2005/06	2009/10	19	32	1	821	148	26.48	1	4	127	4		31.75	3-37	-	-	8	-
	All	2005/06	2009/10	33	57	2	1694	189	30.80	2	9								20	-
D.J.Guthardt	CD	1985/86	1988/89	10	18	2	282	82*	17.62	-	1								20	-
J.W.Guy	CD	1953/54	1962/63	18	31	1	996	115	33.20	3	4	16	1		16.00	1-0	-	-	5	-
	Cant	1957/58	1958/59	10	18	1	486	62	28.58	1	4								7	-
	Otago	1959/60		4	7	0	180	47	25.71	-	2								4	-
	Well	1960/61		5	9	0	290	66	32.22	-	2	4	0		-	-	-	-	6	-
	ND	1964/65	1972/73	11	22	0	279	42	13.28	-	2	4	0		-	-	-	-	6	-
	All	1953/54	1972/73	90	165	13	3923	115	25.80	3	24	82	1		82.00	1-0	-	-	32	2
A.E.Hadden	Auck	1905/06	1910/11	16	29	4	824	84	32.96	-	9	565	25		22.60	5-65	1	-	6	-
	All	1905/06	1910/11	20	37	4	986	84	29.87	-	10	630	25		25.20	5-65	1	-	6	-
G.P.Haddon	CD	1969/70		4	7	1	125	33*	20.83	-	-								4	-

		First	Last	M	I	NO	Runs	HS	Avg	100	50	Runs	Wkts	OW	Avg	Best	5i	10m	ct	st
B.G.Hadlee	Cant	1961/62	1980/81	82	151	11	4428	163*	31.62	6	24	212	4		53.00	2-28	-	-	31	-
	All	1961/62	1980/81	84	155	11	4538	163*	31.51	6	24	212	4		53.00	2-28	-	-	35	-
D.R.Hadlee	Cant	1969/70	1983/84	49	68	22	1115	109*	24.23	-	1	3918	195		20.09	7-55	10	3	20	-
	All	1966/67	1983/84	111	152	39	2113	109*	18.69	-	2	8853	351		25.22	7-55	11	3	40	-
R.J.Hadlee	Cant	1971/72	1988/89	62	100	22	2012	93	25.79	-	4	4600	285		16.14	7-49	19	2	35	-
	All	1971/72	1990	342	473	93	12052	210*	31.71	14	59	26998	1490		18.11	9-52	102	18	198	-
W.A.Hadlee	Cant	1933/34	1951/52	44	80	7	3183	194	43.60	10	13	130	1		130.00	1-20	-	-	25	-
	Otago	1945/46	1946/47	7	12	0	784	198	65.33	3	-	110	4		27.50	3-14	-	-	4	-
	All	1933/34	1951/52	117	203	17	7523	198	40.44	18	31	293	6		48.83	3-14	-	-	70	-
H.E.Haggett	Tara	1894/95	1897/98	2	4	1	15	12	5.00	-	-								-	-
F.H.Haig		1919/20					18	13*	18.00	-	-								-	-
S.B.Haig	Otago	2005/06	2009/10	25	41	2	1229	153	31.51	3	5								22	-
W.S.Haig	Otago	1949/50	1957/58	30	55	1	1048	102	19.40	1	6	351	15		23.40	4-12	-	-	17	-
	All	1949/50	1957/58	31	56	1	1062	102	19.30	1	6	355	15		23.66	4-12	-	-	18	-
S.C.W.Hainsworth	Well	1988/89		1	1	0	6	6	6.00	-	-								-	-
G.Haldane	Well	1885/86		1	2	0	2	2	1.00	-	-	5	2		2.50	2-5	-	-	-	-
E.O.Hales	Well	1896/97	1909/10	19	29	3	213	48	8.19	-	-	1077	59		18.25	6-22	4	-	14	-
	All	1896/97	1909/10	20	31	4	220	48	8.14	-	-	1145	60		19.08	6-22	4	-	14	-
S.G.Haliday	All	1942/43		2	4	0	55	36	13.75	-	-								-	-
P.J.Hall	Otago	1955/56		1	2	0	63	33	31.50	-	-	43	1		43.00	1-36	-	-	-	-
W.K.Hall	HB	1948	1955/56	12	14	3	235	49	21.36	-	1	1045	28		37.32	5-51	1	-	5	-
R.G.Hallamore	HB	1904/05	1905/06	3	6	0	183	93	30.50	-	1								1	-
	HB	1898/99	1906/07	9	16	4	232	35*	19.33	-	-	47	3		15.66	3-27	-	-	5	9
	Sland	1918/19		1	2	0	9	9	9.00	-	-								-	2
	All	1898/99	1918/19	10	18	5	241	35*	18.53	-	-	47	3		15.66	3-27	-	-	5	11
R.Halley	Cant	1886/87	1890/91	7	13	1	126	29	10.50	-	-	385	29		13.27	5-33	2	-	6	-
C.J.Halliday	Nel	1876/77	1886/87	3	6	0	27	10*	9.00	-	-								-	-
H.H.Halliday	Nel	1873/74	1880/81	7	14	0	111	35	7.92	-	-								4	-
T.S.Hambrook	Auck	1951/52	1958/59	32	53	4	1321	104	26.95	2	5	1319	44		29.97	3-9	-	-	21	-
	All	1951/52	1958/59	33	55	4	1333	104	26.13	2	5	1388	44		31.54	3-9	-	-	22	-
A.J.Hamilton	Sland	1914/15	1920/21	5	9	4	82	25	16.40	-	-								1	-
B.G.Hamilton	CD	1953/54		1	1	0	5	5	5.00	-	-								-	-
D.C.Hamilton	Sland	1919/20		1	2	0	32	24	16.00	-	-								1	-
I.M.Hamilton	Cant	1926/27	1932/33	15	30	1	732	80	25.24	-	4								16	-
	All	1926/27	1932/33	17	33	1	788	80	24.62	-	4								16	-
J.J.Hamilton	Well	1877/78	1879/80	3	4	0	4	2	1.00	-	-								-	-
L.J.Hamilton	CD	1996/97	2006/07	57	79	26	258	23	4.86	-	-	5104	198		25.77	6-32	7	-	14	-
	All	1996/97	2006/07	60	83	28	266	23	4.83	-	-	5391	212		25.42	6-32	8	-	16	-
J.E.Hammel	Well	1965/66		1	2	0	8	8	4.00	-	-								-	-
G.Hammond	Sland	1920/21		2	4	0	35	27	8.75	-	-	22	1		22.00	1-22	-	-	-	-
B.L.Hampton	CD	1961/62	1968/69	34	48	6	1140	107	27.14	1	4	1787	72		24.81	6-7	3	-	24	-
	All	1961/62	1968/69	35	49	6	1163	107	24.90	1	4	1843	74		24.90	6-7	3	-	24	-
G.S.Hampton	Auck	1932/33		2	4	3	19	10	19.00	-	-								5	-
I.R.Hampton	CD	1962/63	1965/66	14	21	3	310	62	17.22	-	1	109	1		109.00	1-27	-	-	15	-
K.B.Hancock	ND	1985/86	1986/87	5	8	4	54	31	13.50	-	-	459	9		51.00	3-37	-	-	3	2

		First	Last	M	I	NO	Runs	HS	Avg	100	50	Runs	Wkts	OW	Avg	Best	5i	10m	ct	st
A.Handford	Sland	1914/15	1914/15	1	2	0	4	3	2.00	-	-	1722	60		28.70	7-39	5	-	-	-
B.C.Harbridge	All	1892		26	38	9	275	24*	9.48	-	-								16	1
G.W.Harden	Cant	1939/40	1940/41	3	3	0	41	23	13.66	-	-								5	
R.I.Harden	Tara	1894/95		1	0															
	CD	1987/88		8	14	0	409	82	29.21	-	1	14	0						4	
	All	1985	2000	253	417	63	13336	187	37.67	28	70	124	4		31.00	2-7	-	-	189	
M.G.Harding	ND	1986/87		4	8	0	69	31	8.62	-	-	1023	20		51.15	2-7	-	-	1	
J.Hardstaff	Auck	1948/49	1949/50	5	8	1	437	135	62.42	1	2	4	0							
N.S.Harford	All	1930	1955	517	812	94	31847	266	44.35	83	166	168	1		168.00	1-102	-	-	123	
	CD	1953/54	1958/59	19	34	4	972	91	32.40	1	8	2141	36		59.47	4-43	-	-	14	
	Auck	1963/64	1966/67	13	23	3	614	103*	30.70	1	2	362	14		25.85	3-19	-	-	7	
	All	1953/54	1966/67	74	122	8	3149	158	27.62	3	18								39	
R.I.Harford	Auck	1965/66	1967/68	12	16	5	100	23	9.09	-	-	478	18		26.55	3-19	-	-	26	4
	All	1965/66	1967/68	25	32	14	143	23	7.94	-	-								60	8
J.P.Hargreaves	Cant	1886/87		1	2	1	5	4*	5.00	-	-									
J.T.Harkness	Auck	1892/93		1	2	1	5	5*	5.00	-	-	11	0		-	-	-	-	1	
	Otago	1897/98	1900/01	4	5	1	14	9*	14.00	-	-	87	4		21.75	3-29	-	-	1	
	All	1892/93	1900/01	5	7	2	19	9*	9.50	-	-	98	4		24.50	3-29	-	-	1	
E.S.Harley	Cant	1864/65		3	6	1	22	11	4.40	-	-	95	12		7.91	5-27	1	-	-	
J.A.Harliwich	Cant	1951/52	1868/69	1	1	0	7	7	7.00	-	-	59	1		59.00	1-30	-	-	-	
A.F.G.Harman	Cant	1889/90	1893/94	12	22	0	193	45	8.77	-	-	268	16		16.75	5-43	2	-	8	
R.D.Harman	Cant	1883/84	1896/97	9	16	0	135	61	8.43	-	-	5	0		-	-	-	-	1	
T.D.Harman	Cant	1882/83	1901/02	12	23	0	223	65	11.15	-	2	27	1		27.00	1-1	-	-	7	
F.Harper	Otago	1886/87	1894/95	14	24	1	297	69	12.91	-	2	2	1		2.00	1-2	-	-	7	
G.D.Harper	ND	1958/59		1	1	1	0	0*	-	-	-	23	0		-	-	-	-	4	
T.A.Harpur	Well	1938/39		2	3	0	28	12	9.33	-	-	46	1		46.00	1-28	-	-	1	
A.J.Harris	Otago	2005/06		2	4	0	17	13	4.25	-	-								1	
B.Z.Harris	Cant	1988/89	1994/95	17	29	2	713	133	26.40	2	1	172	3		57.33	3-13	-	-	7	
	Otago	1989/90	1990/91	18	34	2	864	141*	27.00	1	4	121	3		40.33	2-18	-	-	21	
	All	1988/89	1994/95	35	63	4	1577	141*	26.72	3	5	293	6		48.83	3-13	-	-	28	
C.Z.Harris	Cant	1989/90	2009/10	84	125	31	5442	251*	57.89	13	30	3708	126		29.42	4-22	-	-	85	
	All	1989/90	2009/10	131	204	42	7377	251*	45.53	15	41	5720	160		35.75	4-22	-	-	120	
C.M.Harris	Otago	1928/29	1929/30	3	5	0	25	7	5.00	-	-	135	1		135.00	1-9	-	-	-	
J.H.Harris	Otago	1865/66		1	1	0	0	0	0.00	-	-								1	
L.M.Harris	Otago	1881/82	1887/88	9	18	0	272	63	16.00	-	1	24	1		24.00	1-11	-	-	7	
	Well	1891/92	1893/94	2	3	0	76	59	25.33	-	1								1	
	All	1881/82	1893/94	11	21	1	348	63	17.40	-	2	24	1		24.00	1-11	-	-	8	
M.J.Harris	Well	1975/76		7	11	1	376	83	37.60	-	2								13	
	All	1964	1982	344	581	58	19196	201*	36.70	41	98	3459	79		43.78	4-16	-	-	288	14
P.G.Z.Harris	Cant	1949/50	1963/64	38	67	6	1925	118	31.55	4	5	510	16		31.87	3-8	-	-	24	
	All	1949/50	1964/65	69	120	9	3126	118	28.16	5	13	647	21		30.80	3-8	-	-	37	
R.M.Harris	Auck	1955/56	1973/74	67	119	9	3598	157	31.28	3	20	595	14		42.50	4-105	-	-	46	
	All	1955/56	1973/74	73	130	5	3863	157	30.90	3	21	595	14		42.50	4-105	-	-	48	
S.J.Harris	ND	1975/76		1	0														-	
V.Harris	Well	1913/14		1	2	0	29	15	14.50	-	-	31	1		31.00	1-14	-	-	-	
H.J.H.Harrison	Auck	1940/41	1943/44	4	4	1	36	15	12.00	-	-	270	5		54.00	2-44	-	-	3	

185

		First	Last	M	I	NO	Runs	HS	Avg	100	50	Runs	Wkts	OW	Avg	Best	5i	10m	ct	st
A.W.Hart	Cant	1981/82	1985/86	31	44	12	506	70*	15.81	-	-	1	0		-	-	-	-	72	11
B.P.Hart	Otago	1997/98		1	1	0	1	1	1.00	-	-								5	
G.R.J.Hart	CD	1994/95		5	9	2	135	55	16.87	-	1								4	
M.N.Hart	ND	1990/91	2004/05	95	140	16	3398	201*	27.40	4	16	3984	130		30.64	5-37	5	-	81	
	All	1990/91	2004/05	135	198	26	4418	201*	25.68	4	20	7424	212		35.01	6-73	7	-	110	
R.G.Hart	ND	1992/93	2003/04	85	119	19	2135	102*	21.35	2	7								228	15
	All	1992/93	2003/04	110	156	24	2893	127*	21.91	2	12								298	17
R.T.Hart	CD	1982/83	1990/91	37	68	3	2222	207	34.18	5	12	88	0		-	-	-	-	24	
	Well	1992/93	1993/94	10	18	0	400	120	22.22	1	-								4	
	All	1980/81	1993/94	51	94	3	2686	207	29.51	6	12	88	0		-	-	-	-	30	2
B.R.Hartland	Cant	1986/87	1996/97	59	103	7	2771	150	28.86	5	13								34	
	All	1986/87	1996/97	83	150	8	3753	150	26.42	5	19								52	
I.R.Hartland	Cant	1960/61	1965/66	16	26	1	613	60	24.52	-	4	16	0		-	-	-	-	8	
J.F.Hartland	Cant	1877/78	1890/91	5	7	0	48	11	6.85	-	-								4	
D.J.Hartshorn	Cant	1984/85	1987/88	20	37	6	703	103	22.67	1	-	1544	29		53.24	4-45	-	-	13	
	CD	1993/94		6	8	2	160	35	26.66	-	-	585	13		45.00	4-124	-	-	2	
	All	1984/85	1993/94	26	45	8	863	103	23.32	1	-	2129	42		50.69	4-45	-	-	15	
M.J.Harvie	Otago	2003/04	2009/10	26	29	9	233	37*	11.65	-	-	2441	60		40.68	4-73	-	-	8	
W.L.D.Harvie	Auck	1914/15		2	3	2	6	6*	6.00	-	-	292	12		24.33	4-85	-	-	-	
N.J.Harwood	ND	1959/60		1	1	0	11	11	11.00	-	-	35	1		35.00	1-22	-	-	-	
R.C.Harwood	Otago	1944/45	1945/46	5	8	0	60	24	7.50	-	-	222	7		31.71	2-46	-	-	3	
A.S.Hasell	Cant	1894/95	1895/96	2	3	1	26	17*	13.00	-	-	43	2		21.50	1-19	-	-	4	
O.H.Haskell	Otago	1877/78	1889/90	6	12	1	78	34	7.09	-	-	103	3		34.33	2-26	-	-	1	
W.J.R.Haskell	Well	1955/56	1968/69	16	22	8	182	35	13.00	-	-	797	40		19.92	6-6	1	-	10	
M.J.Haslam	Auck	1991/92	2001/02	42	54	17	288	30*	7.78	-	-	2912	80		36.40	4-60	-	-	16	
	All	1991/92	2001/02	63	72	22	389	30*	7.78	-	-	4436	118		37.59	5-25	1	-	22	
B.F.Hastings	Well	1957/58		1	2	0	49	27	24.50	-	-								1	
	CD	1960/61		5	9	0	168	60	18.66	-	1								3	
	Cant	1961/62	1976/77	73	124	9	3607	226	31.36	7	18	102	3		34.00	1-0	-	-	51	
	All	1957/58	1976/77	163	273	32	7686	226	31.89	15	38	139	4		34.75	1-0	-	-	112	
M.A.Hastings	Cant	1992/93	2000/01	10	14	3	206	52	18.72	-	1	512	20		25.60	4-30	-	-	7	
R.K.Hatch	Well	1945/46		5	10	1	64	26	7.11	-	-	454	14		32.42	4-104	-	-	1	
R.J.Hatch	Well	1933/34		3	2	1	11	11*	11.00	-	-	102	2		51.00	2-80	-	-	-	
J.G.Hatwell	ND	2003/04		3	4	1	93	68	31.00	-	1	59	1		59.00	1-20	-	-	1	
J.H.Haughton	Well	1876/77		1	2	0	6	3	3.00	-	-								-	
P.J.Havill	ND	1969/70		2	3	1	46	34*	46.00	-	-								1	
G.Hawke	HB	1900/01	1910/11	14	27	2	580	87	22.30	-	4	127	2		63.50	1-19	-	-	5	
W.H.Hawkins	Auck	1886/87	1896/97	9	13	2	54	20	4.90	-	-	42	1		42.00	1-25	-	-	8	1
W.H.Hawkins	HB	1887/88	1894/95	8	13	3	37	12*	3.70	-	-	247	13		19.00	3-11	-	-	5	3
W.Hawksworth	Otago	1929/30	1933/34	12	22	0	162	27*	14.72	-	1								20	7
B.A.Haworth	Cant	1953/54	1958/59	18	33	4	587	123	20.24	1	2								6	
A.Hawthorne	Well	1906/07	1909/10	4	5	0	29	18	5.80	-	-	14	1		14.00	1-3	-	-	-	
D.Hay	Well	1913/14	1914/15	6	11	1	227	47*	22.70	-	1	38	1		38.00	1-7	-	-	6	
G.R.Hay	CD	2006/07	2008/09	20	34	4	1345	164*	44.83	4	6								12	
	All	2006/07	2008/09	22	38	4	1443	164*	42.44	4	6								12	
J.C.Hay	Cant	1917/18	1918/19	5	10	0	102	30	10.20	-	-								2	

		First	Last	M	I	NO	Runs	HS	Avg	100	50	Runs	Wkts	OW	Avg	Best	5i	10m	ct	st
S.C.Hay	Auck	1931/32		2	4	0	27	11	6.75	-	-	444	19		23.36	5-10	1	-	7	-
T.D.B.Hay	Auck	1893/94	1906/07	21	40	3	631	144	17.05	1	2	444	19		23.36	5-10	1	-	7	-
	All	1893/94	1927	25	47	4	689	144	16.02	1	2	192	18		10.66	8-70	2	1	9	-
W.A.Hay	Otago	1917/18		1	2	0	17	13	8.50	-	-								1	-
W.P.C.Hay	Auck	1893/94		1	2	0	2	2	1.00	-	-								-	-
S.C.Hayden	Auck	1996/97		1	2	0	3	3	1.50	-	-	1	0		-	-	-	-	1	-
W.H.Haydon	Otago	1895/96	1897/98	4	7	0	37	13	5.28	-	-								5	1
J.A.Hayes	Auck	1946/47	1958/59	10	13	6	129	29	18.42	-	-	892	58		15.37	7-28	6	2	5	-
	Cant	1950/51	1954/55	20	31	8	234	36	10.17	-	-	1789	79		22.64	6-26	1	-	5	-
	All	1946/47	1960/61	78	100	36	611	36	9.54	-	-	6759	292		23.14	7-28	12	3	29	-
R.L.Hayes	ND	1991/92	1995/96	29	34	14	52	10	2.60	-	-	2276	78		29.17	4-41	-	-	4	-
	All	1991/92	1995/96	33	39	17	109	33*	4.95	-	-	2560	91		28.13	4-41	-	-	4	-
W.H.J.Hayes	Cant	1909/10	1927/28	24	44	2	708	125	16.85	1	4	210	7		30.00	2-25	-	-	18	-
G.P.Hayne	Auck	2006/07	2007/08	5	7	2	39	18	7.80	-	-	483	9		53.66	3-80	-	-	3	-
G.Hayward	Auck	1910/11		2	3	1	1	1	0.50	-	-								3	-
R.E.Hayward	CD	1982/83	1985/86	27	45	7	1034	102	27.21	1	6	58	0		-	-	-	-	17	-
	All	1979	1985/86	50	80	14	1766	102	26.75	3	9	63	0		-	-	-	-	27	-
W.Hayward	HB	1885/86		2	4	1	32	16*	10.66	-	-	71	1		71.00	1-9	-	-	-	-
W.Hayward	Auck	1935/36		1	1	0	1	1*	-	-	-								2	-
D.Heenan	Otago	1928/29	1929/30	2	2	0	19	14*	9.50	-	-								3	-
G.C.Heenan	Well	1882/83	1887/88	12	21	1	381	146*	19.05	1	2								3	-
	Tara	1891/92	1897/98	4	6	1	49	24*	9.80	-	-								-	-
	All	1882/83	1897/98	16	27	2	430	146*	17.20	1	2								3	-
B.E.Hefford	CD	1999/00	2008/09	48	63	20	358	32*	8.32	-	-	3719	119		31.25	5-50	1	-	12	-
G.J.T.Hegglun	CD	2004/05	2007/08	11	17	3	151	52*	10.78	-	1	840	23		36.52	4-52	-	-	6	-
G.B.Heley	Sland	1917/18		1	2	0	12	10	6.00	-	-	28	0		-	-	-	-	-	-
A.T.R.Hellaby	Auck	1979/80	1987/88	26	39	5	655	62	19.26	-	2	898	33		27.21	4-17	-	-	19	-
A.Hellicar	Otago	1872/73		1	2	0	17	15	8.50	-	-								-	-
G.H.N.Helmore	Cant	1883/84	1891/92	4	7	0	44	22	6.28	-	-								1	-
R.C.Hemi	Auck	1950/51		2	6	0	69	30	11.50	-	-								2	-
F.E.Hemmingson	Auck	1945/46	1949/50	11	16	8	106	34*	13.25	-	-	936	28		33.42	4-35	-	-	6	-
L.G.Hemus	Auck	1904/05	1921/22	39	71	4	2701	148	40.31	8	10	197	3		65.66	1-4	-	-	25	-
	All	1904/05	1921/22	46	85	4	2916	148	36.00	8	10	278	3		92.66	1-4	-	-	26	-
J.D.Henderson	CD	1960/61		3	3	1	13	13	6.50	-	-	267	6		44.50	2-41	-	-	2	-
M.Henderson	Well	1921/22	1931/32	23	37	14	363	47	15.78	-	-	2238	70		31.97	6-70	3	-	5	-
	All	1921/22	1931/32	41	57	22	495	47	14.14	-	-	3200	107		29.90	6-70	5	-	12	-
N.D.Henderson	Otago	1935/36		1	2	1	8	7	8.00	-	-	113	2		56.50	1-54	-	-	2	-
W.Hendley	Otago	1864/65	1872/73	8	13	2	22	11	2.00	-	-	314	37		8.48	8-28	2	1	9	-
R.Hendry	Otago	1961/62	1973/74	33	61	6	1027	87*	18.67	-	5	14	0		-	-	-	-	18	-
	All	1961/62	1973/74	34	63	6	1061	87*	18.61	-	5	14	0		-	-	-	-	18	-
W.J.Hendy	Auck	1927/28		2	4	0	70	38	17.50	-	-								-	-
D.W.Henry	Well	1980/81		6	9	3	153	40*	25.50	-	-	304	5		60.80	2-16	-	-	3	-
G.W.Henry	Cant	1965/66		5	6	0	8	3*	2.00	-	-								11	2
	Otago	1967/68		1	2	0	2	2	1.00	-	-								-	-
	All	1965/66	1967/68	6	8	0	10	3*	1.66	-	-								11	2
P.J.Henry	Otago	1996/97		2	2	0	9	9	4.50	-	-								6	-

		First	Last	M	I	NO	Runs	HS	Avg	100	50	Runs	Wkts	OW	Avg	Best	5i	10m	ct	st
W.F.T.Hepburn	Well	1931/32	1940/41	7	13	0	305	58	23.46	-	3	40	0		-	-	-	-	2	
G.L.Hermansson	All	1962/63		1	2	0	12	12	6.00	-	-								4	
D.F.Hewat	Well	1887/88	1889/90	4	6	0	18	12	3.60	-	-	222	27		8.22	7-30	3	-	1	
R.Hewat	Otago	1889/90		1	2	0	0	0	0.00	-	-	16	1		16.00	1-16	-	-	-	
A.R.Hewson	Well	1978/79		8	11	2	82	25	9.11	-	-								2	
G.A.Hick	ND	1987/88	1988/89	17	30	4	2055	211*	79.03	10	5	183	3		61.00	1-12	-	-	21	
	All	1983/84	2008	526	871	84	41112	405*	52.23	136	158	10308	232		44.43	5-18	1	-	709	3
C.E.H.Hickey	Well	1902/03	1910/11	8	13	4	84	35	9.33	-	-	489	26		18.80	4-50	-	-	5	
R.G.Hickmott	Cant	1911/12	1914/15	11	19	0	623	109	32.78	1	4	192	9		21.33	4-5	-	-	4	
	All	1911/12	1914/15	17	31	0	778	109	25.09	1	4	300	11		27.27	4-5	-	-	7	
H.C.Hickson	Well	1898/99	1911/12	23	43	2	930	135	22.68	1	2	225	10		22.50	7-56	1	-	25	
	All	1898/99	1911/12	25	47	2	973	135	21.62	1	2	225	10		22.50	7-56	1	-	26	
H.S.Hickson	Well	1879/80	1881/82	3	5	0	21	11	4.20	-	-	68	5		13.60	2-8	-	-	-	
W.R.S.Hickson	Well	1896/97	1906/07	12	20	1	236	32	12.42	-	-	53	3		17.66	3-37	-	-	4	
J.S.Hiddleston	Otago	1909/10		3	6	0	51	43	8.50	-	-	9	0		-	-	-	-	-	
	Well	1913/14	1928/29	41	75	1	3413	212	46.12	8	18	2202	85		25.90	8-59	3	1	48	
	All	1909/10	1928/29	52	97	1	3818	212	39.77	8	20	2312	86		26.88	8-59	3	1	55	
B.B.Higgins	ND	1956/57		1	2	0	14	14	7.00	-	-	44	0		-	-	-	-	-	
W.L.Higgins	Otago	1910/11	1920/21	7	13	0	201	67	15.46	-	1								4	
B.C.Hiini	Cant	2005/06	2009/10	32	43	10	910	103*	27.57	2	2	2683	92		29.16	5-32	2	-	15	
A.J.Hill	CD	1975/76	1976/77	2	4	0	36	13	9.00	-	-								2	
D.Hill	Cant	1961/62		5	9	0	176	58	19.55	-	1	21	0		-	-	-	-	5	
	Auck	1967/68		2	4	0	94	66	23.50	-	1								1	
	All	1961/62	1967/68	7	13	0	270	66	20.76	-	2	21	0		-	-	-	-	6	
G.H.F.Hill	HB	1891/92	1901/02	11	18	2	162	27	10.12	-	-								2	
H.P.Hill	Cant	1873/74		1	2	0	0	0	0.00	-	-	2	0		-	-	-	-	-	
J.Hill	Otago	1961/62	1962/63	7	13	8	25	10	5.00	-	-	422	15		28.13	4-76	-	-	2	
	All	1961/62	1962/63	8	15	9	31	10	5.16	-	-	483	19		25.42	4-61	-	-	3	
J.V.Hill	CD	1999/00	2000/01	8	16	1	141	26	9.40	-	-								4	
R.J.Hill	Otago	1976/77	1979/80	9	12	2	93	36	9.30	-	-	250	7		35.71	4-55	-	-	5	
P.W.Hills	Otago	1978/79	1989/90	33	42	8	290	32	8.52	-	-	2196	58		37.86	5-57	2	-	20	
	All	1978/79	1989/90	34	44	8	307	32	8.52	-	-	2232	58		38.48	5-57	2	-	20	
H.S.W.Hindmarsh	HB	1920/21		2	4	0	20	15	5.00	-	-	33	0		-	-	-	-	1	
J.S.Hindmarsh	HB	1907/08	1913/14	8	16	0	207	50	12.93	-	1								4	
S.D.Hinton	Otago	1994/95		1	2	1	8	6	8.00	-	-	68	2		34.00	2-62	-	-	-	
A.J.Hintz	Cant	1985/86	1987/88	6	10	1	108	62	13.50	-	1	365	11		33.18	3-51	-	-	-	
E.Hipkiss	ND	1966/67		6	10	4	24	7*	4.00	-	-	291	10		29.10	4-39	-	-	5	
R.M.Hira	Auck	2006/07	2007/08	4	5	1	106	45*	26.50	-	-	205	1		205.00	1-27	-	-	1	
P.A.Hitchcock	Well	1999/00		1	2	0	1	1	0.50	-	-	51	1		51.00	1-51	-	-	-	
	Auck	2003/04	2008/09	10	14	3	297	51	27.00	-	1	696	13		53.53	3-27	-	-	1	
	All	1999/00	2008/09	11	16	3	298	51	22.92	-	1	747	14		53.35	3-27	-	-	1	
R.E.Hitchcock	Cant	1947/48		2	4	0	42	17	10.50	-	-	161	5		32.20	2-26	-	-	3	
	All	1947/48	1964	323	519	71	12473	153*	27.84	13	65	5845	196		29.82	7-76	7	1	116	
W.H.Hitchens	HB	1913/14		1	2	1	7	7	3.50	-	-	56	1		56.00	1-56	-	-	-	
F.R.Hoar	Well	1928/29		2	2	0	13	13*	13.00	-	-	175	5		35.00	2-77	-	-	2	

		First	Last	M	I	NO	Runs	HS	Avg	100	50	Runs	Wkts	OW	Avg	Best	5i	10m	ct	st
N.R.Hoar	Well	1944/45	1944/45	4	7	2	190	76	38.00	-	1	182	7		26.00	3-68	-	-	3	
R.W.Hodder	All	1942/43	1944/45	6	11	3	264	76	33.00	-	2	334	10		33.40	3-68	-	-	3	
G.Hodge	Nel	1882/83	1886/87	6	11	0	104	18	9.45	-	-								8	
W.G.Hodgson	Well	1907/08		1	1	0	8	8	8.00	-	-								2	
K.W.Hogg	CD	1979/80	1981/82	12	22	1	521	51	24.80	-	2	157	2		78.50	1-29	-	-	12	
	All	1979/80	1981/82	13	24	2	560	51	25.45	-	2	157	2		78.50	1-29	-	-	13	
	Otago	2006/07		4	5	2	170	71	42.50	-	2	313	5		62.60	2-59	-	-	1	
W.A.Holdaway	All	2001	2010	64	78	11	1649	88	24.61	-	11	4406	124		35.53	5-48	1	-	16	
A.C.Holden	Otago	1918/19		1	2	0	9	9	4.50	-	-								1	
W.J.Holden	Otago	1937/38	1939/40	2	4	0	77	36	19.25	-	-								1	
H.V.A.Holderness	Otago	1917/18	1918/19	4	6	1	117	35	23.40	-	-								3	
M.A.Holding	Cant	1918/19		1	2	1	4	4	4.00	-	-									
A.R.Holdship	All	1987/88	1989	7	11	4	62	31	8.85	-	-	39	10		3.90	5-10	2	1	9	
	All	1972/73	1898/99	222	283	43	3600	80	15.00	-	14	488	29		16.82	7-52	3	-	125	
F.Holdsworth	Well	1893/94	1898/99	17	27	1	697	79	26.80	-	6	18233	778		23.43	8-92	39	5	12	
H.W.Hole	All	1893/94	1902/03	21	35	1	801	79	23.55	-	7	374	15		24.93	3-6	-	-	15	
C.A.Holland	Well	1891/92	1924/25	12	19	3	153	32	9.56	-	-	390	15		26.00	6-35	3	-	7	
	Nel	1874/75		1	2	0	10	6	5.00	-	-	575	33		17.42	8-37	1	-		
	Well	1923/24	1924/25	3	6	0	95	54	23.75	-	1	61	10		6.10	2-60	-	-	2	
P.J.Holland	All	1913/14	1977/78	5	10	0	121	54	17.28	-	1	218	4		54.50	2-60	-	-	3	
	CD	1976/77		10	18	0	242	69	15.12	-	1	373	6		62.16					
	ND	1978/79		5	8	0	44	16	8.25	-	-	22	0						4	
R.G.Holland	Well	1979/80	1983/84	23	37	5	739	67	23.09	-	5	485	11		44.00	1-44	-	-	2	
	All	1976/77	1983/84	39	65	7	1047	69	18.05	-	6	551	12		44.09	2-24	-	-	9	
L.D.Hollands	Well	1987/88		7	3	0	9	7	3.00	-	-	738	31		45.91	2-24	2	-	2	
R.L.Holle	All	1978/79	1987/88	95	95	5	706	53	9.67	-	1	9857	316		23.80	7-69	14	3	15	
	Otago	1969/70	1971/72	6	9	2	191	66*	27.28	-	-	193	20		31.19	9-83			3	
	Well	1883/84	1886/87	4	7	0	29	17	4.14	-	-	25	0		9.65	5-22	1	-	54	
	Auck	1893/94		3	6	1	41	9	8.20	-	-								2	
A.M.Hollings	All	1883/84	1893/94	7	13	1	70	17	5.83	-	-	218	20		10.90	5-22	1	-	1	
R.A.Holloway	Well	1926/27	1929/30	8	14	3	330	65*	30.00	-	2	235	5		47.00	2-18	-	-	2	
	Otago	1961/62	1964/65	14	27	2	368	61*	14.72	-	2								9	
	All	1961/62	1964/65	15	29	2	373	61*	13.81	-	2								4	
J.E.Hollywood	Auck	1947/48	1949/50	7	9	5	41	17*	10.25	-	-	722	25		28.88	4-86	-	-	5	
A.Holmes	Otago	1870/71	1873/74	2	3	1	24	12*	12.00	-	-								3	
W.Holmes	Nel	1880/81		1	2	0	3	3	1.50	-	-									
	Well	1882/83	1883/84	2	3	0	10	9	3.33	-	-	20	0			1-5	-	-	4	
	All	1880/81	1883/84	3	5	0	13	9	2.60	-	-	51	3		17.00	1-5	-	-	2	
W.R.Holt	ND	1964/65		2	2	0	37	32	18.50	-	-	71	3		23.66	2-42	-	-	2	
B.L.Hood	ND	2000/01		2	3	0	12	12	4.00	-	-	140	4		35.00					
G.H.Hook	Auck	1935/36	1936/37	5	5	0	126	48	25.20	-	1	42	6		7.00	3-9	-	-	4	
	All	1935/36	1942/43	8	11	0	198	54*	19.80	-	1	54	6		9.00	3-9	-	-	3	
R.C.Hooton	ND	1968/69	1971/72	12	20	0	354	54	17.70	-	2	57	4		14.25	4-38	1	-	4	
	Auck	1979/80		2	6	0	6	6	1.00	-	-	6	1		6.00	1-6	-	-	5	
	All	1968/69	1979/80	19	31	1	598	54	19.93	-	2	63	5		12.60	4-38	1	-	4	
J.Hope	Otago	1885/86	1899/00	22	37	14	243	24	10.56	-	-	958	73		13.12	6-23	7	1	16	

		First	Last	M	I	NO	Runs	HS	Avg	100	50	Runs	Wkts	OW	Avg	Best	5i	10m	ct	st
J.H.Hope	Otago	1863/64	1866/67	4	7	0	84	28	12.00	-	-	155	3		51.66	2-60	-	-	12	
R.W.Hope	Well	1928/29	1929/30	2	1	1	0	0*	-	-	-	382	10		38.20	3-61	-	-	3	
	Cant	1933/34		1								789	16		49.31	3-61	-	-	2	
	All	1925/26	1933/34	3	1	1	0	0*	-	-	-	177	6		29.50	2-20	-	-	5	
B.H.Hopkins	Well	1966/67		3	5	2	63	29											1	
C.C.Hopkins	Otago	1908/09	1912/13	9	17	0	68	29	9.71	-	-	32	0		-	-	-	-	2	
G.J.Hopkins	ND	1997/98		2	3	0	40	21	10.00	-	-	13	0		-	-	-	-	3	
	Cant	1998/99	2002/03	41	68	12	448	132	26.35	1	1								91	10
	Otago	2003/04	2006/07	33	52	10	57	38	19.00	-	-								111	3
	Auck	2007/08	2009/10	20	27	4	1642	175*	29.32	4	4								47	2
	All	1997/98	2009/10	117	181	28	1471	139*	35.02	3	7								304	20
A.J.Hore	Otago	1996/97	2003/04	26	44	2	1370	201	59.56	4	8	36	0		-	-	-	-	24	
M.J.Horne	Auck	1992/93	2005/06	50	80	4	5336	201	34.87	11	23	49	0		-	-	-	-	25	
	Otago	1996/97	2000/01	23	40	2	992	102	23.61	2	5	144	1		144.00	1-77	-	-	23	
	All	1992/93	2005/06	128	219	11	3184	209*	41.89	9	12	283	5		56.60	2-58	-	-	79	
P.A.Horne	Auck	1979/80	1990/91	40	67	4	1977	241	52.02	7	9	176	2		88.00	2-68	-	-	36	
T.B.Horne	All	1979/80	1990/91	53	90	6	8501	241	40.87	24	33	531	7		75.85	2-58	-	-	42	
N.K.W.Horsley	CD	1977/78	1979/80	12	21	0	2380	209	39.01	4	15	16	1		16.00	1-5	-	-	9	
	Auck	2001/02		9	13	6	2879	209	34.27	5	17	16	1		16.00	1-5	-	-	3	
	ND	2002/03	2007/08	35	60	3	422	54	20.09	-	1	0	0		-	-	-	-	14	
	All	2001/02	2007/08	44	73	4	410	106*	34.16	2	2	36	2		18.00	1-5	-	-	17	
E.Horspool	Auck	1909/10	1928/29	38	69	2	2003	159	35.14	3	15	36	2		18.00	1-5	-	-	27	
	All	1909/10	1928/29	39	71	2	2413	159	34.97	3	17	454	9		50.44	2-15	-	-	27	
R.G.Hortin	Cant	1963/64		2	4	1	1665	143	24.85	2	7	454	9		50.44	2-15	-	-	-	
M.J.Horton	ND	1967/68	1970/71	19	34	1	1686	143	24.43	2	7	16	0		-	-	-	-	5	
	All	1952	1970/71	410	724	49	30	16	7.50	-	-	1054	33		31.93	5-35	1	-	166	
D.C.Hoskin	ND	1956/57	1964/65	23	36	20	1090	109	33.03	1	7	22226	825		26.94	9-56	40	7	13	
R.N.Hoskin	Otago	1980/81	1992/93	80	138	6	19949	233	29.55	23	112	1644	60		27.40	7-33	2	-	54	
	All	1980/81	1992/93	81	140	7	126	23	7.87	-	-	109	1		109.00	1-105	-	-	57	
D.R.Hosking	Well	1967/68		1	1	1	3573	157	27.06	6	21	109	1		109.00	1-105	-	-	1	
S.J.Hotter	Well	1988/89	1999/00	21	31	6	3580	157	26.91	6	21	107	0		-	-	-	-	8	
	All	1988/89	1999/00	24	35	9	214	33	8.56	-	-	1837	60		30.61	6-69	3	1	9	
K.W.Hough	ND	1956/57		5	9	0	240	33	9.23	-	-	2048	70		29.25	6-69	4	1	2	
	Auck	1957/58	1959/60	16	26	3	42	11	4.66	-	-	446	12		37.16	4-101	-	-	17	
	All	1956/57	1959/60	28	46	8	420	91	18.26	-	1	1490	86		17.32	7-43	6	3	25	
J.H.P.Houghton	CD	1953/54		3	5	0	624	91	16.42	-	1	2484	119		20.87	7-43	6	3	-	
M.V.Houghton	Well	2007/08	2008/09	9	9	1	5	2	1.00	-	-								2	
A.R.Hounsell	Cant	1969/70	1976/77	18	21	8	192	81	24.00	-	1	612	14		43.71	3-20	-	-	8	
	Well	1972/73		6	6	1	152	27*	11.69	-	-	1152	40		28.80	5-50	1	-	4	
	Auck	1973/74		5	4	3	24	9	4.80	-	-	461	16		28.81	4-35	-	-	4	
	ND	1974/75		5	4	2	13	9	4.33	-	-	288	5		57.60	2-17	-	-	1	
	All	1968/69	1976/77	37	40	15	36	26	18.00	-	-	331	8		41.37	3-32	-	-	14	
P.J.Hounsell	Auck	1987/88	1988/89	4	3	0	250	27*	10.00	-	-	2485	78		31.85	5-50	1	-	3	
D.W.Houpapa	Auck	2006/07		3	5	0	28	22	9.33	-	-	16	0		-	-	-	-	1	
J.M.How	CD	2000/01	2009/10	56	102	9	74	33	14.80	-	-	986	18		54.77	3-57	-	-	68	
	All	2000/01	2009/10	92	161	12	3563	176	38.31	10	18	1202	20		60.10	3-57	-	-	96	

		First	Last	M	I	NO	Runs	HS	Avg	100	50	Runs	Wkts	OW	Avg	Best	5i	10m	ct	st
A.H.S.Howard	Well	1895/96	1897/98	5	9	0	125	51	13.88	-	1	85	5		17.00	3-33	-	-	2	
G.P.Howarth	HB	1904/05	1905/06	2	4	0	28	15	7.00	-	-									
	All	1895/96	1905/06	7	13	0	153	51	11.76	-	1	85	5		17.00	3-33	-	-	2	
	Auck	1972/73	1973/74	11	20	1	443	55	23.31	-	1	604	29		20.82	5-32	1	-	18	
	ND	1974/75	1985/86	58	105	6	3122	151	31.53	5	16	1638	57		28.73	4-43	-	-	42	
	All	1968/69	1985/86	338	584	42	17294	183	31.90	32	88	3596	112		32.10	5-32	1	-	229	
H.J.Howarth	Auck	1963/64	1978/79	80	103	27	1163	56	15.30	-	2	7361	332		22.17	8-75	18	4	87	
	All	1962/63	1978/79	145	179	58	1668	61	13.78	-	3	13674	541		25.27	8-75	31	6	137	
A.M.Howden	Auck	1906/07	1914/15	10	14	3	84	29	7.63	-	-	899	53		16.96	7-87	4	1	4	
C.E.Howden	Otago	1906/07	1914/15	11	16	4	95	29	7.91	-	-	954	53		18.00	7-87	4	-	5	
	All	1902/03	1908/09	11	21	0	341	62	16.23	-	1	7	0		-	-	-	-	5	
C.P.Howden	Otago	1902/03	1908/09	13	25	1	386	62	16.08	-	1	7	0		-	-	-	-	5	
A.G.Howe	HB	1937/38		2	4	0	63	30	15.75	-	-	46	0		-	-	-	-	-	
G.Howe	Well	1886/87		1	2	0	9	9	4.50	-	-									
G.A.Howell	Cant	1913/14		5	9	0	139	31	15.44	-	-								5	
	Well	1998/99		1	1	0	19	19	9.50	-	-								4	
	All	2001/02	2001/02	3	5	2	25	19*	8.33	-	-								10	
J.H.Howell	CD	1998/99	1972/73	4	7	2	44	19*	8.80	-	-	2275	82		27.74	5-56	1	-	14	
L.G.Howell	Cant	1966/67	1998/99	34	41	9	275	32	8.59	-	-	68	0		-	-	-	-	20	
	CD	1990/91	1996/97	36	57	8	1473	112	30.06	1	10	42	0		-	-	-	-	24	
	Auck	1994/95	2003/04	19	32	3	1132	181	39.03	2	5								4	
	ND	1999/00		9	18	3	179	34	11.93	-	-								7	
	All	2004/05		3	6	0	92	35	15.33	-	-								2	
W.B.Howell	Cant	1990/91	2004/05	83	143	16	3586	181	28.23	3	20	110	0		-	-	-	-	48	
	All	1902/03	1918/19	9	15	4	116	20*	10.54	-	-	625	41		15.24	7-32	2	1	5	
J.T.Howlett	Auck	1902/03	1918/19	11	19	5	130	20*	9.28	-	-	729	47		15.51	7-32	2	1	6	
	All	1891/92		1	1	0	33	33	33.00	-	-	32	5		6.40	4-11	-	-	-	
W.J.Hughes	HB	1891/92	1903/04	2	3	0	66	33	33.00	-	-	94	5		18.80	4-11	-	-	-	
J.E.Hume	Otago	1891/92	1905/06	16	25	1	108	21	6.00	-	-	711	34		20.91	6-80	2	-	4	
E.Humphreys	Cant	1880/81		1	2	1	2	1*	2.00	-	-	70	2		35.00	2-70	-	-	-	
	All	1908/09		3	6	0	150	43	25.00	-	-	313	25		12.52	6-23	2	-	1	
C.Humphries	Nel	1899	1920	393	639	45	16603	208	27.95	22	86	9314	379		24.57	7-33	12	-	229	3
A.J.Hunt	Auck	1879/80	1888/89	6	12	0	56	15	4.66	-	-	5			-	-	-	-	2	
H.A.Hunt	All	1981/82	1992/93	65	99	15	2069	102*	24.63	1	13	1099	25		43.96	4-26	-	-	72	
R.T.Hunt	Otago	1980/81	1992/93	67	103	16	2128	102*	24.45	1	13	1226	28		43.78	4-26	-	-	72	
	All	1929/30	1903/04	4	6	3	1	1	0.33	-	-								6	
A.A.Hunter	Cant	1947/48	1930/31	15	27	0	731	75	27.07	-	5								6	
	All	1959/60	1953/54	4	8	0	67	29	8.37	-	-								1	
D.J.Hunter	CD	1947/48	1959/60	19	35	0	798	75	22.80	-	5	3	0		-	-	-	-	7	
R.J.Hunter	All	1951/52	1955/56	15	25	0	698	108	27.92	1	4	3	0		-	-	-	-	5	
R.J.Hunter	Otago	1951/52	1955/56	16	27	0	752	108	27.85	1	4	158	3		52.66	1-14	-	-	5	
H.J.Huntley	Well	1989/90		1	2	0	220	36	14.66	-	-	158	3		52.66	1-14	-	-	5	
	Auck	1884/85	1991/92	16	19	4	42	22	21.00	-	-	1475	43		34.30	4-35	-	-	5	
	Otago	1975/76	1984/85	5	6	4	41	28*	20.50	-	-	411	8		51.37	2-56	-	-	6	
		1912/13		1	2	1	15	8	15.00	-	-	27	0		-	-	-	-	2	

		First	Last	M	I	NO	Runs	HS	Avg	100	50	Runs	Wkts	OW	Avg	Best	5i	10m	ct	st
J.M.Hussey	HB	1901/02		3	5	1	29	8	7.25	-	-	514	24		21.41	4-27	-	-	-	-
	Otago	1902/03		1	2	0	4	3	2.00	-	-	514	24		21.41	4-27	-	-	-	-
	Auck	1904/05		8	14	2	242	74*	20.16	-	1	792	19		41.68	4-102	-	-	5	-
J.H.Hutchings	Well	1901/02	1907/08	12	21	2	275	74*	15.27	-	1								5	-
F.C.Hutchison	Otago	1903/04	1907/08	18	33	7	472	74*	18.15	-	1								5	-
R.W.Hutchison	Otago	1917/18	1924/25	6	9	1	144	85	18.00	-	-								2	-
	CD	1965/66	1919/20	30	54	5	963	66	19.65	-	3	343	0		114.33	2-12	-	-	1	-
		1975/76	1971/72	7	13	1	271	45	22.58	-	3	168	3		56.00	2-41	-	-	14	-
	All	1965/66		37	67	6	1234	66	20.22	-	3	511	3		85.16	2-12	-	-	16	-
N.A.Huxford	Well	1964/65	1975/76	15	15	6	34	8	4.85	-	-	1197	57		21.00	7-95	4	-	9	-
	Cant	1967/68	1966/67	15	13	8	66	19	13.20	-	-	1134	39		29.07	5-25	1	-	4	-
	All	1964/65	1969/70	31	29	16	109	19	8.38	-	-	2419	101		23.95	7-95	5	-	13	-
K.B.K.Ibadulla	Otago	1982/83	1969/70	22	35	4	862	107	27.80	2	3	991	22		45.04	5-22	1	-	11	-
	All	1982/83	1990/91	31	50	8	1131	107	26.92	2	4	1290	29		44.48	5-22	1	-	14	-
K.Ibadulla	Otago	1964/65	1990/91	16	32	8	760	111	33.53	2	4	32	27		28.14	4-38	-	-	9	-
P.A.Iles	All	1951/52	1966/67	417	704	78	17078	171	27.28	22	82	14307	462		30.96	7-22	6	-	337	-
C.D.Ingham	Auck	1946/47	1972	2	3	0	32	20	19.33	-	-	122	3		40.66	3-46	-	-	3	-
W.S.Ingle	CD	1990/91	1951/52	31	58	0	1373	102	24.51	2	5	100	3		33.33	1-11	-	-	14	-
P.J.Ingram	All	1990/91	1994/95	32	60	2	1424	102	24.55	2	6	100	3		33.33	1-11	-	-	14	-
A.E.Irving	Well	1879/80	1994/95		4	0	32	15	8.00	-	-	56	8		7.00	3-8	-	-	9	-
B.C.Irving	CD	2001/02	2009/10	64	117	8	4156	247	38.12	12	14	47	0		-	-	-	-	38	-
	All	2001/02	2009/10	67	122	8	4290	247	37.63	12	15	47	0		-	-	-	-	39	-
R.J.R.Irving	Auck	1917/18	1923/24	7	13	0	206	68	15.84	-	-	38	1		38.00	1-25	-	-	3	-
G.D.Irwin	Cant	1962/63	1972/73	18	24	11	114	17	8.76	-	-	1189	42		28.30	4-32	-	-	6	-
B.P.Isherwood	All	1962/63	1972/73	19	25	11	137	23	9.78	-	-	1264	44		28.72	4-32	-	-	6	-
E.B.Izard	Auck	1996/97	2000/01	3	4	0	22	15	5.50	-	-								6	-
	ND	2002/03		1	2	0	6	4	3.00	-	-								2	-
	Cant	1966/67	1972/73	7	13	2	182	74*	16.54	-	1	63	0		-	-	-	-	14	3
	All	1965/66	1972/73	10	19	3	237	74*	14.81	-	1								20	3
	Well	1890/91	1894/95	5	9	0	106	31	11.77	-	-								3	4
	Tara	1896/97	1897/98	2	3	0	28	24	9.33	-	-									
	All	1890/91	1897/98	7	12	0	134	31	11.16	-	-								3	4
M.W.Jack	Cant	1955/56	1957/58	4	6	4	1	1*	0.50	-	-	238	7		34.00	5-57	1	-	4	-
C.K.Q.Jackman	Cant	1934/35	1936/37	8	13	2	73	17	6.63	-	-								10	17
	Auck	1937/38	1941/42	8	5	1	11	7*	2.75	-	-								8	5
	All	1934/35	1941/42	16	21	4	95	17	5.58	-	-								20	27
H.Jackson	Sland	1918/19		1	2	0	8	6	4.00	-	-								-	-
A.W.Jacobs	Auck	1893/94		3	6	0	60	24	10.00	-	-	46	0		-	-	-	-	-	-
E.L.Jacobs	Well	1873/74		1	2	0	9	6	4.50	-	-								5	1
J.Jacobs	Cant	1927/28	1937/38	11	19	0	420	69	23.33	-	4								5	1
	All	1927/28	1945	12	21	1	464	69	23.20	-	4								5	1
S.Jacobs	Well	1899/00		1	2	0	2	2	1.00	-	-								-	-
N.R.Jacobsen	HB	1919/20	1920/21	5	10	0	172	62	17.20	-	2	136	2		68.00	1-42	-	-	2	-
J.N.Jacomb	Otago	1863/64		1	2	0	2	2	1.00	-	-								1	-
	All	1860/61	1863/64	2	4	0	2	2	0.50	-	-								3	-
H.T.G.James	Cant	1997/98	2000/01	5	10	1	225	65*	25.00	-	2	14	0		-	-	-	-	6	-

		First	Last	M	I	NO	Runs	HS	Avg	100	50	Runs	Wkts	OW	Avg	Best	5i	10m	ct	st
K.C.James	Well	1923/24	1946/47	38	67	11	1908	109*	34.07	5	6	0	0						69	8
K.D.James	All	1923/24	1946/47	205	330	41	6413	109*	22.19	7	23	17	0						311	112
	Well	1982/83	1984/85	8	9	1	144	36	20.57			551	16		34.43	3-52			1	
R.M.James	All	1980	1999	225	337	57	8526	162	30.45	10	42	12607	395		31.91	8-49	11	1	78	
	Well	1964/65		3	6	1	55	20	11.00			113	2		56.50	1-8			1	
S.N.James	All	1956	1964/65	51	90	10	2208	168	27.60	4	5	1356	38		35.68	4-5			16	
	Otago	1953/54		1								73	0		73.00	1-50			2	
V.James	Cant	1939/40	1944/45	6	9	2	248	155*	35.42	1	1								8	
M.D.Jamieson	CD	1980/81	1981/82	5	5	2	84	59	28.00		1	387	8		48.37	2-44			4	1
T.W.Jarvis	Auck	1964/65	1976/77	46	80	3	2403	118*	31.20	2	16	61	0						68	
	Cant	1969/70	1970/71	10	19	0	669	107	39.35		2				-	-			15	
	All	1964/65	1976/77	97	167	8	4666	182	29.34	6	26	89	0		-	-			102	
M.R.Jefferson	Well	1996/97	2002/03	37	52	11	1077	114	26.26	2	4	2656	66		40.24	4-84			8	
	ND	2006/07		2	4	2	57	29	19.00			95	1		95.00	1-95			1	
	All	1996/97	2006/07	48	69	12	1399	114	24.54	2	5	3468	90		38.53	5-42	1		14	
R.G.Jefferson	Otago	1965/66		2	3	0	23	11	7.66			8	0		-	-			2	
	Well	1969/70		3	6	1	71	26*	14.20						-	-			3	
	All	1965/66	1969/70	5	9	1	94	26*	11.75			8	0		-	-			5	
T.E.Jesty	Cant	1979/80		6	10	0	126	32	12.60			265	12		22.08	4-42			1	
	All	1966	1991	490	777	107	21916	248	32.71	35	110	16075	585		27.47	7-75	19		265	1
L.J.Joel	Otago	1899/00		1	1	0	1	1*												
J.Johnson	HB	1919/20		1	2	1	11	11	5.50										2	
V.F.Johnson	Otago	1984/85	1990/91	26	29	12	176	25*	10.35			2219	62		35.79	5-54	1		7	
	All	1984/85	1990/91	27	29	12	176	25*	10.35			2303	64		35.98	5-54	1		7	
C.E.Johnston	HB	1896/97		2	4	0	17	5	4.25			24	0		-	-				
R.J.Johnston	Otago	1872/73	1873/74	2	3	0	7	6	2.33										2	
W.Johnston	Otago	1889/90	1902/03	20	35	2	434	48	13.15										7	
J.L.Jolly	Otago	1933/34		1	2	0	12	10	6.00											
G.R.Jonas	Well	1993/94	1997/98	25	33	7	132	19	5.07			91	0		-	-			9	
	Otago	1998/99	1999/00	7	10	4	62	14	10.33			2154	88		24.47	5-60	1		3	
	All	1993/94	1999/00	35	47	12	212	19	6.05			551	31		17.77	6-35	3	1	12	
A.O.Jones	Auck	1911/12		2	3	0	20	13	6.66			3024	132		22.90	6-35	5		1	
A.H.Jones	CD	1979/80	1995/96	26	46	1	1068	78	23.73		5	80	4		20.00	3-30			16	
	Otago	1983/84	1984/85	13	23	1	771	102*	48.18	1	4	7	0		-	-			10	
	Well	1985/86	1993/94	39	67	7	2978	181*	53.17	7	19	234	9		26.00	4-28			28	
	All	1979/80	1995/96	145	254	33	9180	186	41.53	16	52	908	20		45.40	3-104			91	
B.L.Jones	CD	1954/55		1	2	0	4	3	2.00			1439	34		42.32	4-28			4	
C.Jones	Well	1944/45		1	2	1	9	5	4.50			11	1		11.00	1-11				
G.J.Jones	Auck	1976/77		1	2	1	43	25*	43.00										2	
J.F.Jones	Well	1950/51	1953/54	6	9	3	53	16*	8.83			426	23		18.52	4-39			1	
	CD	1954/55	1956/57	4	5	1	22	12	5.50			262	9		29.11	4-58			3	
	All	1950/51	1956/57	10	14	4	75	16*	7.50			688	32		21.50	4-39			4	
N.H.P.Jones	Cant	1918/19	1920/21	5	10	0	252	88	25.20		3								6	
R.P.Jones	Cant	1980/81	1984/85	5	8	0	150	56	18.75		1	4	0		-	-			2	
	Otago	1982/83		1	2	0	49	45	24.50											
	All	1980/81	1984/85	6	10	0	199	56	19.90		1	4	0		-	-			2	

		First	Last	M	I	NO	Runs	HS	Avg	100	50	Runs	Wkts	OW	Avg	Best	5i	10m	ct	st
R.A.Jones	Auck	1993/94	2009/10	79	137	8	4721	201	36.59	12	23	0	1		0.00	1-0	-	-	70	-
	Well	2000/01	2003/04	36	63	4	2343	188	39.71	7	10	0	1		0.00	1-0	-	-	29	-
	All	1993/94	2009/10	124	215	12	7254	201	35.73	19	33	6	1		6.00	1-6	-	-	105	-
S.P.Jones	Auck	1904/05	1908/09	5	7	1	83	45	11.85	-	-	1844	55		33.52	5-54	1	-	1	-
	All	1880/81	1908/09	152	259	13	5189	151	21.09	5	24	36	2		18.00	2-20	-	-	81	-
S.T.Jones	Otago	1953/54		1	2	0	8	8	4.00	-	-								-	-
F.Joplin	Well	1913/14		4	8	1	162	80	23.14	-	1								1	-
A.B.Jordan	CD	1968/69	1979/80	55	79	32	517	47	11.00	-	-	4431	157		28.22	7-82	7	-	27	-
	All	1968/69	1979/80	58	83	32	560	47	10.98	-	-	4683	165		28.38	7-82	7	-	28	-
W.Judd	Well	1886/87		2	3	0	51	22	17.00	-	-	91	5		18.20	4-58	-	-	1	-
M.O.Kain	Cant	2008/09		1	1	0	24	24	24.00	-	-	121	2		60.50	1-51	-	-	-	-
J.A.Kallendar	Auck	1893/94	1904/05	12	22	1	389	55	18.52	-	1	338	16		21.12	3-7	-	-	5	-
R.J.Kasper	Auck	1966/67	1978/79	32	59	8	1596	102*	31.29	2	8	338	11		30.72	2-7	-	-	12	-
	All	1966/67	1978/79	38	69	10	1742	122*	29.52	3	8	869	23		37.78	6-110	1	-	13	-
E.J.Kavanagh	Sland	1914/15	1920/21	6	11	0	119	33	10.81	-	-	129	7		18.42	3-30	-	-	6	-
V.C.Kavanagh	Auck	1912/13		1	2	0	18	12	9.00	-	-	55	0						-	-
D.J.Kay	CD	1974/75	1977/78	15	22	0	107	39*	8.91	-	-	1076	48		22.41	7-62	3	1	7	-
R.J.Kean	Well	1976/77	1977/78	5	12	1	159	32	14.45	-	-								7	-
A.V.E.M.Keast	Otago	1917/18	1922/23	4	7	0	23	7	3.28	-	-								1	-
S.A.Kellett	Well	1991/92		1	2	0	30	22	15.00	-	-								3	-
D.P.Kelly	All	1989	1995	87	149	10	4234	125*	30.46	2	29	12	0						77	-
	CD	1999/00	2001/02	25	47	2	1349	212*	29.97	3	5	19	0						16	-
	ND	2002/03		3	5	0	50	26	10.00	-	-	239	2		119.50	1-4	-	-	2	-
F.V.Kelly	Auck	1998/99	2002/03	29	54	2	1443	212*	27.75	3	5	239	2		119.50	1-4	-	-	18	-
J.W.H.Kelly	Well	1889/90	1897/98	8	10	2	31	8	4.42	-	-	339	32		10.59	5-30	1	-	5	-
L.E.Kelly	All	1950/51		1	2	0	17	11	8.50	-	-								2	-
P.J.Kelly	Auck	1998/99	1988/89	2	3	1	37	30*	18.50	-	-	117	1		117.00	1-83	-	-	2	-
R.A.Kelly	CD	1981/82	1988/89	48	65	9	834	93	14.89	-	2								140	12
H.J.Kember	Cant	1980/81	1988/89	49	66	10	847	93	15.12	-	2	30	0						140	13
E.J.Kemnitz	All	1990/91	1994/95	4	7	0	100	46	14.28	-	-	532	14		38.00	3-44	-	-	3	-
J.G.Kemp	Sland	1914/15	1994/95	8	11	5	37	16	6.16	-	-	592	17		34.82	3-44	-	-	1	1
R.J.Kemp	Auck	1960/61	1969/70	24	39	0	1076	108	27.58	3	2	5	0						16	-
	Well	1960/61	1969/70	25	41	0	1086	108	27.15	3	2	5	0						16	-
	All	1945/46	1949/50	7	13	1	349	152	29.08	1	1								2	-
K.D.Kennedy	ND	1964/65	1974/75	8	15	1	413	33	29.50	-	2	2315	66		35.07	8-49	2	-	1	-
P.G.Kennedy	Cant	1985/86	1991/92	30	45	12	287	159*	8.69	-	13	169	4		42.25	2-6	-	-	14	-
R.J.Kennedy	Otago	1993/94	1997/98	47	78	6	1944	17*	27.00	-	-	1235	55		22.45	6-61	-	-	25	-
	Well	1998/99	1999/00	17	22	3	69	31	3.63	-	-	569	11		51.72	3-70	-	-	6	-
	All	1993/94	1999/00	38	49	15	306	31	9.00	-	-	2823	91		31.02	6-61	1	-	14	-
R.R.Kennedy	HB	1920/21		1	2	2	4	3*	-	-	-								-	-
W.C.Kennedy	Well	1877/78	1883/84	5	9	0	55	31	6.11	-	-			3					2	-
J.Kenny	Otago	1911/12		1	2	0	11	11	5.50	-	-				2-?				-	-

		First	Last	M	I	NO	Runs	HS	Avg	100	50	Runs	Wkts	OW	Avg	Best	5i	10m	ct	st
L.A.W.Kent	Auck	1943/44	1951/52	30	46	3	568	91	13.20	-	1								46	31
	All	1943/44	1951/52	32	50	3	651	91	13.85	-	1								49	32
A.C.Kerr	Auck	1906/07	1912/13	7	10	0	31	9	4.42	-	-	493	19		25.94	4-24	-	-	9	
A.C.Kerr	Auck	1941/42	1945/46	10	18	2	593	122	37.06	1	3	913	33		27.66	5-55	2	-	9	
	All	1941/42	1945/46	14	24	3	686	122	32.66	1	4	1106	37		29.89	5-55	2	-	10	
F.B.Kerr	Otago	1934/35	1936/37	8	16	2	193	44*	13.78	-	-								-	
J.L.Kerr	Cant	1929/30	1939/40	32	61	3	2228	196	38.41	3	12								13	
	All	1929/30	1942/43	89	157	7	4829	196	32.19	8	22								30	
R.J.Kerr	Well	1993/94	1997/98	4	9	0	102	29	11.33	-	-	46	2		23.00	2-32	-	-	3	
C.C.Kettle	Otago	1868/69	1871/72	7	8	1	67	28*	9.57	-	-	4	0		-	-	-	-	1	1
J.W.Kiddey	Cant	1956/57	1964/65	44	68	11	683	44	11.98	-	-	2845	141		20.17	7-24	5	1	33	
W.A.Kilgour	Otago	1901/02	1907/08	4	7	2	45	11	9.00	-	-								2	
C.B.King	Auck	1893/94		3	6	1	33	17*	6.60	-	-								1	
G.A.King	Auck	1873/74		1	2	0	23	18	11.50	-	-								-	
R.T.King	Otago	1991/92	1995/96	11	22	1	376	117*	17.90	2	1	10	0		-	-	-	-	5	
	Auck	1996/97	2002/03	27	46	1	1303	130*	28.95	6	6	31	0		-	-	-	-	18	
	CD	2001/02		3	6	0	96	31	16.00	-	-	29	0		-	-	-	-	6	
	All	1991/92	2002/03	41	74	2	1775	130*	24.65	8	7	70	0		-	-	-	-	29	3
R.H.King	Cant	1977/78		4	3	2	20	14*	20.00	-	-	212	10		21.20	4-78	-	-	5	
	All	1977/78		5	4	3	23	14*	23.00	-	-	275	12		22.91	4-78	-	-	1	
T.D.Kingsland	Otago	1886/87		2	2	0	40	22	20.00	-	-	16	0		-	-	-	-	-	
G.R.Kingston	Sland	1917/18		1	1	0	20	17	20.00	-	-								-	
C.N.Kingstone	All	1927/28		1	1	0	43	43	43.00	-	-								-	
D.A.Kinsella	CD	1961/62	1965/66	28	34	11	152	25	6.60	-	-	1708	72		23.72	6-25	3	-	12	
A.G.Kinvig	Otago	1893/94	1898/99	7	12	1	190	55	17.27	-	1	87	3		29.00	2-26	-	-	6	
	Cant	1901/02	1903/04	2	5	0	47	38	9.40	-	-								2	
	All	1893/94	1903/04	10	17	1	237	55	14.81	-	1	87	3		29.00	2-26	-	-	3	
J.G.Kinvig	Well	1909/10		2	4	0	40	17	10.00	-	-	70	4		17.50	3-36	-	-	-	
C.M.Kirk	Cant	1969/70	1978/79	27	38	13	406	39	16.24	-	-	2271	79		28.74	7-77	4	-	13	
	Otago	1977/78		8	11	3	81	22*	10.12	-	-	345	17		20.29	5-20	1	-	5	
	All	1969/70	1978/79	35	49	16	487	39	14.75	-	-	2616	96		27.25	7-77	5	-	18	
J.C.Kirkcaldie	Well	1903/04		1	2	0	54	31	27.00	-	-								2	
W.D.R.Kirker	Well	1887/88	1893/94	3	3	1	7	4	3.50	-	-	25	1		25.00	1-17	-	-	1	
J.H.P.Kissling	Nel	1885/86		1	1	0	33	33*	-	-	-								2	
	Auck	1889/90		5	10	1	198	51	22.00	-	1								3	
	All	1885/86	1889/90	6	11	1	231	51	25.66	-	1								-	
A.K.Kitchen	Auck	2008/09	2009/10	15	24	2	878	132	39.90	4	-	88	2		44.00	2-31	-	-	14	
G.A.Kitt	Otago	1886/87		1	2	0	21	17	10.50	-	-	47	1		47.00	1-40	-	-	-	
E.V.M.Kitto	Cant	1894/95		1	2	0	10	7	5.00	-	-								-	
D.S.Kivell	CD	1952/53	1955/56	6	11	0	111	34	10.09	-	-								4	
C.A.Knapp	Well	1873/74	1884/85	9	17	1	124	37	7.75	-	-	105	11		9.54	5-21	1	-	3	
C.H.Knapp	Nel	1873/74	1876/77	4	7	0	48	16	6.85	-	-	63	7		9.00	5-25	1	-	5	
E.C.Knapp	Well	1943/44	1944/45	4	4	0	109	39	27.25	-	1	282	7		40.28	4-57	-	-	4	
K.J.Knapp	Nel	1873/74	1877/78	5	9	3	48	15	5.33	-	-								4	
W.H.Knapp	Nel	1875/76	1876/77	2	4	1	4	3	1.33	-	-								3	
A.R.Knight	Otago	1918/19	1943/44	51	97	4	2245	152	24.13	1	11	377	11		34.27	3-62	-	-	34	

		First	Last	M	I	NO	Runs	HS	Avg	100	50	Runs	Wkts	OW	Avg	Best	5i	10m	ct	st
D.J.Knowles	Auck	1983/84	1964/65	2	2	0	13	13	6.50			5	1		5.00	1-5			1	
S.W.Kohlhase	ND	1963/64	1969/70	3	4	0	12	10	3.00			190	5		38.00	4-47			4	
	Auck	1968/69	1969/70	6	9	2	95	32	13.57			230	8		28.75	3-50			8	
H.H.L.Kortlang	All	1963/64	1926/27	9	13	2	107	32	9.72			420	13		32.30	4-47			11	
	Well	1922/23	1926/27	15	26	2	1240	214*	51.66	4	7								23	
C.V.Kreeft	All	1909/10	1926/27	35	62	8	2688	214*	49.77	6	16								1	
E.A.Kruskopf	Well	1882/83		1	2	1	12	11*	12.00			84	2		42.00	1-32				
G.Kuchen	Otago	1944/45		2	4	0	18	9*	6.00			49	1		49.00	1-39			1	
C.M.Kuggeleijn	Well	1880/81		1	1	1	5	5	5.00			110	1		110.00	1-38				
	ND	1975/76	1990/91	82	138	12	3457	116	27.43	3	16	2057	49		41.97	4-30			71	
D.S.Kulkarni	Well	1975/76	1990/91	89	151	15	3747	116	27.55	4	17	2436	57		42.73	4-30			73	
	Well	2008/09		1	1	1	13	13*				81	3		27.00	3-62				
J.N.Kuru	All	2008/09	2010	29	27	14	411	87	31.61		2	2396	92		26.04	7-50			10	
A.B.M.Labatt	CD	2009/10		4	5	2	18	15*	6.00			316	6		52.66	2-48		6		
	Cant	1887/88	1895/96	17	30	0	486	57	16.20		1	686	39		17.58	5-17			23	
F.H.D.Labatt	Auck	1897/98		2	4	1	32	15	10.66			22	1		22.00	1-22			2	
J.C.Laker	All	1887/88	1897/98	21	38	1	566	57	15.29		1	753	41		18.36	5-17		2	30	
	Cant	1891/92		1	2	0	1	1	0.50			22	2		11.00	2-22				
	Auck	1951/52		4	4	0	77	35	19.25			379	24		15.79	5-44			3	
	All	1946	1964/65	450	548	108	7304	113	16.60	2	18	35791	1944		18.41	10-53	127	32	270	
D.W.Lamason	CD	1990/91	1996/97	5	7	3	20	7*	5.00			363	9		40.33	2-62			1	
J.R.Lamason	Well	1927/28	1946/47	36	67	4	1522	127	24.15	2	9	1108	37		29.94	5-67			34	
	All	1927/28	1946/47	60	106	7	2065	127	20.85	2	11	1476	45		32.80	5-67			61	
A.R.Lamb	Well	2008/09	2009/10	7	7	0	114	28	16.28			632	14		45.14	3-48			2	
H.N.Lambert	All	1917/18	1932/33	36	65	4	1330	107	21.45		6	2000	69		28.98	6-102	3	1	31	
	All	1917/18	1932/33	39	70	4	1455	107	22.04		6	2033	70		29.04	6-102	3	1	33	
S.C.Lambert	Otago	1873/74	1874/75	3	5	0	25	9	5.00			35	3		11.66	3-4			2	
S.O.Lambly	ND	1993/94	1994/95	4	8	0	108	27	13.50										7	
M.J.Lamont	Otago	1990/91	1998/99	32	61	1	1143	127	19.05	1	5	132	2		66.00	1-49			22	
	All	1990/91	1998/99	33	63	1	1202	127	19.38	1	5	132	2		66.00	1-49			22	
H.P.Lance	Cant	1863/64	1864/65	2	4	0	28	13	7.00			35	5		7.00	4-14			2	
M.E.L.Lane	Well	1990/91	1991/92	7	14	0	129	28	11.72										4	
	CD	1993/94		4	4	0	93	84	23.25		1								2	
	Cant	1995/96	1996/97	11	16	0	260	61	16.25		2								4	
	All	1990/91	1996/97	22	34	0	482	84	15.54		3								30	1
M.C.Langdon	ND	1957/58	1964/65	25	46	4	836	77	19.90		5	1466	60		24.43	8-21	3	1	36	1
G.J.Langridge	CD	1976/77	1981/82	30	53	5	1064	76	22.16		7								12	2
J.Langridge	Auck	1927/28		1	2	0	124	78	62.00		1								20	
	All	1924	1953	695	1058	157	31716	167	35.20	42	182	33	0							
M.C.Lankham	Auck	1873/74		3	5	1	2	1*	0.50			34524	1530		22.56	9-34	91	14	380	
W.Lankham	Auck	1882/83	1883/84	5	8	1	90	27	12.85		1	32	3		10.66	3-18			2	
G.R.Larsen	Well	1984/85	1998/99	79	118	25	2938	161	31.59	2	16	373	53		7.03	7-13	6	4	7	
	All	1984/85	1998/99	103	157	35	3491	161	28.61	2	17	3133	105		29.83	6-37	4		56	
E.G.Lash	Tara	1897/98		2	4	0	42	20	10.50			4622	156		29.62	6-37	5		70	
F.W.Lash	Well	1893/94	1896/97	2	2	1	34	25*	34.00											
J.K.Latham	Well	1903/04		1	2	1	23	15	23.00			29	1		29.00	1-16				

		First	Last	M	I	NO	Runs	HS	Avg	100	50	Runs	Wkts	OW	Avg	Best	5i	10m	ct	st
R.T.Latham	Cant	1980/81	1994/95	101	176	17	5919	237*	37.22	8	35	1432	29		49.37	3-20			101	
	All	1980/81	1994/95	108	189	19	6298	237*	37.04	9	36	1532	35		43.77	3-20			106	
W.H.Latthbury	Otago	1875/76		1	2	0	45	42	22.50			74	2		37.00	2-30			1	
C.W.H.Lawrence	Cant	1987/88		8	10	2	95	33	11.87			684	20		34.20	4-43			3	
J.Lawrence	Well	1873/74		1	1	0	1	1	1.00											
J.D.Lawrence	Cant	1891/92	1906/07	28	51	5	1015	167	22.06	1	3	345	9		38.33	2-15			10	
	All	1891/92	1906/07	31	57	5	1124	167	21.61	1	4	345	9		38.33	2-15			12	
F.A.Laws	Well	1896/97	1909/10	11	16	2	228	47	16.28			239	7		34.14	2-30			10	
	HB	1897/98		1	2	0	5	5	2.50			79	2		39.50	1-35				
	All	1896/97	1909/10	12	18	2	233	47	14.56			318	9		35.33	3-20			10	
A.N.Lawson	Otago	1944/45		2	4	0	7	6*	3.50											
H.W.Lawson	Well	1883/84	1889/90	9	17	2	129	38	10.75			442	45		9.82	7-25	5	3	3	
	Auck	1891/92	1897/98	8	13	1	128	25	10.66			256	13		19.69	3-31			3	
	All	1883/84	1897/98	17	30	6	257	38	10.70			698	58		12.03	7-25	5	3	6	
R.A.Lawson	Otago	1992/93	2003/04	66	120	6	2890	200	25.13	2	14	5	1		5.00	1-0			24	
	All	1992/93	2003/04	73	133	6	3278	200	25.81	3	16	18	2		9.00	1-0			28	
J.C.Lawton	Otago	1890/91	1893/94	10	18	1	351	82	20.64		3	621	67		9.26	7-28	4	1	8	
	All	1890/91	1893/94	11	20	1	366	82	19.26		3	695	70		9.92	7-28	4	1	8	
V.V.S.Laxman	Otago	2008/09		1	2	0	64	44	32.00											
	All	1992/93	2010	244	394	49	18154	353	52.62	53	86	754	22		34.27	3-11			260	
W.E.Leach	Cant	1876/77		1	2	0	27	25	13.50										1	
	All	1876/77	1885	6	11	1	235	56	23.50		1	11	0						1	
J.V.Leader	Otago	1928/29	1940/41	11	20	2	292	58	17.17		1	475	18		26.38	6-44	1		2	
C.D.Lee	Well	1991/92	1992/93	2	2	1	12	12*	12.00			146	2		73.00	1-62				
	Auck	1993/94	1996/97	6	10	4	162	111*	27.00			551	15		36.73	3-34				
	All	1991/92	1996/97	9	13	6	174	111*	24.85			786	18		43.66	3-34			5	
G.H.Lee	Cant	1870/71	1875/76	4	5	0	43	25	8.60			150	10		15.00	3-17			3	
J.B.Lee	ND	2003/04		1	2	0	56	46	14.00											
W.K.Lees	Otago	1972/73	1987/88	108	179	31	3754	124	25.36	4	17	105	2		52.50	1-34	1		220	36
	All	1970/71	1987/88	146	243	43	4932	152	24.66	5	18	109	2		54.50	1-34			304	44
R.P.Lefèbvre	Cant	1990/91		7	6	3	65	21*	21.66			493	20		24.65	6-53			3	
I.B.Leggat	All	1990	1995	77	89	16	1494	100	20.46	1	3	5399	149		36.23	6-45	3		36	
	CD	1950/51	1961/62	30	52	3	1163	142*	23.73	2	4	1779	45		39.53	5-60	1		25	
J.G.Leggat	All	1950/51	1961/62	40	69	4	1319	142*	20.29	2	4	2057	58		35.46	5-60	1		37	
	Cant	1944/45	1955/56	35	66	6	2391	166	39.85	5	14	53	1		53.00	1-1			20	
R.I.Leggat	All	1944/45	1955/56	57	106	9	3634	166	37.46	7	23	69	1		69.00	1-1			30	
	Cant	1980/81	1983/84	19	31	5	545	83	20.96		1	650	22		29.54	5-37	1		14	
	All	1979/80	1983/84	22	34	5	563	83	19.41		1	796	24		33.16	5-37	1		14	
J.A.Leigh	ND	1977/78		2	3	1	7	7*	3.50										10	
J.Leith	Otago	1880/81		5	5	1	5	3	5.00											
T.G.F.Lemin	Otago	1929/30	1939/40	8	15	8	63	11	9.00			667	24		27.79	5-21	2		1	
	All	1929/30	1942/43	9	17	8	64	11	7.11			818	29		28.20	5-21	2		2	
B.J.Leonard	ND	2005/06		1	1	1	0	0	0.00			138	0							
D.J.Leonard	CD	1989/90	1993/94	43	54	7	690	67	14.68		3	3087	112		27.56	6-67	4		5	
S.G.Lester	Cant	1929/30	1935/36	16	27	1	595	64	22.88		2	900	26		34.61	4-21			8	

		First	Last	M	I	NO	Runs	HS	Avg	100	50	Runs	Wkts	OW	Avg	Best	5i	10m	ct	st
W.C.S.Levers	Well	1895/96	1896/97	5	8	1	162	57*	23.14	-	1								6	1
	HB	1908/09		1	2	0	14	8	7.00											
M.I.Lewis	All	1895/96	1908/09	6	10	1	176	57*	19.55	-	1								6	
T.W.Lewis	Auck	1949/50		1	2	0	12	9	6.00										1	
F.C.Liggins	HB	1896/97	1898/99	5	8	0	53	31	6.62										2	
J.K.Lindsay	Otago	1900/01		8	13	2	129	24	11.72										4	
A.Lines	Otago	1980/81	1991/92	44	66	8	857	65*	14.77		2	3039	75		40.52	5-48	3	1	20	
W.S.Linn	Nel	1881/82		5	9	2	47	10	6.71			64	4		16.00	2-5				
A.F.Lissette	Auck	1980/81	1891/92	2	5	3	38	23	19.00			85	2		42.50	1-23			1	
	ND	1954/55	1955/56	7	13	6	63	22	9.00			665	34		19.55	7-50	3		5	
	All	1956/57	1962/63	28	46	12	404	27*	11.88			2156	77		28.00	7-45	4		14	
	All	1954/55	1962/63	38	64	20	476	27*	10.81			3004	116		25.89	7-45	5	1	20	
D.S.Little	Well	1998/99		1	1	0	1	1*	-			127	0		-	-				
D.Little	Well	1911/12		1	2	0	1	1	0.50											
J.C.Little	Well	1947/48		2	3	0	2	1	0.66										1	
A.I.Littlejohn	Well	1887/88	1889/90	2	4	2	23	13*	11.50											
W.S.Littlejohn	Nel	1885/86	1886/87	2	3	0	8	8	2.66										1	
T.O.Livingston	Otago	1917/18		3	4	0	14	14	3.50			209	5		41.80	3-41			1	
D.P.Lloyd	ND	1968/69	1980/81	33	61	4	1210	103	21.22	1	3	194	9		21.55	4-33			12	
	All	1968/69	1980/81	34	63	4	1211	103	20.52	1	3	545	6		90.83	2-76			14	
N.A.Lloyd	ND	1990/91		4	4	0	45	33	11.25			545	6		90.83	2-76			9	
D.V.Lobb	Otago	2006/07		1	1	0	4	4	4.00			37	1		37.00	1-37				
J.B.Lockett	Well	1874/75	1877/78	3	6	0	67	31	11.16			29	4		7.25	3-21			1	
	All	1874/75	1879/80	4	7	0	76	31	10.85			42	5		8.40	3-21			1	
G.R.Logan	CD	1986/87	1989/90	22	21	7	115	23*	8.21			1638	45		36.40	5-60	1		8	
M.K.Lohrey	Cant	1943/44		1	1	0	6	6	6.00			57	1		57.00	1-46				
A.L.Lomas	Otago	1919/20		1	2	0	41	39	41.00											
R.P.London	All	1920/21		1	2	0	6	3	3.00											
R.I.Long	Otago	1953/54	1963/64	15	29	0	567	79	19.55		3	226	7		32.28	2-28			4	
A.Longden	Cant	1883/84	1885/86	6	10	1	120	51	13.33		1	13	0		-	-			6	
W.M.Lonsdale	Cant	2006/07	2007/08	5	6	0	14	7	4.66			426	9		47.33	3-57			1	
H.H.Loughnan	Cant	1870/71	1885/86	4	6	2	19	5	4.75			3	0		-	-				
W.J.Love	HB	1920/21		1	2	1	1	1*	1.00											
G.R.Loveridge	CD	1994/95	2002/03	12	21	1	355	49*	17.75		2	777	16		48.56	4-23			1	
	All	1994/95	2002/03	29	43	3	935	126	23.37	1	8	2449	46		53.23	5-59	1		9	
G.E.Lowans	CD	1959/60	1964/65	23	39	7	1053	100	28.45			21	0		-	-			17	
G.E.Lowe	Well	1873/74		2	4	0	19	8*	6.33			5	1		5.00	1-5			10	
P.R.Lowes	CD	1990/91	1874/75	8	7	1	66	27	9.42			539	8		67.37	3-108			1	
T.C.Lowry	Auck	1917/18		2	4	0	48	28	12.00										2	
	Well	1926/27	1932/33	22	40	1	1515	181	38.84	4	6	399	9		44.33	2-15			19	
	All	1917/18	1937/38	198	322	20	9421	181	31.19	18	47	1323	49		27.00	4-14			188	1
T.H.Lowry	HB	1891/92		1	1	0	0	0	0.00										1	
M.B.Loye	Auck	2006/07		2	4	1	51	32*	17.00											49
R.E.Lucena	All	1991	2010	256	410	38	14936	322*	40.15	42	61	61	1		61.00	1-8			119	
	Tara	1891/92		1	1	0	1	1	0.50			34	3		11.33	3-34			1	
M.M.F.Luckie	Well	1891/92	1919/20	2	4	4	22	7*	-			42	2		21.00	2-12			2	

		First	Last	M	I	NO	Runs	HS	Avg	100	50	Runs	Wkts	OW	Avg	Best	5i	10m	ct	st
E.R.Ludbrook	HB	1891/92	1895/96	8	13	2	183	68	16.63	-	1	76	6		12.66	2-1	-	-	4	-
J.R.Lundon	Auck	1892/93	1893/94	4	8	0	86	27	10.75	-	-	158	1		158.00	1-49	-	-	3	-
H.B.Lusk	Auck	1899/00	1920/21	16	31	2	411	45	14.17	-	-	180	7		25.71	4-33	-	-	16	-
	Cant	1906/07	1918/19	16	31	1	934	151*	31.13	2	4								18	-
	Well	1917/18		1	1	0	23	23	23.00	-	-								-	-
	All	1899/00	1920/21	35	67	3	1451	151*	22.67	2	4	338	8		42.25	4-33	-	-	34	-
H.B.Lusk	Auck	1889/90	1908/09	5	9	1	77	32	9.62	-	-	187	11		17.00	5-35	1	-	3	-
	HB	1891/92	1908/09	28	51	0	1395	120	28.46	3	7	914	40		22.85	7-53	1	1	11	-
	All	1889/90	1908/09	38	70	3	1688	120	25.19	3	8	1112	51		21.80	7-53	1	1	14	-
R.B.Lusk	Tara	1891/92	1894/95	3	4	0	47	41	15.66	-	-								1	-
W.N.B.Lusk	Auck	1899/00	1903/04	8	16	0	205	85	12.81	-	1	139	5		27.80	3-48	-	-	9	-
F.H.Luxford	Well	1880/81	1883/84	4	6	1	10	8	1.66	-	-	182	13		14.00	5-40	1	-	-	5
D.J.F.Lynch	Auck	1877/78	1889/90	9	16	1	214	81	14.26	-	1	210	15		14.00	7-31	2	-	9	-
G.Lynch	Otago	1873/74		1	1	0	51	51	51.00	-	1								2	-
R.F.Lynch	Well	1873/74	1883/84	5	10	1	73	32	8.11	-	-	65	6		10.83	3-16	-	-	2	-
R.K.Lynch	Auck	2001/02	2002/03	2	4	0	40	20	10.00	-	-								1	-
S.M.Lynch	Auck	1995/96	1999/00	20	34	3	1141	94	36.80	-	10								13	-
	All	1995/96	1999/00	24	42	3	1263	94	32.38	-	10								19	-
B.J.Lyon	Auck	1997/98		3	5	1	69	38*	17.25	-	-	84	1		84.00	1-62	-	-	9	-
T.D.Lyon	Auck	1931/32		2	4	0	44	18	11.00	-	-	537	9		59.66	2-46	-	-	4	-
T.I.Lythe	Auck	2005/06	2006/07	9	14	1	352	66	27.07	-	3	740	17		43.52	4-89	-	-	4	-
	CD	2007/08		7	12	2	339	75	33.90	-	3	296							9	-
	All	2005/06	2007/08	16	26	3	691	75	30.04	-	6	1277	26		49.11	4-89	-	-	13	-
L.G.McAlevey	Otago	1975/76		3	3	3	60	48	30.00	-	-	31	0						-	-
V.A.C.McArley	Otago	1947/48	1957/58	6	10	3	112	27	16.00	-	-	326	6		54.33	3-41	-	-	1	-
C.G.Macartney	Otago	1909/10		3	6	0	132	45	22.00	-	-	298	17		17.52	7-81	2	1	4	-
	All	1905/06	1935/36	249	360	32	15019	345	45.78	49	53	8782	419		20.95	7-58	17	-	102	-
J.E.Macassey	HB	1900/01	1912/13	7	14	2	192	75	16.00	-	1	189	7		27.00	3-50	-	-	6	-
	All	1900/01	1912/13	8	16	2	219	75	15.64	-	1	189	7		27.00	3-50	-	-	6	-
A.J.McBeath	Sland	1919/20		1	2	0	8	5	4.00	-	-								-	-
D.J.McBeath	Otago	1917/18	1922/23	5	9	3	70	35	11.66	-	-	679	33		20.57	6-52	2	-	7	-
	Cant	1918/19	1926/27	14	25	11	116	20	8.28	-	-	1691	76		22.25	9-56	7	1	9	-
	Sland	1919/20	1920/21	4	7	1	78	32	13.00	-	-	296	35		8.45	8-84	4	2	2	-
	All	1917/18	1926/27	32	56	22	346	35	10.17	-	-	3542	170		20.83	9-56	15	3	19	-
G.McBeath	Sland	1919/20		1	2	0	20	12	10.00	-	-								-	-
V.D.A.McCarten	Otago	1944/45		1	2	0	3	3	1.50	-	-								1	-
B.McCarthy	Tara	1894/95	1897/98	4	7	1	131	52	21.83	-	1	312	17		18.35	5-109	1	-	2	-
	All	1894/95	1902/03	6	11	3	139	52	17.37	-	1	458	20		22.90	5-109	1	-	2	-
C.McCarthy	Well	1941/42		1	2	1	40	23	20.00	-	-								-	-
E.E.M.McCausland	Well	1885/86		1	1	0	2	2	2.00	-	-								1	-
P.M.McCaw	Well	1952/53		3	6	0	115	51	19.16	-	1								3	-
M.J.McClenaghan	CD	2007/08	2008/09	11	13	5	28	6*	3.50	-	-	1374	29		47.37	3-5	-	-	3	-
	All	2007/08	2008/09	12	14	5	29	6*	3.22	-	-	1509	32		47.15	3-5	-	-	3	-
R.J.McCone	Cant	2008/09	2009/10	2	4	0	162	102	27.00	1	-	369	5		73.80	2-39	-	-	1	-
G.T.McConnell	Well	1960/61	1971/72	18	23	8	221	38	14.73	-	-	1098	50		21.96	6-41	4	-	15	-
A.D.MacCormick	Otago	1888/89		1	2	0	1	1	0.50	-	-	52	2		26.00	2-52	-	-	-	-

		First	Last	M	I	NO	Runs	HS	Avg	100	50	Runs	Wkts	OW	Avg	Best	5i	10m	ct	st
C.E.MacCormick	Auck	1884/85	1893/94	5	10	2	65	26	8.12	-	-	12	0			-	-	-	4	-
E.MacCormick	Auck	1900/01	1913/14	13	25	3	329	77	14.95	-	1	500	14		35.71	3-43	-	-	5	-
A.W.McCoy	Auck	1929/30	1934/35	9	16	3	220	68*	16.92	-	1	574	18		31.88	3-43	-	-	6	-
R.B.McCullough	Well	1971/72	1936/37	10	18	3	228	68*	15.20	-	1	93	1		93.00	1-63	-	-	1	-
B.B.McCullum	Otago	1999/00	2009/10	1	2	0	3	3	1.50	-	-					-	-	-	28	2
	Cant	2003/04	2006/07	18	34	1	924	142	28.00	2	4					-	-	-	39	19
	All	1999/00	2009/10	9	15	0	469	80	31.26	2	4					-	-	-	267	
N.L.McCullum	Otago	1999/00	2009/10	95	163	9	5339	185	34.66	9	30	3830	88		43.52	5-28	1	-	49	
S.J.McCullum	Otago	1999/00	2009/10	46	69	9	1794	106*	28.47	1	11	4176	100		41.76	6-90	2	-	51	
E.W.McDermid	All	1999/00	2009/10	48	73	6	1804	106*	26.92	1	11	46	1		46.00	1-0	-	-	69	2
C.J.McDonald	Well	1976/77	1990/91	75	131	0	3174	134	24.41	2	16					-	-	-	2	
F.MacDonald	Otago	1906/07		2	3	0	41	20	13.66	-	-					-	-	-	-	
F.A.MacDonald	Otago	1968/69		2	3	0	9	5	3.00	-	-	201	5		40.20	2-23	-	-	1	
G.K.MacDonald	Cant	1863/64		1	2	0	12	12	6.00	-	-	31	10		3.10	6-17	1	-	-	
J.W.McDonald	Cant	1889/90	1896/97	4	7	0	31	10	4.42	-	-					-	-	-	3	
R.T.McDonnell	Auck	1984/85	1990/91	18	26	10	254	57	15.87	-	1	1137	32		35.53	6-62	1	-	25	
	Cant	1956/57	1957/58	2	4	0	14	6	7.00	-	-	93	2		46.50	1-44	-	-	-	
	Otago	1864/65		1	1	0	6	6	6.00	-	-					-	-	-	1	
J.J.M.McDonogh	All	1867/68	1875/76	7	13	1	144	32	12.00	-	-					-	-	-	3	
A.W.McDougall	All	1864/65	1875/76	8	14	1	150	32	11.53	-	-					-	-	-	4	
W.McDowell	All	1893/94	1908/09	6	12	1	203	86	18.45	-	2	257	10		25.70	4-53	-	-	3	1
C.Mace	Otago	1944/45	1946/47	8	13	0	196	34	19.60	-	-	737	31		23.77	4-44	-	-	7	
	Cant	1883/84		3	3	2	18	9*	18.00	-	-	41	5		8.20	3-9	-	-	2	
	Otago	1863/64		1	2	1	1	1	0.50	-	-					-	-	-	-	
H.Mace	All	1861/62	1863/64	2	3	0	2	1	0.66	-	-					-	-	-	-	
J.Mace	Well	1877/78		1	2	0	27	23	13.50	-	-	36	8		4.50	4-16	-	-	3	
	Otago	1863/64		1	2	0	9	8	4.50	-	-	36	8		4.50	4-16	-	-	1	
M.L.McEwan	All	1860/61	1863/64	1	4	0	16	8	4.00	-	-					-	-	-	2	
P.E.McEwen	Otago	1957/58		1	2	0	9	6	4.50	-	-					-	-	-	-	
J.N.McEwin	Cant	1977/78	1990/91	103	185	11	5940	155	34.13	11	39	1007	27		37.29	3-25	-	-	70	
	All	1976/77	1990/91	115	206	15	6677	155	34.95	12	43	1125	29		38.79	3-25	-	-	82	
J.MacFarlane	Cant	1917/18	1927/28	15	25	5	303	39	17.82	-	-	1303	40		32.57	5-87	2	-	6	
	All	1917/18	1927/28	16	27	5	312	39	16.42	-	-	1347	41		32.85	5-87	2	-	6	
J.H.McFarlane	Otago	1887/88	1895/96	4	7	2	21	6	4.20	-	-	48	0			-	-	-	4	
	Cant	1893/94	1895/96	4	6	3	30	12	10.00	-	-	122	7		17.42	3-12	-	-	-	
T.MacFarlane	ND	1887/88		8	13	1	51	12	6.37	-	-	170	7		24.28	3-12	-	-	4	
T.A.McFarlane	Otago	1964/65		1	2	1	23	23*	23.00	-	-	43	1		43.00	1-43	-	-	-	
A.R.MacGibbon	Otago	1870/71	1873/74	4	8	0	58	16	7.25	-	-	24	2		12.00	1-10	-	-	3	
	All	1909/10	1919/20	12	23	0	426	61	18.52	-	2	532	20		26.60	4-49	-	-	4	
R.McGill	Cant	1947/48	1961/62	49	90	8	1779	94	21.69	-	7	3987	147		27.12	7-56	5	-	35	
	All	1947/48	1961/62	124	206	20	3699	94	19.88	-	14	9301	356		26.11	7-56	8	1	81	
	ND	1970/71	1971/72	3	4	0	81	58	20.25	-	1	169	8		21.12	6-51	1	-	2	
H.M.McGirr	All	1969/70	1971/72	5	8	0	128	58	16.00	-	1	298	11		27.09	6-51	1	-	2	
	Well	1913/14	1932/33	54	97	4	3032	141	32.60	5	17	4326	166		26.06	7-45	7	1	37	
	All	1913/14	1932/33	88	146	7	3992	141	28.71	5	23	6571	239		27.49	7-45	9	-	53	

200

		First	Last	M	I	NO	Runs	HS	Avg	100	50	Runs	Wkts	OW	Avg	Best 6-36	5i	10m	ct	st
W.P.McGirr	Well	1883/84	1889/90	14	23	7	199	47*	12.43	-	1	543	46		11.80		2		5	1
P.D.McGlashan	CD	2000/01	2001/02	5	8	1	125	65	17.85	-	1								4	-
	Otago	2002/03		7	10	2	173	47	21.62	-	-								15	11
	ND	2004/05	2009/10	44	64	5	1900	115	31.66	2	10								122	11
	All	2000/01	2009/10	56	82	7	2198	115	29.30	2	11								141	12
G.G.McGregor	Otago	1935/36	1939/40	4	7	2	67	32*	13.40	-	-	38	0		-	-			-	-
J.McGregor	Otago	1884/85		3	6	1	76	30*	15.20	-	-	7	0		-	-			1	-
P.B.McGregor	Auck	1960/61	1964/65	11	17	4	334	51*	25.69	-	1	117	4		29.25	2-49			7	-
	ND	1962/63	1963/64	11	18	0	466	118	25.88	1	2	314	14		22.42	3-19			8	-
	Well	1968/69	1974/75	13	19	1	401	81	26.73	-	2	351	15		23.40	5-85	1		6	-
	CD	1969/70		5	8	0	104	38	13.00	-	-	20	1		20.00	1-3			3	-
	All	1960/61	1974/75	40	62	5	1305	118	24.16	1	5	802	34		23.58	5-85	1		24	-
S.N.McGregor	Otago	1947/48	1968/69	90	167	13	4259	114*	27.65	3	27	97	1		97.00	1-6			43	-
	All	1947/48	1968/69	148	274	16	6573	114*	25.47	5	38	142	3		47.33	1-5			79	-
T.McGregor	All	1879/80		1	2	1	0	0*	0.00	-	-	37	2		18.50	1-16			1	-
A.J.McGuire	CD	1957/58		4	7	0	82	43	11.71	-	-								-	-
J.McHaffie	Otago	1931/32		1	2	0	19	13	9.50	-	-								2	-
D.S.McHardy	Otago	1991/92	1992/93	12	23	1	649	100	29.50	1	5	115	4		28.75	2-78			11	-
	Well	1993/94	1997/98	9	16	0	241	60	16.06	-	1								13	-
E.J.McInnis	All	1991/92	1997/98	21	39	1	890	100	24.05	1	6	115	4		28.75	2-78				-
	CD	2007/08		2	2	2	47	47	-	-	-	194	7		27.71	4-71			1	-
C.F.McIntosh	All	2003/04	2007/08	4	5	1	77	47	19.25	-	-	304	10		30.40	4-71			-	-
T.G.McIntosh	Auck	1914/15		2	2	0	33	33	16.50	-	-	98	6		16.33	4-59			-	-
	All	1998/99	2009/10	76	128	10	4660	268	39.49	14	19	97	0		-	-			63	-
	Cant	2004/05		6	10	0	49	21	4.90	-	-								9	-
	All	1998/99	2009/10	98	167	12	5459	268	35.21	15	23	97	0		-	-			82	-
J.M.McIntyre	Auck	1961/62	1982/83	77	104	40	1204	87*	18.81	-	2	5447	238		22.88	6-84	8	1	25	-
	Cant	1965/66	1968/69	21	26	8	289	34	16.05	-	-	1337	69		19.37	5-49	1		14	-
	All	1961/62	1982/83	113	148	55	1668	87*	17.93	-	2	7917	336		23.56	6-84	10	1	47	-
P.J.McIntyre	Well	1887/88		1	2	1	1	1	1.00	-	-								-	-
A.J.McKay	Auck	2002/03	2008/09	19	21	8	148	36*	11.38	-	-	1648	54		30.51	4-37			2	-
	Well	2009/10		5	6	4	27	11*	13.50	-	-	600	15		40.00	4-60			-	-
	All	2002/03	2009/10	24	27	12	175	36*	11.66	-	-	2248	69		32.57	4-37			2	-
B.J.McKechnie	Otago	1971/72	1985/86	46	66	8	1057	51	18.22	-	2	2867	97		29.55	4-24			23	-
D.E.C.McKechnie	All	1971/72	1985/86	50	73	9	1169	51	18.26	-	2	3065	100		30.65	4-24			24	-
A.H.McKellar	Well	1975/76	1980/81	17	28	3	278	49*	11.12	-	-	901	37		24.35	6-65			13	-
T.M.McKenna	CD	1919/20		1	2	0	6	4	3.00	-	-	19	0		-	-			-	-
G.W.McKenzie	ND	1987/88	1989/90	12	13	2	54	14	4.90	-	-	777	21		37.00	4-52			5	-
G.J.Mackenzie	Well	1983/84	1990/91	34	58	9	1172	115	23.91	1	3	463	4		115.75	1-12			25	-
H.A.W.McKenzie	Well	1990/91	1992/93	17	20	5	53	8	3.53	-	-	1469	45		32.64	5-41	2		2	-
J.McKenzie	Otago	1876/77	1894/95	3	2	0	5	4	2.50	-	-								2	-
M.N.McKenzie	Cant	1893/94	2001/02	10	4	1	116	74	29.00	-	1								1	-
	Otago	1998/99	2007/08	24	19	0	370	76	20.55	-	2	15	0		-	-			4	-
	All	2002/03	2007/08	34	40	2	685	100	18.02	1	3	15	0		-	-			16	-
M.C.MacKenzie	Otago	1992/93		2	59	3	1055	100	18.83	1	5	218	2		109.00	2-109	-		20	-

Name	Team	First	Last	M	I	NO	Runs	HS	Avg	100	50	Runs	Wkts	OW	Avg	Best	5i	10m	ct	st
N.W.McKenzie	Otago	1972/73	-	1	2	1	63	63*	63.00	-	1	2	0	-	-	-	-	-	2	-
R.H.C.MacKenzie	Well	1929/30	-	1	2	0	40	31	20.00	-	-	-	-	-	-	-	-	-	2	-
J.A.McKeown	Well	1938/39	1954/55	5	7	1	17	9	5.66	-	-	334	9	-	37.11	4-60	-	-	4	-
W.W.Mackersy	Otago	1906/07	1907/08	4	8	0	84	41	10.50	-	-	282	10	-	28.20	4-66	-	-	5	-
R.I.J.MacKinlay	Auck	1986/87	-	2	2	0	9	5	4.50	-	-	-	-	-	-	-	-	-	1	-
M.R.McKinnon	ND	1983/84	1988/89	14	13	5	35	14	4.37	-	-	1304	31	-	42.06	4-27	-	-	2	-
J.M.Mackle	Cant	1980/81	1981/82	10	15	4	108	21*	9.81	-	-	-	-	-	-	-	-	-	24	6
K.J.McKnight	Otago	1987/88	1991/92	8	13	2	172	56*	15.63	-	-	-	-	-	-	-	-	-	15	3
S.G.McKnight	Otago	1958/59	1966/67	7	14	1	123	23	9.46	-	-	-	-	-	-	-	-	-	2	-
D.B.McLachlan	Cant	1912/13	-	1	2	0	1	1	0.50	-	-	-	-	-	-	-	-	-	-	-
A.McLean	Well	1914/15	1921/22	5	7	1	12	10	2.00	-	-	26	2	-	13.00	2-26	-	-	1	-
N.A.M.McLean	Cant	1912/13	1921/22	4	9	1	13	10	1.62	-	-	361	28	-	12.89	7-57	3	2	-	-
	All	1947/48	-	4	6	2	274	86	54.80	1	2	387	30	-	12.90	7-57	3	2	4	-
	Cant	2005/06	-	4	5	2	69	53*	23.00	-	1	304	14	-	21.71	4-25	-	-	1	-
G.W.McLellan	All	1992/93	2005/06	149	221	34	2527	76	13.51	-	4	276	10	-	27.60	4-65	-	-	4	-
W.McLennan	Well	1965/66	1967/68	2	4	0	17	9	4.25	-	-	13925	506	-	27.51	7-28	19	3	41	-
D.N.MacLeod	Otago	1879/80	-	1	1	0	6	6*	-	-	-	37	6	-	6.16	5-34	1	-	1	-
	CD	1956/57	1966/67	30	53	3	1480	135	29.60	3	8	9	0	-	-	-	-	-	15	-
	Well	1958/59	-	2	4	0	33	32	8.25	-	-	-	-	-	-	-	-	-	-	-
	Cant	1967/68	-	1	2	0	18	10	9.00	-	-	-	-	-	-	-	-	-	-	-
E.G.McLeod	All	1956/57	1967/68	34	61	3	1539	135	26.53	3	8	9	0	-	-	-	-	-	16	-
	Auck	1920/21	1923/24	9	16	3	496	56	38.15	-	5	217	6	-	36.16	2-40	-	-	4	-
	Well	1925/26	1940/41	16	31	5	819	102	31.50	1	4	442	14	-	31.57	4-56	-	-	7	-
J.C.McLeod	All	1920/21	1940/41	28	53	10	1407	102	32.72	1	9	664	20	-	33.20	4-56	-	-	11	-
R.J.McLeod	ND	1970/71	1971/72	4	8	2	78	22	13.00	-	-	116	2	-	58.00	1-21	-	-	3	-
F.L.McMahon	CD	1990/91	-	2	4	0	24	14	6.00	-	-	-	-	-	-	-	-	-	1	-
	All	1990/91	-	3	6	0	118	73	19.66	-	1	43	2	-	21.50	2-43	-	-	1	-
	Auck	1908/09	-	1	2	0	15	14	7.50	-	-	74	2	-	37.00	2-43	-	-	-	-
N.A.McMahon	All	1908/09	1913/14	2	4	0	83	68	20.75	-	1	96	3	-	32.00	2-42	-	-	1	-
	Auck	1936/37	1937/38	2	3	1	1	1	0.50	-	-	96	3	-	32.00	2-42	-	-	-	-
T.G.McMahon	All	1936/37	1949/50	3	5	1	13	12	3.25	-	-	-	-	-	-	-	-	-	-	-
	Well	1953/54	1964/65	27	45	8	418	42	11.29	-	-	53	5	-	10.60	4-39	-	-	64	12
G.H.McMaster	Well	1953/54	1964/65	37	57	12	449	42	9.97	-	-	152	0	-	-	-	-	-	84	14
W.McMath	Auck	1891/92	-	3	2	1	5	3	5.00	-	-	-	-	-	-	-	-	-	-	-
C.D.McMillan	Cant	1917/18	1918/19	3	6	3	27	11	9.00	-	-	804	25	-	32.16	3-9	-	-	21	-
	All	1994/95	2006/07	40	65	9	2332	159	41.64	6	9	3167	88	-	35.98	6-71	-	-	58	-
J.M.McMillan	Otago	1994/95	2007	138	226	27	7817	168*	39.28	16	42	3352	95	-	35.28	7-105	1	-	7	-
N.H.McMillan	Auck	2000/01	2009/10	40	49	23	232	21*	8.92	-	-	21	0	-	-	-	-	-	2	-
J.J.M.McMullan	Otago	1931/32	-	1	2	0	12	7	6.00	-	-	13	0	-	-	-	-	-	14	-
S.McMurray	Cant	1917/18	1929/30	32	59	2	1718	157*	30.14	3	9	103	3	-	34.33	2-24	-	-	-	-
S.R.McNally	Cant	1884/85	1896/97	4	6	0	23	12	3.83	-	-	2644	76	-	34.78	4-33	-	-	11	-
	All	1978/79	1985/86	32	46	2	458	47	10.40	-	-	2696	77	-	35.01	4-33	-	-	11	-
F.A.McNeil	Auck	1978/79	1985/86	33	47	2	469	47	10.42	-	-	136	4	-	34.00	2-32	-	-	11	3
H.MacNeil	Otago	1905/06	-	2	4	1	16	11	5.33	-	-	203	15	-	13.53	6-25	1	-	7	-
K.J.McNicholl	Cant	1877/78	1893/94	8	16	0	167	58	10.43	-	1	404	11	-	36.72	4-56	-	-	3	-
	Cant	1952/53	1956/57	6	11	7	42	15	10.50	-	-	-	-	-	-	-	-	-	-	-

		First	Last	M	I	NO	Runs	HS	Avg	100	50	Runs	Wkts	OW	Avg	Best	5i	10m	ct	st
R.McPherson	Auck	1889/90	1970/71	3	5	1	6	4	1.50	-	-	88	4		22.00	3-47	-	-	3	-
R.J.McPherson	ND	1959/60		13	25	1	419	87	17.45	-	1								5	-
D.A.N.McRae	Cant	1937/38	1945/46	15	23	3	336	43	16.80	-	-	1167	50		23.34	4-15	-	-	10	-
	All	1937/38	1945/46	17	26	3	354	43	15.39	-	-	1261	56		22.51	5-20	1	-	11	-
G.P.McRae	CD	1993/94		3	5	0	148	62	29.60	-	1	18	0		-	-	-	-	5	-
W.C.McSkimming	Otago	1999/00	2009/10	58	88	12	1525	111	20.06	1	7	5206	208		25.02	6-39	9	-	25	-
	All	1999/00	2009/10	60	90	13	1548	111	20.10	1	7	5248	210		24.99	6-39	9	-	25	-
E.B.McSweeney	CD	1979/80	1980/81	8	12	3	224	56*	24.88	-	2								23	5
	Well	1981/82	1993/94	102	153	23	4296	205*	33.04	5	20	19	0		-	-	-	-	289	39
	All	1979/80	1993/94	121	177	30	4947	205*	33.65	6	23	19	0		-	-	-	-	340	45
A.C.McVicar	All	1920/21		1	2	0	19	15	9.50	-	-								-	-
C.C.McVicar	CD	1950/51	1951/52	5	9	0	182	42	20.22	-	1								12	-
S.A.McVicar	Well	1943/44	1950/51	10	19	2	269	73*	15.82	-	1	1	0		-	-	-	-	8	-
	All	1943/44	1950/51	11	21	2	322	73*	16.94	-	2								8	-
H.D.Maddock	Otago	1863/64	1869/70	4	7	0	21	10	3.00	-	-	35	6		5.83	4-25	-	-	1	-
S.J.Maguiness	Well	1981/82	1987/88	43	48	10	522	54	13.73	-	1	2848	110		25.89	7-17	2	-	40	-
J.J.Mahoney	Well	1902/03	1911/12	20	37	4	794	84	24.06	-	3	55	1		55.00	1-34	-	-	8	4
	All	1902/03	1911/12	25	47	5	1053	84	25.07	-	5	55	1		55.00	1-34	-	-	16	4
L.A.Mahoney	Cant	1948/49		2	3	1	57	43	28.50	-	-	230	8		28.75	4-52	-	-	2	-
C.T.Maingay	Auck	1970/71		2	3	1	40	31	20.00	-	-								2	-
R.Mainwaring	Cant	1866/67	1870/71	4	6	1	26	14	5.20	-	-	16	0		-	-	-	-	1	-
R.J.Malcolm	Nel	1882/83	1883/84	3	6	1	50	22*	10.00	-	-	6	0		-	-	-	-	1	-
T.J.Malcolm	Well	1885/86		1	2	0	2	2	1.00	-	-								-	-
W.Malcolm	Otago	1914/15		2	4	1	18	16	6.00	-	-								-	1
P.J.Malcon	Well	1972/73		2	4	0	9	6*	3.00	-	-								-	1
F.B.W.Malet	Cant	1883/84		2	4	0	5	3	1.25	-	-								-	-
J.J.Mallard	Otago	1882/83	1884/85	2	4	0	31	18	7.75	-	-								4	-
N.A.Mallender	Otago	1983/84	1992/93	78	112	30	1872	100*	22.82	1	7	5433	268		20.27	7-27	14	3	32	-
	All	1980	1996	345	396	122	4709	100*	17.18	1	10	24654	937		26.31	7-27	36	5	111	-
T.S.Malloch	Well	1953/54		2	3	1	19	12	9.50	-	-	182	6		30.33	2-59	-	-	-	-
T.J.Malone	Cant	1895/96	1908/09	11	19	10	24	7	2.66	-	-	888	39		22.76	7-30	1	-	3	-
C.H.Mansill	Well	1882/83		1	1	0	3	3	3.00	-	-								-	-
E.Maples	Cant	1868/69	1873/74	6	10	1	60	25	6.66	-	-								3	-
W.O.Mapplebeck	Cant	1936/37	1940/41	4	7	1	53	18*	13.25	-	-	457	21		21.76	6-43	2	-	3	-
K.Marc	CD	1999/00		1	1	0	0	0	0.00	-	-	85	6		14.16	3-32	-	-	2	-
	All	1994	1999/00	4	4	0	17	9	4.25	-	-	360	12		30.00	3-32	-	-	-	-
J.W.A.Marchant	Well	1873/74	1881/82	3	6	1	44	20	8.80	-	-	78	9		8.66	5-26	1	-	9	-
W.H.Marcroft	Tara	1894/95		1	0	0						40	0		-	-	-	-	-	-
B.A.Marris	Well	1917/18	1919/20	8	12	5	126	22*	18.00	-	-	489	24		20.37	5-50	1	-	8	-
J.P.Marsdon	Auck	1948/49	1959/60	10	15	2	252	72	19.38	-	2	274	6		45.66	2-21	-	-	4	-
E.J.Marshall	Otago	1991/92	2001/02	25	41	10	457	52	14.74	-	1	1899	70		27.12	6-53	4	-	11	-
	All	1990/91	2001/02	26	42	10	457	52	14.28	-	1	1947	71		27.42	6-53	4	-	12	-
G.Marshall	Cant	1888/89	1890/91	5	9	0	84	30	9.33	-	-	22	2		11.00	2-22	-	-	6	-
	HB	1893/94	1901/02	12	21	1	272	49	13.60	-	-	145	5		29.00	4-46	-	-	5	-
	All	1888/89	1901/02	17	30	1	356	49	12.27	-	-	167	7		23.85	4-46	-	-	10	-

		First	Last	M	I	NO	Runs	HS	Avg	100	50	Runs	Wkts	OW	Avg	Best	5i	10m	ct	st
H.J.H.Marshall	ND	1998/99	2009/10	64	111	8	3250	170	31.55	5	12	606	9		67.33	2-12			33	
J.A.H.Marshall	All	1998/99	2010	153	260	17	8709	170	35.83	18	43	1483	30		49.43	4-24			88	
	ND	1997/98	2009/10	100	171	13	4988	235	31.56	8	24	314	5		62.80	1-5			86	
	All	1997/98	2009/10	121	207	14	5992	235	31.04	11	29	333	5		66.60	1-5			110	
J.M.Marshall	Tara	1891/92		1	2	0	20	19	10.00											
K.B.Marshall	Well	1983/84		1	2	0	8	8	4.00			39	1		39.00	1-30				
P.Marshall	Auck	1900/01		3	6	0	50	17	8.33											
P.G.Marshall	Otago	1991/92		5	6	0	48	12	16.00			402	15		26.80	6-59	1		3	
R.A.Marshall	Auck	1936/37		3	3	0	16	9	5.33											
A.Martin	HB	1896/97	1897/98	2	4	1	5	3	1.66										3	1
B.P.Martin	ND	1999/00	2009/10	77	104	29	1302	62*	17.36		4	6889	192		35.88	7-33	12	2	31	
	All	1999/00	2009/10	89	118	32	1547	113*	17.98		4	7964	220		36.20	7-33	13	2	37	
C.S.Martin	Cant	1997/98	2009/10	49	59	23	170	25	4.72			4445	152		29.24	5-40	3		5	
	Auck	2005/06	2008/09	12	12	8	31	9*	7.75			1270	42		30.23	5-48	3			
	All	1997/98	2010	155	192	95	389	25	4.01			15434	477		32.35	6-54	18	1	30	
G.A.Martin	Otago	1908/09		1	1	0	5	5	5.00											
H.Martin	HB	1883/84	1897/98	8	13	3	77	15*	7.70			30	1		30.00	1-11			2	
J.H.Martin	HB	1883/84	1896/97	10	19	1	180	35*	10.00										6	
K.W.Martin	CD	1984/85	1987/88	16	11	5	123	47*	20.50			1438	53		27.13	6-25	3		11	
W.S.Martin	All	1976/77		1	2	0	33	30	16.50			49	4		12.25	4-49				
R.V.Masefield	Cant	1984/85		1	1	0	8	8	8.00			82	1		82.00	1-59				
F.R.Mason	Auck	1902/03	1914/15	16	27	1	424	81	16.30		1	225	2		112.50	1-23			11	
	All	1902/03	1914/15	19	33	2	520	81	16.77		1	225	2		112.50	1-23			14	
I.R.Mason	Well	1960/61	1965/66	4	8	0	121	39	15.12										2	
	All	1960/61	1965/66	6	12	1	177	39	16.09										2	
M.J.Mason	CD	1997/98	2009/10	69	92	25	965	64*	14.40		1	5621	235		23.91	6-56	10	1	17	
	All	1997/98	2009/10	81	109	33	1194	64*	15.71		1	6474	260		24.90	6-56	11	1	18	
W.F.Mason	Well	1873/74	1875/76	3	6	1	29	13	5.80											
H.B.Massey	Well	1926/27	1932/33	14	23	10	320	64	24.61		2	1013	31		32.67	5-56	1		12	
	All	1926/27	1932/33	15	25	10	331	64	22.06		2	1030	32		32.18	5-56	1		13	
T.C.Masters	ND	1969/70		3	2	1	3	3	3.00			143	3		47.66	2-42			2	
A.M.Matatumua	Otago	1966/67	1967/68	8	15	1	228	69	16.28		1	494	18		27.44	3-38			4	
S.R.Mather	Well	1993/94	2000/01	27	43	4	1059	170	27.15	3	3	351	9		39.00	3-9			21	
	Otago	1998/99	1999/00	11	19	3	503	117*	31.43	1	3	312	11		28.36	3-39			15	
	All	1993/94	2000/01	41	67	7	1606	170	26.76	4	6	740	22		33.63	3-9			40	
A.M.Matheson	Auck	1926/27	1939/40	40	59	9	1370	112	27.40	1	8	3818	120		31.81	5-63	1		29	
	Well	1944/45	1946/47	7	12	0	156	67	13.00			349	14		24.92	3-4			2	
	All	1926/27	1946/47	69	97	19	1844	112	23.64	1	11	5536	194		28.53	5-50	1		44	
H.R.Mathias	Cant	1883/84	1886/87	2	3	0	11	11	3.66			21	1		21.00	1-5				
R.B.Mathias	Cant	1888/89	1893/94	6	11	1	243	48	24.30		1	14	2		7.00	1-0			2	
J.Mathieson	Tara	1882/83		1	2	0	10	8	5.00			55	4		13.75	4-55			1	
P.R.Mathieson	All	1970/71		1	2	0	59	50	29.50		1									
D.N.Matthews	ND	1963/64		5	5	0	38	13	7.60			308	10		30.80	3-44				
	All	1963/64	1964/65	6	6	1	57	19*	11.40			367	10		36.70	3-44				
R.C.Matthews	Auck	1969/70	1975/76	12	10	6	26	7*	6.50			749	25		29.96	6-70	1		8	
S.J.Matthews	All	1942/43		1	2	0	18	15	9.00			32	1		32.00	1-32			1	

Name	Team	First	Last	M	I	NO	Runs	HS	Avg	100	50	Runs	Wkts	OW	Avg	Best	5i	10m	ct	st
P.A.Maunder	CD	1961/62		1	2	0	8	8	4.00	-	-	846	24		35.25	4-51	-	-	-	
R.E.W.Mawhinney	Otago	1983/84	1990/91	18	30	6	615	108	25.62	-	1								8	
	ND	1985/86	1986/87	11	22	1	498	110	23.71	1	1	5	0						8	
	All	1983/84	1990/91	35	62	8	1274	110	23.59	2	3	979	26		37.65	4-51	-	-	17	
D.Mayall	Auck	1913/14		1	2	1	4	3*	4.00	-	-								3	
M.P.Maynard	ND	1990/91	1991/92	19	27	1	1485	195	57.11	5	7	43	0						19	
	Otago	1996/97	1997/98	8	13	0	333	84	27.75	-	1	13	0						7	
	All	1985	2005	395	643	60	24799	243	42.53	59	131	895	6		149.16	3-21	-	-	372	2
N.A.P.Meadows	Well	1980/81		2	3	2	5	5*	5.00	-	-	109	2		54.50	1-38	-	-	-	
T.Meale	Well	1951/52	1953/54	12	23	1	741	130	33.68	2	2	0	0		-	-	-	-	6	
	Well	1951/52	1958	32	54	5	1352	130	27.59	2	5	0	0		-	-	-	-	17	7
W.E.D.Meares	Otago	1873/74	1876/77	2	4	0	19	10	4.75	-	-	3	0		-	-	-	-	5	
J.T.Medlow	Cant	1894/95		1	1	0	5	5	5.00	-	-	4	1		4.00	1-4	-	-	-	
M.D.Meech	Well	1946/47		2	4	0	27	13	6.75	-	-								1	
A.L.Meldrum	Auck	1886/87	1889/90	2	3	0	28	19	9.33	-	-	133	5		26.60	5-130	1	-	1	
D.Meldrum	Auck	1892/93		1	2	0	11	6	5.50	-	-								-	
W.Meldrum	Auck	1884/85	1886/87	4	6	2	26	11*	6.50	-	-	220	22		10.00	7-38	2	-	3	
W.Mendelson	Cant	1893/94		1	1	0	7	7	7.00	-	-								-	
R.E.J.Menzies	Cant	1936/37	1940/41	12	22	1	642	163	30.57	1	3								10	
	Well	1941/42	1946/47	4	8	0	236	76	29.50	-	2								1	
	All	1936/37	1946/47	17	31	1	892	163	29.73	1	5								11	
C.J.Merchant	ND	2007/08	2008/09	8	14	0	394	89	28.14	-	3	6	0		-	-	-	-	5	
	Well	2009/10		2	4	0	108	108		-										11	
	All	2007/08	2009/10	10	20	1	764	108	40.21	2	4	6	0		-	-	-	-	11	
	All	2007/08	2009/10	18	34	1	1158	108	35.09	2	7	6	0		-	-	-	-	5	
R.C.Merrin	Cant	1967/68	1974/75	11	16	5	141	25	12.81	-	-	725	30		24.16	7-61	1	-	4	
W.E.Merritt	Cant	1926/27	1935/36	24	42	3	714	84	18.30	-	3	3559	154		23.11	8-105	15	4	14	
	All	1926/27	1946	125	191	33	3147	87	19.91	-	12	13670	537		25.45	8-41	38	8	58	
C.L.Metge	Auck	1923/24	1924/25	2	4	1	12	12	4.00	-	-								2	
E.M.Meuli	Auck	1945/46		3	5	0	109	56	21.80	-	1								7	
	CD	1950/51	1959/60	38	69	3	1767	154	26.77	2	5	329	11		29.90	6-67	1	-	9	
	All	1945/46	1959/60	42	76	3	1914	154	26.21	2	6	329	11		29.90	6-67	1	-	1	
B.J.Middleton	Well	1973/74		2	3	0	71	24	11.83	-	-								-	
F.S.Middleton	Auck	1917/18		3	6	2	6	6	3.00	-	-	74	2		37.00	1-1	-	-	4	
	Well	1919/20	1921/22	8	14	0	297	70	21.21	-	1	675	50		13.50	7-36	5	2	6	
	All	1905/06	1921/22	14	24	2	355	70	15.43	-	1	912	56		16.28	7-36	5	2	20	
F.A.Midlane	Well	1898/99	1914/15	25	46	0	1399	222*	35.87	3	6								2	
	Auck	1917/18	1918/19	4	8	0	281	126	35.12	1	1	71	2		35.50	2-13	-	-	22	
	All	1898/99	1918/19	30	56	0	1727	222*	35.24	4	7	71	2		35.50	2-13	-	-	148	17
B.D.Milburn	Otago	1963/64	1982/83	60	86	25	697	103	11.42	-	-								176	19
	All	1963/64	1982/83	75	97	33	737	103	11.51	-	-									
C.C.Miles	Well	1883/84		1	2	1	27	25	13.50	-	-								-	
D.J.Millener	Auck	1964/65	1967/68	13	12	0	23	7*	5.75	-	-	727	23		31.60	3-29	-	-	6	
	All	1964/65	1970	26	30	12	176	24	9.77	-	-	1958	57		34.35	4-97	-	-	9	
B.Miller	HB	1914/15		1	2	1	4	4*	4.00	-	-								1	
D.L.Miller	Auck	1892/93		1	2	1	3	2*	3.00	-	-	54	3		18.00	3-43	-	-	2	
	All	1892/93	1905/06	15	25	5	162	21	8.10	-	-	1045	55		19.00	5-38	2	-	11	

		First	Last	M	I	NO	Runs	HS	Avg	100	50	Runs	Wkts	OW	Avg	Best	5i	10m	ct	st
L.S.M.Miller	CD	1950/51	1952/53	8	14	4	661	128*	66.10	2	3	32	1		32.00	1-18	-	-	8	
	Well	1954/55	1959/60	22	41	5	1708	144	47.44	2	15	19	0		-	-	-	-	8	
	All	1950/51	1959/60	82	142	15	4777	144	37.61	5	34	75	3		25.00	1-7	-	-	33	
R.M.Miller	Cant	2002/03		1	2	0	12	9	6.00	-	-								1	
G.I.Millington	Otago	1876/77	1880/81	2	4	0	2	1	0.50	-	-								-	
J.P.Millmow	Well	1986/87	1991/92	28	23	9	102	16*	7.28	-	-	147	10		14.70	6-37	1	-	7	
	All	1986/87	1991/92	37	29	13	129	16*	8.06	-	-	2013	76		26.48	6-13	3	-	10	
A.S.Mills	Otago	1947/48		1	2	0	16	15	8.00	-	-	2789	99		28.17	6-13	4	1	1	
C.Mills	HB	1919/20		1	2	0	21	16	10.50	-	-								-	
E.Mills	Auck	1884/85	1886/87	4	6	0	66	35	13.20	-	-								3	5
G.Mills	Auck	1886/87	1899/00	8	13	1	382	106*	38.20	1	2	133	11		12.09	7-39	1	-	3	
	HB	1894/95		3	5	1	85	49*	21.25	-	-	83	10		8.30	7-36	1	-	7	
	Otago	1900/01		4	7	0	62	39	8.85	-	-	87	6		14.50	5-52	-	-	2	
	All	1886/87	1902/03	17	29	4	551	106*	22.04	1	2	306	26		11.76	7-36	3	-	12	
G.H.Mills	Otago	1935/36	1957/58	55	103	7	1942	121	20.22	2	5	16	0		-	-	-	-	81	29
	All	1935/36	1957/58	59	110	7	2056	121	19.96	2	6	16	0		-	-	-	-	88	34
I.Mills	Auck	1889/90	1903/04	15	27	3	564	88*	23.50	-	3	148	4		37.00	2-17	-	-	10	
	All	1889/90	1903/04	18	33	3	700	88*	23.33	-	3	148	4		37.00	2-17	-	-	13	
J.M.Mills	Auck	1991/92	1998/99	25	39	4	533	73*	15.22	-	1								78	
	All	1991/92	1998/99	27	42	5	585	73*	15.81	-	1								80	
J.E.Mills	Auck	1924/25	1937/38	35	63	1	2126	185	34.29	3	14	100	3		33.33	2-57	-	-	7	
	All	1924/25	1937/38	97	161	8	5025	185	32.84	11	25	123	4		30.75	2-57	-	-	30	
K.D.Mills	Auck	1998/99	2008/09	40	53	14	1369	117*	35.10	1	10	3114	109		28.56	5-33	3	-	14	
	All	1998/99	2008/09	66	94	23	1840	117*	25.91	1	12	5059	176		28.74	5-33	3	-	22	
S.M.Mills	Well	2003/04	2006/07	13	20	4	455	171	28.43	1	2								35	
W.Mills	Tara	1894/95		2	2	0	0	0	0.00	-	-	117	12		9.75	6-35	2	-	6	
	Auck	1900/01	1903/04	6	12	0	198	55	33.00	-	1	284	16		17.75	5-19	1	-	7	
	All	1894/95	1903/04	8	14	0	198	55	24.75	-	1	401	28		14.32	6-35	3	-	7	
W.V.Millton	Cant	1877/78	1886/87	12	21	0	298	57	14.19	-	1								6	
A.F.Milne	CD	2009/10		3	5	0	55	36	55.00	-	1	303	11		27.54	4-49	-	-	-	
J.D.Milne	Well	1985/86	1987/88	8	7	1	92	36	15.00	-	-								20	
G.S.Milnes	CD	1997/98	1999/00	6	11	0	165	107	13.14	-	-								-	1
L.A.Milnes	Otago	1944/45	1948/49	7	14	0	247	46	17.64	-	-	54	2		27.00	2-36	-	-	4	
	All	1942/43	1948/49	9	18	0	354	46	19.66	-	-	54	2		27.00	2-36	-	-	6	
A.Mishra	CD	2008/09		1	1	0	11	11	11.00	-	-	163	3		54.33	3-155	-	-	-	
	All	2000/01	2010	95	127	18	2132	84	19.55	-	10	10019	371		27.00	6-66	19	1	55	
D.Mitchell	Otago	1881/82	1882/83	2	4	1	37	17	12.33	-	-								7	
E.W.Mitchell	Well	1926/27		1	1	0	1	1	1.00	-	-	135	4		33.75	3-82	-	-	-	1
W.J.Mitchell	ND	1964/65	1966/67	10	17	1	431	127*	26.93	-	2	15	1		15.00	1-15	-	-	8	
	Otago	1968/69		2	3	0	99	52	33.00	-	1								-	
	All	1964/65	1968/69	14	24	1	634	127*	27.56	-	4	15	1		15.00	1-15	-	-	8	
Mohammad Wasim	Otago	2002/03	2004/05	26	45	2	1233	108	28.67	1	8	167	2		83.50	1-2	-	-	17	
A.M.Moir	All	1994/95	2009/10	179	284	16	9322	192	34.78	24	43	613	15		40.86	2-12	-	-	184	
	Otago	1949/50	1961/62	54	87	8	1304	66*	16.50	-	5	5926	282		21.01	8-37	20	5	32	5
	All	1949/50	1961/62	97	150	22	2102	70	16.42	-	8	9040	368		24.56	8-37	25	5	44	

		First	Last	M	I	NO	Runs	HS	Avg	100	50	Runs	Wkts	OW	Avg	Best	5i	10m	ct	st
D.A.R.Moloney	Otago	1929/30	1939/40	21	40	2	757	74	19.92	-	3	1208	29		41.65	4-53	-	-	18	
	Well	1935/36	1937/38	7	14	0	596	190	42.57	1	2				-				2	
	Cant	1940/41	1940/41	1	2	0	15	12	7.50	-	-	41	0		-		-	-	2	
	All	1929/30	1940/41	64	119	7	3219	190	28.74	2	16	26	1		26.00	1-26	-	-	35	
D.M.Molony	Well	1985/86	1987/88	10	7	2	41	14*	13.66	-	-	3151	95		33.16	5-23	3	-	4	
D.W.Monaghan	All	1942/43	1910/11	1	2	0	19	10	9.50	-	-	653	18		36.27	3-62	-	-		
H.W.Monaghan	Well	1905/06	1910/11	11	18	4	221	47*	15.78	-	-	877	43		20.39	7-50	2	-	5	
	Cant	1913/14	1913/14	4	7	1	133	46	26.60	-	-	332	16		20.75	4-19	-	-	2	
	All.	1905/06	1913/14	15	25	6	354	47*	18.63	-	-	1209	59		20.49	7-50	2	-	7	
J.S.Monck	Cant	1873/74		1	2	0	9	8	4.50	-	-								-	
L.S.Monk	Otago	1901/02		1	2	1	10	10*	10.00	-	-	46	4		11.50	2-21	-	-	-	
P.G.Monk	Otago	1928/29	1929/30	5	9	2	157	43*	22.42	-	-	256	6		42.66	3-41	-	-	2	
A.P.J.Monteith	Otago	1939/40		2	3	0	14	12	4.66	-	-								1	
L.T.J.Monteith	Auck	1924/25		2	4	1	5	4	1.66	-	-								-	
F.L.H.Mooney	Well	1941/42	1954/55	36	67	2	1474	180	22.67	1	7								66	20
	All	1941/42	1954/55	91	150	14	3143	180	23.11	2	12								168	54
F.E.Moore	Tara	1894/95	1897/98	4	5	0	65	25	13.00	-	-	0	0		-	-	-	-	-	
H.W.Moore	Cant	1876/77	1878/79	3	4	0	173	76	43.25	-	2	3	1		3.00	1-3	-	-	2	
	Tara	1894/95		2	4	2	12	12	6.00	-	-								2	
	All	1876/77	1894/95	5	6	0	185	76	30.83	-	2	3	1		3.00	1-3	-	-	5	
J.G.H.Moore	Otago	1905/06		2	4	0	1	1	0.25	-	-								2	
P.C.E.Moore	Well	1919/20		1	2	0	11	6	5.50	-	-								-	
T.R.Moore	Cant	1866/67	1874/75	6	9	1	36	14*	4.50	-	-	212	15		14.13	4-17	-	-	2	
W.S.Moore	All	1879/80		1	1	0	3	3	3.00	-	-								-	
M.Moorhouse	Cant	1883/84	1907/08	3	5	0	130	86	26.00	-	1	37	1		37.00	1-15	-	-	3	
	Well	1886/87	1890/91	9	16	2	246	63	17.57	-	1	72	2		36.00	1-25	-	-	9	10
	All	1883/84	1907/08	12	21	2	376	86	19.78	-	2	109	3		36.33	1-15	-	-	12	10
T.A.Moresby	Auck	1889/90	1893/94	4	7	0	67	21	9.57	-	-	32	0		-	-	-	-	1	
H.A.T.Morey	Well	1888/89		1	1	0	11	11	11.00	-	-								-	
G.J.Morgan	Auck	2007/08	2009/10	4	4	1	102	83*	34.00	-	1	197	5		39.40	2-46	-	-	3	
H.R.Morgan	Well	2000/01	2001/02	4	4	0	66	35	16.50	-	-								-	
H.J.Morgan	CD	2000/01		2	4	0	11	8	2.75	-	-	157	2		78.50	2-64	-	-	1	
H.A.Morgan	Well	1963/64	1977/78	33	48	7	789	67	19.24	-	4	1914	73		26.21	5-42	1	-	20	
L.J.Morgan	Well	2001/02	2002/03	4	6	0	117	30	19.50	-	-								1	
	Otago	2007/08	2009/10	14	25	1	727	81	30.29	-	7								9	
	All	2001/02	2009/10	18	31	1	844	81	28.13	-	7								10	
R.G.Morgan	ND	1993/94		3	6	1	68	27*	13.60	-	-	285	9		31.66	3-74	-	-	3	
	Auck	1999/00	2001/02	6	8	2	93	26	15.50	-	-	488	20		24.40	5-44	2	-	3	
	All	1993/94	2001/02	9	14	3	161	27*	14.63	-	-	773	29		26.65	5-44	2	-	3	
R.W.Morgan	Auck	1957/58	1976/77	90	154	8	4162	166	28.50	7	20	2290	91		25.16	6-40	4	-	57	
	All	1957/58	1976/77	136	229	13	5940	166	27.50	8	32	3558	108		32.94	6-40	4	-	85	
R.T.Morgan	Well	1932/33	1940/41	10	18	2	328	81	20.50	-	3	371	12		30.91	2-34	-	-	11	
	All	1932/33	1945	11	20	2	374	81	20.77	-	3	384	12		32.00	2-34	-	-	12	
F.H.Morice	Well	1886/87	1889/90	4	6	0	18	10	3.00	-	-								-	
D.M.Morland	CD	1973/74	1973/74	5	10	1	137	40*	15.22	-	-	432	17		25.41	4-98	-	-	1	1
	All	1965/66	1973/74	6	12	1	182	40*	16.54	-	-	432	17		25.41	4-98	-	-	3	1

		First	Last	M	I	NO	Runs	HS	Avg	100	50	Runs	Wkts	OW	Avg	Best	5i	10m	ct	st
N.D.Morland	Otago	1996/97	2003/04	33	48	11	543	56	14.67	-	1	2033	49	-	41.48	4-26	-	-	27	-
	All	1996/97	2003/04	34	50	11	573	56	14.69	-	1	2060	50	-	41.20	4-26	-	-	28	-
A.Morris	Otago	1884/85		1	2	0	2	2	1.00	-	-	12	0						-	
C.Morris	Otago	1863/64		1	2	0	3	2	1.50										-	
J.B.Morris	Auck	1951/52	1956/57	22	41	2	987	103	25.30	2	3	28	1		28.00	1-7	-	-	10	
	All	1951/52	1956/57	23	42	2	1021	103	25.52	2	3	28	1		28.00	1-7	-	-	11	
P.P.W.Morris	Auck	1961/62	1962/63	10	16	2	407	66	29.07	-	3	0	0						5	
P.R.Morris	Otago	1975/76	1976/77	11	13	4	29	12	3.22	-	-	733	16		45.81	3-72	-	-	5	
A.R.Morrison	Auck	1965/66	1966/67	10	17	0	322	53	18.94	-	1								15	
B.D.Morrison	Well	1953/54	1964/65	45	63	27	356	37	9.88	-	-	3858	163		23.66	7-42	7	2	29	
	All	1953/54	1964/65	47	67	27	374	37	9.35	-	-	4036	167		24.16	7-42	7	2	30	
D.K.Morrison	Auck	1985/86	1996/97	49	52	17	434	40*	12.40	-	-	4034	168		24.01	7-82	7	-	16	
	All	1985/86	1996/97	142	161	58	1127	46*	10.94	-	-	13298	440		30.22	7-82	19	-	43	
H.B.Morrison	Otago	1880/81		1	2	0	17	17	8.50			34	0						-	
J.B.Morrison	Well	1958/59	1959/60	3	6	0	28	7	4.66										1	
J.F.M.Morrison	CD	1965/66	1966/67	4	7	0	105	24	15.00			9	0						4	
	Well	1967/68	1983/84	89	160	22	4694	180*	34.01	6	25	1306	43		30.37	5-69	1	-	108	
	All	1965/66	1983/84	126	225	25	6142	180*	30.71	7	32	1607	51		31.50	5-69	1	-	133	
W.Morrison	Otago	1876/77	1880/81	2	4	0	21	15	5.25			102	9		11.33	6-40	1	-	-	
W.E.W.Morrison	Cant	1877/78		1	2	0	22	16	11.00										-	
A.E.Moss	Cant	1889/90		4	8	3	13	8	2.60	-	-	285	26		10.96	10-28	2	1	2	
J.R.Moss	Well	1969/70		5	6	2	7	5	1.75	-	-	399	15		26.60	5-57	1	-	-	
	All	1965/66	1969/70	6	8	2	11	8	1.83	-	-	413	15		27.53	5-57	1	-	2	
R.M.Moss	Well	1903/04		1	2	0	19	10	9.50										1	
A.Motley	All	1886/87	1888/89	5	8	1	96	58*	13.71	-	1								1	
	All	1879	1888/89	7	10	2	106	58*	13.25	-	1								1	
R.C.Motz	Cant	1957/58	1968/69	56	90	10	1535	103*	19.18	1	3	4587	239		19.28	4-48	-	-	19	
	All	1957/58	1969	142	225	21	3494	103*	17.12	1	13	11767	518		19.19	8-61	12	3	41	
L.S.Mountain	ND	1967/68	1973/74	37	66	7	877	51	14.86	-	1	4	0		22.71	8-61	24	4	61	
	All	1967/68	1973/74	38	67	7	892	51	14.86	-	1	4	0						64	
W.Mowatt	Well	1903/04		1	2	0	20	20	10.00										1	
H.Moyle	Auck	1950/51	1956/57	10	11	8	39	10*	13.00	-	-	758	26		29.15	4-110	-	-	1	
T.D.Moynihan	Cant	1940/41	1952/53	5	7	0	138	46	19.71	-	1								1	
C.A.Muir	Well	1943/44		1	2	0	18	18	9.00										-	
F.J.Muir	Otago	1872/73		1	2	0	3	3	1.50			40	0						-	
G.A.Muir	Cant	1995/96	1997/98	6	9	1	127	44	15.87	-	-	279	5		55.80	2-54	-	-	1	
M.F.Muir	Otago	1949/50		1	1	1	0	0*	0.00			20	0						-	
E.Mulcock	Cant	1936/37	1938/39	9	15	10	39	8*	7.80	-	-	896	44		20.36	8-61	4	-	7	
	Otago	1943/44		1	2	1	5	4*	5.00	-	-	166	5		33.20	5-166	1	-	-	
	All	1936/37	1943/44	12	20	13	47	8*	6.71	-	-	1234	55		22.43	8-61	5	-	8	
J.B.Mumford	Auck	1873/74	1877/78	4	7	0	47	22	6.71										8	
E.L.Mummery	CD	1961/62		5	7	1	69	40*	11.50	-	-	355	13		27.30	4-152	-	-	2	
C.Munro	Auck	2006/07	2007/08	4	5	1	76	37	19.00	-	-	375	8		46.87	3-106	-	-	3	
D.H.Murdoch	Cant	1943/44	1944/45	3	6	0	78	28	13.00										2	
G.H.Murdoch	Otago	1974/75		5	7	4	116	34*	38.66	-	-	253	5		50.60	2-58	-	-	8	23
R.L.Murdoch	Otago	1964/65		6	12	0	199	50	16.58	-	1								2	23

		First	Last	M	I	NO	Runs	HS	Avg	100	50	Runs	Wkts	OW	Avg	Best	5i	10m	ct	st
S.J.Murdoch	Well	2009/10		4	8	0	280	88	35.00	-	3	5	0		-	-	-	-	4	-
T.J.Murdoch	All	1977/78		1	2	1	6	5*	6.00	-	-								4	-
W.T.Murdock	CD	1962/63	1974/75	11	20	2	427	55	23.72	-	2	14	0		-	-	-	-	4	-
	All	1962/63	1974/75	12	22	2	473	55	23.65	-	2	14	0		-	-	-	-	5	-
W.D.Murison	Otago	1864/65	1866/67	3	5	0	29	14	5.80	-	-								-	-
A.J.Murphy	CD	1985/86		3	4	1	1	1	0.33	-	-	190	6		31.66	2-31	-	-	17	-
	All	1985	1994	84	86	39	323	38	6.87	-	-	7934	208		38.14	6-97	6	-	75	-
B.A.G.Murray	Well	1958/59	1972/73	64	116	9	3753	213	35.07	3	27	829	26		31.88	4-43	-	-	124	-
	All	1958/59	1972/73	102	187	11	6257	213	35.55	6	43	868	30		28.93	4-43	-	-	19	-
D.J.Murray	Cant	1990/91	1997/98	32	52	4	1619	153	33.72	3	8	85	0		-	-	-	-	36	-
	All	1990/91	1997/98	53	90	6	2907	182	34.60	7	13	85	0		-	-	-	-		
G.B.Murray	Well	2004/05		3	6	0	76	33	12.66	-	-	88	0		-	-	-	-	9	-
R.M.Murray	Well	1946/47	1950/51	15	24	4	351	52*	17.55	-	1	1172	51		22.98	5-85	1	-	10	-
	All	1946/47	1950/51	17	28	5	399	52*	17.34	-	1	1412	59		23.93	5-85	1	-	2	-
J.R.Murtagh	Otago	1988/89		1	1	0	0	0	0.00	-	-								4	-
	Well	1991/92		5	10	0	126	44	12.60	-	-								6	-
	All	1988/89		6	11	0	126	44	11.45	-	-								21	-
J.G.Myburgh	Cant	2007/08	2009/10	25	46	4	2172	199	51.71	7	13	706	19		37.15	4-56	-	-	50	-
	All	1997/98	2009/10	73	132	18	5180	203	45.43	13	30	1326	30		44.20	4-56	-	-		
H.W.Mytton	HB	1863/64	1866/67	2	4	0	13	7	3.25	-	-								2	-
E.J.Napier	HB	1913/14	1920/21	6	12	3	86	24	9.55	-	-	564	22		25.63	5-83	1	-	2	-
G.R.Napier	Well	2008/09		4	4	2	25	20	12.50	-	-	294	14		21.00	4-52	-	-	1	-
D.J.Nash	All	1997	2010	103	142	30	3350	125	29.91	3	20	8134	210		38.73	6-103	3	-	39	-
	ND	1990/91	1997/98	12	19	2	456	125	26.82	1	1	440	8		55.00	2-93	-	-	8	-
	Otago	1992/93	1993/94	10	18	0	343	51	19.05	-	1	499	26		19.19	5-18	1	-	5	-
	Auck	2000/01	2001/02	11	18	2	581	118	36.31	2	2	184	5		36.80	3-16	-	-		
	All	1990/91	2001/02	120	168	37	3555	135*	27.13	5	16	7165	255		28.09	7-39	10	1	46	-
J.A.Nash	Well	1919/20		1	2	0	7	4	3.50	-	-	24	0		-	-	-	-	1	-
R.G.Nash	HB	1886/87		1	2	0	11	7	5.50	-	-									
A.Nathu	Cant	1983/84	1991/92	28	52	2	1354	153	27.08	2	4	41	2		20.50	1-0	-	-	16	-
	All	1980/81	1991/92	29	54	2	1404	153	27.00	2	4	41	2		20.50	1-0	-	-	16	-
D.H.Naughton	Well	1908/09	1911/12	4	7	0	159	97	22.71	-	1	8	0		-	-	-	-	1	-
M.P.Naughton	Well	1897/98		1	1	0	40	40	40.00	-	-								1	-
J.Naylor	Nel	1879/80	1880/81	2	4	0	24	15	8.00	-	-	3	1		3.00	1-3	-	-	-	-
D.W.Neal	CD	1971/72	1976/77	27	50	4	1173	90	24.43	-	5	5	0		-	-	-	-	27	-
E.R.Neale	All	1920/21	1921/22	2	4	0	74	37*	24.66	-	-	6	1		6.00	1-6	-	-	-	-
D.O.Neely	Well	1964/65	1967/68	21	35	3	921	132*	28.78	1	5	11	1		11.00	1-4	-	-	14	-
	Auck	1968/69	1970/71	13	16	3	380	66*	29.23	-	2	18	0		-	-	-	-	3	-
	All	1964/65	1970/71	34	51	6	1301	132*	28.91	1	7	29	1		29.00	1-4	-	-	17	-
J.D.S.Neesham	Auck	2009/10		1	1	0	0	0	0.00	-	-	73	0		-	-	-	-	2	-
R.Neill	Auck	1889/90	1905/06	20	34	4	439	94	14.63	-	1	1772	134		13.22	9-75	16	7	17	-
	All	1889/90	1905/06	21	36	4	460	94	14.37	-	1	1832	138		13.27	9-75	16	7	17	-
T.Neill	Auck	1892/93	1897/98	2	3	0	8	7	2.66	-	-								1	-
W.F.Neilson	Cant	1874/75	1878/79	6	10	1	123	57*	13.66	-	1	67	8		8.37	5-19	1	-	-	-
F.A.Nelson	HB	1908/09	1909/10	2	3	1	5	5*	5.00	-	-	289	9		32.11	4-55	-	-	-	-
F.M.Nelson	HB	1892/93	1897/98	3	5	0	88	49	17.60	-	-								-	-

		First	Last	M	I	NO	Runs	HS	Avg	100	50	Runs	Wkts	OW	Avg	Best	5i	10m	ct	st
J.Nelson	HB	1912/13		1	2	0	7	4	3.50	-	-	77	4		19.25	2-32	-	-	1	-
J.A.Nelson	Otago	1914/15		1	1	0	5	5	5.00	-	-								1	-
T.S.Nethula	Auck	2008/09	2009/10	16	20	5	170	33	11.33	-	-	1782	41		43.46	4-17	-	-	10	-
P.S.Neutze	Otago	1984/85		3	3	2	4	3*	4.00	-	-	312	5		62.40	5-109	1	-	-	-
	Auck	1987/88	1988/89	3	4	0	3	3	0.75	-	-	223	9		24.77	4-41	-	-	2	-
	ND	1989/90		9	9	2	100	40	14.28	-	-	801	16		50.06	3-61	-	-	2	-
	All	1984/85	1989/90	15	16	4	107	40	8.91	-	-	1336	30		44.53	5-109	1	-	5	-
C.J.Nevin	Well	1995/96	2009/10	106	163	26	4882	143*	35.63	4	28								291	9
	All	1995/96	2009/10	112	172	26	5058	143*	34.64	4	28								304	9
E.J.D.Newbigin	Well	1953/54		2	4	2	17	7	8.50	-	-	222	7		31.71	3-37	-	-	-	-
G.A.Newdick	Well	1970/71	1980/81	60	112	6	3236	143	30.52	4	13	134	5		26.80	2-33	-	-	19	-
	All	1970/71	1980/81	61	114	6	3292	143	30.48	4	13	134	5		26.80	2-33	-	-	20	-
A.Newman	Well	1930/31		2	4	0	30	15	7.50	-	-	66	0						3	-
J.Newman	Cant	1922/23		1	1	0	1	1*	1.00	-	-	69	2		34.50	2-54	-	-	2	-
	Well	1930/31	1935/36	13	21	3	172	22*	9.55	-	-	1386	65		21.32	5-45	2	1	4	-
	All	1922/23	1935/36	17	27	3	206	22*	8.95	-	-	1709	69		24.76	5-45	2	1	6	-
J.A.Newman	Cant	1927/28	1928/29	6	12	3	476	112*	52.88	1	2	778	16		48.62	3-88	-	-	3	-
	All	1906	1930	541	841	129	15364	166*	21.57	10	69	51397	2054		25.02	9-131	134	35	318	-
P.A.Newman	CD	1958/59		2	4	2	28	16	7.00	-	-								-	-
S.Newman	Well	1929/30		2	2	0	21	11*	-	-	-								-	-
F.W.Newton	Cant	1938/39		1	1	0	2	2	2.00	-	-	78	3		26.00	2-29	-	-	3	-
G.M.Newton	HB	1883/84	1886/87	4	7	2	30	12	6.00	-	-	235	17		13.82	6-20	2	-	8	2
R.W.Newton	Cant	1973/74		5	9	2	118	29	16.85	-	-								13	1
	Well	1974/75		6	7	1	77	38	12.83	-	-								21	-
	All	1973/74	1974/75	11	16	3	195	38	15.00	-	-								-	3
A.D.Niblett	CD	2006/07		5	9	0	71	22	7.88	-	-	577	10		57.70	3-121	-	-	1	-
J.C.Nicholls	Otago	1876/77		1	2	1	4	3	4.00	-	-								-	-
S.Nicholls	Well	1882/83	1893/94	15	25	2	227	32	9.45	-	-								11	4
C.R.Nicholson	Cant	1959/60		1	2	2	13	9*	-	-	-	42	0						-	-
	Otago	1963/64		2	2	2	1	1*	-	-	-	60	0						-	-
	All	1959/60	1963/64	3	4	4	14	9*	-	-	-	102	0						-	-
J.A.Nicholson	Auck	1893/94		1	2	0	12	8*	12.00	-	-								-	-
K.A.Nicholson	Otago	1971/72		1	1	0	5	5	5.00	-	-	65	4		16.25	4-38	-	-	1	-
V.R.Nicholson	Otago	1914/15		1	1	0	19	19	19.00	-	-								-	-
R.J.Nicol	Auck	2001/02	2008/09	65	100	11	3187	160	35.80	7	16	1070	15		71.33	2-26	-	-	45	-
	Otago	2009/10		10	20	3	545	134	32.05	1	2	598	9		66.44	3-65	-	-	9	-
	All	2001/02	2009/10	76	122	14	3823	160	35.39	8	19	1668	24		69.50	3-65	-	-	54	-
B.J.Nielsen	Auck	2001/02	2002/03	7	12	2	135	42	13.50	-	-	378	6		63.00	2-37	-	-	8	-
A.F.Nightingale	Well	1950/51	1958/59	12	23	0	332	61	14.43	-	1	84	1		84.00	1-57	-	-	8	-
J.R.Nimmo	Otago	1933/34	1936/37	2	4	0	51	42*	17.00	-	-	132	5		26.40	2-35	-	-	1	-
R.C.Niven	Otago	1887/88	1888/89	2	4	1	37	16	9.25	-	-								5	2
	Well	1890/91	1901/02	16	23	7	178	42	11.12	-	-								12	17
	All	1887/88	1901/02	18	27	7	215	42	10.75	-	-								17	19
D.C.Nixon	Cant	1926/27	1927/28	5	10	0	222	81	22.20	-	1	270	8		33.75	4-74	-	-	2	-
	All	1926/27	1927/28	6	12	0	239	81	19.91	-	1	274	8		34.25	4-74	-	-	2	-
K.Noema-Barnett	CD	2008/09	2009/10	4	5	1	54	32*	13.50	-	-	328	1		328.00	1-29	-	-	-	-

Name	Team	First	Last	M	I	NO	Runs	HS	Avg	100	50	Runs	Wkts	OW	Avg	Best	5i	10m	ct	st
W.M.Noon	Cant	1994/95	2003	2	4	-	37	26	9.25	-	-	-	-	-	-	-	-	-	6	-
	All	1989		92	145	23	2527	83	20.71	-	12	34	0		-	-	-	-	195	20
A.D.Norman	Cant	1907/08	1912/13	9	18	2	352	68	22.00	-	1								9	
W.B.Norman	Auck	1959/60	1962/63	20	34	7	522	58*	19.33	-	3	939	40		23.47	5-62	1	-	7	2
W.E.Norris	Well	1940/41	1942/43	4	8	0	141	48	17.62	-	-								10	2
R.H.North	Cant	1940/41		5	10	0	167	48	16.70	-	1								-	
T.H.North	Cant	1917/18		3	6	0	166	75	27.66	-	1	9	0		-	-	-	-	5	
J.Notman	All	1893/94	1896/97	8	13	0	162	62	14.72	-	-	226	13		17.38	5-13	1	-	1	
H.C.Nottman	Auck	1879/80		1	1	0	0	0	0.00	-	-								-	
A.J.Nuttall	Cant	1941/42		1	1	1	24	24*	-	-	-	120	7		17.14	4-60	-	-	-	
	Auck	1982/83	1988/89	17	23	3	170	33	8.50	-	-	1253	26		48.19	4-74	-	-	7	
	All	1977/78	1988/89	19	24	3	181	33	8.61	-	-	1420	33		43.03	4-74	-	-	8	
D.F.Oakley	Well	1980/81	1984/85	5	9	1	90	38*	11.25	-	-								3	
J.H.Oakley	Well	1946/47		2	4	0	74	43	18.50	-	-								3	
A.B.O'Brien	Auck	1882/83	1889/90	8	14	2	135	33	11.25	-	-								2	
F.P.O'Brien	Cant	1932/33	1945/46	23	39	2	1317	164	35.59	4	6	62	1		62.00	1-17	-	-	2	
I.E.O'Brien	All	1932/33	1945/46	66	113	22	2649	164	24.52	4	10	655	14		46.78	2-14	-	-	13	
	Well	2000/01	2009/10	45	50	16	301	44	8.85	-	-	3976	179		22.21	8-55	10	1	34	
J.J.O'Brien	All	2000/01	2010	91	113	26	756	44	8.68	-	-	8392	322		26.06	8-55	14	1	6	
M.A.O'Brien	HB	1905/06	1920/21	14	27	4	314	39	13.65	-	4	735	27		27.22	5-55	1	-	17	
	Well	1932/33	1941/42	13	24	4	637	76*	28.95	-	4	16	0		-	-	-	-	8	
	All	1932/33	1943/44	15	28	2	685	76*	26.34	-	4	39	0		-	-	-	-	9	
W.J.O'Connell	HB	1919/20	1920/21	4	8	0	98	38	12.25	-	-	461	22		20.95	8-48	3	-	11	
K.J.O'Connor	Otago	1969/70	1970/71	6	12	0	252	71	21.00	-	1								5	
L.O'Connor	Well	1876/77		1	2	1	5	3*	5.00	-	-								-	
S.B.O'Connor	Otago	1994/95	2002/03	35	50	16	515	47	15.14	-	-	3321	160		20.75	6-31	11	2	14	
	All	1994/95	2002/03	73	94	31	790	47	12.53	-	-	6582	278		23.67	6-31	16	2	27	
C.S.Odell	Cant	1869/70	1870/71	2	3	0	14	13	4.66	-	-	25	2		12.50	2-25	-	-	1	
A.P.O'Dowd	Auck	1991/92	1993/94	14	23	4	551	113	29.00	1	2								6	
	ND	1996/97		3	6	1	53	31*	10.60	-	-								6	
K.R.O'Dowda	All	1991/92	1996/97	17	29	5	604	113	25.16	1	2								12	
	CD	1988/89		2	2	0	0	0	0.00	-	-	108	2		54.00	2-75	-	-	1	
	Otago	1991/92	2000/01	9	13	5	84	24	10.50	-	-	840	26		32.30	4-67	-	-	2	
	All	1988/89	2000/01	15	15	5	84	24	8.40	-	-	948	28		33.85	4-67	-	-	3	
H.J.Ogier	Cant	1889/90	1891/92	5	10	4	101	27	16.83	-	-								1	
P.H.W.Ogier	Well	1889/90	1891/92	3	6	0	52	36	8.66	-	-	40	4		10.00	3-32	-	-	4	
J.E.Ogilvie	Well	1953/54	1963/64	5	10	0	244	54	24.40	-	2								3	
F.J.Ohlson	Auck	1894/95	1902/03	11	21	0	209	59*	13.06	-	-								5	
C.J.Oliver	Cant	1923/24	1936/37	16	29	1	713	91	25.46	-	5	15	0		-	-	-	-	13	
	All	1923/24	1942/43	35	61	5	1301	91	23.23	-	9	169	1		169.00	1-35	-	-	20	
C.Olliff	Auck	1903/04	1912/13	18	29	4	355	52	14.20	-	1	1558	87		17.90	7-42	6	2	5	4
	All	1903/04	1912/13	23	33	4	411	52	14.17	-	1	1665	90		18.50	7-42	6	2	7	
A.M.Ollivier	Cant	1866/67	1882/83	11	17	2	349	67	23.26	-	3	8	-		-	-	-	-	8	1
F.M.Ollivier	Cant	1867/68		1	2	0	8	7	4.00	-	-								1	
K.M.Ollivier	Cant	1900/01	1911/12	21	41	4	764	83	20.64	-	3	453	29		15.62	6-43	2	1	21	
	All	1900/01	1911/12	24	47	5	928	83	22.09	-	3	698	35		19.94	6-43	3	1	21	

		First	Last	M	I	NO	Runs	HS	Avg	100	50	Runs	Wkts	OW	Avg	Best	5i	10m	ct	st
P.W.O'Malley	Cant	1947/48	1954/55	15	27	1	763	102	29.34	1	5	55	1		55.00	1-28			7	
	All	1947/48	1954/55	17	31	2	945	132*	32.58	2	5	71	1		71.00	1-28			9	
T.P.O'Neil	Well	1965/66		1	2	1	2	1*	2.00			20	0							
S.R.O'Neill	Well	1944/45	1951/52	11	19	4	284	37	18.93			729	27		27.00	5-43	2		8	
A.M.Ongley	HB	1901/02		1	2	2	4	3*	2.00			43	1		43.00	1-14				
	All	1901/02	1903/04	2	4	2	8	3*	1.33			131	4		32.75	2-45			1	
J.A.Ongley	Well	1938/39	1949/50	20	38	1	950	110	25.67	1	5								8	
	CD	1950/51	1951/52	8	16	1	243	51	16.20		1								4	
	All	1938/39	1951/52	30	57	2	1234	110	22.43	1	6								13	
J.D.P.Oram	CD	1997/98	2008/09	35	53	5	1619	155	33.72	1	11	1402	60		23.36	6-45	2		12	
	All	1997/98	2009	85	136	18	3992	155	33.83	8	18	4172	155	3	26.91	6-45	3		36	
M.G.Orchard	ND	2001/02	2007/08	42	71	9	1756	175	28.32	1	12	2648	67		39.52	5-10	1		28	
	All	2001/02	2007/08	44	74	9	1779	175	27.36	1	12	2761	72		38.34	5-10	1		29	
S.A.Orchard	Cant	1894/95	1912/13	29	55	2	1066	83	20.11		6	348	14		24.85	4-67			22	
	All	1894/95	1912/13	31	59	3	1109	83	19.80		6	353	14		25.21	4-67			26	
I.W.Ormiston	Well	1987/88		4	6	2	89	47	22.25			238	4		59.50	2-44			4	
R.W.Ormiston	CD	1975/76	1977/78	9	15	0	169	37	11.26										2	
	Well	1980/81	1985/86	45	75	11	1896	179	29.62	2	8	173	1		173.00	1-26			43	
	All	1975/76	1985/86	56	94	12	2166	179	26.41	2	9	173	1		173.00	1-26			47	
M.H.O'Rourke	Auck	1991/92		1	1	0	5	5	5.00			128	3		42.66	2-79				
P.W.O'Rourke	Well	1989/90	1992/93	29	31	11	140	26	7.00			2214	89		24.87	7-81	4		4	
G.Orr	Well	1923/24	1926/27	3	6	0	187	69	31.16		2								4	
H.W.Osborn	Well	1940/41	1941/42	4	8	0	285	116	35.62	1	1	26	1		26.00	1-26			1	
G.C.Osborne	Otago	1977/78	1981/82	2	2	0	61	53	30.50		1	75	1		75.00	1-10				
C.H.Osmond	Auck	1884/85		2	4	1	43	19	14.33										2	
D.R.O'Sullivan	CD	1972/73	1984/85	90	123	30	1561	70*	16.78		3	9560	392		24.38	6-40	21	3	26	
	All	1971	1984/85	136	187	46	2174	70*	15.41		3	13554	523		25.91	6-26	28	4	46	
J.M.O'Sullivan	Otago	1946/47	1947/48	3	6	1	76	45	15.20			50	0						1	
G.W.F.Overton	Otago	1945/46	1955/56	34	44	21	96	17*	4.17			3013	128		23.53	7-88	5		16	
	All	1945/46	1955/56	51	64	31	137	17*	4.15			4250	169		25.14	7-52	6		21	
M.B.Owens	Cant	1991/92	1995/96	19	24	16	115	18*	14.37			1277	51		25.03	4-18			6	
	All	1991/92	1995/96	34	43	23	133	18*	6.65			2354	86		27.37	5-74			11	
H.E.Owles	Sland	1917/18		1	2	1	0	0	0.00											
B.S.Oxenham	ND	1990/91	1992/93	12	17	0	341	74	21.31		2	134	2		67.00	2-12			13	
	Auck	1993/94		2	4	0	24	19	6.00			52	1		52.00	1-48			1	
	All	1990/91	1993/94	14	21	0	365	74	18.25		2	186	3		62.00	2-12			14	
J.C.Pabst	Auck	1894/95	1897/98	5	8	1	71	20	8.87			6	0						5	
D.L.Paetz	Well	1966/67		1	0	0						60	1		60.00	1-20			1	
A.H.C.Page	Cant	1884/85		1	2	0	3	3	1.50			7	0							
H.Page	Well	1895/96		2	4	0	16	7	4.00											
J.E.Page	Well	1879/80	1880/81	3	6	0	14	10	2.33			48	7		6.85	4-14			1	
M.L.Page	Cant	1920/21	1936/37	41	75	2	2424	206	33.20	2	14	615	14		43.92	2-18			27	
	All	1920/21	1942/43	132	213	17	5857	206	29.88	9	32	2364	73		32.38	4-10			115	
B.H.Pairaudeau	ND	1958/59	1966/67	36	68	3	1970	102	30.30	1	16	32	0						31	1
	All	1946/47	1966/67	89	159	5	4930	163	32.01	11	25	82	0						64	
A.L.Palethorpe	Well	1879/80		1	2	0	0	0	0.00											1

		First	Last	M	I	NO	Runs	HS	Avg	100	50	Runs	Wkts	OW	Avg	Best	5i	10m	ct	st
E.V.Palmer	Cant	1892/93	1893/94	3	4	1	30	19	10.00	-	-	115	12	-	9.58	5-32	1	-	6	-
	All	1892/93	1893/94	4	6	2	38	19	9.50	-	-	156	13	-	12.00	5-32	1	-	7	-
J.I.Pamment	Auck	1993/94	1995/96	14	24	2	351	98	15.95	-	1	53	0	0	-	-	-	-	14	3
M.H.W.Papps	Cant	1998/99	2009/10	86	156	13	6202	192	43.37	19	25	15	0	0	-	-	-	-	104	4
	All	1998/99	2009/10	110	200	16	6996	192	38.02	20	29	17	0	0	-	-	-	-	128	-
T.J.T.Papps	Cant	2003/04	2004/05	7	11	0	117	33	10.63	-	-								8	
G.H.Paramor	Otago	1873/74	1880/81	8	15	0	232	62	15.46	-	1								6	
D.Park	CD	1957/58		3	4	1	17	17	5.66	-	-	521	25	-	20.84	6-45	1	-		
J.M.Parker	ND	1972/73	1983/84	75	139	19	4611	195	38.42	7	25	176	6	-	29.33	2-9	-	-	83	-
	All	1971	1983/84	207	362	39	11254	195	34.84	21	53	345	7	-	49.28	2-43	-	-	177	1
												681	14	-	48.64	3-26	-	-		
K.J.Parker	Auck	1970/71		1	2	0	62	61	31.00	-	1								1	
M.M.Parker	Otago	1996/97		3	6	0	50	14	8.33	-	-								5	
N.M.Parker	Otago	1967/68	1969/70	6	10	0	73	19	7.30	-	-								5	
	Cant	1973/74	1978/79	41	76	12	1870	135	29.21	1	8	6	0	0	-	-	-	-	39	-
	All	1967/68	1978/79	52	96	12	2102	135	25.02	1	8	6	0	0	-	-	-	-	45	-
T.S.Parker	Otago	1864/65	1866/67	2	3	1	5	4	2.50	-	-	12	6	-	2.00	5-6	1	-	-	-
W.H.Parker	Otago	1880/81	1896/97	25	45	5	412	54*	10.30	-	1	510	31	-	16.45	5-31	2	-	11	-
K.Parkin	Well	1945/46		1	2	1	11	11*	11.00	-	-	57	1	-	57.00	1-57	-	-	-	-
	All	1942/43	1945/46	2	4	1	22	11*	7.33	-	-	170	4	-	42.50	2-61	-	-	1	-
J.H.Parks	Cant	1946/47		3	5	0	59	34	11.80	-	-	448	19	-	23.57	5-62	1	-	2	-
		1924	1952	468	758	63	21369	197	30.74	41	95	22789	852	-	26.74	7-17	24	1	326	-
M.E.Parlane	ND	1992/93	2009/10	81	139	12	4108	146	32.34	7	20	21	1	-	21.00	1-14	-	-	48	6
	Well	2003/04	2007/08	40	69	3	2397	203	36.31	7	10	39	-	-	-	-	-	-	27	-
	All	1992/93	2009/10	135	231	15	7204	203	33.35	15	33	60	1	-	60.00	1-14	-	-	87	24
N.R.Parlane	ND	1996/97	2000/01	15	26	2	681	147	28.37	1	4	21	0	-	-	-	-	-	9	-
	Well	2002/03	2009/10	70	112	9	4122	193	40.01	9	25	25	0	0	-	-	-	-	91	-
	All	1996/97	2009/10	85	138	11	4803	193	37.81	10	29	46	0	0	-	-	-	-	100	-
A.C.Parore	Auck	1988/89	1999/00	30	45	9	1675	155*	46.52	4	10	55	0	0	-	-	-	-	64	-
	All	1988/89	2001/02	163	252	43	6826	155*	32.66	10	35	4	0	0	-	-	-	-	367	-
H.R.Parrington	Tara	1875/76		1	2	1	35	26	17.50	-	-	13	0	0	-	-	-	-	1	-
	All	1882/83		1	2	0	12	9	6.00	-	-	57	4	-	14.25	4-28	-	-	3	-
C.K.Parsloe	Well	1875/76	1882/83	3	6	0	53	26	8.83	-	-	1285	60	-	21.41	7-66	2	-	8	-
	All	1932/33	1940/41	16	29	2	391	59	14.48	-	1	1528	69	-	22.14	7-66	3	-	9	-
J.S.Parson	Cant	1932/33	1940/41	19	35	3	427	59	13.34	-	1	37	2	-	18.50	1-7	-	-	1	-
	Well	1960/61		1	1	0	3	3	1.50	-	-	220	11	-	20.00	3-22	-	-	7	-
	All	1961/62	1963/64	5	6	0	36	15	7.20	-	-	536	26	-	20.61	5-80	1	-	9	-
A.E.W.Parsons	Auck	1960/61	1982/83	60	12	2	49	15	4.90	-	-	179	2	-	89.50	1-26	-	-	32	-
	All	1973/74	1982/83	82	113	8	2820	132	26.85	3	13	183	2	-	91.50	1-26	-	-	44	-
L.E.Partridge	Auck	1971/72	1982/83	82	156	10	3847	141	26.34	4	19	396	12	-	33.00	3-39	-	-	2	-
	Auck	1946/47	1950/51	5	8	0	54	29	6.75	-	-	495	15	-	33.00	3-23	-	-	2	-
M.Y.Pasupati	Well	1942/43	1950/51	7	11	0	59	29	5.36	-	-	127	4	-	31.75	3-51	-	-	3	-
	All	1997/98	2000/01	3	3	1	12	6	4.00	-	-	39	4	-	9.75	4-39	-	-	1	-
	Auck	2006/07																		
D.U.Patel	All	1997/98	2006/07	4	4	1	76	76*	29.33	-	1	166	8	-	20.75	4-39	-	-	-	-
	ND	1971/72		2	3	1	88	76*	-	-	-	80	1	-	80.00	1-59	-	-	1	-
	All	1966/67	1971/72	18	33	6	1035	172	38.33	1	7	120	2	-	60.00	1-27	-	-	8	-

		First	Last	M	I	NO	Runs	HS	Avg	100	50	Runs	Wkts	OW	Avg	Best	5i	10m	ct	st
D.N.Patel	Auck	1985/86	1994/95	67	102	9	3648	204	39.22	8	18	4298	184		23.35	7-72	9	2	35	
J.S.Patel	All	1976	1996/97	358	558	51	15188	204	29.95	26	66	21737	654		33.23	7-46	27	2	193	
	Well	1999/00	2009/10	69	83	30	994	71*	18.75		3	5518	138		39.98	6-32	4	-	19	
M.M.Patel	All	1999/00	2009/10	90	109	35	1438	120	19.43	1	4	8237	197		41.81	6-32	5	-	29	
	CD	2005/06		5	6	0	49	20	8.16			505	19		26.57	6-121	2	-	5	
	All	1989	2007	208	278	51	3945	87	17.37		17	19309	630		30.64	8-96	30	9	102	
A.Paterson	Well	1914/15		2	3	1	29	24	14.50										-	
A.T.Paterson	CD	1973/74		1	2	0	79	47	39.50										3	
J.L.Paterson	Cant	1912/13	1913/14	5	8	0	119	71	17.00		1	214	11		19.45	3-26			3	
	HB	1914/15	1920/21	5	10	0	149	57	14.90		1	186	9		20.66	4-60			2	
	Auck	1922/23		3	6	0	96	37	16.00			35	1		35.00	1-5			3	
	All	1912/13	1922/23	13	24	0	364	71	15.82		2	435	21		20.71	4-60			6	
L.Paterson	HB	1886/87	1887/88	2	4	0	86	29	21.50			39	2		19.50	2-28			1	
D.M.Patrick	Well	1907/08	1921/22	12	20	2	197	33	10.94			500	18		27.77	5-13	1		10	
G.M.Patrick	Otago	1918/19		1	2	0	2	2	1.00										2	
W.R.Patrick	Cant	1905/06	1926/27	58	108	7	2803	129	27.75	2	17	712	15		47.46	4-42			36	
	Otago	1917/18		2	4	0	172	107	43.00	1		78	8		9.75	6-36	1		1	
	All	1905/06	1926/27	74	138	8	3536	143	27.20	4	18	1087	34		31.97	6-36	1		38	
L.Pattie	Nel	1884/85		1	2	0	21	13	10.50			50	1		50.00	1-30			1	
B.M.K.Patton	CD	2006/07	2009/10	18	31	3	1041	142	37.17	2	7	238	6		39.66	2-19			12	
J.M.Paul	Otago	1992/93	1994/95	8	15	3	143	23	11.91			267	6		44.50	3-34			1	
J.G.Pawley	CD	1994/95		1	2	0	7	7	3.50			6	0		-				-	
M.J.Pawson	CD	1990/91	1994/95	18	24	10	251	54*	17.92		2	1309	40		32.72	5-41	1		6	
	All	1990/91	1994/95	19	25	11	255	54*	18.21		2	1309	40		32.72	5-41	1		6	
S.J.Pawson	Cant	1995/96	1998/99	11	17	1	212	54*	13.25		2	305	7		43.57	2-40			8	
E.S.J.Payne	Well	1908/09		1	2	1	20	18*	20.00										1	
I.W.Payne	Otago	1947/48	1951/52	5	10	2	51	23*	6.37			83	1		83.00	1-36			4	
D.H.Payton	CD	1965/66	1976/77	49	92	4	2459	145	27.94	3	9	10	1		10.00	1-0			58	
	All	1964/65	1976/77	51	96	4	2475	145	26.90	3	9	10	1		10.00	1-0			64	
G.G.Peacock	HB	1891/92		1	1	0	1	1*											-	
W.C.Pearce	Cant	1893/94	1902/03	12	19	1	317	68	17.61		2	692	55		12.58	6-37	4		8	
	All	1893/94	1902/03	14	23	1	468	68	21.27		3	755	59		12.79	6-37	4		11	
W.H.Pearless	Otago	1904/05		2	3	1	29	17	14.50										1	
F.A.Pearson	Auck	1910/11		3	5	0	48	33	9.60			275	21		13.09	6-10	2		-	
	All	1900	1926	454	811	38	18734	167	24.23	22	82	24715	853		28.97	9-41	38	4	162	
H.T.Pearson	Auck	1932/33	1947/48	28	45	3	1331	172	31.69	2	7	7	0		-				16	
	All	1932/33	1947/48	30	49	3	1392	172	30.26	2	7	7	0		-				18	
L.R.Pearson	Otago	1961/62	1970/71	30	57	2	1332	140	24.21	1	6	70	1		70.00	1-6			26	
	All	1961/62	1970/71	31	59	2	1348	140	23.64	1	6	70	1		70.00	1-6			26	
R.A.Penhearow	ND	1964/65	1975/76	3	4	2	17	8	8.50			218	3		72.66	1-3			-	
	All	1963/64	1975/76	4	5	2	17	8	8.50			410	9		45.55	4-103			-	
A.J.Penn	CD	1994/95	1999/00	25	34	8	344	90	13.23		1	2343	97		24.15	6-36	6	1	6	
	Well	2000/01	2003/04	28	40	11	582	66	20.06		2	2295	107		21.44	8-21	3	2	7	
	All	1994/95	2003/04	66	91	22	1276	90	18.49		6	5806	252		23.03	8-21	11	2	15	
R.W.Percy	HB	1884/85	1892/93	4	7	1	35	9	5.83			29	1		29.00	1-21			3	
W.R.Perkins	Well	1952/53	1953/54	6	10	3	68	22	9.71			277	1		277.00	1-45			2	

		First	Last	M	I	NO	Runs	HS	Avg	100	50	Runs	Wkts	OW	Avg	Best	5i	10m	ct	st
E.G.Perrin	Cant	1917/18	1918/19	4	8	0	130	64	16.25	-	1	46	0		-	-	-	-	1	-
A.Perry	Cant	1877/78		1	2	2	0	0*	-	-	-	23	3		7.66	2-1	-	-	-	-
C.T.H.Perry	Cant	1870/71		1	1	0	10	10	10.00	-	-	56	3		18.66	2-1	-	-	-	-
	All	1868/69	1870/71	2	3	0	23	13	7.66	-	-									
D.L.Perry	Auck	1949/50	1958/59	21	39	1	771	104	20.28	1	2	170	5		34.00	2-42	-	-	7	-
S.J.Peterson	Auck	1989/90	1996/97	26	46	1	1033	77	22.95	-	5	2394	114		21.00	9-93	8	2	26	-
P.J.Petherick	Otago	1975/76	1977/78	26	31	16	75	19*	5.00	-	-	1294	50		25.88	5-48	-	-	15	-
	Well	1978/79	1980/81	17	20	10	90	17	9.00	-	-	4625	189		24.47	9-93	9	2	8	-
	All	1975/76	1980/81	52	65	31	200	19*	5.88	-	-								27	-
E.C.Petrie	Auck	1950/51	1954/55	13	26	1	486	151	19.44	1	4	16	0		-	-	-	-	26	8
	ND	1956/57	1966/67	57	95	17	1625	136	20.83	1	6	16	0		-	-	-	-	90	22
	All	1950/51	1966/67	115	189	34	2788	151	17.98	2									198	37
F.R.S.Petrie	Sland	1920/21		1	1	0	16	16*	-	-	-								1	-
R.G.Petrie	Cant	1988/89	1992/93	22	24	5	303	100	15.94	1	-	2170	67		32.38	5-59	2	-	7	-
	Well	1993/94	1999/00	34	54	6	1278	80	26.62	-	5	1908	67		28.47	5-23	1	-	13	-
	All	1988/89	1999/00	56	78	11	1581	100	23.59	1	5	4078	134		30.43	5-23	3	-	20	-
E.M.Phillips	Well	1911/12	1920/21	8	14	2	171	40	14.25	-	-								1	-
J.Phillips	Cant	1898/99		2	3	1	149	110*	74.50	1	-	165	9		18.33	4-86	-	-	1	-
	All	1885/86	1898/99	124	203	58	1827	110*	12.60	1	3	7102	355		20.00	8-69	30	7	50	-
J.G.Phillips	Cant	1977/78		1	1	0	21	21*	-	-	-								2	-
R.Phillips	Well	1947/48		1	2	0	82	67	41.00	-	1								-	-
P.S.Philpott	Cant	1881/82		1	2	0	7	5	3.50	-	-								1	-
R.A.Pick	Well	1989/90		2	1	1	5	5*	-	-	-	215	12		17.91	5-57	1	-	-	-
	All	1983	1997	195	206	55	2259	65*	14.96	-	5	16454	495		33.24	7-128	16	3	50	-
C.J.Pickett	Well	1983/84		1	2	0	29	23	14.50	-	-	566	14	14	40.42	2-8	-	-	40	-
R.A.Pierce	CD	1971/72	1984/85	53	98	5	2296	100*	24.68			113	13		8.69	5-16	1	-	2	-
W.Pierce	Cant	1869/70	1872/73	4	6	2	38	17	9.50	-	-	909	43		21.13	5-47	2	1	3	-
A.C.S.Pigott	Well	1982/83	1983/84	11	12	0	173	35	14.41	-	-	20831	672	20	30.99	7-74	26	2	121	-
	All	1978	1995	260	317	66	4841	104*	19.28	1		205	5		205.00	1-27	-	-	5	-
R.J.Pither	Well	1976/77	1984/85	7	11	3	165	31	20.62	-	1	301	5		60.20	2-27	-	-	5	-
	All	1976/77	1984/85	8	13	4	192	31	21.33	-	1	2383	89		26.77	6-38	6	-	16	-
A.S.Player	Auck	1919/20	1928/29	27	42	14	572	58	20.42	-	2	6	0		-	-	-	-	45	-
W.R.Playle	Auck	1956/57	1963/64	36	61	7	1316	116*	24.37	2	5	94	1		94.00	1-11	-	-	81	-
	All	1956/57	1967/68	85	145	13	2888	122	21.87	4	9	240	4		60.00	1-7	-	-	20	-
B.A.Pocock	Auck	1990/91	2000/01	39	69	11	1696	167	29.24	4	4								9	-
	ND	1992/93	1996/01	19	29	2	947	137	33.82	2	7	313	4		78.25	1-7	-	-	52	-
	All	1990/91	2000/01	100	176	16	4699	167	29.36	10	22	248	5		49.60	2-49	-	-	4	-
M.G.Pocock	ND	1965/66		4	5	2	20	6*	6.66	-	-	384	39		9.84	6-18	3	-	2	-
W.J.Pocock	Cant	1882/83	1883/84	7	13	1	90	28	7.50	-	-	408	43		9.48	6-18	3	-	3	-
	All	1872/73	1883/84	8	15	1	96	28	6.85	-	-								1	-
M.A.Pollard	Well	2009/10		5	10	1	193	60	21.44	-	1	1488	66	13	22.54	6-37	2	-	27	-
V.Pollard	CD	1964/65	1968/69	29	45	7	1394	146	36.68	1	13	1149	41		28.02	7-76	2	-	8	-
	Cant	1969/70	1974/75	17	31	5	723	107	27.80	2	2	6931	224	30	30.94	7-65	6	1	81	-
	All	1964/65	1974/75	130	207	33	5314	146	30.54	6	30								2	-
W.Pollitt	Cant	1946/47	1947/48	4	6	0	63	40	10.50	-	-	26	0		-	-	-	-	2	-
N.D.Pollock	ND	1981/82	1986/87	7	9	3	107	24	17.83	-	-	600	17		35.29	2-31	-	-	1	-

		First	Last	M	I	NO	Runs	HS	Avg	100	50	Runs	Wkts	OW	Avg	Best	5i	10m	ct	st
A.V.Poole	Sland	1914/15	1920/21	6	11	0	223	77	20.27	-	1	153	7	-	21.85	4-104	-	-	3	-
M.B.Poore	Cant	1950/51	1961/62	27	50	2	1313	142	27.35	2	8	1128	49	-	23.02	4-27	1	-	7	-
	All	1950/51	1961/62	61	108	7	2336	142	23.12	2	11	1813	68	-	26.66	5-27	1	-	14	-
T.R.W.Pope	Sland	1920/21		1	2	1	2	2	2.00	-	-								1	-
M.W.Posa	Auck	1994/95	1938/39	3	4	0	57	29	14.25	-	-	154	4	-	38.50	3-62	-	-	2	-
A.J.Postles	Auck	1924/25	1942/43	29	52	3	1481	103	30.22	3	7	363	8	-	45.37	4-20	-	-	14	-
	All	1924/25		31	56	3	1588	103	29.96	3	7	363	8	-	45.37	4-20	-	-	17	-
B.J.Postles	Auck	1952/53	1956/57	19	37	3	770	80	22.64	-	5								7	-
D.F.Potter	ND	1991/92		9	9	1	44	14*	5.50	-	-								5	-
M.G.Poultney	ND	1972/73	1992/93	1	2	0	22	22	11.00	-	-	502	17	-	29.52	5-69	1	-	-	-
G.A.Powell	Otago	1969/70	1977/78	18	22	3	187	56	9.84	-	1	1305	46	-	28.36	5-45	1	-	9	-
	All	1969/70	1977/78	19	24	3	201	56	9.57	-	1	1387	48	-	28.89	5-45	1	-	9	-
J.L.Powell	Cant	1928/29	1932/33	10	15	4	406	164	36.90	1	1	9	0	-	-	-	-	-	3	-
M.J.Powell	Otago	2005/06		3	5	1	90	61	22.50	-	1	7	0	-	-	-	-	-	4	-
R.F.J.Powell	All	1996	2008	149	246	12	7395	236	31.60	12	40	745	11	-	67.72	2-16	-	-	105	-
S.Powell	Cant	1922/23	1876/77	2	3	1	79	41	39.50	-	1								3	-
T.L.Powell	Nel	1874/75	1976	2	4	1	25	22	8.33	-	-								3	-
A.L.Powys	All	1971/72	1867/68	2	4	0	24	14	6.00	-	-								4	-
R.A.N.Powys	Cant	1863/64	1866/67	4	8	1	27	7	3.85	-	-								3	-
G.Prain	Cant	1865/66		2	4	0	14	12	3.50	-	-								2	-
A.E.Pratt	HB	1887/88		1	2	0	10	8	5.00	-	-	10	1	-	10.00	1-4	-	-	-	-
P.M.Pratt	Auck	1912/13		1	1	0	2	2	2.00	-	-	39	2	-	19.50	2-14	-	-	3	-
E.S.Prentice	Tara	1894/95	1897/98	5	7	1	227	85	32.42	-	1	12	1	-	12.00	1-12	-	-	2	-
C.M.Presland	Auck	1945/46		1	0	0						55	5	-	11.00	3-34	-	-	-	-
A.H.Preston	ND	1982/83	1984/85	14	25	6	503	97*	26.47	-	4	89	2	-	44.50	2-26	-	-	1	-
	Well	1955/56	1962/63	38	65	10	1384	122	25.16	1	8	65	1	-	65.00	1-65	-	-	8	-
	All	1955/56	1962/63	40	69	10	1448	122	24.54	1	8	1008	32	-	31.50	5-49	1	-	29	-
E.W.Prideaux	Well	1885/86		1	2	0	4	4	2.00	-	-	1066	31	-	34.38	3-32	-	-	30	-
M.W.Priest	Cant	1984/85	1998/99	88	130	21	3457	119	31.71	4	24	1103	32	-	34.46	3-32	-	-	1	-
	All	1984/85	1998/99	109	154	25	3945	119	30.58	4	28	8501	290	-	29.31	9-95	12	3	52	-
W.A.Priest	Otago	1907/08	1932/33	2	4	0	6	4	1.50	-	-	10478	329	-	31.84	9-95	12	3	66	-
F.L.Prime	Auck	1931/32		2	3	0	42	25	14.00	-	-								-	-
H.W.Prince	Well	1923/24	1924/25	2	3	0	45	35	15.00	-	-								1	-
C.Pringle	Auck	1989/90	1995/96	32	41	7	510	47	15.00	-	-	2858	126	-	22.68	7-56	5	1	7	-
	All	1989/90	1995/96	63	75	13	795	47	12.82	-	-	5617	194	-	28.95	7-52	7	2	15	-
M.R.Pringle	Auck	1984/85	1991/92	29	42	3	1038	89*	23.92	-	6								23	-
T.L.Pritchard	All	1984/85	1991/92	33	49	3	933	89*	22.56	-	7	1	0	-	-	-	-	-	26	-
	Well	1937/38	1940/41	12	21	0	331	43	20.68	-	-	1293	71	-	18.21	7-32	6	-	7	-
	All	1937/38	1956	200	293	41	3363	81	13.34	-	6	19062	818	-	23.30	8-20	48	11	84	-
R.A.Procter	Otago	1960/61		6	10	0	79	15	7.90	-	-								6	-
R.H.Prouting	Otago	1969/70	2003/04	3	3	1	13	8*	6.50	-	-	107	2	-	53.50	1-12	-	-	2	-
C.R.Pryor	Auck	1997/98	2001/02	15	21	4	342	55*	20.11	-	1	1334	35	-	38.11	5-59	4	-	3	-
	Otago	2000/01	2003/04	21	33	6	648	61	24.00	-	2	1685	61	-	27.62	5-28	4	-	17	-
	All	1997/98		36	54	10	990	61	22.50	-	3	3019	96	-	31.44	5-28	5	-	20	-
R.A.Pudney	Auck	2000/01		2	4	0	33	22	8.25	-	-								-	-
A.Puna	ND	1971/72	1972/73	10	19	1	203	24	11.27	-	-	793	20	-	39.65	5-77	1	-	5	-

		First	Last	M	I	NO	Runs	HS	Avg	100	50	Runs	Wkts	OW	Avg	Best	5i	10m	ct	st
K.N.Puna	ND	1975/76	1978/79	8	15	4	251	41	22.81	-	-	5314	224		23.72	6-25	11	-	9	
N.Puna	All	1971/72	1978/79	9	17	4	291	41	22.38	-	-	5597	229		24.44	6-25	11	-	9	
	ND	1956/57	1968/69	66	105	18	1263	62*	14.51	-	2	194	3		64.66	2-69	-	-	34	
	All	1956/57	1968/69	70	111	22	1305	62*	14.66	-	2								36	
J.W.Purdue	Otago	1938/39		2	4	3	5	3*	5.00	-	-								-	
A.G.Putt	Auck	1947/48	1950/51	2	4	0	51	35	12.75	-	-								-	
F.J.Quarterman	Well	2007/08		3	5	0	70	47	17.50	-	-	140	3		46.66	1-26	-	-	1	
R.W.Quee	Well	1899/00	1904/05	10	19	1	189	51	10.50	-	-	9	0		-	-	-	-	1	
W.G.L.Quentery	Auck	1893/94		1	2	0	18	17	9.00	-	-								-	
J.J.Quinn	Well	1913/14		2	4	0	32	23	8.00	-	-								4	
G.O.Rabone	Well	1940/41	1950/51	18	18	1	377	74	22.17	-	1	508	13		39.07	3-74	-	-	10	
	Auck	1951/52	1959/60	21	36	1	1013	125	28.94	1	7	1392	74		18.81	8-66	4	-	27	2
	All	1940/41	1960/61	82	135	14	3425	125	28.30	3	19	4835	173		27.94	8-66	9	-	76	2
B.J.Rae	Cant	2006/07	2007/08	5	7	0	149	58	21.28	-	1								5	
W.G.Rainbird	Sland	1934/35	1946/47	10	19	0	492	102	25.89	1	2	10	0		-	-	-	-	5	
S.V.Raines	Otago	1919/20		2	3	0	10	7	3.33	-	-								1	
A.G.Rains	Otago	1894/95	1896/97	4	7	0	52	32	7.42	-	-	53	1		53.00	1-16	-	-	4	
	All	1894/95	1896/97	5	9	0	110	55	12.22	-	1	53	1		53.00	1-16	-	-	5	
J.Ramsden	Otago	1909/10	1914/15	10	18	3	189	74*	12.60	-	1	638	23		27.73	4-9	-	-	5	
S.H.A.Rance	CD	2008/09	2009/10	7	9	0	211	71	23.44	-	2	624	9		69.33	2-24	-	-	3	
C.L.W.Randall	Well	1948/49	1950/51	10	15	4	140	36	12.72	-	-	605	31		19.51	3-18	-	-	5	
A.F.Rapley	Cant	1957/58	1959/60	7	10	6	88	40	22.00	-	-	445	21		21.19	6-73	1	-	2	
	All	1957/58	1959/60	8	12	8	102	40	25.50	-	-	470	23		20.43	6-73	1	-	2	
S.Rasmussen	Well	2005/06	2006/07	6	6	1	14	10	2.80	-	-	434	17		25.52	4-39	-	-	2	
D.S.Rathie	Cant	1979/80		6	11	2	183	55	20.33	-	1								5	
	All	1970/71	1980/81	14	26	2	344	55	14.33	-	1	4	0		-	-	-	-	7	
C.W.Rattray	Otago	1883/84	1896/97	12	21	2	153	23	9.56	-	-								4	
P.J.Rattray	Cant	1980/81	1984/85	22	42	5	909	133	22.72	1	3	5	0		-	2-10	-	-	11	
J.A.Raval	Auck	2008/09	2009/10	11	17	1	821	256	51.31	2	4	150	4		37.50	1-90	-	-	6	
D.L.Rayner	CD	2006/07		2	2	1	16	11*	16.00	-	-	90	1		90.00	2-36	-	-	-	
G.L.Rayner	Cant	1884/85	1889/90	9	9	2	123	49*	17.57	-	-	93	2		46.50				1	
	Otago	1887/88		1	2	0	44	33	22.00	-	-								-	
	All	1884/85	1889/90	10	11	2	167	49*	18.55	-	-	93	2		46.50	2-36	-	-	1	
J.Read	Tara	1882/83		1	2	0	16	12	8.00	-	-								-	
R.J.Read	Cant	1904/05	1937/38	44	79	10	1023	50	14.82	-	1	4704	184		25.56	7-24	11	1	29	
	All	1904/05	1937/38	48	85	10	1034	50	13.78	-	1	4994	188		26.56	7-24	11	1	30	
R.Reade	Well	1899/00	1900/01	2	3	1	18	17*	9.00	-	-								-	
L.B.Reade	CD	1958/59	1962/63	24	43	0	1106	163	25.72	1	2	2	0		-	-	-	-	7	
L.E.Reade	Cant	1869/70		1	2	0	1	1	0.50	-	-	59	6		9.83	3-21	-	-	1	
	Otago	1870/71	1876/77	4	7	0	113	38	16.14	-	-	132	5		26.40	4-73	-	-	4	
	All	1869/70	1876/77	5	9	0	114	38	12.66	-	-	191	11		17.36	4-73	-	-	5	
H.E.I.Reaney	Well	1932/33		1	2	0	17	13	8.50	-	-	16	0		-	-	-	-	-	
P.S.Reaney	HB	1905/06		1	2	0	1	1	0.50	-	-	196	4		49.00	2-41	-	-	3	
T.P.L.Reaney	Well	1927/28	1948/49	6	11	0	195	85	17.72	-	1	10	0		-	-	-	-	-	
	CD	1950/51		1	2	0	9	5	4.50	-	-	206	4		51.50	2-41	-	-	3	
	All	1927/28	1950/51	7	13	0	204	85	15.69	-	1									

		First	Last	M	I	NO	Runs	HS	Avg	100	50	Runs	Wkts	OW	Avg	Best	5i	10m	ct	st
G.Reardon	Otago	1903/04	1903/04	1	2	0	0	0	0.00	-	-	23	0		-	-	-	-	-	-
D.J.Reddington	Otago	2002/03		1	1	1	0	0*	-	-	-	82	1		82.00	1-27	-	-	-	-
J.Redfearn	Otago	1863/64	1863/64	1	2	0	27	14	13.50	-	-								2	-
W.P.Redgrave	All	1862/63		2	4	0	32	14	8.00	-	-								4	-
	Well	1903/04	1905/06	6	11	0	331	165	30.09	1	1	188	9		20.88	5-37	1	-	1	-
	HB	1906/07	1908/09	3	6	0	83	44	13.83	-	-	394	11		35.81	3-97	1	-	2	-
	All	1903/04	1908/09	9	17	0	414	165	24.35	1	1	582	20		29.10	5-37	1	-	3	-
A.T.Redmayne	Cant	1880/81		1	1	0	61	61	61.00	-	1								-	-
A.J.Redmond	Cant	1999/00	2003/04	33	54	4	1207	101	24.14	1	4	2379	58		41.01	4-35	1	-	19	-
	Otago	2004/05	2009/10	32	54	5	2102	136	42.89	4	16	1444	27		53.48	4-79	1	-	27	-
	All	1999/00	2009/10	86	147	10	4529	146	33.05	8	27	4314	100		43.14	4-30	-	-	66	-
R.E.Redmond	Well	1966/67	1967/68	8	15	0	283	76	18.86	-	2	296	6		49.33	2-16	-	-	6	-
	Auck	1969/70	1975/76	29	55	4	2004	141*	39.29	4	9	22	0						17	-
	All	1963/64	1975/76	53	100	7	3134	141*	33.69	5	16	481	17		28.29	6-56	1	-	31	-
A.J.Reece	Cant	1947/48		1	2	0	52	26	26.00	-	-		0		-	-	-	-	-	-
F.J.Reeder	Cant	1873/74		1	2	1	2	2	2.00	-	-	9			-	-	-	-	-	-
D.J.Reekers	Otago	1997/98		3	6	1	52	33*	10.40	-	-	89	8		11.12	3-25	-	-	2	-
	All	1997/98	2005/06	6	11	2	129	33*	14.33	-	-	277	12		23.08	3-25	-	-	5	-
A.W.Rees	Auck	1889/90		5	7	2	3	3	0.60	-	-	416	38		10.94	8-36	4	2	4	-
	HB	1896/97		1	2	0	10	6	5.00	-	-	118	3		39.33	3-118	-	-	1	-
	All	1889/90	1896/97	6	9	2	13	6	1.85	-	-	534	41		13.02	8-36	4	2	5	-
W.L.Rees	Auck	1877/78		1	2	0	22	20	11.00	-	-	28	1		28.00	1-16	-	-	1	-
	All	1856/57	1877/78	4	7	0	65	37	9.28	-	-	28	1		28.00	1-16	-	-	2	-
D.Reese	Cant	1895/96	1920/21	47	85	4	2066	111	25.50	2	11	3040	168		18.09	6-43	10	1	28	-
	All	1895/96	1920/21	72	134	8	3182	148	25.25	4	16	3893	196		19.86	7-53	11	1	36	-
D.W.Reese	Cant	1917/18	1920/21	6	11	0	71	27	6.45	-	-	52	5		10.40	5-33	1	-	2	-
J.B.Reese	Cant	1900/01		2	3	0	22	15	7.33	-	-								1	-
T.W.Reese	Cant	1887/88	1917/18	24	44	7	374	53	10.10	-	1	1	0		-	-	-	-	20	-
W.P.Reeves	Cant	1879/80	1887/88	5	9	0	188	54	20.88	-	1								1	-
D.J.Reid	Cant	1953/54	1956/57	7	9	4	28	16	5.60	-	-	453	18		25.16	4-58	-	-	14	-
J.F.Reid	Auck	1975/76	1987/88	69	117	17	3733	173	37.33	5	22	214	6		35.66	2-5	-	-	90	8
	All	1975/76	1987/88	101	170	22	5650	180	38.17	11	29	221	6		36.83	2-5	-	-	116	9
J.R.Reid	Well	1947/48	1964/65	58	102	8	4538	296	48.27	13	16	3115	172		18.11	7-29	10	-	64	-
	Otago	1956/57	1957/58	11	18	0	670	201	37.22	2	3	243	21		11.57	7-20	1	-	9	-
	All	1947/48	1965	246	418	28	16128	296	41.35	39	83	10535	466		22.60	7-20	15	1	240	7
R.B.Reid	Well	1979/80	1991/92	19	34	4	710	88	23.66	-	5	9	0		-	-	-	-	14	-
	Auck	1985/86	1989/90	23	42	2	1060	107	26.50	1	6	14	2		7.00	2-5	-	-	13	-
	All	1979/80	1991/92	43	78	6	1789	107	24.84	1	11	981	33		29.72	6-57	1	-	27	-
R.E.Reid	Well	1958/59	1960/61	13	23	3	205	33*	12.81	-	-								4	-
A.T.Reinholds	Auck	1993/94	1995/96	21	40	4	1207	97	33.52	2	8								21	-
A.E.Relf	Auck	1907/08	1909/10	8	12	0	633	157	52.75	2	3	625	53		11.79	7-42	6	2	8	-
	All	1900	1921	565	900	70	22238	189*	26.79	26	113	39726	1897		20.94	9-95	114	23	533	-
J.R.Renner	Well	1882/83		1	2	0	1	1	1.00	-	-								-	-
C.Renwick	Auck	1959/60		2	4	1	43	19*	14.33	-	-	98	2		49.00	2-80	-	-	-	-
C.Restieaux	Auck	1900/01		3	6	2	14	6*	3.50	-	-	158	5		31.60	2-52	-	-	2	-
L.J.Rewcastle	Auck	1979/80		6	9	2	187	40	26.71	-	-	274	9		30.44	3-69	-	-	2	-

		First	Last	M	I	NO	Runs	HS	Avg	100	50	Runs	Wkts	OW	Avg	Best	5i	10m	ct	st
D.K.Rhodes	Otago	1874/75	1876/77	1	2	1	1	1*	1.00											
H.Rhodes	Otago	1872/73		3	6	1	13	8	2.60			229	5		45.80	2-38			2	
S.J.Rhodes	Well	2009/10		5	10	1	391	142*	43.44	2	1	174	7		24.85	2-11			2	
H.F.Rice	Well	1937/38	1945/46	10	19	0	392	77	20.63		2								8	
	CD	1950/51		1	2	0	2	2	1.00											
	All	1937/38	1950/51	12	23	0	401	77	17.43		2	174	7		24.85	2-11			12	
G.A.Richards	Auck	1955/56		5	9	2	153	53*	21.85		1									
H.M.R.Richards	Cant	1987/88		1	0							65	0							
I.Richards	Auck	1889/90	1893/94	5	10	0	112	29	11.20										2	
K.D.Richards	CD	2007/08		1	2	0	0	0	0.00			75	1		75.00	1-75				
S.J.Richards	Otago	1983/84	1984/85	5	7	0	88	25	12.57										1	
C.A.Richardson	Well	1897/98	1906/07	13	20	2	562	113	31.22	1	2	154	3		51.33	2-12			13	
	All	1886/87	1906/07	30	50	7	1079	113	25.09	1	5	193	3		64.33	2-12			22	
G.R.Richardson	Nel	1884/85	1891/92	5	8	0	12	6	1.50			94	6		15.66	3-3			3	
H.Richardson	Otago	1865/66		1	2	0	33	19	16.50			54	4		13.50	3-30				
M.H.Richardson	Auck	1989/90	2004/05	34	48	8	1411	133	35.27	3	5	586	19		30.84	5-77	1		19	
	Otago	1992/93	2000/01	49	89	10	3089	166	39.10	8	13	912	13		70.15	3-136			34	
	All	1989/90	2004/05	157	264	31	9994	306	42.89	20	48	1911	44		43.43	5-77	1		90	
F.Riddiford	Tara	1882/83	1891/92	3	6	0	21	16	3.50			9	0						2	
A.W.Riddolls	Well	1941/42		1	2	0	30	23	15.00			106	1		106.00	1-36				
J.D.Ridland	All	1945		1	2	0	62	44	31.00		3								1	
A.E.Ridley	Cant	1889/90	1909/10	24	42	4	820	82	21.57		3								24	
	All	1889/90	1909/10	25	44	4	859	82	21.47		3								24	
H.C.Ridley	Cant	1891/92	1904/05	18	34	3	611	52	19.70		1	33	1		33.00	1-11			8	
R.A.Ridley	Cant	1905/06	1906/07	2	4	1	20	12	6.66			31	0						1	
A.A.Rigg	Well	1884/85		1	1	0	1	1	1.00											
J.D.Riley	Cant	1968/69		5	8	2	147	37*	24.50			0	0						4	
	Well	1970/71	1971/72	10	16	3	269	41*	20.69			2	0						11	
	Auck	1973/74	1976/77	24	44	8	1563	130	38.12	3	8	2	0						17	
	All	1968/69	1976/77	40	70	8	1993	130	32.14	3	8								34	
J.P.Riley	HB	1885/86		1	2	0	27	22	13.50											
L.E.Riley	Cant	1933/34		4	7	1	131	67*	21.83		1	538	21		25.61	6-89	2		2	
	Well	1934/35		2	3	0	33	17	11.00			56	0						1	
	All	1933/34	1934/35	6	10	1	164	67*	18.22		1	594	21		28.28	6-89	2		3	
A.W.Ritchie	Auck	1951/52	1959/60	12	17	8	220	44	24.44										17	
B.D.Ritchie	Cant	1979/80	1981/82	17	27	8	559	75*	29.42		2								30	
D.C.Ritchie	Auck	1943/44		2	4	1	115	46*	38.33											
T.D.Ritchie	Well	1982/83	1990/91	58	92	14	2494	106	31.97	3	15	179	4		44.75	1-12			46	
	All	1982/83	1990/91	59	93	14	2509	106	31.75	3	15	195	5		39.00	1-12			47	
C.T.Rix	Cant	1922/23		2	4	1	27	17	9.00			116	2		58.00	2-31			1	
A.W.Roberts	Cant	1927/28	1940/41	35	60	8	2004	181	38.53	2	15	1640	53		30.94	4-49			37	
	Otago	1944/45	1950/51	18	31	2	904	110*	31.17	1	5	1018	35		29.08	5-62	1		15	
	All	1927/28	1950/51	84	135	17	3645	181	30.88	3	28	4762	167		28.51	5-47	3		78	7
A.Roberts	Well	1959/60	1963/64	7	8	0	121	49	15.12			99	1		99.00	1-46			2	1
A.C.Roberts	All	1945	1947/48	2	3	1	26	12	13.00			182	4		45.50	3-83				

		First	Last	M	I	NO	Runs	HS	Avg	100	50	Runs	Wkts	OW	Avg	Best	5i	10m	ct	st
A.D.G.Roberts	ND	1967/68	1983/84	104	192	35	5533	128*	35.24	7	29	2303	79		29.15	5-30	1		68	
A.R.Roberts	All	1967/68	1983/84	112	206	37	5865	128*	34.70	7	31	2520	84		30.00	5-30	1		73	
	Well	1993/94		2	3	0	54	23	18.00			56	0		–	–			1	
B.L.Roberts	All	1989	1996	61	83	18	1173	62	18.04		2	4829	107		45.13	6-72	1		23	
E.J.Roberts	ND	1977/78		2	4	0	40	24	10.00											
H.Roberts	Well	1909/10		3	5	0	111	31	22.20										2	
S.A.Roberts	Well	1882/83	1889/90	12	22	0	213	42	9.68			171	13		13.15	3-22			4	
S.J.Roberts	Auck	1994/95		1	2	1	25	25*	25.00										2	
	Cant	1985/86	1995/96	60	62	12	597	25	11.94		1	5738	193		29.73	5-56	6		16	
	All	1985/86	1995/96	63	66	12	629	55	11.64		1	6001	203		29.56	5-56	6		16	
F.H.Robertson	Tara	1897/98		1	2	0	58	25	14.50										1	
	Well	1898/99		3	4	0	72	25	8.00			28	0		–	–			1	
	All	1897/98	1901/02	6	10	1	130	24	14.44			91	7		13.00	6-23	1		1	
G.K.Robertson	CD	1979/80	1989/90	78	99	22	1727	99*	22.42		10	6573	228		17.00	6-23			22	
	All	1979/80	1989/90	88	111	23	1875	99*	21.30		10	7469	252		28.82	6-47	8	1	20	
G.J.Robertson	Otago	1937/38	1940/41	11	21	1	550	83*	27.50	1	5	545	13		29.63	6-47	9	1	22	
I.A.Robertson	Cant	2005/06	2008/09	20	27	6	721	102*	34.33	1	4	953	17		41.92	3-25			6	
	All	2005/06	2008/09	21	28	7	828	107*	39.42	2	4	953	17		56.05	3-58			15	
S.P.Robertson	CD	1985/86	1987/88	13	24	2	479	94	21.77		2	30	1		56.05	3-58			15	
W.Robertson	Cant	1893/94	1900/01	10	12	6	40	14*	6.66			1005	72		30.00	1-5			10	
	All	1893/94	1900/01	12	16	7	68	15	7.55			1228	85		13.95	9-98	9	3	5	
W.A.Robertson	Otago	1960/61		4	7	0	43	22	6.14						14.44	9-98	10	4	5	
T.P.Robin	CD	1999/00	2000/01	3	3	0	17	14	5.66			286	7		40.85	3-84			2	
C.W.Robinson	Well	1911/12	1914/15	8	15	0	275	45	21.15		1	677	34		19.91	5-63	1		2	
	All	1911/12	1914/15	14	26	3	376	45	16.34		1	1288	53		24.30	5-63	1		4	
G.G.Robinson	ND	2001/02	2007/08	21	35	1	736	125*	21.64	1	2	16	0		–	–			6	
M.Robinson	Cant	1877/78		1	2	0	2	2*	2.00										10	
M.A.Robinson	Cant	1988/89		6	9	3	11	9*	3.66			609	15		40.60	3-52			2	
R.H.Robinson	All	1987	2002	229	259	112	590	27	4.01			17807	584	1	30.49	9-37	13	2	41	
	Otago	1946/47	1948/49	10	18	0	338	74	18.77		1	895	28		31.96	4-45			4	
	All	1934/35	1948/49	46	81	4	2441	163	31.70	4	13	1654	44		37.59	4-45			24	
S.A.Robinson	Otago	1984/85	1996/97	45	78	10	1427	93	20.98		6								118	5
W.Robinson	Auck	1902/03	1912/13	12	18	7	85	20	7.72										12	6
W.W.Robinson	Auck	1873/74	1884/85	12	22	1	248	42*	11.80		1	521	41		12.70	5-13	2		6	
J.Rodgers	Well	1908/09	1914/15	3	6	1	139	62	27.80		1	124	4		31.00	2-37			1	
F.B.Rogers	Well	1941/42		1	2	0	21	21	10.50											
A.J.Rohrs	Well	1987/88		2	2	1	4	4	4.00			9	0		–	–				
A.C.Rolleston	Cant	1889/90	1890/91	2	4	0	16	9*	8.00										1	
R.F.Romanos	Well	1951/52		2	4	0	20	9	5.00										1	
A.Ronaldson	Well	1922/23		1	2	0	16	16	8.00											
T.S.Ronaldson	Well	1883/84		2	4	0	24	20	8.00			116	6		19.33	3-50			1	
G.A.Rose	CD	1958/59		5	10	0	116	33	11.60										4	
	ND	1967/68		4	8	0	58	18	7.25										4	
	All	1958/59	1967/68	9	18	0	174	33	9.66										4	
H.Rose	Otago	1876/77	1883/84	5	9	1	67	15	8.37										1	
W.Rose	Well	1885/86		1	2	1	0	0*	0.00										2	

		First	Last	M	I	NO	Runs	HS	Avg	100	50	Runs	Wkts	OW	Avg	Best	5i	10m	ct	st
B.R.Ross	Well	1929/30	1935/36	2	4	0	11	11	2.75	-	-	58	1		58.00	1-50	-	-	1	-
C.J.Ross	Well	1975/76		7	7	3	21	7*	5.25	-	-	434	9		48.22	2-29	-	-	2	-
C.E.Ross	All	1975/76	1980	31	41	13	132	23*	4.71	-	-	1938	55		35.23	4-34	-	-	8	-
C.W.Ross	Cant	2005/06		2	2	0	34	20	17.00	-	-	172	3		57.33	2-74	-	-	-	-
E.J.Ross	ND	1989/90	1996/97	17	19	5	219	66	15.64	-	1	1337	42		31.83	4-36	-	-	3	-
R.R.Rotch	Cant	1883/84		2	3	2	2	2*	2.00	-	-	81	5		16.20	3-26	-	-	-	-
G.A.Rotherham	Well	1928/29		1	2	0	8	7*	-	-	-	67	3		22.33	3-67	-	-	1	-
	All	1919	1928/29	3	5	0	101	45	20.20	-	-	184	2		92.00	2-60	-	-	1	-
J.Rothwell	Cant	1883/84		65	107	11	1801	84*	18.76	-	7	5105	180		28.36	7-69	8	-	48	-
C.G.Rowe	Well	1944/45	1945/46	1	2	0	7	6	3.50	-	-								2	-
	CD	1952/53		6	12	0	324	72	27.00	-	2	88	3		29.33	2-36	-	-	8	-
	All	1944/45	1952/53	4	5	0	56	35	11.20	-	-	88	3		29.33	2-36	-	-	1	-
R.W.Rowntree	Auck	1914/15	1931/32	11	19	0	380	72	20.00	-	2								10	38
	All	1914/15	1931/32	31	42	11	289	48	9.32	-	-								55	38
R.A.Roy	Otago	1970/71	1971/72	33	45	12	308	48	9.33	-	-	88	6		14.66	3-10	-	-	57	
G.E.Royfee	Cant	1952/53		4	6	1	55	30	11.00	-	-								4	-
P.J.Rugg	Cant	2003/04		3	5	0	75	41	15.00	-	-								1	-
B.J.Rule	Well	1982/83		2	3	0	28	21	9.33	-	-								7	-
N.W.Rushton	Otago	2001/02	2003/04	3	5	2	4	4*	4.00	-	-	131	4		32.75	2-32	-	-	-	-
T.S.Russ	Well	1940/41	1945/46	5	8	2	163	59	27.16	-	1	340	4		85.00	2-49	-	-	3	-
J.M.Ruston	Cant	1962/63		2	5	0	29	24	5.80	-	-								-	-
H.D.Rutherford	Otago	2008/09	2009/10	6	4	0	29	16	7.25	-	-								1	-
I.A.Rutherford	Otago	1974/75	1983/84	63	115	5	131	41	11.90	-	-	41	1		41.00	1-8	-	-	3	-
	CD	1977/78		8	16	3	3122	222	27.87	4	13								40	-
K.R.Rutherford	All	1974/75	1983/84	79	144	4	518	133	34.53	1	2								3	-
	Otago	1982/83	1994/95	68	121	7	3794	222	27.10	5	16	56	2		28.00	1-8	-	-	50	2
	All	1982/83	1999/00	220	383	33	5051	226*	14.30	14	18	486	15		32.40	5-72	1	-	50	-
R.M.Rutherford	Otago	1908/09	1913/14	9	18	1	13974	317	39.92	35	67	1012	22		46.00	5-72	1	-	180	-
P.D.Rutledge	Cant	1982/83		5	9	1	251	42*	14.76	-	-	309	10		30.90	3-52	-	-	4	-
B.Ryan	HB	1903/04	1910/11	2	4	2	33	11	4.71	-	-								7	-
M.L.Ryan	Cant	1965/66	1978/79	45	78	8	2040	129	29.14	2	14	208	5		41.60	3-130	1	-	60	11
	CD	1967/68	1969/70	17	27	1	866	110	33.30	1	4	435	17		25.58	3-30	-	-	22	-
	All	1965/66	1978/79	66	113	9	3022	129	29.05	3	18	259	15		17.26	4-34	-	-	87	11
J.D.Ryder	CD	2002/03	2003/04	8	12	2	446	114*	44.60	1	1	706	33		21.39	4-34	-	-	3	-
	Well	2004/05	2009/10	30	48	2	2010	236	43.69	5	11	51	1		51.00	1-5	-	-	28	-
	All	2002/03	2009/10	53	85	6	3514	236	44.48	8	17	1022	40		25.55	4-23	-	-	44	-
E.A.P.Sainsbury	HB	1893/94	1894/95	5	8	0	18	10	2.25	-	-	1294	45		28.75	4-23	-	-	2	-
D.S.St.John	Otago	1946/47	1950/51	15	28	5	493	85	21.43	-	2	32	0		-	-	-	-	12	-
	Well	1952/53	1955/56	18	34	0	633	88	18.61	-	2	51	0		-	-	-	-	9	-
	All	1946/47	1955/56	34	64	5	1236	88	20.94	-	5								21	-
E.V.Sale	Auck	1904/05	1914/15	19	34	2	762	121	23.81	1	3	51	0		-	-	-	-	16	1
	All	1904/05	1914/15	23	42	3	1012	121	25.94	2	4	22	2		11.00	2-7	-	-	17	1
G.S.Sale	Cant	1863/64	1864/65	2	4	1	38	16	12.66	-	-	22	2		11.00	2-7	-	-	2	-
M.J.Sale	Otago	1997/98		2	4	1	56	38	18.66	-	-								7	1

		First	Last	M	I	NO	Runs	HS	Avg	100	50	Runs	Wkts	OW	Avg	Best	5i	10m	ct	st
V.S.Sale	Auck	1934/35	1939/40	9	13	1	421	106	35.08	1	2	30	1		30.00	1-2			4	
	All	1934/35	1939/40	11	17	1	531	106	33.18	1	2	30	1		30.00	1-2			4	
D.J.G.Sales	Well	2001/02	2010	2	4	0	113	62	28.25		1								2	
	All	1996	2010	204	329	28	12145	303*	40.34	24	59								189	
I.J.Salmon	Well	1873/74	1881/82	6	12	1	62	22	5.63			184	9	4	20.44	4-25			2	
J.A.N.Salmon	Well	1873/74	1880/81	4	7	1	17	7	2.83			106	19	2	5.58	7-36	3	1	3	
W.J.Salmon	Well	1873/74	1889/90	10	18	1	220	50	12.94		1	33	1		33.00	2-?			7	3
	HB	1885/86		1	2	0	6	3	3.00			15	0							
	Tara	1891/92		1	2	0	9	8	4.50											
B.V.Sampson	All	1873/74	1891/92	12	22	1	235	50	11.19		1	15	0						7	3
G.H.Sampson	Cant	1969/70		2	4	2	40	24*	20.00			15	0						7	
H.C.Sampson	Otago	1874/75		1	2	0	10	8	5.00										1	
	CD	1970/71	1972/73	15	29	0	745	119	25.68	1	2	15	0						6	
	Otago	1973/74	1975/76	20	39	4	1133	90	32.37		9								15	
	Cant	1976/77		2	4	0	88	41	22.00										2	
	All	1970/71	1976/77	37	72	4	1966	119	28.91	1	11	15	0						23	
B.Samuels	Well	1919/20		1	2	1	7	7	7.00										1	
I.P.Sandbrook	CD	2002/03		1	2	0	7	7	7.00										1	
D.M.Sandman	Cant	1909/10	1926/27	45	80	8	1508	93	20.94		9	3503	140		25.02	7-30	5	2	21	
	All	1909/10	1926/27	55	99	10	1841	93	20.68		11	4539	170		26.70	7-30	6	9	29	
M.F.Sandri	Otago	1956/57		1	2	0	27	25	13.50			55	0		20.50	2-35			2	
R.Sands	Auck	1905/06		1	1	0	0	0	0.00			82	4						1	
R.E.Satchell	Nel	1884/85		1	2	1	5	5*	5.00											
C.R.Satherley	ND	1959/60	1960/61	2	4	0	62	52	15.50		1	4	1		4.00	1-4			2	
J.V.Saunders	Well	1910/11	1913/14	14	25	5	99	21*	4.95			1480	80		18.50	7-56	8	2	12	
	All	1899/00	1913/14	107	170	47	586	29*	4.76			12064	553		21.81	8-106	48	9	72	
L.H.Saunders	Auck	1925/26		1	1	0	5	5	5.00											
G.Savile	Cant	1871/72		1	2	0	58	58	58.00		1	38	0							
	All	1867	1874	16	24	1	529	105	23.00	1	3								4	1
K.R.J.V.Saxon	Cant	1923/24		1	2	0	43	43	21.50										10	
C.K.Saxton	Otago	1934/35	1938/39	7	14	1	226	37	17.38											
J.C.Scandrett	Otago	1935/36	1943/44	4	7	0	73	22	10.42			20	0						3	
R.J.Schaw	CD	2006/07	2008/09	14	21	2	319	34	16.78		2	1467	26		56.42	5-130	1		3	
	Well	2009/10		4	6	1	38	16	7.60			361	7		51.57	2-44			2	
	All	2006/07	2009/10	18	27	3	357	34	14.87		2	1828	33		55.39	5-130	1		7	
G.E.Schmoll	Auck	1903/04	1905/06	5	9	1	69	28	8.62										2	4
	Well	1910/11	1912/13	2	4	2	15	11	7.50										9	
	All	1903/04	1912/13	7	13	3	84	28	8.40										9	4
J.W.J.Schofer	Well	1969/70		2	4	0	96	43	24.00										10	
P.J.Schofer	Well	1983/84		1	2	1	7	4*	7.00			51	2		25.50	2-45			1	
R.M.Schofield	CD	1959/60	1974/75	53	78	17	1082	55*	17.73		2	162	5		32.40	2-42			110	15
W.J.Schollum	All	1920/21		1	2	1	8	4*	8.00			70	1		70.00	1-70			1	
E.A.A.Schrader	Well	1919/20		3	6	0	56	26	9.33			1	0						2	
H.T.Schuster	Auck	1963/64	1964/65	7	11	2	300	85*	33.33		2	1	0						6	
	ND	1965/66	1971/72	23	44	3	647	95	15.78		2								14	
	All	1963/64	1971/72	30	55	5	947	95	18.94		4								20	

		First	Last	M	I	NO	Runs	HS	Avg	100	50	Runs	Wkts	OW	Avg	Best	5i	10m	ct	st
A.M.Schwass	CD	1998/99	2004/05	29	39	8	558	44	18.00	-	-	2554	109	-	23.43	7-36	6	-	10	1
A.H.Scott	Auck	1925/26	1927/28	5	6	3	30	9*	10.00	-	-	98	2	-	49.00	1-38	-	-	3	-
B.E.Scott	Otago	2000/01	2007/08	43	53	13	892	96	22.30	-	4	3551	142	-	25.00	6-20	5	-	14	-
	ND	2008/09	2009/10	12	17	3	350	65	25.00	-	2	838	12	-	69.83	2-51	-	-	5	-
	All	2000/01	2009/10	56	72	17	1246	96	22.65	-	6	4427	157	-	28.19	6-20	5	-	19	-
D.G.Scott	Auck	1985/86	1986/87	11	21	1	519	79	25.95	-	6	196	4	-	49.00	2-44	-	-	4	-
N.A.Scott	Auck	1980/81	1984/85	16	13	6	99	17*	14.14	-	3								31	4
P.W.Scott		1962/63		1	2	0	20	15	10.00	-	-								1	
R.H.Scott	Cant	1940/41	1954/55	20	31	4	744	86*	27.55	-	6	1948	74	-	26.32	6-99	3	-	10	-
	ND	1940/41	1954/55	25	40	5	874	86*	24.97	-	6	2442	94	-	25.97	6-98	4	-	13	-
S.J.Scott	All	1978/79	1985/86	35	49	11	520	60*	13.68	-	1	2624	73	-	35.94	5-21	3	-	21	-
V.J.Scott	Auck	1937/38	1952/53	44	74	15	3546	204	60.10	11	15	237	9	-	26.33	3-22	-	-	22	-
	All	1937/38	1952/53	80	130	17	5620	204	49.73	16	23	271	10	-	27.10	3-22	-	-	42	-
R.S.Scragg	Auck	1996/97		1	2	0	25	14	12.50	-	-								1	
	CD	2001/02		4	7	0	128	54	18.28	-	1								1	
	All	1996/97	2001/02	5	9	0	153	54	17.00	-	1								-	
M.J.Sears	Well	1990/91	1993/94	20	25	6	243	26*	12.78	-	-	1498	52	-	28.80	6-48	2	-	6	-
H.H.Secretan	Cant	1876/77	1886/87	6	10	0	168	72	16.80	-	1	18	0	-	-	-	-	-	6	-
H.E.Seed	HB	1913/14		1	2	0	6	5	3.00	-	-	20	0	-	-	-	-	-	-	-
M.Sellon	Nel	1873/74	1875/76	2	4	1	28	19*	9.33	-	-								1	
T.Selwood	CD	1972/73		2	4	0	162	89	40.50	-	1								-	
	All	1966	1973	20	35	4	603	89	19.45	-	5	1	0	-	-	-	-	-	9	-
P.C.Semple	Otago	1961/62	1971/72	33	60	5	1188	107	21.60	1	5	109	4	-	27.25	4-76	-	-	12	-
B.W.H.Sergent	Well	1951/52	1952/53	5	9	0	94	39	10.44	-	-	187	4	-	46.75	3-6	-	-	2	-
D.G.Sewell	Otago	1995/96	2005/06	55	75	35	232	24	5.80	-	-	5198	178	-	29.20	8-31	7	1	12	-
	All	1995/96	2005/06	67	91	43	282	24	5.87	-	-	6260	218	-	28.71	8-31	10	1	15	-
F.J.Shacklock	Otago	1903/04	1904/05	4	7	1	73	31	12.16	-	-	396	20	-	19.80	8-136	2	-	5	-
	All	1883	1904/05	156	231	26	2438	77	11.89	-	2	9458	497	-	19.03	8-32	39	8	92	-
R.C.S.A.Shand	Cant	1937/38	1946/47	9	17	0	424	77	24.94	-	4								3	
H.H.Sharp	HB	1904/05		1	2	0	14	13	7.00	-	-								1	
P.A.Sharp	Cant	1964/65	1965/66	8	8	5	19	7*	6.33	-	-	565	21	-	26.90	4-55	-	-	9	-
T.M.Sharp	Cant	1936/37	1945/46	2	4	0	57	28	14.25	-	-	126	4	-	31.50	3-65	-	-	-	-
	All	1934/35	1945/46	4	7	2	74	28	14.80	-	-	222	6	-	37.00	3-65	-	-	-	-
M.F.Sharpe	Cant	1990/91	1996/97	20	22	5	199	33	11.70	-	-	1456	52	-	28.00	4-59	-	-	4	-
	All	1990/91	1996/97	21	22	5	199	33	11.70	-	-	1515	55	-	27.54	4-59	-	-	4	-
G.S.Shaw	Auck	2001/02	2009/10	16	19	8	122	28	11.09	-	-	1551	53	-	29.26	5-73	2	-	4	-
	Otago	2005/06		3	5	1	36	20	9.00	-	-	272	9	-	30.22	5-49	1	-	3	-
	All	2001/02	2009/10	19	24	9	158	28	10.53	-	-	1823	62	-	29.40	5-49	3	-	4	-
H.J.Shaw	Cant	1999/00	2004/05	21	21	5	275	47*	17.18	-	-	1337	36	-	37.13	5-84	1	-	6	-
L.J.Shaw	Auck	2005/06	2009/10	16	33	8	254	52*	10.16	-	1	2381	83	-	28.68	5-59	2	-	5	-
T.E.Shaw	ND	1956/57	1963/64	27	60	11	1083	78	18.35	-	4	567	19	-	29.84	3-52	-	-	14	-
	All	1956/57	1963/64	31	63	11	1096	78	17.67	-	4	567	19	-	29.84	3-52	-	-	14	-
A.G.Sheath	Cant	1879/80		1	1	0	12	12	12.00	-	-								1	
J.W.Sheed	Otago	2001/02	2008/09	43	74	4	1513	89	21.61	-	11	196	2	-	98.00	1-30	-	-	22	-
J.R.Sheffield	Well	1938/39		3	5	0	92	38	18.40	-	-	28	0	-	-	-	-	-	2	-
	All	1929	1938/39	180	277	40	3914	108	16.51	1	16								196	54

223

Name		First	Last	M	I	NO	Runs	HS	Avg	100	50	Runs	Wkts	OW	Avg	Best	5i	10m	ct	st
J.S.F.Shepherd	Otago	1912/13	1930/31	24	46	0	1402	146	30.47	1	8	693	18		38.50	3-19	-	-	7	-
R.R.Sherlock	All	1912/13	1930/31	29	55	3	1686	146	30.65	1	10	777	21		37.00	3-19	-	-	9	-
	CD	2003/04	2008/09	7	10	3	147	64	21.00	-	-	703	23		30.56	4-33	-	-	2	-
	Cant	2005/06		4	5	1	10	4	2.50	-	-	268	7		38.28	3-92	-	-	1	-
	Auck	2009/10		1	1	0	9	9	9.00	-	-	178	7		25.42	7-133	1	-	-	-
	All	2003/04	2009/10	13	18	5	173	64	13.30	-	1	1227	38		32.28	7-133	1	-	3	-
C.V.Shirley	Otago	1945/46		1	2	0	26	16	13.00	-	-								1	-
A.W.Short	CD	2003/04	2009/10	3	5	0	96	33	19.20	-	-								4	-
E.Shove	Tara	1891/92	1979/80	1	2	0	1	1	0.50	-	-	22	0		-	-	-	-	-	-
C.E.Shreck	Well	2005/06	2007/08	11	12	6	21	8	3.50	-	-	1228	45		27.28	5-64	4	-	5	-
	All	2003	2010	85	97	54	154	19	3.58	-	-	9390	307		30.58	8-31	18	2	31	-
M.J.F.Shrimpton	CD	1961/62	1979/80	97	171	15	4551	150	29.17	5	24	1815	57		31.84	6-40	1	-	58	-
	ND	1974/75		5	10	0	254	76*	36.28	-	-	209	10		20.90	5-32	1	-	4	-
	All	1961/62	1979/80	122	218	23	5812	150	29.80	7	29	2386	81		29.45	6-40	2	-	68	-
R.R.Shutte	ND	2004/05		1	2	0	20	12	10.00	-	-	39	2		19.50	2-39	-	-	-	-
H.G.Siedeberg	Otago	1898/99	1921/22	41	74	3	1307	90	18.40	-	5	548	26		21.07	6-30	1	-	20	-
	All	1898/99	1921/22	47	86	4	1420	90	17.31	-	5	568	26		21.84	6-30	1	-	22	-
E.J.Sigley	Well	1959/60	1960/61	5	9	0	140	44	15.55	-	-	175	4		43.75	2-63	-	-	-	-
M.A.Sigley	CD	1994/95	2002/03	44	60	9	832	74*	16.31	-	3								124	4
G.J.Silcock	Nel	1877/78	1885/86	7	13	1	72	30	5.53	-	-								1	-
W.A.S.Silva	CD	2000/01		3	5	0	73	43	36.50	-	-	113	8		14.12	4-11	-	-	1	-
	Auck	2001/02		1	2	0	83	33	16.60	-	-	280	2		140.00	1-39	-	-	-	-
	All	1990/91	2001/02	17	25	2	459	86	19.95	-	2	174	4		43.50	3-74	-	-	15	-
R.C.D.Silver	Otago	1935/36	1945/46	14	25	4	175	37	8.33	-	-	1350	44		30.68	5-27	1	-	11	-
G.W.Simmonds	Cant	1929/30		3	5	0	14	12	7.00	-	-	1334	49		27.22	6-20	2	-	1	-
H.Simpson	Auck	1917/18		1	2	0	17	9	8.50	-	-	268	6		44.66	3-64	-	-	-	-
J.B.Simpson	Auck	1925/26	1937/38	3	5	0	50	29	10.00	-	-	77	5		15.40	4-73	-	-	3	-
	CD	1937/38		1	2	0	29	29	14.50	-	-	312	7		44.57	3-123	1	-	-	-
	All	1925/26	1937/38	4	7	0	50	29	7.14	-	-	376	9		41.77	3-123	1	-	3	-
R.Simpson	CD	1955/56	1957/58	3	6	1	89	56	17.80	-	1	5	0		-	-	-	-	1	-
A.Sims	Cant	1896/97	1912/13	41	78	7	1792	103*	25.23	1	7	391	19		20.57	5-36	1	-	41	-
	All	1896/97	1913/14	53	93	10	2182	184*	26.28	2	8	409	19		21.52	5-36	1	-	51	-
B.W.Sinclair	Well	1955/56	1970/71	68	116	14	3583	148	35.12	2	26	31	0		-	-	-	-	26	-
	All	1955/56	1970/71	118	204	18	6114	148	32.87	6	38	86	2		43.00	2-32	-	-	45	-
I.M.Sinclair	Cant	1953/54	1956/57	13	18	3	239	40	15.93	-	-	1001	40		25.02	5-57	2	-	15	-
	All	1953/54	1956/57	15	22	4	264	40	14.66	-	-	1121	41		27.34	5-57	2	-	16	-
M.S.Sinclair	CD	1995/96	2009/10	89	152	17	7111	243*	52.67	21	40	937	21		44.61	3-29	1	-	91	-
	All	1995/96	2009/10	158	268	28	11680	268	48.66	30	59	955	22		43.40	3-29	1	-	157	1
S.P.L.Singe	Auck	2003/04		2	4	0	62	24	15.50	-	-								1	-
W.R.Skeet	Auck	1938/39		1	1	1	0	0*	-	-	-	5	1		5.00	1-5	-	-	2	-
P.J.Skelton	Otago	1953/54		1	2	1	66	53	33.00	-	1								-	-
	ND	1957/58		2	4	2	17	11	8.50	-	-								-	-
	All	1953/54	1957/58	3	6	3	83	53	20.75	-	1	5	1		5.00	1-5	-	-	-	-
W.H.Skitch	Orago	1883/84		2	3	0	11	6	3.66	-	-								-	-
J.A.Sloman	Auck	1903/04		2	4	0	24	19	6.00	-	-	34	1		34.00	1-9	-	-	5	-
R.G.Sloman	Auck	1913/14	1918/19	4	8	0	185	62	23.12	-	1								-	-
A.G.Small	CD	1955/56		1	2	0	0	0*	0.00	-	-	24	0		-	-	-	-	-	-

		First	Last	M	I	NO	Runs	HS	Avg	100	50	Runs	Wkts	OW	Avg	Best	5i	10m	ct	st
C.A.Small	Cant	2006/07		3	3	2	47	18	47.00	-	-	260	5		52.00	4-50	-	-	1	-
P.A.T.Small	Cant	1946/47	1958/59	12	20	2	305	45	16.94	-	-	912	23		39.65	4-52	-	-	11	-
R.G.Small	All	1946/47	1958/59	13	22	2	317	45	15.85	-	-	1039	26		39.96	4-52	-	-	12	-
H.A.K.Smalley	CD	1958/59	1962/63	8	14	2	146	46	10.42	-	-								5	-
	Auck	1965/66		1	2	0	13	7	6.50	-	-								-	-
	All	1964/65	1965/66	2	4	0	25	7	6.25	-	-								-	-
W.J.Smeeton	Auck	1913/14	1929/30	5	8	0	144	48	18.00	-	-	101	2		50.50	1-12	-	-	2	-
B.F.Smith	CD	2000/01	2001/02	19	33	3	1472	201*	49.06	3	10	52	0				-	-	10	-
	All	1990	2010	334	529	58	18777	204	39.86	40	100	488	4		122.00	1-5	-	-	214	-
B.D.Smith	Well	1966/67	1976/77	41	67	11	1233	76*	22.01	-	4	1358	50		27.16	6-57	1	-	32	-
	All	1965/66	1976/77	42	69	11	1311	76*	22.60	-	5	1358	50		27.16	6-57	1	-	32	-
C.J.P.Smith	CD	1983/84	1990/91	62	118	9	3499	160*	32.10	7	15	20	0		-	-	-	-	42	-
C.R.Smith	HB	1891/92	1892/93	4	6	2	35	15*	8.75	-	-	192	33		5.81	7-20	4	-	-	-
C.M.Smith	Otago	2004/05	2007/08	9	10	1	131	49	14.55	-	-	585	15		39.00	3-74	-	-	4	-
E.H.Smith	Sland	1917/18		1	2	0	8	8	4.00	-	-						-	-	-	-
F.A.Smith	Cant	1922/23		2	4	0	58	39	14.50	-	-						-	-	1	-
F.B.Smith	Cant	1946/47	1952/53	20	36	1	1447	153	41.34	4	7	32	0		-	-	-	-	9	-
	All	1942/43	1952/53	49	85	5	2643	153	33.03	4	14	76	1		76.00	1-6	-	-	21	-
G.B.Smith	Cant	1977/78	1978/79	7	14	1	196	31	14.00	-	-	225	9		25.00	2-9	-	-	4	-
H.D.Smith	Otago	1931/32	1932/33	6	11	1	263	52	26.30	-	1	232	7		33.14	3-41	-	-	3	-
	Cant	1933/34		4	7	0	137	33	19.57	-	-	570	17		33.52	3-41	-	-	3	-
	All	1931/32	1933/34	11	19	1	404	52	22.44	-	1	25	0		-	-	-	-	6	-
I.D.S.Smith	CD	1977/78	1986/87	59	95	12	2265	145	27.28	3	10								140	11
	Auck	1987/88	1991/92	18	19	4	430	72*	28.66	-	4								52	7
	All	1977/78	1991/92	178	250	42	5570	173	26.77	6	24	38	0		-	-	-	-	417	36
J.D.Smith	ND	1967/68	1971/72	15	26	9	211	27*	12.41	-	-	1266	33		38.36	5-80	1	-	6	-
J.M.Smith	Otago	1914/15	1921/22	6	11	1	45	12	4.50	-	-								6	-
J.Smith	Cant	1943/44	1945/46	5	7	0	194	51	27.71	-	1								4	-
J.R.Smith	All	1962/63		1	2	1	16	9*	16.00	-	-	45	4		11.25	2-21	-	-	1	-
K.F.H.Smith	Well	1953/54	1954/55	5	10	1	403	141*	44.77	1	2	21	2		10.50	2-12	-	-	2	-
	CD	1955/56	1960/61	33	60	0	1316	108	22.68	1	5	762	33		23.09	3-0	-	-	13	-
	All	1953/54	1960/61	38	70	1	1719	141*	25.65	2	7	783	35		22.37	3-0	-	-	15	-
K.P.Smith	ND	1993/94		3	5	2	41	18*	13.66	-	-	242	9		26.88	5-39	1	-	2	-
L.D.Smith	Otago	1934/35	1956/57	59	108	16	2277	109	24.75	1	11	3189	82		38.89	5-52	1	-	46	-
	All	1934/35	1956/57	61	110	17	2281	109	24.52	1	11	3250	85		38.23	5-52	1	-	46	-
N.G.S.Smith	Otago	1969/70		1	2	1	3	2*	3.00	-	-	19	0		-	-	-	-	-	-
	Auck	1971/72		1	1	0	0	0	0.00	-	-	124	6		20.66	4-77	-	-	-	-
P.H.Smith	Well	1969/70	1971/72	2	3	0	3	2*	1.50	-	-	143	6		23.83	4-77	-	-	-	-
P.H.Smith	ND	1909/10		1	1	0	12	12	12.00	-	-								1	-
R.A.Smith	Otago	1956/57		4	7	0	84	18	12.00	-	-								-	-
R.G.T.Smith	Otago	1993/94	1995/96	6	10	0	80	25	8.00	-	-	428	8		53.50	2-16	-	-	1	-
R.W.Smith	Well	2001/02		6	10	1	102	21	11.33	-	-	598	12		49.83	3-21	-	-	1	-
S.G.Smith	Auck	1968/69	1976/77	33	56	5	1486	124	29.13	1	9	0	0		-	-	-	-	20	-
	All	1917/18	1925/26	26	46	6	1673	256	41.82	1	12	2980	140		21.28	8-55	14	5	20	-
	All	1899/00	1925/26	211	379	30	10920	256	31.28	14	60	17271	955		18.08	9-34	71	19	156	-

		First	Last	M	I	NO	Runs	HS	Avg	100	50	Runs	Wkts	OW	Avg	Best	5i	10m	ct	st
E.W.Smyrk	HB	1909/10	1912/13	4	7	1	65	30	10.83	-	-	269	9		29.88	3-27	-	-	4	-
	Well	1913/14	1919/20	3	5	0	52	29	10.40	-	-	118	4		29.50	4-45	-	-	1	-
A.N.C.Snedden	All	1909/10	1919/20	7	12	1	117	30	10.63	-	-	387	13		29.76	4-45	-	-	5	-
	Auck	1909/10	1927/28	39	67	3	1997	139	31.20	2	9	2154	87		24.75	5-13	4	-	18	-
C.A.Snedden	All	1909/10	1927/28	49	87	4	2492	139	30.02	2	14	2502	95		26.33	5-13	4	-	20	-
	Auck	1938/39	1947/48	6	8	4	38	14	9.50	-	-	551	25		22.04	6-59	1	-	2	-
	All	1938/39	1948/49	9	11	6	44	14	8.80	-	-	788	31		25.41	6-59	1	-	7	-
C.A.Snedden	Auck	1920/21		4	7	1	234	119	39.00	1	-	55	6		9.16	4-1	-	-	2	-
M.C.Snedden	Auck	1977/78	1989/90	55	62	15	966	64*	20.55	-	3	4631	217		21.34	7-49	10	2	32	-
	All	1977/78	1990	118	124	29	1792	69	18.86	-	6	9918	387		25.62	8-73	15	2	55	-
W.N.Snedden	Auck	1946/47		2	3	0	92	75	30.66	-	1								1	-
C.G.Snook	Cant	1947/48	1949/50	5	8	0	173	62	21.62	-	1	308	7		44.00	3-52	-	-	-	-
I.R.Snook	CD	1972/73	1987/88	39	68	6	1312	100*	21.16	1	5	107	1		107.00	1-8	-	-	22	-
	All	1971/72	1987/88	40	70	6	1344	100*	21.00	1	5	107	1		107.00	1-8	-	-	23	-
G.A.Snowden	Well	1968/69		1	1	0						37	0							
G.Solomon	Well	1966/67		2	2	0	29	21	14.50	-	-	157	5		31.40	3-102	-	-	2	-
A.Somani	ND	1988/89	1993/94	7	10	0	151	40	15.10	-	-	331	7		47.28	2-14	-	-	-	-
	All	1987	1993/94	8	11	0	177	40	17.70	-	-	338	9		37.55	2-7	-	-	-	-
R.C.Somervell	Auck	1911/12	1921/22	8	13	1	270	74*	22.50	-	2	165	3		55.00	1-21	-	-	2	-
	All	1911/12	1921/22	9	15	1	270	74*	19.28	-	2	179	3		59.66	1-21	-	-	2	-
W.E.R.Somerville	Otago	2004/05	2007/08	4	5	2	53	20*	17.66	-	-	264	7		37.71	3-26	-	-	1	-
T.R.Sonntag	Otago	1883/84		1	1	0	2	2	2.00	-	-								-	-
B.J.Sorenson	Auck	1955/56	1957/58	12	20	3	221	48	13.00	-	-								10	6
R.G.Sorenson	Auck	1943/44		2	3	1	58	29	29.00	-	-	190	6		31.66	3-43	-	-	2	-
J.Souter	Cant	1871/72	1873/74	5	9	1	9	4	2.25	-	-	59	5		11.80	4-29	-	-	-	-
T.R.Southall	Well	1912/13	1914/15	7	11	3	28	6*	3.50	-	-	509	24		21.20	7-32	3	-	3	-
T.G.Southee	ND	2006/07	2009/10	18	21	3	234	75*	13.00	-	1	1700	68		25.00	8-27	3	-	4	-
	All	2006/07	2009/10	31	39	6	476	77*	14.42	-	2	3103	106		29.27	8-27	3	-	7	-
R.J.Sowden	Cant	1972/73		1	2	0	34	23	17.00	-	-	72	1		72.00	1-54	-	-	-	-
C.R.Spackman	HB	1913/14	1919/20	3	6	1	29	12*	5.80	-	-								2	-
L.C.Sparks	CD	1967/68	1970/71	9	14	4	109	21	10.90	-	-	445	18		24.72	6-46	1	-	4	-
J.T.Sparling	Auck	1956/57	1970/71	73	123	17	2977	105	28.08	2	20	5327	248		21.47	7-49	17	3	57	-
	All	1956/57	1970/71	127	215	26	4606	105	24.37	2	27	7223	318		22.71	7-49	17	3	86	-
C.M.Spearman	Auck	1993/94	1994/95	13	24	2	654	147	31.14	1	3								11	-
	CD	1996/97	2003/04	44	76	3	3033	144	41.54	8	18	50	1		50.00	1-37	-	-	45	-
	All	1993/94	2009	201	360	16	13021	341	37.85	30	56	55	1		55.00	1-37	-	-	197	-
J.M.Speed	Nel	1874/75		1	2	0	1	1	1.00	-	-								-	-
	Well	1877/78	1879/80	3	6	0	32	15	5.33	-	-								-	-
	All	1874/75	1879/80	4	8	1	33	15	4.71	-	-								-	-
S.R.Speed	Auck	1962/63	1970/71	28	37	7	711	88	23.70	-	3								50	10
	All	1962/63	1970/71	33	44	8	904	88	25.11	-	4								61	12
M.P.Speight	Well	1989/90	1992/93	4	8	1	287	65*	41.00	-	2								4	-
	All	1986	2001	193	323	31	9225	184	31.59	13	48	32	2		16.00	1-2	-	-	292	5
D.V.Spence	CD	1955/56	1961/62	11	18	1	272	61	16.00	-	1	588	14		42.00	5-38	1	-	6	-
J.E.Spice	ND	1993/94	1996/97	5	6	1	77	30*	15.40	-	-	336	3		112.00	2-24	-	-	3	-
J.Spivey	HB	1884/85	1885/86	2	3	0	8	6	2.66	-	-	9	0		-	-	-	-	-	1

		First	Last	M	I	NO	Runs	HS	Avg	100	50	Runs	Wkts	OW	Avg	Best	5i	10m	ct	st
B.T.Spragg	ND	1987/88	1988/89	4	6	0	84	47	14.00	-	-	141	5		28.20	3-28	-	-	3	
R.D.Spraggon	Otago	1894/95	1896/97	6	11	2	125	40*	13.88	-	-	103	6		17.16	5-21	1	-	3	1
J.P.Spring	Otago	1877/78	1884/85	8	16	2	127	18	9.07	-	-								1	
L.R.Spring	Auck	1936/37		3	3	0	48	30	16.00	-	-								-	
C.S.Stafford	Auck	1884/85		3	6	0	128	63	21.33	-	1								2	
G.Staite	HB	1895/96	1897/98	6	12	1	154	54	14.00	-	1								2	
J.A.Standidge	Well	1940/41		1	2	1	29	25	14.50	-	-								3	
P.H.Standidge	Well	1957/58		4	7	0	95	38	13.57	-	-								-	
F.W.Stanley	Otago	1950/51	1953/54	13	21	6	104	28	6.93	-	-	1108	46		24.08	5-25	3	-	8	
A.Staples	Well	1901/02	1903/04	4	8	1	221	78	31.57	-	2	81	5		16.20	3-48	-	-	2	
D.W.Stark	Cant	1953/54		3	4	0	15	11	3.75	-	-	88	2		44.00	2-59	-	-	-	
D.W.Stead	Cant	1969/70	1985/86	77	133	11	3169	193*	25.97	1	20	5009	167		29.99	7-99	6	-	2	
G.R.Stead	All	1968/69	1985/86	80	139	11	3205	193*	25.03	-	20	5063	170		29.78	7-99	6	-	67	
H.K.C.Steele	All	1993/94	2005/06	88	146	10	4410	190	32.42	10	20	475	8		59.37	4-58	-	-	69	
	Auck	1991/92	2005/06	101	165	10	4984	190	32.15	10	24	587	9		65.22	4-58	-	-	37	
	All	1974/75		5	8	1	48	24*	6.85	-	-	374	14		26.71	4-71	-	-	46	
W.I.Stemson		1970	1974/75	26	40	4	711	103*	19.75	-	3	1276	30		42.53	4-71	-	-	3	
M.J.Stephens	Auck	1889/90	1908/09	30	56	4	696	76	13.38	-	2	1764	81		21.77	7-60	3	-	13	
	All	1889/90	1908/09	31	58	4	702	76	13.00	-	2	1880	87		21.60	7-60	3	-	14	
	Auck	1990/91		2	3	2	7	5*	-	-	-	247	8		30.87	3-55	-	-	14	
	ND	1993/94		4	7	2	72	49*	14.40	-	-	394	14		28.14	5-101	1	-	14	
	All	1990/91	1993/94	7	9	2	79	49*	15.80	-	-	641	22		29.13	5-101	1	-	2	
W.B.Stephens	Auck	1899/00	1900/01	5	9	1	37	14	4.62	-	-	444	23		19.30	7-46	1	-	3	
L.Stephen-Smith	Auck	1931/32		2	3	0	26	9*	8.66	-	-								2	1
F.C.Stephenson	Otago	1890/91		1	2	0	20	16	10.00	-	-	0	0		-	-	-	-	-	
C.J.Stevens	Well	1891/92	1904/05	10	18	4	118	34	8.42	-	-	650	27		24.07	7-58	3	-	9	
E.C.J.Stevens	Cant	1895/96	1896/97	3	6	1	17	7	3.40	-	-	35	0		-	-	-	-	2	
G.R.Stevens	All	1890/91	1904/05	14	26	5	155	34	7.38	-	-	685	27		25.37	7-58	3	-	11	
J.Stevens	Cant	1966/67	1967/68	3	6	0	28	13	4.66	-	-								1	
J.A.M.Stevens	Cant	1863/64	1883/84	13	21	1	147	35	7.35	-	-	190	2		95.00	2-128	-	-	2	
G.R.Stewart	HB	1911/12	1920/21	5	9	1	133	37	16.62	-	1	47	0		-	-	-	-	2	
J.A.M.Stewart	HB	1919/20		2	4	0	56	38	14.00	-	-	94	12		7.83	5-17	1	-	1	
B.A.Stewart	Cant	1863/64	1865/66	3	6	1	29	12	5.80	-	-	160	6		26.66	3-40	-	-	3	
G.W.Stewart	CD	1972/73		1	2	0	4	4	2.00	-	-								-	
R.D.Stewart	ND	1968/69		1	2	0	23	12	11.50	-	-								1	
	CD	1963/64	1968/69	6	9	0	78	21	8.66	-	-								2	
	All	1963/64		10	16	0	102	63	20.40	-	1								3	
R.N.Stewart	Otago	1973/74	1977/78	17	29	2	205	63	12.81	-	1	7	0		-	-	-	-	11	
S.L.Stewart	Cant	2001/02	2009/10	64	113	10	451	73	16.70	-	2	344	4		86.00	2-52	-	-	22	
A.J.P.Stimpson	ND	1974/75	1978/79	24	30	6	3870	227*	37.57	7	22	2023	61		33.16	6-46	3	-	7	
D.A.Stirling	CD	1981/82	1987/88	42	55	19	231	36	9.62	-	-	3401	113		30.09	6-75	4	-	14	
	Well	1988/89	1991/92	14	19	3	775	51*	21.52	-	1	1153	27		42.70	4-66	-	-	8	
	All	1981/82	1991/92	84	106	30	394	70	24.62	-	3	6948	206		33.72	6-75	5	-	27	
D.N.Stokes	Cant	1937/38	1938/39	4	8	0	1651	75	21.72	-	5								-	
C.E.Stone	Auck	1894/95	1895/96	2	2	0	226	59	28.25	-	3	62	3		20.66	2-13	-	-	1	

		First	Last	M	I	NO	Runs	HS	Avg	100	50	Runs	Wkts	OW	Avg	Best	5i	10m	ct	st
P.D.Stone	ND	1961/62	1968/69	23	42	2	705	80	17.62	-	4	688	32		21.50	4-42	-	-	11	
L.W.Stott	Auck	1969/70	1983/84	63	68	19	591	50*	12.06	-	1	5341	214		24.95	6-68	8	-	36	
P.A.Stoyanoff	All	1980/81		1			4	4	4.00			15	0		-	-	-	-	-	
W.W.Strang	Otago	1929/30		1	2	0	37	32	18.50										1	
C.Strange	Cant	1884/85		2	2	0	22	13	11.00										-	
R.B.Strange	Cant	1901/02	1903/04	8	15	1	308	52	22.00	-	1	37	1		37.00	1-0	-	-	2	
	All	1901/02	1903/04	9	17	1	320	52	20.00	-	1	99	5		19.80	2-21	-	-	2	
G.H.Stringer	Cant	1933/34		2	4	0	69	29	17.25			3	0		-	-	-	-	1	
	Well	1943/44		2	4	0	90	47	22.50										-	
H.D.Stronach	All	1933/34	1943/44	4	8	0	159	47	19.87	-	1	3	0		-	-	-	-	1	
A.Stubbs	Otago	1892/93	1894/95	6	8	1	31	10	4.42										-	
E.C.Studholme	HB	1887/88		1	2	0	13	11	6.50										2	
W.P.Studholme	Cant	1891/92		1	2	1	4	2*	4.00										1	
S.B.Styris	Cant	1887/88	1888/89	2	3	0	25	15	8.33	-	-	33	2		16.50	2-22	-	-	2	
	ND	1994/95	2004/05	42	70	10	1773	212*	29.55	2	8	2667	106		25.16	6-32	6	-	28	
	Auck	2005/06	2009/10	10	15	1	532	112	38.00	-	4	138	2		69.00	2-51	-	-	12	
	All	1994/95	2009/10	126	210	19	5964	212*	31.22	10	29	6353	203		31.29	6-32	9	1	100	
M.L.Su'a	ND	1988/89	1989/90	5	5	1	72	30	18.00	-	-	380	7		54.28	2-46	-	-	2	
	Auck	1990/91	1994/95	23	27	7	385	52*	19.25	-	1	1995	75		26.60	6-56	5	-	12	
	All	1988/89	1994/95	51	60	15	828	56	18.40	-	2	4794	141		34.00	6-56	6	-	45	
G.P.Sulzberger	CD	1995/96	2004/05	74	120	12	3505	159	32.45	8	16	4458	115		38.76	6-54	4	-	56	
	All	1995/96	2004/05	83	135	12	3836	159	31.18	8	17	5175	147		35.20	6-54	4	-	56	
K.J.Sunderland	Auck	1990/91		4	2	1	6	6*	-	-	-	344	15		22.93	4-42	-	-	1	
B.Sutcliffe	Auck	1941/42	1948/49	13	21	1	1243	146	62.15	4	7	339	9		37.66	2-25	-	-	17	
	Otago	1946/47	1961/62	60	110	8	6028	385	59.09	17	26	982	37		26.54	5-19	2	-	41	
	ND	1962/63	1965/66	22	39	6	1052	77*	31.87	-	10	165	2		82.50	1-8	-	-	14	
	All	1941/42	1965/66	233	407	39	17447	385	47.41	44	83	3273	86		38.05	5-19	2	-	160	1
H.Sutcliffe	Otago	1875/76		1			2	2	1.00										-	
T.D.Sutherland	Otago	1979/80		5	8	1	68	28*	9.71										3	
R.E.Sutton	Auck	1958/59	1973/74	54	74	31	498	39	11.58	-	-	3364	152		22.13	7-64	6	-	14	
	All	1958/59	1973/74	56	76	31	516	39	11.46	-	-	3497	156		22.41	7-64	6	-	14	
T.S.Sweet	Auck	1873/74	1876/77	3	6	1	34	13	6.80			141	21		6.71	5-21	2	-	4	
	Cant	1874/75	1876/77	3	5	0	51	20	10.20			183	27		6.77	7-34	3	1	2	
	All	1873/74	1876/77	6	11	1	85	20	8.50			324	48		6.75	7-34	5	1	6	
G.Syme	Tara	1891/92	1897/98	5	7	0	28	21	4.00										2	
J.R.Syme	All	1965/66	1966/67	2	4	1	21	11	7.00	-	-	231	10		23.10	4-57	-	-	1	
I.A.H.Symes	Well	1934/35	1935/36	2	3	1	15	13*	-	-	-	168	4		42.00	1-25	-	-	3	
A.E.Symonds	Otago	1926/27		1	2	0	5	5	5.00										1	
J.G.Taiaroa	HB	1891/92	1898/99	8	14	4	140	32*	14.00	-	-	43	1		43.00	1-9	-	-	2	
M.P.Taiaroa	CD	2007/08		1	1	0	1	1	1.00										-	
A.R.Tait	ND	1994/95	2000/01	26	33	5	703	77	25.10	-	4	2288	115		19.89	9-48	7	1	8	
	All	1994/95	2000/01	32	42	8	888	77	26.11	-	4	2699	134		20.14	9-48	8	1	11	
W.C.Tait	Otago	1872/73	1874/75	3	5	1	27	21*	6.75			72	6		12.00	4-32	-	-	-	
G.L.Talbot	Cant	1929/30		1		0						28	3		9.33	2-24	-	-	1	

Name	Team	First	Last	M	I	NO	Runs	HS	Avg	100	50	Runs	Wkts	OW	Avg	Best	5i	10m	ct	st
R.O.Talbot	Cant	1922/23	1932/33	22	39	1	1028	117	27.05	3	5	975	33		29.54	5-106	1		14	
	Otago	1933/34	1935/36	4	8	0	151	69	18.87		1	143	4		35.75	2-71			1	
	All	1922/23	1935/36	51	86	7	1946	117	24.63	3	10	2005	54		37.12	5-106	1		31	
E.D.Tanner	HB	1883/84	1885/86	2	4	0	16	8	4.00			59	3		19.66	3-42			2	
C.B.Tapley	Sland	1914/15	1918/19	3	6	0	24	15	4.00											
H.E.Tapping	Auck	1950/51	1952/53	8	14	4	106	38*	10.60			474	20		23.70	4-21			4	
J.W.Tarleton	Well	1884/85		1	2	0	16	8	8.00											
G.M.Tarr	ND	1957/58	1958/59	8	14	1	109	38	8.38										5	
D.R.Tarrant	CD	1954/55	1957/58	9	14	8	20	5	3.33			10	1		10.00	1-0			7	
H.J.Tattersall	Auck	1912/13	1913/14	2	4	2	37	22	18.50			699	28		24.96	4-40			3	4
	Well	1922/23	1927/28	4	7	1	57	24	9.50										3	1
	All	1912/13	1927/28	6	11	3	94	24	11.75										6	5
A.R.Taylor	Well	1963/64	1965/66	12	11	2	115	50	12.77		1	971	44		22.06	6-47	2		11	
	All	1962/63	1965/66	13	13	2	131	50	11.90		1	1056	52		20.30	6-47	3		11	
B.R.Taylor	Cant	1964/65	1969/70	20	31	5	890	82*	34.23	2	5	1454	69		21.07	5-49	3		9	
	Well	1970/71	1979/80	35	54	6	1237	173	25.77	4	5	2291	100		22.91	6-37	5		20	
	All	1963/64	1979/80	141	210	25	4579	173	24.75	4	17	10605	422		25.13	7-74	15		66	
D.D.Taylor	Auck	1946/47	1960/61	43	75	1	1889	143	25.52	2	12	816	21		38.85	2-2			33	
	All	1946/47	1960/61	95	168	6	3772	143	23.28	7	22	1063	32		33.21	4-24			62	
F.J.Taylor	Well	1889/90	1890/91	2	4	1	17	12	5.66			47	2		23.50	1-11			2	
F.A.Taylor	Auck	1909/10	1913/14	6	9	3	92	21	15.33			353	16		22.06	4-45			4	
G.W.Taylor	ND	1973/74	1974/75	7	14	0	260	62	18.57		1								2	
H.M.Taylor	Cant	1919/20	1920/21	3	5	1	40	32	10.00										6	2
J.S.Taylor	Well	1927/28		1	2	0	62	61	31.00			18	0						2	
	All	1911/12	1927/28	3	5	1	108	61	27.00		1	18	0							
K.Taylor	Auck	1963/64		5	10	1	56	17	6.22			28	0						1	
	All	1953	1968	313	524	36	13053	203*	26.74	16	68	3763	131		28.72	6-75	1		150	
K.G.W.Taylor	Cant	1983/84		1	1	0	1	1	1.00			37	1		37.00	1-17				
L.G.Taylor	Auck	1910/11	1917/18	11	20	1	313	92	16.47		2	328	11		29.81	4-35			6	
	All	1910/11	1917/18	14	26	1	419	92	16.76		2	328	11		29.81	4-35			9	
L.R.P.L.Taylor	CD	2002/03	2009/10	35	55	1	2205	217	40.83	4	13	312	4		78.00	2-34			33	
	All	2002/03	2009/10	71	120	3	4774	217	40.80	10	26	330	4		82.50	2-34			89	
R.Taylor	Cant	1863/64	1868/69	2	3	1	5	4	2.50			71	9		7.88	6-21	1		4	
A.E.Tennant	Cant	1863/64	1865/66	3	6	0	31	24	5.16			15	2		7.50	2-7				
R.C.Tennent	Nel	1873/74		2	2	0	24	13	12.00										2	
J.C.Testro	Auck	1882/83	1886/87	9	15	1	149	34	10.64			18	0						2	
I.J.Therkleson	Well	1966/67	1973/74	39	58	12	1004	71	21.82		2								93	7
C.H.Thiele	Cant	1980/81	1985/86	34	46	21	260	49	10.40			2882	107		26.93	6-45	3		11	
A.W.Thomas	Cant	1911/12	1922/23	19	32	4	801	83*	28.60		6	932	35		26.62	8-99	1		11	
B.D.Thomas	Cant	1980/81		1	1	0	74	74	74.00											
M.Thomas	Well	1937/38		1	2	0	14	13	7.00										1	
R.I.Thomas	CD	1975/76	1977/78	16	25	4	137	24	6.52			1009	38		26.55	4-31			9	
W.E.Thomas	CD	1966/67		1	2	0	12	10	6.00											
E.P.Thompson	CD	2000/01	2009/10	51	74	9	1674	126	25.75	3	7	5140	171		30.05	7-55	6	1	17	
	All	2000/01	2009/10	52	75	9	1734	126	26.27	3	8	5310	177		30.00	7-55	6	1	18	

Name	Team	First	Last	M	I	NO	Runs	HS	Avg	100	50	Runs	Wkts	OW	Avg	Best	5i	10m	ct	st
G.J.Thompson	Auck	1911/12		3	6	1	114	54	22.80	-	1	281	22		12.77	7-35	2	-	4	-
H.F.Thompson	All	1897	1922	352	606	60	12018	131*	22.01	9	54	30058	1591		18.89	9-64	147	40	252	-
N.R.Thompson	HB	1885/86		1	2	1	0	0*	0.00	-	-								-	-
G.B.Thomson	Otago	1956/57	1962/63	17	31	5	418	100*	16.07	1	-								5	-
	All	1956/57	1962/63	18	33	5	420	100*	15.00	1	-								5	-
	Otago	1973/74	1980/81	39	54	20	308	34*	9.05	-	-	2576	88		29.27	6-41	21	1	21	-
	All	1973/74	1980/81	47	59	22	340	34*	9.18	-	-	3180	110		28.90	6-41	23	1	23	-
J.C.Thomson	Otago	1873/74		2	3	0	21	10	7.00	-	-								3	-
J.C.A.Thomson	Well	1953/54		5	10	0	73	22	7.30	-	-								2	-
K.Thomson	Cant	1959/60	1973/74	59	104	11	2644	136*	28.43	5	11	412	8		51.50	4-93	-	-	32	-
	All	1959/60	1973/74	71	125	14	3134	136*	28.23	5	15	206	4		51.50	1-14	-	-	35	-
S.A.Thomson	ND	1987/88	1996/97	51	80	20	2530	167	42.16	5	14	246	5		49.20	1-9	-	-	21	-
	All	1987/88	1996/97	90	148	38	4209	167	38.26	6	25	2118	62		34.16	3-1	-	-	37	-
W.A.Thomson	Cant	1973/74		1	1	0	58	55	29.00	-	1	4625	116		39.87	5-49	2	-	-	-
L.D.A.Thorn	All	1964/65	1973/74	2	4	0	79	55	19.75	-	1								1	-
D.J.Tidmarsh	Cant	1978/79	1979/80	7	13	0	216	41	16.61	-	1								1	-
J.T.Tilyard	ND	1992/93		3	3	0	1	1	0.33	-	-	15	0		-	-	-	-	-	-
E.W.T.Tindill	Well	1907/08		1	2	0	40	31	20.00	-	-								-	-
	Well	1932/33	1949/50	39	73	5	2442	149	35.91	6	10								59	15
	All	1932/33	1949/50	69	116	13	3127	149	30.35	6	12								96	33
P.Tindill	Well	1965/66		1	2	1	14	14*	14.00	-	-								1	2
G.R.Todd	CD	2000/01	2002/03	10	18	5	289	61*	22.23	-	2	281	6		46.83	2-34	-	-	4	-
	Otago	2004/05	2009/10	45	79	10	2774	165	40.20	4	16	931	13		71.61	2-26	-	-	18	-
	All	2000/01	2009/10	55	97	15	3063	165	37.35	4	18	1212	19		63.78	2-26	-	-	22	-
K.W.M.Todd	Auck	2004/05	2007/08	5	8	0	129	84	16.12	-	1								2	-
A.S.Tonks	Tara	1891/92		1	2	1	17	16*	17.00	-	-								-	-
C.D.G.Toomey	Otago	1939/40	1945/46	7	14	0	251	51	17.92	-	1	37	1		37.00	1-37	-	-	4	-
	All	1939/40	1945/46	8	16	0	257	51	16.06	-	1	37	1		37.00	1-37	-	-	4	-
F.J.Toomey	Otago	1934/35	1935/36	3	6	1	24	7	4.80	-	-								4	-
J.P.Topp	Well	1978/79		1	2	2	4	4*	-	-	-								1	-
W.Torkington	HB	1904/05		1	2	1	14	14	14.00	-	-	19	0		-	-	-	-	-	-
R.C.Torrance	Otago	1905/06	1927/28	42	78	17	684	43	11.21	-	1	4354	176		24.73	7-21	13	4	17	-
B.Totman	Auck	1897/98		1	2	0	3	2	1.50	-	-								2	-
H.P.L.Tottenham		see H.P.L.Gaussen																		
E.R.Tovey	Auck	1960/61	1963/64	12	20	4	220	62	13.75	-	1	701	40		17.52	7-25	5	1	35	6
	Auck	1957/58	1963/64	13	21	4	238	62	14.00	-	1	22984	1088		21.12	8-26	51	16	35	7
L.F.Townsend	Auck	1934/35	1935/36	7	11	3	343	90*	42.87	-	3								6	-
	All	1922	1939	493	786	75	19555	233	27.50	22	102	2280	74		30.81	6-39	1	-	241	-
M.H.Toynbee	CD	1977/78	1984/85	53	88	13	1859	100	24.78	1	7	2334	77		30.31	6-39	1	-	38	-
	All	1977/78	1984/85	56	92	13	1943	100	24.59	1	7	1226	40		30.65	4-65	1	-	39	-
S.R.Tracy	Auck	1982/83	1984/85	14	13	4	69	33	7.66	-	-	466	13		35.84	5-19	1	-	6	-
	Cant	1985/86		6	10	1	27	7	3.00	-	-	361	14		25.78	5-28	1	-	1	-
	Otago	1990/91		5	7	3	23	12*	5.75	-	-								-	-
	All	1982/83	1990/91	30	34	8	124	33	4.76	-	-	2316	81		28.59	5-19	1	-	7	-
K.Treiber	ND	1979/80	1987/88	26	28	11	172	31	10.11	-	-	2095	72		29.09	7-42	3	-	8	-
	All	1979/80	1987/88	27	29	12	174	31	10.23	-	-	2161	73		29.60	7-42	3	-	8	-

		First	Last	M	I	NO	Runs	HS	Avg	100	50	Runs	Wkts	OW	Avg	Best	5i	10m	ct	st
M.F.Tremlett	CD	1951/52	1960	2	3	0	76	39	25.33	-	-	40	0		30.70	8-31	1	-	2	-
C.Treweek	All	1947		389	681	49	16038	185	25.37	16	83	10778	351		8.00	3-17	11	-	257	-
W.Tricklebank	Cant	1889/90	1894/95	2	3	0	24	0	0.00	-	-	24	3		8.00	3-17	-	-	1	-
	Well	1934/35	1936/37	5	8	3	129	47	25.80	-	-	361	8		45.12	2-19	-	-	3	-
D.G.Trist	All	1934/35	1936/37	6	10	3	136	47	19.42	-	-	443	12		36.91	3-33	-	-	5	-
	Cant	1969/70	1977/78	18	26	4	216	41*	9.81	-	-	1191	45		26.46	5-31	1	-	11	-
A.E.Trott	All	1968/69	1977/78	24	33	6	267	41*	9.88	-	2	1610	57		28.24	5-31	1	-	13	-
	HB	1901/02		5	6	2	261	80*	65.25	-	-	350	23		15.21	7-58	3	1	2	-
I.J.L.Trott	All	1892/93	1911	375	602	53	10696	164	19.48	8	44	35318	1674		21.09	10-42	131	41	452	-
	Otago	2005/06	2010	4	8	1	275	120	39.28	-	1	165	8		20.62	4-35	-	-	3	-
G.B.Troup	All	2000/01		153	257	31	10183	226	45.05	23	51	2471	56		44.12	7-39	1	-	148	-
	Auck	1974/75	1986/87	72	82	25	775	60*	13.59	-	3	5213	200		26.06	6-48	4	1	31	-
P.B.Truscott	All	1974/75	1986/87	100	115	39	925	60*	12.17	-	3	7541	272		27.72	6-48	5	-	39	-
	Cant	1961/62		3	6	0	88	38	14.66	-	-								1	-
K.H.Tucker	Well	1964/65	1965/66	11	21	0	507	77	24.14	-	4	92	2		46.00	2-60	-	-	7	-
	All	1961/62	1965/66	18	35	0	904	165	25.82	1	4	97	2		48.50	2-60	-	-	10	-
S.J.Tucker	Well	1895/96	1919/20	35	62	8	1257	86	23.27	-	7	1649	94		17.54	7-31	7	2	21	-
W.C.Tucker	All	1895/96	1919/20	40	72	8	1460	86	22.81	-	9	1717	97		17.70	7-31	7	2	24	-
B.J.Tuckwell	Well	1892/93	1896/97	4	8	1	109	37	15.57	-	-								1	-
	Tara	1891/92		1	2	0	1	1	0.50	-	-								-	-
D.R.Tuffey	Otago	1912/13	1914/15	2	3	1	181	52	22.62	-	1	45	2		22.50	1-21	-	-	2	-
	Well	1917/18		1	3	1	3	2	1.00	-	-								4	-
	All	1902/03	1917/18	14	26	4	468	93*	18.72	-	3	60	2		30.00	1-21	-	-	12	-
M.J.Tugaga	ND	1996/97	2006/07	33	44	10	451	89*	13.26	-	1	2843	117		24.29	7-12	5	1	11	-
C.L.Tuke	Auck	2008/09	2009/10	9	6	1	158	56	31.60	-	2	685	29		23.62	6-33	1	-	4	-
H.L.Tuke	All	1996/97	2009/10	84	100	25	1232	89*	16.42	-	6	7274	280		25.97	7-12	10	1	37	-
A.J.Turnbull	Well	2008/09	2009/10	11	17	5	204	103	17.00	1	-	1065	26		40.96	5-77	1	-	3	-
	HB	1884/85		1	2	1	10	9	10.00	-	-								1	-
	HB	1904/05		1	2	0	7	4*	7.00	-	-								-	-
J.A.Turnbull	Otago	1896/97		1	2	0	1		0.50	-	-								-	-
P.J.Turnbull	Auck	1955/56	1962/63	6	9	0	46	20	5.11	-	-	624	21		29.71	7-54	2	-	2	-
A.D.Turner	ND	1959/60		2	4	0	32	19	8.00	-	-	87	1		87.00	1-68	-	-	2	-
B.A.Turner	All	1955/56	1962/63	8	13	0	78	20	6.00	-	-	711	22		32.31	7-54	2	-	4	-
G.A.Turner	Otago	1884/85		1	2	1	1	1	0.50	-	-	67	3		22.33	3-30	-	-	-	-
G.M.Turner	Well	2001/02	2004/05	8	7	1	42	16	7.00	-	-	635	17		37.35	5-66	1	-	1	-
	CD	1951/52	1955/56	15	27	2	490	66	19.60	-	3								24	-
	Cant	1878/79	1879/80	2	2	1	16	16	16.00	-	-								2	-
N.M.Turner	Otago	1964/65	1982/83	59	109	14	4439	186*	46.72	13	18	51	5		10.20	3-16	-	-	56	-
	ND	1976/77		7	12	2	672	177*	67.20	1	5	45	0						8	-
	All	1964/65	1982/83	455	792	101	34346	311*	49.70	103	148	189	5		37.80	3-18	-	-	409	-
G.K.Turton	Otago	2006/07		3	4	1	53	27*	26.50	-	-	241	7		34.42	3-57	-	-	1	-
C.H.Twist	Auck	2009/10		1	1	0	0	0	0.00	-	-	97	2		48.50	2-66	-	-	-	-
	All	2006/07	2009/10	4	5	1	53	27*	17.66	-	-	338	9		37.55	3-57	-	-	1	-
	Otago	1863/64	1871/72	6	10	0	79	28	8.77	-	-								-	-
	Well	1882/83	1883/84	4	7	1	91	35	15.16	-	-								-	-

231

		First	Last	M	I	NO	Runs	HS	Avg	100	50	Runs	Wkts	OW	Avg	Best	5i	10m	ct	st
R.G.Twose	ND	1989/90	1993/94	8	15	2	397	61	30.53	-	3	144	1		144.00	1-35	-	-	5	-
	CD	1991/92	2000/01	25	44	4	1484	154	37.10	3	7	1092	40		27.30	4-42	-	-	14	-
	Well	1994/95		27	45	4	1735	163*	45.65	5	9	421	17		24.76	4-24	-	-	17	-
J.C.Tynan	All	1989		178	300	35	9802	277*	36.98	18	53	4237	133		31.85	6-28	2	-	96	-
	Well	1951/52	1953/54	4	7	0	80	29	11.42	-	-	48	2		24.00	1-11	-	-	2	-
N.M.Uluiviti	Auck	1954/55		4	8	2	141	48*	23.50	-	-	157	2		78.50	1-18	-	-	6	-
	All	1953/54	1954/55	8	16	3	210	48*	16.15	-	-	183	3		61.00	1-18	-	-	11	-
H.Unka	ND	1968/69	1975/76	25	31	2	90	16*	6.42	-	-	1793	46		38.97	6-67	3	-	5	-
P.D.Unwin	CD	1986/87	1992/93	29	33	11	324	38	14.72	-	-	2425	54		44.90	6-42	1	-	29	-
	Cant	1993/94		4	5	1	30	18	7.50	-	-	302	6		50.33	2-94	-	-	3	-
E.F.Upham	All	1986/87	1993/94	34	39	13	358	38	13.76	-	-	2843	65		43.73	6-42	1	-	32	-
	Well	1892/93	1909/10	40	62	13	598	52	12.20	-	2	3393	226		15.01	7-24	17	1	35	-
	All	1892/93	1909/10	49	80	20	716	52	11.93	-	2	4414	264		16.71	7-24	19	1	37	-
J.H.W.Uru	Cant	1893/94	1894/95	2	2	0	2	2	1.00	-	-	102	9		11.33	5-43	-	-	4	-
K.F.M.Utley	Otago	1933/34	1938/39	19	38	0	1316	145	36.55	3	8						-	-	14	-
	Cant	1940/41		12	21	2	529	78	26.45	-	3						-	-	3	-
	Well	1951/52	1945/46	2	4	0	55	21	13.75	-	-	4	0				-	-	-	-
	All	1933/34	1951/52	37	69	3	2053	145	31.10	3	12	4	0				-	-	20	-
T.Vaikvee	Well	1973/74	1975/76	11	13	4	157	41*	17.44	-	-	477	14		34.07	4-41	-	-	4	-
W.H.T.C.P.Vallange	Otago	1886/87		1	2	1	30	21	15.00	-	-						-	-	1	-
L.V.van Beek	Cant	2009/10		2	2	0	11	11	11.00	-	-	53	1		53.00	1-30	-	-	-	-
R.A.Vance	Well	1947/48	1961/62	41	71	4	1510	109	21.57	-	7	9	3		3.00	2-8	-	-	34	4
R.H.Vance	Well	1976/77	1990/91	119	205	18	6440	254*	34.43	12	34	231	4		57.75	2-18	-	-	147	4
	All	1976/77	1990/91	135	230	18	6955	254*	32.80	12	36	232	4		58.00	2-18	-	-	150	5
C.F.K.van Wyk	Cant	2006/07	2009/10	35	52	13	1716	178*	44.00	2	9						-	-	101	13
	All	2000/01	2009/10	83	125	26	3466	178*	35.01	4	18	9	1		9.00	1-7	-	-	249	-
J.T.C.Vaughan	Auck	1989/90	1996/97	48	81	14	2269	127	33.86	2	12	2171	99		21.92	8-27	3	3	50	-
	All	1989/90		70	120	20	3159	127	31.59	2	16	3440	132		26.06	8-27	3	3	66	-
D.J.Vear	Otago	1959/60	1960/61	3	4	1	49	22	16.33	-	-	94	1		94.00	1-19	-	-	2	-
J.R.Veitch	Otago	1957/58	1963/64	13	26	0	332	43	12.76	-	-						-	-	8	-
	Cant	1964/65		5	7	0	132	44	18.85	-	-						-	-	1	-
	All	1957/58	1964/65	20	37	0	517	44	13.97	-	-	31	0				-	-	10	-
S.W.Veitch	ND	1960/61	1966/67	7	14	1	182	49*	14.00	-	-	31	0				-	-	1	-
P.J.Verhoek	CD	1978/79	1980/81	7	13	1	171	38	14.25	-	-						-	-	5	-
M.J.Vermeulen	Cant	2009/10		1	2	0	10	10*	-	-	-						-	-	-	-
E.S.Vernon	Otago	1878/79	1879/80	2	4	0	22	10	5.50	-	-	132	4		33.00	2-65	-	-	2	-
J.W.Vernon	CD	1961/62		2	2	0	2	2	1.00	-	-	12	0				-	-	10	-
R.A.Verry	Well	1985/86	1992/93	15	26	4	590	132	26.81	1	3	14	0				-	-	7	-
D.L.Vettori	ND	1996/97	2006/07	14	20	5	475	120	31.66	1	2	1161	46		25.23	5-22	4	-	10	-
	All	1996/97	2009/10	152	220	31	5809	140	30.73	8	32	15920	499		31.90	7-87	28	3	79	-
M.Vijay	CD	2008/09		1	2	0	96	93	48.00	-	-	21	0				-	-	1	-
L.Vincent	All	2006/07	2010	38	61	2	3033	243	51.40	7	14	118	1		118.00	1-16	-	-	39	-
	Auck	1997/98	2006/07	40	61	5	2132	185*	38.07	4	12	367	8		45.87	2-37	-	-	61	-
	All	1997/98	2008	92	151	11	4922	224	35.15	10	29	527	10		52.70	2-37	-	-	109	-
R.B.Vincent	Well	1886/87		1	2	1	9	9	4.50	-	-	79	4		19.75	3-35	-	-	1	-
R.M.Virtue	Well	1891/92		1	1	0	2	2	2.00	-	-						-	-	-	-

Name	Team	First	Last	M	I	NO	Runs	HS	Avg	100	50	Runs	Wkts	OW	Avg	Best	5i	10m	ct	st
P.J.Visser	CD	1983/84	1986/87	19	17	5	11	8	0.91	-	-	1531	50	-	30.62	7-40	2	-	11	-
G.E.Vivian	Auck	1966/67	1978/79	58	98	16	2324	111*	28.34	2	13	1161	36	-	32.25	5-59	1	-	35	-
G.E.Vivian	All	1964/65	1978/79	88	140	25	3259	137*	28.33	3	17	2128	56	-	38.00	5-59	1	-	41	-
H.G.Vivian	Auck	1930/31	1938/39	25	43	3	1461	165	36.52	2	9	2055	90	-	22.83	6-49	8	2	26	-
H.G.Vivian	All	1930/31	1938/39	85	143	15	4443	165	34.71	6	31	6165	223	-	27.64	6-49	12	2	71	-
L.G.Vivian	HB	1912/13		1	1	0	33	28	16.50	-	-	87	2	-	43.50	2-57	-	-	2	-
T.G.Vogel	Well	1980/81	1983/84	4	2	0	1	1	13.40	-	-	266	4	-	66.50	1-7	-	-	-	-
W.N.Vorrath	Otago	1927/28	1929/30	6	11	1	172	41	19.11	-	-								3	-
J.S.Waddingham	Auck	1953/54	1959/60	5	10	2	63	103*	7.00	1	-								2	-
K.J.Wadsworth	CD	1968/69	1971/72	15	23	2	485	37	23.09	-	-								26	5
K.J.Wadsworth	Cant	1972/73	1975/76	19	29	2	668	79	24.74	-	4								54	3
K.J.Wadsworth	All	1968/69	1975/76	118	166	23	3664	117	25.62	2	19								264	27
N.Wagner	Otago	2008/09	2009/10	15	21	1	393	70	19.65	-	1	1747	49	-	35.65	4-62	-	-	5	-
N.Wagner	All	2005/06	2009/10	35	42	9	556	70	16.84	-	1	3376	138	-	24.46	5-28	4	-	8	-
W.G.Wagstaffe	Well	1913/14		4	8	1	77	17	11.00	-	-								5	-
S.J.Waide	Otago	2001/02		3	5	0	57	17	11.40	-	-	108	0	-		-	-	-	2	-
H.C.Waine	Cant	1944/45		3	4	0	44	16	11.00	-	-	78	1	-	78.00	1-18	-	-	3	-
A.J.Walker	Cant	1866/67	1869/70	2	4	0	19	9	4.75	-	-								2	-
B.G.K.Walker	Auck	1997/98	2004/05	61	81	20	1374	107*	22.52	1	3	4025	128	-	31.44	8-107	4	-	31	-
B.G.K.Walker	All	1997/98	2004/05	84	109	27	1769	107*	21.57	1	4	5325	164	-	32.46	8-107	4	-	38	-
D.J.Walker	Otago	1980/81	1987/88	39	65	13	1519	113	29.21	2	8	691	19	-	36.36	4-50	-	-	23	-
D.J.Walker	All	1980/81	1987/88	40	67	13	1562	113	28.92	2	8	691	19	-	36.36	4-50	-	-	25	-
M.D.J.Walker	CD	1995/96	1997/98	14	22	2	558	86	27.90	-	4	220	4	-	55.00	1-24	-	-	9	-
A.Wallace	Well	2000/01	2003/04	34	48	8	1453	126	36.32	2	9	2183	101	-	21.61	6-114	3	-	32	-
A.Wallace	All	1995/96	2003/04	50	73	10	2070	126	32.85	2	13	2474	106	-	23.33	6-114	3	-	42	-
C.L.Wallace	Auck	1910/11	1911/12	3	5	1	102	72	25.50	-	1	19	0	-		-	-	-	2	-
G.F.Wallace	Auck	1978/79		5	3	1	44	27	14.66	-	-								7	-
G.F.Wallace	Auck	1941/42	1945/46	5	8	1	177	62	25.28	-	2								1	-
G.F.Wallace	All	1936/37	1945/46	6	10	1	195	62	21.66	-	2								1	-
G.M.Wallace	Auck	1976/77		1	2	0	62	60	31.00	-	1								-	-
P.E.Wallace	Cant	1973/74		5	10	1	283	140	31.44	1	-	18	0	-		-	-	-	6	-
W.M.Wallace	Auck	1933/34	1956/57	47	73	5	3409	211	50.13	9	18	2	0	-		-	-	-	32	-
W.M.Wallace	All	1933/34	1960/61	121	192	17	7757	211	44.32	17	43								68	-
J.Walls	Otago	1886/87		1	2	1	28	20	14.00	-	-								1	-
J.W.Walmsley	Cant	1889/90		1	1	0	19	16*	19.00	-	-								-	-
K.P.Walmsley	Otago	1994/95	2005/06	33	41	7	335	48	9.85	-	-	3179	122	-	26.05	7-28	6	1	10	-
K.P.Walmsley	Otago	2000/01	2002/03	18	20	3	206	59	12.11	-	1	1805	83	-	21.74	6-74	2	-	4	-
K.P.Walmsley	All	1994/95	2005/06	67	81	19	709	59	11.43	-	1	6302	253	-	24.90	7-28	10	1	20	-
W.T.Walmsley	ND	1959/60		3	4	1	99	37	33.00	-	-	319	12	-	26.58	4-30	-	-	1	-
I.A.Walsh	All	1945/46	1959/60	37	50	11	1064	180*	27.28	2	4	3861	122	-	31.64	6-56	3	-	8	-
C.V.Walter	Otago	1948/49	1949/50	3	4	0	2	2*	1.00	-	-	270	8	-	33.75	5-76	1	-	3	-
H.G.Walters	Cant	1945/46		2	4	0	29	13	7.25	-	-								-	-
G.W.Walton	Auck	1941/42		1	2	0	120	81	60.00	-	1								1	-
H.Walton	CD	1985/86	1987/88	7	10	3	73	36	10.42	-	-	640	6	-	106.66	2-56	-	-	-	-
H.Walton	Auck	1897/98		1	2	0	20	20	10.00	-	-	18	0	-		-	-	-	-	-
B.J.Ward	Cant	1986/87		8	10	2	86	19	10.75	-	-								18	2

		First	Last	M	I	NO	Runs	HS	Avg	100	50	Runs	Wkts	OW	Avg	Best	5i	10m	ct	st
B.P.Ward	ND	1986/87	1987/88	2	3	3	1	1*	-	-	-	234	7		33.42	2-24	-	-	1	-
J.S.Ward	Cant	2000/01	2004/05	4	4	3	13	8*	13.00	-	-	150	4		37.50	3-71	-	-	1	-
J.T.Ward	Cant	1959/60	1970/71	55	75	18	811	54*	14.22	-	1	7	0		-	-	-	-	143	17
	All	1957/58	1970/71	95	129	39	1117	54*	12.41	-	1	7	0		-	-	-	-	227	27
S.W.Ward	Well	1929/30	1937/38	10	20	1	282	61	14.84	-	1	22	0		-	-	-	-	9	
C.P.S.Wareham	Well	1934/35		2	3	0	7	6	2.33	-	-									
W.Warne	Well	1919/20	1920/21	5	9	2	212	55	30.28	-	1								5	1
B.H.Warner	Auck	1944/45		1	2	0	8	8	4.00	-	-								1	
W.F.Warren	Well	1894/95	1896/97	4	6	0	157	50	26.16	-	1	60	5		12.00	3-11	-	-	4	
	Auck	1897/98		1	2	0	27	19	13.50	-	-	12	0		-	-	-	-	1	
	All	1894/95	1897/98	5	8	0	184	50	23.00	-	1	72	5		14.40	3-11	-	-	5	
J.W.Warrington	ND	1973/74		6	12	0	365	84	30.41	-	3								3	
	Auck	1975/76		3	6	0	131	80	21.83	-	1								1	
	All	1973/74	1975/76	9	18	0	496	84	27.55	-	4								4	
A.J.Washer	Sland	1919/20		1	1	0	1	1	1.00	-	-	5	0		-	-	-	-	1	
A.T.Washer	Cant	1884/85		1	2	0	38	31	19.00	-	-	122	6		20.33	3-48	-	-	2	
V.H.Waters	Well	1895/96	1905/06	11	18	2	231	86	14.43	-	1	122	6		20.33	3-48	-	-	2	
	All	1895/96	1905/06	12	20	2	241	86	13.38	-	1								3	
B.J.Watling	ND	2004/05	2009/10	40	74	2	2205	153	30.62	5	10	8	0		-	-	-	-	49	
	All	2004/05	2009/10	47	86	4	2460	153	30.00	5	11	8	0		-	-	-	-	56	
E.A.Watson	Otago	1947/48	1959/60	46	86	3	1779	103	21.43	1	8	1249	41		30.46	4-26	-	-	48	
F.E.Watson	All	1879/80		1	1	0	6	6	6.00	-	-									
G.Watson	Cant	1880/81	1883/84	5	9	0	367	175	40.77	1	2								1	
H.Watson	Cant	1909/10	1920/21	10	17	2	234	45	15.60	-	-	385	20		19.25	6-48	1	-	7	
H.C.Watson	Otago	1907/08	1914/15	9	18	0	198	40	11.00	-	-	58	3		19.33	3-13	-	-	5	
	Cant	1917/18		2	2	0	3	3	1.50	-	-								1	
	Well	1923/24		11	2	0	29	29	14.50	-	-	35	1		35.00	1-16	-	-	7	
	All	1907/08	1923/24	11	22	0	230	40	10.45	-	-	93	4		23.25	3-13	-	-	7	
L.C.Watson	Otago	1911/12		1	2	0	20	10	10.00	-	-								4	
L.F.Watson	Otago	1953/54		3	6	0	96	22	16.00	-	-									
L.T.Watson	Cant	1978/79		1	0	0	0	0*	-	-	-	12	0		-	-	-	-		
T.M.Watson	All	1964/65		1	2	1	0	0*	0.00	-	-	67	2		33.50	2-67	-	0		
W.Watson	Auck	1984/85	1994/95	53	47	17	285	38*	9.50	-	-	4110	176		23.35	7-60	7	0	15	
	All	1984/85	1994/95	93	83	30	472	38*	8.90	-	-	7485	272		27.51	7-60	8	0	23	
D.G.Watt	Otago	1943/44		1	2	0	120	105	60.00	1	-								1	
L.Watt	Otago	1943/44	1962/63	45	84	0	1954	96	23.82	-	10	14	0		-	-	-	-	12	
	All	1942/43	1962/63	48	89	3	2004	96	23.30	-	10	14	0		-	-	-	-	14	
K.A.Wealleans	ND	1988/89	1994/95	41	70	4	2029	112*	30.74	4	11								22	
	All	1988/89	1994/95	43	74	4	2053	112*	29.32	4	11								23	
C.A.Webb	CD	1981/82		5	8	1	188	45	26.85	-	-								3	
G.Webb	Well	1879/80	1896/97	3	5	1	40	26	10.00	-	-	8	1		8.00	1-8	-	-		
M.G.Webb	Otago	1969/70	1973/74	20	23	9	147	20*	10.50	-	-	1947	105		18.54	7-49	9	-	8	
	Cant	1972/73		1	2	1	24	21	24.00	-	-	113	5		22.60	4-102	-	-		
	All	1969/70	1973/74	32	33	13	202	21	10.10	-	-	3112	133		23.39	7-49	10	-	11	
P.N.Webb	Auck	1976/77	1986/87	65	114	18	3307	136	34.44	5	20	177	4		44.25	2-34	-	-	50	2
	All	1976/77	1986/87	75	130	19	3671	136	33.07	5	23	177	4		44.25	2-34	-	-	53	2

		First	Last	M	I	NO	Runs	HS	Avg	100	50	Runs	Wkts	OW	Avg	Best	5i	10m	ct	st
R.J.Webb	Otago	1975/76	1983/84	25	32	14	79	14*	4.38	-	-	1862	67	-	27.79	6-20	2	-	12	-
R.C.Webb	Cant	1937/38	1949/50	12	18	0	161	40	8.94	-	-	341	18	-	18.94	5-42	1	-	17	4
W.A.A.Webb	Otago	1897/98	1900/01	7	12	1	83	28	7.54	-	-	552	23	-	24.00	3-34	-	-	4	-
R.V.Webster	Otago	1966/67	1967/68	7	11	4	135	42*	19.28	-	-	5290	272	-	19.44	8-19	13	4	4	-
S.W.Weenink	All	1961	1967/68	70	82	19	865	47	13.73	-	-	161	4	-	40.25	4-69	-	-	21	-
	Well	1995/96	1996/97	6	10	0	100	40	10.00	-	-	641	10	-	64.10	4-69	-	-	3	-
	All	1995/96	2000	12	19	2	224	72*	13.17	-	1	26	0	-	-	-	-	-	7	-
A.F.Weir	Auck	1927/28		3	5	0	10	10	2.00	-	-								1	-
G.L.Weir	Auck	1927/28	1946/47	42	67	6	2625	191	43.03	7	12	1814	60	-	30.23	6-56	1	-	38	-
	All	1927/28	1946/47	107	172	16	5022	191	32.19	10	26	3992	107	-	37.30	6-56	2	-	68	-
F.L.Wells	Otago	1895/96	1896/97	2	3	0	9	9	3.00	-	-	21	1	-	21.00	1-2	-	-	-	-
J.D.Wells	Well	1989/90	2000/01	72	113	18	3016	143	31.74	5	14	1666	33	-	50.48	6-59	1	-	52	-
	All	1989/90	2000/01	73	115	18	3058	143	31.52	5	14	1666	33	-	50.48	6-59	1	-	52	-
S.R.Wells	Otago	2007/08	2009/10	13	21	5	598	115*	37.37	2	1	758	27	-	28.07	5-26	2	-	5	-
A.F.Wensley	Auck	1929/30	1930/31	7	11	1	238	51*	23.80	-	2	748	32	-	23.37	9-36	3	1	7	-
	All	1922	1947/48	400	595	64	10875	154	20.48	9	45	30251	1142	-	26.48	9-36	56	10	265	-
N.W.Werry	Well	1873/74	1883/84	4	8	0	56	20	7.00	-	-	6	0	-	-	-	-	-	2	1
G.L.West	CD	2000/01		5	7	2	21	10	4.20	-	-	407	14	-	29.07	4-62	1	-	3	-
	ND	2002/03	2003/04	10	12	2	55	31	5.50	-	-	730	22	-	33.18	4-23	-	-	3	-
	All	2000/01	2003/04	15	19	4	76	31	5.06	-	-	1137	36	-	31.58	4-23	-	-	3	-
R.M.West	CD	1996/97	2004/05	13	16	3	211	44	16.23	-	-	1087	25	-	43.48	3-52	-	-	6	-
	Well	2000/01		1	1	0	19	19*	-	-	-	25	0	-	-	-	-	-	-	-
	All	1996/97	2009	20	26	7	352	44*	18.52	-	-	1699	45	-	37.75	7-88	1	-	11	-
R.A.Westbrook	Otago	1914/15	1921/22	11	20	1	282	40	14.84	-	1	14	0	-	-	-	-	-	4	-
	All	1910/11	1921/22	14	26	0	384	41	15.36	-	1	28	0	-	-	-	-	-	6	-
D.L.Weston	Auck	1950/51		1	2	0	9	9	4.50	-	-								-	-
G.T.Weston	Cant	1903/04	1904/05	4	8	0	74	42	9.25	-	-								6	-
T.I.Weston	CD	2005/06	2009/10	36	61	9	2083	152	40.05	1	14								18	-
R.J.Westwood	Cant	1940/41		3	5	1	27	14	6.75	-	-	251	11	-	22.81	4-35	-	-	3	-
B.A.Weyburne	Well	1896/97	1905/06	7	9	0	185	44	20.55	-	-								3	-
J.Wheatley	Cant	1882/83	1903/04	12	20	1	254	53	13.36	-	-	55	3	-	18.33	2-27	-	-	7	-
B.M.Wheeler	CD	2009/10		2	3	1	24	10*	12.00	-	-	167	3	-	55.66	2-67	-	-	3	-
G.P.Wheeler	Well	1981/82		1	1	0	32	32*	-	-	-	30	0	-	-	-	-	-	2	-
W.J.Wheeler	Auck	1944/45		1	2	0	22	22	11.00	-	-	59	2	-	29.50	2-33	-	-	-	-
	All	1944/45		2	4	0	47	25	11.75	-	-	119	7	-	17.00	4-21	-	-	1	-
R.F.W.Whelan	Auck	1922/23		2	4	0	155	57	25.83	-	2	21	0	-	-	-	-	-	3	-
B.H.White	Nel	1876/77	1879/80	2	4	0	18	10	4.50	-	-								1	-
D.J.White	ND	1979/80	1992/93	99	173	15	4656	209	29.46	7	27	1364	33	-	41.33	6-45	1	-	44	2
	All	1979/80	1993/94	106	187	17	4926	209	28.97	7	28	1369	33	-	41.48	6-45	1	-	45	2
G.M.White	HB	1884/85	1905/06	14	24	2	340	87	15.45	-	-	107	8	-	13.37	3-28	-	-	4	-
H.R.White	Well	1923/24		1	2	0	6	5	3.00	-	-	64	0	-	-	-	-	-	-	-
J.S.S.White	ND	1972/73	1973/74	7	12	3	100	34	11.11	-	-	549	13	-	42.23	5-29	1	-	-	-
K.J.White	ND	1978/79		1	1	0	2	2	2.00	-	-	74	1	-	74.00	1-48	-	-	-	-
	CD	1979/80		1	2	1	3	3*	3.00	-	-	31	1	-	31.00	1-31	-	-	-	-
	All	1978/79	1979/80	2	3	1	5	3*	2.50	-	-	105	2	-	52.50	1-31	-	-	-	-
N.M.White	HB	1907/08		1	2	0	34	28	17.00	-	-	15	0	-	-	-	-	-	-	-

		First	Last	M	I	NO	Runs	HS	Avg	100	50	Runs	Wkts	OW	Avg	Best	5i	10m	ct	st
P.C.White	Auck	1906/07	1907/08	2	3	1	4	2*	2.00	-	-	74	7		10.57	6-21	1	-	1	-
P.White	HB	1910/11		1	2	1	0	0	0.00	-	-				-	-	-	-	1	-
P.E.Whitelaw	Auck	1928/29	1946/47	42	68	4	2417	195	37.76	5	13	8	0		-	-	-	-	35	-
	All	1928/29	1946/47	49	80	7	2739	195	37.52	5	15	8	0		-	-	-	-	39	-
S.J.G.Whiteman	Auck	2003/04		2	3	0	23	11	7.66	-	-	20	1		20.00	1-8	-	-	-	-
O.R.D.Whitford	Cant	1947/48		2	2	0	46	25	23.00	-	-				-	-	-	-	4	-
H.B.Whitta	Cant	1903/04	1919/20	18	32	1	684	147	22.06	1	3	22	0		-	-	-	-	5	-
	All	1903/04	1919/20	19	34	1	749	147	22.69	1	4	22	0		-	-	-	-	6	-
G.L.Whyte	Well	1939/40		2	4	0	45	42	22.50	-	-	45	1		45.00	1-45	-	-	-	-
R.A.Whyte	Well	1934/35		2	4	2	29	29	14.75	-	-				-	-	-	-	-	-
P.B.Wight	Cant	1963/64		4	7	2	312	114	62.40	1	2	4	0		-	-	-	-	-	-
	All	1950/51	1965	333	590	53	17773	222*	33.09	28	91	2262	68		33.26	6-29	1	-	203	-
W.C.H.Wigley	Cant	1893/94	1903/04	22	38	0	646	73	17.00	-	2	33	2		16.50	1-4	-	-	14	-
J.Wigzell	Nel	1877/78	1883/84	7	13	4	103	31*	11.44	-	-	87	16		5.44	5-16	2	-	5	-
R.G.Wilde	CD	1951/52		2	4	0	23	15	5.75	-	-			12	-	-	-	-	-	-
A.F.Wilding	Cant	1900/01	1901/02	2	3	0	60	28	20.00	-	-	52	3		17.33	3-22	-	-	-	-
F.Wilding	Cant	1881/82	1899/00	34	60	3	1079	136	18.92	2	2	1318	103		12.79	7-31	6	-	27	-
A.V.Wiles	Auck	1946/47		5	7	1	113	40	18.83	-	-	360	13		27.69	3-32	-	-	4	-
J.L.Wilkie	Otago	1901/02		2	3	0	122	73	40.66	-	1	3	1		3.00	1-3	-	-	1	-
R.A.Wilkie	Otago	1899/00		1	2	0	30	19	15.00	-	-	17	0		-	-	-	-	-	-
A.M.Wilkinson	Otago	2002/03		1	1	0	0	0	0.00	-	-	53	0		-	-	-	-	-	-
G.J.Wilkinson	Well	1996/97		1	2	0	173	96	86.50	-	2	3	0		-	-	-	-	1	-
A.M.Williams	HB	1883/84		1	2	0	34	29	17.00	-	-	81	4		20.25	3-55	-	-	-	-
A.B.Williams	Otago	1886/87	1894/95	8	16	1	112	19	7.46	-	-				-	-	-	-	6	2
	Well	1896/97	1909/10	15	25	2	556	163	22.24	2	1				-	-	-	-	16	11
	All	1886/87	1909/10	26	47	2	785	163	17.44	2	2				-	-	-	-	23	15
A.G.Williams	Auck	1927/28		1	1	0	9	9*	-	-	-	79	2		39.50	1-38	-	-	1	-
B.R.Williams	Well	1987/88	1992/93	22	31	3	440	103*	15.71	1	-	1521	30		50.70	4-60	-	-	12	-
E.H.Williams	HB	1891/92					4	4	4.00											
F.Williams	Otago	1898/99	1908/09	26	48	12	295	39	8.19	-	-				-	-	-	-	32	-
G.J.Williams	Otago	1975/76	1977/78	8	13	3	127	60	12.70	-	1	54	2		27.00	2-26	-	-	2	-
G.C.Williams	HB	1883/84		1	2	0	7	6	3.50	-	-	16	0		-	-	-	-	-	-
H.B.Williams	HB	1891/92	1894/95	10	17	0	170	36	10.00	-	-	346	13		26.61	4-49	-	-	4	-
J.C.Williams	Auck	1970/71	1973/74	6	7	6	19	9	19.00	-	-				-	-	-	-	5	-
J.L.Williams	Cant	1952/53		3	5	1	34	13	8.50	-	-				-	-	-	-	2	-
J.N.Williams	HB	1903/04		3	5	0	21	20	10.50	-	-				-	-	-	-	1	-
	All	1903/04	1908	4	7	2	52	20	7.42	-	-				-	-	-	-	2	-
J.A.Williams	Well	1981/82		7	9	2	74	18*	10.57	-	-	555	22		25.22	4-26	1	-	2	-
	All	1974/75	1982/83	26	36	9	281	33	10.40	-	-	1890	52		36.34	4-26	4	-	1	-
K.S.Williams	Cant	1906/07	1907/08	2	4	0	15	9	3.75	-	-	112	2		56.00	1-39	-	-	4	-
	All	1906/07	1913/14	3	6	0	15	9	2.50	-	-	126	2		63.00	1-39	-	-	2	-
L.G.Williams	Well	1951/52	1953/54	6	12	0	173	64	14.41	-	1		0		-	-	-	-	2	-
N.T.Williams	Auck	1893/94	1894/95	3	5	0	102	82	20.40	-	1	19	0		-	-	-	-	4	-
	Well	1884/85		1	2	0	17	9	8.50	-	-	3	0		-	-	-	-	8	-
O.C.Williams	All	1870/71	1884/85	5	9	0	84	20	9.33	-	-	3	0		-	-	-	-	10	-

		First	Last	M	I	NO	Runs	HS	Avg	100	50	Runs	Wkts	OW	Avg	Best	5i	10m	ct	st
K.S.Williamson	ND	2007/08	2009/10	18	30	2	1323	192	47.25	4	6	1186	29		40.89	5-75	1	-	21	-
	All	2007/08	2009/10	20	33	2	1428	192	46.06	4	6	1282	30		42.73	5-75	1	-	24	-
A.Willis	Well	1946/47		1	2	0	31	22	15.50	-	-	18	0		-	-	-	-	-	-
J.W.Wills	Otago	1869/70		1	2	1	1	1*	1.00	-	-								-	-
A.C.Wilson	Cant	1877/78		1	2	0	18	16	9.00	-	-								-	-
A.M.Wilson	Well	1979/80		5	6	0	57	28	9.50	-	-								4	-
B.M.Wilson	Well	1892/93		1	2	1	2	1*	2.00	-	-								-	-
B.S.Wilson	ND	2004/05	2009/10	32	58	3	1529	109	27.80	4	5	26	0		-	-	-	-	27	-
C.G.Wilson	Otago	1905/06	1911/12	15	27	1	928	188	35.69	3	1	9	0		-	-	-	-	8	-
	Well	1912/13	1919/20	13	24	0	487	61	20.29	-	2								4	-
	All	1894/95	1919/20	32	59	2	1490	188	25.68	3	3	16	0		-	-	-	-	14	-
D.S.Wilson	Well	1935/36	1948/49	24	47	4	1119	90	26.02	-	6	1775	60		29.58	6-44	2	-	18	-
	All	1935/36	1948/49	25	49	4	1158	90	25.73	-	6	1929	65		29.67	6-44	2	-	19	-
E.S.Wilson	Otago	1927/28		1	1	0	8	8*	-	-	-	78	3		26.00	2-29	-	-	-	-
F.E.Wilson	HB	1893/94		2	4	0	22	18	5.50	-	-	678	31		21.87	7-80	4	2	1	-
G.C.L.Wilson	Cant	1913/14		5	8	3	168	64*	33.60	-	1	717	31		23.12	7-80	4	2	1	-
	All	1913/14		6	10	4	186	64*	31.00	-	1								-	-
H.Wilson	Auck	1923/24	1926/27	7	12	3	118	30	13.11	-	-	535	11		48.63	3-60	-	-	8	-
H.C.Wilson	HB	1896/97	1900/01	9	15	0	256	35	21.33	-	-	334	17		19.64	4-22	-	-	7	-
I.D.Wilson	Cant	1977/78	1979/80	8	10	0	42	17	4.20	-	-	439	11		39.90	2-18	-	-	1	-
J.H.Wilson	Well	1883/84	1885/86	3	5	0	72	65	14.40	-	1	18	0		-	-	-	-	-	-
J.W.Wilson	Otago	1991/92	2004/05	38	62	7	1218	78	22.14	-	6	3010	125		24.08	5-34	7	-	29	-
	All	1991/92	2004/05	39	64	7	1245	78	21.84	-	6	3113	129		24.13	5-34	7	-	29	-
M.Wilson	CD	1959/60		1	0	0						30	0		-	-	-	-	-	-
N.R.Wilson	ND	1957/58	1960/61	5	9	0	81	29	9.00	-	-	184	3		61.33	2-49	-	-	1	-
P.D.Wilson	Well	1940/41		3	6	0	96	32	16.00	-	-	9	0		-	-	-	-	-	-
R.S.Wilson	Otago	1971/72	1978/79	2	2	0	73	62	36.50	-	1								1	-
S.Wilson	Sland	1917/18	1918/19	2	4	0	29	16	7.25	-	-								-	-
S.W.J.Wilson	CD	1990/91	1993/94	25	45	4	1108	112	27.02	2	2	97	0		-	-	-	-	12	-
	Cant	1994/95		5	10	0	190	74	19.00	-	2	42	0		-	-	-	-	1	-
	All	1990/91	1994/95	33	61	5	1420	112	25.35	2	4	139	0		-	-	-	-	13	-
T.H.Wilson	Auck	1891/92		3	2	1	9	8	4.50	-	-								-	-
T.J.Wilson	Otago	1984/85	1988/89	31	45	7	528	55	13.89	-	2	2387	85		28.08	7-57	4	-	9	-
	All	1984/85	1988/89	33	46	7	533	55	13.66	-	2	2642	90		29.35	7-57	4	-	10	-
W.C.Wilson	Cant	1863/64	1864/65	4	4	1	7	2*	2.33	-	-	1	0		-	-	-	-	-	-
J.R.Wiltshire	Auck	1974/75	1980/81	30	54	11	1504	100*	34.97	1	7	4	0		-	-	-	-	17	-
	CD	1981/82	1983/84	22	38	5	902	105	27.33	1	3	5	0		-	-	-	-	8	-
	All	1974/75	1983/84	54	94	16	2422	105	31.05	2	10								25	-
A.G.Wiren	Well	1945/46		2	4	0	100	84	25.00	-	1								2	-
P.J.Wiseman	Auck	1991/92	1992/93	3	4	2	69	26	34.50	-	-	166	0		-	-	-	-	1	-
	Otago	1994/95	2000/01	43	62	11	849	77	16.64	-	4	3801	136		27.94	8-66	7	1	28	-
	Cant	2001/02	2005/06	44	65	12	1513	130	28.54	1	8	3613	114		31.69	9-13	5	2	12	-
	All	1991/92	2008	186	254	51	4254	130	20.95	1	16	15727	466		33.74	9-13	18	4	79	-
W.A.Wisneski	CD	1992/93	1995/96	16	22	4	483	86	24.15	-	4	1383	53		26.09	5-21	4	-	9	-
	Cant	1996/97	2003/04	44	55	9	891	89*	19.36	-	4	4092	154		26.57	7-151	4	-	29	-
	All	1992/93	2003/04	71	94	13	1750	89*	21.60	-	9	6467	248		26.07	7-151	12	-	46	-

		First	Last	M	I	NO	Runs	HS	Avg	100	50	Runs	Wkts	OW	Avg	Best	5i	10m	ct	st
A.M.Wix	Nel	1873/74	1874/75	2	4	0	37	24	9.25	-	-	15	0		-	-	-	-	2	-
R.P.Wixon	CD	1991/92	1992/93	4	7	3	23	8	5.75	-	-	299	10		29.90	4-83	-	-	1	-
	Otago	1993/94	1994/95	13	23	1	242	34*	20.16	-	1	845	24		35.20	5-83	2	-	13	-
	All	1991/92	1994/95	17	30	14	265	34*	16.56	-	1	1144	34		33.64	5-83	2	-	14	-
J.Wolstenholme	HB	1886/87	1898/99	10	16	0	280	103	17.50	1	1	137	14		9.78	4-9	-	-	6	-
G.Wontner	Cant	1872/73		1	1	0	9	9	9.00	-	-				-	-	-	-	-	-
B.B.Wood	Cant	1907/08	1918/19	10	19	0	423	108	22.26	1	1	233	17		13.70	4-24	-	-	4	-
J.W.H.Wood	Well	1882/83	1883/84	5	9	1	74	32*	9.25	-	-	57	2		28.50	2-22	-	-	4	-
	HB	1884/85	1886/87	2	4	0	46	39	11.50	-	-				-	-	-	-	2	-
	Nel	1887/88	1888/89	2	3	0	11	11	3.66	-	-	84	1		84.00	1-84	-	-	2	-
	All	1873/74	1888/89	9	16	1	131	39	8.73	-	-	374	20		18.70	4-24	-	-	8	-
J.Wood	Cant	1868/69	1877/78	5	10	1	61	16	6.77	-	-				-	-	-	-	1	-
	Well	1873/74		1	2	1	5	4	2.50	-	-				-	-	-	-	-	-
	All	1868/69	1877/78	6	12	1	66	16	6.00	-	-				-	-	-	-	1	-
L.J.Woodcock	Well	2001/02	2009/10	70	117	15	3427	220*	33.59	4	20	3134	78		40.17	4-3	-	-	34	-
	All	2001/02	2009/10	71	118	15	3433	220*	33.33	4	20	3259	78		41.78	4-3	-	-	34	-
E.R.Woods	Auck	1913/14		2	4	0	10	8	2.50	-	2	226	8		28.25	3-23	-	-	6	-
F.Woods	Cant	1913/14	1926/27	13	23	1	597	124*	27.13	1	2	10	0		-	-	-	-	6	-
	All	1913/14	1926/27	14	25	1	619	124*	25.79	1	2	5	0		-	-	-	-	6	-
N.T.Woods	Otago	1958/59	1965/66	18	26	11	148	31*	9.86	-	-	1046	44		23.77	6-56	1	-	10	-
C.W.Wordsworth	Otago	1908/09	1909/10	4	8	0	56	19	7.00	-	-	335	12		27.91	3-41	-	-	1	-
	All	1907/08	1909/10	5	10	0	72	19	8.00	-	-	407	16		25.43	3-24	-	-	-	-
G.H.Worker	CD	2007/08	2009/10	22	38	1	840	71	22.70	-	6	2016	28		72.00	3-54	-	-	21	-
R.V.D.Worker	Auck	1914/15		1	2	0	5	3	2.50	-	-				-	-	-	-	3	-
	Cant	1919/20	1922/23	11	22	3	478	65	25.15	-	2				-	-	-	-	3	2
	Otago	1923/24	1925/26	9	18	2	961	172	60.06	3	4				-	-	-	-	5	3
	Well	1926/27	1929/30	7	14	1	519	151	39.92	1	4				-	-	-	-	1	-
	All	1914/15	1929/30	37	73	6	2338	172	34.89	4	12				-	-	-	-	9	-
J.H.Worrall	Auck	1951/52	1954/55	9	17	0	275	63	16.17	-	1	34	0		-	-	-	-	7	-
C.Worthington	Otago	1864/65	1865/66	2	4	1	41	14	13.66	-	-	34	0		-	-	-	-	-	-
W.J.Wyatt	Nel	1882/83	1883/84	2	4	0	13	5	3.25	-	-	4	1		4.00	1-4	-	-	-	-
E.L.Wright	Auck	1894/95	1897/98	7	10	1	156	89	17.33	-	1	13	1		13.00	1-13	-	-	7	9
	Well	1898/99	1900/01	4	6	3	24	10*	8.00	-	-	16	0		-	-	-	-	10	1
	Cant	1899/00		1	2	1	12	8*	12.00	-	-				-	-	-	-	-	-
	All	1894/95	1900/01	13	20	5	200	89	13.33	-	1	16	0		-	-	-	-	19	10
G.T.Wright	Well	1955/56		1	2	0	19	19	9.50	-	-				-	-	-	-	1	-
H.Wright	Auck	1912/13	1913/14	3	6	0	142	88	23.66	-	1				-	-	-	-	4	-
J.L.Wright	ND	1958/59		2	3	0	7	6	2.33	-	-				-	-	-	-	2	-
J.G.Wright	ND	1975/76	1983/84	43	84	3	3301	145*	40.75	5	21	288	8		36.00	4-52	-	-	34	-
	Cant	1984/85	1988/89	16	30	4	1555	192	59.80	5	8	13	0		-	-	-	-	4	-
	Auck	1989/90	1992/93	14	23	0	993	118	43.17	2	5	87	0		-	-	-	-	5	-
	All	1975/76	1992/93	366	636	44	25073	192	42.35	59	126	13	0		-	-	-	-	193	-
M.J.E.Wright	ND	1972/73	1983/84	65	114	10	2632	115	25.30	1	10	339	2		169.50	1-4	-	-	110	-
O.L.Wrigley	Well	1939/40	1940/41	3	6	0	27	12	4.50	-	-	94	0		-	-	-	-	3	-
	All	1939/40	1942/43	4	8	0	81	52	10.12	-	1				-	-	-	-	3	-
I.E.Wyatt	Auck	1947/48		4	6	0	202	67	33.66	-	1				-	-	-	-	3	17

		First	Last	M	I	NO	Runs	HS	Avg	100	50	Runs	Wkts	OW	Avg	Best	5i	10m	ct	st
J.L.Wyatt	ND	1956/57	1885/86	4	7	0	163	54	23.28	-	1								1	-
W.Wyinks	Otago	1882/83		2	4	0	17	7	4.25	-	-								1	-
R.N.Wylie	CD	1973/74		5	10	1	142	55*	15.77	-	1	382	10		38.20	3-46	-	-	5	-
W.T.Wynyard	Auck	1882/83	1899/00	8	12	2	182	63	18.20	-	1								5	-
	Well	1890/91	1907/08	4	6	0	49	25	8.16	-	-								3	-
	All	1882/83	1907/08	12	18	2	231	63	14.43	-	1								8	-
R.J.Yates	Auck	1873/74	1893/94	15	27	0	435	50	16.11	-	1								8	-
W.C.Yates	HB	1883/84		2	2	1	2	2	2.00	-	-								1	-
B.A.Yock	Cant	1996/97	1997/98	2	3	0	20	11	6.66	-	-								4	-
B.A.Young	ND	1983/84	1997/98	93	148	36	3853	138*	34.40	5	18								209	11
	Auck	1998/99		3	6	1	143	111	28.60	1	-								5	-
	All	1983/84	1998/99	163	276	43	7489	267*	32.14	10	37								297	11
G.A.Young	Cant	1866/67	1867/68	2	4	1	8	5*	2.66	-	-	76	1		76.00	1-76	-	-	1	-
J.G.Young	Cant	1921/22	1923/24	6	12	3	154	35	17.11	-	-	71	12		5.91	6-27	2	-	-	-
R.A.Young	Auck	1998/99	2009/10	90	120	22	2834	126*	28.91	5	17	68	1		68.00	1-65	-	-	252	5
	All	1998/99	2009/10	94	127	23	3031	126*	29.14	5	19	68	1		68.00	1-65	-	-	265	5
W.H.Young	HB	1896/97	1905/06	6	10	0	30	14	3.00	-	-								-	-
J.A.F.Yovich	ND	1996/97	2009/10	98	150	29	3552	144	29.35	3	20	8432	253		33.32	7-64	8	1	30	-
	All	1996/97	2009/10	99	151	29	3552	144	29.11	3	20	8432	253		33.32	7-64	8	1	30	-
B.W.Yuile	CD	1959/60	1971/72	61	90	10	2190	146	27.37	1	13	4485	233		19.24	9-100	12	2	40	-
	Cant	1967/68		1	1	0	9	9	9.00	-	-	106	2		53.00	2-40	-	-	2	-
	All	1959/60	1971/72	123	187	31	3850	146	24.67	1	22	8209	375		21.89	9-100	17	2	73	-
S.B.Zavos	Well	1958/59		1	2	0	8	5	4.00	-	-	15	0		-	-	-	-	-	-
C.Zimmerman	Otago	1925/26	1929/30	9	15	2	269	77	20.69	-	1	304	8		38.00	3-47	-	-	7	-

Notes:
There is a separate line of first-class career figures for each provincial team with a total for all first-class matches shown for players who did not play all their first-class cricket for one provincial team. The OW column denotes additional wickets taken in innings where no bowling analyses are available. These wickets are ignored when working out the bowling average.

FIRST-CLASS AVERAGES FOR FIJI PLAYERS

	First	Last	M	I	NO	Runs	HS	Avg	100	50	Runs	Wkts	OW	Avg	Best	5i	10m	ct	st
H.J.Apted	1947/48	1953/54	9	18	0	497	97	27.61	-	4	139	5		27.80	2-36	-	-	19	-
W.W.Apted	1953/54		4	8	0	408	102	51.00	1	3								4	-
K.T.Aria	1947/48		3	6	0	114	46	19.00	-	-								4	-
M.Bogisa	1947/48	1953/54	6	12	0	152	33	12.66	-	-	134	3		44.66	3-66	-	-	2	-
I.L. Bula	1947/48	1953/54	9	18	1	702	120	41.29	2	3								8	-
G.K.Cakobau	1947/48		4	8	1	176	67*	25.14	-	1	260	5		52.00	2-48	-	-	3	-
R.Caldwell	1894/95		6	11	2	109	25*	12.11	-	-	453	22		20.59	5-17	2	-	4	-
J.C.Collins	1894/95		6	11	2	249	128*	24.90	1	-	47	4		11.75	3-30	-	-	1	-
A.Driu	1953/54		4	6	2	56	16	14.00	-	-	508	16		31.75	4-98	-	-	2	-
V.Epeli	1894/95		6	7	2	10	5*	2.00	-	-	42	0		-	-	-	-	-	-
M.J.Fenn	1947/48	1953/54	9	16	1	296	44	19.73	-	-	1045	50		20.90	6-94	4	1	1	-
J.W.Gosling	1947/48		1	2	0	5	5	2.50	-	-	117	2		58.50	1-55	-	-	1	-
W.O.Groom	1894/95		6	11	3	75	19	9.37	-	-	94	0		-	-	-	-	1	-
A.B.Joske	1894/95		5	9	0	111	31	12.33	-	-								1	-
P.Kadavulevu	1894/95		6	11	0	52	25	4.72	-	-	87	5		17.40	3-30	-	-	4	-
N.Kavuru	1953/54		2	3	0	41	22	13.66	-	-	85	3		28.33	1-6	-	-	1	-
P.Kubunavanua	1947/48		3	5	2	88	33*	29.33	-	-								-	-
E.Loganimoce	1953/54		3	5	1	31	22	7.75	-	-	177	5		35.40	2-45	-	-	3	-
I.T.Logavatu	1947/48		5	8	2	73	48	12.16	-	-	480	16		30.00	4-46	-	-	3	-
I.McOwan	1894/95		6	11	2	49	22	4.45	-	-	61	4		15.25	2-14	-	-	3	-
K.K.T.Mara	1953/54		2	4	1	64	44	21.33	-	-	137	8		17.12	4-77	-	-	4	-
R.Nailovolovo	1894/95		6	11	0	86	30	7.81	-	-	8	0		-	-	-	-	2	2
P.T.Raddock	1947/48	1953/54	9	16	0	337	89	21.06	-	1								11	10
S.R.Ravouvou	1947/48		1	2	0	8	6	4.00	-	-	28	0		-	-	-	-	-	-
H.M.Scott	1894/95		6	11	3	81	21	10.12	-	-	197	11		17.90	4-19	-	-	2	-
M.F.Simmons	1953/54		4	6	3	44	16	14.66	-	-	304	4		76.00	1-42	-	-	1	-
P.A.Snow	1947/48		5	9	2	121	38	17.28	-	-	101	4		25.25	2-60	-	-	1	-
F.L.Temesia	1894/95		1	1	0	3	3	3.00	-	-								-	-
A.T.Tuidraki	1947/48		2	4	0	53	23	13.25	-	-								4	-
L.B.Tuisavau	1894/95		1	2	0	3	2	1.50	-	-	19	0		-	-	-	-	-	-
W.Tuivanuavou	1894/95		6	10	2	38	12	4.75	-	-	391	37		10.56	5-25	4	1	2	-
N.N.Tuiyau	1953/54		4	8	0	170	33	21.25	-	1	4	0		-	-	-	-	2	-
J.S.Udal	1871	1894/95	9	17	1	215	50	13.43	-	1	5	0		-	-	-	-	4	-
S.M.Viliame	1947/48		3	6	3	50	14*	16.66	-	-	212	11		19.27	6-34	1	-	3	-
A.J Wendt	1947/48		2	4	0	67	41	16.75	-	-	28	0		-	-	-	-	-	-